BEST PRACTICES OF LITERACY LEADERS

Also Available

The Reading Specialist, Third Edition:
Leadership and Coaching for the Classroom,
School, and Community
RITA M. BEAN

Best Practices of Literacy Leaders

Keys to School Improvement

SECOND EDITION

edited by
Allison Swan Dagen
Rita M. Bean

Foreword by Diane Kern

Copublished with

THE GUILFORD PRESS
New York   London

Copyright © 2020 The Guilford Press
A Division of Guilford Publications, Inc.
370 Seventh Avenue, Suite 1200, New York, NY 10001
www.guilford.com

Copublished simultaneously with the
International Literacy Association,
PO Box 8139, Newark, DE, 19714, USA.
www.literacyworldwide.org

Printed in the United States of America

This book is printed on acid-free paper.

Last digit is print number: 9   8   7   6   5   4   3   2   1

Library of Congress Cataloging-in-Publication Data

Names: Swan Dagen, Allison, editor. | Bean, Rita M., editor.
Title: Best practices of literacy leaders : keys to school improvement /
    Edited by Allison Swan Dagen, Rita M. Bean ; Foreword by Diane Kern.
Description: Second edition. | New York : The Guilford Press, 2020. |
    Includes bibliographical references and index. |
Identifiers: LCCN 2019043553 | ISBN 9781462542291 (hardcover) |
    ISBN 9781462542284 (paperback)
Subjects: LCSH: School improvement programs. | Language arts. | Academic
    achievement.
Classification: LCC LB2822.82 .B485 2020 | DDC 371.2/07—dc23
LC record available at *https://lccn.loc.gov/2019043553*

About the Editors

Allison Swan Dagen, PhD, is Professor in the College of Education and Human Services at West Virginia University, where she also serves as Program Coordinator for the Literacy Education/Reading Specialist graduate program. Her research interests include effective professional learning for literacy educators, reading specialist/literacy coach preparation, teachers' literacy leadership, National Board Teaching Certification, and emergent literacy practices. Dr. Swan Dagen was a member of the Standards Committee of the International Literacy Association and serves on the editorial board of *Reading and Writing Quarterly*.

Rita M. Bean, PhD, is Professor Emerita in the School of Education at the University of Pittsburgh. Her research focuses on the roles of the reading specialist and the literacy coach, professional learning for teachers, and the evaluation of large-scale efforts to improve literacy instruction in the elementary school. Dr. Bean served as cochair of the Standards Committee of the International Literacy Association. She is the author of *The Reading Specialist, Third Edition*. Dr. Bean was a member of the board of the International Literacy Association, and is a member of the Reading Hall of Fame.

Contributors

Lisa D. Aker, PhD, College of Education, Clemson University, Clemson, South Carolina

Rita M. Bean, PhD, School of Education (Emerita), University of Pittsburgh, Pittsburgh, Pennsylvania

Jill Castek, PhD, College of Education, University of Arizona, Tucson, Arizona

Megin Charner-Laird, EdD, School of Education, Salem State University, Salem, Massachusetts

Lori Lyman DiGisi, EdD, Wayland Public Schools, Wayland, Massachusetts

Christina L. Dobbs, EdD, Wheelock College of Education and Human Development, Boston University, Boston, Massachusetts

Janice A. Dole, PhD, Department of Educational Psychology, University of Utah, Salt Lake City, Utah

Susan M. Dougherty, EdD, College of Education and Human Services, Rider University, Lawrenceville, New Jersey

Cheryl L. Dozier, PhD, Department of Literacy Teaching and Learning, University at Albany, State University of New York, Albany, New York

Christina Glance, MA, College of Education and Human Services, West Virginia University, Morgantown, West Virginia

Virginia J. Goatley, PhD, Department of Literacy Teaching and Learning, University at Albany, State University of New York, Albany, New York

Carolyn B. Gwinn, PhD, educational consultant, Andover, Minnesota

Lori Helman, PhD, Department of Curriculum and Instruction, University of Minnesota, Minneapolis, Minnesota

Kerry A. Herman, PhD, Department of Educational Psychology, University of Utah, Salt Lake City, Utah

Jacy. Ippolito, EdD, School of Education, Salem State University, Salem, Massachusetts

Carrie L. James, MEd, College of Education, University of Illinois at Urbana–Champaign, Champaign, Illinois

Britney Jones, doctoral student, Neag School of Education, University of Connecticut, Storrs, Connecticut

Jennifer Jones Powell, EdD, School of Education and Teacher Leadership, Radford University, Radford, Virginia

Joanna Lieberman, MEd, Brookline Public Schools, Brookline, Massachusetts

Stephanie Maze-Hsu, MEd, Teaching and Learning Alliance, Inc., Woburn, Massachusetts

Sarah J. McCarthey, PhD, College of Education, University of Illinois at Urbana–Champaign, Champaign, Illinois

Anne McGill-Franzen, PhD, Department of Theory and Practice in Teacher Education, College of Education, Health, and Human Sciences, University of Tennessee, Knoxville, Tennessee

Julie Meltzer, PhD, Mount Desert Island Regional School System, Mount Desert, Maine

Heidi Anne E. Mesmer, PhD, Department of Teaching and Learning, School of Education, Virginia Polytechnic Institute and State University, Blacksburg, Virginia

Aimee L. Morewood, PhD, College of Education and Human Services, West Virginia University, Morgantown, West Virginia

Jeanne R. Paratore, EdD, Wheelock College of Education and Human Development (Emerita), Boston University, Boston, Massachusetts

Katie Pekel, EdD, Department of Organizational Leadership, Policy, and Development, University of Minnesota, Minneapolis, Minnesota

Jaime Puccioni, PhD, Department of Literacy Teaching and Learning, University at Albany, State University of New York, Albany, New York

Victoria J. Risko, EdD, Peabody College of Education (Emerita), Vanderbilt University, Nashville, Tennessee

Donna M. Scanlon, PhD, Department of Literacy Teaching and Learning, University at Albany, State University of New York, Albany, New York

Lynn Schade, MEd, Teaching and Learning Alliance, Inc., Woburn, Massachusetts

Kathleen Spring, PhD, Department of Educational Policy and Leadership, University at Albany, State University of New York, Albany, New York

Sheree E. Springer, PhD, Department of Educational Psychology, University of Utah, Salt Lake City, Utah

Lilly M. Steiner, EdD, School of Education, Monmouth University, West Long Branch, New Jersey

Allison Swan Dagen, PhD, College of Human Resources and Education, West Virginia University, Morgantown, West Virginia

Meaghan N. Vitale, doctoral student, School of Education, University of Delaware, Newark, Delaware

MaryEllen Vogt, EdD, College of Education (Emerita), California State University, Long Beach, Long Beach, California

Doris Walker-Dalhouse, PhD, College of Education, Marquette University, Milwaukee, Wisconsin

Sharon Walpole, PhD, School of Education, University of Delaware, Newark, Delaware

Natalia Ward, PhD, Department of Curriculum and Instruction, East Tennessee State University, Johnson City, Tennessee

Sarah L. Woulfin, PhD, Neag School of Education, University of Connecticut, Storrs, Connecticut

Foreword

Given that the *Standards for the Preparation of Literacy Professionals 2017* (International Literacy Association [ILA], 2018) serves as an important resource for the content in this book, I was asked to write a summary of key concepts addressed in *Standards 2017* to provide foundational knowledge for readers and to set a context for the chapters that follow.

In January 2015, ILA set out to revise its standards, which, over the past 60 years, have guided the design and evaluation of literacy professional preparation programs, national recognition of reading/literacy specialist programs, state standards development for both students and teachers, literacy educator licensure regulations, and ongoing professional learning for literacy professionals in schools. This 3-year revision effort was led by cochairs Dr. Rita M. Bean (coeditor of this book) and me. A team of 26 literacy leaders served as writers, and another 41 professionals were external reviewers. This initiative resulted in a major revision of the earlier *Standards for Reading Professionals—Revised 2010* (International Reading Association, 2010) and culminated in the release of *Standards 2017* in spring 2018. This foreword provides an overview of the roles and content of the 2017 standards, highlighting some of the major shifts or changes.

A DESCRIPTION OF THE ROLES OF LITERACY PROFESSIONALS

Writers of *Standards 2017* reviewed key research on the changing roles of literacy professionals in U.S. PreK–12 schools and developed descriptions of responsibilities and competencies for professionals, as identified in the material that follows.

Specialized Literacy Professionals

The 2017 standards describe three specialized roles of literacy professionals: reading/literacy specialist, literacy coach, and literacy coordinator/supervisor. In *Standards 2017*, ILA separated the roles of reading/literacy specialist and literacy coach. Although there are overlapping functions and responsibilities in these roles, this decision was based on several studies, including a large-scale nationwide survey of specialized literacy professionals (SLPs)—reading/literacy specialists, reading teachers/interventionists, literacy coaches, and literacy coordinators/supervisors—which found distinctions between and among the roles (Bean et al., 2015). The results of this study led to a research brief (ILA, 2015a) and a position statement (ILA, 2015b), both of which guided the work of the Standards committee (both can be accessed at *literacyworldwide.org*).

Classroom Teachers

Titles of classroom teachers in the 2017 standards are as follows: PreK/primary, elementary/intermediate, middle/high school. In *Standards 2010*, PreK and elementary classroom teachers were grouped into one role, and in *Standards 2017*, PreK/primary and elementary/intermediate classroom teachers are now two distinct roles. Although there are overlapping professional knowledge, skills, and dispositions required of these PreK/primary and elementary/intermediate teachers, there are also distinctly different bodies of research-based literacy methods and associated foundational knowledge required for each of these two roles. In *Standards 2017*, the role of middle and high school classroom teachers (of students ages 11–18) describes their responsibilities for teaching language and literacy in the service of learning disciplinary content (National Governors Association Center for Best Practices & Council of Chief State School Officers, 2010). Further, the role of middle and high school reading teacher was deleted because the work of these professionals is best categorized in the description of reading/literacy specialist.

Principals

In *Standards 2010*, the title *administrator* was used. In *Standards 2017,* the focus is on the *principal*, thereby highlighting the importance of the principal as a literacy leader who understands literacy instruction and has a major responsibility for facilitating a schoolwide culture of shared leadership and collaboration that results in a shared vision of literacy teaching and learning.

Teacher Educators

Although the title of *teacher educator* remained the same, the Standards committee, using current research findings, updated the assumptions and responsibilities for this group of literacy professionals.

Literacy Partners

In previous standards, this category was titled *Education Support Personnel*. In *Standards 2017*, ILA describes a much broader schema and developed the title *literacy partners* to include the following groups: parents and families; allied professionals, community agencies, and volunteers; and teaching assistants (formerly *education support personnel*). The goal was to emphasize the importance of a host of people, internal and external to the school, who team with others to make a difference in the literacy lives of PreK–12 learners.

KEY CHANGES IN THE CONTENT OF THE 2017 STANDARDS

Standards 2010 contained six standards; in *Standards 2017* there are seven. For all standards, writers updated the content of the components using current research evidence. The overarching key change across all standards is the emphasis on literacy, which is operationally defined as teaching reading, writing, speaking, listening, viewing, and visually representing. Next I highlight major aspects of each of the standards.

Standard 1: Foundational Knowledge

Although the title remains the same, the content of this standard has changed significantly to reflect the broader notion of literacy and language foundational knowledge rather than reading only. In addition, knowledge of the historical and evidence-based foundations related to the role of the literacy professional was added across roles in *Standards 2017.*

Standard 2: Curriculum and Instruction

Writers attempted to be more explicit about the responsibility of candidates to design, evaluate, and implement not only a reading curriculum but also a broader literacy curriculum. Standard 2 provides research-based guidance on explicit, intense, and systematic instruction as well as whole-class literacy curriculum and instructional methods. The goal was to establish standards that recognized the need for professionals to understand and be able to implement high-level, rigorous instruction that meets the needs of all students.

Standard 3: Assessment and Evaluation

This standard requires candidates to select and use valid, reliable, fair, and appropriate assessment tools for a variety of educational purposes (e.g., to inform instruction; revise curriculum; and screen, diagnose, and measure student literacy achievement). An emphasis was placed on supporting and guiding professionals in the use of assessment to inform instruction and to advocate for appropriate literacy curriculum and instruction.

Standard 4: Diversity and Equity

Standards 2017 adds the term *equity* to the *Standards 2010* diversity standard. Literacy professionals need to demonstrate knowledge of research and pedagogies related to diversity and equity, understand how their cultural experiences affect their own beliefs and values, and continue to learn ways to develop culturally responsive pedagogies and communication. This standard advances the need for literary professionals to situate diversity as a core asset that informs instructional planning and teaching. Literacy professionals, with families and community members, must learn strategies to advocate for student access to excellent and equitable instruction, materials, and opportunities.

Standard 5: Learners and the Literacy Environment

Standards 2010 focused on creating literacy learning environments; the *Standards 2017* revision required significant changes because of advancements in digital literacy and their effects on the literacy learning environment. In addition, writers added *learners* to the title of this standard to align with updated InTASC standards (Council of Chief State Officers, 2013) that emphasize the importance of understanding child and adolescent development and of applying this knowledge to learning experiences that foster student motivation and active engagement.

Standard 6: Professional Learning and Leadership

This standard maintains an emphasis on literacy professionals being lifelong learners as part of their career-long leadership role and responsibility. *Standards 2017* advances the role that literacy professionals have in working collaboratively with colleagues and advocating on behalf of teachers, students, families, and communities.

Standard 7: Practicum/Clinical Experiences

This is a new standard that was created to provide clear expectations for advanced licensure specialized literacy professional programs to ensure that candidates have supervised and meaningful field experiences in schools and university-based literacy clinics. Standard 7 applies only to the three roles of the specialized literacy professionals.

The coeditors of this practical and research-rich volume, Dr. Allison Swan Dagen (a lead writer on *Standards 2017*) and Dr. Rita M. Bean, have a deep knowledge and understanding of *Standards 2017* and how its content can impact literacy teaching and learning in PreK–12 schools today. They have convened an accomplished group of literacy educators and scholars to guide readers in using the evidence-based standards to transform literacy teaching, learning, and leadership.

DIANE KERN, PhD
School of Education, University of Rhode Island

REFERENCES

Bean, R., Kern, D., Goatley, V., Ortlieb, E., Shettel, J., Calo, K., et al. (2015). Specialized literacy professionals as literacy leaders: Results of a national survey. *Literacy Research and Instruction, 54*(2), 83–114.

Council of Chief State School Officers. (2013, April). *Interstate Teacher Assessment and Support Consortium InTASC model core teaching standards and learning progressions for teachers 1.0: A resource for ongoing teacher development.* Washington, DC: Author.

International Literacy Association. (2015a). *Multiple roles of specialized literacy professionals* (Research brief). Newark, DE: Author. Retrieved from *www.literacyworldwide.org/docs/default-source/where-we-stand/literacy-professionals-research brief.pdf?sfvrsn=ff3aa28e_10.*

International Literacy Association. (2015b). *Multiple roles of specialized literacy professionals* (Position statement). Newark, DE: Author. Retrieved from *www.literacyworldwide.org/docs/default-source/where-we-stand/literacy-professionals-position-statement.pdf?sfvrsn=f33aa28e_4.*

International Literacy Association. (2018). *Standards for the preparation of literacy professionals 2017.* Newark, DE: Author.

International Reading Association. (2010). *Standards for reading professionals—revised.* Newark, DE: Author.

National Governors Association Center for Best Practices & Council of Chief State School Officers. (2010). *Common Core State Standards* (English language arts). Washington, DC: Authors.

Preface

The challenges that schools face in the 21st century are many: how to safely and effectively use new and evolving technological tools available to students and teachers; the increasing diversity present in schools and in local communities; the ever-shifting policies of districts, states, or the nation; concerns around funding and the high cost of resources; and the increasing demands for accountability. These challenges, as well as others, have created pressures on schools and especially teachers, who must have the knowledge, skill sets, and dispositions that enable them, with support, to address these challenges and provide a high-quality education for every student.

Those who study schools, school reform, and school improvement highlight the importance of quality teachers and teaching and address issues of how to prepare and then support these professionals. Educators such as Fullan (2001) write about the importance of providing environments and opportunities that help teachers develop "habits of learning" (p. 253) that will prepare them to address the challenges that they face. These new demands and expectations are especially prevalent in the area of literacy and permeate all curricular domains at all grade levels. As is often stated, students must learn not only literacy skills, but they also must be able to use literacy to learn. In other words, literacy provides the foundation for thinking and learning.

There are two major themes in this book that are supported by the research in the field of education and reflect the beliefs and knowledge of the editors and authors of this text. Each theme is summarized in the following sections.

LITERACY LEADERSHIP IS A COLLECTIVE RESPONSIBILITY SHARED BY MANY

Whether one reads research findings, policy briefs, the local newspapers, or a social media thread or blog post, there appears to be an ever-growing awareness of the need for more innovative ways of functioning if schools are to be successful. An emerging message is that leadership should be shared by many professionals in schools in ways that reflect their expertise, unique knowledge, roles, and skills. In addition to traditional administrative leadership, there is a need for leadership by all those who educate students in schools: literacy coaches or facilitators, teachers, and specialized personnel, such as reading/literacy specialists, special educators, speech and language teachers, and content teachers. Such leadership must be seamless; it must flow top-down, bottom-up, and horizontally. Our belief is that effective leadership, especially literacy leadership, can be the catalyst for improving classroom practice and student learning. One of the essential roles of the PreK–12 principal as a designated leader is to maximize opportunities for others to assume leadership roles and to foster their capacity to serve as leaders. Literacy professionals may have formal roles (e.g., literacy coach), or they may serve informally as leaders (e.g., a classroom teacher who serves as chair of the curriculum committee). Special educators, psychologists, guidance counselors, and librarians/media specialists all have specialized knowledge that can enhance the literacy program in schools, and, as such, they too serve as literacy leaders.

LITERACY LEADERSHIP FUNCTIONS MOST EFFECTIVELY IN A CULTURE OF COLLABORATION

Our vision of shared leadership, described above, can happen only in a culture of collaboration that recognizes that each of us has the potential to lead and create an environment where such leadership flourishes. Wenner and Campbell (2017), in their review of research about teacher leadership, identified the following conditions as important for shared leadership and collaboration: encouragement and support from both principal and colleagues, logistical modifications (e.g., time, scheduling), and the nurturing of a culture of collaboration with an explicit shared vision or purpose. When collaboration is encouraged—that is, when schools function in ways in which staff members have opportunities to interact and talk collegially about issues related to their own learning as well as to student learning and are supported by administrators who recognize the importance of such collaboration—then schools can become places of learning for students and teachers. The success of such collaborative initiatives requires that educators serve as leaders; share a vision, common goals, and a common language; are willing to be accountable; and are involved in inquiry and reflection about how best to serve their students.

KEY FEATURES

In this book, our goal is to provide evidence-based information about critical content to support literacy leadership in schools. We begin with an introductory chapter that provides an overview of leadership and its importance to literacy learning for teachers and students. In Part I, authors summarize key research and describe ways by which specific role groups (e.g., teachers, specialists) serve as literacy leaders in schools. In Part II, authors focus on program development, implementation, and evaluation, summarizing key research in specific areas (e.g., writing instruction, digital literacy) and then identifying implications for literacy leaders to consider. In Part III, authors describe the contexts that influence literacy programs (e.g., diversity, special education programs, English learners, parent and community partnerships, policy). We conclude with a final chapter that highlights the importance of professional learning that addresses both personal and organizational goals. In a page before each section, we provide a more in-depth description of the contents of each author's chapter and how the chapters in a section interrelate. There are several key features in this book that contribute to its usefulness and practicality.

- A foreword written by Diane Kern, one of the cochairs of the committee that developed the *Standards for the Preparation of Literacy Professionals 2017* (International Literacy Association, 2018). Diane succinctly describes the essential features of *Standards 2017*. Given that these standards serve as a framework for the contents of each chapter, this foreword provides critical background information for readers.
- Guiding questions that highlight the major concepts of the chapter and serve as an advanced organizer to promote thinking and understanding.
- A chapter about the role of the reading/literacy specialist and another on the role of the literacy coach, aligning contemporary research on the nuanced differences between these specialized roles.
- A focus on literacy leadership spanning a range of grades (PreK–12), with specific chapters for each of the following levels: PreK/primary, elementary/intermediate, and middle/high school literacy programs.
- Case examples that provide specific real-life scenarios and stories to assist readers in understanding the key concepts of a chapter. These case examples can also be used for small-group discussions.
- Specific questions in each chapter, labeled "Think about This,"

which support readers in reflecting on the case examples and making connections to their own situations or contexts.

- Vignettes written by literacy leaders who function in a variety of roles follow many of the chapters. These literacy leaders describe the ways in which they fulfill their roles and the challenges they face. Many discuss their beliefs and values that serve as a foundation for their work as literacy leaders. These vignettes bring to life and support the content presented in chapters and provide opportunities for reflective thinking by individual or groups of readers.
- Engagement activities follow each chapter; often they include an activity related to the case example or vignette presented in that chapter. We also include, when appropriate, an activity that relates to *Standards 2017*, through which readers can investigate further the content of the standards and the ways in which they relate to specific aspects of this book.

For us, this book is the culmination of years of experience, as both of us served in schools as teachers and reading specialists, and then as teacher educators working with teachers, administrators, and literacy professionals to create learning environments that promote high-level student thinking and learning. It has been rewarding to collaborate with chapter authors who, through their writing, have brought to life the themes that permeate this book. We also appreciated the opportunity to expand our own understanding of *Standards 2017* and the ways in which it provides a powerful tool for influencing literacy teaching and learning. The premise of this book, which serves as its framework, is that educators must take collective responsibility for improving student learning in a school and that such responsibility can be enhanced through shared leadership, collaboration, and the development of each school as a place of learning for students and teachers.

REFERENCES

Fullan, M. (2001). *The new meaning of educational change* (3rd ed.). New York: Teachers College Press.

International Literacy Association. (2018). *Standards for the preparation of literacy professionals 2017*. Newark, DE: Author.

Wenner, J. A., & Campbell, T. (2017). The theoretical and empirical basis of teacher leadership. *Review of Educational Research*, 87(1), 134–171.

Contents

15. Culturally Responsive Literacy Instruction   304
Doris Walker-Dalhouse and Victoria J. Risko

VIGNETTE. Literacy Leadership in Action   323
Valerie Kinloch

16. Academic Language and Literacy Development for English Learners   325
MaryEllen Vogt

VIGNETTE. Literacy Leadership in Action   344
Celia Banks

17. Developing Effective Home–School Literacy Partnerships   346
Jeanne R. Paratore, Lilly M. Steiner, and Susan M. Dougherty

VIGNETTE. Literacy Leadership in Action   364
Shawna Zervos

18. Enactment of Reading Policy: Leading and Learning   366
for Literacy and Equity
Sarah L. Woulfin and Britney Jones

PART I

ROLES

This section focuses on the leadership roles of key professionals who have a great impact on the development, implementation, and evaluation of literacy programs. In Chapter 1, Bean unpacks an overarching theme of this edition—the importance of collaborative culture—by defining the who and what of leadership in today's schools. Bean summarizes critical research findings and outlines research-based implications for school improvement. In this chapter, Bean also elaborates on how Standards 2017 provide a framework for the content of this book's chapters. In Chapter 2, Swan Dagen, Morewood, and Glance discuss the critical roles and responsibilities that classroom teachers can assume as informal and formal leaders. They also identify characteristics of teacher leaders and conclude by exploring conditions and outcomes of teacher leadership. In Chapter 3, Bean, after describing the evolution of the role of the reading/literacy specialist, focuses on a discussion of the challenges faced by these professionals and possible solutions for addressing these challenges. Bean also presents a framework for thinking about the multiple roles of specialized literacy professionals. In Chapter 4, Ippolito and Lieberman describe the role of the literacy coach, discussing ways in which coaches might organize their time more efficiently and collaborate with others to develop an effective literacy program. They also describe key mindsets that are important for those serving in this role. In Chapter 5, Helman and Pekel describe ways in which principals can support literacy environments that lead to collective educator efficacy and rigorous student learning. They discuss the importance of principals as leaders who facilitate shared and collective leadership. The final chapter in this section (Chapter 6) provides a synthesis of how various professionals, working together, can develop an effective literacy program in schools. Through a rich narrative, Walpole and Vitale weave together the ways in which collective efficacy can be developed in schools.

CHAPTER 1

Literacy Leadership in a Culture of Collaboration

Rita M. Bean

GUIDING QUESTIONS

➥ Why is leadership so essential in schools, and how is it defined and described in this chapter?

➥ What are the issues faced by literacy leaders in their school improvement efforts (PreK–12)?

➥ How does the framework for leadership described in this chapter align with the *Standards for the Preparation of Literacy Professionals 2017* (International Literacy Association [ILA], 2018b)?

➥ In what ways does literacy leadership serve as a key to school improvement?

➥ What implications does effective literacy leadership in schools have for literacy leaders?

During the past several decades, much has been written about the need for changes in how schools (PreK–12) function; phrases such as *school reform, school restructuring, school improvement,* and *school transformation* are used to describe such initiatives. The demand for such change comes from the recognition that too few schools provide a high-quality education for all the students they serve. There is a need to develop more schools that provide a first-class education for all students, an education that prepares students to be informed citizens who can successfully compete in the globalized, highly technological world in which they live. Many

researchers identify school leadership as a critical feature of school success. Much emphasis has been given to the importance of school principals,
who in their role as leaders are agents of change and major contributors
to school success, especially as measured by student achievement (Bryk,
Sebring, Allensworth, Luppescu, & Easton, 2010; Leithwood, Seashore
Louis, Anderson, & Wahlstrom, 2004; Marzano, Waters, & McNulty,
2005; Supovitz, Sirinides, & May, 2010). At the same time, as highlighted
in this book, others too can serve as leaders in the school (e.g., classroom
teachers, reading/literacy specialists, literacy coaches, special educators) to
improve educational programs for students.

In the case example that follows, I describe the dilemma faced by
Brenda, a reading/literacy specialist in an urban school whose position
changed from working with students experiencing reading difficulties to
one of supporting teachers in their efforts to improve literacy instruction
and student learning.

CASE EXAMPLE ·

THINK ABOUT THIS

1. What major challenges do you think Brenda will face as she changes her
   role and responsibilities?
2. What skill sets does Brenda need to be successful in her new role?

Brenda had served as the reading specialist (K–5) in an urban elementary
school for 6 years. She worked both in the classroom and in a pullout setting with students who had been identified as needing additional reading
support. It had taken Brenda several years to develop a program that, in her
view, was effective. Teachers were comfortable with her being in the classroom, and they had established a routine in which Brenda worked with
specific students during the time that other students were working independently in centers or with the classroom teacher. Brenda felt as though
she knew the students and teachers; moreover, she felt that her students
were making steady progress. However, district administrators, concerned
about the lack of overall student progress, had applied for and received
funding from a state grant that had several stipulations. First, the district
had to agree that it would rethink its approach to reading instruction.
There would be more emphasis on writing and more focus on disciplinary literacy, especially in grades 3–5. Second, each school would employ a
literacy coach to work with teachers to improve overall classroom instruction. Given Brenda's experience and her excellent rapport with teachers, she
was asked to assume this role. After her meeting with the principal and the
assistant superintendent (who told Brenda that they saw great promise in
this new initiative, especially with her involvement), Brenda begin to think

about what this change in role meant. She sighed: What would the teachers who were her colleagues think about this? What did she think about this? What did it mean for her current students? How would she begin? And did she have the knowledge, leadership, communication, and interpersonal skills to effectively handle these new responsibilities?

· · · · · · · · · · · · ·

Many reading/literacy specialists, teachers, principals, or other specialized personnel have faced similar dilemmas as expectations change for how they work to promote student learning. Teachers are expected to work with grade-level or subject-area teams, to discuss their teaching with peers, or to participate as members of professional learning communities to address curricular or instructional challenges. Such expectations are the norm for literacy leaders because literacy cuts across all subject lines and provides a foundation for student learning.

In this chapter, I describe the notion of leadership as advocated in the chapters of this book and provide a summary of the research and literature that undergirds that description. I then focus on literacy leadership, describing some specific aspects of literacy instruction that require the attention of school leaders. I also discuss the *Standards for the Preparation of Literacy Professionals 2017* (ILA, 2018b) and the ways in which the standards provide a foundation for the content in this book. From there, I focus on the major theme of this chapter, outlining the research on the ways that literacy leadership serves as a key to school improvement. Finally, I highlight the practical implications of the findings from research and literature about effective literacy leadership.

WHAT IS LEADERSHIP?

As I reflected on my experiences as a teacher and reading specialist, I realized that I was fortunate to work in a district that believed teachers should be involved in setting goals for the various curricular areas and in making decisions about curriculum and instruction. I served as chair of the Elementary Reading Committee and with representatives from each grade level, developed a proposal for an elementary reading curriculum that was submitted to administration for their review. At the same time, other teacher colleagues were doing the same in the areas of math, social studies, and science. The chairs of these committees also met with principals of the four elementary schools and the assistant superintendent to discuss the relationships between what each team was proposing and the more general goals for the school. In other words, we were leaders in our schools, working in what today might be called a "professional learning community." Although I didn't realize it at the time, those experiences were crucial in helping me learn how to work collegially while also building my understanding of what an effective reading program is, how it relates to the other academic subjects, and the need for helping teachers integrate all they know and do into meaningful learning experiences for students. Fast forward! We now have strong evidence that those schools in which leadership among professional personnel is encouraged and promoted, in which teachers collectively have a voice in what and how they teach, is an important ingredient in increasing student learning (Bryk et al., 2010; DuFour, 2016; Leana & Pil, 2017; Little, 2003; Seashore Louis, Leithwood, Wahlstrom, & Anderson, 2010; Marzano, 2003).

So, on to the question of leadership. Offering a definition of leadership is not easy because of the many ways that leadership is defined within different educational contexts. Some view leadership as a function of *position* (e.g., superintendent, principal); individuals find themselves in positions of power that give them the authority to be leaders. Others describe leadership in terms of *traits*: leaders are flexible, fair, and passionate about what they do; in other words, "leaders are born, not made." Some describe a *style* of leadership (democratic, laissez-faire, authoritative). However, leadership in this book is all of these and more. The research community, including contributing authors of this book, acknowledge that there are many leaders in schools, both formal and informal, who lead by *influence,* that is, they encourage, nudge, and persuade colleagues in ways that effect change in practices and policies.

The specific definition of leadership in this book is similar to that proposed by Kaser, Mundry, Stiles, and Loucks-Horsley (2002): "an individual's ability to work with others to accomplish some agreed-upon end" (p. 2); to do this effectively, leaders must create positive environments in which their members thrive (Murphy & Louis, 2018). Leithwood and Jantzi (2008) describe four key categories of leadership activities or functions: (1) setting goals or directions for the school; (2) developing people, that is, providing professional learning experiences that help individuals grow as professionals; (3) redesigning the organization, that is, changing the school structure so that it better facilitates the work of teachers and promotes student learning; and (4) managing the instructional program, that is, using data to monitor student and school progress, establishing routines and procedures that facilitate efforts to achieve school goals, and selecting approaches that meet the specific needs of students.

Leadership, as described throughout this book, refers to more than traits, style, or position; rather, it describes a set of actions. Teachers serve as leaders: They mentor colleagues; facilitate the work of tutors, volunteers, or student teachers; identify student needs and possible instructional strategies for addressing those needs; work with parents; and so on. Reading/literacy specialists or literacy coaches, although they have a position of leadership, generally don't have the positional authority to require teachers to make changes; rather, they serve as leaders by providing insights and resources, and influencing others to consider ideas for change (Bean, 2010a; Bean, Dagen, Ippolito, & Kern, 2018; Bean et al., 2015; Bean & Lillenstein, 2012; Coburn & Woulfin, 2012). They also lead because of the specific knowledge or expertise that they share with teachers, often working closely with the principal as they consider ideas for improving literacy instruction. Other professionals, such as special educators, psychologists, guidance counselors, and speech and language teachers, given their areas of expertise, provide important information about how to address various challenges (e.g., what are some additional ways of promoting positive behavior in students?) And principals, in addition to their role as designated leader, facilitate the leadership capacity of others by creating conditions that support leadership behavior. Indeed, principals serve as important drivers of leadership by designing structures that provide opportunities for collaboration and collective decision making (Goddard, Goddard, Kim, & Miller, 2015).

As Lambert (1998) describes it, "leadership is about learning together, and constructing meaning and knowledge collectively and collaboratively" (p. 5). Such a definition highlights the importance of building capacity in schools and recognizes the value of multiple leaders in schools, some with positional authority and others without. In schools with such a leadership model, there is the recognition that adults as well as students are learners. Moreover, leadership will not look the same across individuals or schools: some leaders will work with other teachers to improve instruction (i.e., coaching); others will chair committees or serve on task forces; all will lead in their daily work with others by raising questions, identifying possible solutions to problems, suggesting alternatives, and so on.

The concept of leadership reflected in this book is based in a perspective of distributed leadership (Spillane, 2005, 2015; Spillane, Halverson, & Diamond, 2001). In such a perspective, *leadership* does not refer to the actions of an individual, but what various individuals know and do together—in other words, their interactions with each other. A distributed perspective defines leadership as a "system of practice comprised of a collection of interacting components: leaders, followers, and situation" (Spillane, 2005, p. 150). As such, one must understand not only the actions of various individuals but also the interactions among them. For example, in one school, the principal, with little literacy background, might rely greatly on the expertise of the literacy coach in making decisions about instructional approaches, grouping, and scheduling. In another school, the principal, with a master's degree in reading, might work more collaboratively with the literacy coach or reading/literacy specialist, taking on much more responsibility for decision making about instructional approaches, and so on. In both cases, leadership is shared, but the way in which that leadership is distributed is different. In other words, the issue is not that leadership is distributed, but rather *how* it is distributed. This perspective of distributed leadership emphasizes "reciprocal interdependency" (Spillane, 2005, p. 146): that is, one in which leaders, whether formal or informal, are influenced by and influence each other. *Leadership* then "is not simply a function of an individual leader's ability, skill, charisma, and cognition" (Spillane et al., 2001, p. 27).

In a landmark book about leadership in business organizations, *Good to Great* (Collins, 2001), in which companies were identified as moving from "good to great," leadership was noted as an important contributing factor. Unexpectedly, however, these leaders, rather than being charismatic and autocratic, were humble, determined, and modest. They recognized they needed the support and wisdom of those around them. Their leadership emphasized building the leadership capacity of all employees in the organization. Collins's findings have implications for school leaders as they support the notion of *distributed leadership* as a means of improving the organization, teacher practices, and ultimately, the desired outcome: student learning.

Stoelinga (2008) presents examples of three schools to illustrate the relationships among principals, more formal teacher leaders such as literacy coaches or coordinators, and teachers who serve as informal leaders in the school. The findings illustrate the impact of the informal relationships in an organization on the ways in which a formal teacher leader (i.e., the literacy coordinator) enacted his or her role. For example, in one school, where teachers valued autonomy, there were several strong, informal teacher leaders who were resistant to the literacy coordinator in the role of mentor or coach. This literacy coordinator, with only 4 years of teaching experience, had little influence on instructional practices in classrooms. In another school, the literacy coordinator had a well-defined and focused role for mentoring teachers; teachers identified this coordinator, the principal, and the bilingual coordinator as important resources about literacy. In the third school, the literacy coach, the principal, and a sixth-grade teacher were all seen as key resources. However, the literacy coordinator's role was to tie together the many different programs in the school, and this professional spent little time mentoring individuals. These three cases illustrate the different ways in which informal networks can influence the work of colleagues in schools. Stoelinga concludes that informal teacher leaders in schools can have a powerful influence on school improvement or reform in a positive or negative way. Moreover, her work provides a clear illustration about the complexity of leadership and its influence on school change or reform. In discussing or studying leadership, attention must be given to the impact of factors such as school organization or culture, and the experiences, beliefs, and values of school personnel.

Effective school leadership is both forceful and enabling (Kaplan & Kaiser, 2008). Leaders are forceful in that they take stands, set high expectations, stay focused on the goals, and make the tough calls. At the same time, leadership that is enabling empowers people by delegating authority and responsibility, providing support, seeking input, and showing appreciation for the work that has been accomplished. The key is knowing when one form of leadership rather than another might be more beneficial to the growth of the organization.

LITERACY LEADERSHIP IS ESSENTIAL

Although much of the previous discussion addresses leadership in general, this book focuses on *literacy* leadership. Given that literacy—or one's ability to read, write, think, and communicate—is a critical key to future success, all school personnel need to understand how they can support students' literacy learning. In fact, in many schools, the ultimate test of school effectiveness, agree or disagree, is often the school's ability to improve students' performance on one or more standardized test of reading. There are many different topics and issues facing literacy educators in today's schools. For example, respondents to the "What's Hot in Literacy 2018 Report" (ILA, 2018c) survey highlighted as hot or important, topics such as early literacy, community involvement, and differentiation. Three other topics that are of importance in schools today include the emphases on high-level digital literacies, diversity, and equity. All of these topics are addressed in more depth in other chapters in this book. Literacy leaders, to be effective, need to have a vast amount of knowledge and understanding of what is important about literacy, to set into motion actions that improve literacy instruction. Below I highlight some key points about three of these essential topics.

High-Level, Rigorous Expectations for Students

Most states have developed a set of standards regarding students' ability to read, write, and think creatively and critically, and future-ready expectations that students will be capable of succeeding in their workplace and as educated citizens. Many of these state standards are adaptations of the Common Core Standards for English Language Arts and Literacy in History/Social Studies, Science and Technical Subjects (National Governors Association Center for Best Practices & Council of Chief State School Officers, 2010). What is significant is that these recent state standards address literacy not only in the English language arts, but also in the social and natural sciences. In other words, teachers in the academic disciplines have responsibility for providing students with supported experiences and opportunities to read, write, talk, and think deeply in service of content learning. This approach allows students to experience disciplinary literacy as a means of learning content. In order to accomplish the goals of these rigorous standards set by states, schools need to develop a comprehensive, coherent literacy program for a full range of learners, including gifted students, learners who need Title I or compensatory services, and learners requiring special education support.

Digital Literacies

As stated in *Standards 2017,* "teaching and learning must guide learners toward becoming fully literate within a complex, globally connected digital world that revolves around digital devices and tools, use of social media, and digital interactions" (ILA, 2018b, p 16). Teachers must learn new ways of using technology, its limitations, and its benefits. At the same time, students, because of their access to and familiarity with technology, often need instructional support as to how to judge the merit of various resources, and how to use various digital tools appropriately and effectively.

Diversity and Equity

The population in schools and society is changing and requires schools to acknowledge, respect, and value all forms of diversity. Instruction should be relevant and sensitive to students' instructional needs and "embrace their diversity as an asset" (ILA, 2018a, p. 15). Creating environments in which diversity is valued and appreciated requires teachers to reflect on their own beliefs and biases and to gain an understanding of the value of other groups' experiences, beliefs, and identities (ILA, 2018b). Another aspect of this focus on diversity is the emphasis on equity, or providing strategies that enable all learners to be successful.[1]

THE IMPORTANCE OF STANDARDS FOR PREPARING LITERACY PROFESSIONALS

The issues described above have created challenges for teachers, specialized literacy professionals, and administrators, and have stimulated the need for new ways of functioning in order to provide key educational experiences for all students in today's schools. As one of my colleagues said, "Business as usual must give way to unusual business!" *Standards 2017* provides a roadmap for those preparing literacy professionals, for states that have responsibilities for developing standards for teachers and for students, for districts seeking to employ literacy professionals who have the expertise to teach effectively in today's schools, and for literacy professionals themselves. In this book, we capitalize on *Standards 2017,* using the revised standards as a framework that underlies the content in all chapters.

---

[1]See the ILA Literacy Glossary (2018a) at *www.literacyworldwide.org/get-resources/ literacy-glossary.*

LITERACY LEADERSHIP AS A KEY TO SCHOOL IMPROVEMENT

In the following section, I describe and summarize key research studies that address both school and literacy leadership. These findings provide literacy professionals with an understanding of ways they can be involved in developing a climate and implementing learning activities that are conducive to effective teaching and learning. I specifically address three categories of findings: (1) A shared perspective of distributed leadership is a factor in school improvement; (2) colleagues learn from each other; and (3) distributed leadership occurs in a culture of collaboration.

Distributed Leadership Is a Key Factor in School Improvement

Previously, I cited the work of Bryk et al. (2010) that describes the cumulative body of research conducted over a 10-year period in the Chicago public schools. Bryk and colleagues collected and analyzed information from many schools, including some that had substantially improved and others that had not. They identified several critical elements for school success, each of which is essential for student learning. Leadership, however, was identified as the "driving subsystem for improvement" (p. 61). Although they emphasized the importance of the principal as leader, they were clear that the principal cannot transform a school alone, and that there is a need to bring all partners—teachers, parents, and community members—into leadership roles as a means of building school capacity. They highlighted the importance of school leaders in engaging and providing teachers with opportunities for them to lead as well. In other words, they acknowledged the importance of promoting the growth of a professional community that is guided by a shared vision and a coherent strategic plan. Bryk et al. use as their metaphor of school improvement, "baking a cake," to suggest that, just like baking a cake, all the critical ingredients (flour, sugar, eggs, etc.) are important; if any is missing, the result suffers. The five core school-related ingredients include, first, *instructional guidance,* which refers to curricular alignment; in other words, there must be a coordinated set of goals, both vertically (across grades) and horizontally (within a grade). Second, efforts to build *professional capacity* are critical; teachers must be knowledgeable about the subjects they teach, and schools must provide the professional learning activities essential for ongoing teacher learning. Such professional learning includes building a community where teachers interact about their instructional practices and seek solutions for problems that they face. Third, *parent–community–school ties* are essential for school success. Fourth, the *school learning climate* must be one in which students feel safe, experience a sense of order, and value learning. The fifth essential core and the catalyst for school change is *school leadership*—and, according to Bryk and colleagues, some form of distributed leadership is key.

Seashore Louis et al. (2010) conducted an extensive 6-year study of 180 schools in 43 districts across nine states to investigate the influence of school, district, and state leadership on student learning. They found that school leadership was second only to classroom instruction as an influence on student learning and that many different people exercised formal or informal leadership in schools and districts. Specifically, they found that student achievement was linked to what they call *collective leadership*, in which educators, parents, and others have a voice in making school decisions. They found that such leadership can take many forms, determined by the specific personnel and/or situation in the school. They found that the principal not only played an important role as instructional leader but also established conditions that promoted effective instruction. Several key implications include the importance of focusing on specific goals and expectations for student learning by providing professional learning experiences for teachers and creating a structure in which teachers collaborate. They also indicated that less is known about leadership at the secondary level, but that most frequently, department chairs, or those who have special expertise in various content areas, provide important leadership for other teachers. They highlighted the fact that the principal in such a situation cannot possess the knowledge necessary to be an instructional leader for all subject areas, but again must set the conditions for collective leadership among teachers.

Based on principals' perspectives, Bean et al. (2018) compared ways in which specialized literacy professionals functioned at the elementary and secondary levels. They found that there were few differences in the roles of reading/literacy specialists and coaches across these levels, with both groups having specific leadership responsibilities. Both role groups worked extensively to support teachers in understanding how to use student assessment data. Moreover, principals indicated that these specialized literacy professionals greatly influenced the schoolwide literacy program (e.g., teaching practices and student literacy learning).

Colleagues Learn from Each Other

Supovitz (2010) investigated the influence of both principals and peers on teachers' instructional practice and student learning. Survey data to address questions about principal and teacher leadership were collected from teachers in a midsized urban district with many schools. Supovitz et al. (2010) found that principal leadership was critical. These authors "found empirical evidence that principal leadership influences student learning indirectly through teachers' instructional practices" (p. 45). Supovitz et al. highlighted the fact that principals had the greatest impact on learning when they fostered a climate of instructional collaboration and communication; in other words, principals "work through other leaders in schools to influence what goes on inside of classrooms" (p. 47). Also, they found that teacher peers influenced each other's classroom practices through collaborative discussions about teaching and learning, peer coaching, and instructional advice networks. The influence of both principals and peers was also significantly related to students' literacy learning.

The importance of peer interaction is also supported by Leana (2011), who reported that teachers tended to seek advice from their peers to a greater extent than they did from district experts or principals. Such peer interactions were based on a sense of trust among teachers and a focus on substantive issues related to teaching.

One of the approaches to professional learning that provides opportunities for collegial learning is that of professional learning communities (PLCs). Vescio, Ross, and Adams (2008) provided a review of 11 studies that contain empirical evidence about the impact of PLCs on both teaching practice and student learning—and more specifically, on literacy learning. Their findings include the following: (1) Teachers in these studies appreciated and valued PLCs, (2) PLCs had an impact on practice as "teachers became more student centered" (p. 88), and (3) there were improvements in student achievement. According to DuFour (2016, p. 8), there are three elements in effective PLCs: (1) a focus on learning (i.e., all students are expected to achieve at high levels), (2) collaboration in which all educators take collective responsibility for student success, and (3) an emphasis on evidence or results.

Distributed Leadership Occurs in a Culture of Collaboration

Distributed leadership cannot occur in isolation; rather, it requires "creating a common culture, a set of values, symbols, and rituals" (Elmore, 2000, p. 15). Elmore discusses Rosenheltz's (1989) work in which she describes two types of cultures: collegial or teacher autonomy. In a collegial culture, teachers have an agreed-upon and coherent set of goals. In cultures where there is teacher autonomy, the focus is on individual goals, and teachers are accountable to no one; rather, they work in isolation. Working in isolation rather than in collaborative teams "has consistently been cited as a primary obstacle to improving achievement" (DuFour, 2016, p. 9).

Leana and Pil (2006), in their study of schools in a large urban district, found that the interactions and relationships among teachers and administrators, which formed what they termed *social capital,* was essential for improved student achievement. Some of the dimensions of social capital included a shared vision and common goals for student outcomes, a sense of responsibility for all students, high expectations for student learning, and a belief that all students can learn. In their later work, Pil and Leana (2009) found that human capital—teachers' experience and task-specific strengths (e.g., knowledge of teaching math)—were important. At the same time, social capital served as a conduit for helping less able teachers gain greater insights and benefit from the support of their higher-performing colleagues (Pil & Leana, 2009; Leana & Pil, 2014). However, Leana (2011) concluded that an emphasis on human capital alone will not yield the changes needed to improve schools, especially those in urban districts. She suggested that there is "an undervaluing of the benefits that come from teacher collaborations" (p. 30) and that more opportunities should be provided for teachers to talk with each other about substantive issues related to their teaching and student learning.

Creating a collaborative culture is not easy; it requires excellent leadership on the part of the principal and a recognition that the difficult challenges in schools today require a new style of leadership. Heifetz and Laurie (2002) identified several principles related to this new style of leadership:

- View the situation from a distance or, as they state it, "get on the balcony and off the dance floor" (p. 1). In other words, try to see the situation from a different perspective, or step away from the conflict or controversy, thinking about it from an outsider's point of view. What are the beliefs or thoughts of students, parents, or perhaps a small group of teachers that have been identified as resistant or negative?
- Identify the specific challenges and the conflicts that might exist about values and norms.
- Regulate distress by maintaining a balance between pressure and support. Consider the demands that are placed on teachers (i.e., multiple and perhaps conflicting initiatives, overemphasis on test scores). Be deliberate in setting the rate of change. Aim high, but at the same time provide the support needed to achieve the established goals.
- Value the diversity and different perspectives of colleagues. There will always be differences among individuals; effective leaders recognize and value those differences. Moreover, individuals differ in the time they need to adjust to change.
- Instill a sense of self-confidence in the staff members so that they can address challenges. Individuals within the school have different areas of expertise and perspectives to bring to the table.
- Protect those who lead from those who might be negative. Encourage a sense of risk taking among the staff members so that they feel comfortable raising issues.

Vescio et al. (2008), in their study, found that PLCs had an impact on the culture in schools because of the collaboration among teachers, the focus on student learning, and the increased decision-making opportunities for teachers—what Vescio et al. call "teacher authority" (p. 88). Decisions were made based on student data and teachers' knowledge of effective instructional approaches and materials. Likewise, Saunders, Goldenberg, and Gallimore (2009), who were interested in PLCs, conducted a 5-year quasi-experimental study comparing achievement gains among nine experimental and six matched elementary schools. In the experimental schools, grade-level teams were given time to meet, support for their efforts, and explicit protocols that focused on how to meet students' needs. The authors concluded that teachers need to be provided with structural opportunities and skills to focus on improving their practices. They also highlighted the fact that just providing time and support is not enough; collaborative work must take place under the right conditions with appropriate leadership.

In 2012, I had an opportunity to observe in five elementary schools in which I saw distributed leadership in action (Bean & Lillenstein, 2012). Each of these schools was implementing response to instruction and intervention (RTII), which required providing effective core, supplemental, and intensive instruction for students. The purposes of the study were to get a more in-depth picture of how personnel in the school, including specialized literacy professionals, worked together and what skill sets they needed to function effectively. One of the key findings was that these schools functioned effectively because of shared leadership and collaboration among staff. All personnel were involved and represented in instructional goal setting and decision making. Although principals served as central figures for promoting a positive school climate and establishing norms for collaboration, district leadership was important, both in helping to establish goals and to provide support. Moreover, in each school, there was a leadership team that included reading/literacy specialists or coaches, special educators, the principal, and often the psychologist or a teacher of English learners (ELs). This team reviewed schoolwide data, discussed successes and challenges, and made suggestions about ways to support teachers in their efforts to improve student learning. Each school also had teacher groups, generally grade-level teams, which met to discuss student learning and how they might modify instruction to meet student needs. At times, reading/ literacy specialists or coaches met with these teams to facilitate the meetings or simply to gain a better understanding of how they, the specialists, might better support teachers' work. Finally, individual teachers also served as literacy leaders in the schools. Teachers with formal roles—that is, reading/literacy specialists and coaches, special educators, speech and language teachers—often met with classroom teachers on an individual basis to problem-solve or provide guidance. Likewise, classroom teachers with experience or special expertise often functioned informally and were sought out by their peers as a source of information or reassurance. In other words, the culture in these schools was such that collaboration was the norm. The social networking that went on was elaborate; that is, there were opportunities for multiple relationships and interactions. Figure 1.1 provides a graphic of the many relationships evident in these schools.

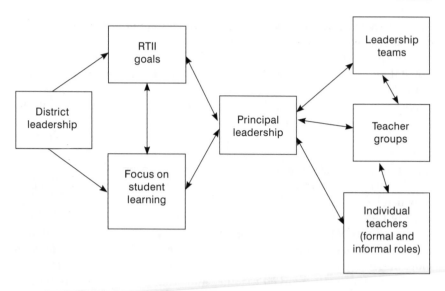

FIGURE 1.1. Shared leadership in RTII schools. Adapted from Bean (2010b) with permission of the Pennsylvania Department of Education.

Bean's findings are similar to those of Leithwood and Jantzi (2008), who in their study addressed several questions about the importance of leadership. They were interested in the extent to which district leadership and district organizational conditions influenced school leader efficacy. They found that the effects of district leadership were largely indirect; that is, district leaders created conditions that were important for enhancing and supporting the work of school leaders. They also found that building a collaborative culture was important. Likewise, Camburn, Kimball, and Lowenhaupt (2008), in a case study of a literacy coach initiative, identified the ways that district guidelines and support can serve to either promote or dilute the potential effectiveness of such an initiative. They highlighted the need for both district guidance and acknowledgment of the specific needs of individual schools. In other words, district guidelines must allow for the individual differences and needs of specific schools in the district.

IMPLICATIONS

The evidence that a culture in which there is distributed and collective leadership contributes to improved teaching practices and student learning is strong. But what does it look like in action? Below I highlight implications of the research that provide some specific conditions and actions for literacy leadership in schools.

- Principals have a key role in establishing conditions for success and involving others in both formal and informal leadership activities. Principals serve as key leaders, not just by facilitating collaboration in schools, but also by developing external relationships with community and families to support teachers' efforts (Dufour & Mattos, 2013; Leana, 2011).

- If teacher leaders (formal and informal) are to be successful, the environment must be one that encourages and promotes teacher leadership; these leaders must be provided with learning opportunities that help them understand what leadership means, how they can develop leadership skills, and how to function as leaders.

- All literacy leaders can influence the behaviors, thoughts, and feelings of those with whom they work if they listen and learn from all those in their schools (e.g., students, paraprofessionals, families, other staff, as well as teachers and others). The time spent in active listening can help leaders develop a better sense of what individuals and groups value, how they view the organization (especially as it relates to literacy instruction), and how it might improve. Such leadership behavior will generate a sense of ownership in those whose advice is being sought (i.e., "My ideas matter").

- Literacy leaders should facilitate the leadership abilities of others. This requires having a solid understanding of how adults learn, accept that they will differ in their responses to various school change initiatives, and provide support as they move forward from where they are to an acceptance and ownership of new ideas.

- Literacy leaders must also possess an in-depth knowledge of literacy that helps them think about goals for the program, appropriate materials and resources, and ways to evaluate the effectiveness of the program. They need to consider what kinds of professional learning experiences might be necessary to support teacher growth.

- Given the importance of literacy instruction across all subject areas, many literacy leaders are needed to improve literacy instruction. Literacy coaches or specialists, for example, can provide important support to principals in analyzing data to inform instruction. At the secondary level, chairs of academic departments as well as coaches or specialists may be responsible for guiding the work of teachers in the academic disciplines. Literacy leadership that enables a school to set a focused, coherent vision and agenda for literacy instruction is critical for school success regardless of level or subject.

- Effective literacy leaders understand that they are there to support the work of others in the school. They care less about control or praise, and are quick to solicit and acknowledge the contributions of others. They concur with the words of Lao-Tzu (n.d.): "A leader is best when people barely know he exists; when his work is done, his aim fulfilled, they will say: we did it ourselves."

In sum, effective literacy leadership can be promoted through the development of a culture in which teachers and administrators work collectively to set goals and establish a vision and common expectations for students. Such a culture can promote the development of staff members as decision makers, professionals, and leaders. Jennifer Allen, in her book *Becoming a Literacy Leader* (2016), describes her work as a literacy specialist, highlighting the importance of what she calls *layered leadership*, and her role at the district, school, and classroom levels. She also discusses collaboration with others as a means of developing shared understanding, and the need for school faculty to strive to achieve common goals, or what she calls, "rowing in the same direction" (p. 6).

CONCLUSION

The message is clear! There is evidence that student learning is enhanced when leadership is shared. Such leadership facilitates the setting of common goals and a shared vision for improved student learning. Such leadership is based on the belief that all students can learn and that as educators we have a responsibility to facilitate students' learning. Such leadership transforms schools so that they are places in which collaboration, interdependence, and professionalism exist. This is the message that is conveyed throughout this book across a variety of contexts (e.g., special education programs, Title 1 programs, preschools) and content-specific literacy foci.

ENGAGEMENT ACTIVITIES

1. Think about the scenario of Brenda described in this chapter and the specific interpersonal, communication, and leadership skills that Brenda might need to be successful in her position. Then individually analyze your own experiences and education: How ready would you be to assume such a position? What skills and abilities would you bring to the position? What types of professional learning experiences would you need or want?

2. Interview a principal at a school and obtain his or her responses to the following questions. Then ask a teacher and a reading/literacy specialist or literacy coach

to respond to the same questions. Finally, analyze the results to determine similarities or differences in responses across the role groups.

   a. In what ways are teachers, literacy coaches, and reading/literacy specialists involved in setting goals for the schools? (Question for teacher/literacy coach or reading/literacy specialist: In what ways have you been involved in setting goals for the school?)

   b. In what ways are teachers, literacy coaches, and reading/literacy specialists involved in making decisions about curriculum and instruction? Professional learning experiences?

   c. What structures are in place that enable teachers and others to participate in shared decision making (common planning time, etc.)?

3. Think about the four categories (goals, people, organizations, programs) of leadership functions described by Leithwood and Janzi on page 6 of this chapter. In what ways are you, in your current role, involved in any of these functions?

Example: Literacy coach	
Function	Identify your role.
Setting goals	As facilitator of a grade-level team, I help teachers set goals for the year for their students. I also work with the leadership team to set schoolwide goals. This year, we are focusing on improving vocabulary instruction in all subjects.

ANNOTATED RESOURCES

Bean, R. M., Dagen, A. S., Ippolito, J., & Kern, D. (2018). Principals' perspectives on the roles of specialized literacy professionals. *Elementary School Journal, 119*(2), 327–350.

The authors describe, as perceived by principals, ways in which specialized literacy professionals function in PreK–12 schools. They also discuss the views of principals about the influence of these professionals on teaching and learning in the school's literacy program.

Ippolito, J., & Bean, R. M. (2018). *Unpacking coaching mindsets: Collaboration between principals and coaches.* West Palm Beach, FL: Learning Sciences International.

The authors provide ideas for how principals and literacy professionals can work collaboratively as leaders to improve literacy instruction. They describe essential concepts of the leadership role for both principals and literacy professionals.

Leana, C. R. (2011, Fall). The missing link in school reform. *Stanford Social Innovation Review,* pp. 30–35. Retrieved from *https://ssir.org/articles/entry/the_missing_link_in_school_reform.*

Leana discusses her research on social capital and its contribution to student learning. She suggests that both human and social capital are keys to school improvement.

REFERENCES

Allen, J. (2016). *Becoming a literacy leader* (2nd ed.). Portland, ME: Stenhouse.

Bean, R. M. (2010a). *The reading specialist: Leadership in the classroom, school, and community* (2nd ed.). New York: Guilford Press.

Bean, R. M. (2010b). Making response to instruction and intervention (RTII) work: What school personnel need to know and be able to do. Retrieved March 30, 2018, from *www.exeter.k12.pa.us/cms/lib/PA01000700/Centricity/Domain/31/PA%20State%20Resource%20Materials/RtII%20Role%20and%20Function. pdf.*

Bean, R. M., Dagen, A. S., Ippolito, J., & Kern, D. (2018). Principals' perspectives on the roles of specialized literacy professionals. *Elementary School Journal, 119*(2), 327–350.

Bean, R. M., Kern, D., Goatley, V., Ortlieb, E., Shettel, J., Calo, K., et al. (2015). Specialized literacy professionals as literacy leaders: Results of a national survey. *Literacy Research and Instruction, 54*(2), 83–114.

Bean, R. M., & Lillenstein, J. (2012). Response to intervention and the changing roles of schoolwide personnel. *The Reading Teacher, 65*(7), 491–501.

Bryk, A. S., Sebring, P. B., Allensworth, E., Luppescu, S., & Easton, J. Q. (2010). *Organizing schools for improvement: Lessons from Chicago.* Chicago: University of Chicago Press.

Camburn, E. M., Kimball, S. M., & Lowenhaupt, R. (2008). Going to scale with teacher leadership: Lessons learned from a districtwide literacy coach initiative. In M. M. Mangin & S. R. Stoelinga (Eds.), *Effective teacher leadership: Using research to inform and reform* (pp. 120–143). New York: Teachers College Press.

Coburn, C. E., & Woulfin, S. L. (2012). Reading coaches and the relationship between policy and practice. *Reading Research Quarterly, 47*(1), 5–30.

Collins, J. (2001). *Good to great: Why some companies make the leap . . . and others don't.* New York: HarperCollins.

DuFour, R. (2016). *ESSA: An opportunity for American education* (White paper). Bloomington, IN: Solution Tree. Retrieved from *https://mkt.solution-tree.com/ opportunity-for-american-education.*

DuFour, R., & Mattos, M. (2013). How do principals really improve schools? *Educational Leadership, 70*(7), 34–40.

Elmore, R. F. (2000, Winter). *Building a new structure for school leadership.* Washington, DC: Albert Shanker Institute. Retrieved November 15, 2010, from *www. ashankerinst.org/Downloads/building.pdf.*

Goddard, R., Goddard, Y., Kim, E. S., & Miller, R. (2015). A theoretical and empirical analysis of the roles of instructional leadership, teacher collaboration, and collective efficacy beliefs in support of student learning. *American Journal of Education, 121*(4), 501–530.

Heifetz, R. A., & Laurie, D. L. (2002, December). The work of leadership. *Harvard Business Review on Point.* Retrieved December 20, 2010, from *www.hbr.org.*

International Literacy Association (ILA). (2018a). *ILA literacy glossary.* Newark, DE: Author.

International Literacy Association (ILA). (2018b). *Standards for the preparation of literacy professionals 2017*. Newark, DE: Author.

International Literacy Association (ILA) 2018 Report. (2018c). *What's hot in literacy 2018 report*. Newark, DE: Author.

Kaplan, B., & Kaiser, R. (2008). Adjusting your leadership volume: When it comes to leadership strengths, more is not always better. In F. Hesselbein & A. Shrader (Eds.), *Leader to leader 2: Enduring insights on leadership from the leader to leader institute's award-winning journal* (pp. 89–97). San Francisco, CA: Jossey-Bass.

Kaser, J., Mundry, S., Stiles, K. E., & Loucks-Horsley, S. (2002). *Leading every day: 124 actions for effective leadership*. Thousand Oaks, CA: Corwin Press.

Lambert, L. (1998). *Building leadership capacity in schools*. Alexandria, VA: Association for Supervision and Curriculum Development.

Lao Tzu (n.d.). Quote. Retrieved from *www.goodreads.com/quotes/46410*.

Leana, C. R. (2011, Fall). The missing link in school reform. *Stanford Social Innovation Review*. Retrieved from *https://ssir.org/articles/entry/the_missing_link_in_school_reform*.

Leana, C. R., & Pil, F. K. (2006). Social capital and organizational performance: Evidence from urban public schools. *Organization Science, 17*(3), 353–366.

Leana, C. R., & Pil, F. K. (2014). The glue that holds schools together—and reformers ignore. *Washington Post*. Retrieved from *www.washingtonpost.com/news/answer-sheet/wp/2014/10/19/the-glue-that-really-holds-a-school-together-and-that-reformers-ignore/?utm_term=.326d8a17abed*.

Leana, C. R., & Pil, F. (2017). Social capital: An untapped resource for educational improvement. In E. Quintero (Ed.), *Teaching in context: How social aspects of schools and school systems shape teachers' development and effectiveness* (pp. 113–130). Cambridge, MA: Harvard University Press.

Leithwood, K., & Jantzi, D. (2008). Linking leadership to student learning: The contributions of leader efficacy. *Educational Administration Quarterly, 44*(4), 496–528.

Leithwood, K., Seashore Louis, K. S., Anderson, S., & Wahlstrom, K. (2004). *How leadership influences student learning*. Minneapolis: University of Minnesota, Center for Applied Research and Educational Improvement.

Little, J. W. (2003). Inside teacher community: Representations of classroom practice. *Teachers College Record, 105*(6) 913–945.

Marzano, R. J. (2003). *What works in schools?: Translating research into action*. Alexandria, VA: Association for Supervision and Curriculum Development.

Marzano, R. J., Waters, T., & McNulty, B. A. (2005). *School leadership that works: From research to results*. Alexandria, VA: Association for Supervision and Curriculum Development.

Murphy, J. F., & Louis, K. S. (2018). *Positive school leadership: Building capacity and strengthening relationships*. New York: Teachers College Press.

National Governors Association Center for Best Practices & Council of Chief State School Officers. (2010). *Common Core Standards for English language arts and literacy in history/social studies, science, and technical subjects*. Washington, DC: Authors.

Pil, F., & Leana, C. R. (2009). Applying organizational research to public school reform: The effects of teacher human and social capital on student performance. *Academy Management Journal, 52*(6), 1101–1124.

Rosenheltz, S. J. (1989). *Teachers' workplace: The social organization of schools*. New York: Teachers College Press.

Saunders, W., Goldenberg, C. N., & Gallimore, R. (2009, December). Increasing achievement by focusing grade-level teams on improving classroom learning: A prospective, quasi-experimental study of Title 1 schools. *American Educational Research Journal, 46*(4), 1006–1033.

Seashore Louis, K., Leithwood, K., Wahlstrom, K. L., & Anderson S. E. (2010). *Investigating the links to improved student learning: Final report of research findings.* Unpublished document, University of Minnesota, Minneapolis.

Spillane, J. P. (2005, Winter). Distributed leadership. *Educational Forum, 69,* 143–150.

Spillane, J. P. (2015). Leadership and learning: Conceptualizing relations between school administrative practice and instructional practice. *Societies, 5,* 277–294.

Spillane, J. P., Halverson, R., & Diamond, J. B. (2001). Investigating school leadership practice: A distributed perspective. *Educational Researcher, 30*(23), 23–28.

Stoelinga, S. R. (2008). Leading from above and below: Formal and informal teacher leadership. In M. M. Mangin & S. R. Stoelinga (Eds.), *Effective teacher leadership: Using research to inform and reform* (pp. 99–119). New York: Teachers College Press.

Supovitz, J., Sirinides, P., & May, H. (2010). How principals and peers influence teaching and learning. *Educational Administration Quarterly, 46*(1), 31–56.

Vescio, V., Ross, D., & Adams, A. (2008). A review of research on the impact of professional learning communities on teaching practice and student learning. *Teaching and Teacher Education, 24,* 80–91.

CHAPTER 2

Teachers as Literacy Leaders

Allison Swan Dagen
Aimee L. Morewood
Christina Glance

GUIDING QUESTIONS

➥ What is teacher leadership?

➥ In what ways do classroom teachers engage in leadership opportunities?

➥ What challenges do teacher leaders experience?

➥ How can schools use the *Standards for the Preparation of Literacy Professionals 2017* (International Literacy Association [ILA], 2018) as a framework, to encourage classroom teachers to also serve as teacher leaders?

In her best-selling book, *Multipliers: How the Best Leaders Make Everyone Smarter,* Liz Wiseman (2010) describes leaders in one of two categories, as multipliers or diminishers. *Multipliers,* she asserts, develop capacity in others by nurturing each person's unique skills, aptitude, and talent. These multipliers "create an atmosphere of genius innovation, productive effort, and collective intelligence" (p. 10). Wiseman's outlook on the traits of leaders who function as multipliers seems remarkably similar to those of classroom teachers. In reality, PreK–12 teachers do function as authentic multipliers within their classroom space; they provide high-quality instruction geared toward promoting students' growth, foster positive literate environments, uphold learning expectations, and motivate students through engaging experiences. This student-centered approach to teaching has certainly been a focal point of university-based teacher education preparation programs as well as school-based ongoing professional experiences for teachers. Today, however, there is an expectation for classroom teachers to assert a different type of multiplier effect by focusing more on assuming leadership responsibilities outside of their classrooms but still within their schools, as teacher leaders. For classroom teachers, leadership opportunities, mainly informal in scope, provide a context to engage and collaborate with peers about matters such as professional learning, reflective practice, inquiry, and advocacy (ILA, 2018).

We strongly support ILA's assertion for "literacy as a foundation for all learning" (2018, p. 65) and uphold the principle that teacher leaders are also literacy leaders. Thus, the focus of this chapter is the "what and how" of teacher leadership and how teachers may function as literacy leaders in PreK–12 schools. We provide a brief synthesis of research describing teacher leadership, elaborate on how standards can support and guide teacher leaders, reveal contexts for leadership opportunities, and share illustrative examples of teacher leaders. Through these examples, we foreground the teacher leaders' day-to-day work in relation to four concepts: learning, reflection, inquiry, and advocacy. These concepts are the focal points of the ILA's *Standards 2017*, Standard 6: Professional Learning and Leadership. We conclude the chapter by addressing challenges teacher leaders face and share recommendations to support teacher leadership efforts. To begin, we share the thoughts of Christina who teaches third grade and is a teacher leader:

> "A few years back, as a first-year teacher in my own classroom, I watched my academic coach and principal provide mentorship to teachers at my school, including myself. By observing, I began to understand what a leader looked like and I knew right then I wanted to be one. The first step I took in my development as a teacher leader was to obtain a master's degree in literacy education and reading specialist certification. This experience broadened my knowledge of the foundations of literacy and instruction and made me more aware of the resources available within my school to improve literacy. This motivated me as I completed my own research in the area of intervention, professional development, and coaching.
>
> "Over the past 3 years, I have also sought leadership opportunities within my school. One of my first leadership roles was that of professional development coordinator within the professional development school (PDS) committee at my school. Each year this role gives me the opportunity to plan meaningful professional development sessions for our faculty. For example, I know that our teachers wanted more opportunities to visit each other's classrooms and observe best

practices so they could implement them in their own classrooms; however, finding the time in the day to allow for this opportunity was extremely difficult. Therefore, using technology with which I was familiar from my degree program (VoiceThread), I developed a framework for teachers to record lessons in their classrooms and make them available for other teachers to both view and comment on in their own time. And they did!

"Most recently, I also became a member of our school's leadership and positive behavior interventions and support (PBIS) team, which consists of a small group of teachers, administrators, and school counselors. We meet as a leadership team quarterly and as a PBIS team monthly to discuss our school's academic and behavioral needs and goals. Being a member of these teams has allowed me the opportunity to show the most growth as a teacher leader. For example, our team discussed a need for more parent involvement at our school. To address this need, a small group of teachers and I decided to lead an initiative called One School, One Book this spring. Through this initiative, we are providing a copy of a high-interest chapter book to every family in the school and all staff members. With nightly reading activities, daily trivia, grade-level projects, and a celebratory family night, we hope the experience will increase parent involvement in the school and promote positive literacy practices. Because of these experiences, I feel more confident being a teacher leader; however, I recognize the role of teacher leader is not static and will continue to evolve as the needs of teachers and students in my school continue to change."

DEFINING TEACHER LEADERSHIP

The concept of school leadership is not radical, but the leveraging of teachers as leaders in schools certainly is. National educational associations (e.g., Learning Forward), Department of Education affiliated partners (e.g., Teach to Lead), educational think tanks (e.g., Learning Policy Institute), researchers, policymakers, and others have advocated for a shift toward increased teacher leadership capacity in schools. Much of the focus on teacher leadership has been situated within school reform efforts calling for teacher professionalism, performance-based compensation, site-based management, and professional development schools (York-Barr & Duke, 2004). More recently, this focus on teacher leadership has also been associated with trends of integrating leadership criteria into teacher evaluations and utilizing teacher leadership opportunities as a possible solution to high teacher attrition rates (Wenner & Campbell, 2017). The two-word term *teacher leadership* is complex. In order to understand how teacher leadership may influence school culture, teachers, and students, it is imperative to clarify this term. The concept has traditionally been defined by role (e.g., department chair), by demographics (e.g., experienced educator), by personal characteristics (e.g., collaborator), or through actions (e.g., mentoring). Although there is no single standard definition, many researchers have attempted to unpack the term (Cosenza, 2015; Curtis, 2013; Killion et al., 2016; Katzenmeyer & Moller, 2009; Mangin & Stoelinga, 2008; Neumerski, 2013; Wenner & Campbell, 2017; York-Barr & Duke, 2004). The concepts outlined in this chapter align most closely with York-Barr and Duke (2004), who define teacher leadership as "the process by which teachers, individually or collectively, influence their colleagues, principals, and other members of school communities to improve teaching and learning practices with the aim of increased student learning and achievement" (p. 287).

Current data indicate there are approximately 3.2 million classroom teachers in U.S. schools and a little over 90,000 principals (Riser-Kositsky, 2019). In these numbers, we see much leadership capacity, both from the formal leaders (e.g., principals) and the millions of informal leaders (e.g., teachers). Exactly how many teachers engage in leadership responsibilities and how their principals support or impede this engagement are unknown. However, research indicates that teachers are engaged in some form of leadership responsibilities (MetLife, 2013), and many consider themselves leaders (Curtis, 2013). These teacher leaders may choose to engage in varying degrees of formal and informal leadership, serving as coordinators, literacy coaches, specialists, instructional leaders, mentors, data analysts, curriculum developers, and school–parent advocates (Harrison & Killion, 2007).

Who are these classroom teachers who engage in leadership and why are they inclined to do so? In addition to feelings of satisfaction, those who engage in leadership responsibilities find the work empowering and an incentive for continuing in the profession. Teacher leaders are often experienced, with deep pedagogical knowledge and a well-developed personal philosophy of education. These teachers are confident in their teaching ability, which allows them to grow and effectively fulfill such leadership responsibilities. Teacher leaders also desire to collaborate—to form solid, collegial relationships with their colleagues (Cooper et al., 2016; Katzenmeyer & Moller, 2009; York-Barr & Duke, 2004). Engaging in leadership opportunities, however, is not for everyone. For example, teachers may choose to pursue other educational challenges by pursuing content-area specializations, research opportunities, or advanced graduate work (Crowther, Ferguson, & Hann, 2009).

STANDARDS AND TEACHER LEADERSHIP

Since the 1990s, ILA has advocated for classroom teachers and specialized literacy professionals to contribute to leadership efforts in their schools (International Reading Association, 1998, 2003, 2010; ILA, 2018).

Standards 2010 represent the organization's most notable and explicit shift toward leadership. Shortly after the release of *Standards 2010*, the Teacher Leadership Exploratory Consortium (TLEC), a group representing state education departments, higher education institutions, and national associations, created and released the Teacher Leader Model Standards (TLMS). The intention of this document was "to stimulate dialogue among stakeholders of the teaching profession about what constitutes the knowledge, skills, and competencies that teachers need to assume leadership roles in their schools, districts, and the profession" (Teacher Leadership Exploratory Consortium, n.d., p. 3). Since their release, the TLMS have served as a framework to support licensure and certification in Michigan, and then in Illinois, Georgia, and New York (Killion et al., 2016). In addition, the content of the TLMS has also been analyzed (Berg, Carver, & Mangin, 2014) against well-known leadership preparation programs (e.g., Boston Teacher Leadership Certificate Program) and used as a framework for preschool educator leadership studies (Swan Dagen, Morewood, & Loomis, 2016; Swan Dagen, Morewood, & Smith, 2017).

Most recently, the leadership responsibilities of classroom teachers were again revised and amplified in *Standards 2017*. In this iteration of the standards, the classroom teacher role, divided into three grade bands—preschool/primary, elementary/intermediate, and middle/high school—is clearly focused on leadership development. While collaborative engagement is evident throughout the content of the entire *Standards 2017*, Standard 6 specifically hones in on actions to ground and support professional learning and leadership. Standard 6 includes four components, described later in this chapter: learning, reflection, inquiry, and advocacy. In reviewing the content of Standard 6 across the three classroom teacher grades, we notice shifts toward:

- More authentic job-embedded collaborative engagement with peers.
- Classroom teachers exploring individualized professional learning opportunities.
- Move from participating in to leading professional learning opportunities.
- Leadership work through a schoolwide cultural lens.
- Expanded role as an advocate for families, communities, and profession.

CONTEXTS FOR TEACHER LEADER ENGAGEMENT

The variables that contribute to an effective school environment, discussed later in this chapter, are the most critical variables for the success, or failure, of teacher leadership initiatives (Barth, 2013; Crowther et al., 2009; Wenner & Campbell, 2017; York-Barr & Duke, 2004). As mentioned previously, in some schools, leadership opportunities for classroom teachers sometimes include a change in title or position type, and at other times, include new responsibilities that permit the teacher to remain in the classroom with K–12 students. Depending on how school culture recognizes (and supports) such opportunities, teachers may need to seek additional leadership both outside and inside of the school. Examples of contexts that support such leadership may include action research, National Board Certification, professional development schools, and professional networks (Katzenmeyer & Moller, 2009).

Action Research

Action research, or practitioner research, involves an inquiry stance, which is an important attribute of any teacher leader. Cochran-Smith and Lytle (1993) state, "An inquiry stance provides a kind of grounding within the changing cultures of school reform and competing political agendas" (p. 289). Practitioner research is a systematic way for teacher leaders to support their colleagues' understanding of specific questions about instruction and student learning. This systematic process involves (1) defining a question about localized educational practice, (2) grounding the question(s) in the field's research, (3) implementing a change, (4) systematically collecting data to study the instructional intervention, (5) analyzing the data, (6) reflecting on the data, and (7) presenting the findings to others (Fichtman Dana & Yendol-Silva, 2003; Hirschy, 2008). Since so much emphasis has been placed on data-driven instruction across classrooms from PreK to grade 12, teachers now have a greater opportunity to engage in action research and better meet their students' needs as they reflect on their instruction and adapt it based on analysis of student assessment data.

National Board Certification

The National Board for Professional Teacher Standards (NBPTS) certification is widely recognized as a high-quality professional learning experience for teachers who choose to pursue this credential. To certify, teachers focus on one of 25 content areas (e.g., literacy: reading–language arts, exceptional needs specialist) and complete four "components," including a content knowledge assessment and three narrative entries centered on student work samples, a videotaped reflection on teaching, professional contributions, and impact in the field. The certification requires teachers to engage in rigorous reflection on their understanding of pedagogy, student achievement, and content knowledge. This work is guided by a content-specific set of standards. The process is challenging, and candidate attrition rates range from 37 to 55% (Coskie & Place, 2008; Sato, Wei, & Darling-Hammond, 2008). Since 1993, 122,000 teachers in the United States have earned this prestigious certification (National Board for Professional Teacher Standards, 2018).

Professional Development Schools

Professional development schools (PDSs) are not new to the educational landscape; they have been around for decades, sometimes geographically close to colleges and universities. As Zenkov, Shiveley, and Clark (2016) note, these partnerships involve faculty at PreK–12 schools and universities working collaboratively around student learning with preservice teachers, providing professional learning opportunities to inservice teachers, and engaging in educational research. Originally, the Holmes Group (1990) articulated four areas of PDS work: preservice teacher education, PreK–12 student learning, educational research areas in which university and school partners collaborate, and opportunities for all PDS partners to engage in professional learning opportunities. Then the National Association of Professional Development Schools (NAPDS) established the *Nine Essentials* (2008) to serve as a framework of PDS characteristics. NAPDS uses *this framework* to define school–university partnerships/PDS work by breaking down the intricacies of partnership work into discrete points that guide all educational stakeholders as they build and sustain a PDS school and/or network.

Professional Networks

Collaboration with peers, outside and inside of school, can include a focus on professional learning, reflection, inquiry, and advocacy. Research on effective schools tells us that collaborating and interacting with colleagues improve teacher confidence, pedagogy, student achievement, and school culture (Reeves, Pun, & Chung, 2017). In a national survey, Bean et al. (2015) reported that 89% of the literacy professionals (including reading teachers) indicated that they collaborate, coach, or support professionals in their schools. Given the "full plate" of many school professionals, finding time to engage in a professional network is a challenge, especially within the school day. As gleaned from the most recent national survey of its kind, K–12 teachers in the United States collaborate an average of only 2.7 hours per week (MetLife, 2010). Currently, social media platforms (e.g., Twitter, Facebook) are widely popular in promoting professional networking among educators and allow teachers more time to connect with a larger network of educators—albeit on their time outside of school.

TEACHER LEADERS IN ACTION

What does teacher leadership look like in action? To answer this question, we asked teacher leaders with whom we collaborate (see Table 2.1) to share some of their ideas with us about their experiences, thoughts, and beliefs on teacher leadership. The case examples we share below present a

TABLE 2.1 **Classroom Teacher Leaders**

Teacher	Teaching position	Specialized educator certification	Years teaching experience
Laura	Kindergarten	National Board Certified Teacher	31
Christina	Third grade	Reading Specialist	5
Kristen	Fifth grade	Reading Specialist	13
Adam	Middle/high school	Reading Specialist Special Education	11
Teresa	High school	Reading Specialist National Board Certified Teacher	26

mini-snapshot of their work with PreK–12 students, peers, and other key stakeholders. We present these narratives organized around the four key components identified in *Standards 2017,* Standard 6: learning, reflection, inquiry, and advocacy.

CASE EXAMPLES ·

Learning

> **THINK ABOUT THIS**
>
> 1. What commonalities do the following teacher leaders exhibit?
> 2. In what ways are these teacher leaders' experiences, along with Christina's earlier in the chapter, different/similar from your school experiences?

Adam Shickley is a secondary reading and social studies teacher in a center-based educational program serving grades 6–12. He collaborates with his three co-teachers and is also responsible for instructional planning, delivering materials, benchmarking, and progress monitoring. We met Adam while he was completing his reading specialist certification and special education master's degree. Adam is an adjunct instructor for West Virginia University's (WVU) special education master's program. Here he shares information on his professional learning and how he collaborates with peers:

> "As an educator committed to learning, I continually challenge myself to grow, and it pays off. Recently I took advantage of a free online professional learning opportunity and became a Newsela Certified Educator. Through the Newsela platform, I was able to gain some new knowledge and approaches regarding how to use expository texts to motivate adolescent readers. While integrating leveled reading in

multiple classrooms at our school, I noticed our school data showed an overall deficit in reading comprehension. My colleagues were noticing that students' comprehension of text was improving in my classroom and asked me for advice. I took on an informal coaching role, and suggested we read and discuss selections from Tovani's *I Read It, but I Don't Get It* (2000) to help my peers connect to their students. After this, my co-teachers began to integrate some of these practices in their classrooms. Since we are a small school setting, we were able to discuss the new practices and even co-plan and co-teach together. While reflecting on literacy practices, we discussed some options and also decided to use the Google Classroom format as well to help integrate technology skills within content reading classes.

"Also, through the use of social media (i.e., Twitter), I have been able to collaborate with a large network of literacy professionals outside of my school setting. I found input and connections from those who inspire me. I was able to engage and exchange ideas with some of the most influential people in the field and keep up on what's trending in literacy education. I use technology to shape my professional learning and to network for continued growth."

Reading Adam's story, it is clear he is a self-motivated lifelong learner. As a teacher leader, he has chosen to engage in professional learning opportunities outside of his school, on his own time. This has allowed him to continue to grow in the areas of literacy instruction (e.g., Newsela certification) and effective pedagogical uses of technology (e.g., Google Classroom). As a teacher leader and collaborator, Adam uses this knowledge as a context in which to collaborate with peers within his school and a network of literacy professionals outside of the school. Adam relies on technology to connect with teacher leaders, researchers, authors, and educators locally and from around the country. His experiences demonstrate that teacher leaders continue to learn and grow as professionals through traditional and technology-enhanced learning opportunities. This learning has supported his work in collaborating and coaching his peers.

Reflection

Kristen Blum is a fifth-grade English language arts (ELA) teacher in a large suburban school district. We met Kristen while she was on an educational sabbatical earning her master's degree and reading specialist certification in our online program. After graduation, Kristen has continued to partner with our graduate program as an adjunct instructor. Here, Kristen discusses two projects that required her to implement findings from classroom and school data sets and how those projects have contributed to her role as a reflective practitioner/teacher leader:

"Leadership opportunities can be found in classrooms throughout any school on any given day. My course work in action research and schoolwide literacy leadership allowed me to more fully grasp this concept. Based on the needs of the students and teachers in my school, I was able to uncover different strategies and resources to develop and grow my "teacher toolbox," while facilitating learning at both levels. Both projects required me to gather multiple data sources and analyze these findings at the classroom level as well as with multiple sources of schoolwide data.

"Working with these data gave me a different perspective on how to take the initiative in creating new and effective learning opportunities for both students and teachers. I found myself in uncharted territory, having the responsibility of using these data results and leading professional development with my peers, though my familiarity of the content and curriculum served as a strong foundation. Having a solid understanding of our school culture and structure, I was able to provide several different instructional strategies, activities, and resources that could be incorporated in the classroom. Thinking about how these instructional practices fit within our existing curriculum was an ongoing process. Working collaboratively with peers was not a new concept, though guiding them in their new learning and providing feedback was unfamiliar and a challenge initially."

In this snapshot, Kristen describes how her experiences with two field-based course assignments strengthened her self-efficacy in the area of teacher leadership. Through action research, using both an individual class as well as schoolwide information, Kristen was able to systematically reflect on instructional practices for increasing student interest, motivation, and engagement in reading. During this project, she engaged in the iterative cycle of instructional intervention, reflected on student learning, and was able to share her findings and discuss them with her school colleagues. In addition to focusing on student learning, Kristen was also able to support teachers and observe learning through this lens as well. In her schoolwide literacy improvement project, Kristen was able to investigate, design, implement, and evaluate a school-based professional learning project at her own school. She analyzed school data, collaborated with school administrators and peers, created a professional development plan, and engaged in levels of literacy coaching (ILA, 2015).

Collaboration/Inquiry

Teresa Campbell is a high school ELA teacher in a midsized rural school. Teresa is a National Board Certified Teacher (NBCT) whom we met years ago when she was part of a regional cohort of teachers working toward reading specialist certification. In addition to teaching high school students, she serves as an adjunct instructor for WVU's literacy education master's program and is actively involved in her county's efforts to support teachers' interest in National Board Certification. Here, Teresa discusses how she uses technology to collaborate with peers/colleagues across the state:

> "As an English teacher of 26 years, I have learned to use words like *Google* and *Skype* as verbs and to use this technology daily. My teaching has evolved from using a filmstrip of a famous author to actually Skyping with a famous author! The use of technology has become a strength of mine as I support my high school students' learning. Mentoring other teachers has also become a highlight of my work as a teacher. And in recent experiences, using technology has been a central part of the mentoring. Being a National Board Certified teacher, I was able to take on the role of lead mentor through a statewide, grant-funded initiative. My role was vital, as I engaged with almost 80 PreK teachers as they reflected on their practice. Technology allowed these teachers, who were located in 55 different counties covering 24,000 square miles, to pursue advanced credentials that otherwise would not have occurred. Through the Google Cloud Platform I was able to chat with, email, and conduct virtual face-to-face meetings and office hours. I was able to mentor these teachers both individually and in groups to explain the process of reflection through examples via video and writing samples. As a mentor, using Google Cloud Platform was a very positive educational experience for me because I was able to collaborate with teachers and support their work toward National Board Certification through a virtual space. Witnessing these teachers realize that lifelong learning and collaboration are possible, even in remote rural areas, added to this already rich experience."

As a teacher leader, Teresa mentored the PreK teachers as they worked with their focused inquiry around emergent literacy practices. Teresa recognized that teachers needed opportunities to collaborate, and through the use of technology, she was able to create a collaborative working environment so that her colleagues were able to view, respond, and engage in meaningful conversations. Teachers in her network engaged in asynchronous and synchronous conversations that were flexible and convenient to their schedules, thereby supporting teachers' abilities to participate.

Advocacy

Laura VanHorn is a kindergarten teacher at a suburban elementary school that serves as a university PDS partner. We have worked with her for over a decade through this network as PDS coordinator and most recently through a statewide grant supporting PreK teachers. In addition, Laura is an adjunct instructor for WVU's Five-Year Teacher Education Preparation Program. Below she reflects on her advocacy work with community, university, and school partnerships anchored in a garden-based learning initiative (*https://stemedu.cehs.wvu.edu/funded/garden-based-learning*). She describes how the initiative enables her to serve as an advocate as she engages with a variety of stakeholders both inside and outside of school:

> "I've taken an active role in making our school's large garden visible to the general community and also to specific stakeholders who can make a difference in the future of the garden. The school's presence at the Morgantown farmers market in the summer provides us with the opportunity to raise funds and receive small donations, but more importantly spreads the word about what we're doing. People are amazed at the range of opportunities that we're giving our students, and generally they express the wish that 'their kids' school did this.' Parents of our students become engaged by the connections our garden program makes with the academic curriculum and the learning experience we provide our students.
>
> "There are many ways that I facilitate our garden program, including advertising all of our garden-based learning efforts. For example, I invited our newly appointed superintendent to do a read-aloud for my students. His time at my school included a tour of the garden to introduce him to what we were doing at the school. I helped plan and facilitate a showcase of our program and invited local politicians and university stakeholders. I've also been involved in using the GigaPan platform to create educational content to be used by others. Working with a proactive administration allows the garden-based learning project to remain at the forefront of our school agenda and helps it continue to be a vital part of our community."

As a teacher leader Laura is an advocate for her school and multiple partners, such as teachers, administrators, parents, university, and community. The multiple foci of the garden-based learning curricula allowed students in her school to engage in disciplinary-based literacy opportunities. Through this initiative the school community has been able to successfully engage with the educational community (e.g., university, principal) and community (e.g., farmers market). Laura also advocates for her students and her schoolwide program by inviting administrators and parents to participate in the initiative program. Through this project she has used technology (e.g., the GigiPan website) to support her role as a school advocate.

CHALLENGES FOR TEACHER LEADERS

In this chapter we have described teacher leadership, suggested standards-based guidelines, discussed contexts, and provided examples of successful teacher leaders. The experiences described by Christina, Adam, Kristen, Teresa, and Laura demonstrate how teachers are able to take on leadership responsibilities for the benefit of their students, peers, schools, and themselves. And still, engaging in teacher leadership is challenging. Decades of research have identified school culture, relationship, and time as factors that may challenge teacher leadership (York-Barr & Duke, 2004; Wenner & Campbell, 2017).

School Culture and Organization

For teachers to engage in leadership, school administrators need to support a culture conducive for teacher learning, risk taking, collaboration, shared decision making, and critical reflection. Cultivating this type of culture should be a priority of those who have formal leadership roles in the school. Unfortunately, many schools simply are not designed around a "teacher as leader" model and the cliché—principals lead and teachers follow—is alive and well in too many of today's schools. Top-down hierarchical models of principal as leader and teachers as workers serve to marginalize teachers from the hub of meaningful, democratic participation in the day-to-day operations of educating students. Current calls for universal programmatic fidelity further remove the teacher from the instructional decision-making process. Instead of turning to teachers for input and to help improve the system, the system is telling teachers what to do and then pointing the finger of blame their way if student achievement goals are not met. Simply stated, without an accepting school culture, teacher leadership initiatives are likely to fail.

The teacher leaders introduced above are fortunate and describe (to us) working in schools with supportive principals who encourage their role as teacher leaders. They engage in leadership opportunities in areas that they feel comfortable leading. They are able exert some autonomy and navigate their new responsibilities, though much of this work is carried out on their own time.

Relationships

As related earlier, a receptive culture is a necessary component for teacher leadership opportunities. Equally important are the relationships that exist among key stakeholders who work in the schools—more specifically, *trusting* relationships. In the best situation, these relationships are respectful, productive, and collaborative. However, negative relationships that exist between school administrators and teaches, or among fellow teachers, may serve as an obstacle for teacher leadership. School administrators need to trust and respect the fact that teachers, because of their daily interaction with students, are many times in the best position to make critical decisions about curriculum and instruction. Consequently, they (the administrators) must be willing to relinquish some of their control and allow teacher leaders to assume additional responsibilities. Barth (2013) asserts that lack of support by school principals may be an indication that they want to keep a stronghold on the decision-making process, may prefer a top-down hierarchical model of leadership, or feel that teacher leadership is time-consuming and only creates division among teachers.

Relationships among fellow teachers are also a critical dimension of teacher leadership initiatives. Issues of perceived equity within the ranks of teachers crop up when the responsibilities of teachers shift (Katzenmeyer & Moller, 2009; York-Barr & Duke, 2004). The egalitarian view, which espouses the notion that all teachers are equal, stands to take a direct hit when one of their own is promoted or granted leadership roles and responsibilities. Danielson (2007) refers to this situation as the "tall poppy syndrome," wherein "those who stick their heads up risk being cut down to size" (p. 18). Whereas informal leadership assignments might not confuse the existing hierarchy, formal leadership role designations almost certainly create a division that can result in conflict among teachers or at the very least, create friction (York-Barr & Duke, 2004).

The teacher leaders we describe in this chapter share positive dispositions and openness to collaboration that seem to have a knack of moving people forward (i.e., they are multipliers [Wiseman, 2010]); thus, they continually build trusting relationships. This positive cycle has allowed them to assume leadership responsibilities.

Time

Lack of time within the structure of the school day is most certainly a barrier for teacher engagement in a variety of opportunities. Barth (2013) states that teachers' "plates are full"; we cannot imagine a teacher we know disagreeing with this assertion. Demands on a teacher's time, both in and outside of school, are great. Teacher leaders, who take on additional informal leadership responsibilities while staying in the classroom, experience even greater demands on their time. In addition to crafting lesson plans, teaching a full day, providing student feedback, handling student issues, and other related teaching duties, teacher leaders are also dealing with a wide array of other responsibilities that require extensive amounts of time, typically extending beyond the structured school day. Recently, during the implementation of the statewide PreK grant project, we were reminded how "time" can be such a constricting issue for teachers (Swan Dagen & Morewood, 2016). The teacher leaders described above overcome the barrier of time by doing much of this work "off the clock" on their own time or creatively using social media and technology to get around the issue of time.

SUPPORTING TEACHER LEADERS

After completing an extensive review of research pertaining to teacher leaders, studies conclude that the most obvious impact of teacher leadership is growth and learning among teachers themselves (York-Barr & Duke, 2004; Wenner & Campbell, 2017). In this way, teacher leadership can be viewed as a pathway to empowerment (Morewood & Swan Dagen, 2018). Teachers who partake in leadership roles report professional growth, a break from the routine of the classroom in order to engage with colleagues and administrators, increased satisfaction and retention, a chance to learn more about the *big picture* of the school, and the ability to exercise creativity through collegial and administrative work (Curtis, 2013; Killion et al., 2016). Teacher leadership, as an initiative, requires us to think about issues such as evaluation, compensation, distributed leadership, and redefining the role of classroom teacher (Curtis, 2013).

In this chapter we have shared snapshots of the experiences of the five teacher leaders—classroom teachers who have progressed from being multipliers within their own classrooms with their students to multipliers within their schools with fellow teachers. The teacher leaders we describe represent a range of teaching experiences (5–31 years). They work in schools with supportive principals who encourage their role as teacher leaders. These teacher leaders leverage the professional learning and leadership activities outlined in *Standards 2017,* including learning, reflection, inquiry, and advocacy, to engage in leadership opportunities at their schools in areas where they feel comfortable leading. They are able to leverage their social capital to navigate these new roles. As teacher leaders, these educators have created opportunities to become engaged beyond their classrooms, fostering an empowering sense of ownership in their schools.

For teachers who would like to take on informal leadership roles, or for principals/administrators who lead efforts to cultivate teacher leadership, we provide the following recommendations to support learning, inquiry, reflection, and advocacy.

- Use technology tools to alleviate time and proximity/location barriers.
- Create opportunities for web-based learning and sharing (e.g., webinars, podcasts, social media, online coursework).
- Collaborate with a variety of partners (school, administrator, university, community).

- Provide time for co-planning, co-teaching, and observing in each others' classrooms.
- Create university partnerships (even if at a distance via technology).
- Create a private virtual space for teachers (at the school) to collaborate and share ideas (e.g., Google Cloud Platform).
- Allow teachers input in creating schoolwide professional learning content.
- Use data to support teacher and student learning needs.
- Use teacher leaders as facilitators of inservice day/professional learning agenda.
- Create collaboration zones of inviting spaces in which teachers can work together.
- Invite community members to serve as school liaisons.
- Identify a teacher leader to serve as community liaison.
- Identify positive (celebrate) and negative aspects of school culture that support and inhibit teacher literacy leadership. Start the conversation.
- Make professional learning job-embedded and relevant!

CONCLUSION

In this era of increased accountability and in order to retain highly qualified teachers, we need to rethink the role and responsibilities of classroom teachers—both operationally and conceptually—and focus on initiatives that will make teacher leadership the norm rather than the exception. The role of teacher leader is an evolving one whose description and responsibilities need to be regularly revisited or reshaped by the changing context of the school and educational reform initiatives. In this chapter, we have leaned on *Standards 2017* to help create a roadmap for teacher leaders' ongoing work with professional learning, reflection, inquiry, and advocacy. For the teachers who function as leaders, including those we describe, the work they do, the efforts to collaborate, create change, and lead are for the benefit of their schools and their students' success. To close, we share a key observation of Wiseman, who wrote, "There is more intelligence inside our organizations than we are using" (2017, p. xvii). We wholeheartedly support this assertion. We need schools where teachers are encouraged to function as leaders, as multipliers.

ENGAGEMENT ACTIVITIES

1. Identify, observe, and interview a teacher leader in a school. These questions can be used as a guide or you may develop your own. What are his or her roles and

responsibilities? Is the position an informal or formal one? What aspects of the position seem the most rewarding? What professional and personal traits does he or she demonstrate? How has this teacher leader been prepared for these responsibilities?

2. What do you know about yourself and your leadership abilities? Identity a reputable resource and complete a self-assessment as a (a) reflective tool and (b) focus for wider discussion with teaching peers and teacher leadership opportunities. Two possibilities include Glanz's *Finding Your Leadership Style* (2002) and Clifton's Strength Finder (*www.gallupstrengthscenter.com*).

3. Using the *Standards 2017* professional learning and leadership framework outlined in this chapter (learning, reflection, inquiry, advocacy), review the examples of evidence under each of the four components for your specific grade band (pp.67–93). With the teachers in your school, discuss opportunities you have, both individually and collectively, in your school setting to engage in learning, reflection, inquiry, and advocacy.

ANNOTATED RESOURCES

Teacher Leadership Exploratory Consortium. (n.d.). Teacher leader model standards. Retrieved from *www.teacherleaderstandards.org/downloads/TLS_Brochure.pdf.*

The multipage TLMS document identifies seven domains representing both formal and informal leadership opportunities, such as creating collaborative culture, promoting professional learning, and improving collaboration with families and communities.

Cult of Pedagogy (*www.cultofpedagogy.com*)
Learning Forward (*https://learningforward.org*)
National Board for Professional Teaching Standards (*www.nbpts.org/national-board-certification*)
Teach to Lead (*http://teachtolead.org*)

These selected web resources for teacher leadership—representing national organizations, an individual, and an advanced certification opportunity—provide support for and demystify teacher leadership. The key concepts identified in this chapter (learning, reflection, inquiry, and advocacy) are addressed in these resources through blog posts, webinars, publications, and social media.

REFERENCES

Barth, R. S. (2013). The time is ripe (again). *Educational Leadership, 71*(2), 10–17.

Bean, R., Kern, D., Goatley, V., Ortlieb, E., Shettel, J., Calo, K., et al. (2015). Specialized literacy professionals as literacy leaders: Results of a national survey. *Literacy Research and Instruction, 54*(2), 83–114.

Berg, J. H., Carver, C. L., & Mangin, M. M. (2014). Teacher leader model standards: Implications for preparation, policy, and practice. *Journal of Research on Leadership Education, 9*(2), 195–217.

Cochran-Smith, M., & Lytle, S. L. (1993). *Inside/outside: Teacher research and knowledge*. New York: Teachers College Press.

Cooper, K., Stanulius, R., Brondyk, S., Hamilton, E., Macaluso, M., & Meier, M. (2016). The teacher leadership process: Attempting change within embedded systems. *Journal of Educational Change, 17*, 85–113.

Cosenza, M. N. (2015). Defining teacher leadership: Affirming the teacher leader model standards. *Issues in Teacher Education, 24*(2), 79–99.

Coskie, T. L., & Place, N. A. (2008). The national board certification process as professional development: The potential for changed literacy practice. *Teaching and Teacher Education, 24*(7), 1893–1906.

Crowther, F., Ferguson, M., & Hann, L. (2009). *Developing teacher leaders: How teacher leadership enhances school success* (2nd ed.). Thousand Oaks, CA: Corwin Press.

Curtis, R. (2013) *Finding a new way: Leveraging teacher leadership to meet unprecedented demands*. Washington, DC: Aspen Institute.

Danielson, C. (2007). The many faces of leadership. *Educational Leadership, 65*(1), 14–19.

Fichtman Dana, N., & Yendol-Silva, D. (2003). *The reflective educator's guide to classroom research: Learning to teach and teaching to learn through practitioner inquiry*. Thousand Oaks, CA: Corwin Press.

Harrison, C., & Killion, J. (2007). Ten roles for teacher leaders. *Educational Leadership, 65*(1), 74–77.

Hirschy, S. T. (2008). Action research: A valuable framework for developing staff training and solving administrative problems. *Action Research Exchange, 180*, 74–76.

Holmes Group. (1990). *Tomorrow's schools: Principles for the design of professional development schools*. Lansing, MI: Author.

International Literacy Association (ILA). (2015). *The multiple roles of school-based specialized literacy professionals* (Research brief). Newark, DE: Author.

International Literacy Association (ILA). (2018). *Standards for the preparation of literacy professionals* 2017. Newark, DE: Author.

International Reading Association. (1998). *Standards for reading professionals*. Newark, DE: Author.

International Reading Association. (2003). *Standards for reading professionals*. Newark, DE: Author.

International Reading Association. (2010). *Standards for reading professionals—revised 2010*. Newark, DE: Author.

Katzenmeyer, M., & Moller, G. (2009). *Awaking the sleeping giant: Helping teachers develop as leaders* (3rd ed.). Thousand Oaks, CA: Corwin Press.

Killion, J., Harrison, C., Colton, A., Bryan, C., Delehant, A., & Cooke, D. (2016). *A systemic approach to elevating teacher leadership*. Oxford, OH: Learning Forward.

Mangin, M. M., & Stoelinga, S. R. (Eds.). (2008). *Effective teacher leadership: Using research to inform and reform*. New York: Teachers College Press.

MetLife. (2010). *MetLife survey of the American teacher: Collaborating for student success*. New York: Author

MetLife. (2013). *MetLife survey of the American teacher: Challenges for school leadership*. New York: Author.

Morewood, A., & Swan Dagen, A. (2018). Empowering early educators: Promotion of literacy learning and leadership opportunities at the pre-K level. *Literacy Today, 35*(6), 12–13.

National Association for Professional Development Schools. (2008). What it means to be a professional development school. Retrieved from *https://napds.org/nine-essentials*.

National Board for Professional Teacher Standards (2018). *2018 state rankings by total number of National Board Certified Teachers*. Arlington, VA: Author. Retrieved from *www.nbpts.org/wp-content/uploads/StateRankings_All_NBCTs.pdf*.

Neumerski, C. (2013). Rethinking instructional leadership, a review: What do we know about principal, teacher, and instructional leadership, and where should we go from here? *Educational Administration Quarterly, 49*(2), 310–347.

Reeves, P. M., Pun, W. H., & Chung, K. S. (2017). Influence of teacher collaboration on job satisfaction and student achievement. *Teaching and Teacher Education, 67*, 227–236.

Riser-Kositsky, M. (2019). Educational statistics: Facts about American schools. Retrieved from *www.edweek.org/ew/issues/education-statistics/index.html*.

Sato, M., Wei, R. C., & Darling-Hammond, L. (2008). Improving teachers' assessment practices through professional development: The case of National Board Certification. *American Educational Research Journal, 45*(3), 669–700.

Swan Dagen, A., & Morewood, A. (2016). Strengthening early literacy through online collaboration and mentoring. *Young Children, 71*(4), 20–25.

Swan Dagen, A., Morewood, A., & Loomis, D. (2016). Leadership functions of National Board Certified Teachers and teachers certification candidates. In R. D. Johnson, S. Vasinda, & S. Szabo (Eds.), *Association of Literacy Educators Yearbook: Vol. 38. Literacy educators and researchers: Making a difference in our diverse communities* (pp. 161–177). Richmond, KY: Association of Literacy Educators and Researchers.

Swan Dagen, A., Morewood, A., & Smith, M. (2017). Teacher leader model standards and the functions assumed by National Board Certified Teachers. *The Educational Forum, 81*(3), 322–338.

Teacher Leadership Exploratory Consortium. (n.d.). Teacher leader model standards. Retrieved from *www.teacherleaderstandards.org/downloads/TLS_Brochure.pdf*.

Tovani, C. (2000). *I read it, but I don't get it: Comprehension strategies for adolescent readers*. Portland, ME: Stenhouse.

Wenner, J. A., & Campbell, T. (2017). The theoretical and empirical basis of teacher leadership. *Review of Educational Research, 87*(1), 134–171.

Wiseman, E. (2010). *Multipliers: How the best leaders make everyone smarter*. New York: HarperCollins.

Wiseman, E. (2017). *Multipliers: How the best leaders make everyone smarter—revised*. New York: HarperCollins.

York-Barr, J., & Duke, K. (2004). What do we know about teacher leadership?: Findings from two decades of scholarship. *Review of Educational Research, 74*(3), 255–316.

Zenkov, K., Shiveley, J., & Clark, E. (2016). Why we must answer the question "What is a professional development school?" *School–University Partnerships, 9*(3), 1–9.

Literacy Leadership in Action

Katy Carroll, EdD
Kindergarten teacher, Pittsburgh Public Schools,
Pittsburgh, Pennsylvania

THINK ABOUT THIS

1. In what ways does Katy serve as a literacy leader?
2. What lessons can be learned about the role of teacher leader?
3. What questions come to mind while reading this vignette?

I have just begun my 29th year of teaching in Pittsburgh Public Schools, and I have alternated between teaching at various grade levels and working as a literacy coach. I have been a kindergarten teacher for the last 8 years.

My Thoughts about Teacher Leadership

I am the leader for my kindergarten team. I have been assigned to work with a first-year teacher who is currently back in school working toward her reading specialist certification. Also, I have preservice teachers in my classroom throughout the school year.

I approach my work with each group differently, but all the work requires me to remember that not only are children on journeys to celebrate, so are teachers. Our work begins enthusiastically. Everyone has ideas, expectations, and goals. Some teachers succeed easily. Others need more guidance and support. My job is to figure out how to help them move forward on their journey. Below I share examples of my leadership work (the teacher names are pseudonyms).

Sara has been teaching for 3 years. She is enthusiastic about her work, and she has many questions when we meet at our weekly team meeting. She tries to take what she hears at the meetings and replicate it in her classroom. It doesn't always work out the way she wants. She needs to see it in action with children. Because time and scheduling are always an issue, we decided to combine my class with hers, and I teach while she observes. This allows us to have sidebar conversations in which I explain my rationale for doing something or she asks clarifying questions. It can be a little hectic, but it has strengthened our bond as teammates, and she feels much more confident to do the work in her own classroom.

Reba went directly from getting her bachelor's degree to entering a master's program for reading specialists. She has never had her own classroom. She had only one class on the teaching of reading and did not understand any of the reading terms I used when talking with her—*guided reading, shared reading, encoding, decoding.* Once I realized that, I knew we had to develop some common ground. I found articles that we both read and discussed. Time being an issue again (isn't it always?), I asked her to keep a journal of questions, thoughts, and experiences she had with children, anything she wanted me to know. I respond to her in writing, in our weekly meetings, and, at times, on our way down the hall. I can preplan for our time together because she has shared her thoughts with me. It makes our meetings much more productive.

My work with teachers has taught me that I need to be available. It's not always easy because there is always so much to do, but we can multitask while I answer questions, talk through a lesson, or listen to their thoughts.

Teachers need time to assimilate knowledge and find their rhythm. As a result, my best advice is to relax and enjoy the process of each teacher. I know if I am consistent, patient, and trust the process, the magic of learning will happen. And when it does, we celebrate and celebrate and celebrate!

CHAPTER 3

The Reading/Literacy Specialist

Still a Multifaceted Role

Rita M. Bean

GUIDING QUESTIONS

➥ In what ways has the role of the reading/literacy specialist evolved over years?

➥ What research has contributed to knowledge about the multifaceted dimensions of the role?

➥ How have the *Standards for the Preparation of Literacy Professionals 2017* (International Literacy Association [ILA], 2018) influenced the development of a framework for the role of the reading/literacy specialist?

➥ What are key challenges that reading/literacy specialists face in today's schools and how can they address these challenges?

As schools struggle to adjust to the demands of high-level standards, differentiate instruction to meet the literacy needs of learners, and meet the accountability requirements of their districts and states, many rely on the services of reading/literacy specialists both to work with students and to collaborate with teachers to improve overall literacy learning in schools. Although the title *reading/literacy specialist* is a new term that acknowledges a shift from a narrow perspective on reading to a broader emphasis on literacy instruction (ILA, 2018), reading specialists as literacy professionals have been in existence for many years, even though titles have varied (e.g., remedial reading teacher, Title I or Chapter 1 teacher, reading specialist). In addition to differences in titles, so too have role expectations evolved. In discussing past research, I use the term *reading specialist* given its prevalence in early studies and papers describing the role. When I discuss the role as described in *Standards 2017*, I switch to the new title, *reading/literacy specialist*. I begin by discussing the evolution of the role and the research and literature that influenced changes over time.

EVOLUTION OF THE READING SPECIALIST ROLE

In 1940, Dolch described the need for schools to consider employing remedial reading specialists, professionals who had a deep interest in working with students experiencing difficulties with reading. These individuals were to assess the reading strengths and needs of students and then develop or select appropriate methods for working with these students. This focus on remediation continued through the 1960s and 1970s, with the passage of the Elementary and Secondary Education Act (1965), which funded supplemental support for students identified as economically deprived. The regulations of this large-scale, federally funded program (i.e., Title I) required that monies be used to support eligible students only. This requirement led to a proliferation of programs in which reading specialists taught students in pullout contexts as a means of ensuring that materials and resources purchased with these funds were being used by these students only.

Unfortunately, this large-scale compensatory program did not achieve the expected results (Borman & D'Agostino, 2001; Kennedy, Birman, & Demaline, 1986; Slavin, 1987), and researchers highlighted several factors that they believed contributed to these mediocre results: lack of congruence between classroom instruction and compensatory instruction (Allington, 1986; Allington & Shake, 1986; Walp & Walmsley, 1989) and an emphasis on skill-related and workbook-type activities (Allington & McGill-Franzen, 1989; Bean, Cooley, Eichelberger, Lazar, & Zigmond, 1991).

Pullout or in Class: Is That the Question?

One solution to the lack of congruence between classroom and pullout instruction was an increased emphasis on in-class instruction; reading specialists moved from working in isolation "down the hall" to working in the classrooms alongside the teachers. Further, there was more emphasis on the sharing of approaches, materials, and resources with classroom teachers. Unfortunately, given that neither reading specialists nor classroom teachers were prepared for this implementation change, several problems arose. Some reading specialists found themselves functioning as aides, with classroom teachers making the decisions about what and how these reading specialists would teach (Bean, 2001; Bean, Trovato, & Hamilton, 1995). Other classroom teachers and specialists had difficulties because of the differences in their philosophical approach to literacy instruction or classroom management (Walp & Walmsley, 1989). This change from pullout to in-class instruction required reading specialists to be knowledgeable not only about how to work with students experiencing reading difficulties, but also how to effectively collaborate and cooperate with their peers. Models for working collaboratively in the classroom were developed and shared with those being prepared to be reading specialists and with those in the field (Bean, 2001; Bean et al., 1995; Cook & Friend, 1995).

Supporting Classroom Instruction

Another shift in the evolution of the role occurred in 1998, supported by the publication of a landmark text, *Preventing Reading Difficulties* (Snow, Burns, & Griffin, 1998), which highlighted the importance of improving primary teachers' ability to teach reading. These researchers recommended that, in addition to providing instructional support to students, reading specialists provide professional development for teachers to help them develop expertise and competence in teaching classroom reading instruction.

This focus on a dual role was supported by the International Reading Association (IRA—now the ILA) in its position statement *Teaching All Children to Read: The Roles of the Reading Specialist* (2000). Three major roles of the reading specialist were identified: instruction, diagnosis and assessment, and leadership. This position statement was based on the results of several key studies (Bean, Cassidy, Grumet, Shelton, & Wallis, 2002; Bean, Swan, & Knaub, 2003; Quatroche, Bean, & Hamilton, 2001) on the roles of reading specialists, which corroborated the notion that reading specialists had multiple responsibilities. In the Bean et al., 2003 study, principals in exemplary schools indicated that they perceived reading specialists to be instrumental in the improvement of literacy learning in their schools, an important finding. In 2014, Galloway and Lesaux (2014), based on a synthesis of the research on the reading specialist, identified four major roles of this specialized position: a student-oriented role, a teacher-oriented role, a managerial role, and a data-oriented role. This framework is similar to the International Reading Association's 2000 position statement and substantiates the notion that reading specialists have multiple roles.

Thus, although instruction is often a primary focus of the role, to be effective, reading/literacy specialists must also know how to collaborate with teachers in ways that improve literacy achievement for all students in the school. Below, Katie Regner, a reading specialist in a K–3 primary school, describes a typical day in her professional life. Katie exemplifies the role of many reading specialists in today's schools; they have both instructional responsibilities and they support teachers' efforts to provide quality-first teaching.

> "Although there is not really a typical day, I do have a daily schedule that gives me time to work with students, do assessments, plan, and work with teachers. Teachers use a sign-up sheet that tells me when I can be helpful to them and not interfere with their whole-class instruction. Teachers were open to the sign-up sheet and seem to prefer this over having a regularly scheduled session. Further, given my schedule, I can't get into every classroom. In the afternoon, when students are in their special classes, I meet with teachers to talk about instruction or assessment results. Students benefit from seeing us work together; they see the same topic presented in different ways."

Given the premise that reading/literacy specialists have a multifaceted role, in the remainder of the chapter I focus on two major topics: a framework that describes the multiple roles of specialized literacy professionals, including the reading/literacy specialist; and key challenges that reading/literacy specialists face in today's schools, followed by ideas for how they might address these challenges.

A FRAMEWORK DESCRIBING THE MULTIPLE ROLES OF SPECIALIZED LITERACY PROFESSIONALS

In *Standards 2017,* the title *specialized literacy professionals* was used as an overarching term to describe the roles of various literacy professionals (i.e., reading/literacy specialist, literacy coach, literacy coordinator). Further, in these standards the primary role of the reading/literacy specialist was identified as that of instruction, and at the same time, it was acknowledged that these specialists also had responsibilities for working with teachers and at the school or system level. In Figure 3.1 (ILA, 2018), the pertinent levels of emphases for the roles of reading/literacy specialist, literacy coach, and literacy coordinator are summarized; note, however, that there are no distinct lines between the three levels. Rather the figure highlights the fact that most often reading/literacy specialists spend most of their time working with students, with less time devoted to working with teachers and school systems. This means that the *frequency* as well as the *nature* of responsibilities may differ from those of coaches or coordinators who spend more time with teachers or have system-level responsibilities. However, the context in which reading/specialists work does influence their role and responsibilities.

As a means of thinking about the three roles of the specialized literacy professional addressed throughout this book, I describe a framework, as

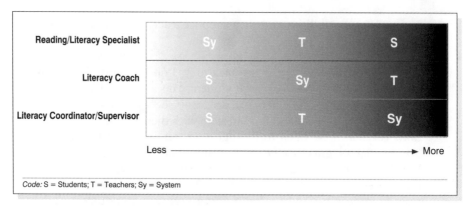

FIGURE 3.1. Levels of emphasis in *Standards 2017*. From ILA (2018). Copyright © 2018 International Literacy Association. Reprinted by permission.

summarized in Figure 3.2, that builds on the Galloway and Lesaux framework (2014) and the content of *Standards 2017*. This framework identifies three major areas of focus: the student, the teacher, and the system. In this chapter, I specifically address these three areas of focus as they relate to reading/literacy specialists as literacy leaders in all aspects of their role (i.e., their work with students, teachers, and the system). In Chapter 4, Ippolito and Lieberman describe the role of the literacy coach more specifically. Note that the lines in the circle between each of the areas of focus are dotted, indicating that there is often overlap in responsibilities for these specialized literacy professionals.

Student-Focused Area

Reading/literacy specialists are responsible for assessing the literacy strengths and needs of students, and they must be able to share that information in a meaningful way with their teaching colleagues, administrators, and families. As exemplified previously by Katie Regner, they may work in both in class and pullout contexts to provide instruction. When working in the classroom, they often co-plan and co-teach with teachers, which requires collaboration, leadership, and communication skills. They may also model specific instructional strategies while the teacher watches or assists. Although most frequently they provide intervention-type instruction for students experiencing reading or writing difficulties, they may also develop and implement instruction for other students. Katie, for example, described her work with an enrichment group of 12 students in which they read challenging texts and then participated in follow-up discussions that emphasized critical thinking. As Katie mentioned, this was an exciting

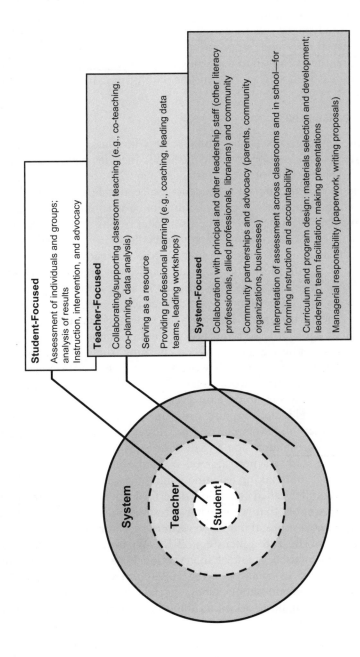

Student-Focused

Assessment of individuals and groups; analysis of results

Instruction, intervention, and advocacy

Teacher-Focused

Collaborating/supporting classroom teaching (e.g., co-teaching, co-planning, data analysis)

Serving as a resource

Providing professional learning (e.g., coaching, leading data teams, leading workshops)

System-Focused

Collaboration with principal and other leadership staff (other literacy professionals, allied professionals, librarians) and community

Community partnerships and advocacy (parents, community organizations, businesses)

Interpretation of assessment across classrooms and in school—for informing instruction and accountability

Curriculum and program design: materials selection and development; leadership team facilitation; making presentations

Managerial responsibility (paperwork, writing proposals)

System

Teacher

Student

FIGURE 3.2. Framework for specialized literacy professionals as literacy leaders: Areas of focus.

opportunity for her; moreover, students began to realize that there was no stigma attached to working with her. Reading/literacy specialists also have an important advocacy role,: That is, they do all they can to ensure that their students are receiving appropriate and effective instruction. To do that, they are often involved in collecting and analyzing assessment results that they discuss with teachers as a means of informing instruction.

Teacher-Focused Area

Reading/literacy specialists must collaborate with classroom teachers to develop effective instruction for students. This includes having conversations with teachers about possible strategies, materials, or approaches that can be used to provide support to students, especially those who need specific intervention support. When co-planning or co-teaching, they will need to problem-solve with teachers, using assessment results to make decisions about instruction. Some reading/literacy specialists may be asked to lead workshops or make presentations about specific instructional approaches or strategies (e.g., talk to the fourth-grade team about implementing writing workshops) or model a specific approach in a classroom. Experienced reading/literacy specialists may be asked to coach teachers; for example, watching a teacher try a new instructional approach and then having a conversation about that lesson and how it might be modified or adapted for the students in that classroom. When coaching, these reading/literacy specialists most likely focus on what Bean and Ippolito (2015) identify in their levels of intensity framework as level 1; that is, they work informally with teachers, making sure to develop a trusting relationship. Examples of coaching at this level include holding problem-solving conversations about students or instruction, developing and providing materials for colleagues, and developing curriculum. Some reading/literacy specialists may, however, be working with teachers at level 2 (analyzing practice) or level 3 (changing practice and making teaching public).[1]

In 2012, Jennifer Lillenstein and I described the results of our observations in five schools that were using a response-to-intervention (RTI) framework to learn more about how various specialized literacy professionals functioned (Bean & Lillenstein, 2012). We found that reading specialists provided focused, frequent intervention for selected students and informal support to teachers, working collaboratively with them. They also functioned as a team with coaches, special educators, a psychologist, and the principal in making decisions about how to support instruction at

---

[1] A free, reproducible copy of the levels of intensity is available at *www.learningsciences. com/media/wysiwyg/Study-Guides/Cultivating-Coaching-Mindsets/CCMch1. Coaching_Activities_of_Specialized_Literacy_Professionals.pdf.*

all levels (e.g., Tiers 1, 2, and 3). These responsibilities required reading/literacy specialists to be especially knowledgeable about literacy acquisition, instruction, and assessment. Again, reading/literacy specialists were expected to advocate for teachers to ensure that they have the resources, time, and professional support to teach effectively.

System-Focused Area

Reading/literacy specialists may have some responsibility for working at a school or systemwide level. A key task is that of working closely with the principal and other leadership staff to ensure that there is a coherent, comprehensive literacy program in the school, both horizontally (within grade levels) and vertically (from grade to grade). Some reading/literacy specialists also have responsibilities for reviewing assessment data across grades and the school. They may serve as members or even lead literacy leadership data meetings. They are often responsible for developing programs to encourage parent involvement in the school; often this is a requirement of those who work with Title I programs. At times, they may have responsibilities that require them to lead efforts to develop curriculum and select or design materials. Advocacy for the literacy program, the school, and its programmatic efforts is also a key role for some reading/literacy specialists. Further, reading/literacy specialists often have managerial responsibilities that require them to write proposals (e.g., a proposal to receive Every Student Succeeds Act funds) and to handle the paperwork that often accompanies these responsibilities.

It is obvious, then, that the reading/literacy specialist does have a multifaceted role, one with a myriad of responsibilities. As Katie stated, "I work with so many different people—all stakeholders. I love working with teachers, administrators, kids, and parents, even though they are looking for different things." This brings me to the next section of this chapter, which highlights key challenges faced by those serving as reading/literacy specialists.

CHALLENGES FACED BY READING/LITERACY SPECIALISTS IN TODAY'S SCHOOLS

Although all educators face issues related to their work, reading/literacy specialists often have unique challenges that require them to be especially knowledgeable about how to address their multifaceted role. Some of these challenges are specific to the context of the schools in which they work; others are related to current policy requirements of districts, states, or the federal government. Before addressing these challenges, I present a fictional case example that puts them into perspective or describes what I call a "reality-based picture." Think about the following questions as you read this scenario.

CASE EXAMPLE ·

THINK ABOUT THIS

1. What specific challenges does Frank face?
2. How comfortable would you be if your principal asked you to change your role to include more work with teachers? What would be your concerns?
3. What do you think about Frank's ideas for addressing this issue of change? Are they realistic? Do you have other ideas you might suggest?

On Tuesday, Frank, a reading/literacy specialist, met with his principal to discuss the state test scores, which indicated that the fourth graders were not doing well on the reading comprehension section of the test. The principal asked Frank if he could rearrange his schedule to meet with the fourth-grade teachers and provide them with the professional learning they needed to help them make some changes in their instruction. Although Frank thought this was probably a good idea, he wasn't quite sure how to manage another responsibility. His schedule was already full: He worked with fourth-, fifth-, and sixth-grade students experiencing reading difficulties in a pullout context and had only two free periods each day. In addition, Frank anticipated that some teachers would be unhappy if he reduced or eliminated the time he spent working with their students. For example, Jessica counted on him pulling out six students for 45 minutes 2 days a week; during that time, she had the remaining students read, discuss, and write about challenging informational text. On the other hand, there was Mrs. Hanover. Frank chuckled as he thought of how she always complained when he came to the classroom door to get the assigned four students from her room. "Now I'll have to help them catch up on what they are missing." She was not a fan of pullout instruction! She'd probably be delighted if he stopped working with her students.

As an experienced reading specialist, Frank was also concerned about the district's recent adoption of a scripted program that was to be used by all reading/literacy specialists for their intervention work. Frank was ambivalent about this change because he knew that many of his students had unique and specific needs that would not be addressed by this program. Frank acknowledged tweaking some of the lessons so that they were more appropriate for his students.

As Frank left the building that Tuesday, his head was spinning. Perhaps he should consider going back to the classroom where he could just be responsible for the 25 students assigned to him! On second thought, Frank loved his role as a reading/literacy specialist, not only the work with students, but the opportunity to collaborate with teachers to develop strong classroom literacy programs for students. He also knew that he wasn't afraid of change, enjoyed problem solving, and realized that he did not have to address these issues by himself. He would sit down with the leadership team to tackle each of these challenges and ask this group to help him think about possible options that might improve the current ways in which he worked.

. . . .

The story of Frank is not an unusual one; it highlights several of the challenges that reading/literacy specialists face. In the next section I elaborate on these challenges and provide some suggestions that reading/specialists might consider for addressing them.

Meeting Expectations of Different Stakeholders: Different Strokes for Different Folks

Those who earn reading/literacy specialist certification often have specific expectations about what their responsibilities might be. Many have become specialists because they have a commitment and passion for working with students experiencing difficulties, and they expect to spend most of their days teaching these students. However, as illustrated in the case example of Frank, administrators from either the school or district also have expectations for the role (e.g., Frank's principal wants him to help fourth-grade teachers implement strategies for enhancing students' reading comprehension). Also, as described above, the expectations of teachers may differ from that of the administrator, and as well, individual teachers may differ in their expectations. Further, reading/literacy specialists themselves have their own personal beliefs about what they do best and how they view the role. There are reading/literacy specialists who are passionate about their work with students and much less enthusiastic about working with teachers! Some, especially those new to the reading/specialist position, don't feel as though they have the knowledge to work with more experienced teachers.

Reading/literacy specialists then must be able to think creatively about how to deal with the differing expectations of stakeholders. Becoming knowledgeable about adult learning theory and system-level change can help them understand not only why perspectives and differences exist, but also how to address those differences. Reading/literacy specialists might also ask themselves the following questions as they think about this issue of differing expectations.

- Is there a written job description? Such a description can be helpful as a means of setting parameters for the role. Moreover, candidates for a position can decide whether the emphases of that position are something with which they are comfortable. In other words, is there a match between the role expectations and the candidate's knowledge, skills, and expectations?

- Taking this to a personal level, how comfortable are you with the role as described? If you are expected to collaborate with teachers, how much experience do you have in that area? Do you recognize the importance of being a good listener, of helping teachers solve problems, and working collaboratively with them? Where can you go to learn more about how to collaborate with the teachers in your school?

- How flexible are you? Are you aware that professionals in a school may have philosophies about teaching, learning, and literacy that may differ from yours? Can you make the adjustments needed to work effectively with these teachers? Consider the fact that you need to work with teachers in a respectful way and, at the same time, stand up for what you believe is important in helping students become effective literacy learners. For example, if students haven't finished their classroom assignments because of their work with you, and are expected to give up their recess break to complete it, in what ways can you help teachers understand how detrimental that might be to the emotional growth of their students?

- Do teachers view you as credible, as someone who works effectively with students and also understands classroom challenges and dilemmas? Your work with students can help you develop that credibility; that is, you can speak from experience (e.g., "I have been using Readers' Theatre with your students in a small group, and it really seemed to help them develop fluency. Would it be possible for us to try this in your classroom?").

Wearing Many Hats: The Multiple Dimensions of the Role

As described above, results of various surveys have substantiated the many different tasks that reading/literacy specialists are expected to assume. Recently, I talked with an elementary reading/literacy specialist whose job description indicated that she was to work as an interventionist for 50% of her time and as a coach for 50% of her time. As she stated, however, she spends about 70% or more of her time with students, and the remainder with teachers. Given the numbers of students with whom she works, coaching receives less emphasis. Likewise, Mike Henry, a high school literacy professional who has written a vignette for this book (see pp. 89–91), indicates that his workload is distributed between his teaching responsibilities (60%) and coaching (40%). This is a great example of what is summarized in Figure 3.1; although Mike has important instructional responsibilities, he also has a key coaching role, although he spends less time in that role. Many reading/literacies specialists (as well as coaches) are faced with "wearing several hats," sometimes because they are the only specialized literacy professional in the school and sometimes because of role expectations. As Hudson and Pletcher (2016) state, often the reading specialist moves back and forth from an instructional role to one of coaching. Pletcher, Hudson, John, and Scott (2018) call this a *hybrid role,* and indicate it is not for the "faint of heart" (p. 1). Regardless, here are some thoughts to consider when faced with responsibilities that include working with both students and teachers:

- *Work smart!* It's often difficult to make time for collaborating with teachers (e.g., co-planning, coaching), given their busy schedules. You will need to find creative ways of connecting with teachers. For example, is there some scheduled time between periods for a short, focused conversation? Would the principal be willing to arrange schedules so that a group of teachers have time to meet while their students are attending special-subject classes? In some schools, the schedule provides for a weekly or monthly meeting of grade-level or departmental-area teachers with the reading/literacy specialist. Flexibility is key; when an opportunity to collaborate arises, seize it!

- *Set priorities by focusing on students and their needs.* In planning your intervention work, think about which students need more intervention and how often you need to meet with them. Which students would benefit from pullout instruction, and are there some with whom you might work in their classroom? Are there other students whom classroom teachers might instruct, especially if teachers were given specific instructional suggestions?

- *Focus on student learning to support teacher learning.* How aware are you of what your students are learning in their classrooms and where they might be experiencing difficulties? Do you know what topics they are studying or what books they are reading? In Figure 3.3, I list questions you may want to use when you meet with teachers about their students. Such discussions can help you become more intentional in making instructional decisions, and at the same time, you may be able to support what the teacher is doing in the classroom—an informal and nonthreatening way to address the teacher-focused responsibilities of your role. Your work with teachers may reduce the necessity for you to provide intervention for some of the students.

- *Discuss your schedule with the principal.* He or she needs to be aware of what you are doing and any challenges you face in meeting your responsibilities. Your principal is an important ally, and you need his or her support if you are to be effective in your role.

A. Learning more about students and their success in the classroom
1. What do you see as the major needs of this student in reading? Writing? Other related literacy skills?
2. What do you see as some strengths of this student in the literacy area (that we can build on)?
3. To what degree is this student succeeding in the activities that he or she is being asked to do?
4. How well does he or she work in group activities? Individual activities?
5. What other things can you tell me about this student that will help me in my instructional planning? For example, does he or she enjoy reading or writing tasks? Avoid them? Any behavioral issues?
B. Planning for student work
6. What unit or topic are you currently working on in your classroom? How might I use what you are teaching to help me plan my instruction?
7. How can I work with you to support your classroom instruction for this student? What specific skills/strategies might you want me to address?
8. How might we work together (e.g., co-plan, co-teach) to support this student?

FIGURE 3.3. Teacher–specialist conversation about students.

Addressing Both Student Needs and Classroom Requirements

As stated in *The Role of the Reading Specialist: Leadership and Coaching for Classroom, School, and Community* (Bean, 2015), reading/literacy specialists must be able to design instruction that (1) meets the needs of students and (2) helps them succeed in their classrooms. The effective specialist can identify students' strengths and needs and use that knowledge to develop instruction to improve their literacy learning. Specialists may work on specific skills (e.g., structural analysis, phonics) or focus on instruction that helps students develop strategies for learning (e.g., summarizing). At the same time, regardless of grade level, reading/literacy specialists have a responsibility to help students achieve success in their classrooms. When students can apply what they are learning in a pullout supplemental class to their classroom assignments, they may become more motivated to participate in reading and writing activities and gain a greater sense of self-confidence and self-efficacy. For example, students in the early grades may benefit from additional fluency practice (e.g., rereading of text) with the reading/literacy specialist, so that they can then participate successfully when reading the same text aloud in their classrooms. At later grades, students may need additional practice and support to learn specific academic vocabulary or to learn strategies for developing word knowledge, both keys for learning in a content area. Think about the following:

- *Knowledge of strengths and needs.* What measures or tools can be used to determine students' strengths and needs and to make decisions about instruction? What materials, strategies, and grouping plans should be considered?

- *Knowledge of classroom assignments and activities.* As mentioned, reading/literacy specialists who know what students are experiencing in their classrooms can develop, much more successfully, lessons that reinforce what students are learning in the classroom. Also, a discussion with teachers can help you learn a great deal about how students are perceived by a specific teacher and by other students (see Figure 3.3).

Time and Scheduling

When I talked with Katie Regner, she indicated that her greatest challenge was "time to do everything that I wanted to do." I have heard this concern many times from reading/literacy specialists with whom I have talked, and the reading/literacy specialists interviewed in previous studies (Bean et al., 2003; Bean et al., 2015) also identified time as a concern. If specialists are assigned to teach students for six of the seven daily periods, it is difficult to provide much support to teachers. Specialists in such a position most often have to talk with teachers "on the fly"; some schedule brief meetings before and after school. At times, there may be opportunities, while teaching in the classroom, to talk briefly with teachers about students, grouping, or instruction. Even if reading/literacy specialists have some flexible time to meet with teachers about students, teachers may not be available, given their many responsibilities. Several suggestions for addressing these issues of time and scheduling follow:

- *Use student needs to set priorities.* You can ask yourself how and where you can make the greatest difference. Perhaps, early in the year, it might be better to focus on those first graders who are having difficulties with phonemic awareness or phonics. Later in the year, you might want to work more intensely with a group of fourth graders who are experiencing difficulties with reading comprehension. Some reading/literacy specialists have found that they can be more effective if they work with a specific grade level (or levels) for a month or 6 weeks and then move on to another grade level. Scheduling flexibly requires that you have a relationship with the principal that allows you to request such scheduling modifications.

- *Get advice and support.* When you have difficulties meeting with teachers or even scheduling time to teach students who need instruction, it's wise to seek advice from others (e.g., teachers. principals, supervisor). Be sure to have a rationale for any suggestions you want to make. If the issue is meeting with teachers, the principal might be able to provide a substitute to take over a classroom while you meet with teachers. Teachers may be able to make suggestions about when they are available and willing to meet.

● *Work with the willing!* Often, reading/literacy specialists try to work collaboratively in the same way with all teachers whose students they teach. Yet, it might be better to begin by working in classrooms with those teachers who indicated an interest and receptivity to working more closely with you. You will probably be more successful by doing this rather than "requiring" all teachers to include you in their planning. Often, your success with this initial group of teachers will lead others to request your support and involvement. Katie Regner, for example, indicated that in the past, she tried to "see every teacher, but found that if a teacher wasn't doing something that lent itself to my being there [in the classroom], it was not useful."

The Importance of Working Collaboratively

Collaboration among school personnel has been found to be key to overall school improvement. As stated by DuFour (2016), "The fact that American educators work in isolation rather than in collaborative teams has consistently been cited as a primary obstacle to improving student achievement since the 1970s" (p. 9). Indeed, the word *collaborate* is found throughout *Standards 2017* for reading/literacy specialists (e.g., Standard 2: Collaborate with teachers to implement effective literacy practices; Standard 5: Collaborate with school personnel to use a variety of print and digital materials).

As mentioned previously, in the Bean and Lillenstein (2012) study of five elementary schools using an RTI model, reading specialists and coaches collaborated to make instructional and grouping decisions based on various assessment results, including informal teacher observations. Reading specialists and coaches functioned as a team; most often the coach had both coordination and coaching responsibilities, while the reading specialist provided instruction to students. However, "reading specialists were often involved in informal coaching" (Bean & Lillenstein, 2012, p. 499). Think about the following as ways to enhance collaborative efforts in the school:

● *Beyond labels!* As Cozart (2018) notes, too often students are categorized as being the responsibility of a specific teacher (e.g., special educator, Title I teacher). She describes the ways in her school in which all teachers as a team assumed responsibility for successfully teaching a specific student. Cozart describes teachers working together to teach students, of "looking beyond a label" (p. 261; that is, students in the school were viewed as the responsibility of all teachers).

 • *Sharing of data.* When teachers at a specific grade level or content-area department share assessment results that include informal observations by teachers and student work samples, they gain a better understanding of which instructional strategies are working—and which are not. They identify possible grouping arrangements not only within a specific classroom but across classrooms, to better meet the needs of students. And they learn from each other, asking questions and sharing ideas that enable them to solve instructional dilemmas.

 • *System supports.* When there is collaboration across classrooms, teachers are better able to determine what types of supports a particular student needs (e.g., Tier 2 or Tier 3 interventions, counseling). They can also collaboratively identify what they might do to modify and improve instruction and what support they need to accomplish their goals. For example, if teachers realize that they need to know more about how to teach writing, reading/literacy specialists, coaches, and teacher leaders can work together to make decisions about how to make the desired improvements. Perhaps there is a need to consider different instructional approaches, increase the time allocated for writing, or enhance teacher knowledge.

Scripted or Responsive Instruction

THINK ABOUT THIS

1. If you are required to use a scripted program, how can you make modifications in the lessons to address individual student needs? In what ways can you design more intense, explicit instruction or provide additional scaffolding for specific students?

2. Have you thought about raising questions about the use of such programs with your administrators, indicating your concerns and suggesting ideas for how to provide alternatives or modifications to the program?

During the past decade and a half, there has been an emphasis on using core, often scripted programs to improve reading achievement. Reading First, with its emphasis on teaching with fidelity (Dewitz & Jones, 2013), and initiatives such as RTI and multi-tiered systems of support (MTSS) have led districts to search for programs that provide targeted interventions to specific groups of students. Such programs too often focus on constrained skills (Dewitz & Jones, 2013; Dougherty Stahl, 2011), with an emphasis on phonics and decoding, and fewer opportunities for active engagement with reading and writing. Such programs may limit teachers' initiative to think about what worked in a specific lesson, what did not work, and what modifications might be necessary if students are to be successful. Reading/ literacy specialists may be put in the position of following the script, rather than designing intentional and responsive instruction. Although scripted programs can provide a general roadmap, reading/literacy specialists must think about the detours they need to take if students are not successful with a specific lesson or lessons. Responsive instruction requires reading/literacy specialists to be reflective practitioners who can pinpoint what students need and design instruction that addresses those needs; it requires that they know their students, what they can and cannot do. As Katie Regner stated, "My principal allows me to have an overview/agenda of my plan for the week with each group, but I'm not required to have specific lesson plans. He realizes that something may come up one day that requires that I change or slow down my lesson for the next day."

Keeping Abreast of Policy and Legislative Requirements

Previously, I discussed the huge effect that federal legislation has had on reading instruction and the role of the reading specialist. Current initiatives such as RTI and MTSS have also had an impact on how reading/ literacy specialists' function in schools. The most recent federal legislation, Every Student Succeeds Act (2015), which replaced No Child Left Behind, provides more flexibility to states in developing their plans for receiving federal funds. For example, although states are accountable for student learning, they can set their own long-term achievement goals, and there is no requirement that 100% of the students score at proficiency or above. Reading/literacy specialists need to be aware of (1) state requirements regarding standards, testing, and accountability, and (2) efforts to reform and improve instruction, especially in low-achieving schools. Here are some questions to consider as you think about state and federal requirements and how they influence your work.

- To what extent are you aware of any federal, state, or district regulations that affect your role? Does your school district provide you with information about various policy initiatives or changes?
- Does your district make it possible for you to attend key workshops in which you can learn more about these initiatives? Do you share your knowledge with other professionals in your school?

Serving as an Advocate

As indicated in *Standards 2017* (Standard 6), reading/literacy specialists have an important advocacy role, especially for the students they serve. I have known reading specialists who served as advocates in many creative ways: for example, taking their students to a local bookstore and letting them choose and purchase a book that they especially liked, promoting self-confidence in older students by arranging for them to tutor or read to younger ones. At times, their student advocacy role is demonstrated in their work with teachers; for example, making suggestions about strategies for promoting the self-confidence and sense of self-worth of these students in the classroom.

In addition, reading/literacy specialists can advocate for teachers. They can encourage administrators to schedule times for teachers to plan collaboratively with them, ask that teachers be permitted to attend conferences, and support teachers who want to make justifiable modifications in their instructional plans so that they can better meet student needs. Further, effective reading/literacy specialists are always looking for ways to advocate for the families of the students with whom they work. They provide them with resources, help them obtain any additional support their children might need, and represent them when there are conflicts related to issues that affect their children (e.g., assessment, instruction, grouping). Most of all, they are good listeners who learn much from their interactions with families.

Finally, reading/literacy specialists advocate for effective literacy instruction. When they know that specific literacy practices in the school do not reflect effective literacy instruction, they are willing to step forward and share evidence that illustrates why such practices might need to be modified (Bean & Ippolito, 2015). Some thoughts to consider:

- *Student advocacy.* In what ways do I work with my students so that they feel good about who they are and what they can do? Can I identify their specific strengths and competencies, beyond those related to literacy? In what ways do I help them develop a motivation to read? In what ways do I support efforts to provide these students with the very best literacy instruction?

- *Promoting literacy in the school.* Reading/literacy specialists who are effective advocates find ways to illustrate to the community the many ways that school professionals are working to provide an excellent education for students. They share test results and results of student work. They work with their colleagues to develop a school environment that highlights student work and pride in what is being accomplished.

Evaluating Your Work

Effective reading/literacy specialists are always thinking about ways to improve, and to do that, they must consider what information might be useful to them in making changes in how they work. For example, results of student assessment can be one indicator of whether they have had any effect on literacy learning. However, these test results, although important, are limited by several factors (e.g., students receive instruction from more than the reading/literacy specialist; test results are limited in what they measure). Often, an evaluation of one's work is related to specific goals, generally set in collaboration with the principal. These goals are often accompanied by examples of how they are to be measured. Reading/literacy specialists might consider some of the following ideas for assessing their own performance.

They might ask teachers to complete a survey about ways in which the reading/literacy specialist has helped them or their students (Bean, 2015). Reading/literacy specialists might also keep a journal or diary of their everyday activities, which they can then share with administrators as evidence of the numbers of students and teachers with whom they have worked and the specific activities in which they engaged. Those reading/literacy specialists who keep a journal of their successes or challenges can also use this as a self-assessment tool, reminding them of what they did that was effective, what concerns or problems arose, and whether there is a need for change. I'm reminded of the words of John Gardner, a well-known social scientist, who many years ago in his book *Self-Renewal* (1964/1995) described the need to "repot" oneself as a means of remaining innovative and staying engaged—that is, to embrace change as necessary for self-growth. Questions to ask include:

- In what ways do I keep track of my responsibilities and how I meet them? Do I share what I have learned with the principal as a means of making changes in my position (e.g., need for more time to meet with teachers)?
- Have I worked with my principal to set goals and determine ways in which I can assess the accomplishment of those goals?
- Am I willing to consider changes in how I work? What might I do to improve my effectiveness?

Being Nimble Requires Being a Lifelong Learner

There is nothing more constant than change! Think about the many ways in which schools have had to change during the past decade: increase in technology use, changes in teaching beginning reading, the emphasis on disciplinary literacy, and so on. And, as mentioned previously, the role of reading/literacy specialists has changed over time. To adjust to these changes, reading/literacy specialists (and all professionals) must be lifelong learners, that is, they need to stay abreast of new evidence about literacy and learning. They can accomplish this in many ways: reading professional articles, attending conferences, joining book clubs, and so on. I know of a group of reading/literacy specialists who meet once a month on a Friday evening to share ideas and discuss dilemmas and challenges. They go home with new ideas and are inspired to continue their difficult but rewarding work. They also enjoy an evening with colleagues who are passionate about their work!

By keeping current, they are better prepared to adjust when they are required to make changes in roles or responsibilities. For example, they may be able to lead a workshop with teachers in their school about new ideas for promoting the reading of informational text in the primary grades or developing strategies for improving higher-order thinking skills of intermediate students. In addition to gaining new knowledge about literacy teaching and learning, however, reading/literacy specialists, given their leadership role, have a responsibility to learn more about adult learning and system-level change. It is this knowledge that often can guide reading/literacy specialists in developing the ability to work well with teachers. Which of the following applies to you as a lifelong learner?

- To what organizations do I belong? What professional journals do I read? What conferences do I attend?
- Do I belong to a network of colleagues who are eager to share successes and dilemmas and to problem-solve as a means of continual self-renewal?
- In what ways do I share my knowledge and expertise with others (e.g., presenting at conferences, writing brief pieces for the teachers in my school, writing a blog?

CONCLUSION

Although the reading/literacy specialist role is a complex one, those who serve in this role can be assured that they can make a difference in the teaching and learning that take place in the schools in which they work. To be effective, they must understand and value their role as literacy leaders. Such a role requires that they work collaboratively with teachers and others in the school to design, implement, and evaluate literacy instruction that addresses the needs of the students in their schools. They must take advantage of the opportunities they have to work intentionally and yet flexibly with both students and teachers. Most of all, they need to view themselves and be viewed by others as key members of the school team, working toward a common vision: that of improving literacy instruction for all students in the school.

1. Read the ILA brief *Multiple Roles of Specialized Literacy Professionals*[2] to learn more about how each of the specialized literacy roles is defined and described. These role definitions were used to develop standards for each of the role groups in *Standards 2017.*

2. Interview a reading/literacy specialist to learn more about how that individual functions in his or her role. Use Figure 3.2, the *framework for specialized literacy professionals as literacy leaders,* to guide your discussion.

3. Observe a reading/literacy specialist working in a pullout setting and then in an in-class setting. What do you see that is similar about the two teaching situations? Different?

ANNOTATED RESOURCES

Bean, R. M., & Goatley, V. (in press). *The literacy specialist: Leadership and coaching for the classroom, school, and community* (4th ed.). New York: Guilford Press.

In this book, each of the multiple roles that literacy specialists (PreK–12) are asked to fulfill is described. Ideas for working with students experiencing reading difficulties and supporting teachers through collaboration and coaching are offered. An emphasis is placed on the importance of the leadership role, and ideas presented for how literacy specialists can develop essential communication and facilitation skills.

Bean, R. M., & Kern, D. (2018). Multiple roles of specialized literacy professionals: The ILA 2017 Standards. *The Reading Teacher, 71*(5), 615–621.

The authors describe the distinctions that these standards make in setting expectations, and what these expectations mean in relation to what specialized literacy professionals need to know and be able to do.

Galloway, E. P., & Lesaux, N. K. (2014). Leader, teacher, diagnostician, colleague, and change agent: A synthesis of the research on the role of the reading specialist in this era of RTI-based literacy reform. *The Reading Teacher, 67*(7), 517–526.

In this synthesis of the research, the authors describe three key themes: the multiple roles and the comfort in meeting them, the different expectations of various stakeholders, and the importance of context in setting role expectations.

REFERENCES

Allington, R. L. (1986). Policy constraints and effective compensatory reading instruction: A review. In J. Hoffman (Ed.), *Effective teaching of reading and research and practice* (pp. 261–289). Newark, DE: International Reading Association.

---

[2] Available at *www.literacyworldwide.org/docs/default-source/where-we-stand/literacy-professionals-research-brief.pdf.*

Allington, R. L., & McGill-Franzen, A. (1989). School response to reading failure: Instruction for Chapter 1 and special education students in grades 2, 4, and 8. *Elementary School Journal, 89*, 529–542.

Allington, R. L., & Shake, M. C. (1986). Remedial reading: Achieving curricular congruence in classroom and clinic. *The Reading Teacher, 39*(7), 648–654.

Bean, R. M. (2001). Classroom teachers and reading specialists working together to improve student achievement. In V. Risko & K. Bromley (Eds.), *Collaboration for diverse learners: Viewpoints and practices* (pp. 348–368). Newark, DE: International Reading Association.

Bean, R. M. (2015). *The reading specialist: Leadership and coaching for the classroom, school, and community* (3rd ed.). New York: Guilford Press.

Bean, R. M., Cassidy, J., Grumet, J. V., Shelton, D., & Wallis, S. R. (2002). What do reading specialists do?: Results from a national survey. *The Reading Teacher, 55*(8), 2–10.

Bean, R. M., Cooley, W., Eichelberger, R. T., Lazar, M., & Zigmond, N. (1991). In-class or pullout: Effects of setting on the remedial reading program. *Journal of Reading Behavior, 23*(4), 445–464.

Bean, R. M., & Ippolito, J. (2015). *Cultivating coaching mindsets: An action guide for literacy leaders*. West Palm Beach, FL: Learning Sciences International.

Bean, R. M., Kern, D., Goatley, V., Ortlieb, E., Shettel, J., Calo, K., et al. (2015). Specialized literacy professionals as literacy leaders: Results of a national survey. *Literacy Research and Instruction, 54*(2), 83–114.

Bean, R. M., & Lillenstein, J. (2012). Response to intervention and the changing roles of schoolwide personnel. *The Reading Teacher, 65*(7), 491–501.

Bean, R. M., Swan, A. L., & Knaub, R. (2003). Reading specialists in schools with exemplary reading programs: Functional, versatile, and prepared. *The Reading Teacher, 56*(5), 446–455.

Bean, R. M., Trovato, C., & Hamilton, R. (1995). Focus on Chapter 1 reading programs: Views of reading specialists, classroom teachers, and principals. *Reading Research and Instruction, 35*(3), 204–221.

Borman, G. D., & D'Agostino, V. (2001). Title 1 and student achievement: A quantitative synthesis. In G. D. Borman, S. C. Stringfield, & R. E. Slavin (Eds.), *Title I: Compensatory education at the crossroads* (pp. 25–57). Hillsdale, NJ: Erlbaum.

Cook, L., & Friend, M. (1995). Co-teaching: Guidelines for creating effective practices. *Exceptional Children, 28*(3), 1–16.

Cozart, T. J. (2018). Looking beyond a label. *The Reading Teacher, 72*(2), 261.

Dewitz, P., & Jones, J. (2013). Using basal readers: From dutiful fidelity to intelligence decision making. *The Reading Teacher, 66*(5), 391–400.

Dolch, E. (1940). A remedial-reading specialist in every school. *Elementary School Journal, 41*(3), 206–209. Retrieved from *www.jstor.org/stable*.

Dougherty Stahl, K. A. (2011). Applying new visions of reading development in today's classrooms. *The Reading Teacher, 65*(1), 52–56.

DuFour, R. (2016). *ESSA: An opportunity for American education*. Bloomington, IN: Solution Tree Press.

Elementary and Secondary Education Act of 1965, Pub.L.No. 89-10, 29 Stat.27.

Every Student Succeeds Act of 2015, Pub.L.No. 114-95 &114 Stat.1177 (2015). 116, 33–37.

Galloway, E. P., & Lesaux, N. K. (2014). Leader, teacher, diagnostician, colleague, and change agent: A synthesis of the research on the role of the reading specialist in this era of RTI-based literacy reform. *The Reading Teacher, 67*(7), 517–526.

Gardner, J. W. (1995). *Self-renewal: The individual and the innovative society*. New York: Norton. (Original work published 1964)

Hudson, A., & Pletcher, B. C. (2016). From reading specialist to coach and back again: Considering coaching conversations with teachers. *Texas Journal of Literacy Education, 4*(2), 126–129.

International Literacy Association (ILA). (2018). *Standards for the preparation of literacy professionals 2017*. Newark, DE: Author.

International Reading Association. (2000). *Teaching all children to read: The roles of the reading specialist*. Newark, DE: Author.

Kennedy, M. M., Birman, B. F., & Demaline, R. E. (1986). *The effectiveness of Chapter services: Second interim report from the national assessment of Chapter 1*. Washington, DC: Office of Educational Research and Improvement.

Pletcher, B. C., Hudson, A. K., John, L., & Scott, A. (2018). Coaching on borrowed time: Balancing the roles of the literacy professional. *The Reading Teacher, 72*(6), 689–699.

Quatroche, D. J., Bean, R. M., & Hamilton, R. L. (2001). The role of the reading specialist: A review of research. *The Reading Teacher, 55*(3), 282–294.

Slavin, R. E. (1987). Making Chapter 1 make a difference. *Phi Delta Kappan, 69*(2), 110–119.

Snow, C., Burns, N. S., & Griffin, P. (1998). *Preventing reading difficulties in young children*. Washington, DC: National Research Council.

Walp, T. P., & Walmsley, S. A. (1989). Instructional and philosophical congruence: Neglected aspects of coordination. *The Reading Teacher, 42*(6), 364–368.

Literacy Leadership in Action

Susan Porter, MEd
Literacy Specialist, Fall-Hamilton Enhanced Option School,
Nashville, Tennessee

THINK ABOUT THIS

1. In what ways does Susan serve as a literacy leader?
2. What lessons can be learned about Susan in her multifaceted role as a literacy/reading specialist?
3. What questions come to mind while reading this vignette?

Currently, I serve as the literacy teacher development specialist (LTDS) in an elementary school in a large urban district. My school, a PreK–4 building, serves a diverse student body with over half of our students qualifying for free or reduced lunch and almost 20% eligible for special education. In my district, the reading professional role has changed from reading specialist to literacy coach to LTDS. As part of my role, I administer our universal screening assessments, teach small groups of students identified for Tier 3 reading support, and assist the administration in making decisions related to instruction and intervention. My primary responsibilities, however, are coaching classroom teachers and providing professional learning on high-quality literacy instruction. In addition to these responsibilities, I serve on our state's Dyslexia Advisory Council.

At my school, we established shared leadership through collaborative weekly planning around rich, complex texts. For example, the first-grade teachers were doing a unit on plants and chose to use the texts *Sunflower House* by Eve Bunting and *The Dandelion Seed* by Joseph Anthony and Cris Arbo. During weekly planning sessions, grade-level teams and I discussed the author's key understandings of a preselected complex text and drafted a focus question to guide our students in uncovering those key ideas. The focus question also served as the summative writing task at the end of the week. After the focus question was drafted, we discussed (1) what meaning, structural, vocabulary, and language demands made the text complex for our students; (2) what kinds of knowledge our students could bring to the text; and (3) what kinds of knowledge and skills they needed to be successful in understanding the text. We also considered what connections students could make between their lives or previous texts that would enhance their comprehension of the new text. We noted these complexities and addressed them through the text-based questions we wrote to guide our students to a deeper understanding of the author's message. We chose Tennessee reading standards that paired well with the text, always including Standards 1 (key ideas and details) and 10 (text complexity). By the end of our planning sessions, we had created a rich progression of literacy instruction based on our knowledge of our students and the high expectations of the literacy standards. Throughout the year, teachers visit each other's classrooms to provide feedback about their instruction based on their collaborative planning. This collaborative planning process has empowered teachers to take the lead in planning their literacy instruction.

Data from our district and state assessments provide evidence of the efficacy of this collaboration. Last year, our students improved 10 percentage points on the state reading assessment. More importantly, we have watched our students grow in perseverance and stamina when engaging with complex texts. Further evidence of the positive impact of this collaborative work is the shifting mindsets of teachers. In the beginning, many teachers were hesitant to shift to text-based planning. Some felt that the process was time-consuming; others believed strongly in a standards-first approach. Teachers were concerned about how our students would respond to being asked to read challenging texts. As they have become comfortable with the process, those same teachers now see how their students can be successful with complex texts when supported by rich instructional support and discussions. Teachers have also commented that the joy of teaching and learning has returned to their classrooms with the use of engaging texts and rich discussions with their students.

Despite the changing title, I have learned that being a school-based literacy professional is a multifaceted role that can vary based on the context. I realize that flexibility and adaptability are keys for positively impacting students' literacy success in our schools. I strive to recognize the strengths and needs of the teachers and students with whom I work and draw on my ever-growing understanding of the complexities of literacy. As a literacy specialist, it is important to grow alongside the teachers and learn from them, just as you want them to learn from you. Building trusting relationships situated in goals to deepen knowledge around using complex texts with rigorous standards is one of the ways I serve as a literacy leader in my school.

CHAPTER 4

Literacy Coaches as Literacy Leaders

Jacy Ippolito
Joanna Lieberman

GUIDING QUESTIONS

⤳ How can literacy coaches:

> ⤳ Organize their time to work with both individual teachers and larger systems within the school?
> ⤳ Work with principals, teacher leaders, and community stakeholders to create a coherent culture of literacy teaching and learning?
> ⤳ Adopt the mindsets of leader, facilitator, designer, and advocate to support continual improvement?
> ⤳ Differentiate professional learning experiences for teachers to support targeted adult learning?

⤳ How can the *Standards for the Preparation of Literacy Professionals 2017* guide the preparation and work of literacy coaches?

Research, practice, and policy focused on the work of literacy coaches have evolved steadily over the past few decades in the United States. We have witnessed a shift from early research and descriptions of teacher collaboration within *peer-coaching* models (Joyce & Showers, 1996), to one-on-one mentoring within *cognitive coaching* models (Costa & Garmston, 2002), to more content-focused and programmatic coaching models associated with initiatives such as Reading First (Bean, Draper, Hall, Vandermolen, & Zigmond, 2010; Deussen, Coskie, Robinson, & Autio, 2007). Research into coaches' relationships with teachers has described a variety of stances and ways of working that coaches might adopt (Ippolito, 2010a, 2010b; Moran, 2007; Rainville & Jones, 2008), and distinctions have been made between coaching in the early grades versus coaching in secondary school settings (Blamey, Meyer, & Walpole, 2008; L'Allier, Elish-Piper, & Bean, 2010; Lent, 2007). Research on the impact of coaching on teacher beliefs, practices, and associated student achievement has shown modest success (Biancarosa, Bryk, & Dexter, 2010; Elish-Piper & L'Allier, 2011; Marsh et al., 2008; Stephens et al., 2011), but also has left just enough doubt to afford states and school districts wiggle room to dismantle coaching models when budgets become tight. Now, in the age of the Common Core State Standards (CCSS), coaching has focused on standards-based curricular work (Elish-Piper & L'Allier, 2014), student-centered coaching (Sweeney, 2010), and refining disciplinary literacy instruction (Elish-Piper, L'Allier, Manderino, & Di Domenico, 2016). Most recently, researchers and educators have acknowledged the critical relationships between coaches and principals, and the important role of literacy leadership teams in guiding schoolwide cultural changes around literacy instruction (Bean, Swan Dagen, Ippolito, & Kern, 2018).

Given these many and shifting characterizations of literacy coaching, it is perhaps no surprise that educators—and coaches most of all—have historically struggled to articulate their roles and responsibilities. Consider the case example that follows as an illustration of both the possibilities and challenges that many coaches face in schools today.[1]

CASE EXAMPLE ·

THINK ABOUT THIS

1. What are the individual and organizational dilemmas confronting Jessica?
2. What actions might Jessica consider to promote shared responsibility for literacy learning in her building, including the pros and cons of each?

Jessica, a successful eighth-grade English language arts (ELA) teacher in an urban middle school, enrolled in a university-directed literacy coaching program sponsored by her district. After completing the program, Jessica became a coach in her own building and worked with colleagues one-on-one and in small groups regularly. Inspired by the reading and writing

---

[1]This case is a composite of several literacy professionals, with personal details obscured to protect privacy.

workshop models, Jessica worked diligently to share her knowledge with teachers and leaders. Although she wanted to coach in all middle school ELA classrooms, she struggled to reach reluctant teachers, and she had little to no luck connecting with math, science, and social studies content-area teachers.

Working with the willing, Jessica helped ELA teachers plan units of study, and she set up occasional meetings with her principal to report on progress; however, his feedback remained minimal: "You're doing a great job; just keep going." At the urging of district administrators, she taught her colleagues how to incorporate assessment data into their instructional decision making. After 4 years of coaching, Jessica believed that differentiated workshop instruction had mostly taken root in ELA classrooms, replacing more traditional stand-and-deliver pedagogy. Then a medical issue forced Jessica to vacate her position for 6 months. When she returned, Jessica was dismayed. Many of her colleagues had abandoned workshop teaching. Her principal shrugged and suggested that Jessica would simply need to start again. Jessica was deeply troubled that without her daily presence, none of the work seemed to stick. She questioned her abilities and worried that no one was sharing responsibility for literacy leadership.

. . . .

Jessica's dilemmas are common for coaches across all grade levels. In the early stages of her work, she met with teachers, discussed pedagogy, and saw student achievement increase. However, Jessica remained the sole change agent in her building—the only *literacy leader* responsible for a schoolwide literacy plan. Jessica and her colleagues might do well to examine approaches that encourage collaborative and collective literacy leadership work. In short, Jessica needs not only to clarify her own roles and responsibilities, but also to support others (leaders and teachers alike) in adopting *coaching mindsets* (Bean & Ippolito, 2016) in order to create collective ownership of literacy improvement work (Bean et al., 2018). It is not enough to introduce coaching roles into schools that have few support systems established (Biancarosa et al., 2010; Blachowicz, Obrochta, & Fogelberg, 2005; Marsh et al., 2008; Resnick, 2009; Steckel, 2009). Without appropriate supports or adequate attention to factors that encourage building-wide growth, literacy coaches will continue to struggle.

While acknowledging that coaching work is highly context-specific, we share widely agreed-upon, research-based frameworks and resources in this chapter that have helped to clarify the roles and responsibilities of those who coach. We use the guiding questions outlined at the beginning of this chapter to explore the work of literacy coaches. Literacy coaches who can answer these guiding questions are well positioned to make lasting changes in their schools.

DEFINING THE LITERACY COACHING ROLE IN RESPONSE TO *STANDARDS 2017*

First, it is important to situate this discussion within the context of newly released standards for specialized literacy professionals. For this chapter we have adopted the term *literacy coach* as defined in the ILA's *Standards 2017*: "The primary role of *literacy coaches* is to work with individual and groups of teachers and to facilitate schoolwide improvement of literacy teaching and learning (pre-K–12)" (ILA, 2018a, p. 43). To fulfill the expectations in *Standards 2017,* we rely on Bean and Ippolito's (2016) work on coaching *mindsets*. Effective coaching requires attending to individuals and systems simultaneously, collaborating with leaders and peers to shape school culture, adopting coaching mindsets, and differentiating professional learning to meet teachers' needs (see Figure 4.1).

Given these distinctions and definitions, this chapter focuses mainly on best practices for those specialized literacy professionals, such as Jessica, who spend most of their time coaching teachers across grade levels. We use *coach* throughout this chapter as a blanket term for these professionals, acknowledging that those who coach may hold a variety of formal job titles.

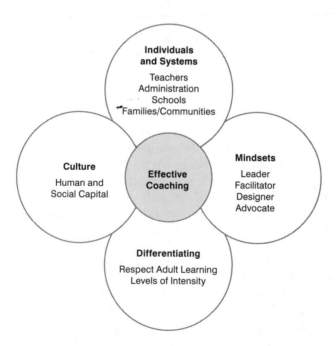

FIGURE 4.1. Framework for thinking and working like a coach. From Bean and Ippolito (2016, p. 6). Reprinted with permission of Learning Sciences International.

ELEMENTARY VERSUS SECONDARY COACHING: DIFFERENCES AS A MATTER OF DEGREE

Before moving on, one debate that deserves attention concerns coaching in elementary versus secondary settings. Educators often wonder and worry about coaching differences across the two settings. However, we prefer to ask: Are the differences between elementary and secondary organizational structures and norms *different enough* to require fundamentally different ways of working?

As a coach working in a K–8 school, Jessica has often considered both the supposed and real differences between working in elementary and middle grades. She is not alone in thinking about this dichotomy. Differences between the roles, responsibilities, and challenges of coaches at elementary versus secondary levels have been noted across sources (Bean, 2015; International Reading Association, 2006; McKenna & Walpole, 2008; Shanklin, 2010; Snow, Ippolito, & Schwartz, 2006; Sturtevant, 2003). Building on distinctions made in the *Standards for Middle and High School Literacy Coaches* (International Reading Association, 2006; Snow et al., 2006), McKenna and Walpole (2008) have provided a table that succinctly compares major differences in elementary versus secondary school settings (p. 150). Key differences for coaches often include the larger number of teachers at the secondary level, shorter blocks of instructional time, departmentalization and teacher specialization by discipline, lack of focus on literacy issues embedded in content-area demands, and teacher resistance to literacy professional development (McKenna & Walpole, 2008, 2010). Beyond organizational and cultural differences, differences in students' skills and needs are also noted, with students beyond elementary school often possessing a wider range of literacy skills and facing dwindling motivation to read, complicated social pressures, and complex content-area texts (McKenna & Walpole, 2008, p. 150). These hypothesized differences between coaching at elementary and secondary levels are certainly important, and few would argue that these differences do not exist to some extent. Yet it is critical for researchers to identify which differences matter the most, and which are simply a matter of degree.

For instance, take the common assertion that secondary coaches have less time than their elementary counterparts to work with teachers. This notion makes intuitive sense considering the long literacy blocks (e.g., 60–90 minutes) present in many high-functioning elementary schools compared to the shorter instructional blocks (e.g., 45–55 minutes) often found in secondary schools. However, research indicates that coaches across all grade levels struggle to find time to work with teachers (Deussen et al., 2007; Marsh et al., 2008). This finding is important because it suggests a slight shift in the conversation about differences between elementary and secondary coaching work. A recent statewide survey of principals in

Pennsylvania supports this notion, with principals reporting that elementary and secondary coaches have more in common than not (Bean et al., 2018). It may be the case that perceived differences between elementary and secondary coaching are not differences in *kind*, but more accurately differences in *degree*.

This is yet another area that *Standards 2017* helps to clarify. Although the standards acknowledge legitimate differences between coaching in early versus later grades (e.g., greater attention to disciplinary literacy in later grades), they do not craft separate roles and goals for coaches working at different levels. Instead, the emphasis is squarely placed on what *all* coaches have in common: "Regardless of the level at which literacy coaches work, they must be able to establish credibility, a trusting relationship, and the ability to work collaboratively with teachers" (ILA, 2018a, p. 43). By highlighting this debate, we hope to temporarily diffuse it and instead focus attention on common ways of working for all who coach.

CONSIDERING AND APPLYING OUR GUIDING QUESTIONS

Finding Time to Meet Individual and System Needs: Research and Recommendations

How coaches spend their time is of utmost importance. Foundational studies have repeatedly shown that coaches across levels struggle to spend time working directly with teachers—arguably the primary role for any specialized literacy professional working as a coach. In the RAND study of literacy coaching in Florida middle schools (Marsh et al., 2008), the 124 coaches reported, on average, spending less than half their time in coaching sessions and cited the lack of time to meet with teachers as a major impediment to greater success. This concern about lack of time and how time is utilized is echoed across studies at both elementary and secondary levels (Bean et al., 2010; Calo, 2008; Deussen et al., 2007; L'Allier et al., 2010; Marsh et al., 2008; Smith, 2007).

Lack of coaching time is noteworthy because connections have been found between the amount of time coaches and teachers spend together, shifts in teacher practice, and gains in student achievement (Hough & Bryk, 2010; L'Allier et al., 2010). Moreover, principals in the recent statewide study of how Pennsylvania principals viewed the roles of specialized literacy professionals (Bean et al., 2018) noted that the most important roles coaches play include coaching teachers, helping teachers understand data, and providing professional learning opportunities for groups of teachers. If coaches are unable to find time to engage in all of these activities, with individuals and groups, then their efficacy may be severely constrained.

Both *Standards 2017* and Bean and Ippolito (2016) argue that the individual coaching of teachers is an essential part of the role. However, they also note that in order to shift schoolwide literacy teaching and learning, coaches must find additional time to coach at the system level. This idea of balancing work with individual teachers and larger systems (e.g., working with groups of teachers, meeting with leaders to craft schoolwide literacy plans, reviewing assessment data, and so on) also reflects the framework outlined earlier in this book, suggesting that specialized literacy professionals all balance working with students, teachers, and systems (see Chapter 3 of this volume, and Figure 3.2).

Mangin and Dunsmore (2015) found that coaches assumed that "the sum of individual changes across teachers [might be] equivalent to systemic reform" (p. 203), and yet this is rarely the case. Systemic reform only occurs when educators work intentionally to build system-level understandings of and capacity for making changes in literacy instruction. Bean and Ippolito (2016) note that "while coaches and literacy leaders are often asked to support system-wide instructional change, coach preparation and support more often prepares them to work with individuals" (p. 7).

This is one reason that *Standards 2017* clearly states that in addition to working closely with individual teachers, coaches must also be able to "design, facilitate, and lead professional learning experiences that support the ongoing improvement of literacy teaching and learning at the classroom, department/grade level, and school levels" (ILA, 2018a, Standard 6.2, p. 51). Similarly, turning to coach preparation programs, *Standards 2017* recommends that preparation programs help coach candidates "develop expertise in collaborative and coaching roles at the schoolwide level" (ILA, 2018a, Standard 7.2, p. 53). Once again, the emphasis is squarely placed on working beyond one-on-one, with larger groups and schoolwide.

A promising approach to working at the system level (and organizing time) has been outlined by Saphier and West (2009/2010), who describe a teacher leader model of coaching. In this format, the coach works within the building to identify teachers willing to open their practice to colleagues in the role of teacher leaders. These teacher leaders are willing to share their instruction and reflections on practices with colleagues, thereby forging a larger culture that values collaborative work and promotes a shared understanding of literacy practices. In this model, coaches spend a significant amount of their time working with lead teachers. Together they build a welcoming, inquiry-focused school culture where lead teachers' classrooms become places where colleagues study and learn from one another. (See Chapter 2 for more about teacher leaders.)

Thinking about how Jessica might spend her time differently to simultaneously work with individuals and influence the entire school, one clear recommendation emerges. Following Bean and Ippolito's guidelines, Jessica could work closely with her principal to outline specific coaching cycles. During any given month she would be working one-on-one with a handful of individuals, with one or two groups of teachers (e.g., grade-level teams, cross-grade study groups), and then also delivering schoolwide professional learning sessions once or twice per month. In this way, Jessica would attend to individual and larger schoolwide needs simultaneously. For more guidance on establishing coaching cycles, see Bean and Ippolito (2016) and Sweeney (2010).

Collaborating to Shape School Culture: Research and Recommendations

A solid relationship between the principal and literacy coach is a critical component of successful literacy leadership (Bean et al., 2018; Matsumura, Sartoris, Bickel, & Garnier, 2009). Current research on coaching at all levels points to the need for three key elements in this relationship: a clear vision or plan for literacy learning in the school, the principal's support for the coach's work, and time for the principal and coach to plan together (Bean et al., 2018; Ippolito, 2009; Ippolito & Bean, 2018; Kral, 2007; Matsumura et al., 2009; Shanklin, 2007).

For coaching to take root and flourish in a school, not to mention shape and shift school culture, the principal and coach must co-construct a clear plan for literacy professional learning. Ippolito and Bean (2018) outline several facets of this work. A clear description of the coach's roles, responsibilities, and expectations is an important starting point. Once agreed upon, the principal and coach can clearly communicate role expectations to community members, thereby reducing confusion and avoiding loss of work time.

Matsumura et al. (2009) describe additional ways in which principals can productively support their coaches: by "publicly identifying the coach as a source of literacy expertise" (p. 685), by "actively participat[ing] in literacy reform activities" (p. 685), and by conceptualizing coaches as professionals who "[help] teachers improve their instruction" (p. 686). Each of these identified leadership behaviors may greatly increase the chances of coaching success.

Another factor to consider in building principal–coach rapport and a larger shared culture of continual improvement is finding the time to collaborate. From his portrayal of three principal prototypes, Ippolito (2009) highlights principal behaviors that contribute to success in coach–teacher relationships (2010a, 2010b). One such behavior is establishing a regular meeting time between principal and coach. If they can do so, they may more easily engage in "collaboration and collective decision-making," factors that may support a successful coaching program (Ippolito, 2009, p. 4).

Principal support of literacy leadership work can take a myriad of forms, from participation in professional learning to providing regular constructive feedback to coaches. Bean et al. (2018), Ippolito and Bean (2018), and Matsumura et al. (2009) all signal that principals' regular engagement in literacy professional learning work bolsters systemic improvement efforts and increases leaders' understandings of best practices. Coaching can be isolating, and principals can provide a much-needed sounding board both to celebrate progress and to plan for the next phase of the work. In Jessica's case, she and her principal might need to share goals and reflect on progress more regularly. Her principal might have considered how to support and promote the coaching work while Jessica was away.

Finally, coaches and teachers can work together to foster a culture of shared literacy leadership, beyond working directly with the principal. One method is to institute learning walks or instructional rounds. Fink and Resnick (2001) describe this procedure as a systematic tour of the school with attention to teaching and learning. Researchers have built upon and described similar walk-through models (City, Elmore, Fiarman, & Teitel, 2009; Rissman, Miller, & Torgesen, 2009; Roberts, 2012). Roberts (2012) recently described instructional rounds in which stakeholders in a school develop a problem of practice, use classroom observations to gather data about this issue, and ultimately make informed decisions about needed change. For coaches, regular walk-throughs with the principal and teacher leaders provide an opportunity for all to analyze practice and fine-tune related professional learning.

Were Jessica and her principal able to conduct learning walks during her previous 4 years of coaching, the principal and literacy leadership team may have been able to play a greater role in sustaining the work during Jessica's leave. Armed with data from learning walks, they might have been able to ask other teachers to take on leadership roles in team meetings. Finally, the principal's presence during learning walks would have emphasized that workshop literacy practices were a building priority, not just Jessica's preference. Although it takes time to establish, the resulting culture of continual improvement and shared responsibility of literacy leadership is worth the investment. In Jessica's case, these suggestions may have helped her colleagues and principal clarify areas of need and related next steps, even in her absence.

Adopting Coaching Mindsets: Research and Recommendations

Both Bean and Ippolito (2016) and *Standards 2017* point to at least four core "mindsets" that coaches must adopt and enact in order to shape literacy teaching and learning in schools. We review each next.

Thinking and Working Like a Leader

Bean and Ippolito (2016) describe how coaching is inherently leadership work. When coaches think and work like leaders, they attend to solving both technical and adaptive instructional dilemmas (Heifetz, Grashow,

& Linsky, 2009). Technical dilemmas are challenges for which we have known solutions, such as how to support a young learner in identifying letter–sound connections; known solutions need to be identified, implemented, and monitored. Meanwhile, adaptive dilemmas are those for which we don't have ready solutions. These are dilemmas that require new adult learning and perhaps the challenging of existing assumptions, norms, and long-held beliefs (e.g., how best to meet the needs of English learners [ELs]). Although recommended practices and suggestions may exist, adaptive challenges have no specific or easily implemented solutions per se. The real solution to an adaptive dilemma will likely emerge from years of collective work in surfacing assumptions and adjusting practices.

When a coach like Jessica begins to think like a *leader,* she is partly parsing the world of organizational and classroom dilemmas into adaptive and technical categories. By sorting her mountain of dilemmas into these categories, she then can decide which technical dilemmas can be solved by providing teachers with resources and targeted professional learning experiences, and which adaptive dilemmas will require longer coaching cycles, with individuals and groups focused on surfacing, addressing, and shifting beliefs, assumptions, and practices.

Increasingly, coaches are being asked to share leadership roles in their schools, such as serving on instructional leadership teams or co-crafting schoolwide literacy plans (Bean et al., 2018). The ILA Standard 6, focused on professional learning and leadership, makes it clear that leadership work is one of the defining characteristics of coaching. The components of Standard 6 describe how coaches "lead" professional learning work for teachers in their buildings, how they wield their knowledge of adult learning and leadership literature and processes to guide teacher inquiry, and how they "lead" collaborative decision-making work with colleagues in order to productively advocate for effective literacy teaching and learning practices within and beyond school walls.

To successfully enact multiple leadership roles, coaches might wish to familiarize themselves with the literature on both adult learning and adult development. Breidenstein, Fahey, Glickman, and Hensley (2012) provide a guide for coaches, principals, and teacher leaders who want to differentiate professional learning, building on Robert Kegan's (1998) constructive developmental theory. Breidenstein et al. (2012) suggest that school leaders (such as coaches!) can organize their work by focusing on instrumental, socializing, and self-authoring professional learning activities (mapping roughly onto Kegan's different stages of adult knowing and learning). Coaches who are thinking and working as leaders will want to consider when it is appropriate to engage colleagues in addressing technical dilemmas through instrumental learning activities. At other times, socializing learning activities that allow for sharing and aligning practices are more desirable. Finally, self-authoring work is needed when teachers need support in defining their own values, interrogating their own assumptions, and crafting new ways of working in response to adaptive dilemmas. Using this framework, and the many discussion-based protocols and professional learning structures outlined both by Breidenstein et al. (2012) and Ippolito and Bean (2018), coaches can begin acting as leaders by more adeptly identifying and responding to adult learning needs in their buildings.

Thinking and Working Like a Facilitator

Standards 2017 prominently highlights the need for coaches to be able to think and work like *facilitators*. Following the work of researcher-practitioners who have spent much of their professional lives studying and designing facilitative routines for adult learning (Allen & Blythe, 2015; Kaner, 2014; McDonald, Mohr, Dichter, & McDonald, 2013), effective coaches must learn how to support adult learners by matching learning purposes with related processes. All too often when we engage in professional learning work in schools, we tackle large adaptive learning challenges (e.g., meeting the needs of ELs) with instrumental, technical learning processes (e.g., reviewing lists of general literacy strategies and expecting dramatic improvement). Instead, when coaches think and work like facilitators, they carefully select learning routines and structures that match the type of learning that adults need at any given time.

The use of formal or informal discussion-based protocols for observing instruction, discussing best practices, and conducting learning walks has been identified as a key factor in helping coaches balance the competing pressures of instituting particular practices while simultaneously helping teachers develop skills and practices of their own choosing (Ippolito, 2010a). For our purposes, protocols are any agreed-upon set of rules that guide coach/teacher/student work, discussion, observation, and interactions. Many useful protocols are freely available online through the School Reform Initiative (*www.schoolreforminitiative.org*) and are also found in numerous books (Allen & Blythe, 2015; Bean & Ippolito, 2016; Breidenstein et al., 2012; Kaner, 2014; McDonald et al., 2013). McDonald et al. (2013) assert that protocols provide "transparency by segmenting elements of a conversation whose boundaries otherwise blur . . . for example, the boundaries between describing and judging, or supporting and critiquing" (p. 8). By using discussion protocols, coaches can help teachers and administrators respectfully share ownership of an improvement effort, reflect on their own practices, and closely examine the many factors in schools that perpetuate poor achievement (Breidenstein et al., 2012). Whether exploring a professional text, examining samples of student work, or scrutinizing a lesson plan gone awry, all participants, not just the coach, contribute. By engaging in protocol-based discussions early in her coaching work, Jessica could have established structures for teachers to use in her absence.

Additionally, we might have advised Jessica to consult the Continuum of Discussion-Based Protocols[2] to help her consider which protocols to use for a variety of adult learning purposes (Ippolito, 2013).

Thinking and Working Like a Designer

Standards 2017 also emphasizes the need for coaches to work as *designers*: designing curriculum for students, designing learning experiences for adults, and collaboratively designing solutions to complex classroom dilemmas.

To think and work like a designer, coaches would be well served to familiarize themselves with resources such as *Data Wise* (Boudett, City, & Murnane, 2013) or the Design Thinking for Educators toolkit (freely available from *https://designthinkingforeducators.com/toolkit*). Each of these resources supports coaches in adopting the mindset of a designer who responds to classroom instructional dilemmas as if they were design problems to be solved (not as innate deficiencies in teachers or students).

When coaches like Jessica treat classroom dilemmas as design problems, they focus on collecting and analyzing data to better understand the problem; collaboratively and iteratively designing and piloting new instructional practices; collecting information on the result of pilot work; and iterating, until desired results are reached. By adopting the mindset of working like a designer, coaches fundamentally shift the way they interact with teachers. They position themselves as design consultants, as opposed to all-knowing experts. If Jessica had functioned more like a designer, she might have modeled collaborative problem-solving methods for teachers to adopt and use, even in her absence.

Thinking and Working Like an Advocate

Finally, *Standards 2017* suggests that *advocacy* work is a major part of effective coaching initiatives. Coaches who are able to successfully *advocate* for student, teacher, and community needs around literacy teaching and learning are coaching not just at the individual level, but they are also coaching at the system level. This element of coaching work involves coaches in both the active work of seeking and securing grant funding to support the implementation of new initiatives, as well as the work of familiarizing themselves and their colleagues with in-depth knowledge of the students and families they serve. Bean and Ippolito (2016) subdivide advocacy work into four main categories: advocating for students; teachers;

---

[2] Available at *www.schoolreforminitiative.org/doc/continuum_discussion_protocols.pdf*.

community partnerships; and particular practices, models, and programs. Each of these advocacy categories requires coaches to (1) continually survey the literature for emerging research and best practices, (2) work toward building shared understandings and consensus across stakeholder groups, and (3) act with great awareness of and sensitivity to all community members' funds of knowledge and unique perspectives. If she had been thinking and working like an advocate, Jessica might have been better positioned to lobby her principal (on behalf of teachers and students) to ensure that the changes accrued across her 4 years of coaching work would remain intact (perhaps through a short-term coach replacement) while she was absent.

Importantly, these research- and standards-based ways of thinking and working are meant to cut across all coaching roles and contexts. Whether coaching in early grades or later grades, coaching for content or coaching for individual teacher growth, coaching in urban or rural settings—these ways of thinking and working are meant to provide a basis from which all coaches can effectively shape school culture and differentiate learning experiences for the adults they serve.

Differentiating Professional Learning Work: Research and Recommendations

Just as *Standards 2017* requires literacy professionals to have broad and deep knowledge of the many ways students acquire and use literacy skills to help them progress, so too must coaches understand teachers' different professional learning needs when it comes to supporting them. Coaches responsible for adult learning experiences must differentiate that learning across time and context so that professional learning is dynamic, flexible, and serves a coherent set of values. Here we discuss professional learning through the two main lenses of professional learning and coaching.

As a professional meeting the expectations of *Standards 2017,* a coach is poised to share deep knowledge about the reading, writing, and language acquisition processes for a variety of diverse learners. Often this happens through structured professional learning opportunities. Ongoing, job-embedded professional learning can be one of the highest-leverage tools to shape and shift literacy teaching and learning in a school. Bates and Morgan (2018) recognize that professional learning can "positively influence teacher knowledge and practice and, in turn, student knowledge" when it incorporates such design elements as content learning, collaboration, and sustained duration (p. 623). Leaders at the Center for Reading Recovery and Literacy Collaborative consider professional learning a cornerstone of their comprehensive school improvement model. In their Literacy Leadership Guide (Center for Reading Recovery and Literacy Collaborative, 2016), the authors write: "This work expands teachers' understanding of theory and practice and provides new thinking about literacy teaching and learning" (p. 38). Clearly, providing professional learning is a critical component of a coach's work. However, professional learning does not follow a singular formula for success. It must respond to educators' shifting needs.

In the literacy collaborative (LC) model, coaches begin their work by offering a substantive initial course of study comprised of up to 60 hours (Center for Reading Recovery and Literacy Collaborative, 2016). In these first 60 hours, educators read professional texts, reflect on their practice, examine student data, and build a collegial community to expand "teachers' understanding of theory and practice and [provide] new thinking about literacy teaching and learning" (p. 38). Next, the professional learning continues as "the coach and the teachers work together . . . to determine the ongoing professional needs of the school" (p. 38). As Bates and Morgan (2018) write, "Sustained focus over time is a hallmark of effective professional development and should be considered in terms of weeks, months, and years" (p. 625). In other words, once teachers have acquired a solid foundation of literacy practices, the nature of the professional learning evolves and becomes more differentiated.

One of the ways in which coaching work begins to differentiate adult learning is through an inquiry approach (Boudett, 2013; Toll, 2016). Using an inquiry method, the coach supports teachers in identifying areas of focus; collects data to help define, understand, and shape a dilemma; designs an action plan; and then reflects on the success of that plan to make adjustments. Toll (2016) suggests that by engaging teachers in this problem-solving model, they may feel increasingly empowered because their needs and interests are driving their learning. For teachers who have been engaged in a longer coaching relationship, this model offers a sense of shared responsibility for the learning and helps sustain teachers' engagement.

Beyond inquiry models, coaching work can be differentiated in a variety of other ways. Perhaps the most recognizable structure is the coaching cycle, with the coach working individually with a teacher, reflecting on an element of practice, co-planning a lesson, or looking at student work. Coaches can rely on this structure to focus on specific needs or to build a trusting relationship with newer teachers or those newer to coaching. This process can evolve over time. Early on, the coach may take the lead, but over time, the teacher may begin to guide conversations. One-on-one coaching affords important flexibility.

The leaders at the Center for Reading Recovery and Literacy Collaborative (2016) also suggest that a coach may consider demonstration coaching, in which "the coach and the teacher plan a lesson together, and the literacy coach teaches the lesson while the classroom teacher observes and takes notes" (p. 40). A coach may adopt this more hands-on method

(1) to support a newer teacher who might want to see a particular practice in action or (2) to help a more veteran teacher consider another approach. Finally, some LC coaches embrace cluster coaching, wherein the coach and a group of teachers "discuss the students, the teacher's goals, and the plan for the lesson," after which the entire group observes the lesson and debriefs (p. 40). Because teachers are working together rather than in a coach–teacher pairing, cluster coaching can build community among colleagues and create space for shared practice. When members of a teaching team trust one another enough to engage in shared conversation, cluster coaching can be both an efficient means of working with more than one teacher at a time and a way to create common language around teaching and learning.

Along with different structures, coaches also vary the purpose and intensity of their work. A recent leadership brief (ILA, 2018b) identifies three purposes for coaching: coaching to conform, coaching into practice, and coaching for transformation. Each model offers a different form of support. *Coaching to conform* helps teachers meet state or district teaching expectations; *coaching into practice* promotes "self-reflection through practice"; and *coaching for transformation* enables teachers to "challenge the fundamental processes of schooling and literacy instruction" (pp. 4–6). Skilled coaches read the school or district context as well as the teachers' goals to set the purpose for the collaborative work they do. Similarly, Bean and Ippolito (2016) describe varying "levels of intensity" (pp. 10–11) in the work coaches do with teachers. From less-intense relationship-building work to the more formal analysis of practice, to the high-intensity work of "transforming practice and making teaching public," they argue that effective coaches "take into consideration the type of learning experiences best suited" for certain teachers at certain points in their professional lives (p. 9). By varying coaching work by structure, purpose, and intensity, coaches have a greater hope of meeting the divergent needs of the teachers they support.

As Jessica contemplates her next steps, for example, she would likely benefit from factoring differentiated professional learning into her work with teachers. Jessica may need to take stock of the teachers in her coaching cohort and adjust intensity and structure. Some teachers may benefit from a focus on building relationships and implementing the workshop model. Other teachers may be ready to engage in conversation alone or with colleagues about how to use their time to reflect together and transform practice. Jessica may also want to change her approach to professional development by using an inquiry model that shifts the responsibility of the literacy learning away from her and helps keep the collective focus on what the chosen data source tells the group about student learning. These efforts may enable Jessica to help build a healthy culture in which "teachers . . .

take pride in being lifelong learners; everyone has goals and is not afraid to ask colleagues for help" (Fountas & Pinnell, 2018, p. 17).

CONCLUSION

As we consider the next iteration of literacy coaching work, we need to develop practices that enable us to build the capacity of coaches, specialists, teacher leaders, and principals to adopt *coaching mindsets*. In many ways, the next wave of work runs parallel to the gradual release of responsibility we see in our strongest literacy classrooms. As the teacher models, scaffolds, and supports student learning, that teacher gradually releases support to determine the extent to which students can navigate on their own. Literacy coaches must do the same. The coach cannot be the sole purveyor of literacy expertise; that expertise must be shared among the principal, teachers, and specialists.

Jessica's case arises at an interesting time in the history of literacy coaching. Coaching is no longer a novel phenomenon, and research is beginning to offer valuable insights. We know that coaches struggle to find enough time to do their work, hope to shape school culture through better relationships with administrators, seek to adopt and perform many varied roles, and strive to differentiate their work with adults to meet many assorted needs. Yet, professionals like Jessica are still facing uncharted waters. They do not always know or cannot always put into action the steps that will transform teacher practice, build community, and raise student achievement. By highlighting research and best practices related to our guiding questions, we offer literacy coaches a means of analyzing their practice and experimenting with new ideas—first steps to help make coaching "stick."

ENGAGEMENT ACTIVITIES

1. Reread the "Adopting Coaching Mindsets" section of this chapter. Which mindsets (and related standards) do you feel the most comfortable adopting? Which will require more professional learning?

2. Reread the questions and case of Jessica. What advice might you offer Jessica as she considers reorganizing her time; forging a stronger relationship with her principal in order to deliberately shape school culture; adopting coaching mindsets and working as a leader, designer, facilitator, and advocate; and differentiating her coaching work to best meet the needs of adult learners?

3. After reading Chapters 3 and 4, discuss with peers the following questions: What are your thoughts about the similarities and differences in the roles and responsibilities of reading/literacy *specialists* versus literacy *coaches*? Which roles and responsibilities feel more comfortable to you—and why?

ANNOTATED RESOURCES

Allen, D., & Blythe, T. (2015). *Facilitating for learning: Tools for teacher groups of all kinds*. New York: Teachers College Press.

This book is written for all educators who are interested in improving their facilitative skills in supporting groups of adult learners. Although not explicitly written for literacy coaches, any specialized literacy professional, teacher leader, or formal leader who coaches others will appreciate the research, wisdom, and practical tools that Allen and Blythe provide.

International Literacy Association. (2018). *Literacy coaching for change*. Newark, DE: Author.

This position statement from the International Literacy Association presents three coaching models: coaching to conform, coaching into practice and coaching for transformation.

Shearer, B. A., Carr, D. A., & Vogt, M. (2018). *Reading specialists and literacy coaches in the real world* (4th ed.). Long Grove, IL: Waveland Press.

A one-stop research and practice reference for reading/literacy specialists and coaches. This book is filled with practical advice, sample templates for coaching work (e.g., needs assessments), and a strong focus on working both one-on-one with teachers and at the systems level.

REFERENCES

Allen, D., & Blythe, T. (2015). *Facilitating for learning: Tools for teacher groups of all kinds*. New York: Teachers College Press.

Bates, C. B., & Morgan, D. N. (2018). Seven elements of effective professional development. *The Reading Teacher, 71*(5), 623–626.

Bean, R. M. (2015). *The reading specialist: Leadership and coaching for the classroom, school, and community* (3rd ed.). New York: Guilford Press.

Bean, R. M., Draper, J. A., Hall, V., Vandermolen, J., & Zigmond, N. (2010). Coaches and coaching in Reading First schools. *Elementary School Journal, 111*(1), 87–114.

Bean, R. M., & Ippolito, J. (2016). *Cultivating coaching mindsets: An action guide for literacy leaders*. West Palm Beach, FL: Learning Sciences International.

Bean, R. M., Swan Dagen, A., Ippolito, J., & Kern, D. (2018). Principals' perspectives on the roles of specialized literacy professionals. *Elementary School Journal, 119*(2), 327–350.

Biancarosa, G., Bryk, A. S., & Dexter, E. R. (2010). Assessing the value-added effects of literacy collaborative professional development on student learning. *Elementary School Journal, 111*(1), 7–34.

Blachowicz, C. L. Z., Obrochta, C., & Fogelberg, E. (2005). Literacy coaching for change. *Educational Leadership, 62*(6), 55–58.

Blamey, K. L., Meyer, C. K., & Walpole, S. (2008). Middle and high school literacy coaches: A national survey. *Journal of Adolescent and Adult Literacy, 52*(4), 310–323.

Boudett, K. P., City, E. A., & Murnane, R. J. (Eds.). (2013). *Data wise: A step-by-step guide to using assessment results to improve teaching and learning.* Cambridge, MA: Harvard Education Press.

Breidenstein, A., Fahey, K., Glickman, C., & Hensley, F. (2012). *Leading for powerful learning: A guide for instructional leaders.* New York: Teachers College Press.

Calo, K. M. (2008). *An exploration of middle school literacy coaching across the United States.* Doctoral dissertation, George Mason University, Fairfax, VA. Retrieved June 15, 2010, from *http://digilib.gmu.edu:8080/bitstream/1920/3086/1/Calo_Kristine.pdf.*

Center for Reading Recovery and Literacy Collaborative. (2016). *A literacy leadership guide: Developing and sustaining comprehensive literacy learning* (3rd ed.). Cambridge, MA: Lesley University.

City, E. A., Elmore, R. F., Fiarman, S. E., & Teitel, L. (2009). *Instructional rounds in education: A network approach to improving teaching and learning.* Cambridge, MA: Harvard Education Press.

Costa, A., & Garmston, R. (2002). *Cognitive coaching: A foundation for Renaissance schools* (2nd ed.). Norwood, MA: Christopher-Gordon.

Deussen, T., Coskie, T., Robinson, L., & Autio, E. (2007). *"Coach" can mean many things: Five categories of literacy coaches in Reading First* (Issues & Answers Report, REL 2007-No. 005). Washington, DC: United States Department of Education, Institute of Education Sciences, National Center for Education Evaluation and Regional Assistance, Regional Educational Laboratory Northwest.

Elish-Piper, L., & L'Allier, S. K. (2011). Examining the relationship between literacy coaching and student reading gains in grades K–3. *Elementary School Journal, 112*(1), 83–106.

Elish-Piper, L., & L'Allier, S. K. (2014). *The Common Core coaching book: Strategies to help teachers address the K–5 ELA Standards.* New York: Guilford Press.

Elish-Piper, L., L'Allier, S. K., Manderino, M., & Di Domenico, P. (2016). *Collaborative coaching for disciplinary literacy: Strategies to support teachers in grades 6–12.* New York: Guilford Press.

Fink, E., & Resnick, L. B. (2001). Developing principals as instructional leaders. *Phi Delta Kappan, 82*(8), 598–606.

Fountas, I. C., & Pinnell, G. S. (2018). Every child, every classroom, every day: From vision to action in literacy learning. *The Reading Teacher, 72*(1), 7–19.

Heifetz, R., Grashow, A., & Linsky, M. (2009). *The practice of adaptive leadership: Tools and tactics for changing your organization and the world.* Cambridge, MA: Harvard Business Press.

Hough, H. J., & Bryk, A. S. (2010, May). *The effects of literacy coaching on teacher practice.* Paper presented at the annual conference of the American Educational Research Association, Denver, CO.

International Literacy Association (ILA). (2018a). *Standards for the preparation of literacy professionals 2017.* Newark, DE: Author.

International Literacy Association (ILA). (2018b). *Literacy coaching for change: Choices matter.* Newark, DE: Author.

International Reading Association. (2006). *Standards for middle and high school literacy coaches.* Newark, DE: Author. Retrieved October 14, 2018, from *www.literacyworldwide.org/get-resources/standards/standards-for-literacy-coaches.*

Ippolito, J. (2009). Principals as partners with literacy coaches: Striking a balance between neglect and interference. *Literacy Coaching Clearinghouse.* Retrieved October 14, 2018, from *https://eric.ed.gov/?id=ED530261.*

Ippolito, J. (2010a). Three ways that literacy coaches balance responsive and directive relationships with teachers. *Elementary School Journal, 111*(1), 164–190.

Ippolito, J. (2010b). Investigating how literacy coaches understand and balance responsive and directive relationships with teachers. In J. Cassidy, S. D. Garrett, & M. Sailors (Eds.), *Literacy coaching: Research and practice: 2009 CEDER yearbook* (pp. 45–66). Corpus Christi: Center for Educational Development, Evaluation, and Research—Texas A&M University–Corpus Christi College of Education.

Ippolito, J. (2013). Professional learning as the key to linking content and literacy instruction. In J. Ippolito, J. F. Lawrence, & C. Zaller (Eds.), *Adolescent literacy in the era of the common core: From research into practice* (pp. 215–234). Cambridge, MA: Harvard Education Press.

Ippolito, J., & Bean, R. M. (2018). *Unpacking coaching mindsets: Collaboration between principals and coaches.* West Palm Beach, FL: Learning Sciences International.

Joyce, B., & Showers, B. (1996). The evolution of peer coaching. *Educational Leadership, 53*(6), 12–16.

Kaner, S. (2014). *The facilitator's guide to participatory decision-making* (3rd ed.). San Francisco: Jossey-Bass.

Kegan, R. (1998). *In over our heads: The mental demands of modern life.* Cambridge, MA: Harvard University Press.

Kral, C. (2007). Principal support for literacy coaches. *Literacy Coaching Clearinghouse.* Retrieved June 15, 2010, from *www.literacycoachingonline.org/briefs/PrincipalSupportFinal3-22-07.pdf.*

L'Allier, S., Elish-Piper, L., & Bean, R. M. (2010). What matters for elementary literacy coaching?: Guiding principles for instructional improvement and student achievement. *The Reading Teacher, 63*(7), 544–554.

Lent, R. C. (2007). *Literacy learning communities: A guide for creating sustainable change in secondary schools.* Portsmouth, NH: Heinemann.

Mangin, M. M., & Dunsmore, K. (2015). How the framing of instructional coaching as a lever for systemic or individual reform influences the enactment of coaching. *Educational Administration Quarterly, 51*(2), 179–213.

Marsh, J. A., McCombs, J. S., Lockwood, J. R., Martorell, F., Gershwin, D., Naftel, S., et al. (2008). *Supporting literacy across the sunshine state: A study of Florida middle school reading coaches* (Prepared for the Carnegie Corporation of New York). Santa Monica, CA: RAND Corporation.

Matsumura, L. C., Sartoris, M., Bickel, D. D., & Garnier, H. (2009). Leadership for literacy coaching: The principal's role in launching a new coaching program. *Educational Administration Quarterly, 45*(5), 655–693.

McDonald, J. P., Mohr, N., Dichter, A., & McDonald, E. C. (2013). *The power of protocols: An educator's guide to better practice* (3rd ed.). New York: Teachers College Press.

McKenna, M. C., & Walpole, S. (2008). *The literacy coaching challenge: Models and methods for grades K–8.* New York: Guilford Press.

McKenna, M. C., & Walpole, S. (2010). *Literacy coaching in the middle grades.* Retrieved October 6, 2018, from *www.adlit.org/article/36143.*

Moran, M. C. (2007). *Differentiated literacy coaching: Scaffolding for student and teacher success.* Alexandria, VA: Association for Supervision and Curriculum Development.

Rainville, K. N., & Jones, S. (2008). Situated identities: Power and positioning in the work of a literacy coach. *The Reading Teacher, 61*(6), 440–448.

Resnick, L. B. (2009). Nested learning systems for the thinking curriculum. *Educational Researcher, 39*(3), 183–197.

Rissman, L. M., Miller, D. H., & Torgesen, J. K. (2009). *Adolescent literacy walkthrough for principals: A guide for instructional leaders.* Portsmouth, NH: RMC Research Corporation, Center on Instruction.

Roberts, J. E. (2012). *Instructional rounds in action.* Cambridge, MA: Harvard Education Press.

Saphier, J., & West, L. (2009/2010). How coaches can maximize student learning. *Phi Delta Kappan, 91*(4), 46–50.

Shanklin, N. (2007). What supports do literacy coaches need from administrators in order to succeed? *Literacy Coaching Clearinghouse.* Retrieved June 15, 2010, from *www.literacycoachingonline.org/briefs/LCSupportsNSBrief.pdf.*

Shanklin, N. (2010, April). *Middle school and high school coaching: What can we learn from the current research?* Paper presented at the 2nd annual International Literacy Coaching Summit, Texas A&M University–Corpus Christi, TX.

Smith, A. T. (2007). The middle school literacy coach: Considering roles in context. In D. W. Rowe et al. (Eds.), *56th yearbook of the National Reading Conference* (pp. 53–67). Oak Creek, WI: National Reading Conference.

Snow, C., Ippolito, J., & Schwartz, R. (2006). What we know and what we need to know about literacy coaches in middle and high schools: A research synthesis and proposed research agenda. In International Reading Association *Standards for middle and high school literacy coaches* (pp. 35–49). Newark, DE: Author. Retrieved June 15, 2010, from *www.reading.org/downloads/resources/597coaching_standards.pdf.*

Steckel, B. (2009). Fulfilling the promise of literacy coaches in urban schools: What does it take to make an impact? *The Reading Teacher, 63*(1), 14–23.

Stephens, D., Morgan, D. N., DeFord, D. E., Donnelly, A., Hamel, E., Keith, K. J., et al. (2011). The impact of literacy coaches on teachers' beliefs and practices. *Journal of Literacy Research, 43*(3), 215–249.

Sturtevant, E. G. (2003). *The literacy coach: A key to improving teaching and learning in secondary schools.* Washington, DC: Alliance for Excellent Education. Retrieved June 15, 2010, from *www.all4ed.org/publications/LiteracyCoach.pdf.*

Sweeney, D. (2010). *Student-centered coaching: A guide for K–8 coaches and principals.* Thousand Oaks, CA: Corwin Press.

Toll, C. A. (2016). A problem-solving model for literacy coaching practice. *The Reading Teacher, 70*(4), 413–421.

Literacy Leadership in Action

Michael P. Henry, EdD

Reading Intervention Teacher and Literacy Coach,
Reavis High School District 220, Burbank, Illinois

THINK ABOUT THIS

1. In what ways does Michael serve as a literacy leader?
2. What lessons can be learned about the role of reading intervention teacher/literacy coach?
3. What questions come to mind while reading this vignette?

I am a reading intervention teacher and literacy coach at a culturally and linguistically diverse high school in Burbank, IL—a collar suburb of Chicago's South Side. About 60% of my time is dedicated to my instructional role and 40% to coaching. At my high school, 51.8% of the 1,823 students are classified as from low-income families. Born in 28 different countries and speaking 24 different languages, about 62% of our students come from multilingual homes with the majority being Spanish-speaking (55%), Arabic-speaking (21%), and Polish-speaking (21%). To provide quality literacy instruction for this large multilingual population, each year over 50% of the freshmen take the reading workshop intervention class that I teach. Also, in my role as literacy coach, I have worked with over 55% of the 112 teachers in the school. In the following, I write about my role, emphasizing the work that I do with teachers.

High school literacy coach—a literacy specialist tasked with leading educated, intelligent teachers toward improving their pedagogy and practice through literacy; many also teach students. I am a teacher and high school literacy coach. How do I lead? I see. I ask questions. I write frameworks and protocols. I count what matters. And it works.

I see. In the ninth-grade reading intervention class at my school, students choose 100% of the books they read. They read, write responses, and discuss their books voluminously during class each week. As their teacher, I see students' literacy preferences. I see them choose reading, writing, and discussing text in personally meaningful ways. I see accomplishments. I see potential. As a literacy coach, I ask teachers to see the same.

I ask questions:

> What do they think . . . ?
> Did you hear them say . . . ?
> Do you think they really understand . . . ?
> Are they ready for . . . ?
> Should we try . . . ?
> What would happen if they . . . ?

I ask questions because purposeful questioning helps teachers. What happens when a literacy coach asks questions? Teachers assume control, opening the door for authentic collaboration. Why questions? Because questions show that I am there to support and guide, not evaluate. It's safe. Teachers love that.

Where do I get the questions? During classes, I talk to as many students as possible, asking them about the tasks and their ability to articulate their understanding. I ask the teacher questions about pacing, effectiveness, and next steps. I ask for their expertise. Then the teacher and I reflect, revise, and plan during the 6-minute passing period when students change classes. It's fast. The questions I ask, however, sit with the teacher for much longer. What do I do when our conversation is over?

I write. I think about what I observed, what the students did and said, and about the teacher's answers or the questions that he or she asked. I take that information, and I write a framework for the teacher to consider. Why frameworks? Frameworks allow teachers to visualize opportunities, to choose which components they would like to try and which components may not fit.

The instructional frameworks that teachers and I design allow students the opportunities to engage in authentic reading, writing, speaking, listening, and text-generation tasks. Teachers commit to the same "literacy" days each week. Frameworks include student work protocols designed around research regarding adolescent cognition, motivation, identity, social relationships, disciplinary literacy, and language. That's the hard part. Then I work to fit each framework to each teacher's style and dispositions, while at the same time allowing for open-ended student choice and self-direction. That's the harder part. Finally, I ask questions, so teachers lead the development of each framework; I keep them tied to the research. That's the hardest, yet most successful part. How do I measure success?

I count. I count library circulation numbers—15,000 books per year in a school of 1,800. Students are choosing to read. I count the number of teachers

I have worked with over the past 10 years: 54. Teachers value the work we do. I count the number of presentations I have done with teachers: 23. Teachers are proud of our work and want to share it. I count the number of publications I have written: 11. Our work has merit. I count the number of student publications: 27. Students are doing authentic work that matters beyond the classroom. I count the number of questions students ask about the content: 20–30 per class period usually. Students are thinking deeply. I count the frameworks and protocols that take off and those that continue long after I stop working directly with teachers: too many to count at this point.

How can a high school literacy coach lead? Allow students to make their own literacy choices. Learn from those students. Ask teachers thoughtful questions. Work within frameworks and protocols. And count what matters.

CHAPTER 5

The Principal's Role in Literacy Leadership

Lori Helman
Katie Pekel

Lori Helman
Katie Pekel

GUIDING QUESTIONS

⇥ How do principals design literacy environments that lead to collective educator efficacy and rigorous student learning?

⇥ Which aspects of the *Standards for the Preparation of Literacy Professionals 2017* (International Literacy Association [ILA], 2018) address principals' participation in the literacy improvement process?

⇥ How do principals, in a shared leadership model, ensure a system of continuous improvement in literacy learning in their schools?

Leadership matters. By now, most have read the oft-quoted statistic highlighting that principal leadership accounts for 25% of the effect on student learning (Marzano, Waters, & McNulty, 2005). Principals are responsible for a myriad of leadership tasks in their day-to-day work—so many, in fact, that Richard Elmore (2000) has described how the role of principal leadership perhaps has been "romanticized." Teachers, parents, community members, and students often look to principals to solve problems. This problem-solving orientation of school principals may allow schools to run smoothly in the moment, yet perhaps it inadvertently detracts from the core purpose of school: learning. In fact, the most important role principals may have is to facilitate collective leadership focused primarily on literacy learning. Developing literacy and using it to access and engage with disciplinary content is one of the chief missions of schooling in the elementary and secondary grades. Principals have a key role in achieving this objective, but it requires thoughtful, long-term planning and follow-through.

The ILA's *Standards 2017* serves as a guiding document for educators of literacy professionals (teachers, specialists) and those who support them in schools, including principals. *Standards 2017* can also assist principals by providing them with the knowledge and understandings they need to work with their colleagues in developing schoolwide literacy programs (ILA, 2018, pp. 96–100). Specifically, principals can take responsibility for creating not only the structures to drive effective literacy teaching, but also a culture wherein collaborative, data-based, continuous improvement practices and learning are the norm.

In this chapter, we provide a brief overview of the research on leadership as it relates to literacy instruction in elementary and secondary classrooms, highlighting connections to standards for professional learning and leadership. Following this foundational information, we outline a framework for conceptualizing and implementing a literacy plan that leads to continuous learning and student growth. In the process, we share several examples of how the steps in this plan have taken shape in real educational settings. The information we present will be useful to principals and other administrators, as well as to literacy professionals who work in partnership with school leaders to help students succeed in literacy. At the end of the chapter, we provide some easy-to-access, practitioner-friendly resources for further exploration.

WHAT PRINCIPALS NEED TO DO TO ENSURE SUCCESS

It has become the expectation that principals will serve as instructional leaders in today's schools, developing, supporting, and promoting "coherent systems of curriculum, instruction and assessment" (National Policy Board for Educational Administration, 2015, p. 12). In order to accomplish these critical tasks, principals must:

- ensure that current, research-based information on literacy teaching and learning is put into practice by the teaching staff,
- provide opportunities for the teaching staff to examine student learning data and address inequities,
- interact intentionally with literacy professionals to prioritize and achieve schoolwide goals,
- create a community in which everyone works together and takes responsibility for each student's literacy success,
- hire, develop, and oversee staff who continuously improve literacy instruction on site.

Standards 2017 (ILA, 2018)

Create a Culture of Collective Leadership

How principals approach the leadership of instruction was the focus of the largest study of educational leadership to date, *Learning from Leadership: Investigating the Links to Improved Student Learning* (Wahlstrom, Seashore Louis, Leithwood, & Anderson, 2010). In the executive summary of their 6 years of research, Wahlstrom and colleagues define three approaches to instructional leadership: *collective leadership* (the engagement of all participants in the educational system in shared decision making), *shared leadership* (principals and teachers sharing responsibility for leading schoolwide decisions and programs, and *distributed leadership* (principals enacting or distributing particular leadership practices related to a specific goal or task).

It is within the realm of shared leadership that Wahlstrom and colleagues identify the role of professional community as a significant factor in bringing about improved student outcomes. They found that "when principals and teachers share leadership, teachers' working relationships are stronger and student achievement is higher" (Wahlstrom et al., 2010, p. 10). It is precisely this shared leadership that *Standards 2017* encourages and, in addition, provides a vision of how the roles of educational professionals (e.g., teachers, specialists, coaches, and principals) support each other to improve literacy outcomes for all their learners (ILA, 2018). In this chapter, we focus most heavily on the principal's role related to Standard 6—Professional Learning and Leadership—but also make connections to other standards outlined by the ILA as well. *Standards 2017* describes the foundational knowledge needed to oversee effective differentiated literacy instruction, provides an understanding of the standards and research base for literacy learning, identifies the uses and limitations of various assessment practices, advocates for equity across diverse school populations, and describes how to support learning environments that engage literacy learners (ILA, 2018). The comprehensive nature of ILA's standards provides a framework for all members of the shared leadership team, including the principal, to collaborate around, thereby contributing to an increased sense of professional community and trust (ILA, 2018).

Trust in the principal and his or her caring leadership is an important predictor of how others in the professional community will view their own work and ultimately their engagement in improvement activities (Seashore Louis & Murphy, 2017). Principals can enhance trust in a shared leadership model by providing support for change as well as assuming leadership of the change process. A study of 165 Reading First schools in Michigan investigated teacher perceptions of principal support in relation to teacher collaboration around literacy instruction and found that, when principals are perceived as supportive of change, teachers' regular collaboration and communication about reading instruction improves (Berebitsky, Goddard,

& Carlisle, 2014). Fixsen, Blase, Naoom, and Duda (2015), in their study of best practices for implementing change initiatives, found that facilitative administration that provides leadership around data-based decision making, procedural implementation, culture, and climate is a key driver of an initiative's success. While the literature is clear that shared leadership, trust, and support all contribute to a more effective professional learning environment, *Standards 2017* provides the content on which collaboration needs to be based.

Provide a Clear Vision and Prioritize

Principals likely will not have the same depth of literacy background as the school literacy specialists or potentially even teachers in their schools; however, they should have experience in setting a vision and direction for the school they lead. The role of the principal in creating a literacy learning environment requires the development of a shared vision focused on student learning and shared instructional values (Fullan, 2005; New Leaders for New Schools, 2009). To do this, principals must ensure that new and relevant research on literacy and culturally and linguistically relevant curriculum are making their way to the professional community (Murrell, 2006). Principals must also be responsible for creating and sustaining a structure for staff members to meet regularly in order to engage in a continuous improvement process where their own professional learning is tended to, while also examining the curriculum, instruction, and assessment of the literacy program to ensure success for students (Au, Strode, Vasquez, & Raphael, 2014; Joyce & Showers, 2002). These structures in which staff meet to consider data, learn specific evidence-based teaching practices, and share what is working in their classrooms are called *professional learning communities* or *PLCs* (Dufour & Dufour, 2012). In addition, principals must be integrally involved in developing an academic plan for improving literacy success at the school. Principals will need to set up the structures, including monitoring the data that will be collected and their analysis to enact the plan in a thorough way (Harn, Basaraba, Chard, & Fritz, 2015; ILA, 2018).

Oversee the Literacy Improvement Process

Creating a culture of collective leadership and providing a clear vision and prioritizing are two foundational steps that will prepare the landscape on a school campus to reap growth in literacy for students. Without a well thought-out plan of action, however, the fertile ground on site may not produce the desired results. The involvement of the principal in overseeing and shepherding the school plan is critical to its comprehensive implementation and overall success (Elmore, 2000; Fixsen et al., 2015; Marzano et al.,

2005; New Leaders for New Schools, 2009). Research (Fixsen et al., 2015; ILA, 2018; Joyce & Showers, 2002; Larson, Cooke, Fiat, & Lyon, 2018; Lesaux & Marietta, 2012; Mead, 2011) has documented the key roles that principals play on a number of fronts, including:

- Guiding the alignment of standards, curriculum, instruction, and assessment on site.
- Overseeing data collection on which to base ongoing change.
- Selecting, developing, and evaluating staff who can improve site literacy instruction.
- Supporting staff efficacy by tending to teacher stress and considering teachers' perceptions of acceptability, feasibility, and usability of the initiative.
- Providing both facilitative and adaptive leadership throughout the initiative.

Throughout the change process, principals support progress by structuring frequent and ongoing opportunities for instructional staff to analyze student progress and adapt instruction (Dufour & Dufour, 2012; ILA, 2018; Raphael, Au, & Goldman, 2009). For example, during the grade-level team meetings or PLCs noted previously, groups of teachers can examine artifacts from common assignments they have given in their classrooms (e.g., writing samples or other student work), match expectations to grade-level or content-area standards, and collectively discuss to what degree the students demonstrate proficiency toward the standard (Blythe, Allen, & Powell, 1999). Where gaps exist in student knowledge or performance, teachers collectively design instruction to support the learning, try it out in their classrooms, and, if possible, observe each other's teaching. Then new student work is brought to another team meeting for analysis and the discussion continues on ways to support students' growth.

Harn and colleagues (2015) found that common features that support implementing academic and behavioral support systems include schoolwide coordination, universal screening and progress monitoring, implementing evidence-based practices, professional learning of the evidence-based practices, data-based evaluation, and commitment to schoolwide implementation from administrators and leadership teams. Principals enhance collective teacher efficacy—the belief that the staff working together have increased power to affect student learning—a factor that is at the top of John Hattie's (2015) actions that influence student learning. Throughout the instructional improvement process, staff need to know that what they are doing is making a difference. An ongoing focus on data to document progress is highly motivating for both teachers and students. Key to enacting these processes is the principal's productive and supportive relationship with content-area leaders such as reading/literacy specialists and instructional coaches (ILA, 2018). Such relationships require an understanding of the roles of the specialized literacy professionals and a willingness to support them to work effectively with teachers (Ippolito & Bean, 2018).

A principal cannot be the manager of every aspect of the multitude of projects and goals that are enacted on site. Based on this brief review of the literature, however, it is clear that for literacy improvement initiatives to take root and grow, the principal needs to be involved, provide direction and support, work collaboratively with literacy leaders, and hold all staff accountable for project objectives (ILA, 2018). In the next section, we describe a model of continuous improvement in literacy instruction and share how the examples of leadership skills outlined in the previous section take shape in the real world of four principals working to enhance their students' literacy achievement.

CREATING CONTINUOUS IMPROVEMENT IN LITERACY LEARNING

Stepping into a dynamic school or classroom where students are engaged and content is being learned, an astute observer will immediately notice that there are numerous interactions taking place on multiple levels. Classrooms and schools are complicated social settings in which the people (students, teachers, principals, specialists, other school or volunteer personnel) work with learning content (curriculum, texts, ideas, etc.) to achieve agreed-upon goals. Much of the action occurs in the educational "moment," but it is based on planning and preparation that took place ahead of time. For classroom environments and instruction to successfully support all students' literacy growth and motivation, a structure for creating continuous improvement must be in place. In other words, the leadership and collaboration described previously in our review of the research need to be embodied in an ongoing structure that personnel understand and of which they feel ownership. In this section, we present an example of such a continuous improvement cycle, sharing case examples of how four principals make this work real in their schools.

Although a variety of terms are used to describe the *action–reflection–revision* cycle for instructional improvement, we present a sequence that consists of four components: *design, apply, analyze,* and *adapt.* Figure 5.1 presents these key elements and highlights the cyclical nature of their implementation.

The structure begins with a new idea or plan that has been co-created (*design*), and then is put into action in a learning setting (*apply*). Informal or formal data are collected to evaluate the implementation and collaboratively review its success (*analyze*). Based on the data analysis, adaptations are made that support ongoing improvement to enhance effectiveness (*adapt*). Information from the effects, feasibility, and evolving school goals

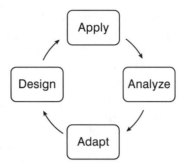

FIGURE 5.1. Phases in the continuous improvement cycle.

converge to provide input into a new *design* phase that is co-created by leaders, staff members, and other stakeholders. Finally, the cycle begins anew as a revised plan of action is put into place that builds upon data and collective knowledge from the previous iteration. The plan continually evolves; it is not thrown out when completed, but rather kept to reflect the learning of school personnel that has just taken place. For this reason, collective knowledge moves forward, and continuous improvement in the school site takes place.

In the next sections we more fully describe each step in the cycle of continuous improvement and share examples of how principals led the implementation.

CASE EXAMPLES ·

THINK ABOUT THIS

What knowledge, skills, and dispositions do the following principals demonstrate that support continuous improvement?

Design

For effective literacy teaching and learning to occur, structures need to be in place that support staff learning, provide for common planning, ensure that the curriculum is well researched, and establish adequate systems for collecting evidence of student learning. Justin Tiarks is the principal of an urban elementary school (K–5) of about 500 students who primarily come from Latino, African American, and Hmong families. About 98% of students receive free or reduced lunch subsidies, and 60% of students are learning English as a new language (EL). Principal Tiarks believes that the key to school improvement is "people before policy." He has worked hard to transform the culture of the school so that it is collaborative and inclusive, and where planning that is sensitive to students who have experienced trauma is the umbrella under which all initiatives fall (Cole, Eisner, Gregory, & Ristuccia, 2013). Leading in a context where there are no easy answers has pushed him to start by building partnerships.

Principal Tiarks notes that educators who serve students living with trauma and poverty face predictable challenges such as burnout, limited resources, and a sense that problems are just too big to solve. When he moved from being a teacher at the school to being its principal, Principal Tiarks began by focusing on building staff capacity. This took place by supporting effective teaching practices, highlighting the message that good language instruction is important for all students, and finding leadership among the staff. Principal Tiarks aims to support a cultural transformation; he demonstrates trust with the adults in the school community, including staff and families. He makes budget decisions that prioritize supporting families, and this has allowed him to have three parent liaisons on site, as well as two social workers and a therapist to help students deal with trauma. Principal Tiarks says that he is asking for the hearts of his staff as they work together to provide outstanding education to their community and nurture healthy families.

Building on this foundation of trust and a shared mission, Principal Tiarks works with school leaders and other staff to take ownership for instructional efficacy. He constantly asks himself, "How can I develop leaders and then give them autonomy in the moment?" He is conscientious about developing leaders and systems so they can run independently. Using a sports metaphor, he describes a system of shared leadership for him and a set of excellent school leaders he has nurtured who "run the balls in all my academic pieces." In their trauma-informed design for school improvement, success goes beyond scores on the yearly statewide exam. Principal Tiarks aims to tell a more complex story by using data that include information about the social–emotional aspects of learning for children and that help families get healthier. One way to do this is to structure regular weekly reframing meetings that help staff reconnect with school goals and not succumb to stress and burnout.

School sites are unique settings composed of students with cultural, linguistic, and academic resources; instructional staff with particular knowledge, skills, and experiences; resources for enacting responsive literacy instruction; and structures within which all of the people can interact and learn with and from each other. At Principal Tiarks' school, the design component of the continuous learning cycle needed to incorporate involvement of all staff, including social workers and community liaisons, because the 8 hours in which students are at school are strongly impacted by the 16 hours a day they are not. Once Principal Tiarks focused on how to support the mindset and dispositions for creating a relationship-based learning community that empowers staff to share leadership for academic and social–emotional learning, he helped create a culture in which "I'm going to have your back and I know you will have mine."

We have just described Principal Tiarks's first step in designing a plan for continuous learning at his school, founded on trauma-sensitive principles and the goal of building community (Cole et al., 2013). With this firm foundation in place, details of the design are co-constructed by members of a shared leadership team. They include:

- *Attending to what new information needs to be introduced into the system.* In other words, how will staff participants share their knowledge and learn not only the language and literacy practices they hope to foster in students, but also acquire the related teaching practices necessary?
- *Focusing on how to build staff capacity.* Who will facilitate the staff learning that needs to take place, how will it be differentiated for staff at a variety of starting points, and how will that learning be checked for understanding?
- *Conceptualizing the needed structures for implementation.* The following are potential questions for discussion and planning: How will common planning time or professional learning events be put into place? How will coaches work with staff? How will observational feedback be set up and shared? How will data be collected, analyzed, and shared?
- *Planning for data collection.* What data will be collected relating to student learning, implementation of the initiative, and staff perception? What will success look like?

The *design* phase of the continuous improvement cycle involves building a strong representative leadership team that will work to help all staff understand the plan's worthiness. The next step is to *apply* the plan in the real world of the school. We present another principal's example of putting a plan into action in the next section.

Apply

As principals move from designing a plan to applying it to the actual work within buildings, they need to rely on two important factors: the plan itself and the people needed to bring it into action. Principal Doug Revsbeck leads a large urban high school where over 75% of the students receive free or reduced lunch, 93% are students of color, 34% are classified as EL, over 80% of the students graduate on time, and 70% enroll in postsecondary education. They have achieved this success largely because of how they have applied their plan for literacy instruction buildingwide. The plan Principal Revsbeck implements relies heavily upon the people implementing it.

When Principal Revsbeck joined Harding High School 11 years ago, he recognized that, in high school, content is king, but literacy must also be a top priority. To ensure that both were addressed, he formulated an approach to reach all 120 of his teachers and make literacy the top priority. In a large secondary setting, this approach required working closely with literacy coaches, department leaders, and PLC leaders.

Principal Revsbeck established a leadership model in which teachers engaged in both content PLCs and interdisciplinary inquiry teams. At the heart of both of these professional learning groups was literacy. To engage teachers in this work and to help them see the urgent need for teaching literacy with a content-area focus in their classrooms, Principal Revsbeck and his team of instructional coaches enacted a schoolwide writing event. All students in the school responded to a writing prompt similar to the one on the state test. The faculty then engaged in learning the rubric used to score the state test. They worked collaboratively to agree on quality via anchor papers, and then collectively scored all of the student essays and provided feedback to the students. This process was good practice for the students, but was even more powerful for the teachers who realized they would need to dramatically change their instruction to include writing if their school was to see improvement and their students were going to graduate. Professional development on writing and reading strategies was implemented through both the content-focused PLCs and the inquiry teams. This design was intended to bring about a cohesive approach to literacy across the building. More than 10 years later, the schoolwide writing event still occurs, though now it is targeted to the real-life application of students depending on their grade level. All 9th and 10th graders respond to global context questions aligned to their International Baccalaureate® programming; 11th graders respond to a sample American College Testing (ACT) writing prompt; and 12th graders respond to a college essay question. The plan of centering on literacy in all they do at Harding High School is carried out through cohesive professional development in content-specific and interdisciplinary teams, ensuring that students get rigorous coursework with consistent expectations.

Principal Revsbeck is a voracious reader himself, though he is quick to point out that the only way this plan works is through the shared leadership across the building. Working with Principal Revsbeck in setting direction is his literacy instructional coach, Louie Francisco. Francisco leads a team of about ten learning team facilitators, teacher leaders who guide the PLCs and inquiry teams. While principal Revsbeck works closely with Francisco on setting direction, he also has an assistant principal of curriculum and instruction who lends further administrative support because, similar to Principal Tiarks in the previous example, Revsbeck recognizes the importance of maintaining trust in these collaborative teams. He knows that Francisco balances two important tasks: how he supports the teacher leaders and simultaneously holds high expectations for their work. This layered structure of people is what Wahlstrom et al. describe as *shared leadership* (Wahlstrom et al., 2010). Revsbeck uses this model so that the entire staff is engaged in the collective work and a cohesive focus on student learning does not waiver. This is challenging in a large urban high school where silos of content-area teachers can often challenge schoolwide initiatives.

The plan, and many of the people, have now been in place in an adaptive way at Harding High School for just over a decade. For seven years there have been incremental gains in reading on the state assessment, though the real outcome Principal Revsbeck notes is the shift to an asset-based mindset across the building. Teachers now recognize the strengths students bring to the classroom and build off those rather than focusing on remediating what they had previously seen as student deficits. The students are more confident and willing to take more risks, as evidenced by the increase in advanced course taking. Principal Revsbeck is proud of the accomplishments of the students and staff at Harding High School, which seem to be fueled by a clear vision that literacy is their top priority. This vision is enacted by a plan collectively carried out by the people who share in the ownership and leadership of student learning.

Analyze

Analyzing the implementation of any initiative or change in practice is key in helping school leadership determine whether the plan is successful and what ongoing professional learning will need to take place to keep it working.

Melissa Sonnek is a principal of an elementary school of 500 students in Minnesota, where the school's demographics do not fit the traditional image of the state. In her K–6 building 79% of the students are students of color, nearly 70% are identified as receiving free or reduced lunch, and 34% are classified as English learners (ELs). Principal Sonnek saw a disturbing move away from writing in her building as a result of what she saw as an overemphasis on the state tested areas of reading, math, and science. Knowing the impact writing has on reading, she and a team of 13 K–6 teachers embarked on a project they called "We Are Writers; Therefore, We Are Readers." Through this project, school staff focused on the implementation of a writer's workshop model in an effort to not only improve writing, but also reading, scores. As they collaboratively learned, practiced, and implemented the writer's workshop, they focused on analyzing their progress by intentionally measuring student learning data, implementation fidelity data, and staff perception data. (Read more about Melissa in her vignette on pp. 111–112.)

- *Student learning data.* Principal Sonnek and her team had baseline data in reading from curriculum-based measures (CBMs) and standardized literacy assessments, but they lacked data on writing. They began by gathering baseline student data of first-draft writing using a common prompt with a 10 minute pre- and postassessment for three types of writing: narrative, informational, and opinion/argumentative (Calkins, 2014). These writings were normed by the teachers using rubrics included in their writing program (Calkins, 2014). Later, the project led to creating rubrics in student-friendly language that were shared during writing conferences with students.

- *Implementation fidelity data.* In an effort to support the quality of the delivery of writing instruction, the team focused on *how* to teach, rather than just *what* to teach, in their PLCs. Principal Sonnek and teachers modeled lessons, teachers co-taught and co-conferred with students, and then the teachers in the pilot program observed each other. In collaborative groups, they conducted walk-throughs to measure the effectiveness of each teacher's implementation and gathered student writing samples to discuss their outcomes. All of these activities generated data that allowed the staff to monitor and discuss the implementation fidelity of their new writing practices.

- *Staff perception data.* Prior to beginning this work, Principal Sonnek surveyed staff members on their perceptions of the importance of explicitly teaching writing. As the learning and implementation of a writer's workshop model progressed, she gathered perception feedback from the teachers following each professional learning session to help guide the next steps in each PLC's learning.

While the ongoing focus of this pilot group was on instructional practice, Principal Sonnek continued to monitor three types of available data to answer their self-study questions:

- Does the pilot seem to be having a positive impact on student writing samples?
- Does the pilot seem to be increasing the reading achievement of students?
- Do teachers see the benefit of balanced literacy instruction that specifically includes writer's workshop?

Through their analysis of the data, Principal Sonnek and her staff found that the answer to all three of their questions was "Yes!" Reading scores of students in Principal Sonnek's building increased by 6% in the last 2 years and scores for ELs went up by 10%. By analyzing these three types of data through ongoing data review cycles, Principal Sonnek and her team were able to build a coalition for schoolwide change with solid evidence through their triangulation of data.

Adapt

The *adapt* phase of the continuous improvement cycle occurs when members of the shared leadership team reflect on the data that have been collected and then adjust the plan. The data tell the principal and leadership team:

- What is working and should be maintained.
- What is not having the hoped-for effect.
- What challenges exist to implementing the plan the way it was intended.
- How we will adapt our literacy improvement actions in the school.

To highlight the work of a principal leading her school through adaptation of the current school literacy plan, we call upon the work of Jenna Peters, principal of a PreK through fifth-grade school that is experiencing rapid demographic diversification.

In Principal Peters's K–5 building, 73% are students of color, 68% are identified as receiving free or reduced lunch, and 17% are classified as ELs. Principal Peters leads one of the most racially diverse schools in her metro suburban district, with the largest percentage of students from Hmong backgrounds, about 25% each coming from African American and European American backgrounds, and a small percentage of students from Latinx or Native American families. Principal Peters sees her school as a culturally rich community, where diversity is viewed as a strength. She is thrilled that her students have the opportunity to engage with peers in a "real-world experience." Principal Peters describes the school staff as highly motivated and says that they find fulfillment in their professional work.

Staff and leadership at the school had been working hard at their literacy improvement plan for several years, but had yet to see changes in their reading proficiency scores on the statewide assessment. Approximately 50% of the students were meeting benchmark goals, but the other 50% were not. These data did not change from year to year. The leadership team thought, "If we keep doing the same thing, we are going to get the same results." Principal Peters had many conversations with the instructional coach to analyze what the data told them. They saw that most of the small-group reading instruction was not taking place in regular classrooms, but primarily happened with Title I specialists in pullout programs. They realized that, with half of all students not meeting benchmark goals, any adaptations to the literacy plan would need to address teaching within the core program, not through interventions.

Providing small-group instruction helps teachers to learn about and apply instruction that is connected to their students' resources—that is, connected to their academic skills and vocabulary, background experiences, language and cultural knowledge, motivation, and interests (Bailey & Heritage, 2008). Small-group reading instruction has been shown to increase the reading skills of students at risk for falling behind their peers (Mathes et al., 2005; Reutzel & Clark, 2019). The principal and instructional coach began to theorize about why teachers weren't consistently providing small-group instruction throughout the building. A couple of reasons surfaced: (1) Because the Title I teachers did do small-group work, some teachers felt that it was already happening; and (2) some teachers felt overwhelmed with the challenge of having so many of their students not yet meeting benchmarks. Teachers wondered, "How can I possibly do this? How do I meet with 15 of 25 kids who are below grade level? How can I manage this?"

Adaptations to the plan took the form of affirming the teachers and providing concrete ways for small-group instruction to be implemented. These adaptations involved:

- Providing professional development on how to manage small groups; for example, how to reinforce independent routines and hold students accountable for their reading when they weren't in the teacher-led small group.
- Setting up collaborative structures with the Title I teachers. Title I teachers began to push in to classrooms so that there were more adults available for small-group instruction during the literacy block. In addition, both Title I and classroom teachers conducted standardized and informal reading assessments and collectively organized the small groups based on these multiple measures.
- Aligning teacher prep times so that collaboration happened regularly and the coach and principal could get to every single meeting and support the professional learning work of the general education and specialist teachers.

Principal Peters attributes the success of the updated plan to the fact that they adjusted, rather than tossed out, the old plan:

"We've learned that if we can give this time, we can build so much more capacity in our teachers. . . . I think because we've continued to adjust, there has been more ownership and willingness to keep going at it. Had we thrown out that plan Year 1, it would have just been frustrating to everyone involved. . . . There's a sense of—it's not going away . . . each year we've been able to drill down and uncover, 'How do we support kids better?' It has been exciting because we are seeing some nice results."

Principal Peters describes the results that are coming in: The scores of the cohorts are higher and higher each year. For example, the data for the current fifth-grade cohort are positive. In second grade that group only met grade-level benchmarks at a rate of 34%. This year, that same group of students has met benchmark at a rate of 65%. On last spring's state reading test, only three of the fifth-grade students who had spent multiple years at the school did not meet proficiency. This success is feeding teachers' desire to keep pushing forward. Principal Peters states, "Had we not stuck with it, those things would not have happened." She highlights the importance of the principal and coach working in tandem:

"We are constantly kind of pushing each other—what are we noticing? Where do we see things going well? How do we highlight those things in our staff meetings? What are broad things we see across our building that could inform us about future learning we could be doing at our staff meetings or through other building professional development time? . . . I think you help support teachers by meeting them where they're at. We're really careful not to ever make teachers feel bad about where they are at. Where you are at is where you are at. We want to meet you where you are at so you feel supported and give you the things you need to grow. So, that whole growth mindset piece is obviously huge, too. As professionals we need to continue to grow, and we'll support you in that work however we can."

Principal Peters does not doubt that next year she and her leadership team will still be asking, "What else can we adjust? Where are we seeing things that could be better?" That is the nature of the continuous cycle of *design—apply—analyze—adapt*; improvement is enhanced by building on what has been demonstrated to be working in the particular settings of educators and students at each school site.

CONCLUSION

Principals play an essential role in the literacy success of students at their schools. They create a learning community for teaching staff that allows for collaboration in a trusting environment; ensure that current, evidence-based practices are identified and implemented in classrooms and supplementary programs; oversee systems for assessment and analysis to support data-based decision making; support and evaluate teaching personnel who are responsible for enacting the literacy curriculum; maintain the focus on the short- and long-term goals of the plan; and highlight successes in the work to increase the staff's collective sense of efficacy. Principals must work closely with specialized literacy professionals because the partnership increases knowledge and perspectives on how to improve student literacy achievement and shows the staff that the school leader is fully committed to the literacy plan. In this chapter we shared the theory behind the key role of the principal in literacy leadership and provided four cases as examples of principals who demonstrate literacy leadership as they engage in the continuous improvement cycle of *design–apply–analyze–adapt*.

ENGAGEMENT ACTIVITIES

1. **Buildingwide literacy plan analysis**. This chapter outlines how to go about creating continuous improvement in literacy learning. Think of ways to transfer this process to your own school site by using the following chart to analyze where your building is in the school improvement process.

	Evidence: What work has been done in each of the stages?	**Needs:** What potential data or professional development may be needed?	**Leadership:** Who can be helpful at each of these stages in improving processes and strategies?
Design			
Apply			
Analyze			
Adapt			

2. **Assessing PLCs.** The publishers of *Learning by Doing: A Handbook for Professional Learning Communities at Work* (DuFour, DuFour, Eaker, Many, & Mattos, 2016) offer a free online self-assessment quiz to assist in determining your current strengths and opportunities for improving your PLC work. The self-assessment provides feedback and recommended resources (it can be found at *www.solutiontree.com/plc-navigator*). This tool may be useful for your building leadership to engage with as a group to see if teachers and leaders have similar perceptions on their strengths and needs. If results differ, this information provides a concrete place to begin discussions.

3. **Self and system assessment using *Standards 2017*.** One way principals can begin to determine where their own strengths and opportunities for improvement

lie is through self-assessment. Using the *Standards for the Preparation of Literacy Professionals 2017* (ILA, 2018), review the recommended competencies for principals (pp. 97–100) to self-assess your knowledge and actions. This may lead to potential next steps in your own professional learning.

ANNOTATED RESOURCES

The Institute of Education Sciences conducts rigorous research and evaluation of educational programs and practices and disseminates their findings through the What Works Clearinghouse website. Here practitioner-friendly *Practice Guides* can be found. These guides make recommendations for educators on a number of topics, based on reviews of research, experiences of practitioners, and input of experts. We have listed a few guides that may be helpful to literacy leaders and teachers:

Foundational Skills to Support Reading for Understanding in Kindergarten through 3rd Grade: *https://ies.ed.gov/ncee/wwc/PracticeGuide/21*
Improving Reading Comprehension in Kindergarten Through 3rd Grade: *https://ies.ed.gov/ncee/wwc/PracticeGuide/14*
Teaching Elementary School Students to Be Effective Writers: *https://ies.ed.gov/ncee/wwc/PracticeGuide/17*
Teaching Secondary Students to Write Effectively: *https://ies.ed.gov/ncee/wwc/PracticeGuide/22*

REFERENCES

Au, K. H., Strode, E. V., Vasquez, J. M., & Raphael, T. E. (2014). Improving literacy achievement in elementary schools: The standards-based change process and the Common Core. In S. B. Wepner, D. S. Strickland, & D. J. Quatroche (Eds.), *The administration and supervision of reading programs* (5th ed., pp. 74–84). New York: Teachers College Press.

Bailey, A., & Heritage, M. (2008). *Formative assessment for literacy grades K–6.* Thousand Oaks, CA: Corwin Press.

Berebitsky, D., Goddard, R. D., & Carlisle, J. F. (2014). An examination of teachers' perceptions of principal support for change and teachers' collaboration and communication around literacy instruction in Reading First schools. *Teachers College Record, 116,* 28.

Blythe, T., Allen, D., & Powell, B. S. (1999). *Looking together at student work: A companion guide to assessing student learning.* New York: Teachers College Press.

Calkins, L. (2014). *Writing pathways: Performance assessments and learning progressions, grades K–8.* Portsmouth, NH: Heinemann.

Cole, S. F., Eisner, A., Gregory, M., & Ristuccia, J. (2013). *Creating and advocating for trauma-sensitive schools* (Trauma and Learning Policy Initiative [TLPI], a partnership of Massachusetts Advocates for Children and Harvard Law School). Boston: TLPI.

Dufour, R., & Dufour, R. (2012). *The school leader's guide to professional learning communities at work (essentials for principals).* Bloomington, IN: Solution Tree.

DuFour, R., DuFour, R., Eaker, R., Many, T. W., & Mattos, M. (2016). *Learning by doing: A handbook for professional learning communities at work*. Bloomington, IN: Solution Tree.

Elmore, R. F. (2000). *Building a new structure for school leadership*. Washington, DC: Albert Shanker Institute.

Fixsen, D. L., Blase, K. A., Naoom, S. F., & Duda, M. (2015). *Implementation drivers: Assessing best practices* (National Implementation Science Network [NIRN]). Chapel Hill: Frank Porter Graham Child Development Institute, University of North Carolina.

Fullan, M. (2005). *Leadership and sustainability: System thinkers in action*. Thousand Oaks, CA: Corwin Press.

Harn, B., Basaraba, D., Chard, D., & Fritz, R. (2015). The impact of schoolwide prevention efforts: Lessons learned from implementing independent academic and behavior support systems. *Learning Disabilities: A Contemporary Journal, 13*(1), 3–20.

Hattie, J. (2015). The applicability of visible learning to higher education. *Scholarship of Teaching and Learning in Psychology, 1*(1), 79–91.

International Literacy Association (ILA). (2018). *Standards for the preparation of literacy professionals 2017*. Newark, DE: Author.

Ippolito, J., & Bean, R. M. (2018). *Unpacking coaching mindsets: Collaboration between principals and coaches*. West Palm Beach, FL: Learning Sciences International.

Joyce, B., & Showers, B. (2002). *Student achievement through staff development* (3rd ed.). Alexandria, VA: Association for Supervision and Curriculum Development.

Larson, M., Cook, C. R., Fiat, A., & Lyon, A. R. (2018). Stressed teachers don't make good implementers: Examining the interplay between stress reduction and intervention fidelity. *School Mental Health, 10*(1), 61–76.

Lesaux, N. K., & Marietta, S. H. (2012). *Making assessment matter: Using test results to differentiate reading instruction*. New York: Guilford Press.

Marzano, R. J., Waters, T., & McNulty, B. (2005). *School leadership that works: From research to results*. Alexandria, VA: Association for Supervision and Curriculum Development.

Mathes, P. G., Denton, C. A., Fletcher, J. M., Anthongy, J. L., Francis, D. J., & Schatschneider, C. (2005). The effects of theoretically different instruction and student characteristics on the skills of struggling readers. *Reading Research Quarterly, 40*(2), 148–182.

Mead, S. (2011). *PreK–3rd: Principals as crucial instructional leaders*. New York: Foundation for Child Development. Retrieved from *www.fcd-us.org/assets/2016/04/FCD-PrincipalsBrief7.pdf*.

Murrell, P. C., Jr. (2006). Toward social justice in urban education: A model of collaborative cultural inquiry in urban schools. *Equity and Excellence in Education, 39*(1), 81–90.

National Policy Board for Educational Administration. (2015). *Professional standards for educational leaders 2015*. Reston, VA: Author.

New Leaders for New Schools. (2009). *Principal effectiveness: A new principalship to drive student achievement, teacher effectiveness, and school turnarounds with key insights from the Urban Excellence Framework*. New York: Author. Retrieved from *https://files.eric.ed.gov/fulltext/ED532064.pdf*.

Raphael, T., Au, K., & Goldman, S. (2009). Whole school instructional improvement through the standards-based change process. In J. Hoffman & Y. Goodman (Eds.),

Changing literacies for changing times (pp. 198–229). New York: Routledge/Taylor & Francis.

Reutzel, D. R., & Clark, S. K. (2019). Organizing effective literacy instruction: Differentiating instruction to meet student needs. In L. M. Morrow & L. B. Gambrell (Eds.), *Best practices in literacy instruction* (6th ed., pp. 359–385). New York: Guilford Press.

Seashore Louis, K., & Murphy, J. (2017). Trust, caring and organizational learning: The leader's role. *Journal of Educational Administration, 55*(1), 103–126.

Wahlstrom, K. L., Seashore Louis, K., Leithwood, K., & Anderson, S. E. (2010). *Investigating the links to improved student learning: Executive summary of research findings.* New York: Wallace Foundation.

Literacy Leadership in Action

Melissa Sonnek, MS

Principal, Edgerton Elementary School,
Maplewood, Minnesota

THINK ABOUT THIS

1. In what ways does Melissa serve as a literacy leader?
2. What lessons can be learned about the role of the principal?
3. What questions come to mind while reading this vignette?

I serve as Principal at Edgerton Elementary, a K–6 neighborhood school with roughly 500 students; 80% are students of color, and 75% qualify for free and reduced-priced lunch. I've had many experiences with literacy instruction, having been an educator for almost 20 years, as a classroom teacher, Reading Recovery teacher, literacy specialist, and instructional coach.

So when my assistant superintendent and I had a conversation about the current reality of our school's literacy instruction, I was eager to share my knowledge and understandings. The two of us began to dream about what effective literacy instruction could look like. I described a list of components for the program:

- Mini-lessons that use a gradual release-of-responsibility model.
- Lessons that include clear learning targets, modeling, think-alouds, and teacher demonstrations.
- Effective writing instruction.
- Formative assessments and feedback as a daily part of lesson writing to carry equal weight as reading.
- Classrooms filled with high-interest books at different student levels and multiple opportunities to read and write.

- Students of color to have access to books and curriculum that serve as mirrors for them.
- Interventions that match students' needs.
- Teacher choice within the structure of reading interventions.
- Students' access to grade-level standards regardless of their reading level.

My supervisor suggested, to my surprise, that because of my background in literacy, I be given some autonomy to put together a proposal for a pilot and present it to key leaders in the district. This was unexpected but exciting.

It's how our Balanced Literacy Pilot began. I spent a year on this pilot with teachers who volunteered to participate. We had ongoing professional development, opportunities for co-teaching, observations, conferencing, and visits to other schools, particularly about writing instruction. We focused on teaching using metacognition. We conferenced daily with student writers to assess their writing and give them feedback. We learned how conferring can evolve into strategy groups and how conferring notes can be used as formative assessment. As we worked, we also kept in mind the reciprocity between reading and writing. We know children show us in their writing what they attend to in their reading. We learned instructional strategies on not just *what* to teach but *how* to teach it.

A year later the outcomes for students included increased achievement that interrupted the race-based achievement gap. The first year the Balanced Literacy Pilot was implemented, and comparing students grade to grade, we saw positive increases for our Hispanic, Black, and White students but more so for our Hispanic and Black students.

So, here's my advice to principals and other instructional leaders: Sometimes you have to rock the boat. When you see a better way for students to learn and teachers to teach, lean into it. And don't be afraid to roll up your sleeves and teach in front of your teachers. You also may wonder, how to take this on if literacy is not your area of expertise? Simple: Find someone on your staff or in your district with whom to partner. We are not meant to do this work alone. Even in our pilot, I partnered with a teacher leader who had a strong background in literacy. Shared leadership is powerful! Finally, although I've focused on sharing effective literacy practices, it's important to note, if love and relationships aren't the foundation of your school—start there first. It's what will make your strategies and initiatives stick. I vow to love people before I lead them. This is my leadership mantra.

CHAPTER 6

PreK–12 Literacy Programs

Moving from Curriculum to Collaboration to Collective Efficacy

Sharon Walpole
Meaghan N. Vitale

➥ How can we leverage the work of all literacy leaders to serve teachers and children?

➥ How can we make the development of teacher efficacy central to our schoolwide literacy efforts?

➥ How can literacy leaders attend to the components of the *Standards for the Preparation of Literacy Professionals 2017* (International Literacy Association [ILA], 2018)—in particular, Standard 6—as they build collaborative learning communities?

As daunting as it seems, changing PreK–12 literacy programs must be a districtwide endeavor with effects in every classroom. Think about it. Districts have schools with feeder patterns, with families sending their young children to elementary schools. Those schools must build competence and confidence for the work that will be required of those children in middle school. High school freshmen have to have a fair chance at a successful experience that leads to choices in college and career. The stakes are high. And schooling is always a PreK–12 endeavor. For many of the central office professionals we know, it's a birth through grade 12 endeavor. And for the policymakers we know, it extends from birth through postsecondary experiences.

In this chapter we describe some of the choices that school leaders make to strengthen their literacy programs and create environments for student success. We draw on research, incorporate the challenging call for high standards for all literacy professionals, and do that in the context of the standards that states have adopted for college and career. We have come to believe that a truly PreK–12 literacy program rests on a foundation of teacher efficacy; that is, on teachers' beliefs that they have the competence to teach literacy effectively, and that the actions of teachers and leaders can nurture those beliefs. We begin with a review of the efficacy work and then contextualize the information in an elementary school and in a middle school to illustrate the efforts required for success in those two settings. We touch on implications for high school, because we know that what is built in elementary and middle school lays the groundwork for advanced disciplinary literacy work.

Successfully building, implementing, and rebuilding literacy programs are always challenging. It takes time—time that is already allocated to other extremely important tasks, and time in the sense that the change will not occur overnight. It also takes attention to collaboration as individuals in the organization work together during the sticky installation and initial implementation phases. Although those stages are not central to this chapter, we give a nod to implementation science as a framework that literacy leaders can consult when creating and nurturing a schoolwide literacy program (Fixsen, Naoom, Blase, Friedman, & Wallace, 2005). In the context of school reform, one of the barriers to acknowledge is the role of teacher motivation and teacher efficacy.

FACILITATING LITERACY LEADERSHIP ROLES AND GOALS

Strong instructional leadership matters because it facilitates greater teacher collaboration and collective efficacy. It is that collective belief that together, teachers can ultimately increase student achievement (Goddard, Goddard, Kim, & Miller, 2015). We use the next few pages to show you what we mean and why it matters. We are well beyond the days when a principal can be held solely responsible for leading a school. The reality is that instructional leadership is important *and* management of day-to-day operations of a school is important. Today, each is more than a full-time job. The responsibility for designing and supporting high-quality instruction must be shared among individuals with varying roles and responsibilities; Bean, Dagen, Ippolito, and Kern (2018) found that not only do most principals involve specialized literacy professionals in decision-making processes, but also that they identify these partners as central to the success of their schools. Although the characteristics or influences of a principal's instructional leadership may be a frequent research topic, we argue that instructional leadership is instructional leadership—regardless of its source. When literacy coordinators, coaches, specialists, and teacher leaders work together to build and implement new literacy programs, they are demonstrating collective instructional leadership.

Such participatory leadership may be attractive on paper, but it is nearly always difficult to achieve. It requires coherence, communication, and collaboration among principals, specialized literacy professionals, and teachers. Each of these individuals must have a publicly defined role and must respect the roles and responsibilities of the other leaders. Figure 6.1 represents the nested leadership support structures that we believe could support teachers. Although the roles and responsibilities of specialized literacy professionals may overlap, they can also be made distinct (ILA, 2015). *Standards 2017* should guide construction of job-specific descriptions. At a cursory level, literacy coaches support teachers and guide school-based initiatives; reading/literacy specialists design and implement interventions for students, and coordinators and supervisors coordinate and evaluate school and district programs (Bean & Kern, 2018). All of these literacy leaders must be able to work together and with their principal, now recognized formally in *Standards 2017* as a literacy leader. When literacy leaders work together optimally, they create an environment that includes both autonomy and collective responsibility. That environment fosters trust. And trust in leaders is positively related to teacher professionalism, academic press, and student achievement (Tschannen-Moran & Gareis, 2015).

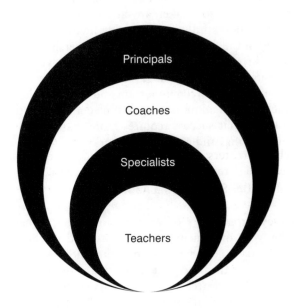

FIGURE 6.1. Nested supports for teachers.

The leadership structure of schools is a complex system. Schools are organizations, and, much like any organization, they tend to have both formal and informal leadership networks (Stoelinga, 2008). The formal organizational structure is apparent in a school's administrative organizational chart. Although the formal system may not be completely identical across schools, it is typically quite similar. One or more administrators lead teachers, who are organized in grade-level teams, usually with a grade-level or content-area leader. They share a group of cross-grade teachers (some combination of media specialists, technology specialists, physical education teachers, art teachers, music teachers). Other specialists may include support staff (counselors, nurses) and sometimes instructional specialists (literacy and mathematics specialists, literacy and mathematics coaches, special educators, teachers of English as a second language).

Informal leadership structures arise organically from within this formal system. For example, teachers turn to one another to solve problems within their classrooms, even when there is a specialist to whom they could reach out. This is normal and natural when it is a matter of immediacy; it is problematic when it is a matter of trust. Not including literacy professionals in literacy problem solving may be a symptom of lack of trust. Ideally the formal and informal structures will overlap. In healthy schools, individuals who are expected to be experts in their job descriptions and titles are the ones teachers contact for help. When the structures are not aligned—when individuals build personal networks such that their colleagues turn to them to sidestep their literacy leaders—organizational effectiveness may suffer.

Misalignment can also weaken any attempt to implement schoolwide change. Therefore, successfully implementing literacy programs requires a connection between the formal and informal leadership structures, which can be achieved through a "deep dive" into the context of the school and the concerns of its teachers (Stoelinga, 2008). We believe that alignment requires the boundaries between important and distinct roles (e.g., coaches, specialists, teachers, and administrators) to be defined and then respected. However, we know that success requires more than clearly defined roles and alignment of formal and informal networks.

MOVING FROM LEADERSHIP TO COLLABORATION

Effective literacy programs require communication, collaboration, and cohesion in the work of principals, specialists, and teachers. Rather than identifying a unitary role for a principal, the findings of Goddard et al. (2015) highlight for us the need for teamwork and help explain why it may be so important. The research team used surveys to gather data on a set of potential levers: elementary school principals' instructional leadership, teacher collaboration for instructional improvement, and collective efficacy beliefs. Then the researchers used multilevel structural equation modeling to examine relationships. There were a series of dominoes. A principal's leadership was related to student achievement, but indirectly. What leadership influenced directly, though, was teacher collaboration. And teacher collaboration was related directly to collective efficacy beliefs. Finally, it was those collective efficacy beliefs that influenced student achievement directly. Goddard et al. theorize that collaborations provide the experiences that strengthen collective efficacy beliefs. That potential explanation of these complex relationships makes good sense to us. We represent the relationships in Figure 6.2.

There is other empirical evidence for the importance of collaboration. Researchers have investigated the power of professional learning communities (PLCs). PLCs are more than meetings. They are formal structures for teacher collaboration and require collegial learning (Hord & Sommers, 2008). PLCs go well beyond teachers' sharing of ideas and finding "magic bullet" solutions; teachers in a PLC work together to set and achieve a goal and are collectively responsible for results as they grapple with adaptive challenges (Dobbs, Ippolito, & Charner-Laird, 2017; Hargreaves & O'Connor, 2017). The functioning of PLCs predicts collective efficacy among teachers (Voelkel & Chrispeels, 2017). Principals who are knowledgeable about effective literacy practices themselves *and also* allow teachers to collaborate frequently in formal settings can influence literacy achievement through their teachers. But not all PLCs work. PLCs require shared goals, supportive leadership, a culture of trust, and a commitment to continuous improvement (Hord & Sommers, 2008). In short, these successful collaborations are both a cause and consequence of collective teacher efficacy.

Building Efficacy through Professional Learning

The *Standards 2017* document includes a four-component standard foregrounded in professional learning and leadership across multiple literacy leader position types (e.g., reading/literacy specialist, classroom teacher). Ongoing professional learning is a critical element of schoolwide literacy programs. When literacy leaders work together to build something new, they will have to confront a difficult reality: Teachers will have to change what they have done previously. The degree to which that change is radical will vary from teacher to teacher and school to school, but it is important

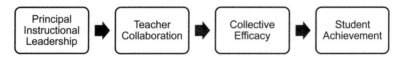

FIGURE 6.2. An overview of the findings of Goddard et al. (2015).

to acknowledge that change is hard. At least some teachers are likely to have to come to grips with the fact that the change goal requires that they replace, rather than revisit or revise, some instructional practices. The strength of their beliefs in those practices, as well as their motivation to learn, will influence their experience of professional learning (Kennedy, 2016). Research on teacher efficacy provides important guidance.

There are positive relationships between teacher efficacy and both engagement in professional learning and improvements in student achievement. Teachers certainly have personal efficacy beliefs. But efficacy also applies to groups. Collective efficacy is the belief that a group of individuals in an organization has the capability to affect outcomes for students. The relationship between efficacy beliefs and success is easy to imagine: Teachers with strong efficacy beliefs are more likely to experiment and persist when faced with challenges (Thoonen, Sleegers, Oort, Peetsma, & Geijsel, 2011; Tschannen-Moran & McMaster, 2009). But how can teachers feel a sense of efficacy in a period of change?

Fostering both change and efficacy requires careful attention to design, and that design can be influenced by both research and theory. Bandura's seminal work (1977) posited that efficacy beliefs have four sources: mastery experiences, vicarious experiences, verbal persuasion, and emotional or physiological states. Each of those sources can be considered in the design of practical professional learning opportunities. We can start with verbal persuasion and modeling and progress to mastery experiences, including actual, physical practice of new routines, which are worth the time they take in collaborative professional learning sessions. They provide a safe and necessary scaffold for teachers before they implement the new routines with their students. When teachers take a try at a new practice first in a role play with colleagues, they can work out some of the kinks and deepen their understanding. After this collegial trial, a reasonable classroom trial schedule, interspersed with additional chances for collaboration and peer support, safe from any administrative evaluation, can keep the change target on track. This careful planning may mitigate the natural negative emotions and fear associated with trying something new. Not surprisingly, Cantrell and Hughes (2008) found that yearlong professional development, coupled with coaching, increased self-efficacy and collective efficacy beliefs in content literacy instruction. From this we can conclude that professional learning opportunities can increase self-efficacy, but it must be sustained and ongoing.

Linking Efforts for Leadership, Collaboration, and Efficacy

In schools where a dynamic new literacy program is enacted successfully, leaders tend to take specific actions that can be replicated or adapted. They create a climate that puts students (and their literacy achievement) first.

That leads them to a careful study of standards and then to selection and/ or creation of curriculum and materials aligned with standards. Leaders provide extensive professional support to teachers in workshops when that is appropriate, and then in collaborations that are designed to foster efficacy. And finally, they collect evidence of their work: specifically, the extent to which teachers are able to implement new ideas, and whether students are building literacy achievement and motivation as a result. All of these actions are grounded in efforts to build teacher efficacy. Figure 6.3 provides a preview.

LAYING THE FOUNDATION IN ELEMENTARY SCHOOL

Challenging standards that enhance choices for college and career are exciting. We look at them as goals worthy of intense and long-term commitment. In the elementary schools where we work currently, the overwhelming challenge to teacher efficacy in the new standards' environment is that the national, state, or local standards require an overhaul of nearly everything: curriculum, texts, assessments, and pedagogy. When new

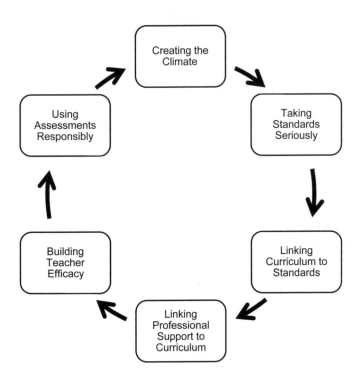

FIGURE 6.3. Targets for schoolwide change.

standards (e.g., National Governors Association Center for Best Practices and Council of Chief State School Officers, 2010) were first released, many school districts simply could not afford a substantial financial investment immediately, so they worked in dribs and drabs. They engaged teachers in intensive collaborative efforts to rework their current curriculum materials to be more rigorous. Because the standards defined and accelerated goals for text difficulty, literacy leaders in these schools realized gradually that they had to embrace (and finance) changes in texts in order to achieve their curricular goals. Schools that did this put teachers in a precarious efficacy position. Absolutely everything was new. But we have worked with teams that leaned in, stayed the course, and created collective teacher efficacy. We draw on our experiences with them in the case example that follows, describing a multistep process of schoolwide literacy leadership. We weave guiding concepts throughout Kim and Tonya's story.

CASE EXAMPLE •

THINK ABOUT THIS

1. How does the principal in this example construct and enable a leadership team that increases collective efficacy?
2. To what extent would these actions make sense in your school?

Creating the Climate

Tonya had followed a relatively familiar leadership career ladder. She was a successful middle school English language arts (ELA) teacher, earned a master's degree in leadership, and became a middle school principal. She was hardworking, organized, positive, and collaborative. The district continued to recognize her talents and moved her to a central office curriculum position. She hated it. She had too few opportunities for directly influencing teachers and students. She asked to be reassigned back to a principalship. Only an elementary position was open—in a school that had recently been awarded federal moneys to improve teaching and learning, so she would have resources to support change.

Establishing a new schoolwide climate is a tall order for any leader, and Tonya had her hands full. The district carefully protected teacher autonomy in a union contract. For many years, her school had performed more poorly than the others in the district, but the differences were not dramatic. Then outcome assessments yoked to the new standards widened the achievement disparities. As in many districts, her teachers were satisfied attributing that fact to demographics over which they had no control. They had the largest percentage of students receiving lunch subsidies.

But Tonya was not willing to see things that way. She needed a leadership team that went beyond herself and her assistant principal. She first tapped her school counselor, a professional with strong relationships with the district's families. She also included her school's union representative to signal her commitment to union concerns. She reviewed her enrollments and saw that she could increase third-grade class size slightly to create a position for a literacy leader. She considered hiring a reading/literacy specialist whose direct daily work would support struggling readers and writers. Then she realized that she really needed a literacy coach. She needed a leadership partner to help her understand the strengths and weaknesses of current instruction, and to plan and implement changes in instruction and the professional learning to support it. She hired Kim, previously a fourth-grade teacher at the school, whose master's degree in reading education and advanced understanding of reading pedagogy would be an important asset.

Taking Standards Seriously

Kim told Tonya that the school's current resources were inconsistent with the standards' requirements for text difficulty and variety, a fact that had long concerned Kim, but was not necessarily on the radar of most teachers. Tonya had been a middle school teacher, so the standards were new to her anyway, and she used that fact to her advantage. The first thing that she did was ask her grade-level teams to evaluate their text resources, and to provide her with a text scope and sequence so that she could better understand their work. The teachers reported that they picked and chose from a commercial core program, augmenting with teacher-created projects and units. Kim then met with each team to investigate measures of text difficulty for each of the texts they were using. Together they documented that the current texts were inconsistent with the standards' text difficulty demands. In fact, beginning in the second half of second grade, nearly all of the texts that students were reading were more appropriate for the previous grade. They needed new materials.

Tonya formed a cross-grade adoption team chaired by Kim, with representatives from each grade level, and a special educator. The team surveyed all teachers, who reported that they wanted to adopt the newer imprint of the curriculum they were using. The adoption team researched it, and they turned to EdReports, a nonprofit whose mission includes review of resources. They found that the new imprint was rated poorly on EdReports for alignment with the standards. In fact, it had almost identical texts to the older imprint they were currently using. This choice would be comfortable for teachers, but not likely to change their practices very much. Tonya decided that she would be the one to remove it from the table. She used the scope and sequence document that the teachers had constructed and prepared a comparison to the texts in the new program. She said that she would not be able to use grant funds to finance this curriculum because it did not solve their standards alignment problem.

Tonya's leadership freed the adoption team. They had to agree on a timeline and a process. Kim introduced a tool that she hoped could guide selection and increase understanding of the need for new pedagogies among the team. Kim had learned to access resources from the Institute of Education Sciences (IES) in her graduate program, and she had been intrigued with Foorman, Smith, and Kosanovich's (2017) *Rubric for Evaluating Reading/Language Arts Instructional Materials for Kindergarten to Grade 5*. It was designed to organize ideas from IES practice guides so that they could inform curriculum selection. The team members agreed that they would act as lead reviewer for their own grade level, and second reviewer for the grade levels above and below.

Linking Curriculum to Standards

The timeline that the adoption team set spanned all the fall term. Kim contacted publishers to get materials for review, and team members had substitutes cover their classes for 3 hours a week to do the work. By the end of the fall, they had two final contenders: a commercial core program with challenging text excerpts, and an open education resource (OER) that used only intact trade books. They decided that team members would each pilot materials for 6 weeks in their own classrooms, beginning at their return from winter break. Because they only had one representative from each grade level, they decided to assign the pilot to alternating grades. Kindergarten, second grade, and fourth grade would try one of the new curricula, and first, third, and fourth would use the other.

Pilot teachers were wary of their responsibilities. They decided to document their pilot each day in a diary so that they could track their own experiences as novice users. They also agreed that Kim would observe them for the purpose of understanding the design differences in their two choices. Since the problem that they were trying to solve was about experience in difficult text, she would observe each of the pilot teachers once each week to document the total number of minutes each day that students were engaged in reading complex text.

The pilot data were clear but troubling. The OER curriculum was providing more time in text, but the teachers' diary entries indicated that they felt less competent in their instruction. The curriculum was so different from their past practices that they wondered, collectively, if it would be associated with better achievement. Kim and Tonya summarized the data from both the diaries and the observations. They decided to bring the adoption group back together with a new charge: to propose a professional development design that they thought could help them develop competence in the OER curriculum.

Linking Professional Support to Curriculum

The team members were clear that in order to feel competent with the new curriculum, they would have to see it in action, learn each of its new routines separately, and then have an internal system of peer coaching to maximize their collaborative support and commitment. They drafted a professional learning syllabus that would begin in the late spring, just after state testing. Their syllabus is presented in Figure 6.4.

To enact this proposal, Kim and Tonya had to be proactive. They scheduled 3-hour workshops with substitutes to cover a morning in one grade level and an afternoon in another, finishing all grade levels in 3 days. They budgeted for stipend funding for preplanning. They scheduled dates for peer coaching (Showers & Joyce, 1996), with substitutes to cover teachers' observations of one another. They agreed that Kim would assign the coaching partners and prepare descriptions to ensure that the classroom host would coach by demonstrating, and the pair would switch roles during the second meeting of the month. Finally, Kim blocked her own calendar to be sure that she could meet the video requirement.

Kim and Tonya went back to the adoption team with concrete evidence that they would be able to enact their professional learning proposal. With all their resources organized, the adoption team presented their

Spring Goals	Summer Goals	Fall Goals
1. Adoption team visits a site implementing the curriculum. 2. Kim takes a second team of grade-level teachers to visit. 3. All teachers have an initial 3-hour grade-level training from the curriculum designers.	1. All teachers have access to the entire curriculum. 2. All teachers attend a daylong training during post planning. 3. All teachers have 2 extra paid preplanning days to work in PLCs to plan fall implementation.	1. No administrative observations will occur during ELA for 9 weeks. 2. All teachers will engage in peer coaching twice each month. 3. Kim will model and videotape one segment of the curriculum at each grade level each week from weeks 3 through 9 of the school year.

FIGURE 6.4. Professional development proposal.

recommendation for curriculum change and professional learning support to the full faculty. Some teachers were excited at the possibilities. Others were not.

Building Teacher Efficacy

Although she had engaged a team, Tonya knew that she would be responsible for the success or failure of the new initiative. She also knew that to lead it, she had to know it. She decided to start in fifth grade (closest to her own middle school wheelhouse) and work backward. She asked to teach a segment in a classroom, and she videotaped herself. Then she brought the video to Kim for coaching support. She continued to teach herself once each week until she could understand the design of the new curriculum. She shared short clips (including bloopers) at faculty meetings, and teachers began to see that she was committed to really understanding the challenges they faced.

By the end of the teachers' fall embargo on formal observations, Tonya knew what she was observing. Her observations revealed that most teachers had relatively strong initial implementation and that students were, in fact, spending more time reading complex text than they had previously. But some teachers were still struggling mightily, and there were too many for Kim's coaching support alone. Tonya decided to leverage her own video coaching. She asked each grade level to collect a five-minute video clip of each member of their team teaching some aspect of the new curriculum particularly well. She set a 6-week goal. At the end of 6 weeks, they would upload their sequence of video examples to a school-based video library to showcase their strengths.

Assigning teachers the task of identifying a personal area of expertise within their grade-level teams encouraged those who were struggling to engage in greater levels of reflection and inquiry and to seek the support of their peers. And their peers were eager to give support, including by identifying and explaining those parts of the new plans that seemed easiest to implement. Teachers who were struggling had a way to develop their instructional comfort gradually, and grade-level teams had access to models of the curriculum in use across grades.

Using Assessments Responsibly

Anyone who has engaged in schoolwide work like this will know that none of this was accomplished entirely smoothly or to plan. However, data revealed, over time, that meaningful changes in instruction were associated with meaningful changes in achievement. The data were complex. They included screening data to track growth for cohorts of children across the year, outcome data to show progress in attaining challenging standards compared with achievement the previous year, and disaggregated data to identify effects on particular groups of children.

None of these student data sets would make sense at all, though, if they were not coupled with observational data. Two independent sets of observations allowed both Tonya and Kim to design and fulfill their leadership roles. Tonya had her formal, confidential observations to provide feedback to individuals and to set goals. For a few teachers, these observations revealed that they were not successfully making the transition to the new literacy curriculum. Tonya helped them to enact improvement plans, and in one case, to switch grade-level placement. Kim used her observations to move from initial implementation of the new curriculum to individualized coaching goals for each teacher. It took both leaders, working towards the same goal but using different strategies, to provide teachers the support they needed.

As statewide outcome data became available, these data helped the staff to tell a story of steady improvement. Tonya began to receive requests from other schools for visits; her team was seen as new experts who could help other schools. Although teachers balked at the idea of visitors at first, they came to welcome these opportunities to showcase their practices. Tonya and Kim both saw this trend as evidence that teachers were building the individual and collective efficacy that would allow them to sustain their efforts.

MOVING TO MIDDLE SCHOOL

One of the most reliable levers for middle school change efforts are changes enacted in elementary school. Once fifth-grade has adopted instruction consistent with standards, literacy leaders seem to naturally begin worrying about sixth grade. In the following case example, Cathy represents a middle school principal, and Tammy represents the literacy coordinators and supervisors we have helped make this transition.

CASE EXAMPLE •

THINK ABOUT THIS

1. How is this middle school change story different from the elementary one?
2. To what extent would these actions make sense in your school?

Creating the Climate

Cathy's district is large, with 17 elementary schools feeding six middle schools and three high schools. Each school had a reading specialist to implement tiered instruction for struggling students, but their student rosters were large and growing. Initial results of new testing shone negative light on the district as one of the weakest-performing schools in the entire state. Rather than accept that designation, the district's leadership team totally upended elementary instruction with rapid and wholesale curriculum replacement. As the stress of that change receded, and the first-year outcome data provided initial evidence of effects on achievement, Cathy and the district's reading coordinator, Tammy, worried about the middle school.

ELA teachers in her middle school formed a strong six-person team. Instead of beginning by examining their own curriculum and instruction, Cathy decided to send them to visit one of the elementary schools to observe in fifth grade. The middle school teachers were surprised to see students spending much more time reading complex text than their own students typically did in a class period. They were also surprised to see some of the novels that they had traditionally used late in middle school were already being read in fourth and fifth grades. The teachers claimed, though, that their students were processing these texts on a much higher level and that the need for depth in middle school ELA precluded a move to increased reading volume.

Taking Standards Seriously

These beliefs were deeply held. Cathy knew that she needed to bring in an outsider to help her team review the standards and challenge them. She consulted with Tammy, and they chose a professor from a local university who was a well-respected literacy leader. John started by reviewing with the team the middle school anchor standards for reading literature, for reading informational text, and for writing. He shared what he considered to be challenges and opportunities presented by the standards. Next, he asked the team members about their current instruction and text choices. He learned that they typically alternated a large writing unit, a novel unit, and an informational text unit each quarter. They used a stand-alone vocabulary-building workbook and a set of grammar worksheets that they had gathered over the years.

John asked the team about student achievement, and the teachers were quick to describe the demographics of their district. They also praised the special educators who co-taught and provided interventions for their support of the many struggling students in their classes. John and Tammy worked together to move the conversation toward things that could change, rather than student characteristics. John guided them to consider streamlining their approach to curriculum so that they could incorporate shorter, more frequent writing assignments, change from decontextualized to contextualized vocabulary and grammar instruction, and examine their text selections to ensure that they were rich enough. Needless to say, this was a heavy lift.

Linking Curriculum to Standards

Before moving forward, Cathy, Tammy, and John had to present a clear framework for reworking the curriculum. John shared an article that he had seen recently in the *Journal of Adolescent and Adult Literacy* about the creation of text sets (Lupo, Strong, Lewis, Walpole, & McKenna, 2018). (Refer to Chapter 8, this volume, for examples of text sets for younger learners.) These text sets would allow the team to use informational texts and other short texts to build background knowledge for more challenging literature. They could easily form the backbone of a new approach to middle school literacy.

Cathy knew that she needed to be specific about how the team would enact the changes that John had revealed to be necessary. Tammy had the deepest understanding of current reading and writing research, and she did not have formal classroom teaching or supervision responsibilities. Cathy asked Tammy to create a model unit to be used schoolwide. She chose *The Boy in the Striped Pajamas* (Boyne, 2006) because of its excellent reviews and its potential to be augmented by historical informational text. Tammy wrote a unit plan that included multiple texts and a small number of before-, during-, and after-reading instructional routines (Lewis, Walpole, & McKenna, 2014). She also designed three research units, one for each grade level, that would be done after the novel was completed.

Linking Professional Support to Curriculum

Because the approach was new, and the teachers needed time with Tammy to learn the routines, Cathy arranged for three consecutive days of substitutes for the team to co-plan with Tammy. They role-played, created visuals to support the instruction, and gathered and organized all the materials they would need. Then the teachers agreed to engage in peer coaching (Showers & Joyce, 1996). Tammy drew pairs out of a hat, and Cathy arranged coverage so that each teacher could watch a partner teach twice. They established norms that these visits would be nonevaluative and that the coach would be the partner doing the teaching.

Peer coaching had some unintended consequences. Since teachers only taught in one of the middle school grades, they had not previously seen differences in achievement, self-regulation, and maturity that come as students move across the grades. The chance to watch the same lesson for multiple ages increased their understanding of literacy development and the potential to engage students in higher-volume, more complex reading and writing tasks. The fact that the lessons were provided helped the teachers concentrate on how to implement them well rather than how to plan them.

Building Teacher Efficacy

Teachers were convinced that text sets could work for them, but now they had to plan them. Tammy provided templates and advice, and she said she would be available to consult. Her expertise as a literacy professional had been bolstered in the eyes of the teachers; she had made their pilot relatively easy, and most of the lessons were well received by the students. But Cathy wanted the teachers to do the rest of the planning so that they could understand the design more deeply.

Tammy and Cathy were not finished. They had to start to engage the rest of the teachers in disciplinary literacy practices. Tammy had some knowledge about these, but she felt ill-equipped to choose texts or build units. Instead, Cathy asked her to lead after-school professional learning in a core set of practices that teachers could use with texts in their discipline. Luckily, the ELA team had already used these practices, so they were also available as on-site experts. Cathy formed peer coaching teams with an ELA teacher and a science or social studies teacher. Because their own trial of peer coaching had been successful, the ELA teachers were able to share how it had been helpful to them.

Using Assessments Responsibly

Cathy and Tammy could see that they had begun a shift toward a school-wide literacy focus in the teachers' reading practices. Writing proved a harder nut to crack. Although knowledge of evidence-based writing instruction was clearly identified as a standard for classroom teachers, her teachers had not come from undergraduate programs that emphasized writing. And since writing was also clearly implicated in the state's standards, this deficit was important to address. Data revealed that students were making gains in their reading comprehension measured in Lexile scores, but the state outcome test required greater proficiency in writing, and the staff had much to learn about how to teach and evaluate writing. Tammy suggested that they try one of the open-access on-demand writing tasks at Achieve the Core (achievethecore.org). All students would complete the same task, and PLC time could be devoted to scoring the samples.

Cathy decided that she should lead these PLCs herself. She wanted teachers to see that she was willing to learn this new content alongside them. They used a protocol for scoring a small set of examples together so that they could establish norms for understanding a standards-based rubric. When they had all the samples scored, the data revealed that there was one seventh-grade teacher and one eighth-grade teacher whose students' essays were longer and better structured than the rest. Cathy asked these two teachers to unpack their approach to teaching writing so that all teachers could use it. Because Cathy took responsibility to serve as both a principal and a literacy leader, and because she leveraged Tammy's expertise as a literacy supervisor and her ELA team to lead by example, this middle school was on its way to a real schoolwide sense of agency and efficacy.

Tammy, of course, had her work cut out for her. She had to start the same ball rolling in the other two middle schools. At least she already had a model unit to start and the other plans that Cathy's teachers were writing. She also had a sense that she could move from reading to writing and then to disciplinary literacy. She thought ninth grade would be her next target.

CONCLUSION

Schoolwide approaches to literacy across the years of formal schooling are key to student's college and career choices. We see the potential for new *ILA Standards for Literacy Professionals 2017* to reinvigorate these efforts by helping all of us to sort and define the powerful roles that principals, reading/literacy specialists, literacy coaches, and literacy coordinators can have in building confident, competent teachers of reading and writing. Together, literacy leaders can help ensure that their teachers have the curricular tools they need and ongoing, meaningful professional development. It's always an issue of coherence and relevance. Individual teachers will build their personal efficacy and groups of teachers will build their collective efficacy when we listen to them, provide them with relentless support, and leverage the potential of literacy leaders to make their day-to-day work more effective. Schools where adults learn together with strong literacy leadership teams become schools where students learn together. This work is not easy, certainly, but its rewards are substantial.

ENGAGEMENT ACTIVITIES

1. Use the free rubric for *Evaluating Reading/Language Arts Instructional Materials for Kindergarten to Grade 5* (Foorman et al., 2017) to review current or potential materials for their match to standards and evidence.

2. Review the list of free Practice Guides available from the Institute of Education Sciences (*https://ies.ed.gov/ncee/wwc/PracticeGuides*). Select one that addresses a need in your school, elementary or secondary level, and form a study group to read it and identify targets for change in curriculum and instruction.

3. Use the new ILA *Standards for the Preparation of Literacy Professionals 2017* to write short- and long-term professional development goals for the improvement of curriculum and instruction relevant to your role.

ANNOTATED RESOURCES

The Center on School Turnaround. (2018). *Four domains for rapid school improvement: Indicators of effective practice.* San Francisco: WestEd.

This free resource from the Center on School Turnaround at WestEd introduces a series of actions that schools can engage for turnaround. It provides useful process guides in four domains: leadership, talent development, instructional transformation, and culture shift. Thinking about transformation broadly can inform the design of targeted literacy transformation.

International Literacy Association. (2016). *Frameworks for literacy education reform* (White paper). Newark, DE: Author.

This white paper from the International Literacy Association presents evidence-based frameworks that consider teachers and teaching, schools and schooling, student support, and families and communities. The paper includes references that can be used to deepen understanding of key conceptual issues in building literacy programs.

REFERENCES

Bandura, A. (1977). Self-efficacy: Toward a unifying theory of behavioral change. *Psychological Review, 84*(2), 191–215.

Bean, R. M., Dagen, A. S., Ippolito, J., & Kern, D. (2018). Principals' perspectives on the roles of specialized literacy professionals. *The Elementary School Journal, 119*(2), 327–350.

Bean, R. M., & Kern, D. (2018). Multiple roles of specialized literacy professionals: The ILA 2017 Standards. *The Reading Teacher, 71*(5), 615–621.

Boyne, J. (2006). *The boy in the striped pajamas.* New York: David Fickling Books.

Cantrell, S. C., & Hughes, H. K. (2008). Teacher efficacy and content literacy implementation: An exploration of the effects of extended professional development with coaching. *Journal of Literacy Research, 40*(1), 95–127.

Dobbs, C. L., Ippolito, J., & Charner-Laird, M. (2017). Scaling up professional learning: Technical expectations and adaptive challenges. *Professional Development in Education, 43*(5), 729–748.

Fixsen, D. L., Naoom, S. F., Blase, K. A., Friedman, R. M., & Wallace, F. (2005). *Implementation research: A synthesis of the literature* (National Implementation Research Network [FMHI Publication #231]). Tampa: University of South Florida, Louis de la Parte Florida Mental Health Institute.

Foorman, B. R., Smith, K. G., & Kosanovich, M. L. (2017). *Rubric for evaluating reading/language arts instructional materials for kindergarten to grade 5* (REL 2017-219). Washington, DC: U.S. Department of Education, Institute of Education Sciences, National Center for Education Evaluation and Regional Assistance, Regional Educational Laboratory Southeast. Retrieved from *http://ies.ed.gov/ncee/edlabs.*

Goddard, R., Goddard, Y., Kim, E. S., & Miller, R. (2015). A theoretical and empirical analysis of the roles of instructional leadership, teacher collaboration, and collective efficacy beliefs in support of student learning. *American Journal of Education, 121*(4), 501–530.

Hargreaves, A., & O'Connor, M. T. (2017). Cultures of professional collaboration: Their origins and opponents. *Journal of Professional Capital and Community, 2*(2), 74–85.

Hord, S. M., & Sommers, W. A. (Eds.). (2008). *Leading professional learning communities: Voices from research and practice.* Thousand Oaks, CA: Corwin Press.

International Literacy Association (ILA). (2015). *The multiple roles of school-based specialized literacy professionals* [Research brief]. Newark, DE: Author.

International Literacy Association (ILA). (2018). *Standards for the preparation of literacy professionals 2017.* Newark, DE: Author.

Kennedy, M. M. (2016). How does professional development improve teaching? *Review of Educational Research, 86*(4), 945–980.

Lewis, W. E., Walpole, S., & McKenna, M. C. (2014). *Cracking the Common Core: Choosing and using texts in grades 6–12.* New York: Guilford Press.

Lupo, S. M., Strong, J. Z., Lewis, W. E., & McKenna, M. C. (2018). Building background knowledge through reading: Rethinking text sets. *Journal of Adolescent and Adult Literacy, 61,* 433–444.

National Governors Association Center for Best Practices & Council of Chief State School Officers. (2010). *Common Core State Standards for English language arts and literacy in history/social studies, science, and technical subjects.* Washington, DC: Authors.

Showers, B., & Joyce, B. (1996). The evolution of peer coaching. *Educational Leadership, 53*(6), 12–16.

Stoelinga, S. R. (2008). Leading from above and below: Formal and informal teacher leadership. In M. M. Mangin & S. R. Stoelinga (Eds.), *Effective teacher leadership: Using research to inform and reform* (pp. 99–119). New York: Teachers College Press.

Thoonen, E. E. J., Sleegers, P. J. C., Oort, F. J., Peetsma, T. T. D., & Geijsel, F. P. (2011). How to improve teaching practices: The role of teacher motivation, organizational factors, and leadership practices. *Educational Administration Quarterly, 47*(3), 496–536.

Tschannen-Moran, M., & Gareis, C. R. (2015). Faculty trust in the principal: An essential ingredient in high-performing schools. *Journal of Educational Administration, 53*(1), 66–92.

Tschannen-Moran, M., & McMaster, P. (2009). Sources of self-efficacy: Four professional development formats and their relationship to self-efficacy and implementation of a new teaching strategy. *Elementary School Journal, 110*(2), 228–245.

Voelkel, R. H., & Chrispeels, J. H. (2017). Understanding the link between professional learning communities and teacher collective efficacy. *School Effectiveness and School Improvement, 28*(4), 505–526.

PART II

PROGRAM DEVELOPMENT, IMPLEMENTATION, AND EVALUATION

In Part II, we focus on key aspects of school-based literacy programs; that is, we describe considerations important for the development of literacy learning (PreK–12). Goatley, Dozier, and Puccioni, in Chapter 7, address the importance of using literacy assessment as a means of informing instruction and highlight the need for multiple measures. In Chapter 8, McGill-Franzen and Ward focus on PreK–primary literacy programs; they describe the importance of oral language as a foundation for later literacy growth and discuss activities important for developing literacy learning of young children. In Chapter 9, Dole, Springer, and Herman, after discussing the literacy needs of elementary and intermediate students, focus on describing core classroom practices to develop the literacy learning of these students. In Chapter 10, Ippolito, Dobbs, and Charner-Laird depict the needs of adolescents and then highlight the importance of both content and disciplinary literacy instruction for middle/high school learners. In Chapter 11, Jones Powell, Aker, and Mesmer describe research that establishes the importance of differentiation. They follow with explicit and pragmatic suggestions for helping teachers differentiate instruction in their classrooms. In Chapter 12, McCarthey and James discuss teachers and students' attitudes about writing and then describe promising practices for improving writing instruction in schools. In the concluding chapter in this section (Chapter 13), Castek and Gwinn explore the expanding notion of literacy, and how technologies are changing the ways in which we address literacy instruction, especially that of online reading comprehension.

CHAPTER 7

Using Literacy Assessments to Improve Student Learning

Virginia J. Goatley
Cheryl L. Dozier
Jaime Puccioni

GUIDING QUESTIONS

⇥ In what ways do the *Standards for the Preparation of Literacy Professionals 2017* (International Literacy Association [ILA], 2018a) assist literacy leaders to:

↪ Facilitate and use a range of assessments to identify areas of strengths and difficulty for learners?

↪ Engage in assessment practices to develop teacher expertise and support student learning?

↪ Support collaborative efforts to engage in data-based decision making to improve literacy teaching and learning?

↪ Use their knowledge of assessments to advocate for learners and communicate with stakeholders?

Assessments have a major impact on the literacy learning of any child or young adult—for better or for worse. Literacy leaders have a responsibility to know and understand both the strengths and concerns about a range of assessments, know how to use them appropriately, and then how to advocate for students for best instructional practices based on a range of data sources. Literacy professionals often take leadership roles for individual, group, classroom, schoolwide, and district-level assessments, creating a need for flexible systems that address both assessment and instruction. Although this chapter has a focus on assessment, the assessment practices discussed are interwoven with instruction, as detailed in other chapters within this book.

Here we draw on several major assumptions about assessment (Afflerbach, 2017; ILA, 2018a; Paratore & McCormack, 2007). First, a major goal of assessment is to inform and improve student learning. Second, assessment tools should be critically evaluated for appropriate use. Third, assessment should draw on a wide range of data sources, including classroom observations, book reading assessments, interest inventories, standardized tests, and writing samples. Fourth, assessment decisions should draw on collaborative conversations among educators to explore and understand the range of available data at classroom, school, and district levels. Fifth, systematic assessment explores student growth over time and draws on both formative and summative assessment processes for overall accountability purposes. Finally, student, classroom, and school literacy profiles should be easily accessible to stakeholders, including families, teachers, and community members.

Each day, educators use informal and formal assessments to make critical instructional decisions about learners. For example, a classroom teacher observes a student to determine the strategies that he or she uses to identify an unknown word, and then makes a further instructional decision about when/how to step in for support. In addition, teachers and/or learners may complete a monthly assessment to monitor progress on specific literacy goals, with schoolwide results discussed among colleagues to evaluate effectiveness of instructional approaches. Further, statewide results on standardized English language arts (ELA) exams may be published in the newspaper, yet another level and type of assessment. Throughout all of these examples, the expertise and ongoing professional learning of the educators are critical to how and why they use a range of assessments to make informed decisions about student learning.

Literacy leaders make many assessment decisions every day. Bethany Nazarian, a teacher at the South Colonie School District, New York, shared the following reflection after reading an article by Bean and Kern (2018) in a literacy specialist graduate course. Bethany's response illustrates the complexity of decisions made about assessments.

CASE EXAMPLE •

THINK ABOUT THIS

1. In what ways does Bethany demonstrate knowledge of assessments and collaborative leadership in strategically using a range of assessments to support a learner?

2. How does this teacher recognize a range of assessment goals to address both instructional needs and accountability?

"Literacy professionals need an extensive understanding of what assessments provide in terms of data regarding students' literacy strengths and needs (Bean & Kern, 2018). There is a wide range of literacy assessments to choose from, and we as teachers must be familiar with which assessment will yield the most useful information based on our learners. As an academic intervention specialist (AIS) provider, I refer to a series of triangulated data when planning my instruction with each one of my groups. The assessments that I gather data from include New York State tests; beginning, middle, and end-of-year exams; and a computer program that is utilized throughout our district called *iReady*. I also write detailed notes about observations that I am making regarding each of my learners every day. Looking at a variety of data can help me understand my learner as a whole. If a student is not familiar with computer-based testing, he or she may not score well on the iReady assessment. I keep this in mind when analyzing computer-based testing data and look to other sources to identify each learner's strengths."

USING ASSESSMENTS

Literacy specialists need to know how and when to use various assessment tools. They also advocate for appropriate use of literacy and language assessments. To do so, they need comprehensive literacy content knowledge and a strategy for evaluating assessments. As ILA (2018a) points out in *Standards 2017,* literacy leaders need to "understand the purposes, attributes, formats, strengths/limitations (including validity, reliability, inherent language, dialect, cultural bias), and influences of various types of tools in a comprehensive literacy and language assessment system and apply that knowledge to using assessment tools" (Standard 3.1, p. 37). When schools consider adding or replacing literacy assessment tools within their assessment system, literacy leaders play an important role in the evaluation process for each potential assessment. Figure 7.1 suggests questions to use when making decisions about assessment tools.

The questions in Figure 7.1 are a starting place for selecting and using assessment tools effectively, including how to evaluate the intent of each assessment relative to goals for student learning.

Selecting Appropriate Tools

Assessment is a complex process, in which educators carefully select tools that best inform them about their own practice and to what degree students are learning literacy components. A systematic approach can successfully generate literacy profiles for districts, schools, and individuals that impact

The following list of questions is a framework for making decisions about assessment tools:

1. What would we learn about a student or students from the assessment selected to inform instruction?
2. What are the literacy components assessed in the tool (e.g., comprehension, writing, word knowledge, motivation)? Which standards does the assessment inform?
3. Does a potential new assessment tool duplicate and/or expand on other assessment tools the school uses?
4. How is the assessment administered? Is the assessment intended for individual, small-group, classroom, schoolwide, or state-level administration?
5. In what ways does the assessment tool inform formative or summative goals?
6. Is there any potential harm associated with the assessment tool?
7. How does the assessment tool address issues of bias?
8. What information is available about the reliability and validity of the assessment tool?
9. How is technology a component of the assessment (e.g., computer, paper, tablet)? Are students already familiar with that technology?

FIGURE 7.1. Decision making about using assessment tools.

instruction. An overarching goal is for literacy leaders to "systematically use assessment data to plan instruction for individuals and groups, select specific strategies for a given context or content, evaluate students' responses to instruction/intervention, engage their learners in self-appraisal, and critically reflect on practice" (ILA, 2018a, p. 29). Within this goal, selecting, using, and analyzing assessment data are all components of evaluating the intent of each assessment.

Formative and Summative Assessments

The title of ILA Standard 3 is Assessment and Evaluation, recognizing the centrality of both components. Although there is a range of definitions for these terms, educators often use formative or ongoing assessments in making *immediate* decisions to inform instruction, such as progress monitoring and teaching observations. Summative evaluation often involves standardized tests for *summaries* and *comparison* to other groups, such as state tests and end-of-year benchmark assessments. Formal definitions of these terms, according to the International Literacy Association Glossary of terms,[1] follow:

---

[1] Available at *www.literacyworldwide.org/get-resources/literacy-glossary*.

Formative assessment: The continuing study of student learning in an instructional program as it moves toward its goals and objectives by monitoring the learning progress of its participants. Diagnostic testing and various formal and informal assessment procedures can be used to identify needed adjustments to the teaching and learning activities.

Summative assessment: The final evaluation, usually quantitative, of the degree to which the goals and objectives of a program have been attained. Different types of evidence, such as the final test scores of students and the statistical analysis of program results, may enter into summative evaluation.

Both types of assessment and evaluations are typically key components of a systematic literacy framework. Literacy leaders benefit from recognizing the reasons for the assessment they are using, including when an assessment might be most appropriate and for what reason (for more examples, see Afflerbach, 2017; ILA, 2017a, 2017b; Roskos & Neuman, 2012).

Validity, Reliability, Bias, and Accessibility

When selecting a potential new assessment, it is important to ask questions about validity, reliability, bias, and accessibility, such as the following:

Does the assessment address a literacy component taught at the grade level?

Is the assessment valid for specific literacy uses and contexts?

Does the assessment reflect the diversity of students taking the test?

Does the assessment demonstrate cultural sensitivity and fairness?

What claims does the assessment make about reliability and validity relative to the intended use of the assessment within the school?

What accommodations, if any, are provided for English learners (ELs) and students in special education settings?

Literacy leaders need to understand the reliability and validity of each assessment they use (for information on assessment reliability and validity, see Afflerbach, 2017; Lane & Moore, 2012). Further, literacy leaders need to ask critical questions about cultural and racial bias and about adaptations or accommodations for certain student populations (Ascenzi-Moreno, 2018; Willner & Mokhtari, 2018).

Technology

In recent years, educators have raised questions about how students read in online areas, including social media, Internet sites, and phone apps. Concurrently, there has been an increasing use of technology platforms for assessment purposes (e.g., computers, tablets, phones) and questions about assessing online reading (Castek & Coiro, 2015; Kervin & Mantei, 2016). When selecting assessments, it is essential to understand the technical aspects required, such as computer-based models, to engage students with technology on a regular basis for familiarity. For example, young children may be more familiar with a tablet than how to use a mouse associated with a computer—a skill needed for some assessments.

Benefits of Multiple Assessments

Just as the expectations for K–12 state or national literacy standards for any grade level can be overwhelming at first, so can the range of assessments available to monitor student progress in learning those standards. Literacy is a broad, encompassing term, with expectations for numerous components: phonemic awareness, phonics, comprehension, fluency, vocabulary, writing, motivation, content learning, spelling, listening, and so forth. As school leaders sort through the best curricular and instructional practices, assessment is closely interwoven to address these various components of literacy. Drawing on a variety of assessments provides multiple data sources and also recognizes that learners may show their strengths and needs in different ways, depending on the type of assessment. Using formative assessment during instructional moments to inform next instructional steps can help minimize the need for numerous additional assessments. Further, assessing students in literacy events that draw on multiple literacy areas can streamline assessment processes. For example, analysis of a writing sample can inform progress in multiple literacy areas (e.g., sense of audience, voice, form, word choice, conventions).

There are numerous assessment and evaluation options available. In a conversation with nine elementary teachers in a small regional geographic area, the teachers shared the multiple assessments required in their schools (see Figure 7.2). Even with only nine teachers from the same state, there was a wide range of assessments with varied goals and purposes. Such diversity of assessments and purpose likely reflects the local nature of curriculum, instruction, and assessment, even when associated with one set of state standards. Further, the range illustrates the need for teachers to critically review and carefully select appropriate assessments within their schools and across literacy areas (e.g., comprehension, writing, phonological awareness). Each assessment has the potential to inform instruction, if used in a valid and reliable manner that also considers cultural bias.

Learning about Students

An ultimate goal of any assessment is to learn more about students, whether individually or as a group. In doing so, it is important to keep the context of the assessment in mind and draw on a range of assessments. To illustrate the complex conditions in which teachers learn about their students from

- Renaissance STAR 360 (*www.renaissance.com*)
- NWEA (*www.nwea.org*)
- AIMS Web (*www.aimsweb.com*)
- iReady (*www.curriculumassociates.com/Products/i-Ready*)
- Fountas and Pinnell Leveled Literacy Intervention (*www.fountasandpinnell.com/lli*)
- New York State ELA test (*www.engageny.org/3-8*)
- New York State ELA Regents Exams (*www.nysedregents.org/hsela*)
- Scholastic Next Step Guided Reading Assessment (*http://teacher.scholastic.com/products/next-step-guided-reading-assessment/program_overview.htm*)
- Read 180 (*www.hmhco.com/products/read-180*)
- *Assessment for Reading Instruction* (McKenna & Stahl, 2015)
- Reading Program Benchmarks/unit tests (Pearson Reading Street Program, McGraw-Hill Wonders Program, Houghton-Mifflin Harcourt Journeys)
- Online fluency assessments
- Interest inventories
- Anecdotal notes
- Running records
- Entrance/exit tickets

FIGURE 7.2. Sample assessments used in New York school districts.

assessments, we share a brief scenario about Wonare, a sixth grader, and her experience with her school-based assessments.

CASE EXAMPLE •

THINK ABOUT THIS

1. In what ways does this scenario capture the complexity of a student learner and the way in which literacy leaders use long-term data and a range of assessments to make instructional decisions?

2. How might you use a similar approach to analyze your assessment practice and instructional implications to identify strengths and needs of a learner in your school, including discussion of complex situations?

Throughout elementary school, Wonare often performed at the below-average range across the schoolwide, computer-based reading and writing assessments given three times per year. At the same time, she was an avid reader and writer, often choosing to read and write at home and during free time in school. When Wonare moved from elementary school to middle school, the teachers placed her in honors courses, including ELA and mathematics, despite her continued low-to-average standardized assessment scores. Drawing on their observations, informal assessments, and analysis of writing products, the mismatch across assessments led to puzzlement for teachers as well as Wonare's parents. She joined an afterschool writing club and continued with daily reading to maintain and improve her literacy skills and strategies. Wonare is a complex learner, and her teachers triangulated across data sources to make instructional choices based on a range of assessments and their knowledge of her as a learner, rather than relying solely on the standardized assessments.

. . . .

It is also important not to administer too many assessments; the goal to keep a focus on instructional time for students. As literacy leaders make decisions for all students, they need to continually ask what they are learning from each assessment and what the assessments do and do not tell them about student learning. As literacy leaders examine what is being assessed across the range of assessments, Afflerbach (2016) cautions educators not to "over assess" specific areas of reading (p. 414). To minimize excessive assessment, evaluate how the assessments represent the K–12 standards and associated instruction. What are the overlaps in literacy components and how valid are the assessments for the intended purposes of that instruction? Further, how do the assessments capitalize on student diversity to demonstrate the many uses of literacy for students? In all of these questions, the focus remains on the learners: what we learn about students and their literacy and language development. (See Chapter 11, this volume, for more information about the use of assessment data to inform instruction.)

DEVELOPING TEACHER KNOWLEDGE ABOUT ASSESSMENT

In this section, we turn to the development of teacher expertise with more informal assessment practices for individual students and groups of students. To support teachers in developing complex individual student literacy profiles, literacy leaders can focus on student strengths and possibilities, advocate for students, celebrate progress, and set meaningful goals with teachers. In these collaborations, the group perceived value of the curriculum and the way instruction is assessed become interwoven. As Teale noted (2008), "Count everything that counts," since "there is no faster way to guarantee that something will be excluded from the curriculum than for teachers to perceive that it doesn't really count" (pp. 360–361). Given this point, literacy leaders want to consider and select the most effective combination of literacy assessments for learners in their district (Afflerbach, 2016). As literacy leaders support teachers to recognize what they know, and still need to discover about learners, teachers develop expertise and come to know and understand learners in more complex ways.

Placing the Learner at the Center of Assessment Conversations

By placing learners at the center of the considerations during data team meetings and asking powerful questions about what is valued in terms of the assessments selected and used, literacy leaders foster continuous learning, inquiry, and a strengths-based focus in the school culture. With an emphasis in some school districts on color-coded spreadsheets, charts, graphs, grades, and increasing reading levels, Howard (2018a) advocates bringing a photograph of each learner to data team meetings to keep the emphasis and focus on the learner. When literacy leaders engage with teachers and analyze assessments used by districts, it is essential not to "lose sight of the child beneath the spreadsheet" (Howard, 2018b). Placing the child at the center of conversations becomes the centerpiece of data team meetings. As literacy leaders lead conversations to interpret data and identify school-wide strengths, needs, and gaps, they might ask, "Are we currently assessing everything that matters, or only those things that are easiest to test and grade?" (McTighe, 2018, p. 16). As shown earlier, Wonare's teachers moved beyond what was easy to test and grade, and sought to understand her strengths and complexities as a learner.

Literacy leaders invite teachers to begin assessment conversations by asking these questions: "What do I know about this learner? What do I still need to know to guide this learner forward? What can assessments tell me about this learner?" Beginning with a lens that is focused on strengths (Dozier, Johnston, & Rogers, 2006) supports teachers in noticing what students are doing well and to build upon these strengths and competencies. Donald Graves (2004) reminds educators that we teach what we value; likewise, we assess what we value. In determining what we want to discover about our learners, literacy leaders guide teachers to approach assessments through a lens of strengths and possibilities, rather than a deficit lens, so that students develop agency as learners.

Assessment Learning Experiences

When literacy leaders and teachers engage in formative assessments, teachers see how a range of these assessments become a part of the classroom fabric and integrated into their instructional practices. Johnston (2012) reminds educators, "The heart of formative assessment is finding the edge of students' learning and helping them to take up possibilities for growth. Assessment isn't formative if it doesn't influence learning in a positive way" (p. 49). The following assessment learning experiences explore several ways literacy leaders and teachers can come to know learners in more complex and nuanced ways to improve/guide student learning.

Observations/Anecdotal Notes

To model how to become careful observers of students and then to systematically document these observations, literacy leaders sit side by side with teachers and take notes while conferring with readers and writers. Together, they notice and name (Johnston, 2004) the range of literate behaviors learners engage in during book discussions, guided reading book introductions, and engagement with texts. Teachers may say to a student, "Wait a moment, I want to write down what you just said." Students see that teachers value their words and their thinking as teachers document students' learning. Likewise, during writing conferences, teachers observe and document students' engagement, decisions, and progress as writers. By routinely documenting their observations, literacy leaders then help teachers reflect and consider these questions: "When you confer with writers, what do you notice? What areas of writing are you most confident documenting: content, voice, or conventions?" Through this discovery, teachers assess the development of student writing and strengthen their teaching strategies (Anderson, 2018).

These "in-the-moment" observation notes can then be analyzed for patterns and trends. First-grade teacher Michelle commented:

> "I just knew that I focused on the content of the writing when I conferred with writers. When we confer, we talk about details, descriptive language, places where I saw student voice. I thought that's what I documented, until I looked across my notes. When I revisited and reflected on my anecdotal notes, I focused primarily on writing conventions. Now, I want my notes to better reflect my conversations with writers."

Michelle's analysis revealed that she did not yet document students' exploration of craft features or content in their writing pieces, areas she wanted to assess. After this analysis, Michelle expanded her documentation to better capture the complexities of each writer.

Analysis of Writing Samples

Discussing writing samples at and across grade levels and content areas helps teachers understand writers and writing development. Through collaborative conversations, scaffolded by literacy leaders, teachers analyze on-demand as well as writer's portfolio pieces. Teachers identify how they score writing pieces, what they notice about writers, and areas in which they are more or less confident. By analyzing student writing across content areas and grade levels together, teachers see the range of genre demands, as well as teacher expectations. In a cycle of inquiry and continuous growth, literacy leaders and teachers analyze expectations and demands, look for patterns and trends, and set future goals. Literacy leaders can then invite writers to share their insights about their growth to set future writing goals.

Running Records

By analyzing running records, teachers and literacy leaders see how children problem solve as they engage with texts. Through running records *need to be transitional*

(Clay, 2000), literacy leaders help teachers notice and document reading behaviors. They support teachers to notice areas such as: When do readers self-correct? Do readers self-correct directly after the word or after re-reading a sentence? What types of errors do readers make and at what part of the text? Do readers repeat lines? Do readers use multiple cueing systems, or over-rely on one cueing system? These detailed understandings build teacher expertise and help teachers make informed decisions as they differentiate their instructional language to guide student learning.

Together, literacy leaders and teachers look across running records for patterns and trends to help teachers reflect on what students learned today that will help them be better readers tomorrow (Lipp & Helfrich, 2016). Katie, an early-career teacher, noted, "When I put all of Lucas's running records side by side and looked across them, I saw all of his self-corrections. I didn't see these day to day. Looking across the array of running records, it was powerful to see how many times he self-corrected when he read." Lipp and Helfrich (2016) also remind teachers to document how they prompt readers, since these notes help teachers decide how to make instructional prompting more effective. When teachers analyze running records, they learn which cueing systems they tend to focus on and address with their readers. Fourth-grade teacher Gabby found this analysis powerful and commented: "Even though my analysis showed my student already focused on the visual cueing system, my praise point and teaching point [instructional prompts after the running record] focused on visuals, too. To help my reader, I need to change my language and help her focus on meaning as well. I'm more comfortable prompting for the visual cueing system, but she needs support with meaning."

When teachers share running records with students, readers have an opportunity to name their literate behaviors and become partners in goal setting. For example, after a recent running record, first grader Jaylee asked her teacher, "Did you get that self-correction? I'm getting better at those. You should write how I did with that goat situation [conversation in text], and how many checks I have each day." As students become an integral part of the assessment process, they become aware of their own learning (Garcia & DeNicolo, 2016).

Exit Tickets/Entrance Tickets

When teachers and literacy leaders ask students to take a moment after a class or lesson to document their learning, teachers discover what students have learned and what might need to be retaught. Entrance and exit tickets make student learning visible and also provide a space for self-assessment. Similarly, when teachers begin a class session with an entrance ticket, they discover what students learned the previous day. As students look across their entrance/exit tickets, they, too, can look for patterns and trends in their learning.

Literacy leaders and classroom teachers advocate for learners by engaging in conversations to decide the value of assessments, carefully observing and describing each child's strengths, analyzing patterns and trends, and reflecting on what students are learning and the instructional practices to best support them. This self-assessment further supports decision making about which assessments to use and for what purpose.

COLLABORATION

In this section, we focus on ways in which literacy leaders can support collaborative efforts to engage in data-based decision making to improve literacy teaching and learning. The first subsection explores collaborative efforts among educators to promote effective uses of assessment data.

Building and Facilitating Collaborative Efforts: Data-Based Decision Making

Literacy leaders develop a school culture in which teachers work collaboratively to analyze data in a continuous process (Datnow & Park, 2014). This work begins by developing a set of structures that will support a culture of collaboration among teachers engaging in data-based decision making (Boudett & Moody, 2013; Cosner, 2011). As such, literacy leaders work with school and district administrators to build a system of teams within a school to facilitate collaborative efforts among teachers as they engage in the analysis of assessment data. Although there are various team configurations within a school, most schools will have teams consisting of school leaders, specialized literacy professionals, grade-level teachers, content-area teachers, and teachers across specializations (e.g., teachers of ELs, special educators).

As literacy leaders it is important to schedule specific time for educators to engage in the collaborative data-based decision-making processes. Often, these collaborative meetings are organized by grade-level teams (horizontal alignment) or content areas (vertical alignment), and special education and EL teachers also participate. A meeting agenda, with clearly defined objectives and measurable tasks that participants complete within that meeting or over a series of meetings, is essential. Since analyzing data may create feelings of anxiety and trepidation among teachers (Price & Koretz, 2013), it is important to begin by taking an inquiry-oriented approach to data analysis and resist the temptation to assign blame (Valencia, 2007). In order to create an inclusive and inquiry-oriented collaborative community, we recommend that teams adopt a set of protocols, in addition to norms and expectations, to guide these meetings.

Facilitating Collaborative Efforts:
Multiple Sources of Data for Literacy Profiles

Educators often feel overwhelmed by the increasing amounts of assessment data available and the lack of opportunities to analyze data collaboratively (Roderick, 2012). One role of literacy leaders is to facilitate collaborative efforts to analyze multiple sources of data to identify learners' strengths and needs to inform the creation of literacy profiles within classes, schools, and districts. It is important for schools to utilize a comprehensive assessment system that consists of a battery of core assessments as well as a battery of literacy diagnostic assessments at each grade level that represent students' progress toward mastery of state standards and district-level expectations (Dorn & Coman Henderson, 2010). Literacy leaders help facilitate the creation of data inventories, which may consist of formative, summative, benchmark, and diagnostic assessments as well as other student-level data, to summarize all of the data available for analysis within a district and schools (Boudett & Moody, 2013; Hodge & Willet, 2013). Ultimately, the purpose of the data overview is to provide a focal area for educators to engage in data-based decision making across multiple data sources.

While it is important to analyze multiple data sources to identify learners' strengths and needs, it is helpful to begin the process of data-based decision making by analyzing a single source of data closely. In general, the single source of data should provide teachers with information at the student level on specific individual items on the assessment. After a single source of data has been selected, literacy leaders facilitate collaborative discussions in which teachers typically articulate learners' strengths and needs based on evidence from the data. After identifying the learners' needs, teachers should examine additional sources of assessment data to triangulate their findings, thereby ensuring that literacy learner profiles are accurate. Most importantly, literacy leaders must continuously encourage teachers to recognize that problems learners experience on any assessment lie within instruction rather than the learner, and that educators must adjust instruction accordingly.

Using Peer Collaboration to Analyze Literacy Instruction
and Develop an Action Plan

In order to address learners' needs, educators should link learning and teaching. One way to do this is by reframing literacy learners' needs as a problem of practice (City, Kagle, & Teoh, 2013). The problem of practice should be based upon evidence from a thorough analysis of instruction as it specifically relates to literacy learners' needs. In other words, if children are having difficulty identifying and analyzing details to determine the main idea within a text, educators can analyze their literacy instruction specifically related to those skills. Developing a shared understanding about what effective literacy instruction looks like, particularly as it relates to literacy learners' needs, is an important next step in the process. Once teachers have a shared understanding and language about what comprises effective literacy instruction, teachers can not only reflect and analyze their own teaching but also to learn to objectively analyze the instruction of their peers. As such, peer assessment is a useful component of the broader assessment system. After teachers (1) engage in collaborative discussions about what effective literacy instruction looks like, (2) reflect on their own practice, and (3) participate in peer observations, literacy leaders can help teachers identify and clearly articulate the problem of practice. Once the problem of practice is determined, literacy leaders help teachers identify potential shifts in their instruction to specifically address literacy learners' needs.

Once teachers have identified and articulated necessary shifts in instruction, the next step involves developing an action plan to address literacy learners' needs. Literacy leaders can facilitate collaborative efforts for teachers to consider a wide range of resources when developing an action plan. These resources should include internal resources from peers (DuFour, 2015) as well as external resources from literacy research (Duke & Martin, 2011) and the What Works Clearinghouse (2018). After reviewing a wide range of resources, leaders help teachers identify a range of literacy instructional strategies for developing an action plan that addresses the problem of practice and ultimately literacy learners' needs. Teachers should select or develop a range of corresponding common assessments to determine the effectiveness of the action plan and literacy learning more specifically. After implementing the action plan and assessing student progress, literacy leaders should continue to facilitate the ongoing collaborative process of data-based decision making.

ADVOCACY: UNDERSTANDING AND DISSEMINATING ASSESSMENT RESULTS

In this final section, we consider how literacy leaders use their knowledge of assessments to advocate for learners and communicate with stakeholders, and we raise questions about the use of advocacy on behalf of learners in understanding and disseminating assessment results.

Creating Bridges in Community and Conversation

Placing learners at the center of assessment conversations develops a more complex portrait of learners. To better understand family literacy practices, literacy leaders seek to learn what goals families have for their children (Garcia & Kleifgen, 2010) and what goals students set for themselves.

As literacy leaders learn from families and students about their hopes and expectations, they facilitate communication pathways that focus on students' growth in areas important to academic, social, and cultural expectations. Such conversations may include home literacy practices, community literacy practices, expectations for school-based literacy, and potential career paths (for examples, see Pierce & Ordoñez-Jasis, 2018).

Using Assessments to Discuss Student Learning

One way to build these conversational bridges between home, school, and community is to enrich opportunities for connections. In many cases, it is family–teacher conferences and school events (e.g., opening orientation, activities, sporting events) that facilitate such discussion in both informal and formal ways. Within the formal settings, teachers can use assessments with students and families to show examples of what students are learning in school, their progress across time (e.g., show three writing samples, test scores), current text reading level (e.g., show recent books read successfully), and explain the meaning of standardized test scores. A goal is to focus on the strengths of the learner, including what the learner can do independently or with support, to help the families understand how they might support literacy areas for student growth, and to learn from the families about student interests and community.

Stakeholders routinely raise questions about assessments, likely because assessments provide a window into what and how students learn. Stakeholders include a range of individuals, including the students themselves, families, guardians, policymakers, teachers, administrators, the general public, and so forth. Each of these stakeholders has a vested interest in the accomplishments of students, whether to see an individual student thrive, a school of students perform well on a state assessment, or to consider how schools are preparing the next generation for the current workforce for accountability purposes.

Whereas it is critically important for literacy leaders and classroom teachers to understand what and how an assessment connects to instructional plans, it is not always the case that other stakeholders have shared understandings of the intent and use of certain assessments. Multiple forms of communication can facilitate conversations across groups, from parent–teacher conferences, newsletter, newspaper articles, and other means of private and public discussion of the implications of assessment data. At the local level, a key goal is to advocate for the students and their learning based on these assessments, which often involves conversations with others (e.g., families) about an assessment and implications for instructional change. At the state and national levels, many public discussions focus on accountability of the education system. For example, since 1969, the National Assessment of Educational Progress (NAEP) has used a nationwide representative sample of students in grades 4, 8, and 12. The 2017 results suggested that the scores showed little change across the last decade. Systemic reform to improve such results needs to incorporate literacy leaders within schools, in collaboration with other stakeholders, to address complex curricular, instructional, and organizational approaches (for suggestions and resources, see ILA, 2018b, 2018c).

CONCLUSION

Literacy standards, curriculum, instruction, and assessment are complex. Every day, every teacher needs to make multiple decisions about how to spend instructional time, interwoven with assessments that inform the instructional practices. Assessment, when used thoughtfully and intentionally, can inform knowledge about individual learners as well as classroom, schoolwide, and district efforts. Using a wide range of assessments will provide multiple sources of data to triangulate, revealing a broad array of literacy accomplishments. Such systematic assessment needs to be carefully monitored to ensure the inclusion of key literacy areas and to avoid too much assessment. In the end, assessment has great potential for informing literacy leaders about students and making critical instructional decisions.

ENGAGEMENT ACTIVITIES

1. Create a time and place for ongoing collaborative assessment discussions across your grade level, content area, or school. Develop an agenda using a specific assessment and associated data for the group to analyze. Generate a protocol with a range of questions to facilitate a discussion among the educators that focuses on student learning goals.

2. Create a data inventory of assessments used within your school and/or district. Use the questions from Figure 7.1 to evaluate the assessments and develop an action plan to focus on the needs of your learners.

3. Consider how you and your school district communicate assessment results to families and how to improve this process. Take an inventory of strategies you use to inform families and then speak with them about how they perceive the results. Also, discuss the specialist's role in communication with families.

ANNOTATED RESOURCES

Afflerbach, P. (2017). *Understanding and using reading assessment K–12* (3nd ed.). Alexandria, VA: ASCD.

In the third edition of this reading assessment book, Afflerbach offers a framework for assessments and raises vital questions that teachers should consider.

He provides detailed information on various types of assessments and specific topics.

Boudett, K. P., City, E. A., & Murnane, R. J . (Eds.). (2013). *Data wise* (2nd ed.). Cambridge, MA: Harvard Education Press.

The revised and expanded second edition of this edited book offers a step-by-step approach to analyzing a range of student assessment data to improve teaching and learning. This text provides school leaders with information about how to develop collaborative professional learning communities, analyze data, and create action plans.

International Literacy Association. (2018). *Literacy leadership brief: Literacy assessment: What everyone needs to know.* Newark, DE: Author.

This position statement from the International Literacy Association explains the importance for both summative and ongoing literacy assessments.

Pierce, K. M., & Ordoñez-Jasis, R. (2018). *Going public with assessment: A community practice approach.* Urbana, IL: National Council of Teachers of English.

The two main sections in this book about assessment practices are (1) teachers collaborating with one another, and (2) teachers collaborating with families and communities. Drawing on extensive examples, specific suggestions, and resources, the authors share a framework involving collaboration among multiple stakeholders to inform student learning and assessment practices.

REFERENCES

Afflerbach, P. (2016). Reading assessment: Looking ahead. *The Reading Teacher, 69*(4), 413–419.

Afflerbach, P. (2017). *Understanding and using reading assessment K–12* (3nd ed.). Alexandria, VA: ASCD.

Anderson, C. (2018). *A teacher's guide to writing conferences K–8.* Portsmouth, NH: Heinemann.

Ascenzi-Moreno, L. (2018). Translanguaging and responsive assessment adaptations: Emergent bilingual readers through the lens of possibility. *Language Arts, 95*(6), 355–367.

Bean, R., & Kern, D. (2018). Multiple roles of specialized literacy professionals: The ILA 2017 standards. *The Reading Teacher, 71*(5), 615–621.

Boudett, K. P., City, E. A., & Murnane, R. J. (Eds.). (2013). *Data wise.* Cambridge, MA: Harvard Education Press.

Boudett, K. P., & Moody, L. (2013). Organizing for collaborative work. In K. P. Boudett, E. A. City, & R. J. Murnane (Eds.), *Data wise* (2nd ed., pp. 13–33). Cambridge, MA: Harvard Education Press.

Castek, J., & Coiro, J. (2015). Understanding what students know: Evaluating their online research and reading comprehension skills. *Journal of Adolescent and Adult Literacy, 58*(7), 546–549.

City, E. A., Kagle, M., & Teoh, M. B. (2013). Examining instruction. In K. P. Boudett, E. A. City, & R. Murnane (Eds.), *Data wise* (pp. 109–131). Cambridge, MA: Harvard Education Press.

Clay, M. M. (2000). *Running records for classroom teachers*. Portsmouth, NH: Heinemann.

Cosner, S. (2011). Supporting the initiation and early development of evidence-based grade-level collaboration in urban elementary schools: Key roles and strategies of principals and literacy coordinators. *Urban Education, 46*(4), 786–827.

Datnow, A., & Park, H. (2014). *Data-driven leadership*. San Francisco: Jossey Bass.

Dorn, L. J., & Coman Henderson, S. (2010). A comprehensive assessment system as a response to intervention process. In P. Johnston (Ed.), *RTI in literacy: Responsive and comprehensive* (pp. 133–153). Newark, DE: International Reading Association.

Dozier, C., Johnston, P., & Rogers, R. (2006). *Critical literacy/critical teaching: Tools for preparing responsive teachers*. New York: Teachers College Press.

DuFour, R. (2015). How PLCs do data right. *Educational Leadership, 73*(3), 22–26.

Duke, N. K., & Martin, N. M. (2011). 10 things every literacy educator should know about research. *The Reading Teacher, 65*(1), 9–22.

Garcia, G., & DeNicolo, C. (2016). Improving the language and literacy assessment of emergent bilinguals. In L. Helman (Ed.), *Literacy development with English learners* (pp. 78–108). New York: Guilford Press.

Garcia, O., & Kleifgen, J. A. (2010). *Educating emergent bilinguals*. New York: Teachers College Press.

Graves, D. (2004). What I've learned from teachers of writing. *Language Arts, 82*(2), 88–94.

Hodge, S. T., & Willett, J. B. (2013). Creating a data overview. In K. P. Boudett, E. A. City, & R. Murname (Eds.), *Data wise* (pp. 67–88). Cambridge, MA: Harvard Education Press.

Howard, M. (2018a, October 13). Maximizing our potential: Assessment that informs. Retrieved from *http://literacylenses.com/2018/10/maximizing-our-potential-part-5-assessment-that-informs*.

Howard, M. (2018b, October 11). G2great Twitter chat, 10/11/18. Retrieved from *https://wakelet.com/wake/1d50e040-7128-4e3c-9266-9a96874446b6*.

International Literacy Association (ILA). (2017a). *Literacy assessment: What everyone needs to know* [Literacy leadership brief]. Newark, DE: Author.

International Literacy Association (ILA). (2017b). *The roles of standardized reading tests in schools* [Literacy leadership brief]. Newark, DE: Author.

International Literacy Association (ILA). (2018a). *Standards for the preparation of literacy professionals 2017*. Newark, DE: Author.

International Literacy Association (ILA). (2018b). *Beyond the numbers: Using data for instructional decision making* [Literacy leadership brief]. Newark, DE: Author.

International Literacy Association (ILA). (2018c). *Exploring the 2017 NAEP reading results: Systemic reforms beat simplistic solutions* [Literacy leadership brief]. Newark, DE: Author.

Johnston, P. (2004). *Choice words: How our language affects children's learning*. Portland, ME: Stenhouse.

Johnston, P. (2012). *Opening minds: Using language to change lives*. Portland, ME: Stenhouse.

Kervin, L., & Mantei, J. (2016). Assessing emergent readers' knowledge about online reading. *The Reading Teacher, 69*(6), 647–651.

Lane, S., & Moore, D. (2012). Literacy assessment in schools. In R. M. Bean & A. S. Dagen (Eds.). *Best practices of literacy leaders* (pp. 261–294). New York: Guilford Press.

Lipp, J., & Helfrich, S. (2016). Key Reading Recovery strategies to support classroom guided reading instruction. *The Reading Teacher, 69*(6), 639–646.

McKenna, M. C., & Stahl, K. A. D. (2015). *Assessment for reading instruction* (3rd ed.). New York: Guilford Press.

McTighe, J. (2018). Three key questions on measuring learning. *Educational Leadership, 75*(5), 14–20.

Paratore, J. R., & McCormack, R. L. (2007). *Classroom literacy assessment: Making sense of what students know and do.* New York: Guilford Press.

Pierce, K. M., & Ordoñez-Jasis, R. (2018). *Going public with assessment: A community practice approach.* Urbana, IL: National Council of Teachers of English.

Price, J., & Koretz, D. (2013). Building assessment literacy. In K. P. Boudett, E. A. City, & R. J. Murnane (Eds.), *Data wise* (pp. 35–63). Cambridge, MA: Harvard Education Press.

Roderick, M. (2012). Drowning in data but thirsty for analysis. *Teachers College Record, 114,* 1–9.

Roskos, K., & Neuman, S. B. (2012). Formative assessment: Simply, no additives. *The Reading Teacher, 65*(8), 534–538.

Teale, W. (2008). What counts?: Literacy assessment in urban schools. *The Reading Teacher, 62*(4), 358–361.

Valencia, S. (2007). Inquiry-oriented assessment. In J. R. Paratore & R. L. McCormack (Eds.), *Classroom literacy assessment: Making sense of what students know and do* (pp. 3–20). New York: Guilford Press.

What Works Clearinghouse. (2018). Find what works based on the evidence. Washington, DC: U.S. Department of Education, Institute of Education Sciences, National Center for Education Evaluation and Regional Assistance. Retrieved from *https://ies.ed.gov/ncee/wwc.*

Willner, L. S., Mokhtari, K. (2018). Improving meaningful use of accommodations by multilingual learners. *The Reading Teacher, 71*(4), 431–439.

CHAPTER 8

PreK/Primary Schoolwide Literacy Programs

Anne McGill-Franzen
Natalia Ward

GUIDING QUESTIONS

➡ What does developmentally appropriate instruction in PreK/primary grades look like?

➡ What skills embedded in national standards as well as the *Standards for the Preparation of Literacy Professionals 2017* (International Literacy Association [ILA], 2018) are precursors to children's beginning or early reading achievement?

➡ What do PreK and primary grade teachers need to know and be able to do in order to support children's early literacy development?

➡ What kinds of activities bring oral language modeling, literacy strategies, materials, and approaches into sharp focus for preschool and primary grade learners?

Concern about the literacy achievement gap between poor and marginalized students and their more advantaged peers has intensified over the past decade, leading to unprecedented scrutiny of teachers and teaching, and this scrutiny has extended to teaching our youngest children. In this chapter, we discuss first the various iterations of developmentally appropriate instruction, a theoretical construct that is central to any examination of what literacy leaders need to know about early literacy. Next, we describe the constellation of student skills, embedded in national standards as well as those in *Standards 2017* (ILA, 2018), which researchers have identified as precursors to later reading achievement. Given the focus of this chapter, we attend particularly to the knowledge and instructional repertoires that teachers of preschool and the early elementary grades must develop to support literacy of all learners. We explain the assumptions and the research base that underpin our current understandings about early literacy development and the teaching practices that sustain and nourish early learners. We examine in detail activities that provide supportive contexts for classroom talk, high-quality language modeling, vocabulary development, and focused literacy instruction—deep, multitext reading of topics, genres, or series; and interactive writing to support the foundational print and phonics skills and genre knowledge that are critical for literacy acquisition. We conclude our chapter with several recommendations for personalized professional learning experiences that enable teachers to observe good examples of high-quality interactions and obtain feedback on their own discourse with students.

WHAT IS "DEVELOPMENTALLY APPROPRIATE PRACTICE"?

In 2009, the National Association for the Education of Young Children (NAEYC) revised the position statement, Developmentally Appropriate Practice (DAP) in Early Childhood Programs, defined by the organization as birth through 8 years old (typically third grade). In current state and federal administrations, as in the previous ones, concerns for achievement and accountability have encompassed younger and younger grade levels. As a long-standing and highly influential professional organization that deals with accreditation and curriculum development issues for early childhood and kindergarten programs and makes recommendations for children through age 8, the NAEYC recently has become a voice to be reckoned with in K–12 policy. According to the National Center for Education Statistics[1] (2018, April), 86% of 5-year-olds, 66% of 4-year-olds, and 42% of 3-year-olds were enrolled in preprimary programs, including kindergarten, in 2016, and another 900,000 or so were enrolled in Head Start,[2] making it critical that early childhood programs be philosophically aligned with the early grades in school so that teachers of children at varying developmental levels can build on what children know and are able to do.

The NAEYC has come a long way in its thinking about literacy and the young child since the first formal DAP position paper appeared in 1987,

---

[1] Available at *https://nces.ed.gov/programs/coe/indicator_cfa.asp.*

[2] Available at *https://eclkc.ohs.acf.hhs.gov/about-us/article/head-start-program-facts-fiscal-year-2017.*

which listed "singing the alphabet song" and holding pencils to write, among other literacy activities, as inappropriate (National Association for the Education of Young Children, 1987). Taken to task for disadvantaging poor children, or second-language learners, who depend on early childhood programs to level the playing field and provide a "head start" for success in school, the NAEYC revised the DAP position in 1996 in response to equity concerns. In its 1996 revision, the association welcomed the conversation with educators outside the early childhood domain and developed language that reflected sensitivity toward poverty and cultural and linguistic diversity. Along the way, the International Reading Association (IRA—now the ILA) joined the conversation with NAEYC, and together created a statement of developmentally appropriate practice that spanned the continuum of literacy development from preschool through third grade (International Reading Association & National Association for the Education of Young Children, 1998). The IRA/NAEYC joint statement, like the Snow, Burns, and Griffin (1998) publication *Preventing Reading Difficulties in Young Children,* released at about the same time, identified not only specific teaching activities to promote phonemic awareness, but also invented spelling as a way for children to develop an understanding of the way sound maps onto print. The joint statement marked a stunning departure in philosophy and practice on the part of NAEYC that, in the past, had held to a maturational view of literacy acquisition: That is, when "ready," children will discover the conventions of print and learn to read. Rather than eschew explicit teaching as "didactic" and hence inappropriate, the joint position statement acknowledged that adults can and should scaffold development: "IRA and NAEYC believe that goals and expectations for young children's achievement in reading and writing should be developmentally appropriate, that is, challenging but achievable, with sufficient adult support" (1998, p. 8).

Several trends prompted the 2009 revision of DAP: the standards and accountability movements, increasing linguistic and cultural diversity, growing consensus on the importance of early schooling to mediate the deleterious effects of poverty on achievement, and the knowledge gained over the past decade about early cognitive development. Embedded within the 2009 position statement are specific recommendations for language and literacy practice. Vocabulary development within storybook reading and other contexts for extended discourse are emphasized, as is alphabet knowledge and phonological awareness. In an explicit reference to past prohibitions about literacy instruction, the position statement acknowledged the following:

> A decade ago, many preschool teachers did not perceive it as their role—or even see it as appropriate—to launch young children on early steps toward literacy, including familiarizing them with the world of print and the sounds of language. The early childhood profession now recognizes that gaining literacy

foundations is an important facet of children's experience before kindergarten, although the early literacy component still needs substantial improvement in many classrooms. (p. 7)

Indeed, research such as the Head Start Impact Study (Puma et al., 2012) and the evaluation of Tennessee's Voluntary Prekindergarten (TN-VPK) program (Lipsey, Farnum, & Hofer, 2016) found positive gains for those participating in these programs, but these gains were not sustained, and were often reversed, beyond the preschool year.

Clearly, then, children need high-quality support not only in preschool but throughout all of the primary grades. Large-scale studies of achievement trajectories in two national databases (National Longitudinal Survey of Youth—Children and Young Adults and the Early Childhood Longitudinal Study of Kindergarten) of over 30,000 children from school entry to eighth grade found that children experienced their most rapid growth early in elementary school—before third grade—after which their rate of growth slowed (Cameron, Grimm, Steele, Castro-Schilo, & Grissmer, 2015). In reading, children demonstrated their fastest rate of growth in mid-first grade! Unfortunately, the results of this analysis also replicated the well-documented and untoward effects of poverty on children's achievement trajectories, and the researchers used the results of their work to call attention, once again, to the potential of early schooling to mitigate disadvantage. However, the quality of teachers' interactions with children is highly variable, and, as the work of the National Institute of Child Health and Human Development (NICHD) early childhood research network has demonstrated (2000, 2002, 2005; see also Pianta et al., 2005; Justice, Mashburn, Hamre, & Pianta, 2008), many teachers are unlikely to meet the literacy and language needs of high-risk children in particular. The heart of DAP, according to the NAEYC and the NICHD research network, lies in the quality of teachers' interactions—the ways in which teachers implement activities and respond to individual children moment by moment (National Association for the Education of Young Children, 2015). NAEYC refers to this quality as the *intentionality* that is embedded in the "knowledge that practitioners consider when they are making decisions, and in always aiming for goals that are both challenging and achievable for children" (National Association for the Education of Young Children, 2009, p. 9).

WHAT SHOULD EARLY LITERACY EDUCATORS KNOW ABOUT LITERACY DEVELOPMENT?

One way to answer this question is to consult the early learning standards for literacy outcomes for children, either those developed by states or nationally. Presumably, the standards are aligned not only with our best research and thinking about early literacy development but also with the way students and, more recently, teachers, are evaluated. The 2010 Common Core State Standards (CCSS) Initiative, developed by the National Governors Association and the Council of Chief State Schools Officers (NGA & CCSSO), presents a developmental progression of skills in essential literacy domains (NGA & CCSSO, 2010). Adopted by over 40 states, the CCSS are organized by grade, starting with kindergarten, with one section devoted to grades K–5. The standards emphasize key features of the English language arts (ELA) curriculum across the grades and provide particular focus on the connections between reading, writing, and language development.

Aspects of text complexity and the growth of comprehension jointly comprise the reading standards, from beginning reading to proficient levels. At all levels, the expectation holds that students "make fuller use of text," demonstrating increasing ability to make inferences within and across texts and read texts with a discerning and critical stance. The Common Core writing standards consider not only the process of writing—that is, the ability to plan, draft, revise, and edit—but also the specific kinds of writing required within different text types. Also expected is the ability to develop written responses to literary and informational texts and draw upon these texts to study topics of interest. The language standards frame speaking and listening in terms of peer collaboration and effective communication that may include drawing and digital media, depending on the nature of the task and levels of the children. The language standards also include the ability to learn the meanings of new words as well as the conventions of oral and written language.

Central to our discussion on emergent literacy are the foundational skills that are not an "end" in themselves but necessary elements in a comprehensive literacy program that ultimately enables understanding and composition of text. Among these foundational skills are understanding the organization and basic features of print (alphabet knowledge, directionality and linearity, concept of word in text); understanding of spoken words, syllables, and sounds (rhyme, segmentation, and blending); knowing and applying grade-level phonics and word-analysis skills in decoding words; and ability to read grade-appropriate texts with fluency (NGA & CCSSO, 2010). See Chapter 14 of this volume for a more extended discussion of these foundational skills.

Although preschool is not included in the CCSS, 50 states and Head Start have developed early learning standards for children before kindergarten age (DeBruin-Parecki & Slutzky, 2016). Early literacy learning standards typically include the domains of social, emotional, and motor development but recently have included early literacy domains similar to those articulated for the CCSS (Scott-Little, Kagan, & Frelow, 2006). For example, the state of Wisconsin expects that preschool children will show "an appreciation of books and understand[ing of] how print works"; develop alphabetic awareness, phonological awareness, and phonemic awareness; and use "writing to represent thoughts or ideas" (Wisconsin Model Early Learning Standards, 2013, p. 43). Likewise, the first two of eight domains in the Head Start Outcomes Framework (2011) are language and literacy standards. In this document, language is broadly construed as listening and understanding, and speaking and communicating, whereas the literacy outcomes are more specific and reflective of the core standards of foundational knowledge: phonological awareness, book knowledge and appreciation, print awareness and concepts, early writing, and alphabet knowledge.

Finally, to underscore the critical importance of literacy in every child's present and future and the diverse socioeconomic, cultural, and multilingual contexts in which the teachers of today work, *Standards 2017* (ILA, 2018) make explicit the pedagogical and content knowledge required of those who teach literacy, and affirm the centrality of literacy educators in the quest for equity. Of special importance to the teacher of preschool, kindergarten, and the primary grades is the broader focus of the revised *Standards 2017* to include the teaching and support of oral language development and writing as well as reading—a focus that aligns with the national outcome standards for student development.

Besides the recently promulgated standards described above, the National Early Literacy Panel (2009) released the results of research syntheses of approximately 500 empirical studies on early literacy development. Although the content of the report, *Developing Early Literacy,* is less accessible to the practitioner than either state early-learning standards or the CCSS, the report affirms the centrality of early literacy skills in later academic achievement. Among the questions posed by the panel and elaborated in the report were two of interest to readers of this chapter: What are the precursor or emergent literacy abilities that are linked to later reading, writing, and spelling achievement? Which interventions support the development of these precursor abilities?

The panel identified several strong or moderate correlates of later reading achievement from these analyses, among them alphabet knowledge, phonological awareness, name writing, oral language, and print knowledge. (Note: Other variables were identified, but for the purposes of this chapter are not elaborated upon here [e.g., automaticity in letter, digit, and object naming]). Oral language emerged as a potentially important variable in later reading comprehension, particularly if the researchers employed complex or composite measures of oral language in the studies. In fact, studies that used the most complex measures of oral language (e.g., listening comprehension, the ability to define words or understand grammatical constructions) obtained the highest correlation with reading comprehension of any measure (Shanahan & Lonigan, 2010). Not surprisingly, the panel also found that children learned what they were taught: Instruction that focused on shared reading improved children's oral language abilities; a focus on the alphabetic code improved children's letter knowledge, phonological awareness, and spelling.

BRINGING LANGUAGE AND LITERACY TOGETHER: SCHOOLWIDE PRACTICES THAT MATTER

Besides knowledge of children's literacy development and the research that underpins national standards for what children at different ages and grades should be able to do, teachers should be able to evaluate, implement, and adapt literacy curricula to meet the needs of learners at diverse levels of proficiency (for examples of literacy practices appropriate in a schoolwide preschool program, see Beauchat, Blamey, & Walpole, 2010). Literacy approaches that emphasize fidelity of implementation basically require teachers to follow a set of procedures rather than engage in the "moment-by-moment" decision making that is essential for high-quality interactions with children. In fact, researchers have demonstrated that teachers can implement most well-sequenced programs with near perfect fidelity after minimal training, yet these highly faithful implementations may make no difference whatsoever in the achievement of children (Justice & Ezell, 2002; Justice et al., 2008). Instead, it is not the prescriptive use of materials or implementation of a script, per se, that constitutes quality instruction; rather, it is the moment-by-moment interactions during which teachers respond to cues by children and adjust their teaching accordingly (Minervino & Pianta, 2013; Henry & Pianta, 2011; Clay, 1998). Often called *professional noticing*, it is the ability of the teacher to notice and judge "student understanding during instruction itself" (Hill & Chin, 2018, p. 31), and it is related both to the teacher's content knowledge and to his or her knowledge of students.

High-quality instructional practices that enable language and literacy competence include such traditional classroom activities as reading aloud, shared reading, using multiple informational texts leveled for difficulty and focused on a single topic, using series books or author studies, writing a shared narrative or informational text, or participating in inquiry circles to study and explaining historical or scientific concepts. Because reading and writing are reciprocal language processes, teachers can support vocabulary development, print and genre knowledge, and the conventions of writing by integrating reading and language arts instruction. For example, *Teaching Literacy in Tennessee,* a document developed and published by the Tennessee Department of Education (2017) as part of the Read to be Ready initiative, provides guidance for K–3 administrators and literacy leaders, as well as teachers, on a programmatic approach to early literacy development that builds foundational reading and writing skills within authentic and engaging texts. In the next section we discuss the importance of classroom talk and the ways that it facilitates learning and builds the literacy identities of young children. Then, drawing on several classroom examples, we describe two important activities—text sets and interactive writing—that are powerful catalysts for student language and literacy development.

Classroom Talk

Although instructional support that teachers provide is important, children's opportunity and motivation to learn are also powerfully mediated by the way teachers talk to them. Researchers involved with the National Center for Research on Early Childhood Education developed a rubric to scale the quality of teachers' interactions with children (Henry & Pianta, 2011; Justice et al., 2008). The rubric emphasizes *language modeling* and *literacy focus* (p. 59), so that observers may identify the kinds of instruction that enhances children's development in these areas (Justice et al., 2008), and where lacking, provide professional learning experiences to support teachers' development of these interactional and knowledge repertoires. In language modeling, teachers:

- Engage children in extensive conversation and open-ended questioning.
- Repeat and extend children's responses (also known as "uptake").
- Use language to describe or "map" their actions.
- Use complex language and encourage their students to do the same.

Literacy focus is conceptualized as "explicit, purposeful, and systematic" (Justice et al., 2008, p. 59) in that teachers use terms that "make clear the relation between oral and written language" (p. 59); define abstract terms such as sound, letter, word, sentence, paragraph; relate code-based instruction to purposeful and authentic reading and writing in different genres; and organize instruction according to developmental progressions of skills (p. 59). Teachers can mediate children's understandings of the way reading and writing works and model for them meaning making from text by elaborating on the meanings of unfamiliar words during read-alouds (Justice & Ezell, 2002); engaging children in extended conversation about the motivation of characters, or similarity of events across stories (McGill-Franzen & Ward, 2018; McGill-Franzen, Lanford, & Adams, 2002; McGill-Franzen, Allington, Brooks, & Yokoi, 1999); or "sharing the pen" with children to jointly compose and write a text (Jordan, 2009),

Language *on the run* can be a productive tool for teachers if used to acknowledge children's agency and shape children's identity as readers and writers, even at the earliest ages. As Johnston (2004, 2011) pointed out, language is constitutive—it limits or extends children's potential (for example, think about the difference between telling a child that he's so smart versus he's so thoughtful). If teachers tell children the answer to something that they can figure out independently, they may be communicating to the children that they are not capable learners. In early CIERA studies (Taylor, Peterson, Pearson, & Rodriguez, 2002), for example, researchers found a negative association between children's reading achievement and "telling" in classroom observations. Rather, effective teachers privilege the process of learning by noticing and naming what children know and encouraging them to share problem-solving strategies. Johnston, Ivey, and Faulkner (2011) captured this sentiment exactly: "If we intend to capitalize on the possibilities that social spaces offer for learning, we can say things to help children attend to each other, see each other as resources, and build relationships" (p. 237).

We now describe two broad sets of activities—using *text sets* and engaging in *interactive writing*—that are especially important for the development of both language and literacy skills in young children. We also provide examples of how several teachers in different grades have put these activities into practice in their classrooms.

CASE EXAMPLES

THINK ABOUT THIS

1. In what ways do teachers in the classroom examples capitalize on what the text set presents in terms of teaching science vocabulary, text organization, and making connections to student writing? How can text sets be implemented in your school?
2. How can interactive writing be incorporated in your literacy instruction?

Text Sets

Text sets are a flexible collection of materials unified by topic that include books of the same or different genres, art, charts, technology or other media, at different levels of difficulty to accommodate a variety of learners. Text sets are suitable for read-alouds and for shared, guided, and independent reading. They can build knowledge, allow for vocabulary repetition and learning, create a platform for authentic reading and writing across disciplines and proficiency levels, and scaffold new learning in other topics or content areas. Most important, text sets are motivating. Providing access to interesting texts and opportunities to become expert and collaborate with peers are classroom practices that engage children and promote achievement (Guthrie & Humenick, 2004).

Cappiello and Dawes (2012) describe several models for teaching with text sets, including paired texts and the solar system model. As the name implies, *paired texts* include two texts paired together to serve a particular teaching goal. For example, the Magic Tree House series and Magic Tree House Fact Tracker books present systematically aligned pairs of fiction and informational texts. The solar system model is a collection of texts that work together to support students' understanding of a particular topic or theme. During a third-grade interdisciplinary unit on animal adaptations, for example, teachers can include a variety of traditional fiction and nonfiction texts about ways animals adapt to survive (e.g., *What If You Had an Animal Nose?* [Markle, 2016] and *What Do You Do with a Tail Like This?* [Jenkins & Page, 2008]), as well as digital texts from online sources (e.g., *https://kids.nationalgeographic.com* and *www.dkfindout. com/us*).

In the early grades, teachers can develop text sets by gathering a number of texts about the same story character (e.g., Pete the Cat, Biscuit, Clifford), or they can gather informational books by different authors and publishers organized around the same topic. To illustrate, we use a text set example from *Kindergarten Literacy: Matching Assessment and Instruction in Kindergarten* (McGill-Franzen, 2006), which describes 16 books on the topic of "animal babies"—several read-aloud big books and some leveled books for guided reading. The titles included *Animal Babies in Grasslands* (Schofield, 2004), *Watch Me Grow: Turtle* (Magloff, 2006), and *Animal Babies: A Counting Book* (Moreton, 1998), among many others. Reading specialists Suzanne Worth, Ruth Lindsey, and Theresa Wishart gathered these related books to illustrate for teachers how a text set can be used for conceptual development of science vocabulary, guided and independent reading, and as a springboard for shared and interactive writing. One of the read-aloud books, *Watch Me Grow: Duckling* (Magloff, 2003), which is part of the *DK Watch Me Grow* series on animal development, presents the timeline of a duckling's growth across several days. During professional learning session, the reading specialists demonstrated for teachers how to make the timeline explicit through discussion and shared writing:

Day 1: Duckling hatches
Day 2: First waddle
Day 3: First swim and paddle
Week 2: Beak growing, losing soft yellow feathers
Week 4: Dabbling (e.g., ducks dabble their feet in the water)
Week 8: Flying

The timeline demonstrates for children one of the ways that information is organized in text; it makes the information more memorable, and it provides support for independent writing. Figure 8.1 illustrates how one first-grade teacher used the information from the animal babies text set to construct shared writing and interactive writing experiences that helped

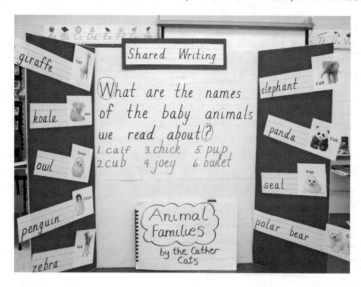

FIGURE 8.1. Writing about animal babies.

consolidate content vocabulary and develop print conventions and more fluent word recognition.

Camille Mason, a preservice teacher, created a text set around ocean life to engage and support a second grader, Ana, an English learner, who had expressed interest in that topic. Camille's text set consisted of three books: one of the *Magic Tree House* narrative series books, *Dolphins at Daybreak* (Osborne, 1997); and two informational series texts from DK Publishing, *Ocean: A Visual Encyclopedia* (DK Children's Books, 2015) and *Why Is the Ocean Salty and Other Questions about Oceans* (Richmond, 2014). To enrich Ana's vocabulary as well as support comprehension of narrative and expository text, Camille created authentic opportunities for Ana to read and to write about what she was learning. Questions about the ocean often peaked Ana's curiosity about some aspect of ocean life and motivated her to consult the encyclopedia, which she and Camille read as a shared reading activity. Ana maintained an ocean dictionary section of her notebook, where she entered new vocabulary words, composed a sentence, and illustrated its meaning with a drawing. The dictionary became a reference that she consulted when that word or a related one appeared in her reading of the book of questions or the series book. In addition to the informational text and writing, Ana also independently read and summarized each chapter from *Dolphins at Daybreak*. Besides the dictionary, Ana jotted ideas for writing in her notebook and clarified events or references from the series book that confused her or gave her clues to the mystery. To further support her understanding of narrative structure, Camille provided a story structure framework in which Ana could record the main and supporting characters, setting, problem, and the solution to the riddle ("It was an oyster!").

Third-grade teachers Kelly Spurgeon and Megan Lamb gathered a set of five books at different levels of difficulty to teach students to identify character traits and corresponding evidence from the text to support these interpretations. After first reading aloud *Henry's Freedom Box* (Levine, 2007), the mentor text, the students discussed and referred to the text to identify which of Henry's traits were prominent. The teachers and students then shared in the writing of a graphic organizer that connected the traits with the explicit evidence in the text. This step served as a model for the small-group collaborative work that followed. For example, one group of four students created a graphic organizer about Hank Aaron after reading *Scraps of Time: The Home Run King* (McKissack, 2008). Through whole-group discussion, led by the teacher, students generated a list of such traits as "hero," "athletic," and "strong" and provided the following evidence: "He broke the home run record," "People love him because he is athletic," and "He is strong because he hit home runs."

Because the topic of weather appears in the Tennessee science standards for the early grades (e.g., the Tennessee Department of Education, 2018, developed an interdisciplinary kindergarten unit starter about weather[3]), teachers often integrate weather with their language arts instruction. In doing so, they use multiple opportunities to teach not only weather-related concepts but also to have students read, write, and discuss weather during interactive read-alouds, with an emphasis on vocabulary, shared reading of newsworthy weather topics in accessible newspaper formats, and small-group guided reading of leveled texts about weather. As an example, kindergarten teacher Allison Riddle used several texts to integrate the topic of weather with literacy development. Allison posted sticky notes throughout the mentor text, *I Can Read about: Weather* (Supraner, 2001), which she read aloud to develop not only weather concepts, but also the vocabulary that represents them.

Deep reading on a topic in different genres enables children (1) to develop expertise in particular areas that can be shared with peers and (2) to experience firsthand the function and supports offered by different multimedia and print formats. In addition, cross-genre reading provides conceptual frameworks for tackling other topics, and most important, helps to sustain engagement with learning from text. A fifth-grade student in a rural county in Tennessee, for example, was so intrigued by learning about tectonic plates and geology in her classroom that she started researching

---

[3] Available at *www.tn.gov/content/dam/tn/readready/documents/unit-starters-2018-2019/earth-science/R1_GK_Final.pdf.*

and taking notes on her own in a small notebook she carried with her. She was eager to share her notebook contents and talk about each page of science drawings, diagrams, and notes. "I want to show you one more thing! Can you believe this? Last year, I would not believe that the Earth was like that!"

Interactive Writing

Interactive writing is poorly understood and underutilized, yet is a powerful instructional context for language modeling and explicit, purposeful, and systematic literacy focus. The teacher and students "share the pen" or "share the keyboard" to construct a meaningful message during this dynamic process of interactive writing (Roth & Dabrowski, 2016). Typically, there are eight recursive steps in this process (McCarrier, Pinnell, & Fountas, 2000): provide a base of active learning experiences; talk to establish purpose; compose the text; construct the text; reread, revise, and proofread the text; revisit the text to support word solving; summarize the learning; and extend the learning (p. 73).

"Interactive writing provides a means for teachers to engage in effective literacy instruction, not through isolated skills lessons, but within the framework of constructing texts filled with personal and collective meaning" (Button, Johnson, & Furgeson, 1996, p. 446). Students and their teacher can engage in interactive writing in conjunction with various activities in the classroom (e.g., read-alouds, content learning, labeling classroom items, field trips/events, classroom routines). Karen Cobble, teacher of 4- and 5-year-olds, uses interactive writing on her smart board to develop emergent literacy skills in the context of a traditional calendar and weather activity (see Figure 8.2). As Karen and her students collectively compose their weather morning message, they count words in their sentences; stretch out words; attend to sounds in each word; and discuss punctuation, capitalization, and spaces between words. Karen references her word wall and students' names posted on a wall nearby throughout the process to demonstrate to the children the relationship between sounds, letters, and spelling patterns and to solidify children's understanding of concepts of print. By using students' names during interactive writing, Karen builds on what students already know to figure out what they need to learn. In addition, by making use of her word wall and name charts, Karen teaches her students how to use their environment effectively as they begin to write independently. While individual students come to the active board to write a letter or a word, other children can practice writing in the air, on small white boards, or personal electronic devices (e.g., iPads). This interactive writing lesson allows students "to reach far beyond their present skills so that they could participate in the construction of a text, using words and conventions that they could not have controlled while working alone" (McCarrier et

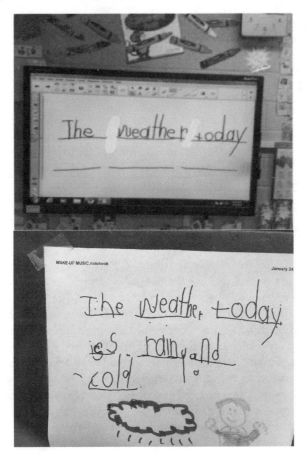

FIGURE 8.2. Interactive writing.

al., 2000, p. 9). Because the smart board has functions that allow erasures and highlighting, it is the perfect venue for sharing the pen with emergent readers and writers. Not only can the teacher and children jointly contribute to the text to be read, reread, revised, and illustrated, the finished and conventionally spelled and punctuated text can be printed and displayed on the wall for use during center time.

Although the process of interactive writing is infused with meaningful conversations about the topic and the purpose of writing, about orthography and interesting features of words, and about other important observations concerning reading and writing, one recent study argued for a closer look at the concepts that get privileged in teacher talk around interactive writing (Williams, 2018). Determining the right amount of instructional talk on craft and conventions of writing is a pedagogical balancing act that requires continuous practice to reap the full benefits of the interactive writing process with young children.

CONCLUSION

As noted in a recent Gates Foundation Report, "Quality of instruction is the primary mechanism responsible for cognitive achievement gains in early learning settings" (Minervino & Pianta, 2013, p. 12). Professional learning activities should target the early literacy skills that are related to reading achievement, and most important, the kinds of instructional interactions that enable children to learn these skills. Further, early literacy educators and those who provide leadership for early literacy programs should emphasize the quality of the interactions between children and those who teach them.

Teachers need to observe firsthand effective language modeling and focused literacy instruction with children of diverse developmental levels; they need to receive feedback from colleagues and literacy leaders on the quality of their own instructional interactions. Given the advances in technology and digital media, such personalized approaches may not be out of reach for literacy leaders and the practitioners whose professional learning they support. Finally, even though we provided a detailed description of interactive writing to demonstrate the reciprocity of reading and writing for the youngest learners and the use of text sets across the grades to support integration of reading, writing, and conceptual development in the content areas, all of the traditional activities of the reading and writing block can also become the context for high-quality language and literacy interactions. To support high-quality interactions across literacy and disciplinary domains, we need to provide opportunities for teachers to reflect on the language they use to communicate content and approval to children and improve their "capacity to notice performance in situ and make corresponding adjustments to instruction" (Hill & Chin, 2018, p. 31).

ENGAGEMENT ACTIVITIES

1. Visit an early childhood setting or kindergarten classroom and describe the nature of children's writing and/or reading. What were children asked to do?

   a. Interview the teacher. What did he or she hope to accomplish in the instructional activity you observed?

   b. Observe the teacher. What did you notice about the teacher's interactions? How do the observed interactions align with high-quality instructional support that includes knowledge of literacy content and pedagogy and knowledge of children's development?

2. Download the free ILA position statement on PreK literacy. Review the examples of teachers' use of text sets. Discuss with your peers the ways in which these activities align with the instructional practices cited in the position statement. How might one of the text set activities be modified to include a missing component?

ANNOTATED RESOURCES

International Literacy Association. (2018). *What effective PreK literacy instruction looks like* (Literacy leadership brief). Newark, DE: Author. Retrieved from *www.literacyworldwide.org/docs/default-source/where-we-stand/ila-what-effective-PreK-literacy-instruction-looks-like.pdf*.

This brief summarizes the tenets of excellent instruction for young children and provides policy recommendations. The authors highlight such essential strategies for building literacy skills as shared reading, drawing and writing on paper, developing verbal reasoning skills and conceptual knowledge, as well as building procedural skills (e.g., alphabet knowledge).

McCarrier, A., Pinnell, G. S., & Fountas, I. C. (2000). *Interactive writing: How language and literacy come together, K–2*. Portsmouth, NH: Heinemann.

The book provides explicit guidance on how to share the pen with young children who are learning how oral language is connected to print. Classroom examples of pieces produced through interactive writing demonstrate the potential of interactive writing in early grades.

McGill-Franzen, A., & Ward, N. (2018). To develop proficiency and engagement, give series books to novice readers! In D. Wooten, L. Liang, & B. Cullinan (Eds.), *Children's literature in the reading program* (5th ed., pp. 153–168). New York: Guilford Press.

The chapter describes how series books can provide support to novice readers through redundancy and formulaic patterns. In addition to being an engaging social activity, reading series books builds larger vocabulary, develops sensitivity to complex syntactical structures of the English language, and ultimately improves comprehension.

REFERENCES

Beauchat, K. A., Blamey, K. L., & Walpole, S. (2010). *The building blocks of preschool success*. New York: Guilford Press.

Button, K., Johnson, M., & Furgeson, P. (1996). Interactive writing in a primary classroom. *The Reading Teacher, 49*(6), 446–454.

Cameron, C. E., Grimm, K. J., Steele, J. S., Castro-Schilo, L., & Grissmer, D. W. (2015). Nonlinear Gompertz curve models of achievement gaps in mathematics and reading. *Journal of Educational Psychology, 107*(3), 789–804.

Cappiello, M. A., & Dawes, E. T. (2012). *Teaching with text sets*. Huntington Beach, CA: Shell Education.

Clay, M. (1998). *By different paths to common outcomes*. York, ME: Stenhouse.

DeBruin-Parecki, A., & Slutzky, C. (2016). *Exploring PreK age 4 learning standards and their role in early childhood education: Research and policy implications.* Princeton, NJ: Educational Teaching Service.

Guthrie, J. T., & Humenick, N. M. (2004). Motivating students to read: Evidence for classroom practices that increase reading motivation and achievement. In P. McCardle & V. Chhabra (Eds.), *The voice of evidence in reading research* (pp. 329–354). Baltimore: Brookes.

Henry, A. E., & Pianta, R. C. (2011). Effective teacher–child interactions and children's literacy: Evidence for scalable, aligned approaches to professional development. In S. D. Neuman & D. K. Dickinson (Eds.), *Handbook of early literacy research* (Vol. 3, pp. 308–321). New York: Guilford Press.

Hill, H. C., & Chin, M. (2018). Connections between teachers' knowledge of students, instruction, and achievement outcomes. *American Educational Research Journal, 20*(10), 1–37.

International Literacy Association (ILA). (2018). *Standards for the preparation of literacy professionals 2017.* Newark, DE: Author.

International Reading Association and National Association for the Education of Young Children. (1998). Learning to read and write: Developmentally appropriate practices for young children. Retrieved November 23, 2010, from *www.reading. org/General/AboutIRA/PositionStatements/DevelopmentallyApropriatePosition.*

Johnston, P. H. (2004). *Choice words: How our language affects children's learning.* Portland, ME: Stenhouse.

Johnston, P. H. (2011). *Opening minds: Using language to change lives.* Portsmouth, NH: Stenhouse.

Johnston, P. H., Ivey, G., & Faulkner, A. (2011). Talking in class: Remembering what is important about classroom talk. *The Reading Teacher, 65*(4), 232–237.

Jordan, J. (2009). *Beyond sharing the pen: Dialogue in the context of interactive writing.* Unpublished doctoral dissertation, University of Tennessee at Knoxville, Knoxville, TN.

Justice, L., & Ezell, H. K. (2002). Use of storybook reading to increase print awareness in at-risk children. *American Journal of Speech–Language Pathology, 11*(1), 17–32.

Justice, L., Mashburn, A. J., Hamre, B. K., & Pianta, R. C. (2008). Quality of language and literacy instruction in preschool classrooms serving at-risk pupils. *Early Childhood Research Quarterly, 23*(1), 51–68.

Lipsey, M. W., Farran, D. C., & Hofer, K. G. (2015a). *Evaluation of the Tennessee Voluntary Prekindergarten Program: Kindergarten and first grade followup results from the randomized control design* (Research report). Nashville, TN: Peabody Research Institute, Vanderbilt University.

McCarrier, A., Pinnell, G. S., & Fountas, I. C. (2000). *Interactive writing: How language and literacy come together, K–2.* Portsmouth, NH: Heinemann.

McGill-Franzen, A., Allington, R. L., Brooks, G., & Yokoi, L. (1999). Putting books in their hands is necessary but not sufficient. *Journal of Educational Research, 93*(2), 67–74.

McGill-Franzen, A., Lanford, C., & Adams, E. (2002). Learning to be literate: A comparison of five early childhood programs. *Journal of Educational Psychology, 94*(3), 443–464.

McGill-Franzen, A., & Ward, N. (2018). To develop proficiency and engagement, give series books to novice readers! In D. Wooten, L. Liang, & B. Cullinan (Eds.),

Children's literature in the reading program (5th ed., pp. 153–168). New York: Guilford Press.

Minervino, J., & Pianta, R. (2013, September). *Early learning: The new fact base and cost sustainability.* Seattle, WA: Bill & Melinda Gates Foundation. Retrieved from *docs.gatesfoundation.org.*

National Association for the Education of Young Children. (1987). *NAEYC position statement on licensing and other forms of regulation of early childhood programs in centers and family day care.* Washington, DC: Author.

National Association for the Education of Young Children. (1996). NAEYC position statement: Responding to linguistic and cultural diversity recommendations for effective early childhood education. *Young Children, 51*(2), 4–12.

National Association for the Education of Young Children. (2009). Developmentally appropriate practice in early childhood programs serving children from birth through age 8. Retrieved November 23, 2010, from *www.naeyc.org/files/naeyc/file/positions/PSDAP.*

National Association for the Education of Young Children. (2015). *Developmentally appropriate practice and the Common Core State Standards: Framing the issues* (Research brief). Washington, DC: Author.

National Early Literacy Panel. (2009). *Developing early literacy: Report of the National Early Literacy Panel.* Jessup, MD: National Institute for Literacy.

National Governors Association Center for Best Practices & Council of Chief State School Officers (NGA & CCSSO). (2010). *Common Core Standards for English language arts and literacy in history/social studies, science, and technical subjects.* Washington, DC: Authors.

National Institute of Child Health and Human Development, Early Child Care Research Network. (2000). The relation of child care to cognitive and language development. *Child Development, 71*(4), 960–980.

National Institute of Child Health and Human Development, Early Child Care Research Network. (2002). Child care structure–process–outcome: Direct and indirect effects of child care quality on young children's development. *Psychological Science, 13*(3), 199–206.

National Institute of Child Health and Human Development, Early Child Care Research Network. (2005). Early child care and children's development in the primary grades: Follow-up results from the NICHD study of early child care. *American Educational Research Journal, 42*(3), 537–570.

Pianta, R. C., Howes, C., Burchinal, M., Bryant, D., Clifford, R., & Early, D. (2005). Features of PreKindergarten programs, classrooms, and teachers: Do they predict observed classroom quality and child–teacher interactions? *Applied Developmental Science, 9*(3), 144–159.

Puma, M., Bell, S., Cook, R., Heid, C., Broene, P., Jenkins, F., et al. (2012). *Third grade follow-up to the Head Start Impact Study final report* (OPRE Report #2012-45). Washington, DC: Office of Planning, Research and Evaluation, Administration for Children and Families, U.S. Department of Health and Human Services.

Roth, K., & Dabrowski, J. (2016). *Interactive writing across grades: A small practice with big results, PreK–5.* Portsmouth, NH: Stenhouse.

Scott-Little, C., Kagan, S. L., & Frelow, V. S. (2006). Conceptualization of readiness and the content of early learning standards: The intersection of policy and research? *Early Childhood Research Quarterly, 21,* 153.

Shanahan, T. (1984). Nature of the reading–writing relation: An exploratory multivariate analysis. *Journal of Educational Psychology, 76*(3), 466–477.

Shanahan, T. (2005). Relations among oral language, reading, and writing development. In C. A. MacArthur, S. Graham, & J. Fitzgerald (Eds.), *Handbook of writing research* (pp. 171–183). New York: Guilford Press.

Shanahan, T., & Lomax, R. G. (1986). An analysis and comparison of theoretical models of the reading–writing relationship. *Journal of Educational Psychology, 78*(2), 116–123.

Shanahan, T., & Lonigan, C. (2010). The National Early Literacy Panel: A summary of the process and the report. *Educational Researcher, 39*(4), 279–285.

Snow, C. E., Burns, M. S., & Griffin, P. (1998). *Preventing reading difficulties in young children.* Washington, DC: National Academy Press.

Taylor, B., Peterson, D., Pearson, P. D., & Rodriguez, M. (2002). Looking inside classrooms: Reflecting on the "how" as well as the "what" in effective reading instruction. *The Reading Teacher, 56*(3), 270–279.

Tennessee Department of Education. (2017). Teaching literacy in Tennessee: Practical guidance for developing proficient readers, writers, and thinkers, K–3. Retrieved from *www.tn.gov/readtobeready/just-for-educators/summer-learning-series.html.*

Tennessee Department of Education. (2018). Unit starters. Retrieved from *www.tn.gov/readtobeready/just-for-educators/summer-learning-series.html.*

Williams, C. (2018). Learning to write with interactive writing instruction. *The Reading Teacher, 71*(5), 523–532.

Wisconsin Model Early Learning Standards (4th ed.). (2013). Available from Wisconsin Child Care Information Center, 2109 South Stoughton Road, Madison, WI 53716. Retrieved January 22, 2019, from *https://dpi.wi.gov/sites/default/files/imce/fscp/pdf/ec-wmels-rev2013.pdf.*

CHILDREN'S LITERATURE

DK Children's Books. (2015). *Ocean: A visual encyclopedia.* New York: DK Children.

Jenkins, S., & Page, R. (2008). *What do you do with a tail like this?* Boston: Houghton Mifflin.

Levine, E. (2007). *Henry's freedom box.* New York: Scholastic.

Magloff, L. (2003). *Duckling: Watch me grow.* New York: DK Children.

Magloff, L. (2006). *Turtle: Watch me grow.* New York: DK Children.

Markle, S. (2016). *What if you had animal nose?* New York: Scholastic.

McKissack, P. (2008). *Scraps of time: The home run king.* New York: Puffin.

Moreton, D. (1998). *Animal babies: A counting book.* New York: Scholastic.

Osborne, M. P. (1997). *Dolphins at daybreak (Magic Tree House #9).* Toronto: Random House Books for Young Readers.

Richmond, B. (2014). *Why is the ocean salty and other questions about oceans: Good questions.* New York: Sterling.

Schofield, J. (2004). *Animal babies in grasslands.* Boston: Kingfisher.

Supraner, R. (2001). *I can read about: Weather.* Mahwah, NJ: Troll.

CHAPTER 9

Literacy Leadership in the Elementary/Intermediate School Reading Program

Janice A. Dole
Sheree E. Springer
Kerry A. Herman

GUIDING QUESTIONS

➥ What do literacy leaders need to know about the reading needs of intermediate grade students?

➥ What are effective core classroom practices in the intermediate grades, and how are they aligned with the *Standards for the Preparation of Literacy Professionals 2017* (International Literacy Association [ILA], 2018)?

➥ What is important to know about the use of reading materials in the intermediate grades in effective school reading programs?

This chapter focuses specifically on intermediate grade students, grades 4–6, most of whom have mastered the foundational skills of reading. Reading at grades 4–6 and beyond requires many additional skills and strategies beyond what students have already learned in the primary grades.

THE READING NEEDS OF INTERMEDIATE GRADE STUDENTS

The end of third grade marks a significant change in how students read and write. Literacy leaders need to be clear about the important milestones that take place once average-achieving students begin fourth grade, and the resulting challenges for students who are not yet reading at the fourth-grade level.

Chall (1983) famously called students reading on the fourth-grade reading level as "unglued from print." These students no longer cling to each word on the page, and they no longer "bark" at the words. They can decode most elementary words effortlessly and automatically. They can read simple stories and informational pieces fluently, with accuracy and good expression.

Concurrently, the Common Core State Standards (CCSS; National Governors Association Center for Best Practices & Council of Chief State School Officers (NGA & CCSSO, 2010) demonstrate the increasing difficulty of reading tasks for intermediate grade students. For example, at grade 4, students need to be able to read narrative stories and "compare and contrast the treatment of similar themes and topics (e.g., opposition of good and evil) and patterns of events (e.g., the quest) in stories, myths, and traditional literature from different cultures" (CCSS, ELA Literacy, RL 4.7). At grade 5, students need to be able to read informational selections and "explain how an author uses reasons and evidence to support particular points in a text, identifying which reasons and evidence support which point(s)" (CCSS, ELA Literacy, RI 5.8). These standards require students to think deeply and strategically about written texts and to perform complex tasks with the material they read. The resources listed in Figure 9.1 will

---

Beck, I. L., McKeown, M. G., & Kucan, L. (2013). *Bringing words to life: Robust vocabulary instruction* (2nd ed.). New York: Guilford Press.

Beers, C. S., Beers, J. W., & Smith, J. O. (2010). *A principal's guide to literacy instruction.* New York: Guilford Press.

Cobb, C., & Blachowicz, C. (2014). *No more "look up the list" vocabulary instruction (not this, but that).* Portsmouth, NH: Heinemann.

Fisher, D., Frey, N., & Hattie, J. (2017). *Teaching literacy in the visible learning classroom, grades K–5.* Thousand Oaks, CA: Corwin Press.

Miller, D., & Moss, B. (2013). *No more independent reading without support (not this, but that).* Portsmouth, NH: Heinemann.

Ness, M. K. (2017). *Think big with think alouds, grades K–5: A three-step planning process that develops strategic readers.* Thousand Oaks, CA: Corwin Press.

Razinski, T. V., & Smith, M. C. (2018). *The megabook of fluency: Strategies and texts to engage all readers.* New York: Scholastic.

Serravallo, J. (2013). *The literacy teacher's playbook, grades 3–6: Four steps for turning assessment data into goal-directed instruction.* Portsmouth, NH: Heinemann.

FIGURE 9.1. Suggested resources for elementary/intermediate reading curriculum and instruction.

assist literacy leaders in understanding issues related to the CCSS and the tasks required of intermediate grade students.

Literacy leaders and teachers, however, know the wide range of reading needs that exist in intermediate grade classrooms. Whereas average and high-achieving readers may be ready for the more difficult reading demands and tasks required of them, many of their peers are not. Some students will not be reading on grade level at the beginning of the intermediate grades because they have not yet mastered the foundational skills of reading. They often have lingering deficiencies in phonics and fluency. Other students *have* mastered decoding and fluency, but they start to fall behind and continue to do so as more advanced vocabulary and academic language are introduced. Chall refers to this downward trend as the "fourth-grade slump" (Chall & Jacobs, 2003).

Literacy leaders need to understand the broad range of intermediate grade students' reading needs and support teachers in advocating to assist these teachers in addressing those needs.

Begin with Assessment

The ILA's *Standards 2017* calls for literacy programs at the elementary/intermediate grades to be developmentally appropriate and guided by assessment: "Research-supported practices should vary according to where students reside across the developmental continuum of literacy, determined through assessment" (ILA, 2018, p. 98). Effective literacy instruction begins with assessment. Research has established the critical roles of *assessment* and *instruction* in the teaching and learning cycle (Brunner et al., 2005; Forman, 2007). Studies in school improvement also point to the positive effect on student learning outcomes when instructional decisions are based upon the analysis of assessment results (e.g., see Howe, Scierka, Gibbons, & Silbertlit, 2003). In essence, the process of data-based decision making is at the core of this cycle. For additional detailed information, refer to Chapter 6 in this volume.

EFFECTIVE CORE CLASSROOM PRACTICES IN THE INTERMEDIATE GRADES

This chapter focuses on the need for elementary/intermediate grade literacy programs to provide "research-supported practices for developing the foundational skills (concepts of print, phonological awareness, phonics, fluency) as well as vocabulary, comprehension, and writing, along with a focus on engagement and motivation" (ILA, 2018, p. 99). Because concepts of print, phonological awareness, phonics, and fluency are typically mastered by the end of the third grade, we begin this section with a discussion of research-based best practices in vocabulary, comprehension, writing, engagement, and motivation. For additional information and ideas for working with intermediate level students, see Table 10.1, Considering Intermediate versus Disciplinary Literacy Questions and Strategies, in Chapter 10 (pp. 198–201).

Please note, however, that all students reading *below the third-grade level* will need small-group instruction in the foundational skills of reading, perhaps phonemic awareness, but definitely phonics and fluency. The most severely struggling readers will need extra support from a reading/literacy specialist or perhaps a special education teacher. In terms of instructional delivery, the *frequency, intensity,* and *time* of the targeted instruction are all significant.

CASE EXAMPLES

Vocabulary

> **THINK ABOUT THIS**
>
> The word *maladaptive* stumped Ms. Greene's fifth graders as they were reading their latest novel. Ms. Greene told one student to look up the word on the Internet and report to the class.
>
> How could the literacy leader who observed this lesson work with Ms. Greene to help her learn a better way to teach vocabulary?

Most of us know, and research supports, the clear connection between vocabulary knowledge and reading comprehension (Wagner, Muse, & Tannenbaum, 2007). Students who have a wide and thorough understanding of a variety of words are more likely to understand what they read (Baumann, 2009). However, the vocabulary knowledge students have when they enter the intermediate grades can vary widely depending on the amount of reading to which they have been exposed (Adams, 1990) and their native language (Carlo et al., 2009). The best evidence-based practices in vocabulary instruction include the following.

- *Explicit instruction in important academic and content-specific words.* Effective teachers select a *small* number of valuable vocabulary words each week and devote instructional time to teaching those words (Beck, McKeown, & Kucan, 2013). These words are introduced using student-friendly definitions, and students are given multiple opportunities to use the words in meaningful contexts during the week. Word walls and charts with academic words written on them assist students in learning vocabulary.

- *Word-learning strategies.* Students need to learn how to use strategies to determine the meanings of new words (Manyak, Baumann, & Manyak, 2018). Effective teachers assist students by teaching them how to break up multisyllabic words through morphology (i.e., prefixes, suffixes, Greek and Latin roots). For example, it is possible to determine the meaning of the word "maladaptive" by knowing that (1) the Latin root *mal* means bad, (2) the root word of *adaptive* is *adapt,* and (3) *adapt* means to adjust or alter. Therefore *maladaptive* means something that does a bad job of adjusting or altering. This definition will help almost all students who come across the word *maladaptive.* Examples of how to incorporate morphology into a literacy curriculum can be found at WordWorks Literacy Center Online (*www.wordworkskingston.com*).

Comprehension

> **THINK ABOUT THIS**
>
> Ms. Ashford used a document camera to show her sixth graders how she would summarize the last chapter in the novel they were reading. For homework, she asked them to summarize the chapter they were to read next.
>
> How would a literacy coach work with Ms. Ashford to help her improve her comprehension instruction in summarizing?

Comprehension is the sine qua non of reading achievement. Learning how to comprehend the more complex texts to which students are exposed in the intermediate grades does not come naturally to students; moreover, it is more than "oral language written down," as the classic simple model of reading suggested (Gough, 1972). Students need assistance and support as they navigate the more complex narrative and informational texts and perform more complex tasks with these texts, such as those identified in the CCSS. The best evidence-based practices in comprehension instruction include the following.

- *The integration of reading with students' daily lives and experiences.* During whole-class and small-group reading, effective teachers promote reading comprehension by helping students relate the content of their reading to their daily lives and experiences. Relating new information to students' existing knowledge helps them integrate what they are learning with their existing knowledge base and builds motivation and stamina for further learning.

- *Explicit instruction in comprehension strategies.* Effective teachers assist students in learning how to read complex texts through extensive modeling and guided practice with them and other students. Over time, teachers gradually increase students' responsibility as they gain more control over the strategies they are taught (Pearson & Gallagher, 1983). For example, teachers model how to summarize a text. Next, teachers assist the whole class as they summarize a different text. Then students work together in teams of four to summarize. Students might then work in pairs before finally summarizing on their own (Dole, Nokes, & Drits, 2009).

• *Higher-order thinking and reasoning skills established through questions and discussions.* The CCSS's (NGA & CCSSO, 2010) emphasis on the importance of higher-order thinking and reasoning skills for intermediate grade students can guide teachers' instruction of close reading using short, complex texts. Such reading helps build reading strength and prepares students for reading grade-level content (Fisher & Frey, 2013). High-level discussions about texts are another important instructional tool when building students' reasoning skills (Kamil et al., 2008).

Writing

> **THINK ABOUT THIS**
>
> In a professional development meeting, Mr. Locke admits that he does not have his students write more because he is not confident in his ability to teach writing, especially when using his own writing as a model. Several other teachers nod in agreement.
>
> How would an instructional leader address teachers' lack of confidence in their ability to teach and model writing?

Applebee and Langer (2006, 2011) found that, like Mr. Locke's students, students in most American schools do not write for a sufficient amount of time each day. Although students do write to fill in the blanks and answer brief questions, writing a paragraph or more does not happen as often as it should.

The CCSS (NGA & CCSSO, 2010) identifies the different kinds of writing students need to practice in the intermediate grades: narratives, opinion pieces, and informative/explanatory. The best evidence-based practices in writing instruction include the following.

• *Teachers teach writing strategies every day, and students write every day.* Students should be writing every day and learning writing strategies to help them become better writers (Harris, Graham, Friedlander, & Laud, 2013). Effective teachers teach these writing strategies explicitly and then provide a sufficient amount of time each day for students to practice by writing narrative, opinion, and informational texts.

• *An engaged community of readers and writers in classrooms.* Students benefit from teachers who are excited about reading and writing and relay that excitement to their students. Allowing students to read and write each day can become addictive to students when their teachers convey a passion for books and for writing (Graham et al., 2012).

Motivation and Engagement

> **THINK ABOUT THIS**
>
> When Ms. Smith visits Mr. Older's sixth-grade classroom, she notices that too many students do not read during independent reading time. Instead, they talk, they flip pages, or they select a book and then quickly place it back on the shelf and select another one.
>
> How would Ms. Smith work with Mr. Older to engage his students in reading?

Research has consistently demonstrated that motivation for literacy begins to wane in the later elementary grades (Baker & Wigfield, 1999; Guthrie et al., 2007; Sainsbury & Schagen, 2004). This has become a particular problem as students' use of technology has increased dramatically over the last decade (McKenna, Conradi, Lawrence, Jang, & Meyer, 2012). The best evidence-based practices in motivation and engagement include the following.

- *Peer collaboration.* Research continues to show the valuable benefits that can come from including meaningful peer collaboration in literacy instruction, particularly as students approach adolescence (Johnson & Johnson, 1999, 2014; Slavin, 2014). Peer work—through partner reading, turn and talk, or cooperative learning groups—promotes engagement in literacy tasks.

- *Choice.* Choice is an important yet often overlooked instructional strategy that promotes engagement (Guthrie et al., 2007). There are many ways meaningful choice can be integrated into the curriculum; for example, effective teachers offer students a choice between two tasks, activities, or writing prompts; students select their next novel through a vote on three books introduced by the teacher; or students select from a number of topics to conduct their research.

THE USE OF READING MATERIALS IN EFFECTIVE SCHOOL READING PROGRAMS

Many school districts adopt core reading programs for their entire district and organize their literacy programs around these programs. In other districts, teachers use a literature-based curriculum in which they exclusively use sets of novels for their intermediate grade students. In addition, digital materials are now used in many classrooms. Regardless of the materials used, it is useful for literacy leaders to be aware of how the materials are used to forward literacy learning. As well, regardless of the materials used, there are several instructional strategies that should be seen in all reading programs (see Figure 9.2).

Core Reading Programs

According to Education Market Research, over 70% of school districts in American elementary classrooms use basal reading programs (Dewitz, Jones, & Leahy, 2009). These programs offer students excerpts from children's literature and a plethora of methods, materials, and activities for teachers to use to teach students to read and write. Foorman, Smith, and Kosanovich (2017) provide an excellent rubric to use to evaluate current core reading programs. When using a core reading program:

- *Maintain consistency within and across grade levels in the use of core reading programs within a school.* If a school district requires the use of a core reading program, then all teachers in the school should use it. Consistency among grades and between one grade level and the next ensures an overall cohesive and coherent school literacy program (Montgomery, Ilk, & Moats, 2013).

- *Increase the amount of modeling and guided practice for struggling readers and English learners (ELs).* Core reading programs are tools, and they do not replace the expertise of teachers. Students who struggle with reading, including students with learning disabilities, will require more explicit instruction, more assistance, and more practice than can be found in core programs (Reutzel, Child, Jones, & Clark, 2014).

- *Save phonics and fluency instruction for lower-achieving students, and teach average and high-achieving students how to decode multisyllabic words.* Phonics and fluency should continue to be taught *only* to students who are reading below the third-grade level (Ivey & Baker, 2004), even though many core programs continue to teach phonics. For average and above readers in grades 4–6, focus on the core program's teaching of multisyllabic words.

- *Include an extensive classroom library full of books.* Effective teachers support students' reading performance by ensuring that they read widely and extensively to practice their newly mastered reading skills in real texts (Hiebert, 2014). It is not enough to read a selection in a core reading program each day. Therefore, all classrooms need classroom libraries (Pikulski & Chard, 2005). Time spent reading each day builds students' stamina in reading (Hiebert, 2014), a skill that becomes more important as students progress through the grades. Time spent reading also builds students' vocabulary knowledge and is one way to reduce the vocabulary

Instructional Strategy	How the Strategy Is Helpful	Comments on Using the Strategy
Think–Pair–Share	All students have an opportunity to talk	Role-play *how* to do a think–pair–share with students. Show *how to do it* and *how not to do it.*
Multimodal Connections	Adds the important visual and auditory information to learn new content, new words, new ideas	Teach words using the Internet—e.g., pull up pictures and sounds of a *meadow.* Teach about art and artists by exploring museums online. Teach about famous people using pictures, videos, and audiotapes.
Graphic Organizers	Excellent visual way to organize and categorize information. Drawing assists in learning.	Conduct a Google search using *graphic organizers* as the subject. You will see multiple examples of different types of organizers for all age groups. There is also a host of resource books on graphic organizers.
Cooperative Learning Groups	Students learn from each other in effective cooperative learning groups.	There is a great deal of research supporting cooperative learning groups, but they must be assigned and managed carefully, with a mix of high and low achievers and a diversity of students in each foursome.
Writing to Learn	Students learn through the tactile experience of writing—not to produce a product, but to learn content more deeply.	Students benefit from using individual white boards on which to write responses, as well as other writing activities that require students to think through their writing. The mechanics of writing don't matter; students benefit and learn through the process of writing.
Jigsaw	Jigsaw assists students in learning content through peer interaction and presentations.	Students must work together to learn the content and be able to present that content to others in effective ways.
Choice	An important component in motivation is choice. Allowing students choice in tasks and activities improves their motivation to perform the tasks and activities.	Choice can be given to students in simple ways. Provide two learning tasks or activities and tell students they can choose which one to do. Provide two stories or informational articles and allow students to choose which one to read.

FIGURE 9.2. Seven important instructional strategies literacy leaders should know and look for.

gap between students who have been exposed to more vocabulary as well as those who have not, and ELs as well (Carlo et al., 2009).

Literature-Based Approaches

The whole-language movement in the 1980s and 1990s ushered in a complete rejection of core reading programs and promoted the use of "authentic" literature in what is called a literature-based approach to reading instruction (Altwerger, Edelsky, & Flores, 1987; Goodman, 1987). Authentic literature is defined as the trade books, chapter books, and novels typically found in libraries. Small groups of students read a shared novel or chapter book in literature circles. When using a literature-based program . . .

- *Continue to instruct every day.* Compared to the systematic instructional approach embedded within core reading programs, literature-based programs offer limited guidance to teachers. Therefore, in order to facilitate and maximize student learning, effective teachers develop a scope and sequence that aligns with their district or state standards. Based on this scope and sequence, effective teachers create engaging vocabulary and comprehension lessons designed around clear learning objectives.

- *Continue to use assessment data.* Effective teachers incorporating literature-based programs still use assessment data to determine their students' reading levels and the specific skills and strategies they need to make steady progress. Day, Spiegel, McLellan, and Brown (2012) address how to facilitate rich discussion using literature circles as well as specific strategy lessons to teach. In addition, Honig, Diamond, and Gotlohn (2012) offer excellent lessons for teachers to use with average and struggling readers to supplement a literature-based program.

- *Develop thematic units.* Literature-based programs afford students the opportunity to learn from a rich array of texts. By creating instructional units centered upon topics related to science and social studies district or state standards, effective teachers build students' background knowledge (Adams, 2010–2011). Reading multiple texts on specific topics has also been shown to increase student content knowledge, reading achievement, motivation, and engagement (Guthrie, Anderson, Aloa, & Rinehart, 1999; Guthrie et al., 2007).

- *Continue to assist struggling readers.* Students reading below grade level will not necessarily improve their reading skills just by reading chapter books and novels and learning strategies from teachers. Most still need the foundational skills of reading, and effective teachers continue to teach these skills in small groups (Wanzek, Wexler, Vaughn, & Cuillo, 2010). Valencia and Buly (2004) can be a particular assistance to teachers in understanding struggling readers.

Digital Materials

In order to prepare students for an increasingly connected world, current literacy instruction must not only include digital materials but also explicit instruction on how to search, read, analyze, create, and communicate in multimodal ways. Effective teachers teach students how to find, use, and evaluate websites and other technologies in meaningful ways. ILA's Digital Literacies blog (*www.literacyworldwide.org/blog/digital-literacies*) is an excellent resource for teachers looking to incorporate more digital materials into their curriculum. See Chapter 13, this volume, for more on this topic.

CONCLUSION

The core of a successful intermediate grade literacy program lies in the ability of literacy leaders and teachers to develop an effective assessment–instructional cycle and provide an evidence-based literacy curriculum and instruction to all students. Such an endeavor is not easy, but the rewards are great. Nothing motivates literacy leaders more than watching and supporting teachers in their implementation of a successful literacy program. Nothing motivates teachers more than watching their students succeed.

ENGAGEMENT ACTIVITIES

1. Based on the findings of effective curriculum and instruction discussed in the chapter, create a brief classroom observation tool that addresses these findings. Using this tool, conduct instructional rounds with your faculty members and design professional development to meet their needs.

2. With your faculty, facilitate a discussion about the importance of consistency in the reading materials used in the school literacy program. Why is consistency important? What happens when the reading materials change from one grade to another? What happens when instructional materials use different terms from one grade to the next? Why is vertical alignment important to a school literacy program?

3. *Standards 2017* calls for elementary and intermediate teachers to be able to provide high-quality teaching and comprehensive reading experiences. Discuss with your peers at schools ways in which your school literacy program is aligned with the recommendations in *Standards 2017.*

ANNOTATED RESOURCES

Gelzheiser, L. M., Scanlon, D. M., Hallgren-Flynn, L., & Conners, P. (2018). *Comprehensive reading intervention in grades 3–8: Fostering word learning, comprehension, and motivation.* New York: Guilford Press.

The text includes strategies for reading interventions with students in grades 3–8. The instructional recommendations inform educators about how to work with whole-group, small-group, and individualized intervention/instruction.

International Literacy Association. (2019). *Creating passionate readers through independent reading* (Literacy leadership brief). Newark, DE: Author.

This position brief provides information on motivation to read and student self-selected reading materials.

What Should a Coach Do in the First Few Weeks of School?

In this excellent 7-minute video, an instructional coach specifically defines a coach's activities during the first few weeks of school. Helpful for all instructional coaches. Retrieved from *www.youtube.com/watch?v=C9AsKF9WH7o&list=PLb5RXypPqP5vDdh-i4XB13cQooyPk1k2E.*

REFERENCES

Adams, M. J. (1990). *Beginning to read: Thinking and learning about print.* Cambridge, MA: MIT Press.

Adams, M. J. (2010–2011). Advancing our students' language and literacy: The challenge of complex texts. *American Educator, 34*(4), 3–11, 53.

Altwerger, B., Edelsky, C., & Flores, B. M. (1987). Whole language: What's new? *The Reading Teacher, 41*(2), 144–154.

Applebee, A. N., & Langer, J. A. (2006). *The state of writing instruction in America's schools: What existing data tell us.* Albany, NY: Center on English Learning and Achievement.

Applebee, A. N., & Langer, J. A. (2011). A snapshot of writing instruction in middle and high schools. *English Journal, 100*(6), 14–27.

Baker, L., & Wigfield, A. (1999). Dimensions of children's motivation for reading and their relations to reading activity and reading achievement. *Reading Research Quarterly, 34*(4), 452–477.

Beck, I. L., McKeown, M. G., & Kucan, L. (2013). *Bringing words to life: Robust vocabulary instruction.* New York: Guilford Press.

Baumann, J. F. (2009). Vocabulary and reading comprehension: The nexus of meaning. In S. E. Israel & G. G. Duffy (Eds.), *Handbook of research on reading comprehension* (pp. 323–346). New York: Routledge.

Brunner, C., Fasca, C., Heinze, J., Honey, M., Light, D., Mardinach, E., et al. (2005). Linking data and learning: The Grow Network study. *Journal of Education for Students Placed at Risk, 10*(3), 241–267.

Carlo, M. S., August, D., McLaughlin, B., Snow, C., Dressler, C., Lippman, D., et al. (2009). Closing the gap: Addressing the vocabulary needs of English-language learners in bilingual and mainstream classrooms. *Journal of Education, 189*(1–2), 57–76.

Chall, J. S. (1983). *Stages of reading development.* New York: McGraw-Hill.

Chall, J. S., & Jacobs, V. A. (2003). Poor children's fourth-grade slump. *American Educator, 27*(1), 14–15.

Day, J. P., Spiegel, D. L., McLellan, J., & Brown, V. B. (2012). *Moving forward with literature circles.* New York: Scholastic.

Dewitz, P., Jones, J., & Leahy, S. (2009). Comprehension strategy instruction in core reading programs. *Reading Research Quarterly, 44*(2), 102–126.

Dole, J. A., Nokes, J. D., & Drits, D. (2009). Cognitive strategy instruction. In G. G. Duffy & S. E. Israel (Eds.), *Handbook of research on reading comprehension* (pp. 347–372). Mahwah, NJ: Erlbaum.

Fisher, D., & Frey, N. (2013). *Better learning through structured teaching: A framework for the gradual release of responsibility.* Washington, DC: ASCD

Foorman, B. R., Smith, K. G., & Kosanovich, M. L. (2017). *Rubric for evaluating reading/language arts instructional materials for kindergarten to grade 5* (REL 2017-219). Washington, DC: U.S. Department of Education, Institute of Education Sciences, National Center for Education Evaluation and Regional Assistance, Regional Educational Laboratory Southeast. Retrieved from *http://ies.ed.gov/ncee/edlabs.*

Forman, M. L. (2007). Developing an action plan: Two Rivers Public Charter School focuses on instruction. In K. P. Boudett & J. L. Steele (Eds.), *Data wise in action: Stories of schools using data to improve teaching and learning* (pp. 107–124). Cambridge, MA: Harvard Education Press.

Goodman, K. S. (1987). *Language and thinking in school: A whole-language curriculum.* New York: Richard C. Owen.

Gough, P. B. (1972). One second of reading. *Visible Language, 6*(4), 291–320.

Guthrie, J. T., Anderson, E., Aloa, S., & Rinehart, J. (1999). Influences of concept-oriented reading instruction on strategy use and conceptual learning from text. *Elementary School Journal, 99*(4), 343–366.

Guthrie, J. T., Hoa, L. W., Wigfield, A., Tonks, S. M., Humenick, N. M., & Littles, E. (2007). Reading motivation and reading comprehension growth in the later elementary years. *Contemporary Educational Psychology, 32*(3), 282–313.

Graham, S., Bollinger, A., Booth Olson, C., D'Aoust, C., MacArthur, C., McCutchen, D., et al. (2012). *Teaching elementary school students to be effective writers: A practice guide* (NCEE 2012-4058). Washington, DC: National Center for Education Evaluation and Regional Assistance, Institute of Education Sciences, U.S. Department of Education. Retrieved from *http://ies.ed.gov/ncee/wwc/publications_reviews.aspx#pubsearch.*

Harris, K. R., Graham, S., Friedlander, B., & Laud, L. (2013). Bring powerful writing strategies into your classroom!: Why and how. *The Reading Teacher, 66*(7), 538–542.

Hiebert, E. H. (2014). The forgotten reading proficiency: Stamina in silent reading. In E. H. Hiebert (Ed.), *Stamina, silent reading, and the Common Core State Standards* (pp. 2–25). Santa Cruz, CA: Text Project.

Honig, B., & Diamond, L., & Gotlohn, L. (2012). *Teaching reading sourcebook* (2nd ed.). Novato, CA: Academic Therapy.

Howe, K. B., Scierka, B. J., Gibbons, K. A., & Silberglitt, B. (2003). A schoolwide organization system for raising reading achievement using general outcome measures and evidence-based instruction: One education district's experience. *Assessment for Effective Intervention, 28*(3–4), 59–71.

International Literacy Association (ILA). (2018). *Standards for the preparation of literacy professionals 2017.* Newark, DE: Author.

Ivey, G., & Baker, M. I. (2004). Phonics instruction for older students?: Just say no. *Educational Leadership, 61*(6), 35–39.

Johnson, D. W., & Johnson, R. T. (1999). Making cooperative learning work. *Theory Into Practice, 38*(2), 67–73.

Johnson, D. W., & Johnson, R. T. (2014). Cooperative learning in 21st century. *Anales de Psicología/Annals of Psychology, 30*(3), 841–851.

Kamil, M. L., Borman, G. D., Dole, J., Kral, C. C., Salinger, T., & Torgesen, J. (2008). *Improving adolescent literacy: Effective classroom and intervention practices: A practice guide* (NCEE #2008-4027). Washington, DC: National Center for Education Evaluation and Regional Assistance, Institute of Education Sciences, U.S. Department of Education. Retrieved from *http://ies.ed.gov/ncee/wwc.*

Manyak, P. C., Baumann, J. F., & Manyak, A. (2018). Morphological analysis instruction in the elementary grades: Which morphemes to teach and how to teach them. *The Reading Teacher, 72*(3), 289–300.

McKenna, M. C., Conradi, K., Lawrence, C., Jang, B. G., & Meyer, J. P. (2012). Reading attitudes of middle school students: Results of a U.S. survey. *Reading Research Quarterly, 47*(3), 283–306.

Montgomery, P., Ilk, M., & Moats, L. (2013). *A principal's primer for raising reading achievement.* Longmont, CO: Sopris Learning.

National Governors Association Center for Best Practices & Council of Chief State School Officers (NGA & CCSSO). (2010). *Common Core Standards for English language arts and literacy in history/social studies, science, and technical subjects.* Washington, DC: Authors.

Pearson, P. D., & Gallagher, M. C. (1983). The instruction of reading comprehension. *Contemporary Educational Psychology, 8*(3), 317–344.

Pikulski, J. J., & Chard, D. J. (2005). Fluency: Bridge between decoding and reading comprehension. *The Reading Teacher, 58*(6), 510–519.

Reutzel, R. D., Child, A., Jones, C. D., & Clark, S. K. (2014). Explicit instruction in core reading programs. *Elementary School Journal, 114*(3), 406–430.

Sainsbury, M., & Schagen, I. (2004). Attitudes to reading at ages nine and eleven. *Journal of Research in Reading, 27*(4), 373–386.

Slavin, R. E. (2014). Making cooperative learning powerful. *Educational Leadership, 72*(2), 22–26.

Valencia, S. W., & Buly, M. R. (2004). Behind test scores: What struggling readers really need. *The Reading Teacher, 57*(6), 520–531.

Wagner, R. K., Muse, A. E., & Tannenbaum, K. R. (2007). *Vocabulary acquisition: Implications for reading comprehension.* New York: Guilford Press.

Wanzek, J., Wexler, J., Vaughn, S., & Ciullo, S. (2010). Reading interventions for struggling readers in the upper elementary grades: A synthesis of 20 years of research. *Reading and Writing, 23*(8), 889–912.

CHAPTER 10

Middle and High School Literacy Programs

Attending to Both Instructional and Organizational Challenges

Jacy Ippolito
Christina L. Dobbs
Megin Charner-Laird

GUIDING QUESTIONS

⇝ What do leaders need to know about the literacy needs of adolescent learners?

⇝ What are the differences between content-area and disciplinary literacy frameworks?

⇝ How can the integration of content-area and disciplinary literacy instruction support adolescents' literacy development? What are the instructional implications for classroom teachers as outlined in the *Standards for the Preparation of Literacy Professionals 2017*?

⇝ How can intentional organizational supports, such as professional learning communities and teacher leaders, support adolescents' literacy development?

LITERACY LEADERSHIP IN MIDDLE AND HIGH SCHOOL SETTINGS: NOT FOR THE FAINT OF HEART

Literacy leaders across all grade levels and school settings face enormous challenges and rewards; however, literacy leaders working in middle and high school settings face a number of unique organizational and instructional dilemmas. Structurally, middle and high schools are often much larger than their elementary counterparts, especially in districts where multiple elementary schools funnel into a few or just one middle or high school setting. At the same time that we find large numbers of students, teachers, and administrators in middle and high school buildings, we also often see a decrease in the number of literacy specialists and literacy coaches. It is not uncommon to see high schools filled with thousands of students being served by only one or two literacy specialists or coaches. Moreover, most middle and high schools adopt a departmental structure, providing content-area teachers with opportunities to meet frequently with role-alike colleagues (e.g., biology teachers meeting with other biology teachers). This structure can be powerful, but all too often it can also mean sacrificing frequent teacher communication and collaboration across content-area boundaries or with specialists, such as literacy coaches.

Layers of leadership emerge in secondary settings—team leaders, coaches, content-area coordinators, department chairs, assistant principals, principals—creating a complex tapestry of leadership that we rarely see in elementary schools. Again, this is a double-edged sword. With more formal and informal leaders on staff, literacy leadership work can potentially be distributed in ways that support rich professional learning and classroom instruction. Alternately, sometimes having more leaders on hand simply means more confusion and murkiness around the vision for and execution of a coherent literacy program.

Beyond organizational challenges, secondary schools face a number of literacy instructional challenges. The range in students' skills and experiences grows ever wider as we move from elementary, to middle, to high school settings. It is not uncommon to find a high school classroom filled with students whose reading skills range from elementary to college levels. At the secondary level, across all literacy domains, we see great differences in what students can and choose to do—with variations in background knowledge, vocabulary, fluency, motivation, writing skills, and so on— all contributing to the overarching challenge of teaching high-level content through challenging texts. Which brings us to another important point: At secondary levels, the concepts, vocabulary, and texts that students encounter across subject areas all increase in complexity (Lee & Spratley, 2010). Lastly, many secondary teachers assume that their job is to teach students particular content, not specifically how to become better readers or writers (Jacobs, 2008). All these challenges, and more, rest at the feet of secondary literacy leaders—the middle and high school specialists, coaches, teacher leaders, department chairs, and principals who are tasked with crafting and implementing a coherent schoolwide vision for literacy and content learning and for how the two work in tandem.

Given these challenges, what then must secondary literacy leaders know and be able to do in order to support adolescent learners' literacy development? In this chapter, following the guidance of recent research and the ILA's (2018) *Standards for the Preparation of Specialized Literacy Professionals 2017,* we assert that the answer lies in strategically connecting organizational and instructional decisions. If secondary literacy leaders simply address classroom-level instructional dilemmas without attending to larger organizational concerns (e.g., how to structure professional learning to simultaneously honor a schoolwide vision of literacy and teachers' content-specific expertise), then schoolwide improvement is unlikely to occur. Similarly, if organizational and structural challenges are addressed without paying close attention to the details of classroom-level instruction, then students may still struggle. Consider the following brief case example that illustrates just a few of the aforementioned challenges.

CASE EXAMPLE

THINK ABOUT THIS

1. What are the organizational and instructional dilemmas Andrea is facing?
2. What kinds of professional learning experiences might benefit Andrea most at this point in her career, and given her particular instructional questions?
3. Who else in Andrea's school is likely best positioned to collaborate with her on solving some of these dilemmas?

Andrea[1] had been teaching high school biology for 10 years in the Murky Falls school district. Although Murky Falls wasn't the wealthiest district in the state, Andrea was lucky to have a reasonably updated lab space and new textbooks that even included online links and interactive extensions for students. Andrea prided herself on preparing students for college and hopefully careers in the sciences. To do this, Andrea frequently tasked her students with a mixture of lab experiments to complete in partners or small groups, and in-class as well as take-home readings, short essays, and of course regular exams. Andrea taught her classes the same way that her own high school biology teacher had taught almost two decades ago: lecture, lab, homework, exam, repeat.

While Andrea was a confident teacher, a good colleague, and had received nothing but positive feedback from her formal principal evaluations, Andrea had noticed in the past few years that her time-tested techniques were not necessarily translating into successful outcomes for all students. In fact, Andrea's department chair had been talking a great deal about how students were increasingly struggling to navigate their textbooks across science classes. In a recent classroom observation, the

---

[1]This case is a composite of several teachers, with personal details obscured to protect privacy.

principal noted that students seemed to be struggling to write coherent lab reports and use scientific terminology in class discussions. Andrea agreed. Some students seemed to know all the content ahead of time, whereas others struggled to even pronounce common biology terms like *mitochondria* and *endocrine*. District-level science coordinators had been asking all science teachers to help students "read, write, and talk like scientists." This sounded good to Andrea, with a focus on more authentic and "real-world" tasks, but she also was being told by a schoolwide literacy coach that what students really needed were more graphic organizers, sentence starters, and comprehension strategies.

All of this left Andrea's head spinning. She was supposed to teach biology, right? But if students were struggling with reading the textbook and writing lab reports, did she need to focus more on basic literacy skills? Also, was the answer to break all the reading and writing tasks down into smaller, bite-size assignments, or to instead go the other way and assign more authentic tasks that asked students to really think and work like biologists? Andrea asked her biology colleagues these questions, and ultimately asked her department chair and then the principal. Unfortunately, everyone gave her slightly different answers and pointed her back to the one overworked literacy coach in the building who didn't have a background in science (Andrea was skeptical that she would be of much assistance). Andrea thought to herself: Maybe next summer's professional learning workshops might help?

Andrea's dilemmas are quite common across middle and high school settings. Content-area teachers, who for most of their professional careers have been steeped in content learning, suddenly are faced with the challenge of supporting adolescents' literacy development. Also, to truly prepare students for "what's next" (i.e., college and the workplace) in the 21st century, simply teaching the way "her own high school biology teacher had" is unlikely to meet the high expectations of current standards such as the Common Core State Standards (CCSS) (National Governors Association Center for Best Practices & Council of Chief State School Officers, 2010) or the Next Generation Science Standards (NGSS) (NGSS Lead States, 2013).

Having outlined some of the oft-cited, literacy-focused organizational and instructional challenges encountered in middle and high school settings, we now turn to four areas of consideration that might provide support and insight for current and future secondary literacy leaders. First, we look a bit more closely at the literacy needs of adolescent learners, including a snapshot of how organizational and instructional issues related to literacy improvement have been previously framed. We then turn to a description of the two prevailing ways that researchers have talked about supporting adolescents' literacy learning: content-area literacy instruction and disciplinary literacy instruction. Next, we discuss critical connections between professional learning and literacy instruction, as bridges between organizational and instructional solutions. Finally, we end with a brief review of how both formal and informal literacy leaders can collaborate to bolster adolescents' literacy skills.

THE LITERACY NEEDS OF ADOLESCENT LEARNERS

The literacy needs of adolescent learners (defined here as students in grades 6–12) have gained worldwide attention during the first two decades of the 21st century. While the literacy learning needs of adolescents have been of interest for over a hundred years in the United States (Jacobs, 2008), new concerns arose in response to decades of lackluster achievement scores for adolescents on national and international literacy assessments directly before and after the turn of the century (National Center for Education Statistics, 2013). Biancarosa and Snow's (2006) seminal report to the Carnegie Corporation of New York, *Reading Next*, prominently labeled this trend an adolescent "literacy crisis" (p. 7). Soon to follow, *Time to Act* (Carnegie Council on Advancing Adolescent Literacy, 2010) and *Reading in the Disciplines* (Lee & Spratley, 2010) were released, emphasizing that the adolescent "literacy crisis" identified earlier in the decade was not going to resolve without shifts in policy, practice, and research.

Importantly, *Reading Next* outlined not just the case for why adolescent literacy needed more attention across policy, practice, and research arenas, but it also synthesized a great deal of the available research to suggest fifteen elements that showed great promise to support effective secondary literacy programs (pp. 4–5). Notably, these elements were divided neatly into two categories: instruction and infrastructure. *Instructional elements* included concrete recommendations such as focusing on "direct, explicit comprehension instruction," embedding "effective instructional principles . . . in content," including "diverse texts" in classroom instruction, fostering "intensive writing," and attending to "motivation and self-directed learning," to name just a few (Biancarosa & Snow, 2006, p. 12). Meanwhile, by highlighting the importance of *infrastructure elements* such as "extended time for literacy," the roles of "teacher teams" and "leadership," and the need for "a comprehensive and coordinated literacy program" (p. 12), Biancarosa and Snow rightly indicated that adolescent literacy achievement would be unlikely to improve across secondary grade levels without explicit attention paid to school- and districtwide structural elements beyond the classroom. This was one of the most prominent calls of the early 21st century suggesting that *literacy leadership* in multiple forms would be needed to improve literacy teaching and learning for adolescents.

The call for literacy leadership and the notion that improving adolescent literacy achievement would require school- and district-level changes as well as shifts in classroom practice were reiterated and strengthened in *Time to Act* (Carnegie Council on Advancing Adolescent Literacy, 2010). The authors of *Time to Act* clearly juxtaposed rapid societal change with the widespread stagnation of secondary school structures and instruction. *Time to Act* reviewed how literacy demands in school and society were increasing dramatically at the outset of the century, due partly to technological advancements and the rise of a new global economy. Moreover, student populations were also rapidly diversifying along all dimensions as a result of increased information and communication opportunities, new waves of immigration, and shifting societal norms that offered more ways for students to express themselves and their intersectional identities than ever before. Despite these wide-scale shifts, most secondary schools remained relatively unchanged in their structures and modes of instruction. A time traveler visiting a U.S. high school classroom in 1956 and then again in 2006 might have been surprised by how little had changed—a single teacher still leading a lesson with a large group of students seated at individual desks and mostly completing the exact same reading or writing task.

Time to Act went further by detailing the many ways in which literacy demands shift for students as they move into secondary levels. Whereas it was once assumed that early literacy skills and achievement would naturally translate into adolescent literacy success, *Time to Act* reviewed why the literacy demands of secondary school classrooms (and then later college and workplace settings) required a different and more advanced set of skills. For example, *Time to Act* listed the following challenges that adolescents face when reading and writing at the secondary level:

- "Texts become longer" (p. 10).
- "Word complexity increases" (p. 10).
- "Sentence complexity increases" (p. 10).
- "Structural complexity increases" (p. 12).
- "Graphic representations become more important" (p. 12).
- "Conceptual challenge increases" (p. 12).
- "Texts begin to vary widely across content areas" (p. 13).

Time to Act served as a powerful reminder, and synthesis, of the challenges that adolescents face when acquiring advanced literacy skills in middle and high school and beyond.

A NEED TO FOCUS ON DISCIPLINARY LITERACY

At the same time that *Time to Act* was released, an additional Carnegie report titled *Reading in the Disciplines* (Lee & Spratley, 2010) outlined the specific ways in which reading comprehension might vary according to disciplinary focus. In other words, the report argued that the ways in which texts vary follow particular patterns along disciplinary lines, with English, history, math, and science classroom and professional texts all sharing discipline-specific characteristics that influence how students both engage with and understand them. Moreover, many have argued that these disciplinary differences are not just superficial differences in textual features, but instead, reflect deeper sociocultural norms, ways of knowing, and ways of generating knowledge within the respective disciplines (Moje, 2015).

This notion of disciplinary differences in texts and adolescents' reading comprehension experiences has been termed *disciplinary literacy* and was prominently described in some depth by a small group of researchers around the same time as the release of the multiple Carnegie reports (McConachie & Petrosky, 2010; Moje, 2007, 2008; Shanahan & Shanahan, 2008). Shanahan and Shanahan (2008) famously articulated a continuum of students' literacy learning needs, from basic skills (e.g., decoding), to intermediate skills (e.g., fluency, general comprehension strategies), to disciplinary literacy skills or the "literacy skills specialized to history, science, mathematics, literature, or other subject matter" (2008, p. 44). As we entered the second decade of the 21st century, the concept of disciplinary literacy caught fire and spread far and wide, influencing the CCSS and spurring dozens of books and hundreds of peer-reviewed articles on the topic (Dobbs, Ippolito, & Charner-Laird, 2018).

Most recently, disciplinary literacy theory and instructional ideas have influenced *Standards 2017* for the preparation of literacy professionals, teachers, and leaders. In fact, early in the standards, the authors state clearly: "Given the emphasis on learning from informational text and the need for associated high-level skills and knowledge of academic vocabulary, disciplinary literacy in the service of content learning is now embedded in these standards" (2018, p. 5). The standards go further by specifying two major ways in which middle and high school classroom teachers must be prepared to support adolescents' literacy work. First, the standards articulate how secondary teachers must simultaneously attend to content and literacy instruction:

> These teachers teach the content of the discipline and are responsible for helping students not only engage in and learn the content but also develop the skills and strategies necessary to read, write, and communicate in discipline-specific ways, as an initial induction into various professional disciplinary communities. (ILA, 2018, p. 85)

This is one of the clearest standards-based statements to date articulating how secondary teachers must assume responsibility for the induction of adolescents into various "professional disciplinary communities," including apprenticeship in the particular reading, writing, and communication norms associated with each academic discipline and related professions.

Secondly, *Standards 2017* takes an additional step forward by suggesting that secondary disciplinary literacy instructional work is best carried out through collaboration among classroom content-area teachers, literacy leaders, and specialized literacy professionals: "Middle and high school content classroom teachers collaborate with specialized literacy and other professionals to improve instruction and to modify the physical and social learning environments as needed" (ILA, 2018, p. 85). In these concise and bold statements from *Standards 2017,* we see once again the suggestion that secondary schools interested in literacy improvement must focus equal attention on instructional and organizational elements.

Following this notion, the next two sections of this chapter offer instructional and then organizational frameworks aimed at improving secondary adolescent literacy work. We begin by considering how the idea of disciplinary literacy may help answer larger questions of how to support adolescents' literacy growth in middle and high school settings. Thinking back to Andrea at the outset of this chapter, we provide ideas for how she (and other teachers and literacy leaders like her) might begin to make sense of disciplinary literacy instructional practices as different than what she (or her former high school biology teacher) has been doing for decades. We do this in part by contrasting disciplinary literacy with earlier content-area literacy theories and instructional practices, ultimately arguing for a layering of intermediate and disciplinary literacy instructional strategies as one potential framework to guide middle and high school literacy leaders.

LAYERING CONTENT-AREA AND DISCIPLINARY LITERACY INSTRUCTION

Thinking back to Andrea, we can understand her concerns about how much reading and writing she might need to teach in her biology classroom so that her students might effectively learn and communicate science concepts. Historically, secondary content-area teachers have received less preparation than their elementary counterparts regarding teaching reading, writing, and discussion, taking perhaps one education course on adolescent literacy at most (Fang, 2014). Across the last century, debates arose about whose job it was to teach literacy beyond elementary school settings. The prevailing viewpoints suggested that either students would enter high school fully prepared or that high school English teachers would bolster the skills of students in need (Lester, 2000; Spencer, Garcia-Simpson, Carter, & Boon, 2008).

However, in the age of CCSS, and given major reports such as *Reading Next* that highlighted the adolescent literacy crisis, more emphasis has recently been placed on how all secondary teachers must apprentice students into the literacies of their disciplines. In fact, *Standards 2017* goes so far as to suggest that all middle and high school classroom teachers across content areas should "demonstrate knowledge of major theoretical, conceptual, and evidence-based components of academic vocabulary, reading comprehension, and critical thinking, with specific emphasis on content area and discipline-specific literacy instruction" (2018, p. 85). The standards continue by suggesting that secondary teachers must understand "writing development, processes, and instruction in their specific discipline" (p. 86), as well as be able to "describe the interrelated components of general literacy and discipline-specific literacy processes that serve as a foundation for all learning" (p. 86). In other words, *Standards 2017* makes it clear that in the 21st century, secondary teachers must understand and be able to support both general and discipline-specific literacy work for their students. But this was not always the focus.

In the 20th century, a focus on content-area literacy was popular and thought to improve student literacy across subjects and grades (Jacobs, 2008). The general idea of content-area literacy was that instructing students in using general comprehension strategies (e.g., questioning, summarizing, inferencing) would support higher achievement across all subjects and content areas (Bean & Readence, 1989, 2002; Vacca & Vacca, 1989). This approach showed promise in improving literacy skills for some students, though it was never quite the panacea that was hoped for (Bos, Anders, Filip, & Jaffe, 1989; Moore, Readence, & Rickleman, 1983). As attention has shifted toward disciplinary literacy over the past two decades, notably in teacher preparation programs (Conley, 2012; Fang, 2014), some are left wondering about content-area literacy approaches and whether and how they might still be used to support students.

Disciplinary literacy is a relatively newer idea than content-area literacy; many seminal works laying out this theory emerged in the mid- to late 2000s (McConachie & Petrosky, 2010; Moje, 2008; Shanahan & Shanahan, 2008). Most often, *disciplinary literacy* is defined as the specialized literacy habits and ways of communicating in particular academic communities (for various definitions, see McConachie & Petrosky, 2010; Moje, 2015; Shanahan & Shanahan, 2008, 2012). Disciplinary literacy focuses on the differences in how experts in various disciplines use literacy to generate and communicate subject-specific knowledge. For example, consider how an environmental microbiologist might ask questions, conduct experiments, and communicate findings about a contaminated freshwater lake versus how an industrial water engineer might think and talk about the same water systems. The differences in the specialized knowledge, language, and ways of communicating would be considered differences in disciplinary literacy.

The overarching argument of disciplinary literacy proponents is that specialized ways of knowing, reading, writing, and communicating must be explicitly identified and taught in secondary schools and beyond in order to fully prepare students to succeed in college and the workplace. This reframing toward teaching more specialized ways of knowing and communicating, rather than the more general ones advocated in a content-area literacy approach, has gained a great deal of attention and offered fodder for much debate about which approach is better or whether the approaches might be combined (Brozo, Moorman, Meyer, & Stewart, 2013; Heller & Greenleaf, 2007). For more extensive reviews of similarities and differences between content-area literacy and disciplinary literacy approaches to teaching and learning, see Ippolito, Dobbs, and Charner-Laird, 2019, as well as Shanahan and Shanahan, 2012.

Having observed high school social studies teachers and other educators working within disciplinary literacy professional learning projects, we argue that the debate over content-area versus disciplinary literacy is perhaps not as productive as thinking carefully about how to "layer" both types of instruction together (Dobbs, Ippolito, & Charner-Laird, 2016, 2017; Ippolito et al., 2019). It seems more likely that instruction that uses the best of both approaches might support students in different subject areas. Shanahan and Shanahan (2008), whose conception of disciplinary literacy is often cited, frame it as one part of a larger theory of literacy specialization. They posit that the early years of schooling are focused on basic literacy development (including skills such as phonics, basic vocabulary, and initial fluency). Then they reframe the content-area literacy approach of focusing on general comprehension strategies as intermediate literacy (including comprehension strategies as well as skills such as the acquisition of general academic vocabulary). Finally, as students progress into secondary school, Shanahan and Shanahan (2008) hypothesize that students should be working increasingly on disciplinary literacy skills, those specialized skills unique to particular disciplines.

Although we agree with the theory outlined by Shanahan and Shanahan, our own work has revealed a much more complex picture of literacy teaching and learning for students in middle and high school settings. Students' literacy development may not always be quite so linear or lockstep as the theory of disciplinary literacy might first suggest. In other words, students may need intermediate and disciplinary skill instruction to be layered together in order to both meet students where they are at, skill-wise, and also support them in learning the particular habits of various disciplines (Dobbs et al., 2016). This layering relies on putting tasks in place that will give teachers insight into where students are at and what they already know, and this can be supported by administrative and teacher leadership in a variety of ways. We offer Figure 10.1 as a visual indication of how teachers and leaders across grade levels might consider layering basic, intermediate, and disciplinary literacy instruction over time.

Returning to Andrea from our case example, we can see a few avenues forward for her, all of which include careful consideration of when and how

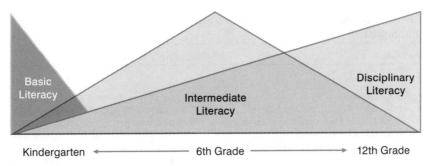

Kindergarten ◄─────────── 6th Grade ──────────► 12th Grade

FIGURE 10.1. Disciplinary literacy instructional focus across the grades. From Ippolito, Dobbs, and Charner-Laird (2019, p. 16). Reprinted with permission of Learning Sciences International.

her students might be best supported by both literacy strategy instruction and more specialized disciplinary literacy instruction. This layering might take place strategically over time, as Andrea's own professional inquiry into different instructional practices shifts from intermediate to disciplinary literacy work. For instance, Andrea might start by considering which domains of literacy (e.g., vocabulary, reading comprehension, fluency, digital literacy, discussion, writing) she might want to explore individually or with colleagues. She might look to a professional text for inspiration, such as *Adolescent Literacy in the Era of the Common Core* (Ippolito, Lawrence, & Zaller, 2013), *Developing Readers in the Academic Disciplines* (Buehl, 2017), or *Strategies That Work* (Harvey & Goudvis, 2017). Andrea then might choose a few general comprehension strategies (e.g., previewing and summarizing routines) from either a core professional text or from a reliable online source (e.g., *www.adlit.org/strategy_library*) to assist students in gaining broad access to texts in her classroom.

Over time, Andrea may then begin to consider a disciplinary literacy framework in which she apprentices students into a deeper analysis of the academic language of their biology texts, the text structures and rhetorical styles, and the broader habits of mind and questions with which biologists are concerned. For Andrea, this might look like designing text-specific interactive reading guides that support students in tracking text structures and complex language as they read (for more about how to create discipline-specific interactive reading guides, see Buehl, 2017). Andrea might also ask students to keep biology journals in which they ask and answer discipline-specific questions while reading, in preparation for asking and answering larger questions through lab experiments—all in service of helping students to adopt certain ways of thinking and working like biologists. See Table 10.1 for a few additional suggestions of how Andrea might ask pertinent inquiry questions and select or design related intermediate

TABLE 10.1. Considering Intermediate versus Disciplinary Literacy Questions and Strategies

Intermediate work	Disciplinary work

Reading

Examples of questions:

- Are students struggling to understand general content in instructional texts (e.g., as evidenced in class discussions, one-on-one conversations, homework, written work)?
- When students face a breakdown in comprehension, are they able to flexibly choose and use general fix-up strategies (e.g., asking questions, summarizing, visualizing)?
- Are students confused about how texts are organized (e.g., headers, sidebars, bolded terms, guiding questions)?
- Are students reading very slowly, or trying to read a dense informational text as if it had a classic narrative/story structure?

Things to try:

- Across several mini-lessons, explicitly teach common text features of informational texts and how they support comprehension.
- Create short text structure "scavenger hunts" to help familiarize students with textbook and informational text structural features.
- Ask students to partner-read for short amounts of time in class, to build fluency and allow for partner questioning strategies as a comprehension check.
- Introduce and model a handful of common comprehension strategies that might be useful across many texts and disciplines (e.g., predicting, summarizing, questioning).
- Create new note-taking organizers to support students as they capture and retain information that they have read.

Examples of questions:

- Are students struggling to understand how and why professionals might communicate differently across genres within a particular academic area?
- Are students using general comprehension strategies, but still struggling to connect information in texts with larger themes, patterns, tropes, and discipline-specific ways of analyzing information in the academic field?
- Are students unable to name and demonstrate at least two or three ways in which reading like a _____ (e.g., historian, mathematician, scientist) differs from more general reading practices?

Things to try:

- Explicitly name, teach, and model reading practices that are discipline-specific (e.g., sourcing and corroborating while reading like a historian).
- Create interactive reading guides that support students in practicing discipline-specific reading strategies (e.g., close reading for symbols in an ELA classroom), with interactive guides being tailored to both the text at hand and the target strategies.
- Create and utilize text sets with a wide variety of instructional texts (e.g., textbooks) and professional texts (e.g., field guides, primary sources, professional articles) to help students better understand the range of texts and their different purposes within each academic area

Writing

Examples of questions:

- Are students struggling to put ideas down on paper in ways that accurately reflect the content learned?

Examples of questions:

- Are students writing accurately about the content but not mirroring the genre, tone, style, and language of the discipline (e.g.,

(continued)

TABLE 10.1. *(continued)*

Intermediate work	Disciplinary work
• Are students struggling with general summaries of content? • Is student writing completely disorganized? • Are students not varying sentence length and word choice?	not using succinct language and shorter factual statements in scientific and mathematical writing)? • Is student writing organized but not following disciplinary organizational patterns (e.g., not following a claim–evidence–reasoning format)? • Are students varying sentence length and word choice but not using these variations in discipline-appropriate ways? • Is writing overly formal or informal for the genre at hand?
Things to try: • Utilize graphic organizers and clear note-taking structures to support students in refining their general writing skills, including summarizing and making arguments. • Adopt, adapt, and teach writing rubrics so that students have a clearer understanding of targets for written products. • Help students distinguish writing-to-learn (informal writing designed to support learning) from writing-to-demonstrate-knowledge (more formal, summative written products demonstrating student understanding). • Provide direct instruction around sentence combining and varying word choice to increase students' general writing skills.	*Things to try:* • Provide opportunities for students to dissect and analyze a wide range of instructional and professional disciplinary written products (e.g., scientific articles, textbooks, various literary and scientific journals) for students to mirror and use as models of discipline-specific writing practices. • Create and use discipline-specific writing templates that highlight particular disciplinary conventions in writing. • Support students as they capture first-draft thinking in writing-to-learn—informal ways (e.g., journals, science notebooks)—and then help students translate that informal writing into more formal, discipline-specific genre structures (e.g., lab reports, analytic essays, research poster presentations).

Discussion

Examples of questions: • Are students not talking with one another about academic content during class sessions? • During academic discussions, are students not using effective talk moves, sentence stems, and connectives (e.g., linking to each other's thinking, reiterating peers' comments before offering contrasting ideas, using connectives such as *however* to signal a shift in an argument)? • Are students relying on classic	*Examples of questions:* • Are students talking regularly with one another about academic content but not using specialized language mirroring the ways that professionals in the discipline might speak? • Are students utilizing talk moves, sentence stems, and connectives but not adopting the specialized and traditional rhetorical styles most prized by various disciplines? • Are students utilizing general discussion structures and protocols but not yet using

(continued)

TABLE 10.1. *(continued)*

Intermediate work	Disciplinary work
argumentative structures and templates to guide their academic discussions? • Are students utilizing general discussion structures and protocols to guide academic discussions (e.g., continuum dialogues, four-corner debates, Socratic seminars)?	the specialized discussion formats prized by the various disciplines (e.g., research poster presentations, formal debates)?
Things to try: • As often as possible, set aside small amounts of time for students to engage with each other in authentic discussion, building slowly to longer stretches of student-led discussions. • Provide opportunities for students to learn and practice classic discussion-based structures and protocols. • Explicitly teach students how to use productive talk moves and language (e.g., revoicing, repeating, probing questions, using connectives, turn-and-talks). • Teach and utilize general discussion structures and protocols that encourage deeper academic thinking (e.g., continuum dialogues, four-corner debates, Socratic seminars).	*Things to try:* • Create discipline-specific sentence stems and conversation starters that students can use to jumpstart more advanced academic discussions. • Modify general talk moves and discussion stems to serve more discipline-specific purposes. • Design and teach discipline-specific discussion structures and protocols that encourage disciplinary thinking (e.g., a peer-to-peer protocol talking through a scientific research poster presentation; small-group opportunities to collaboratively talk through the logic of a document-based question in a history class)

Vocabulary and academic language

Examples of questions: • Are students using a wide range of vocabulary that would be considered Tier 2 or general academic vocabulary? • Are students expressing themselves clearly, or are students using general language like *thing* and *stuff* in oral and written language? • Are students producing the vocabulary and academic language that they are encountering in their academic readings? • Are students able to flexibly use word-learning strategies when they encounter unfamiliar vocabulary?	*Examples of questions:* • Are students using a wide range of vocabulary that would be considered Tier 3 or discipline-specific vocabulary? • Are students using the most precise, discipline-specific language possible when discussing technical content? • Are students toggling back and forth between informal language and more formal, technical language when they shift between writing-to-learn and writing-to-demonstrate knowledge tasks? • Can students vary the level of their academic language in response to different audiences?
Things to try: • Explicitly teach Tier 2 and general academic vocabulary words that appear on the Academic Word List and that appear frequently across all informational texts.	*Things to try:* • Explicitly teach Tier 3 and specialized academic vocabulary words that appear frequently in particular disciplinary texts. • Model for students how to revise their writing with attention to the precise and

(continued)

TABLE 10.1. *(continued)*

Intermediate work	Disciplinary work
• Model for students how to revise their informal writing to make it more formal, with attention to using more formal and precise language. • Ask students to keep vocabulary journals, in which they track new words they encounter in their readings; students can deconstruct and define the words, write sample sentences, and connect the words with others by meaning and/or structure. • Explicitly introduce and model general word-learning strategies (e.g., looking for meaningful chunks in prefixes, roots, and suffixes; relying on contextual clues; considering cognates), and support students through the use of graphic organizers such as Frayer models or vocabulary journals.	unique academic language structures and words associated with specific disciplines. • Provide students with technical word lists and discipline-specific writing models and templates that encourage student experimentation with advanced language and structures. • Using interactive reading guides, ask students to read discipline-specific texts with particular attention to vocabulary and academic language structures; then ask students to write in the same style using discipline-specific templates.

and disciplinary literacy instructional tasks to support student learning across literacy domains.

While Andrea might begin by considering and introducing a few consistent intermediate comprehension strategy routines in her biology classes, we would hope that, over time, she would also layer more discipline-specific practices into her work. Asking questions and trying related practices like those outlined in Table 10.1 provide teachers like Andrea with multiple entry points for tinkering with instruction along the intermediate to disciplinary literacy continuum. While we acknowledge introducing disciplinary literacy teaching and learning practices alone surely will not solve all secondary literacy dilemmas, the framework does reposition secondary content-area teachers like Andrea as experts who are able to apprentice students into the particular literacy practices of their subjects. As new illustrations of the power of disciplinary literacy in secondary classrooms emerge (e.g., Rainey, Maher, Coupland, Franchi, & Moje, 2018), it becomes ever clearer that disciplinary literacy instruction may pave the way to improved literacy outcomes for adolescents.

However, adopting and adapting disciplinary literacy instructional routines is no simple feat. Literacy leaders in secondary schools must plan and implement professional learning structures that support the sophisticated design work that teachers will need to undertake to make disciplinary literacy work successful. In the next section, we turn from an instructional frame to an organizational frame, suggesting a few ways in which secondary leaders might productively create a context for disciplinary literacy design and instructional efforts.

ORGANIZING OURSELVES TO BEST SUPPORT
ADOLESCENTS' LITERACY LEARNING

As literacy leaders consider how best to support middle and high school teachers in adopting and adapting content-area and disciplinary literacy practices, time and resources should be set aside for the intentional planning and refinement of related professional learning structures. The intentional design of ongoing literacy professional learning is one of the key levers for bolstering literacy teaching and learning across content-area classrooms at the secondary level. This means considering how best to structure ongoing professional learning for teachers such that they can invent, test, refine, and enact new practices focused on integrating disciplinary literacy instruction into their practice (Dobbs et al., 2017).

Gone are the days of isolated workshops or 1-day site visits by experts from the field (Borko, 2004). Such traditional professional development offerings fail to attend to the context in which teachers carry out their work and thus fall short on supporting teachers in transferring new knowledge (Borko, 2004; Elmore, 2004; Wilson & Berne, 1999). Ultimately, researchers have found that professional learning that is site-specific, ongoing, and that allows teachers to build on existing expertise in order to generate new knowledge and practices, provides teachers with the type of learning that has a deep and lasting effect on practice (Bill & Melinda Gates Foundation, 2014; Borko, 2004; Darling-Hammond, Hyler, & Gardner, 2017; Darling-Hammond, Wei, Andree, Richardson, & Orphanos, 2009; Elmore, 2004; Garet, Porter, Desimone, Birman, & Yoon, 2001; Jensen, Sonnemann, Roberts-Hull, & Hunter, 2016).

Given that a shift toward disciplinary literacy instruction will likely require significant and context-specific professional learning, literacy leaders are uniquely situated to design and enact such learning opportunities. As experts embedded within school contexts, literacy leaders such as literacy coaches, literacy specialists, or department chairs can pair the knowledge that they bring about effective literacy teaching and learning with their knowledge of the school context and teachers' particular learning needs. Leading this learning, which builds on the expertise of literacy leaders but also includes teachers in the further development of new instructional ideas, centers teachers as agents of reform. Lee and Spratley (2010) note that such models of literacy professional learning are likely to lead to hoped-for improved outcomes in adolescent literacy.

However, merely considering the specific tenets of effective professional learning is often not enough to catalyze the design of effective professional learning processes by literacy leaders. Instead, literacy leaders would benefit from considering the structures and processes that have led to powerful learning among teachers regarding disciplinary literacy practices. In our own work (e.g., Dobbs et al., 2017), we have found that the interaction among a few particular structures and practices can create the ideal conditions for professional learning in the area of disciplinary literacy.

Specifically, we recommend that school leaders look toward the use of professional learning communities (PLCs), teacher leadership, and collaborative inquiry as organizational structures to support learning that can lead to instructional change. As an organizational structure, PLCs provide teachers with ongoing opportunities to learn more about discipline-specific literacy practices from colleagues, teacher leaders, coaches, and professional resources. Such focused PLCs have been shown to lead to the development of context-specific new practices tailored to student needs (Dana & Yendol-Hoppey, 2008; Jacobson, 2010; Servage, 2008; Wood, 2009). Moreover, researchers have found that without a leader present or without clear guidance, teachers do not always know what to do when they find themselves within collaborative structures such as PLCs (Troen & Boles, 2012). This is where teacher leadership can play a key role in school improvement processes and in teacher learning (Fairman & Mackenzie, 2012, 2015; Smylie, Conley, & Marks, 2002; York-Barr & Duke, 2004). A content-area teacher leader guiding a disciplinary literacy-focused PLC can catalyze and support teachers' professional learning, all from the stance of lead learner (Charner-Laird, Ippolito, & Dobbs, 2016). Lastly, by adopting an inquiry focus, teacher-led PLCs adopt a procedural structure that they can rely on over time: defining an inquiry question, building background knowledge, crafting new instructional ideas and routines, testing those ideas in the classroom, and then reflecting on and refining the work. Such teacher-led inquiry has been shown to generate useful knowledge that ultimately can lead to important changes in teachers' instructional practice (Cochran-Smith & Lytle, 2009; Charner-Laird et al., 2016; Dobbs et al., 2017).

Returning once more to Andrea's questions about how best to support her high school biology students, we would not only want to provide her with guidance about productive instructional ideas, but we would also want to talk directly with her principal, literacy coach, and department chair. We would recommend that these literacy leaders create or bolster content-area PLCs focused on collaborative inquiry into science-specific disciplinary literacy practices. We would recommend that a well-respected science teacher (perhaps Andrea herself) serve as team leader of the science PLC, working as lead learner who has in-depth knowledge of the content and the ways in which students struggle to learn, share, and create science-specific content. Andrea might receive support in this role through a one-course release from teaching so that she could visit colleagues' classrooms, meet with the school's literacy coach, review resources around disciplinary learning, and bolster her own knowledge of literacy instructional practices. The PLC could learn about and pilot new science-focused disciplinary literacy practices, then share their work with their department chair and department colleagues as they refine their routines. Ultimately, the principal would want to bring together similarly focused PLCs from across content areas, to align practices and craft a larger schoolwide vision for disciplinary literacy instruction. This is the kind of theory of action for professional learning that the literacy leaders in Andrea's school will need if they wish to truly support teachers in learning and designing context- and content-specific disciplinary literacy practices.

CONCLUSION

While improving literacy teaching and learning processes in middle and high settings can be complex and challenging work, we hope that this chapter has provided a few key guiding principles to follow and resources to consult. If we were to advise Andrea and her school's leadership team, we would recommend, as described in this chapter, attending to both organizational and instructional elements of the dilemma. We would identify potential literacy leaders such as the school's literacy coach, Andrea's department chair, or even Andrea herself as possible leaders of a science-specific team of teachers. We would encourage that team to form a PLC and engage in collaborative inquiry over a period of at least 2 years, asking and answering some of the fruitful questions that Andrea herself outlined about the right balance of intermediate and disciplinary literacy instructional strategies, advancing students' discipline-specific and general academic vocabulary, zooming-in on best practices for honing students' scientific writing skills, and so on. And following the guidance of the ILA's *Standards 2017*, which is rightly "grounded in research related to adult learning and organizational change as well as research on literacy acquisition, development, assessment, and instruction" (p. 19), we would argue that Andrea should be working closely with her department and schoolwide literacy leaders to attend equally to professional learning processes and specific changes in classroom instruction. We would hope that, together, Andrea and her building's leaders could develop and sustain the ongoing professional learning structures teachers need to adopt, adapt, and refine discipline-specific literacy instruction over time.

   This work is not easy. Yet this is the work needed to steadily increase adolescents' general and disciplinary literacy skills, to prepare them for college and the workplace in the 21st century.

ENGAGEMENT ACTIVITIES

1. As you consider the literacy teaching and learning challenges in your classroom, content area, grade level, and school, look at Figure 10.1, illustrating the amount

of disciplinary literacy instructional focus across the grades. What do you see as the implications for layering intermediate or general content-area literacy strategies with more specialized disciplinary literacy strategies for particular grade levels and content areas?

2. Reread the case example featuring Andrea and discuss with colleagues the following questions: What instructional challenges do you see in this scenario? What organizational challenges are apparent? Given the frameworks presented in this chapter, what advice might you offer Andrea as she considers:

   a. finding the right balance of new content-area and disciplinary literacy strategies for her biology classroom;

   b. collaborating more closely with her biology colleagues; and

   c. working more productively with her school's literacy coach to test and assess the efficacy of new literacy-focused instructional practices?

3. After reading this chapter, discuss with teachers in role-alike and then cross-grade/cross-content-area groups the following questions: Which literacy-focused teaching and learning challenges seem most pressing in your classrooms? What are your thoughts about the similarities and differences in pursuing content-area versus disciplinary literacy instructional approaches? Which organizational structures might need to be created or refined in order to best support your instructional design work?

ANNOTATED RESOURCES

Annenberg Foundation. (2017). Reading and writing in the disciplines. Retrieved from *www.learner.org/courses/readwrite*.

These free online, multimedia modules were created to support teachers and leaders in understanding both the challenges of adolescent literacy and the promises of content-area and disciplinary literacy instructional approaches. Filled with short, pragmatic readings; reflection questions; research connections; and illustrative videos of real teachers in classrooms, these modules are a perfect starting place for literacy leaders wanting to think more about supporting adolescent literacy learning.

Dobbs, C. L., Ippolito, J., & Charner-Laird, M. (2017). *Investigating disciplinary literacy: A framework for collaborative professional learning.* Cambridge, MA: Harvard Education Press.

Ippolito, J., Dobbs, C. L., & Charner-Laird, M. (2019). *Disciplinary literacy inquiry and instruction.* West Palm Beach, FL: Learning Sciences International.

Taken together, these two books provide a roadmap for school leaders and teachers interested in building their own robust disciplinary literacy schoolwide instructional model. The authors outline two interconnected frameworks for disciplinary literacy professional learning and connecting teacher inquiry with teacher practice. The 2017 book describes a seven-step process for planning, implementing, and assessing a disciplinary literacy professional learning initiative. The 2019 book focuses on a simple and powerful framework that can guide both teacher collaborative inquiry and instructional design, providing more guidance for teachers engaged in collaborative inquiry around disciplinary literacy.

REFERENCES

Bean, T. W., & Readence, J. E. (1989). Content area reading: Current state of the art. In D. Lapp, J. Flood, & N. Farnan (Eds.), *Content area reading and learning: Instructional strategies* (pp. 14–23). Englewood Cliffs, NJ: Prentice Hall.

Bean, T. W., & Readence, J. E. (2002). Adolescent literacy: Charting a course for successful futures as lifelong learners. *Reading Research and Instruction, 41*(3), 203–209.

Biancarosa, C., & Snow, C. E. (2006). *Reading next—a vision for action and research in middle and high school literacy: A report to Carnegie Corporation of New York* (2nd ed.). Washington, DC: Alliance for Excellent Education.

Bill & Melinda Gates Foundation. (2014). *Teachers know best: Teachers' views on professional development.* Seattle, WA: Author.

Borko, H. (2004). Professional development and teacher learning: Mapping the terrain. *Educational Researcher, 33*(8), 3–15.

Bos, C. S., Anders, P. L., Filip, D., & Jaffe, L. E. (1989). The effects of an interactive instructional strategy for enhancing reading comprehension and content area learning for students with learning disabilities. *Journal of Learning Disabilities, 22*(6), 384–390.

Brozo, W. G., Moorman, G., Meyer, C., & Stewart, T. (2013). Content area reading and disciplinary literacy: A case for the radical center. *Journal of Adolescent and Adult Literacy, 56*(5), 353–357.

Buehl, D. (2017). *Developing readers in the academic disciplines.* Portland, ME: Stenhouse.

Carnegie Council on Advancing Adolescent Literacy. (2010). *Time to act: An agenda for advancing adolescent literacy for college and career success.* New York, NY: Carnegie Corporation of New York. Retrieved from *www.carnegie.org/publications/time-to-act-an-agenda-for-advancing-adolescent-literacy-for-college-and-career-success.*

Charner-Laird, M., Ippolito, J., & Dobbs, C. L. (2016). The roles of teacher leaders in guiding PLCs focused on disciplinary literacy. *Journal of School Leadership, 26*(6), 975–1001.

Cochran-Smith, M., & Lytle, S. L. (2009). *Inquiry as stance: Practitioner research for the next generation.* New York: Teachers College Press.

Conley, M. W. (2012). Foregrounding the disciplines for teacher preparation in secondary literacy. *Journal of Adolescent and Adult Literacy, 56*(2), 141–150.

Dana, N. F., & Yendol-Hoppey, D. (2008). *The reflective educator's guide to professional development: Coaching inquiry-oriented learning communities.* Thousand Oaks, CA: Corwin Press.

Darling-Hammond, L., Hyler, M. E., & Gardner, M. (2017). *Effective teacher professional development.* Palo Alto, CA: Learning Policy Institute.

Darling-Hammond, L., Wei, R. C., Andree, A., Richardson, N., & Orphanos, S. (2009). *Professional learning in the learning profession: A status report on teacher learning in the United States and abroad.* Stanford, CA: National Staff Development Council.

Dobbs, C. L., Ippolito, J., & Charner-Laird, M. (2016). Layering intermediate and disciplinary literacy work: Lessons learned from a secondary social studies teacher team. *Journal of Adolescent and Adult Literacy, 60*(2), 131–139.

Dobbs, C. L., Ippolito, J., & Charner-Laird, M. (2017). *Investigating disciplinary literacy: A framework for collaborative professional learning.* Cambridge, MA: Harvard Education Press.

Dobbs, C. L., Ippolito, J., & Charner-Laird, M. (2018, April). *What do we mean when we say disciplinary literacy?: Exploring a messy construct.* Paper presented at the annual meeting of the American Educational Research Association, New York.

Elmore, R. F. (2004). *School reform from the inside out: Policy, practice, and performance.* Cambridge, MA: Harvard Education Press.

Fairman, J. C., & Mackenzie, S. V. (2012). Spheres of teacher leadership action for learning. *Professional Development in Education, 38*(2), 229–246.

Fairman, J. C., & Mackenzie, S. V. (2015). How teacher leaders influence others and understand their leadership. *International Journal of Leadership in Education, 18*(1), 61–87.

Fang, Z. (2014). Preparing content area teachers for disciplinary literacy instruction. *Journal of Adolescent and Adult Literacy, 57*(6), 444–448.

Garet, M. S., Porter, A. C., Desimone, L., Birman, B. F., & Yoon, K. S. (2001). What makes professional development effective?: Results from a national sample of teachers. *American Educational Research Journal, 38*(4), 915–945.

Harvey, S., & Goudvis, A. (2017). *Strategies that work: Teaching comprehension for understanding and engagement* (3rd ed.). Portland, ME: Stenhouse.

Heller, R., & Greenleaf, C. L. (2007). *Literacy instruction in the content areas: Getting to the core of middle and high school improvement.* Washington, DC: Alliance for Excellent Education.

International Literacy Association (ILA). (2018). *Standards for the preparation of literacy professionals 2017.* Newark, DE: Author.

Ippolito, J., Dobbs, C. L., & Charner-Laird, M. (2019). *Disciplinary literacy inquiry and instruction.* West Palm Beach, FL: Learning Sciences International.

Ippolito, J., Lawrence, J. F., & Zaller, C. (Eds.). (2013). *Adolescent literacy in the era of the Common Core: From research into practice.* Cambridge, MA: Harvard Education Press.

Jacobs, V. A. (2008). Adolescent literacy: Putting the crisis in context. *Harvard Educational Review, 78*(1), 7–39.

Jacobson, D. (2010). Coherent instructional improvement and PLCs: Is it possible to do both? *Phi Delta Kappan, 91*(6), 38–45.

Jensen, B., Sonnemann, J., Roberts-Hull, K., & Hunter, A. (2016). *Beyond PD: Teacher professional learning in high-performing systems.* Washington, DC: National Center on Education and the Economy.

Lee, C. D., & Spratley, A. (2010). *Reading in the disciplines: The challenges of adolescent literacy.* New York: Carnegie Corporation of New York. Retrieved from *www.issuelab.org/resource/reading-in-the-disciplines-the-challenges-of-adolescent-literacy.html.*

Lester, J. H. (2000). Secondary instruction: Does literacy fit in? *The High School Journal, 83*(3), 10–16.

McConachie, S. M., & Petrosky, T. (Eds.). (2010). *Content matters: A disciplinary literacy approach to improving student learning.* San Francisco: Jossey-Bass.

Moje, E. B. (2007). Developing socially just subject-matter instruction: A review of the literature on disciplinary literacy teaching. *Review of Research in Education, 31*(1), 1–44.

Moje, E. B. (2008). Foregrounding the disciplines in secondary literacy teaching and learning: A call for change. *Journal of Adolescent and Adult Literacy, 52*(2), 96–107.

Moje, E. B. (2015). Doing and teaching disciplinary literacy with adolescent learners: A social and cultural enterprise. *Harvard Educational Review, 85*(2), 254–278.

Moore, D. W., Readence, J. E., & Rickelman, R. J. (1983). An historical exploration of content area reading instruction. *Reading Research Quarterly, 18*(4), 419–438.

National Center for Education Statistics. (2013). *The nation's report card: Trends in academic progress 2012* (NCES 2013-456). Washington, DC: Institute of Education Sciences, U.S. Department of Education.

National Governors Association Center for Best Practices & Council of Chief State School Officers. (2010). *Common Core Standards for English language arts and literacy in history/social studies, science, and technical subjects.* Washington, DC: Authors.

Rainey, E. C., Maher, B. L., Coupland, D., Franchi, R., & Moje, E. B. (2018). But what does it look like?: Illustrations of disciplinary literacy teaching in two content areas. *Journal of Adolescent and Adult Literacy, 61*(4), 371–379.

Servage, L. (2008). Critical and transformative practices in professional learning communities. *Teacher Education Quarterly, 35*(1), 63–77.

Shanahan, T., & Shanahan, C. (2008). Teaching disciplinary literacy to adolescents: Rethinking content-area literacy. *Harvard Educational Review, 78*(1), 40–59.

Shanahan, T., & Shanahan, C. (2012). What is disciplinary literacy and why does it matter? *Topics in Language Disorders, 32*(1), 7–18.

Smylie, M. A., Conley, S., & Marks, H. M. (2002). Reshaping leadership in action. In J. Murphy (Ed.), *The educational leadership challenge: Redefining leadership for the 21st century* (pp. 162–188). Chicago: National Society for the Study of Education.

Spencer, V. G., Garcia-Simpson, C., Carter, B. B., & Boon, R. T. (2008). If you teach—you teach reading. *International Journal of Special Education, 23*(2), 1–7.

Troen, V., & Boles, K. C. (2012). *The power of teacher teams: With cases, analyses, and strategies for success.* Thousand Oaks, CA: Corwin Press.

Vacca, R. T., & Vacca, J. L. (1989). *Content area reading* (3rd ed.). New York: Harper Collins.

Wilson, S. M., & Berne, J. (1999). Teacher learning and the acquisition of professional knowledge: An examination of research on contemporary professional development. *Review of Research in Education, 24*(1999), 173–209.

Wood, D. R. (2009). Professional learning communities: Teachers, knowledge, and knowing. *Theory into Practice, 46*(4), 281–290.

York-Barr, J., & Duke, K. (2004). What do we know about teacher leadership?: Findings from two decades of scholarship. *Review of Educational Research, 74*(3), 255–316.

CHAPTER 11

Differentiated Literacy Instruction

Jennifer Jones Powell

Lisa D. Aker

Heidi Anne E. Mesmer

GUIDING QUESTIONS

➥ What is *differentiation*? Is differentiation just a buzzword in education and in what ways is it relevant to our work in classrooms?

➥ Does every aspect of instruction that involves literacy have to be differentiated? What parts of our instruction should be differentiated and why?

➥ What are some examples of differentiation in a literacy classroom? What makes differentiation in these classrooms successful?

Imagine being on a quest to learn something new, perhaps chess. You decide to take a class with your friends, and you expect that you will learn to play the game. Once enrolled, however you discover that you are struggling from week to week. You listen carefully to the instructor. You observe as she explains the rules and details of how to play strategically. You work to apply these strategies, and you even try to practice by playing with others outside of the class. The bottom line, however, is the instruction is above your level. You leave each class frustrated, wondering if something is wrong with you because you struggle. You think about dropping out.

Your friend Katie, who has played chess for years, also joins the class hoping to improve and sharpen her skills. As an experienced player, Katie finds the class to be quite easy. Nonetheless, she participates and goes through the motions. She answers many of the instructor's questions and, at times, "overly" participates. As a result, the instructor compliments Katie and uses her to help with demonstrations. The instructor also partners Katie with those who need help, but this is not what Katie signed up to do. Katie signed up to improve her game. She begins to feel that the class is a waste of her time, and she loses her excitement to attend each week. She is bored—almost to the point of not wanting to play chess any longer.

Consider the above scenario and replace chess with literacy instruction in school. Every day students experience frustration, often rooted in reading instruction that is beyond their current level. Others wrestle with boredom because they are required to read and practice strategies that are already innate. A healthy, growth-fostering challenge is lacking for these students. Such scenarios lead us to ponder with a spirit of equity, *how do we meet the literacy needs of* all *students in our classrooms?*

In this chapter, we discuss differentiation in the literacy classroom as it aligns with Standard 2 (curriculum and instruction) and Standard 5 (learners and the literacy environment) of the International Literacy Association (ILA) *Standards for the Preparation of Literacy Professionals 2017* (2018b). In the first section, we define differentiation, including the integral role of data. In the second section, we address whether or not differentiation is worth the effort. Next, we identify how to determine which elements of the curriculum should be differentiated, and then we examine steps for differentiation—steps that make it possible in the real-world classroom. The concluding section highlights the importance of collaboration throughout the process.

WHAT IS DIFFERENTIATION?

Differentiation is the process of making adjustments to meet the differing needs of students. "Differentiated instruction allows all students to access the same classroom curriculum by providing entry points, learning tasks, and outcomes tailored to students' learning needs" (Hall, Strangman, & Meyer, 2003, as cited in Watts-Taffe et al., 2012, p. 304). Important to note, differentiated instruction is *not* personalized instruction, in which the *student* designs his or her own learning path. Differentiated instruction involves the *teacher*'s adjustments to instruction to meet the needs of students.

Long before the term *differentiated instruction* was coined, it has been practiced in schools. Teachers in one-room schoolhouses differentiated instruction to meet the needs of various ages and stages of learning with leveled readers, whole- and small-group instruction, and assignment adjustments (Birnie, 2015). Beyond the one-room schoolhouse and into our modern-day world, teachers understand that every classroom has a range of reading levels, skills, and abilities that must be addressed.

Researchers during the 1970s such as Vygotsky blazed the trail for the concept of differentiation by placing attention on the *zone of proximal development*. More recently, Tomlinson's work (2000, 2014) in gifted education has highlighted the need for differentiated instruction. A robust line of research points to how exemplary schools and teachers differentiate instruction (Adler & Fisher, 2001; Taylor, Pearson, Clark, & Walpole, 1999; Pressley, 1998; Hoffman, 1991; Weber, 1971). Findings across time highlight literacy instruction that is informed by data, responds to students' needs, and builds instruction on what is unknown (Connor, 2011). Thus, today the ILA's *Standards 2017* identifies differentiation as a key component of effective and high-quality literacy programs.

Inherent in the term *differentiation* is the word *different*. Thus, differentiated instruction is based on what students *know*, what they *need*, and their abilities to *demonstrate* what they know (Tomlinson, 2000, 2014). According to *Standards 2017*, Tomlinson (2001) and other researchers identified the essential components of differentiated instruction as including *process, materials, environment,* and *product* (Watts-Taffe et al., 2012; Walpole & McKenna, 2017). *Process* is "how" students learn and practice targeted literacy-learning goals. The process by which students achieve the learning goals may be differentiated through grouping formats and/or the instruction within each. *Materials* include the texts we use within the process, which can be differentiated by level and text complexity. *Environment* includes both materials and process, providing opportunities to promote and foster success within these settings. Finally, *product* refers to the ways students demonstrate their learning. Products can be differentiated by having students engage in different types of writing, sorts, or projects to assess their knowledge of particular literacy-related skills.

Differentiated instruction is instruction that *responds to* and *connects with* three key components: (1) assessment data to *inform* instruction, (2) instruction that *responds* to the data, and (3) classroom routines and structures that *support* and *connect* with students' needs. We must use data to *respond* to students with *connected* instruction. Instruction is *informed* by data, which then directs the use of materials/texts and the teaching process. All of these components work in tandem to *connect* the unknown to the known and to provide opportunities for students to demonstrate what they know in various ways. Note that curriculum has not been mentioned. Differentiated instruction always begins with the *student*, not the mandated curriculum (Tomlinson & Allan, 2000).

Differentiated instruction in the literacy classroom may take many forms. Some classrooms may utilize *teaching up*, where specific grade-level content is taught to every student (aimed at those who are advanced), but with varying levels of scaffolding and practice opportunities (Tomlinson, 2014, 2015). For example, Ms. Jones teaches informational text structures with the whole class from a common text, targeting her advanced students.

Students then engage in partner and small-group practice as they identify text structures. Advanced students may apply this knowledge by using various text structures in their writing. Students reading on grade level may use grade-level texts to identify various text structures. Struggling readers may use texts on lower reading levels with graphic organizers to identify text structures in their leveled texts.

Here, whole-group instruction *exposes* everyone to district- and grade-level expectations (equal access); however, small-group instruction targets different skills specific to students' stages of literacy development. In other situations, small groups may become intervention, honing specific areas of need (e.g., fluency, phonics, comprehension, phonemic awareness).

In these examples, teachers are using data in the planning and teaching process. Teachers *respond* to data as they determine the content, materials, and the teaching processes utilized each day. Materials and process work to connect what students need to know with what they already know. The teacher meets students where they are at and builds a trajectory of instruction toward where they need to be. As described next, data-informed teaching requires (1) knowledge of students via assessment data, (2) knowledge of literacy development, and (3) the use of strong organizational structures at the macro (classroom) and micro (small-group/individual) levels.

Assessment and Differentiation

Effective teachers do not differentiate based on opinions, a child's behavior, or the feelings of other staff members. They collect data and use that data to tailor instruction. Use of data to inform instruction is a distinguishing characteristic that sets effective schools apart from ineffective schools, especially high-needs school that are *beating the odds* (Taylor et al., 1999). Such schools do not just gather data, they *use* it. In fact, these schools approach and utilize data in systemic ways, which promotes a common language about assessment and instruction at the school level, rather than single classrooms doing things individualistically.

Weber (1971) identified *continuous evaluation of pupil progress* as a key factor among successful schools. Edmonds (1979) gleaned that *systematic evaluation* of student progress as a key factor for student achievement. In the 1990s, Hoffman (1991) explored the attributes of effective schools, identifying *frequent monitoring of student progress* as a key attribute. Clearly, *systematic use of data* for instructional decision making is an integral part of student and school-wide success in reading achievement.

Taylor and colleagues (1999) studied *beating-the-odds* schools and found that these schools used *data to make instructional decisions* based on students' needs, as well as to *monitor student progress* (Taylor et al., 1999). Cunningham, Hall, and Defee's (1998) case studies of beating-the-odds schools found the *use of data to establish instructional goals* to be a hallmark of success for such schools. Further, Booker, Invernizzi, and McCormick (2007) pinpointed *monitoring of student progress* as a key use of data in beating-the-odds schools. This remains true in middle and secondary schools; Langer (2001) studied successful schools and found that data were used to inform instruction and test preparation efforts in these upper grades. Exemplary schools and teachers at all levels, from elementary, middle, to high school, purposefully use data to inform instruction.

Frequently data guide the formation of small groups. There is no "one-size-fits-all" approach to small-group instruction (Adler & Fisher, 2001); we do know, however, that effective small-group instruction uses student data coupled with research-supported instruction (Shanahan, 2004). Data pinpoint students' strengths and needs, inform instructional goals (literacy focus), teaching process (teacher modeling, guided practice, mini-lessons) and materials (levels, complexity, content).

Knowledge of Literacy Development and Specific Literacy Needs Must Be Applied to Differentiate Instruction

When teachers collect data to differentiate instruction, it should yield two important pieces of information for every child. First, teachers should learn students' reading levels and stages of literacy development. Reading levels and stages should be gleaned as early and quickly as possible in the school year. All learners are progressing from some point on a literacy continuum (Bear, Invernizzi, Templeton, & Johnston, 2015; Chall, 1983; Fountas & Pinnell, 2017; Henderson, 1981), which is often defined by a stage of literacy development. Table 11.1 highlights stages of literacy development, typical behaviors, and shifting literacy goals as students move across the continuum of literacy development. Note how needs shift and change.

Secondly, data should be used to identify specific literacy strengths and areas of need for each student *within* the literacy stage. Stage knowledge informs the instruction of specific literacy components. Table 11.1 illustrates how teacher knowledge of literacy development is integrated with student data to determine the construct-specific appropriate reading instruction for students. With a quick glance at Table 11.1, it is easy to see how instruction will differ for beginning readers who have oral reading and fluency issues from transitional readers who need to work on fluency.

Organizational Structures

Usually, differentiated instruction involves teacher-guided small groups, which requires organizational structures that allow the teacher to devote focused time to a small group without distractions from other students. As the teacher works with small groups, the class must have meaningful, engaging, and productive independent work facilitated through a series of

TABLE 11.1. Stages of Literacy Development, Typical Behaviors, and Literacy Goals

Stage	Typical literacy behaviors	Oral reading and fluency goals	Phonics goals	Comprehension goals
Emergent (birth–5 years)	• Developing concepts of print • Incomplete knowledge of the alphabet • Developing oral language skills and vocabulary • Developing listening comprehension	Concepts of print; concept of word	Alphabet knowledge; phonological awareness	Oral language development; vocabulary development
Early/ beginning	• Developing alphabetic principle • Concept of word, finger-point, oral reading • Slow, word-by-word reading • Basic high-frequency words • Learning to spell with short vowels, consonant blends, and digraphs	Supported reading (echo, choral, partner)/rereading; high frequency-word knowledge	Decoding simple word with short vowels, consonant blends, digraphs; building a bank of known words	Retelling; story elements
Transitional/ intermediate	• Increased fluency • Begin to silent read • Increased vocabulary and language skills • Spelling focuses on long vowels, diphthongs, and multisyllabic words • Focus on building comprehension skills and engaging with the text	Improving reading rate and reading expression	Decoding words with long-vowel patterns and some multisyllable words	Comprehension strategies; chapter books
Fluent/ advanced	• Fluent reading • Silent read • Deeper comprehension (linked to background knowledge) • Spelling using word derivations	Prosody	Decoding multisyllabic words and those with meaningful units (morphemes)	Strategic, deep comprehension

routines. What to do with the rest of the class when a teacher is working with a small group remains an enduring question (Cambourne, 2001).

There are many templates for organizing literacy blocks (Boushey & Moser, 2006; Calkins & Tolan, 2010; Diller, 2003). Some teachers use independent literacy work/stations to engage students when they are not in a small group (Diller, 2003). Students rotate through work stations while they are not with the teacher. Effective literacy stations are simple and have clear routines so that students can be successful. Daily Five (Boushey & Moser, 2006) is another literacy block structure in which students rotate across five activities, several of which are teacher-directed: (1) read to self, (2) writing, (3) read to someone, (4) word work, and (5) listen to reading. Reading workshop is another structure. Here, the teacher delivers minilessons to the whole class and then students read and engage in comprehension activities independently while the teacher confers with individual students.

Whatever the choices are, teachers need to have a system in place that will free them to work with small groups. Importantly, independent work should not introduce new material but provide students with opportunities to revisit previously taught material or continue honing skills they have already mastered. Independent time does *not* include art projects or puzzles; rather, it focuses on literacy rich activities aligned with the stages and components of literacy within the classroom.

IS DIFFERENTIATION WORTH THE TIME AND EFFORT?

A wide body of research suggests that differentiated instruction is, indeed, worth the time and effort (Tomlinson, 2000, 2014; Vygotsky, 1978). In addition to being instructionally effective, differentiated instruction reduces behavioral issues, boredom, and frustration while enhancing self-esteem and self-efficacy. In a differentiated classroom, students are learning what they need to learn in order to thrive as literacy learners. Less time is spent reteaching. Students remain on a forward-moving trajectory.

Differentiation is particularly worth it for students who may have special learning needs, and it has actually been written into special education law. In 2004, the reauthorization of the Individuals with Disabilities Education Act Amendment (IDEAA) introduced response to intervention (RTI) as a way of providing differentiated and responsive instruction for every child. RTI and multi-tiered systems of support (MTSS) are general education problem-solving frameworks for differentiated instruction that assess, identify, instruct, and monitor students' progress. RTI/MTSS addresses students' needs based upon data-driven decision making. Students' responses to instruction are monitored on an ongoing basis and adjustments to instruction and/or grouping configurations take place based upon that data. The International Reading Association (2010) identified six guiding principles for RTI, with differentiation included. The first "tier" of instruction within an RTI/MTSS framework is exemplary differentiated instruction for all students at the classroom level. When a student does not respond to core classroom instruction, intervention is provided in varying amounts of intensity (Tiers 2 and 3). Without thoughtful differentiated instruction at Tier 1, all students would need Tiers 2 and 3!

How Do You Determine Which Components of Literacy Instruction to Differentiate?

It is clear that differentiated instruction is worth the time; yet, does all literacy instruction need to be differentiated? The answer is *no*. Student needs should guide decisions on where to differentiate instruction. Where the students are the most different, as indicated by assessment data, the instruction must be differentiated. When data suggest that it would be ineffective and nearly impossible to meet the needs of all students with the same *process, materials, environment,* and/or *products*, then differentiation should be applied.

To understand where to differentiate, we address the parts of the language arts classroom. A comprehensive model of language arts includes the following components: (1) comprehension, (2) fluency, (3) phonemic awareness, (4) phonics, (5) vocabulary, and (6) writing (ILA, 2018b; Mathes et al., 2005; National Reading Panel, 2000; Shanahan, 2004). We call this a "literacy diet." It ensures that students are exposed to everything they need to develop as healthy and thriving readers and writers.

The term *balanced literacy* is often used to refer to such comprehensive models, but this does not mean that all components should be offered in equal portions. Rather, a balanced reader is fostered by adjusting components as they intersect with individual needs or developmental levels. For example, the following are components of literacy instruction in grades K–2: (1) shared reading or interactive read-aloud; (2) guided, small-group reading; (3) shared writing; (4) writing; (5) word study, phonics, and phonemic awareness; and (6) independent reading. The following are components of literacy instruction in grades 3–5: (1) interactive read-aloud, (2) small-group reading/novel groups, (3) shared writing, (4) writing, (5) word study and phonics, and (6) independent reading. Consider: How does each of these teaching processes support the components of literacy instruction?

In our experiences with students, we find that individual and developmental needs tend to be the most different in the areas of (1) reading level; (2) phonics, phonemic awareness, or word study; (3) fluency; and/or (4) writing (expressively). Therefore, these areas are frequently (but not always) differentiated in the classroom. We have never seen a classroom in which all students are reading on the same level and so, in order for students to have practice in appropriate texts, they must be instructed in differentiated small groups with different leveled texts (Clay, 1998; Fountas & Pinnell, 2017). Similarly, students at different reading levels can also be served in novel or literature groups with chapter books written at different levels or by using a Readers' Workshop in which students read in selected texts that match their interests and reading level. We also find that assessed word study, phonics, and/or phonemic awareness can be quite different as early as kindergarten. For this reason, differentiated small-group phonics instruction, different spelling lists, and/or different word sorts are frequently needed in classrooms.

It has been our experience that most students have similar needs in terms of learning new concepts and vocabulary, comprehension strategies, and/or writing genres, mechanics, and revisions. Thus, it is common for teachers to provide undifferentiated whole-group instruction in comprehension and vocabulary through interactive read-alouds. A teacher might also use a whole-group read-aloud to teach a specific comprehension strategy in a mini-lesson that students at various reading levels can apply across texts during small-group instruction. Similarly, a teacher might use a mentor text, such as a biography, to illustrate particular features of a genre that students are learning how to write during a writers' workshop.

As mentioned, students are quite different in both reading levels and interests, and we find that a time to read student-selected books (e.g., "independent reading"), with some type of teacher supervision and accountability, is another way to support differentiated reading instruction (see Kelley & Clausen-Grace, 2006; Miller & Moss, 2013). Fountas and Pinnell (2019) purport that students should not be restricted to leveled text during independent reading time. This makes sense. How would you feel if you walked into a library and were only allowed to choose the books from two shelves marked level R? A reading level is not designed to be a label for a child (Fountas & Pinnell, 2019); rather, it is a guidepost for teachers in the selection of materials and design of instruction.

We caution teachers to not get too focused on one type of instruction (whole or small group). Rather, consider what instructional practices fit the whole class and the best fits for small-group contexts. For example, it often feels as if leveled text is overtaking many of our elementary education classrooms. Interactive read-alouds are not a good fit for leveled texts, and doing so would be a missed opportunity to expose students to a high-quality literature beyond their reading levels. Using whole-group, higher-level, high-quality texts for interactive read-alouds exposes students to new writing styles, vocabulary, and an opportunity to model comprehension at a higher level. Thinking about this section, which of these layers of instruction are best fits for whole-group instruction? Small-group instruction?

HOW DO I BEGIN TO DIFFERENTIATE IN THE REAL-WORLD CLASSROOM?

In this section, we provide four steps for differentiating instruction in the classroom that we have used in our work with schools. These steps are (1) assessment, (2) analysis, (3) grouping and instruction, and (4) progress monitoring for instructional response and regrouping.

Step 1: Assessment

Assessment is the first step in a cycle designed to inform differentiated instruction. As described in Chapter 7 of this volume, assessment can have many different purposes ranging from summarizing the performance of a school or district, to clarifying if a student has met a grade-level criterion, and to screening students to see who might be at risk.

From a differentiation standpoint, diagnostic assessments are particularly critical. A *diagnostic assessment* is one that directly tells a teacher what to teach—both the content and the level. Without a diagnostic assessment, a teacher literally has no roadmap for differentiation. Whereas screenings flag students who may struggle with literacy, diagnostic assessments dig deeper to pinpoint where students have specific literacy needs. Diagnostic assessments help determine the stage of literacy development for each child, as well as strengths and areas of need regarding specific literacy components (fluency, word knowledge, comprehension). Diagnostics may serve to inform both flexible grouping at the Tier 1 classroom level, as well as interventions received in addition to classroom-level instruction.

Start the process of differentiation by identifying the diagnostic assessments that you will use, focusing on the purpose and content of each assessment. In many cases, there is a "buffet plate" full of assessments piled high with redundant measures. Using an assessment inventory helps to determine which assessments are being administered, whom they are benefiting, and if too many different assessments are being used. Figure 11.1 shows one example of an assessment inventory. Added to the inventory could be columns for "Person Who Administers" to determine who is responsible for communicating and collaborating about the results. Use the inventory to identify only the most useful assessments that will reflect where student-learning needs are the most likely to be different. Be aware of where you might be double-dipping.

Because we have so often seen assessment interfere with the purposes of differentiated instruction, we offer two caveats. First, balance the need to assess with instructional urgency. The more time students spend reading, the greater the opportunity to grow and flourish as readers. Assessments must be efficient and useful (ILA, 2018b). Second, recognize that data come in many forms, not always in numbers (e.g., observations, writing samples)

Grade Level	Assessment Name	Frequency of Use	Component of Literacy/Instructional Connection						
			Alphabet Knowledge	Phonemic Awareness	Spelling	Decoding	Fluency	Comprehension	Other:

FIGURE 11.1. Assessment inventory.

(ILA, 2018a). Consider: How many days of literacy instruction will be lost for assessment purposes this grading period? This year? How can this number be reduced to maintain instructional urgency, while gleaning the data needed to engage in differentiated instruction?

Step 2: Analysis of Data and Making Informed Decisions

Data collected by literacy educators are only as good as the analysis, and it is often the part of the process that is shortchanged given time constraints. For the purposes of differentiation, we suggest that teachers analyze their data in a particular way. First, we suggest that they only use three or four pieces of data as they are thinking about differentiation and that they use the pieces of data reflecting the most *difference* among students. There is no point in entering information that is nearly the same for each student. If the data are all the same, then the message is that differentiation is likely *not* needed because either everyone completely knows something, or everyone does not know it.

Tables 11.2 and 11.3 show data from Kristen's class, discussed in detail later in the chapter. These data include an instructional reading level for every student, information about the letters and letter sounds known, and each student's spelling stage. In order to analyze data, we suggest teachers identify a main assessment on which students display the most varied results. Create a list of students in order from those performing highest to lowest on your main assignment (e.g., reading level, spelling stage, phonics screener). This main assessment provides the first data point for forming groups and will provide some degree of sense to multiple pieces of data.

In this example, Table 11.2 orders the students by instructional reading level, and Table 11.3 orders students by spelling stage. The tables and data reflect a number of important points. First, note that the students are not very different with respect to letters and letter sounds. There are a few students at the very lower reading levels who do not know all of their letters and letter sounds, but the majority, letters and letter sounds are completely known. If the teacher used Table 11.2, with the reading levels to form groups, there would be a reasonable distribution of students since the reading levels appear to increase in equal steps. However, if this teacher were to use spelling stage, as shown in Table 11.3, there would be a very large group of students together in the Letter Name stage. By going back and looking at where students are within the stage (early, middle, or late), the spelling stage becomes more useful for identifying necessary instruction.

Our approach to analysis is only one of many approaches. Some schools write students' scores on cards and use those notes as they discuss needs. Our overarching point here is to *not* allow a computer to do that analytical work. Take time to really analyze data carefully.

TABLE 11.2. **Kristen's Classroom Organized by Instructional Reading Level**

Instructional reading level	Student name	Spelling stage (Developmental Spelling Assessment)	Letter–sound knowledge
PPA	Teandra	Emergent	10 letters/8 sounds
PPA	Anita	Emergent	14 letters/10 sounds
PPA	Rachel	Emergent	18 letters/15 sounds
PPA	Kwuan	Letter name	12 letters/11 sounds
PPB	Jarrett	Letter name	22 letters/21 sounds
PPC	Josiah	Letter name	23 letters/22 sounds
PPC	Emilia	Letter name	25 letters/26 sounds
Primer	Taylor	Letter name	26 letters/26 sounds
Primer	Jon	Letter name	26 letters/26 sounds
Primer	Heather	Letter name	26 letters/26 sounds
Primer	Kaitlyn	Letter name	26 letters/26 sounds
Primer	Darrel	Letter name	26 letters/26 sounds
1	Maria	Letter name	26 letters/26 sounds
1	Cal	Letter name	26 letters/26 sounds
1	Emily	Letter name	26 letters/26 sounds
1	Jacobe	Letter name	26 letters/26 sounds
1	Britany	Letter name	26 letters/26 sounds
2	Leandra	Within word	26 letters/26 sounds
2	Tom	Within word	26 letters/26 sounds
2	Divonta	Within word	26 letters/26 sounds
3	Hunter	Within word	26 letters/26 sounds
4	Stephanie	Syllables and affixes	26 letters/26 sounds

Step 3: Grouping and Instruction

After data have been analyzed and organized for students' strengths and areas of need, they may be placed in small groups for differentiated instruction. Such routines and grouping configurations are consistent with the content of ILA Standard 5.4. Typically, teachers create small groups for guided or small-group reading, word study, and possibly even writing groups. As Tables 11.2 and 11.3 illustrate, there are different ways to group students.

One obstacle teachers often encounter is the data-based suggestion of *too many groups,* given the range of abilities in a single classroom. In Table 11.2, if reading level were used strictly, then there would be eight groups!

It is necessary and acceptable to make some compromises in grouping students, and this can be done by considering the additional measures. For example, using Table 11.2 you could form a group of students with a reading level of preprimer A (PPA) because all of these students also need to learn letters and letter sounds. Students in level preprimer B (PPB) through primer are similar because all know their letter/sounds and are in the same spelling stage. A third large group of students reading at the first-grade level would work, and then a fourth group of second- and third-grade-level readers could be formed. Stephanie, the student reading at a fourth-grade level, will need additional resources or grouping (perhaps in other grade groups) to meet her needs.

TABLE 11.3. Kristen's Classroom Organized by Spelling Stage

Spelling stage (Developmental Spelling Assessment)	Student name	Instructional reading level	Letter–sound knowledge
	Teandra	PPA	10 letters/8 sounds
Emergent	Anita	PPA	14 letters/10 sounds
Emergent	Rachel	PPA	18 letters/15 sounds
Letter Name (Early)	Kwuan	PPA	12 letters/11 sounds
Letter Name (Early)	Jarrett	PPB	22 letters/21 sounds
Letter Name (Early)	Josiah	PPC	23 letters/22 sounds
Letter Name (Mid)	Emilia	PPC	25 letters/26 sounds
Letter Name (Mid)	Taylor	Primer	26 letters/26 sounds
Letter Name (Mid)	Jon	Primer	26 letters/26 sounds
Letter Name (Mid)	Heather	Primer	26 letters/26 sounds
Letter Name (Mid)	Kaitlyn	Primer	26 letters/26 sounds
Letter Name (Mid)	Darrel	Primer	26 letters/26 sounds
Letter Name (Late)	Maria	1	26 letters/26 sounds
Letter Name (Late)	Cal	1	26 letters/26 sounds
Letter Name (Late)	Emily	1	26 letters/26 sounds
Letter Name (Late)	Jacobe	1	26 letters/26 sounds
Letter Name (Late)	Britany	1	26 letters/26 sounds
Within Word	Leandra	2	26 letters/26 sounds
Within Word	Tom	2	26 letters/26 sounds
Within Word	Divonta	2	26 letters/26 sounds
Within Word	Hunter	3	26 letters/26 sounds
Syllables and Affixes	Stephanie	4	26 letters/26 sounds

Step 4: Progress Monitoring for Instructional Response and Regrouping

The other important component in differentiation is understanding that groups should be *flexible,* which is why we have Step 4, progress monitoring for instructional response and regrouping. Progress monitoring is a quick assessment, administered frequently, that targets specific content. Whenever a teacher is working with a small group, we suggest that he or she identify a specific progress monitoring measure that matches the focus of the group (e.g., running records, spelling assessments, decoding inventories). We monitor student progress in order to tweak and adjust instruction according to how well students respond to the instruction. Progress monitoring affirms when instruction is meeting the needs of students and lets us know when instruction is not moving students forward. We do not wait until the end of the school year to find out that our instruction has not made a difference. Effective, *beating-the-odds* school research showcases schools that employ regular monitoring of student progress (Taylor et al., 1999).

Importantly, progress monitoring also tells us when students need to change groups. Students may be shifted to better-fit groups whenever a teacher has assessment patterns indicating that students have made progress or have additional needs to be addressed. This assessment can occur within a matter of weeks, rather than waiting until the middle or end of the school year (i.e., instructional urgency). Macro-level restructuring should take place at the beginning of the year, November/December, and then February/March.

COLLABORATION TOWARD DIFFERENTIATED LITERACY INSTRUCTION

Some schools utilize a framework in which one teacher works with a partner for literacy instruction, or where grade-level teams share students for the literacy block. In these contexts, the teacher typically engages students in whole-group instruction to address grade-level material, and then students move into other classrooms for small-group/differentiated work. In these scenarios, the teaching partners and teams typically share their assessment data across the grade and flexibly group students. Grouping this way works exceptionally well in ensuring that students receive appropriate interventions, supports, and opportunities to work with peers at their levels.

The following scenario shows one example of how a first-grade teacher works toward differentiated instruction both before the school year begins and as soon as students enter the classroom.

CASE EXAMPLE ·

THINK ABOUT THIS

1. How does Kristen take initiative in setting up her classroom and selecting her literacy assessments?
2. In what ways do the reading specialist and coach support and collaborate with Kristen?
3. How does Kristen ensure that her literacy block addresses all the components of literacy?

Kristen is a new first-grade teacher who previously taught third grade. Prior to the beginning of the school year, Kristen decides to meet with a reading specialist to figure out what she needs to do to ensure that her language arts block addresses all the components of literacy while also meeting the school, district, and state expectations. Together, Kristen and the reading specialist design a block with the following components: interactive read-aloud, small-group reading, word study, and writing workshop. They determine the assessments that will best inform her student grouping while also informing her instruction. A reading benchmark assessment is selected to find her students' reading levels. Kristen decides to use a developmental spelling inventory, a phonics screening, and a writing prompt to gather information about her students' strengths and weaknesses in literacy.

Within the first 2 weeks of school, Kristen and her reading specialist meet to analyze her data and determine which students may need additional support beyond Tier 1 classroom instruction. In the meantime, Kristen establishes her routines and begins the assessments. At this point in the year, most instruction is whole group so she can review material; in addition, Kristen begins introducing independent literacy stations and provides positive reinforcement for students who are remaining on task. With assessment data in hand (Table 11.2), Kristen meets with the reading specialist to determine students' literacy needs and develop groups for differentiating instruction.

In looking at the data, Kristen is concerned about her most struggling students. The reading specialist provides Kristen with some interventions that will foster students' basic phonics skills. Kristen will use these intervention strategies in her small-group/guided reading time along with leveled text and shared writing. For students who are meeting grade-level expectations, Kristen will work to build their automaticity with high-frequency words, comprehension, and fluency. She will also work on connecting word study to their writing during small group by writing about what they read. Those students performing above level will focus on developing implicit comprehension skills and fluency. They will engage in wide reading with a variety of texts that will also foster vocabulary.

Kristen plans to meet with the reading specialist again in 4 weeks to assess the data she is collecting through her phonics intervention, informal running records, and the writing samples completed during small-group time. Kristen will add the books they use together in small groups to her students' book boxes, so her lower readers have access to text with which they are familiar. The students who are on and above level will have access to texts and be prompted to work on comprehension and fluency skills through interactive read-alouds; they will also have an opportunity to apply implicit comprehension strategies to their independent reading.

Kristen uses a developmental spelling inventory to place her students into differentiated groups and provide small-group instruction a couple of times a week around word sorting. Students also work on their word sorts during their independent station time outside of her mini-lessons. Kristen fosters the bridge between sorting words and writing through small-group writing about reading and during her separate writing workshop time. By separating her students into smaller groups, Kristen is also able to spend additional time focusing on developing the basic phonics skills her below-level students need as well as addressing her above-level students' need to develop understandings of long vowel patterns.

Finally, writing workshop allows Kristen a chance to provide students support in their writing development through mini-lessons and individual or small-groups meetings. This structure allows students to work with their peers to deepen understandings of writing, and to analyze and critique one another. After a few weeks, Kristen realizes that writing is the most difficult area for her to provide support and differentiated instruction because her students are performing on many different levels. Kristen reaches out to her school literacy coach for help in establishing clear routines and a manageable plan for students to confer with peers and her. The literacy coach plans to co-teach a unit on informational text with Kristen, in which she will model management, use of routines, and student conferencing.

CONCLUSION: FUTURE DIRECTIONS FOR DIFFERENTIATION

Fine-tuned research on differentiated instruction in the field of literacy calls for pointed efforts investigating the effects of various structures of differentiation on students' literacy learning. For example, how does the teaching-up approach compare to mini-lessons with small groups to follow? How do various stages of literacy development respond to various forms of differentiation? What are the effects of various forms of differentiated instruction on the learning of various literacy components? For example, does differentiation have a greater effect on improving fluid skills, such as comprehension, compared to finite skills, such as the concept of word?

Differentiated instruction works to meet students where they are at, providing access to content, while concurrently providing what students need to grow as readers. There is a long-standing history of differentiation in our schools, and there is a wide body of research supporting the elements of differentiated instruction. Educators can always grow and learn more.

ENGAGEMENT ACTIVITIES

1. Using Table 11.1, which provides an overview of typical literacy behaviors and goals across the stages, what stages are evident in your classroom? Which assessment is your main tool for decision making? What assessment practices do you have in place to (a) determine the stages in your classroom, (b) determine the components of literacy in which students exhibit strengths and areas of need, and (c) monitor students' progress? Use the assessment inventory to determine where overassessment/double-dipping might be taking place.

2. What grouping structures and routines do you use in your classroom? How do these routines promote independent learning? Collaborative learning? Using the following annotated resources, explore some different ways to group students.

ANNOTATED RESOURCES

International Literacy Association (ILA). (2018a). *Beyond the numbers: Using data for instructional decision making.* Newark, DE: Author.

This leadership brief provides a fresh look at data as a portrait, highlighter, and springboard.

Boushey, G., & Moser, J. (2006). *The daily five: Fostering independence in the elementary grades.* Portland, ME: Stenhouse.

Fountas, I. C., & Pinnell, G. S. (2017). *Guided reading: Responsive reading across the grades.* Portsmouth, NH: Heinemann.

Richardson, J. (2016). *The next step forward in guided reading: An assess–decide–guide framework for supporting every reader: Grades K–8.* New York: Scholastic.

Walpole, S., & McKenna, M. C. (2017). *How to plan differentiated reading instruction: Resources for grades K–3* (2nd ed.). New York: Guilford Press.

Each of the preceding texts provides valuable insight and resources for providing high-quality differentiated small-group instruction using various routines and models.

REFERENCES

Adler, M. A., & Fisher, C. W. (2001). Early reading programs in high-poverty schools: A case study of beating the odds. *The Reading Teacher, 54*(6), 616–619.

Bear, D., Invernizzi, M. A., Templeton, S., & Johnston, F. (2015). *Words their way:*

Word study for phonics, vocabulary and spelling instruction (6th ed.). Essex, UK: Pearson Education.

Birnie, B. F. (2015). Making the case for differentiation. *Clearing House, 88*(2), 62–65.

Booker, K. C., Invernizzi, M. A., & McCormick, M. (2007). "Kiss your brain": A closer look at flourishing literacy gains in impoverished elementary schools. *Reading Research and Instruction, 46*(4), 315–339.

Boushey, G., & Moser, J. (2006). *The daily five: Fostering independence in the elementary grades.* Portland, ME: Stenhouse.

Calkins, L., & Tolan, K. (2010). *A guide to the reading workshop, grades 3–5.* Portsmouth, NH: First Hand/Heinemann.

Cambourne, B. (2001). What do I do with the rest of the class?: The nature of teaching–learning activities. *Language Arts, 79*(2), 124–135.

Chall, J. S. (1983). *Stages of reading development.* New York: McGraw-Hill.

Clay, M. (1998). *By different paths to common outcomes.* York, ME: Stenhouse.

Connor, C. M. (2011). Child by instruction interactions: Language and literacy connections. In S. B. Neuman & D. K. Dickinson (Eds.), *Handbook on early literacy research* (3rd ed., pp. 256–275). New York: Guilford Press.

Cunningham, P. M., Hall, D. P., & Defee, M. (1998). Nonability-grouped, multilevel instruction: Eight years later. *The Reading Teacher, 51*(8), 652–664.

Diller, D. (2003). *Literacy work stations: Making centers work.* York, ME: Stenhouse.

Edmonds, R. (1979). Effective schools for the urban poor. *Educational Leadership, 37,* 15–27.

Fountas, I. C., & Pinnell, G. S. (2017). *Guided reading: Responsive teaching across the grades* (2nd ed.). Portsmouth, NH: Heinemann.

Fountas, I. C., & Pinnell, G. S. (2019). Level books, not children: The role of text levels in literacy instruction. *Literacy Today, 36*(4), 12–13.

Hall, T., Strangman, N., & Meyer, A. (2003). *Differentiated instruction and implications for UDL implementation.* Wakefield, MA: National Center on Accessing the General Curriculum.

Henderson, E. H. (1981). *Learning to read and spell: The child's knowledge of words.* DeKalb: Northern Illinois Press.

Hoffman, J. V. (1991). Teacher and school effects in learning to read. In R. Barr, M. L. Kamil, P. B. Mosenthal, & P. D. Pearson (Eds.), *Handbook of reading research* (Vol. 2, pp. 911–950). New York: Longman.

International Literacy Association (ILA). (2018a). *Beyond the numbers: Using data for instructional decision making.* Newark, DE: Author.

International Literacy Association (ILA). (2018b). *Standards for the preparation of literacy professionals 2017.* Newark, DE: Author.

International Reading Association. (2010). *Response to intervention: Guiding principles for educators.* Newark, DE: Author.

Kelley, M., & Clausen-Grace, N. (2006). R5: The sustained silent reading makeover that transformed readers. *The Reading Teacher, 60*(2), 148–156.

Langer, J. A. (2001). Beating the odds: Teaching middle and high school students to read and write well. *American Educational Research Journal, 38*(4), 837–880.

Mathes, P. G., Denton, C. A., Fletcher, J. M., Anthony, J. L., Francis, D. J., & Schatschneider, C. (2005). The effects of theoretically different instruction and student characteristics on the skills of struggling readers. *Reading Research Quarterly, 40*(2), 148–183.

Miller, D., & Moss, B. (2013). *No more independent reading without support (not this, but that).* Portsmouth, NH: Heinemann.

National Reading Panel. (2000). *Teaching children to read: An evidence-based assessment of the scientific research literature on reading and its implications for reading instruction: Reports of the subgroups.* Washington, DC: National Institute of Child Health and Human Development.

Pressley, M. (1998). *Reading instruction that works: The case for balanced teaching.* New York: Guilford Press.

Richardson, J. (2016). *The next step forward in guided reading: An assess–decide–guide framework for supporting every reader: Grades K–8.* New York: Scholastic.

Shanahan, T. (2004, November). *How do you raise reading achievement?* Paper presented at the Utah Council of the International Reading Association meeting, Salt Lake City, UT.

Taylor, B. M., Pearson, P. D., Clark, K. F., & Walpole, S. (1999). *Beating the odds in teaching all children to read* (R305R70004). Ann Arbor, MI: Center for the Improvement of Early Reading Achievement.

Tomlinson, C. A. (2000). Reconcilably different?: Standards-based teaching and differentiation. *Education Leadership, 58*(1), 6–11.

Tomlinson, C. A. (2001). *Differentiation of instruction in the elementary grades.* Champaign, IL: ERIC Clearinghouse on Elementary and Early Childhood Education.

Tomlinson, C. A. (2014). *The differentiated classroom: Responding to the needs of all learners.* Arlington, VA: Association of Supervision and Curriculum Development.

Tomlinson, C. A. (2015). *Effective differentiation: A guide for teachers and leaders* (Regional Educational Laboratory Mid-Atlantic Educator Effectiveness Webinar Series). Calverton, MD: ICF International.

Tomlinson, C. A., & Allan, S. D. (2000). *Leadership for differentiating schools and classrooms.* Alexandria, VA: Association for Supervision and Curriculum Development.

Vygotsky, L. S. (1978). *Mind in society: The development of higher psychological processes,* Cambridge, MA: Harvard University Press.

Walpole, S., & McKenna, M. C. (2017). *How to plan differentiated reading instruction: Resources for grades K–3* (2nd ed.). New York: Guilford Press.

Watts-Taffe, S., Laster, B. P., Broach, L., Marinak, B., McDonald Connor, C., & Walker-Dalhouse, D. (2012). Differentiated instruction: Making informed teacher decisions. *The Reading Teacher, 66*(4), 303–314.

Weber, G. (1971). *Inner city children can be taught to read: Four successful schools* (CGE Occasional papers No. 18). Washington, DC: Council for Basic Education.

Literacy Leadership in Action

Sheri Vasinda, EdD

University Professor, Oklahoma State University,
Stillwater, Oklahoma

THINK ABOUT THIS

1. In what ways does Sheri serve as a literacy leader?
2. What lessons can be learned about the leadership role of a university faculty member?
3. What questions come to mind while reading this vignette?

As a former K–12 district literacy leader, I have always been passionate about supporting striving readers and writers. As a university literacy leader, I still am. As a teacher educator, I support readers and writers indirectly by preparing their teachers. Over the past decade, my work has included purposeful use of technology tools to mediate traditional reading and writing processes, providing new entry points for student success. The guiding question that influences the practices I model and promote is, How do we make literacy accessible to all learners? As a literacy leader, this question is still central to my work as I prepare teachers to support the variabilities of all learners while understanding typically developing readers and writers.

Preparing new teachers by modeling effective processes and practices of foundational knowledge of reading and writing is at the core of my work as a teacher educator. I also support teachers' implementation of these practices in our reading clinic, where they each work with a student from the community near the university. This clinic also serves as a lab in which we consider new ways to implement effective literacy strategies. Future teachers and reading specialists learn to administer and interpret comprehensive assessments that identify their students' strengths and needs. Then they plan and implement both effective evidence-based practices and new promising practices to support student needs. Our teacher candidates explore literacy teaching as researchers, problem solvers, and designers, and I serve as an experienced mentor.

As a university literacy coach, I engage with teachers in problem-solving cycles to find creative and innovative ways to help them achieve their goals. These school-based partnerships provide valuable opportunities to work together in a spirit of reciprocity to address current literacy challenges and goals. Together, we collaborate in thinking of new possibilities for strengthening practices with a shared goal of better access to literacy for students.

To extend the reach of the university, I advocated for and led the effort to collaboratively develop an online master's program for practicing teachers in any corner of our rural state, or beyond. Just as with any program or school-wide change, I collaborated and engaged in a problem-solving model with my peers to facilitate this undertaking. Through partnerships with other universities, we have learned together and created a dynamic hybrid type of online program.

This exciting new territory is rich with possibilities. I now pair digital tools with effective engagement strategies to supervise clinical practica, form small study groups across geographically distant professionals, or provide more options for supportive coaching groups. For example, pairing Harvard's Visible Thinking routines with new digital tools amplifies the effects of both. Using reflective video to support clinical supervision of practica provides greater depth and insight into promising practices and goal setting that was not possible in face-to-face contexts. Using VoiceThread (online learning tool) and structured protocols provides opportunities for literacy leader candidates to analyze student work or case studies in small groups that provide a more democratic space for all to be heard. My colleagues and I could not have imagined many of these formats, tools, and "classroom" spaces even a dozen years ago. As I continue to focus on my guiding question of access to literacy for all learners and extend it to literacy education practices, the university continues to be a place of possibilities.

CHAPTER 12

Fostering Effective Writing Instruction across the Grades

Sarah J. McCarthey
Carrie L. James

GUIDING QUESTIONS

➥ What are current instructional practices in writing in K–12 classrooms? What are teachers' and students' attitudes about writing and
how do these attitudes influence writing instruction?

➥ What approaches are most promising to improve writing instruction
and in what ways are they aligned with *Standards for the Preparation
of Literacy Professionals 2017* (International Literacy Association
[ILA], 2018)?

➥ How might we foster student growth as writers through effective
feedback and assessment practices? How might we foster this growth
through the use of technology?

➥ How might professional learning enhance the quality of writing
instruction?

As teachers grapple with implementing the Common Core State Standards
(CCSS; National Governors Association Center for Best Practices & Council of Chief State School Officers, 2010) or their own state standards across
grade levels, they have to consider attitudes toward writing and the state of
current writing practices as they seek ways to foster student growth. Additionally, teachers seek to understand what professional learning resources
are available to them as they implement high-quality writing instruction.
The ILA's *Standards 2017* provides a literacy framework by which we

address writing and provide guidance as to what is important for teachers to know and be able to do to improve writing instruction in their classrooms.

CURRENT STATE OF WRITING PRACTICES: FOUNDATIONAL KNOWLEDGE

For teachers to have a deep grasp of writing practices, they need to understand current writing instruction, teachers' attitudes toward writing, and students' attitudes about writing. With attention to current and best practices, teachers can select appropriate approaches to writing, consider feedback about writing, and understand how technology fits into instruction.

Writing Instruction

The CCSS offered a means to rethink the ways that writing was taught in K–12 classrooms; as Applebee (2013) articulated, they offered both "promise and perils." Promises included higher expectations for writing across disciplines, whereas perils consisted of an overemphasis on informational genres, composing in a linear manner, a disregard for developmental writing, and potential risks of high-stakes testing. Despite the lack of consistency in implementation of the CCSS in K–12 schools, several patterns have emerged: the lack of extended writing on a frequent basis, mundane writing tasks, on-demand writing to prepare for high-stakes tests, and teachers feeling underprepared to teach writing.

Using the National Assessment of Educational Progress (NAEP) writing assessment data for 35 years, Applebee and Langer (2009) identified trends in writing instruction and achievement in secondary schools. In 2007, fewer than 32% of students were identified as "proficient"; however, there were significant gains from the previous years in writing at grades 8 and 12. Students reported making changes in their writing to address errors, but rarely wrote more than one draft. Teachers did not see state assessments as valid measures of students' abilities and believed that preparing for assessments consumed too much instructional time. Applebee and Langer (2011) found that in middle schools, little writing of extended texts took place across the curriculum, and external exams shaped teachers' writing practices. Surveying 285 middle school teachers, Graham and colleagues (Graham, Gillespie, & McKeown, 2013; Graham, Capizzi, Harris, Hebert, & Morphy, 2014) found that language arts teachers provided more opportunities for writing than social studies or science teachers. However, the average amount of time devoted to writing daily ranged from a mere 2 to 11 minutes. Language arts teachers reported using evidence-based practices, but often sparingly. In his synthesis of the major studies surveying current writing instruction in secondary schools, Sundeen (2015) found the following trends: students were writing infrequently; tasks consisted primarily of note taking, short answers, and summaries rather than lengthy essays or stories; exams shaped teaching with a preponderance of on-demand writing occurring in a single setting; and teachers reported little preparation to teach writing.

Researchers conducting smaller-scale studies have documented similar patterns. Lawrence, Galloway, Yim, and Lin's (2013) study of writing tasks showed that students were asked to write in many genres but were provided little scaffolding or opportunities to practice. Brimi's (2012) interviews with teachers found that there was much emphasis on teaching the five-paragraph essay; the teachers valued writing as a process, but there were few examples of planning, drafting or publishing texts.

Might there be more writing opportunities with teachers providing explicit instruction in elementary than in secondary schools? In their national survey of third- and fourth-grade teachers' classroom practices in writing, Brindle, Graham, Harris, and Hebert (2015) found that teachers spent only 15 minutes a day teaching writing, students spent only 25 minutes a day writing, and teachers reported using evidence-based writing practices, but infrequently. What these findings signal is that across the K–12 spectrum, little time is spent on writing instruction, and researchers generally are calling for this to change.

Testing has had a major influence on teachers' writing instruction as the result of the implementation of No Child Left Behind (No Child Left Behind [NCLB], 2002). McCarthey (2008) found that teachers in high-income schools had fewer constraints on their writing curriculum, whereas teachers in low-income schools had little control over writing curriculum, had low morale, and felt pressure to raise test scores. Yet, the CCSS intended to create common standards and lessen differences between schools in different income areas. Comparing six elementary schools with above-performance and six schools with typical performance after implementation of the CCSS, Wilcox, Jeffrey, and Gardner-Bixler (2016) found that teachers were using evidence-based practices, including prewriting/planning, drafting cycles, peer collaboration, rubrics, and writing to learn. Data suggested that teachers used modules developed by the state, resulting in higher expectations for writing; however, typically performing schools reported a loss of creative writing and independent thinking in students resulting from scripted lessons. It is clear that most teachers are experiencing constraints from testing; nevertheless, students in higher-performing schools have access to more evidence-based practices. However, it is incumbent for teachers who will be leaders in teaching writing to consider how to implement evidence-based practices in all schools.

Teacher Attitudes

One of the reasons teachers may have resisted implementing evidence-based practices and maintained traditional instruction is the lack of preparation, and hence, a lack of confidence about teaching writing. Although the CCSS are intended to shed a renewed light on the importance of writing instruction, many university teacher education programs focus more on strategies for teaching reading than for writing; they often embed writing methods within a general course on literacy rather than having a specific course dedicated to writing (Hall, 2016). It is no wonder, then, that many teachers feel underprepared to teach writing, have a negative or indifferent view of writing, and feel less than confident as writers themselves (Bausch, 2010; Cremin & Baker, 2010; Gardner, 2014; Harward et al., 2014). Carrie (second author) surveyed her students early in the writing methods course to ask about their confidence levels in teaching students to be strategic writers. Here are some of their responses:

- "I feel I'm not as creative as I'd like to be, so I wouldn't be able to give students much guidance."
- "I need to become an intentional strategic writer first."
- "Not very confident yet, and I think that's because I do not believe that I am a strategic writer."
- "I'm just not really a confident writer."
- "I don't feel confident in creating strategic writers because I don't know if I am one myself."

These self-efficacy issues impact teachers' instructional practices regarding writing. Harward and colleagues (2014) examined the reasons K–6 teachers engaged (or not) in writing practices with their students. They found that teachers who had low self-efficacy were less likely to engage their students in writing activities and practices. Low implementers were more likely to focus on the mechanics of writing over content, less likely to differentiate, less able to recognize strategies to help alleviate hindrances (e.g., lack of time, diversity of students), and did not have (or recognize) mentors that could guide them. High implementers (and those with higher self-efficacy), on the other hand, recognized many ways to work around those hindrances, scaffolded writing instruction, implemented writing daily, and ultimately enjoyed teaching writing. Brindle and colleagues (2015) found that teachers who were better prepared and more positive about teaching writing were more likely to spend time teaching writing and use evidence-based practices than others. Teachers' lack of feeling prepared to teach writing is reflected in a study conducted by Myers and colleagues (2016) that found that 37% of surveyed teachers expressed feeling a lack of confidence because they were not required or offered a writing methods course in their teacher preparation program.

In addition to self-efficacy, context plays a major role in teachers' attitudes and beliefs about writing. McCarthey and Mkhize (2013) interviewed 29 third- and fourth-grade teachers, who worked either in high-income or low-income schools, about their beliefs and practices. They found that teachers who worked at high-income schools attended to rhetorical choices, voice, and connections between reading and writing; they also referred to a wide variety of programs or materials that shaped their instructional practice. In contrast, teachers at low-income schools who aligned with a "correct writing" mindset focused on skills such as grammar, mechanics and correct sentence structure, and relied on mandated programs and basal materials. Differences in teachers' beliefs were shaped by the environment where they taught, including the program and materials at their disposal and the impact of high-stakes assessments. Low-income schools, in particular, were impacted by the shadow of high-stakes testing, and teachers felt the pressure to help their students be successful, leading to the focus on correctness. This focus, unfortunately, leads to curriculum that does not allow students to experience authentic, rich writing opportunities.

It is important for literacy leaders to know that meaningful professional learning can impact teachers' sense of self-efficacy and their consideration of contextual factors. Hall and Grisham-Brown (2011) found that preservice teachers' attitudes about writing changed as they participated in writing projects. Publishing or sharing their writing and engaging with "creative opportunities and process-oriented teaching strategies" led to more positive views of themselves as writers and writing teachers. Hall (2016) noted that focusing on writing methods that include reflective practices and specific instructional practices help teachers to see the importance of writing and self-efficacy. Gardner (2014) found similar results when teachers participated in a teacher-as-writer experience; teachers shifted their attitudes about writing from a predominantly negative view to a more positive perception. Graham et al. (2013) sum up why it is important to change teachers' attitudes. They argue that if teachers know why writing is important and gain a sense of self-efficacy in their own writing abilities, then they are more likely to invest energy and time to learn how to teach writing.

Student Attitudes

It should come as no surprise that students' attitudes about writing mirror those of most teachers. Erdogan and Erdogan (2013) found that although many elementary students (fifth graders) created positive metaphors to describe their attitudes toward writing, about one in seven students described writing as "boring," "tiring," or "horrible." In her study of 10- to 13-year-olds, Ryan (2014) found that the majority of her student participants (16 out of 24) were "school writers." These 16 students did not write outside of school, saw it as a mandate rather than a benefit, and lacked engagement in writing because of these views. These same students, while being able to talk the talk of writing, lacked effective qualities in their texts. On the other end of the spectrum, reflexive writers loved to write, wrote for their own purposes outside of school in addition to school writing, and made many strategic choices in their writing resulting in more effective texts. Graham, Berninger, and Fan (2007) found a statistically significant link between students' attitudes about writing and the impact of those attitudes on writing achievement in first and third graders. They went so far as to hypothesize that these links strengthen and become bidirectional in older grades as students' sense of self-efficacy is impacted by their writing achievement.

It is important, then, that teachers and literacy leaders find early opportunities to develop strategies to support students in shifting their attitudes about writing. Hawthorne (2008) examined the differences between highly engaged and less engaged high school students to explore their reasons for engaging (or not) in writing activities. She found that students' interest in a topic and the topic's relevance to their lives played the most significant role in student engagement, regardless of ability. Reluctant writers were also heavily influenced by their impressions of the teacher as helpful or not, their own self-efficacy as writers, and whether they felt knowledgeable. Hawthorne suggests that teachers examine these reasons and create shifts in their practice that include more choice and relevance in the types of writing required, scaffolding learning so that students feel knowledgeable in their writing, and fostering a safe place that nurtures writers.

A focus on content rather than conventions is essential in the teaching of writing. Wolsey, Lapp, and Fisher (2012) found that students in high school tended to focus more on "local operations" of writing, such as grammar, mechanics, and usage, as well as structural or formatting concerns. This focus differed from what teachers expected when it comes to academic writing: content and digging deeply into their writing by synthesizing ideas. What accounted for the discrepancy? In part, they found that teachers focused their early instruction on the local operations for engaging students as a bridge to the richness of academic writing. Students didn't make that connection. The researchers made the case for explicit modeling of academic writing to help students make that shift.

There is some evidence, though, that instructional practices can influence students positively in shifting their emphases. Seban and Tavsanli (2015) explored elementary students' identity construction through writers' workshop practices and demonstrated that many students made the shift away from local operations. Most students, whether high or low achieving, made connections between reading and writing. Struggling writers recognized the role of personal abilities and hard work on writing success, as well as participating in writing activities like those in the writers' workshop. Therefore, literacy leaders can help foster writing instruction that allows struggling writers to make these connections as well. Implementing evidence-based practices can address the needs of all students, including struggling writers as they develop skills, strategies, and more positive attitudes towards writing.

CURRICULUM AND INSTRUCTION

What are evidence-based practices? *Standards 2017* addresses teachers' writing needs from multiple lenses: foundational knowledge, curriculum and instruction, assessment, motivation, and use of digital tools. In this section, we focus on curriculum and instruction while embedding some of the other concepts included in *Standards 2017*. What does effective curriculum and instruction in writing look like? Following an extensive review of evidence-based practice and writing instruction across grade levels, Graham and Harris (2016) made several recommendations for teachers. First, they argue that engaging students in more writing (45 minutes daily) for different purposes and audiences increases achievement. Second, they point out that writing to comprehend and learn, including note taking, summarizing, and making arguments, helps students understand the value of writing. Third, teachers need to provide pleasant and motivating environments for writing; classrooms should support opportunities for writing that connect to students' interests, establish classroom routines, and deliver feedback to individual students. Teachers' roles include facilitating student writing by setting goals, generating ideas, and encouraging students to collaborate. Explicitly teaching students skills—such as handwriting, spelling, and typing as well as strategies such as planning, revising, and editing—is also critical. Finally, they argue that students need to use 21st-century technology in the service of writing, such as making writing easier by using word-processing programs.

The findings from studies of effective teachers of writing have aligned well with the practices identified by Graham and Harris (2016). For example, Parr and Limbrick (2010) found that effective teachers of writing have explicit learning aims, align those aims with writing activities, use deliberate teaching, provide feedback, and establish a supportive classroom environment. Zumbrunn and Krause (2012) discovered that writing experts (e.g., Flowers, Hillocks, Newkirk, Smagorinsky) understand the impact of teachers' beliefs about the value of writing on their own practices; teachers need to encourage student motivation, plan for daily writing instruction, and scaffold students' writing. Studies taking up one or more of these practices have found positive results. Corden (2007) found that reading, discussing, and evaluating mentor texts improved children's narratives. Flanagan and Bouck (2015) demonstrated how concept mapping can lead to higher-quality writing, especially in terms of cohesion and the inclusion of relevant ideas. Teacher modeling and writing collaboratively were effective in Read, Landon-Hays, and Martin Rivas's (2014) study with first graders; journal writing with teacher support allowed children to gain authority and write meaningful texts.

Classroom practices and teachers' attitudes toward writing are rooted in teachers' epistemological and ideological views of writing (Ivanic, 2004). Identifying instructional approaches and locating effective practices within them have the potential to assist teachers in working with leaders to challenge current practices and promote innovative writing instruction in PreK–12 classrooms.

Instructional Approaches

In their study of writing instruction across four states, McCarthey and Ro (2011) identified four instructional approaches: writer's workshop (process), traditional skills, genre-specific, and hybrid/eclectic. *Writer's workshop* included allowing students to select their own topics and a format of mini-lesson, writing time, conferences, and sharing. *Traditional skills* focused on grammar and punctuation using mandated programs, whereas a focus on narrative, expository, or descriptive writing with specific, teacher-led prompts characterized the genre approach. *Hybrid* included teachers drawing from many sources without a specific focus. Each approach had strengths and weaknesses, yet effective strategies were embedded within the process and genre approaches more intentionally than in traditional or hybrid practices. The following example from Martha's classroom demonstrates a writing workshop in a third-grade classroom.

CASE EXAMPLE •

THINK ABOUT THIS

1. In what ways does this classroom teacher demonstrate effective writing instruction?

2. How can this teacher's example be implemented in your school?

Students were seated on the carpet for the mini-lesson on introductions or "leads." Martha began by reading aloud a section of Judy Blume's (1972) *Tales of a Fourth Grade Nothing* and asked students to discuss the lead in the chapter. Two students provided the leads they used for their narratives on the previous day. Martha told students before they returned to their desks, "If you have not tried to make an interesting lead, try to do a catchy one, get your reader interested." She then took the "status of the class," asking each student to announce what he or she was working on. As students worked on their narratives (either fictional or personal narratives), she walked around the room and held individual conferences with students, asking them questions about their topics, indicating where they might add details, or providing suggestions about punctuation. After about 15 minutes of writing time, students came back to the circle to share. Each student read aloud a part of the written text and both the teacher and students make comments about it. The teacher's comments included "I like how she has a repeated pattern about her character" and "I like the humor." She also asked questions such as "Where did you get the idea of using letters in the story?" and "Did this happen or was it a dream?" Martha made suggestions such as "You might want to add a part between the two dreams."

During the workshop, the teacher focused on a particular writer's craft of using effective leads by starting with a mentor text. Students selected their own topics and the teacher facilitated their narrative writing through individual conferences. Students had opportunities to share their writing and get feedback by reading aloud their texts. Martha was an experienced teacher who had used workshop methods for several years; she gained confidence in teaching writing by participating in professional development sessions and was supported by both the principal and her colleagues.

• • • • • • • • • • •

The writing workshop reflects the process approach (Bazerman, 2016; Beach, Newell, & VanDerHeide, 2016), focusing on writing for an audience and the author's craft. Laman (2011) studied fourth graders in a writing workshop structure and the functions of their talk during writing conferences, author celebrations, and author sharing. Students' talk helped create a shared learning space, developed meta-awareness of processes and practices, and built writing identities. Dunn and Finley (2010) found that using storytelling and the visual arts helped to encourage struggling students to write narratives. Hovan (2012) used writing groups in middle schools to help students consider audience. In their observational study of 15 classrooms, Jesson and Rosedale (2016) focused on how teachers can facilitate voice, especially cultivating students' textual histories.

Current research on process writing approaches has looked to bestselling authors to understand how their practices might translate to classroom practices. Sampson, Ortlieb, and Leung (2016) found that successful writers maintain flexibility in content and voice, and they do not progress in a linear fashion through prewriting, drafting, and revision. This suggests that teachers may be too rigid when implementing a workshop approach. In her comparative study of three approaches with young children—writing workshop (e.g., mini-lesson, conferences, sharing), interactive writing (e.g., teacher-led whole class using the shared pen and co-constructing texts), and control group using prompts—Jones (2015) found distinct advantages of the writing workshop and the interactive writing over the control group. She then identified the features of these effective classrooms, including teacher explanations with think-alouds and modeling, using the writing process, and establishing a community of learners. Based on these studies, we argue that teachers need to have a fundamental understanding of the principles behind the approaches and the alignment of practices to approaches to become effective, reflective writing teachers.

Graham, McKeown, Kiuhara, and Harris (2012) concur that, as a result of a series of intervention studies on effective instructional strategies, teachers need to be reflective. Additionally, other scholars have identified the benefits of explicit teaching through strategy instruction, as Table 12.1 demonstrates.

FEEDBACK AND ASSESSMENT PRACTICES

"As American schools implement the Common Core Standards Initiative . . . teachers have braced themselves for higher expectations . . . by clearly articulated skill sets that their students must demonstrate at various stages" (DelleBovi, 2012, p. 273). With new attention on writing from the CCSS and other state standards, there is even more attention on teachers' feedback and assessment practices, specifically, which ones support students' growth and development as writers. A key question for literacy leaders, then, is how to support teachers in developing effective feedback and assessment practices.

What makes writing good? This is a question that Nauman, Stirling, and Borthwick (2011) address when they argue that teachers should question and critique literacy experts' views of what makes writing good (e.g., Lucy Calkins, Nancie Atwell, Jim Burke). Nauman and colleagues remind us that what is defined as good writing is constantly in flux. In their survey, they found that teachers valued writing that illustrated good thinking and communication; in essence, good writing was seen as interpersonal. Teachers also saw good writing as being structured, with a clear purpose conveyed through voice and correctness of writing. Most disagreed with the current emphasis on good writing as an economy of words or light on adjective and adverb use.

Many teacher education programs do not focus on assessing writing, according to both DelleBovi (2012) and Dempsey, PytlikZillig, and Bruning (2009). They argue for the importance of providing teachers with practical ways to develop effective feedback and assessment practices. For example, DelleBovi (2012) engaged students in developing criteria-based (analytic) assessment rubrics for writing assignments. These rubrics clearly articulated assigned goals and purposes for a writing task. She found that

TABLE 12.1. Summary of Research-Based Strategy Instruction

Authors (year)	Strategies researched	Instructional implications
Tracy, Graham, & Reid (2009)	Researched impact of general and genre-specific strategies for writing narratives using SRSD.	Students using these strategies effectively write longer, stronger narratives and maintain these strategies over time. Some strategies transfer to new tasks.
Mason, Harris, & Graham (2011)	Explored SRSD and its impact on students with writing difficulties, including students with learning disabilities.	Students improved in what they wrote, as well as how they wrote and perceived the writing process.
Hacker et al. (2015)	Examined short-term and maintenance effects of SRSD on argumentative writing. Strategies included topic sentence development, using supporting details, constructing counterclaims, and concluding.	Students who self-regulated their use of strategies were more likely to maintain these skills over time. Students were able to transfer learning to new tasks.
Idalgo, Torrance, & Garcia (2009)	They explored CSRI through a scaffolded approach that taught students to use cognitive strategies for planning, drafting, and revising their writing.	Students in the CSRI condition spent more time planning, produced better texts, and had fewer negative statements about their abilities as writers.
Koster, Tribushinina, De Jong, & van den Bergh (2015)	They conducted a meta-analysis of the writing intervention studies to examine the impact writing intervention strategies have on students.	Students most benefited from goal setting and strategy instruction, text structure instruction, feedback, and peer assistance. They did not benefit from grammar instruction.

Note. CSRI, cognitive self-regulation instruction; SRSD, self-regulated strategy development.

when preservice teachers used these rubrics, they more effectively assessed student writing. Additionally, by engaging in learning about writing assessment, preservice teachers better understood practices associated with assessing students' writing. Dempsey et al. (2009) supported teachers' writing assessment skills through an online platform where they participated in learning and practicing their assessment skills with authentic student work. Teachers were able to see how experts graded the text as well as how their peers assessed it, thereby helping to develop their own self-efficacy in assessment. These two studies highlight the need for literacy leaders to support teachers in learning about writing assessment and fostering self-efficacy in giving feedback and assessing writing.

In establishing professional learning that supports teachers in their feedback and assessment practices, literacy leaders can highlight best practices that foster students' writing development. For example, in Carrie's (second author) former high school classroom, students often engaged in peer and self-assessment during their writing process using 21st-century technology tools.

CASE EXAMPLE •

THINK ABOUT THIS

1. How does a digital platform support effective feedback and assessment practices?

2. How can you encourage teachers to use digital spaces for composing and assessing?

Students huddled in front of laptop computers composing and revising texts using Google Docs. They were able to ask for and receive feedback on their work more easily than in more traditional ways. Through a few taps of the keyboard, a peer could access the document, suggest changes, and ask questions or provide feedback using the comments feature. When a student wanted feedback or had a question, Carrie would jump into the document so they could collaborate on the writing or engage in a conversation. By using the Google Classroom platform, students also could check for task expectations and complete self-evaluations. In the end, students uploaded their final projects and submitted them through the Google Classroom platform, saving paper and time collecting hard copies. Carrie was then able to use the "version history" to explore how the students' texts changed over time.

Using this digital platform for feedback and assessment allowed for more student interaction such as choosing multiple peers to provide feedback. The digital platform saves all feedback automatically, allowing for easy access later. It also allows the teacher to get a sense of each child's writing process so that more than just the final product is assessed.

• • • • • • • • • • • • •

One key aspect in the above example is that students received feedback during the writing process (formative) rather than at the end (summative). By giving them feedback during the process, students have the ability to act on the feedback within their current writing task. Research evidence supports the benefit of using feedback as part of formative assessment rather than summative. Baxa (2015) focused on fifth graders' use of self-assessment during their writing process to argue for a shift toward using rubrics as a formative assessment tool while students are still writing. These fifth graders were able to use a rubric to self-assess their writing, which enhanced their reflective thinking about their writing, their ability to talk about strengths and weaknesses, and ultimately supported their revision practices. Boon (2016) found that elementary students made good use of feedback if they had the time to discuss it and act on suggestions they received from others. Graham, Hebert, and Harris (2015) found that feedback during the process provides positive results in students' writing skills and strategy use regardless of where the feedback is coming from (e.g., teacher, self, peer, or computer).

Graham et al. (2015) remind us there are many ways to provide feedback and ultimately assess students' writing. Peterson and McClay (2010) established that the fourth- through eighth-grade teachers they surveyed valued feedback as critical for developing students' writer identities and self-efficacy. The challenge, particularly for middle school and high school teachers, is finding the time to provide teacher feedback to all students during the writing process. Peer feedback and self-assessment practices can help to alleviate these pressures and are backed by research as well. Early and Saidy (2014) engaged high school students in a multiple-component feedback approach to revision workshop where they provided direct instruction on how to assess writing by using model texts. Students then engaged in self-assessment and peer-feedback sessions. Students shifted their view of revision from focusing on surface issues (e.g., grammar and mechanics) to more substantive issues (e.g., content and organization). Self and peer feedback also helped students see themselves as writers. Loretto, DeMartino, and Godley (2016) suggested that sometimes peer feedback works best when it is anonymous, particularly in older grades where students might want to save face. High school students valued receiving feedback from multiple people, but struggled with how to respond to conflicting feedback, suggesting that part of engaging students in feedback practices is that we need to teach them how to assess, make sense of, and respond to feedback.

Hawe and Dixon (2014) go even further by arguing that it is imperative that students engage fully in the assessment process. By learning about the assessment process, including examining assignment criteria, students will develop autonomy and self-regulation strategies. When students evaluate their own and others' work during the process, they develop abilities to make judgments about their writing. Perhaps this is why both Lundstrom and Baker (2009) and Crinon (2012) found that those students who reviewed peers' work made more improvements in their own writing than those students who only received feedback. In Crinon's study, elementary students gained a deeper understanding of genre and the ability to self-reflect on their own writing based on their need to provide advice and suggestions to peers.

Another key element of successful writing assessment is allowing students to have input in the writing criteria used to assess their writing. Andrade, Du, and Wang (2008) found that if they engaged third and fourth graders in generating criteria based on a model text, students were better able to use that rubric for self-assessment. This then led students to produce more effective writing. Andrade, Du, and Mycek (2010) found the same to be true for middle school students when they replicated these activities of establishing criteria with a model. By engaging students in rubric creation or even talking through the criteria early in the process, it might be possible to avoid what Varner, Roscoe, and McNamara (2013) called misalignment between how teachers and students view an assignment's criteria. They found that students tended to focus more on surface features, whereas teachers valued more text features and complexity. They argued for student involvement in understanding the systematic criteria used to evaluate writing.

DIGITAL SPACES FOR DIGITAL TEXTS

The students currently in our classrooms have often been described as *digital natives*. While Martin and Lambert's (2015) study demonstrates the complications of labeling all students this way, clearly literacy practices have expanded into digital spaces and the creation of digital and multimodal compositions. As literacy leaders, we can take steps to both support our literacy teachers in fostering collaborative digital spaces and our students in taking up multimodal composing practices successfully.

Martin and Lambert (2015) argue that not all students are digital natives, instead falling into one of three categories: digital passenger, digital navigator, and digital driver. The *digital passenger* does not frequently consume digital texts, needs support to use technology, and has only minimally engaged in digital text creation. He or she is most likely to create digital texts that resemble paper-based texts. *Digital navigators* use technology more frequently, but struggle with digital text creation, particularly project management. These students stay safe when it comes to digital text creation. Finally, *digital drivers* highly engage in both digital text consumption and creation; they navigate digital composition (e.g., posting on and designing websites or creating videos) with ease. Martin and Lambert argue that their findings demonstrate how important it is that literacy teachers differentiate their instruction so that all three types of digital users develop familiarity with digital tools, genres, and interactional conventions (e.g., how different modes support each other). They suggest surveying students at the start of the year to get a sense of the skills and experiences they bring to the table.

Just like our students, many of our literacy teachers are digital users (see Chapter 13, this volume). Research shows, however, that teachers are reluctant to bring digital composing practices into their classrooms. Traditional literacy values get in the way, as some studies show, causing both teachers and students to not always view digital writing as "real writing" (Dredger, Woods, Beach, & Sagstetter, 2010; Edwards-Groves, 2011; Pytash, Testa, & Nigh, 2015). This perspective frequently leads to teachers' use of technology to support print-based text creation. For instance, Peterson and McClay (2012) interviewed 216 fourth- through eighth-grade teachers about the use of digital tools in their classrooms, later observing 21 of them. They found that teachers viewed computers as a tool to extend and support mini-lessons for themselves but allowed students to use the computers only when they were making a "good copy" or for Internet research. Similarly, Dredger et al. (2010) make the case for bringing in Web 2.0 practices to build on existing uses for computers in classrooms: word processing and PowerPoint creation. "Web 2.0 consists of tools that allow students to find and publish to authentic audiences, communicate with experts and enthusiasts, collaborate with geographically distant peers, and to make their place in the world, are yet to be widely-accepted as educationally-beneficial" (p. 85). Literacy leaders can support their colleagues as they explore Web 2.0 environments and develop ways of bringing these spaces into the classroom. Pytash et al. (2015) encourage teachers to engage in their own creation of digital texts, thereby getting both a sense of how they can bring these ideas into the classroom as well as how best to support their students in creating texts. These lived experiences, fostered by literacy leaders, can help teachers see that digital spaces can foster writing habits and digital writing communities.

A good first step in fostering Web 2.0 environments is exploring specific digital texts through the lens of mentor texts (Werderich, Manderino, & Godinez, 2017). In their study, Godinez—a seventh-grade literacy teacher—reflected on her own digital creation, a digital memoir, and explored the effects of the various modes (i.e., visual, linguistic, aural, gestural, spatial) she used to compose it. By treating a digital text as a mentor text, students and teachers can discuss which modalities they noticed being used, the affordances and limitations of each of these modes, and the features that are associated with each mode (i.e., color, size, or composition in a visual element). They can also consider other digital texts that informed this mentor text or how this text might inform future compositions. Finally, students can collaborate and envision ways to integrate a multimodal format into their own composing projects. All of these experiences can take place in digital spaces.

Creating digital spaces, typically cloud-based ones such as Google Docs or Wiki sites, fosters a collaborative environment that can support students' digital abilities and help them grow as composers of digital texts. Nobles and Paganucci (2015) surveyed high school students about their perceptions of using digital writing spaces and tools compared to traditional pen and paper. Not surprisingly, students saw their writing as stronger, in part due to digital platforms providing more opportunities for feedback from authentic audiences. Other studies (Pifarré & Fisher, 2011; Yim, Warschauer, Zheng, & Lawrence, 2014) show that cloud-based platforms allow students to engage in digital composing and can facilitate peer collaboration, the development of revision strategies, and an expansion of their experiences with the composing process. Mills and Exley (2014) found that these spaces also foster a distributed expertise, where expertise about construction and digital spaces is diffused throughout the participants in the classroom. They reported that students spent more time on task in digital spaces as opposed to traditional pen and paper settings. Finally, digital spaces expand learning beyond the four walls of the classroom, as illustrated in the following example in which eighth graders use the online learning environment Scholar, developed at the University of Illinois at Urbana–Champaign, to compose and respond to texts.

Mrs. M, an eighth-grade English language arts teacher, logs onto Scholar (*https://cgscholar.com*) to post her assignment with the directions to create an informative/explanatory text about "an ordinary person who has led an extraordinary life." She writes the goals, which include learning about the qualities of ordinary people who have led extraordinary lives as well as the structure and language features of informative/explanatory writing. She adds directions for the writing process, including drafting, getting feedback from peers, and revising their work before publication. She also provides questions about qualities of ordinary people to prompt their thinking, a rubric to guide their writing, and a model text about Dr. Hawa Abdi, a Somalian obstetrician, lawyer, and human rights activist. Orally, she encourages them to add multimedia to their texts and to use the structure feature of Scholar to organize their writing. When students complete their drafts, they respond to their peers' texts using the annotation tool and commenting feature with the rubric as a guide. Once they have received their comments, students have the opportunity to revise their texts several times before submitting it to "publisher." The teacher uses the analytics function to track where students are in the writing process, the amount of revision performed, and the peers' ratings.

This example shows the intersection of several innovative practices: students using an online environment capable of showcasing multimodality as well as peers providing feedback to one another. When students engage with digital spaces, including but not limited to Scholar, they develop almost a designer or composer mindset, expanding the writing process beyond traditional, linear text creation. Edwards-Groves (2011) provided inservice teachers with strategies to support students' digital composing in elementary school settings. In addition to supporting teachers in creating collaborative digital spaces, Edwards-Groves encouraged teachers to teach design principles that would enhance students' digital text creation, thereby broadening the writing process to include a multimodality approach. "Retheorizing writing in new times demands that pedagogical practices and understandings incorporate 'designing,' 'producing' and 'presenting' as key elements of the writing process. . . . These new dimensions of writing and text construction need to sit beside 'planning,' 'drafting,' 'editing,' 'redrafting' and 'proofreading'" (p. 62). These ideas have much in common with a multiliteracies pedagogy (Kalantzis, Cope, Chan, & Dalley-Trim, 2016) that fosters students' abilities to apply concepts about digital texts to create their own.

So far, we have argued that digital spaces and digital composing support all students in developing their authorial stance through collaboration that fosters revision, addressing authentic audiences that gives their writing real purpose, and using skills and strategies for composing across modes. This is particularly true for students who are non-native English speakers. Several studies (e.g., Brown, 2016; Lenters & Winters, 2013; Smythe & Neufeld, 2010) point to the benefits of multimodal composing. It allows students to communicate their conceptual understandings using modes that are not language-based. It has also been found to help them develop literacy skills in their new language.

PROFESSIONAL LEARNING AND LEADERSHIP

How might teachers become more knowledgeable about best practices for teaching writing and implementing innovative instruction in their classrooms? In particular, because preservice teachers are not receiving sufficient exposure to theories, approaches, and methods of teaching writing, inservice teachers should be provided with ongoing opportunities to gain expertise by engaging in professional learning activities. The models discussed next come from McCarthey and Geoghegan's (2016) review of professional learning in writing. The intervention studies align with the self-regulated strategies development (SRSD) model by using similar strategies with teachers and students. The professional networks, learning communities, and coaching models embrace collaboration among teachers to develop distributed leadership (see Chapter 1, this volume).

Intervention Studies

Intervention studies linking professional learning to teacher change and/ or student learning are relatively rare; however, both experimental and multimethodological studies have indicated the positive impact of such efforts. Interventions have also been conducted across multiple sites and within a single school. Olson and her colleagues (Olson & Land, 2007; Olson et al., 2012) began the Pathway project, providing teachers with a set of curricular materials and exposing them to a set of cognitive strategies with English learners (ELs). After participating in professional learning, the key factors in teachers' success with students were setting high expectations, providing exposure to a rigorous curriculum, and explicit teaching of strategies. Harris and her colleagues (2012) conducted a study with 20 second- and third-grade teachers from rural schools, providing them and their students with 2 days of intensive professional learning in SRSD, using explicit, interactive strategies for story writing and opinion essays. Both teachers and students found the intervention to be helpful, and students in the SRSD group produced higher-quality texts than other groups. Conducting a mixed multimethods design over 1 school year, Troia, Lin, Cohen, and Monroe (2011) investigated six teachers' knowledge, beliefs, and practices about writing instruction. They found that teachers used critical workshop elements, including daily workshop time, student-centered assignments, and teacher modeling and feedback. The studies show how focusing on particular strategies or methods of writing can have a positive effect on teachers' instruction.

Professional Networks, Learning Communities, and Online Professional Development

Two nationally recognized sites for professional learning operate as networks for teachers to learn more about the teaching of writing: the National Writing Project (NWP) and the Reading & Writing Project at Teachers College, Columbia University. These networks engage teachers in active learning through writing and demonstrations (NWP), employ summer institutes with follow-up activities for sustained engagement with colleagues, link teacher and student learning, and connect teachers to their colleagues through professional learning communities. Across quasi-experimental and qualitative studies it is clear that the NWP has had a major impact on teachers' philosophies of writing; willingness to take on leadership roles; and sense of self-efficacy, agency, and autonomy. Students in classrooms of NWP teachers have shown strong performance on writing assessments, and the data support the process approach to writing embedded within the network models (Lieberman & Friedrich, 2007; Whitney & Friedrich, 2013).

Professional learning communities (PLCs) consist of a group of individuals who work toward a shared goal, hold themselves accountable for the goal, assess their progress, and make connections to practice (Hargreaves, 1992; Lieberman & Miller, 2011; McLaughlin & Talbert, 2010). The small-scale, mostly qualitative investigations have demonstrated that PLCs provide opportunities for collaboration, inquiry, and conversations about students, curriculum, and policies related to writing (Pella, 2011). PLCs have an impact on teachers' self-efficacy, can increase awareness of research-based practices, and help teachers solve problems (Curry, 2008).

Online professional learning is becoming increasingly more important, particularly to address the needs of rural teachers (Hunt-Barron, Kaminski, Howell, & Tracy, 2013). It affords teachers opportunities to work on their own time *and* to communicate with and learn from peers (Beach, 2012). As noted previously, the NWP has developed online summer institutes, and the National Council of Teachers of English provides extensive resources through readwritethink (*www.readwritethink.org*) and many opportunities for webinars. Online resources, especially blogs and Google resources, can link teachers to one another through professional networks and may be especially valuable as follow-up to face-to-face interactions.

CONCLUSION AND RECOMMENDATIONS

To communicate effectively in the 21st century, students need effective writing strategies and composing practices. Literacy leaders can help facilitate students' writing development by supporting teachers as they:

- Engage students in authentic writing activities more frequently through effective instructional practices, including using the writing process and employing explicit strategy instruction.
- Support students in developing their writing identities, strengthen their writing abilities, and engage more fully in writing tasks by increasing the amount of time spent on in-class writing.
- Develop effective assessment and feedback practices, including student self-assessment, peer feedback, and teacher–student conferences.
- Foster multimodal composing practices, digital composing spaces, and generally engaging students in 21st-century composing practices.

By interacting with the research-based practices outlined in this chapter, teachers are primed to facilitate students' self-efficacy and foster lifelong writing habits.

ENGAGEMENT ACTIVITIES

1. Discuss with peers how these instructional practices support literacy teachers in fostering their ability to "design, implement, and evaluate" writing instruction that meets the needs of all learners. How do the ideas in this chapter help teachers "create classrooms and schools that are inclusive and affirming"? How can we learn from what researchers have found in terms of helping our students understand the assessment process?

2. One of the main concerns highlighted at the start of this chapter is how little time students engage in writing throughout their school day. Brainstorm and develop an action plan to foster more composing time within and across disciplinary classes. In your action plan, consider the type of writing instruction you want to incorporate, including feedback and assessment practices, digital composing opportunities, and how you will support teachers in feeling prepared for this shift.

ANNOTATED RESOURCES

Elementary School Journal, 115(4) (June 2015)

This special issue of the *Elementary School Journal* focuses on writing and the CCSS. It includes an article we reference here by Steve Graham, Michael Hebert, and Karen R. Harris that outlines formative assessment practices for writing. There are many other great articles that serve as excellent resources for exploring how to navigate writing instruction after the implementation of the CCSS.

MacArthur, C. A., Graham, S., & Fitzgerald, J. (Eds.). (2016). *Handbook of writing research* (2nd ed.). New York: Guilford Press.

Edited by Charles MacArthur, Steve Graham, and Jill Fitzgerald, this cornerstone text compiles and synthesizes current research in writing instruction across all grade levels. Experts in the field explore many aspects of writing instruction, including sociocultural, cognitive, linguistic, neuroscience, and new literacy/technological perspectives. Several of the chapters have been cited in this paper and can be a key tool in supporting individuals' development as teachers of writing.

The National Writing Project (and local chapters)

The NWP's mission is to support the development of knowledge, expertise, and leadership of teachers in their efforts to improve writing and writing instruction. Their vision is to help all students become effective communicators through writing. The organization "envisions a future where every person is an accomplished writer, engaged learner, and active participant in a digital, interconnected world." To check it out, visit *www.nwp.org.*

REFERENCES

Andrade, H. L., Du, Y., & Mycek, K. (2010). Rubric-referenced self-assessment and middle school students' writing. *Assessment in Education: Principles, Policy and Practice, 17*(2), 199–214.

Andrade, H. L., Du, Y., & Wang, X. (2008). Putting rubrics to the test: The effect of a model, criteria generation, and rubric-referenced self-assessment on elementary school students' writing. *Educational Measurement, 27*(2), 3–13.

Applebee, A. N. (2013). Common Core State Standards: The promise and the peril in a national palimpsest. *English Journal, 103*(1), 25–33.

Applebee, A. N., & Langer, J. A. (2009). What is happening in the teaching of writing? *English Journal, 98*(5), 18–28.

Applebee, A. N., & Langer, J. (2011). A snapshot of writing instruction in middle schools and high schools. *English Journal, 100*(6), 14–27.

Bausch, L. S. (2010). The power of teachers' writing stories: Exploring multiple layers of reflective inquiry in writing process education. *Journal of Language and Literacy Education, 6*(1), 20–39.

Baxa, S. (2015). Enhancing students' understanding and revision of narrative writing through self-assessment and dialogue: A qualitative multi-case study. *Qualitative Report, 20,* 1682–1708.

Bazerman, C. (2016). What do sociocultural studies of writing tell us about learning to write? In C. A. MacArthur, S. Graham, & J. Fitzgerald (Eds.), *Handbook of writing research* (2nd ed., pp. 11–23). New York: Guilford Press.

Beach, R. (2012). Can online learning communities foster professional development? *Language Arts, 89*(4), 256–262.

Beach, R., Newell, G. E., & VanDerHeide, J. (2016). A sociocultural perspective on writing development: Toward an agenda for classroom research on students' use of social practices. In C. A. MacArthur, S. Graham, & J. Fitzgerald (Eds.), *Handbook of writing research* (2nd ed., pp. 88–101). New York: Guilford Press.

Blume, J. (1972). *Tales of a fourth grade nothing.* New York: Dutton.

Boon, S. I. (2016). Increasing the uptake of peer feedback in primary school writing: Findings from an action research enquiry. *Education 3–13, 44*(2), 212–225.

Brimi, H. (2012). Teaching writing in the shadow of standardized writing assessment: An exploratory study. *American Secondary Education, 41*(1), 52–77.

Brindle, M., Graham, S., Harris, K. R., & Hebert, M. (2015). Third and fourth grade teachers' classroom practices in writing: A national survey. *Reading and Writing, 29,* 929–954.

Brown, S. (2016). E-journaling in response to digital texts. In L. C. de Oliveira & T. Silva (Eds.), *Second language writing in elementary classrooms* (pp. 13–32). New York: Palgrave.

Corden, R. (2007). Developing reading–writing connections: The impact of explicit instruction of literary devices on the quality of children's narrative writing. *Journal of Research in Childhood Education, 21*(3), 269–289.

Cremin, T., & Baker, S. (2010). Exploring teacher-writer identities in the classroom: Conceptualising the struggle. *English Teaching: Practice and Critique, 9*(3), 8–25.

Crinon, J. (2012). The dynamics of writing and peer review at primary school. *Journal of Writing Research, 4*(2), 121–154.

Curry, M. (2008). Critical friends groups: The possibilities and limitations embedded in teacher professional communities aimed at instructional improvement and school reform. *Teachers College Record, 110,* 733–774.

DelleBovi, B. M. (2012). Literacy instruction: From assignment to assessment. *Assessing Writing, 17,* 271–292.

Dempsey, M. S., PytlikZillig, L. M., & Bruning, R. H. (2009). Helping preservice teachers learn to assess writing: Practice and feedback in a Web-based environment. *Assessing Writing, 14*(1), 38–61.

Dredger, K., Woods, D., Beach, C., & Sagstetter, V. (2010). Engage me: Using new literacies to create third space classrooms that engage student writers. *Journal of Media Literacy Education, 2*(2), 85–101.

Dunn, M. W., & Finley, S. (2010). Children's struggles with the writing process: Exploring storytelling, visual arts, and keyboarding to promote narrative story writing. *Multicultural Education, 18*(1), 33–42.

Early, J. S., & Saidy, C. (2014). Uncovering substance: Teaching revision in high school classrooms. *Journal of Adolescent and Adult Literacy, 58,* 209–218.

Edwards-Groves, C. J. (2011). The multimodal writing process: Changing practices in contemporary classrooms. *Language and Education, 25*(1), 49–64.

Erdogan, T., & Erdogan, O. (2013). A metaphor analysis of the fifth grade students' perceptions about writing. *The Asia–Pacific Education Researcher, 22*, 347–355.

Flanagan, S. M., & Bouck, E. C. (2015). Mapping out the details: Supporting struggling writers' written expression with concept mapping. *Alternative Education for Children and Youth, 59*, 244–252.

Gardner, P. (2014). Becoming a teacher of writing: Primary student teachers reviewing their relationship with writing. *English in Education, 48*, 128–148.

Graham, S., Berninger, V., & Fan, W. (2007). The structural relationship between writing attitude and writing achievement in first and third grade students. *Contemporary Educational Psychology, 32*(3), 516–536.

Graham, S., Capizzi, A., Harris, K. R., Hebert, M., & Morphy, P. (2014). Teaching writing to middle school students: A national survey. *Reading and Writing, 27*, 1015–1042.

Graham, S., Gillespie, A., & McKeown, D. (2013). Writing: Importance, development, and instruction. *Reading and Writing, 26*, 1–15.

Graham, S., & Harris, K. R. (2016). A path to better writing: Evidence-based practices in the classroom. *The Reading Teacher, 69*(4), 359–365.

Graham, S., Hebert, M., & Harris, K. R. (2015). Formative assessment and writing. *Elementary School Journal, 115*, 523–547.

Graham, S., McKeown, D., Kiuhara, S., & Harris, K. R. (2012). A meta-analysis of writing instruction for students in the elementary grades. *Journal of Educational Psychology, 104*(4), 879–896.

Hacker, D. J., Dole, J., Ferguson, M., Adamson, S., Roundy, L., & Scarpulla, L. (2015). The short-term and maintenance effects of self-regulated strategy development in writing for middle school students. *Reading and Writing Quarterly, 31*, 351–372.

Hall, A. H. (2016). Examining shifts in preservice teachers' beliefs and attitudes toward writing instruction. *Journal of Early Childhood Teacher Education, 37*(2), 142–156.

Hall, A. H., & Grisham-Brown, J. (2011). Writing development over time: Examining preservice teachers' attitudes and beliefs about writing. *Journal of Early Childhood Teacher Education, 32*(2), 148–158.

Hargreaves, A. (1992). Cultures of teaching: A focus for change. In A. Hargreaves & M. B. Fullan (Eds.), *Understanding teacher development* (pp. 216–236). New York: Teachers College Press.

Harris, K. R., Lane, K. L., Graham, S., Driscoll, S. A., Sandmel, K., Brindel, M., et al. (2012). Practice-based professional development for self-regulated strategies development in writing: A randomized controlled study. *Journal of Teacher Education, 63*(2), 103–119.

Harward, S., Peterson, N., Korth, B., Wimmer, J., Wilcox, B., Morrison, T., et al. (2014). Writing instruction in elementary classrooms: Why teachers engage or do not engage students in writing. *Literacy Research and Instruction, 53*, 205–224.

Hawe, E. M., & Dixon, H. R. (2014). Building students' evaluative and productive expertise in the writing classroom. *Assessing Writing, 19*, 66–79.

Hawthorne, S. (2008). Students' beliefs about barriers to engagement with writing in secondary school English: A focus group study. *Australian Journal of Language and Literacy, 31*(1), 30–42.

Hovan, G. (2012). Writing for a built-in audience: Writing groups in the middle school classroom. *Voices from the Middle, 20*(2), 49–53.

Hunt-Barron, S., Kaminski, R., Howell, E., & Tracy, K. (2013, December). *Conquering the divide: Infusing new literacies into professional development for the Common Core Standards.* Paper presented at the Literacy Research Association, Dallas, TX.

Idalgo, R., Torrance, M., & Garcia, J. N. (2009). The long-term effects of strategy focused writing instruction for grade six students. *Contemporary Educational Psychology, 33*(4), 672–693.

International Literacy Association (ILA). (2018). *Standards for the preparation of literacy professionals 2017.* Newark, DE: Author.

Ivanic, R. (2004). Discourses of writing and learning to write. *Language and Education, 18*(3), 220–245.

Jesson, R., & Rosedale, N. (2016). How teachers might open dialogic spaces in writing instruction. *International Journal of Educational Research, 80,* 164–176.

Jones, C. D. O. (2015). Effects of writing instruction on kindergarten students' writing achievement: An experimental study. *Journal of Educational Research, 108,* 35–44.

Kalantzis, M., Cope, B., Chan, E., & Dalley-Trim, L. (2016). *Literacies.* Port Melbourne, Australia: Cambridge University Press.

Koster, M. P., Tribushinina, E., De Jong, P., & van den Bergh, H. H. (2015). Teaching children to write: A meta-analysis of writing intervention research. *Journal of Writing Research, 7,* 299–324.

Laman, T. T. (2011). The functions of talk within a 4th-grade writing workshop: Insights into understanding. *Journal of Research in Childhood Education, 25*(2), 133–144.

Lawrence, J. F., Galloway, E. P., Yim, S., & Lin, A. (2013). Learning to write in middle school? *Journal of Adolescent and Adult Literacy, 57,* 151–161.

Lenters, K., & Winters, K.-L. (2013). Fracturing writing spaces. *The Reading Teacher, 67*(3), 227–237.

Lieberman, A., & Friedrich, L. (2007). Teachers, writers, leaders. *Educational Leadership, 65*(1), 42–47.

Lieberman, A., & Miller, L. (2011). Learning communities: The starting point for professional learning is in schools and classrooms. *Journal of Staff Development, 32*(4), 16–20.

Loretto, A., DeMartino, S., & Godley, A. (2016). Secondary students' perceptions of peer review of writing. *Research in the Teaching of English, 51*(2), 134–161.

Lundstrom, K., & Baker, W. (2009). To give is better than to receive: The benefits of peer review to the reviewer's own writing. *Journal of Second Language Writing, 18,* 30–43.

Martin, N. M., & Lambert, C. (2015). Differentiating digital writing instruction. *Journal of Adolescent and Adult Literacy, 59,* 217–227.

Mason, L. H., Harris, K. R., & Graham, S. (2011). Self-regulated strategy development for students with writing difficulties. *Theory into Practice, 50,* 20–27.

McCarthey, S. J. (2008). The impact of No Child Left Behind on teachers' writing instruction. *Written Communication, 25*(4), 462–505.

McCarthey, S. J., & Geoghegan, C. M. (2016). The role of professional development for enhancing writing instruction. In C. A. MacArthur, S. Graham, & J. Fitzgerald (Eds.), *Handbook of writing research* (2nd ed., pp. 330–345). New York: Guilford Press.

McCarthey, S. J., & Mkhize, D. (2013). Teachers' orientations towards writing. *Journal of Writing Research, 5*(1), 1–33.

McCarthey, S. J., & Ro, Y. S. (2011). Approaches to writing instruction. *Pedagogies: An International Journal, 6*(4), 273–295.

McLaughlin, M. W., & Talbert, J. E. (2010). Professional learning communities: Building blocks for school culture and student learning. *Voices in Urban Education, 27,* 35–45.

Mills, K. A., & Exley, B. (2014). Time, space and text in the elementary school digital writing classroom. *Written Communication, 31,* 434–469.

Myers, J., Scales, R. Q., Grisham, D. L., Wolsey, T. D., Dismuke, S., Smetana, L., et al. (2016). What about writing?: A national exploratory study of writing instruction in teacher preparation programs. *Literacy Research and Instruction, 55,* 309–330.

National Governors Association Center for Best Practices & Council of Chief State School Officers. (2010). *Common Core Standards for English language arts and literacy in history/social studies, science, and technical subjects.* Washington, DC: Authors.

Nauman, A. D., Stirling, T., & Borthwick, A. (2011). What makes writing good?: An essential question for teachers. *The Reading Teacher, 64*(5), 318–328.

No Child Left Behind Act of 2001, P.L. 107-110, 20 U.S.C. § 6319 (2002).

Nobles, S., & Paganucci, L. (2015). Do digital writing tools deliver?: Student perceptions of writing quality using digital tools and online writing environments. *Computers and Composition, 38,* 16–31.

Olson, C. B., Kim, J. S., Scarcella, R., Kramer, J., Pearson, M., van Dyk, D., et al. (2012). Enhancing the interpretive reading and analytical writing of mainstreamed English learners in secondary school: Results from a randomized field trial using a cognitive strategies approach. *American Educational Research Journal, 49*(2), 323–355.

Olson, C. B., & Land, R. (2007). A cognitive strategies approach to reading and writing instruction for English language learners in secondary school. *Research in the Teaching of English, 41*(3), 269–303.

Parr, J. M., & Limbrick, L. (2010). Contextualising practice: Hallmarks of effective teachers of writing. *Teaching and Teacher Education, 26*(3), 583–590.

Pella, S. (2011). A situative perspective on developing writing pedagogy in a teacher professional learning community. *Teacher Education Quarterly, 38*(1), 107–125.

Peterson, S. S., & McClay, J. (2010). Assessing and providing feedback for student writing in Canadian classrooms. *Assessing Writing, 15*(2), 86–99.

Peterson, S. S., & McClay, J. K. (2012). Assumptions and practices in using digital technologies to teach writing in middle-level classrooms across Canada. *Literacy, 46*(3), 140–146.

Pifarré, M., & Fisher, R. (2011). Breaking up the writing process: How wikis can support understanding the composition and revision strategies of young writers. *Language and Education, 25*(5), 451–466.

Pytash, K. E., Testa, E., & Nigh, J. (2015). Writing the world: Preservice teachers' perceptions of 21st century writing instruction. *Teaching/Writing, 4*(1), 142–163.

Read, S., Landon-Hays, M., & Martin Rivas, A. (2014). Gradually releasing responsibility to students writing persuasive text. *The Reading Teacher, 67,* 469–477.

Ryan, M. (2014). Writers as performers: Developing reflexive and creative writing identities. *English Teaching: Practice and Critique, 13*(3), 130–148.

Sampson, M. R., Ortlieb, E., & Leung, C. B. (2016). Rethinking the writing process: What bestselling and award-winning authors have to say. *Journal of Adolescent and Adult Literacy, 60,* 265–274.

Seban, D., & Tavsanli, Ö. F. (2015). Children's sense of being a writer: Identity construction in second grade writers workshop. *International Electronic Journal of Elementary Education, 7*, 217–234.

Smythe, S., & Neufeld, P. (2010). "Podcast time": Negotiating digital literacies and communities of learning in a middle years ELL classroom. *Journal of Adolescent and Adult Literacy, 53*(6), 488–496.

Sundeen, T. H. (2015). Writing instruction for adolescents in the shadow of the Common Core State Standards. *Journal of Adolescent and Adult Literacy, 59*, 197–206.

Tracy, B., Graham, S., & Reid, R. (2009). Teaching young students strategies for planning and drafting stories: The impact of self-regulated strategy development. *Journal of Educational Research, 102*(5), 323–332.

Troia, G. A., Lin, C. S., Cohen, S., & Monroe, B. W. (2011). A year in the writing workshop: Linking instructional practices and teachers' epistemologies and beliefs about writing instruction. *Elementary School Journal, 112*(1), 155–182.

Varner, L. K., Roscoe, R. D., & McNamara, D. S. (2013). Evaluative misalignment of 10th-grade student and teacher criteria for essay quality: An automated textual analysis. *Journal of Writing Research, 5*(1), 35–59.

Werderich, D. E., Manderino, M., & Godinez, G. (2017). Leveraging digital mentor texts to write like a digital writer. *Journal of Adolescent and Adult Literacy, 60*, 537–546.

Whitney, A. E., & Friedrich, L. (2013). Orientations for the teaching of writing: A legacy of the National Writing Project. *Teachers College Record, 115*, 1–37.

Wilcox, K. C., Jeffery, J. V., & Gardner-Bixler, A. (2016). Writing to the Common Core: Teachers' responses to changes in standards and assessments for writing in elementary schools. *Reading and Writing, 29*, 903–928.

Wolsey, T. D., Lapp, D., & Fisher, D. (2012). Students' and teachers' perceptions: An inquiry into academic writing. *Journal of Adolescent and Adult Literacy, 55*(8), 714–724.

Yim, S., Warschauer, M., Zheng, B., & Lawrence, J. F. (2014). Cloud-based collaborative writing and the Common Core standards. *Journal of Adolescent & Adult Literacy, 58*, 243–254.

Zumbrunn, S., & Krause, K. (2012). Conversations with leaders: Principles of effective writing instruction. *The Reading Teacher, 65*(5), 346–353.

Literacy Leadership in Action

Mellinee Lesley, PhD
Professor and Associate Dean, Texas Tech University,
Lubbock, Texas

THINK ABOUT THIS

1. In what ways does Mellinee serve as a literacy leader?
2. What lessons can be learned about the role of university faculty?
3. What questions come to mind while reading this vignette?

For the past 4 years, I have served as a "literacy champion" at an underperforming high school in the Southwestern United States. This work was funded through a large-scale community-based Department of Education grant. The term *literacy champion* was coined by the Director of Literacy for this local school district to represent a nonthreatening and positive collaboration with a university. This role grew out of a school–university partnership where I was asked to help implement a writing workshop approach with English teachers in the high school in order to increase students' writing skills. Each year in my role, I worked with different classroom teachers and the English language arts and reading (ELAR) instructional coach. Over the years, my role has evolved from a consultant to the leader of an engaged research project. My presence in the school started on the periphery of curriculum with several writing enrichment activities, but through ongoing collaboration has blossomed into a position where I have been entrusted with providing evaluative feedback.

The greatest success of my work has been the extent to which I have nurtured collaboration at the school while attending to multiple stakeholders. My work is intermingled with learning from high school students, reflecting with teachers, collaborating with the instructional coach, meeting with campus and district leadership, and guiding graduate students. Currently, I am helping the instructional coach study the implementation of a process approach to writing instruction and the effects it has on student writing achievement. I am also studying the cultivation of teacher leaders through this work.

On my first day in Ms. Jenkins's ninth-grade English class, I sat in the back of the room and watched students slowly organize notebooks, backpacks, tissues, and pencils. As I waited for the lesson to begin, a pastiche of students and staff stumbled through the morning announcements. Although they did not ask many questions about what I was doing in the classroom, students quickly became used to my presence. They responded to my questions and asked me for assistance with various literacy tasks. I was assigned to work with Ms. Jenkins to help her integrate a process approach to writing instruction with ninth-grade students who had failed, or almost failed, the previous year's state mandated exam in ELA, but our work together quickly became much more complicated.

When the class ended, Ms. Jenkins and I gathered artifacts of student writing from the day's lesson and compared notes. We scoured student writing for evidence of growth and read excerpts to one another that delighted and terrified us. I asked about the instructional decisions she made and how she planned to modify the lesson for the next class. We talked about critical literacy, student engagement, annotation, and building students' stamina. We worried about students who were living without electricity. We problem-solved about students who provoked tears in other students. In tandem to this classroom support, I also worked with the instructional coach, carefully sharing insights about the importance of feedback in writing and teaching revision. Through persistence, we forged a relationship and a shared set of goals.

Some of the key ingredients to this partnership are embedded within attributes such as patience, flexibility, and communication. These traits are essential in fostering collaboration with multiple stakeholders. Teacher leaders must value collaborative learning and empowering peers to be successful. Teacher leaders must also understand that improvement in instruction is a lifelong pursuit that requires continuous learning. Teacher leaders must model what learning together looks like for other professionals in the school. These are ideals I strive for on a daily basis as a literacy champion.

CHAPTER 13

Literacy and Leadership in the Digital Age

Jill Castek
Carolyn B. Gwinn

GUIDING QUESTIONS

↪ How is the widespread use of technologies shifting and expanding notions of literacy and how must our instruction be reconceptualized to address this broader notion of literacy?

↪ In what ways are new technologies transforming how we teach reading, writing, and communication in PreK–12 classrooms?

↪ In what ways do the Common Core State Standards for English Language Arts (National Governors Association Center for Best Practices & Council of Chief State School Officers [NGA & CCSSO], 2010) and the *Standards for the Preparation of Literacy Professionals 2017* (International Literacy Association [ILA], 2018a) create new opportunities for teaching literacy using the Internet and new technologies?

↪ How can professional learning efforts help cultivate literacy leaders who address digital literacies and online reading comprehension instruction?

SHIFTING AND EXPANDING NOTIONS OF LITERACY

The use of digital technologies has grown rapidly in the United States, with nearly 89% of adults reporting that they own or use smartphones, Internet, computers, social media, and tablets (Hitlan, 2018). The four elements of literacy (reading, writing, listening, and speaking) are no longer enough to navigate complex online interfaces, access reliable information resources, network with learners and colleagues, and design and create digitally in multiple forms.

The Internet has become increasingly central to our daily lives and is changing the way we read, interact, teach, and learn. The emergence of new technologies and the rapid shift in literacy practices from page to screen require literacy leaders to think differently about the ways that literacy is taught and practiced in school classrooms (National Council of Teachers of English, 2018).

In today's world, digital devices are an important means of accessing and sharing information through online networks. *Digital devices* include computers, tablets, and smartphones. To use these digital devices to navigate online resources requires literacies that involve critical evaluation of online information. Learners must examine the texts they consume, produce, and distribute online for bias and commercial interests. The American Library Association refers to digital literacies as "the ability to find, evaluate, create, and communicate information, requiring both cognitive and technical skills" (American Library Association, 2013, p. 2). Digital literacies represent the multitude of ways people collaborate, create, and communicate using digital texts and tools. These literacies are multiple and encompass the socially mediated ways of generating and interpreting online content through multiple modes (e.g., video, audio, still and moving images, sounds, gestures, performances) (ILA Literacy Glossary, n.d.) These literacies are necessary to engage in all aspects of life in a digital age. They are needed to access a range of information resources, interact globally, and participate in a variety of learning events.

Many educators are expanding literacy contexts for instruction to include digital texts, tools, and networks. Digital texts incorporate features such as the ability to scan or search within a document, highlight text, copy sections to save them elsewhere, or to click on a link that brings one to another text. Digital tools aid readers in interacting with digital texts and each other by offering visual and collaborative potentials for idea creation and sharing. Networks expand learning beyond the four walls of the classroom and connect learners across contexts and continents. Digital tools, texts, and networks can be used to support students with learning challenges because they offer flexible accommodations and personalization opportunities (e.g., making print larger for vision impairments, offering audio support to aid reading, text-to-speech and speech-to-text functionality). They create open spaces to participate in more authentic literacies than ever before, as learners of all ages develop the mindsets and competencies needed to make choices, interact, and engage in a networked society that is constantly changing in the face of new innovations (Phillips & Manderino, 2015).

Today's students have spent their lives surrounded by technology—using computers, playing online games, listening to digital music, sharing YouTube videos, social networking on sites like Facebook, and texting on smartphones. They have grown up in a networked world in which texts are multimodal, interactive, and socially distributed (Coiro, Knobel, Lankshear, & Leu, 2008). As a result of ubiquitous interactions with new technologies, Prensky (2001) suggests that young people's online immersion has made this generation of "digital natives" think and process information differently.

Although students are skilled with social networking, texting, video, and music downloads, most students are less skilled with online information use, including locating and critically evaluating information (Leu, O'Byrne, Zawilinski, McVerry, & Everett-Cocapardo, 2009). Digital literacies and learning with technologies require skills and strategies that are complex, and in some cases unique, to online reading and writing contexts (Coiro & Dobler, 2007).

While some might conceptualize the use of new technologies in classrooms as a natural outgrowth of the use of technology in our daily lives, few school stakeholders (e.g., teachers, administrators) are knowledgeable about how to guide students in developing online reading skills and strategies in today's networked world. We need to cultivate leaders who understand the profound changes taking place in literacy and its ripple effect on educational settings spanning preschool to grades K–12 and beyond (ILA, 2018a).

This chapter is designed to inform literacy leaders about ways to expand literacy teaching and learning and inspire educators to make the most of the Internet, digital texts, and tools in their literacy and content-area instruction. We begin by introducing a case example that illustrates the dynamic, creative, and innovative ways teachers are using the Internet to support new forms of reading comprehension in today's networked world. Next, we discuss how new technologies are redefining literacy, ways that technology use creates motivation for literacy learning, and essential strategies involved in online reading comprehension. Finally, we suggest ways to cultivate literacy leaders who support online reading comprehension and offer suggestions for implementation.

As teachers come in contact with new ideas, and as illustrated in Mrs. Rodriguez's example that follows, they move across a developmental continuum as they progress in their thoughts and actions regarding the implementation of digital literacies and online reading. More specifically, continuum stages include (1) *adoption,* with technology used to support traditional instruction; (2) *adaptation,* with technology embedded within current classroom practices; (3) *appropriation,* with strengths of technology capitalized on as new instructional approaches are used; and (4) *innovation,* with technology used in new ways. It is critically important to recognize that all levels of change take time and support to take hold. Educators begin their journeys at various points on the continuum and travel across it at varying paces. Research suggests it takes time and ongoing support for teachers to move from novices to experts who support students' digital literacies acquisition and learning (Cennamo, Ross, & Ertmer, 2009; McKenney & Visscher, 2019). Likewise, the process of school-level change is one that takes time and coordination across all levels of the school system from the district level, to administration, to support personnel, to literacy leaders, classroom teachers, and literacy partners, as described in *Standards 2017* (ILA, 2018a).

CASE EXAMPLE

THINK ABOUT THIS

1. In what ways does Mrs. Rodriguez demonstrate tangible ways to teach digital literacies given the range of abilities in her classroom?

2. How can Mrs. Rodriquez's teaching become an example for implementation in your school setting?

3. What might Mrs. Rodriguez and her school leadership team consider as they expand professional learning opportunities for both bold and reluctant teachers?

Mrs. Rodriguez's fifth-grade class consists of a wide range of academically diverse learners. She collaborates with her school's literacy coach and reading specialist to plan digital literacies instruction so that students have opportunities to acquire the digital literacies needed to navigate and learn within the digital information age. Mrs. Rodriguez has been designing instructional sequences in her classroom that provide opportunities for purposefully accessing, shaping, sharing, and exchanging information online. Creating an instructional chain of nested activities allows us to examine, in a principled way, the moments of instruction that are linked together to maximize students' learning.

Mrs. Rodriguez begins a climate change unit by administering two short formative assessments: one informs her about her students' experience using the Internet, and the other addresses students' background knowledge about the content they are preparing to learn. During the first week of instruction, she introduces the 350.org website (see *https://350.org/science/*) and Climate Kids (*https://climatekids.nasa.gov*). After debriefing the content and the authorship of these websites to examine scientific expertise, students are given time to engage in small-group discussions. Marcelina, a Spanish-speaking English learner (EL), and three other students discuss what they have learned about long- and short-term patterns in the weather and climate. Students are organized into small groups to create concept maps that compare the differences. Each group takes a turn on the classroom's Internet-connected computer, replaying sections of the video and searching for interactive online resources to extend their understanding.

Marcelina and her group locate the video and poster labeled *What's the Difference between Weather and Climate?* (*https://climatekids.nasa. gov/weather-climate*). After evaluating these resources for quality and veracity, a process modeled by Mrs. Rodriguez, the group saves them on Diigo (*www.diigo.com/education*), a suite of collaboration tools for use in schools, so they can be shared with everyone in the class. Then, Marcelina's group shares the comparisons on Mindmeister (*www.mindmeister.com*), a collaborative platform for creating concept maps that encourages learners to use images together with words to illustrate key ideas and logical relationships for critical thinking. Marcelina shares, "It helps you organize your thinking. When you put in bubbles, you can show the difference on each side." For more about the use of digital texts and tools within this climate change unit, see Castek and Dwyer (2018).

As is typical in classrooms nationwide, Mrs. Rodriguez integrates literacy and disciplinary learning. What is less typical is her strategic use of the Internet to address literacy, language learning, and disciplinary goals in tandem. As a result of Mrs. Rodriguez's efforts, her students have learned how to search for Web resources that match their learning needs, navigate within websites to locate the information they need, critically evaluate the reliability of these websites, and synthesize key ideas from the many resources they have read. In addition to the literacy skills commonly taught in schools, these skills are essential for full participation in higher education and the workplace. Mrs. Rodriguez goes on to create an instructional chain of learning activities that helps her students read, share ideas, and interact digitally while developing voice and choice in their learning. During their collaborative inquiry, learners bring different perspectives and critical analysis to the same topic or issue, resulting in a wider range of critical questions and stances.

Mrs. Rodriguez was not always this skilled in using the Internet to support teaching and learning. In fact, she considered herself a casual technology user until her school took part in professional learning efforts that introduced ways to incorporate digital literacies and online reading comprehension into classroom instruction. To date, Mrs. Rodriguez has spent 2 years with her professional learning community (PLC), refining her implementation of instructional approaches. The PLC includes four grade-level teachers, a literacy specialist, a literacy coach, a library media teacher, literacy partner, and her principal. This group meets face-to-face monthly and regularly dialogues in their shared virtual discussion space—a teaching literacy with technology blog they created as a means to pose questions and share ideas. This digital community offers expanded contact hours, sustained opportunities to problem-solve implementation issues, and it promotes engagement in active learning with peers.

Mrs. Rodriguez's confidence in teaching online reading comprehension has grown exponentially, not only because of sustained interactions with her PLC, but also due to her willingness to learn from the interactions among students that regularly take place within her own classroom. She provides time and opportunity for students to share and exchange online reading comprehension strategies.

* * * * * * * * * * * *

As Mrs. Rodriguez demonstrates, integrating the Internet into literacy and content learning opens doors that make it possible for her students to realize their learning potential. Recognizing the changing literacy landscape that is emerging with the spread and use of new technologies requires teachers to teach in new ways and fully incorporate online reading comprehension into the curriculum.

In this chapter, we introduce ways that teachers like Mrs. Rodriguez can expand students' literacy experiences and make use of new technologies for reading, writing, communication, and collaboration in PreK–12 classrooms. We contend that implementing a lasting approach to professional learning will aid teachers in transforming their teaching and those efforts will go a long way toward preparing students to effectively engage in literacy and content learning in the 21st century.

DIGITAL LITERACIES AND INSTRUCTION

As mentioned at the start of this chapter and exemplified in the case example, digital technologies are transforming the ways we access, use, and exchange information. To maximize the potential of the Internet as an educational context, we need to ensure that all students have opportunities to develop the literacy skills required in today's networked world (Watts-Taffe & Gwinn, 2007). We also need to support teachers in designing and delivering instruction that makes the most of what the Internet has to offer. Implementation requires the development of a new generation of literacy leaders who can support their students in learning and their colleagues in teaching new forms of literacy essential for Internet use. Making online reading an integral part of classroom instruction motivates students to access information quickly, explore a range of multimedia resources, and share ideas as part of a socially networked classroom community.

Reading online requires additional skills beyond those needed for traditional print reading (Leu, Kinzer, Coiro, Castek, & Henry, 2019; Coiro & Dobler, 2007). Many of these higher-order, online reading comprehension skills appear in the Common Core State Standards (NGA & CCSSO, 2010) and are essential for success in both literacy and content-area classrooms (International Reading Association, 2009; ILA, 2018b).

The Common Core State Standards (NGA & CCSSO, 2010) provide an overview of the capacities of 21st-century-literate individuals. These standards assert that students are expected to use technology and digital media strategically and capably and employ technology thoughtfully to enhance their reading, writing, speaking, listening, and language use. For example, students are expected to (1) conduct online searches to acquire useful information; (2) draw information from multiple print or digital sources to locate an answer or solve a problem; (3) gather relevant information from multiple print and digital sources and assess the credibility and accuracy of each source; (4) use technology, including the Internet, to produce, publish, and interact with others, while also recognizing the strengths and limitations of various technological tools; and (5) select digital tools that are suited to meeting specific communication goals. Research-based models of professional learning are needed to support literacy professionals' important work in developing students' skills in these areas (Desimone, 2009), especially as classrooms address the new reading, writing, and communication demands required by the Internet.

Standards 2017, especially Standard 5, addresses the developmental needs of all learners and describes how school personnel can collaborate to (1) use a variety of print and digital materials to engage and motivate all learners; (2) integrate digital technologies in appropriate, safe, and effective ways; (3) foster a positive climate that supports a literacy-rich learning environment; and (4) implement instruction that develops learners' critical thinking, research, and inquiry skills. Mrs. Rodriguez's well-designed instruction in the climate change instructional vignette illustrates the careful thinking and planning she engaged in to address each of these components within *Standards 2017*. It is important to note, however, that she was not alone in her efforts. She worked collaboratively with the literacy professionals and literacy partners at her school to amplify efforts to address her students' needs.

ESSENTIAL LITERACIES STRATEGIES

To fully participate in a globally networked society, every student needs to develop strategies for locating, comprehending, and responding to text in ways that take advantage of the devices, digital texts, and tools that surround us. Most of these literacy strategies cluster in four areas: (1) reading to locate online information; (2) reading to critically evaluate online information; (3) reading to synthesize online information, often from multiple media sources; and (4) reading to communicate information, often in social networks (Leu et al., 2009). The sections that follow briefly outline these areas.

Reading to Locate Online Information

One component of successful Internet reading is the ability to read and locate information that meets one's needs. New online reading skills and strategies are required to generate effective keyword search strategies (Kuiper, 2007), to infer which link may be most useful within a set of search engine results (Henry, 2006), and to efficiently locate relevant information within websites. To accomplish these goals, students need to learn strategies that will help them become flexible and adaptable searchers. These strategies include selecting appropriate key words, determining whether searches are yielding pertinent results, and knowing when to revise search terms to arrive at a more targeted set of results. Effective searching allows students to navigate to useful websites efficiently so time can be spent reading, discussing, and learning from the information found on the sites located (Dwyer, 2011).

Reading to Evaluate Online Information

A second component of successful Internet use is the ability to critically evaluate information encountered on the Internet. Such evaluation presents challenges greater than traditional print and media sources (Burbules & Callister, 2000). The content of online information is even more diverse, often driven by commercial purposes. Source information about authorship and expertise is frequently difficult to determine. Reading online materials requires skillful recognition and interpretation of potential bias. Political campaigns, different newspapers reporting on the same event, or seemingly neutral advertisements introduce understated commercial motives and stances that students must navigate, negotiate, and sort. Reading to critically evaluate information is an important area in which to target instruction because students are typically unskilled (Henry, 2006).

Reading to Synthesize Online Information

A third strategy requires learners to develop the ability to read and synthesize information from different online sources, often with multiple media (Goldman, Wiley, & Graesser, 2005). Innovative teachers are tackling synthesis by expecting that students will draw information from more than one online source. Providing several articles on the same subject, some expository and others narrative, and asking students to read across them to inform their own perspective is one way to promote this important skill. The ability to manage, process, and filter multiple resources is a key component of digital literacy and is another challenging aspect of online reading comprehension (Goldman et al., 2005).

Reading to Communicate Online Information

A fourth component is the ability to read and respond via the Internet while seeking information or sharing what has been learned. The interactive processes of reading and communicating have become so intertwined on the Internet that they often happen simultaneously (Leu et al., 2009). Thus, the communication processes involved in using online tools to ask and answer questions on the Internet appear to be inextricably linked to aspects of online reading comprehension. Moreover, each communication tool on the Internet has different affordances and presents a range of necessary new skills, strategies, and social practices to use them effectively (Greenhow, Robelia, & Hughes, 2009).

DIGITAL LITERACIES AND MOTIVATION

Although the research regarding the relationship between technology use and academic achievement is limited, working with a range of digital technologies appears to increase motivation (International Reading Association, 2009; National Council of Teachers of English, 2018). Most teachers who have used the Internet to extend literacy learning can attest to the positive relationship between technology use and student engagement. Projects and group work that include digital literacies instruction seem to increase engagement in schoolwork (Castek, 2008; Dwyer, 2010) and provide a context in which students produce work they care about and in which they take pride (Castek & Dwyer, 2018). Digital technologies also offer expanded access to content through multimedia such as video, visual representations, and text-to-speech options, as well as opportunities for learners to create their own texts.

Technology use for literacy and content learning extends new social contexts for developing knowledge (Dalton & Proctor, 2008). These social contexts influence how learners make sense of, interpret, and share understandings. Participation in these social contexts motivates students to read for a range of purposes, use knowledge gained from previous experiences to generate new understandings, and actively engage in meaningful literacy interactions. Incorporating collaborative learning experiences that make use of digital technologies in classrooms fulfills an important need, given that many students, especially adolescents, are driven by social interaction.

Henry, Castek, Zawilinski, and O'Byrne (2012) found that using the Internet and creating digital projects such as podcasts, videos, and digital inquiry projects appeared to engage students who were considered struggling readers in digital literacies in ways that helped reshape their identities as learners. Given their technology expertise, these often-marginalized students became valued collaborators and contributors in digital literacies activities. Working in groups appeared to encourage active participation and created community among learners who worked toward a common purpose. Drawing all students into learning with high levels of engagement, if sustained over time, may lead to improved literacy and content learning (Castek, 2008).

Not only is using technology motivational, it also forges a tangible connection to students' out-of-school lives. By drawing in and making use of the technology experiences students bring to the classroom from outside of school, we acknowledge students as valuable contributors to learning. This recognition has the potential to transform the classroom learning environment by encouraging students to collaborate, guide one another, and engage fully in literacy activities. As teachers, we need to tap into this powerful potential and provide students with the means for such strategic engagement.

DIGITAL LITERACIES: PRINCIPLES AND IMPLEMENTATION

Standards 2017 suggests that "although reading is important to core beliefs and values, literacy educators today have responsibilities for oral language development, writing, *digital and multiple literacies,* visual literacy, and the power of literacy learning to change lives" (International Literacy Association, 2018a, p. 11; italics added for emphasis). As teachers, we must create conditions for students in our classrooms to use technologies in ways that mirror the purposes for real-world use in the digital world around us. In doing so, we as educators widen students' access to a range of texts and tools and provide multiple means, modes, and ways to demonstrate their learning. In doing so, we help learners to engage in a complex, globally connected, digital world, which brings together physical, social, and virtual spaces.

While these purposes reflect the changing nature of literacy in the 21st century, what specifically do literacy professionals need to know and be able to do to support the learners they work with, including their colleagues, students, school leadership, and professional learning colleagues? In short, we must implement increased opportunities for flexible and expanded communication, and students must be provided with numerous opportunities to learn and experiment with these vital and essential digital and multiple literacies across the curriculum.

As reflected in *Standards 2017,* Standard 5 states that literacy professionals must provide a literate environment that incorporates multiple dimensions of learning, including instructional routines, modeling, interactions, time, and opportunities to acquire digital literacies across the curriculum. Teaching online reading introduces a new way of delivering comprehension instruction for nearly every teacher. Instruction begins with a solid foundation of inquiry, with teacher modeling and opportunities to engage in personal digital inquiry both individually and in collaboration with others (see Coiro, Castek, & Quinn, 2016). The dimensions of inquiry deepen purposes for reading and communicate and provide opportunities for student voice and choice in learning.

DIGITAL LITERACIES: RECOMMENDATIONS FOR PROFESSIONAL LEARNING

Professional learning is a gatekeeper to meaningful educational implementations designed to impact student learning; this aspect becomes increasingly complex with the infusion of technology into learning opportunities. Thus, what characterized more traditional professional development must now be reexamined in relation to the changing landscape of learning. The impact of technology on learning is noted in the IRA Position Statement addressing "New Literacies and 21st-Century Technologies" (International Reading Association, 2009). This document calls for professional learning that provides opportunities for teachers to explore online tools and resources expected for use with students, suggesting it isn't enough to just make new technologies available. *Standards 2017* encourages teachers to integrate technology into student learning experiences across planning, implementing, assessing, and reflecting, which Watts-Taffe and Gwinn (2007) refer to as the *instructional cycle.* More specifically, learners are expected to engage in learning with traditional print, digital, and online resources from various genres and perspectives, as well as media and communication technologies. The integration of technology into literacy learning is called for in the Common Core State Standards (NGA & CCSSO, 2010) and in similar rigorous state standards. Students who meet these standards can use technology and digital media strategically and capably.

With the call for students to develop a full range of digital literacies, including online reading skills and strategies, we are challenged to consider the impact of these new forms of literacy on reading professionals, as they must be competent in this area (ILA, 2018a). In response to this charge, we address the following questions:

1. What characterizes effective professional learning in general?
2. How are these characteristics infused into effective professional

learning when preparing teachers to engage students in digital literacy and online reading comprehension?

High-quality professional learning seeks to increase teacher knowledge and skills, change teacher practice, and improve student achievement (Borko, 2004). The design of such professional learning is characterized by (1) expanded contact hours; (2) sustained opportunities across time; (3) shared engagement by teachers from the same grade, school, or subject; (4) active learning experiences; (5) connections to various reform efforts; and (6) a focus on subject-matter content (Desimone, 2009). Opportunities to collaborate with others around tangible implementation of new pedagogical practices solidify learning and can create a lasting effect.

Job-embedded professional learning, described by DuFour, DuFour, Eaker, and Many (2010) as essential for improved student learning, is a meaningful alternative to presentations delivered to large groups. More specifically, a PLC is an "ongoing process in which educators work collaboratively in recurring cycles of collective inquiry and action research to achieve better results for the students they serve" (p. 11). Such a community is characterized by members who commit to a focus on learning, collaborative teams, collective inquiry, an action orientation, and continuous improvement, all of which are assessed based on results, not objectives (DuFour et al., 2010). An integral way to embed new literacies within a PLC is to test the potential of digital technologies (e.g., Moodle, wikis, social networking forums, blogs, and digital tools yet to be conceptualized) to expand collective inquiry. These tools provide opportunities for teachers to collaborate, share, and develop content (Huber, 2010). Communities such as the ILA publish a regular series called Teaching with Tech.[1] It provides teachers with an extended network of resources, teaching tips, and colleagues with whom to discuss instructional approaches, share resources, and collaborate.

Professional learning efforts, such as the Summer Institute in Digital Literacy (see Hobbs & Coiro, 2016, 2018), offer transformative models that expand beyond the school level and help build extended learning communities that promote lasting change. This weeklong institute addresses ways that new digital tools can create challenging and engaging learning opportunities for students and teachers in K–12 and higher education. Participants come together to network, share ideas, boost their leadership skills, and create technology-infused curriculum units that they can implement in their own classrooms. For teachers who are unable to attend such an institute in person, online resources can be explored and discussed with colleagues to support implementation. Available resources include videos, instructional suggestions, readings that link theory to practice, and online

---

[1] Available at *www.literacyworldwide.org/blog/digital-literacies/teaching-with-tech*.

networking tools that allow teachers to connect with others who have similar goals and interests.

Despite growing interest and participation in these online professional learning networks, many educators lack familiarity with or preparation in teaching the skills and strategies required for online reading, writing, and collaboration (Wallace, 2004). Even those who consider themselves experienced in this arena recognize that the online literacy landscape is complex and constantly changing. Barone and Wright (2008) suggest that teachers face many challenges, including a lack of resources (e.g., technology, time, technical support), a lack of knowledge and skills (insufficient technological and pedagogical knowledge), and a lack of school leadership (e.g., inadequate planning or scheduling). In addition, teachers' attitudes and beliefs are often limiting. Some educators are fearful of the use of new technologies. A lack of valid and reliable assessments that match the skills and strategies for online reading comprehension also present limitations (Leu et al., 2019). To offer support to educators at primary, intermediate, and secondary levels, we turn our attention to discussing job-embedded professional learning activities for teachers who seek to engage students in digital literacy and online reading comprehension.

Primary/Elementary Level

Given primary students' needs, early-grade teachers, in particular, may identify strongly with traditional notions of literacy. However, incorporating new technologies and digital resources in literacy and content instruction involves adopting expanded views of reading, writing, and communicating. Professional development efforts that emphasize how teachers can model the skills and strategies involved in using the Internet and demonstrate ways to locate information online, evaluate Internet sources, synthesize information found across sites, and communicate with digital tools such as email, blogs, and wikis are critically important (see Moss & Lapp, 2009). Not only does this exposure support teachers' pedagogical knowledge, it expands their vision of literacy. Teachers can provide targeted instruction in the early grades to help students learn to read critically online (Assaf & Adonyi, 2009; Zhang & Duke, 2011). Specific focus areas might include strategies for (1) identifying the author or sponsor of a website, (2) determining how current the information is, (3) integrating website content together with background knowledge to judge the usefulness and veracity of the information, and (4) examining the URL to determine whether a site serves commercial or educational interests.

Providing opportunities for students to create digital stories with sound and images, record podcasts, and use the Internet to locate information enriches students' literacy experiences while fostering both traditional and digital literacies. In addition, a variety of digital tools can be widely used in primary classrooms: touch screen tablets now include digital cameras that can capture photographs, videos, and audio clips together with students' drawings. These pieces can be sequenced and produced to archive learning in the form of digital stories. Based on this information, we recommend that professional learning include strategies that promote active participation, inclusion, and diverse roles for working collaboratively in groups with teachers, leaders, and other literacy partners.

The relationship between digital literacy and offline literacy is complex; we suggest that a useful approach for teaching young learners is to consider how digital literacies and offline reading and writing skills are connected in everyday use. Offering primary grade students access to online resources to develop their literacy skills is a tangible way for teachers to aid them in learning about the Internet and will promote their independent use of it in the upper grades. Incorporating online reading within learning experiences fosters both traditional and new literacies. Tumblebooks (*www.tumblebooks.com*) and Starfall (*www.starfall.com/h/*) offer students short fiction and nonfiction books, early scaffolded literacy experiences, and multimodal interactives that support reading and writing. Guiding students' use of this site by exploring resources as a class, before offering access to students individually, will make the most of these highly scaffolded digital literacy experiences. These teacher-directed activities will set the stage for future online reading comprehension activities, in which teachers model effective search strategies, Web evaluation techniques, and synthesis across sites.

Intermediate and Secondary Levels

In light of the increased expectations of technology-infused literacy teaching and learning at the intermediate and secondary levels, teachers may find it useful to participate in a regular, ongoing learning experience supported by the building-level instructional coach, instructional technology teacher, and/or principal. The focus of the learning experience is to increase teacher understanding of the ways in which to expand students' familiarity with online reading comprehension and to support the teacher as technology is infused into the curriculum in increasing amounts. At the onset of the experience, teachers are reminded of the connections between online reading comprehension and district literacy efforts. Teachers assume the role of learner as they collaboratively engage in online reading comprehension; they read to locate information, evaluate information, synthesize information, and to communicate information. Then, building on instruction that occurred at the primary level, they teach students the same process gradually, moving from modeled to guided and beyond to independent practice. Across this process, teachers participate in meaningful conversations, some online and others offline, to ponder critical questions key to learning in professional communities including:

1. What do we want all students to know and be able to do?
2. How will we know if they have learned it?
3. How will we respond when students have not learned it?
4. What will we do if they already know it? (DuFour et al., 2010).

REMAINING CHALLENGES

Despite the fact that schools have made great strides in student-to-computer ratios with the affordability of Chromebooks and iPads, the digital divide— a situation in which different groups do not have the same degree of access to digital information and communication technologies—is still prevalent and, for this reason, some groups do not have the same opportunities for social and economic development (ILA, 2017). However, digital divide discussions among educators are moving beyond physical access to computers and are paying closer attention to equity and inclusion (ILA, 2017, 2018b). The emergence of this second wave of attention to issues of digital inequality has been called the *second-level digital divide*. We interpret this emerging research to suggest that simply providing schools with funds to purchase updated equipment, software, and reliable Internet access in schools does not go far enough, because extending access does not mean that students will become skilled at online reading comprehension. We believe that investing in sustained professional learning for teachers is an essential and integral part of providing high-quality and relevant instructional experiences for students. This sentiment is strongly echoed in ILA (2018b). These priorities were identified a decade earlier in a 2008 survey of 111 middle school teachers: 66% indicated a need for professional development in "integrating technology within the existing curriculum"—the highest self-identified need (Silvernail & Buffington, 2009). These results suggest that when funds are available, professional development and coaches are more of a priority than hardware and software.

CONCLUSION

In this chapter, we have introduced ways that digital literacies can be taught to support online reading comprehension and offered suggestions for designing professional development experiences that support teaching and learning in this important area. We suggest that teaching digital literacies provides many opportunities to engage students with content and develop reading and writing, communicating, and learning strategies for a digital age. However, as important as these multiple literacies are, there are few professional learning models that support teachers in teaching online reading comprehension. As school communities work toward designing meaningful teacher learning experiences, capitalizing in part on the afore-mentioned characteristics of high-quality professional learning, we encourage teachers to embrace students and colleagues as collaborative learning partners. In collaboration with their colleagues, students and teachers, acting as literacy partners, will make strides in generating new and innovative ways to teach digital literacies and online reading comprehension. In the process, they will explore a growing range of digital resources that extend literacy and learning in the digital age.

ENGAGEMENT ACTIVITIES

Reflect on Mrs. Rodriguez's journey toward developing instructional sequences that nest digital literacies instruction across multiple lessons and units throughout the school year.

1. Discuss with colleagues how Mrs. Rodriguez, described in this chapter, might continue to extend students' literacy and content learning with technology. What have you learned from Mrs. Rodriguez and her students? How might you apply this learning to your own work with students, colleagues, and literacy partners?

2. As a means to extending your learning, visit a classroom during the implementation of digital literacies instruction. Engage in a postvisit conversation to reflect on what was observed. Discuss specific implementation ideas that help literacy professionals at all levels make connections that support implementation in their settings. Discuss insights gained within your professional learning community.

ANNOTATED RESOURCES

Casey, H., Lenski, S., & Hryniuk-Adamov, C. (2015). Literacy practices that adolescents deserve: Access to a wide variety of print and nonprint materials (International Literacy Association E-ssentials Series). Newark, DE: International Literacy Association. Retrieved from *https://www.literacyworldwide.org/get-resources/ila-e-ssentials/8059*.

This article explores multiple literacies and the use of technology and digital devices in school. The authors describe instructional opportunities that open up possibilities for students to construct meaning in new ways.

Castek, J. (2015). *Literacy practices that adolescents deserve: Instruction with multimodal, multiple texts* (International Literacy Association E-ssentials Series). Newark, DE: International Literacy Association. Retrieved from *www.literacyworldwide.org/get-resources/ila-e-ssentials/8064*.

This article showcases ways to put digital tools in the hands of adolescents, and the adults who work with them, to transform literacy learning. The classroom examples and resources included demonstrate ways to help ensure that *all* students become skilled in the digital literacies that are a vital part of our 21st-century world.

International Literacy Association. (2017). *Overcoming the digital divide: Four critical steps* (Literacy Leadership Brief). Newark, DE: Author. Retrieved from *www.literacyworldwide.org/docs/default-source/where-we-stand/ila-overcoming-digital-divide-brief.pdf.*

This literacy leadership brief from the International Literacy Association describes the challenge of digital access for people living in poverty. The paper includes four actionable steps for overcoming the digital divide.

Laird, S. (2015). *Sharing student writing with the world* (International Literacy Association E-ssentials Series). Newark, DE: International Literacy Association. Retrieved from *www.literacyworldwide.org/get-resources/ila-e-ssentials/8072.*

This article provides ways to motivate students to write for an authentic audience outside the four walls of your classroom. It introduces ways in which students can use blogging, website creation, e-books, and digital stories to share their voices with the world.

REFERENCES

American Library Association. (2013). Digital literacy, libraries, and public policy. Report of the Office for Information Technology Policy's Digital Literacy Task Force. Retrieved March 7, 2019, from *www.districtdispatch.org/2013/01/on-the-front-lines-of-digital-inclusion.*

Assaf, C. L., & Adonyi, A. (2009). Critically reading advertisements: Examining visual images and persuasive language. In B. Moss & D. Lapp (Eds.), *Teaching new literacies in grades K–3* (pp. 209–220). New York: Guilford Press.

Barone, D., & Wright, T. E. (2008). Literacy instruction with digital and media technologies. *The Reading Teacher, 62*(4), 292–302.

Borko, H. (2004). Professional development and teacher learning: Mapping the terrain. *Educational Researcher, 33*(8), 3–15.

Burbules, N. C., & Callister, T. A. (2000). *Watch IT: The risks and promises of information technologies for education.* Boulder, CO: Westview Press.

Castek, J. (2008). *How do 4th and 5th grade students acquire the new literacies of online reading comprehension?: Exploring the contexts that facilitate learning.* Unpublished doctoral dissertation, University of Connecticut, Storrs, CT.

Castek, J., & Dwyer, B. (2018). Think globally act locally: Teaching climate change through digital inquiry. *The Reading Teacher, 71*(6), 755–761.

Castek, J., Zawilinski, L., McVerry, G., O'Byrne, I., & Leu, D. J. (2011). The new literacies of online reading comprehension: New opportunities and challenges for students with learning difficulties. In C. Wyatt-Smith, J. Elkins, & S. Gunn (Eds.), *Multiple perspectives on difficulties in learning literacy and numeracy* (pp. 91–110). New York: Springer.

Cennamo, K., Ross, J., & Ertmer, P. (2009). *Technology integration for meaningful classroom use: A standards-based approach.* Belmont, CA: Wadsworth, Cengage Learning.

Coiro, J., Castek, J., & Quinn, D. (2016). Personal inquiry and online research: Connecting learners in ways that matter. *The Reading Teacher, 69*(5), 483–492.

Coiro, J., & Dobler, E. (2007). Exploring the online comprehension strategies used by sixth-grade skilled readers to search for and locate information on the Internet. *Reading Research Quarterly, 42,* 214–257.

Coiro, J., Knobel, M., Lankshear, M., & Leu, D. J. (2008). Central issues in new literacies and new literacies research. In J. Coiro, M. Knobel, C. Lankshear, & D. J. Leu (Eds.), *Handbook of research on new literacies* (pp. 17–49). Mahwah, NJ: Erlbaum.

Dalton, B., & Proctor, C. P. (2008). The changing landscape of text and comprehension in the age of new literacies. In J. Coiro, M. Knobel, C. Lankshear, & D. J. Leu (Eds.), *Handbook of research on new literacies.* Mahwah, NJ: Erlbaum.

Desimone, L. M. (2009). Improving impact studies of teachers' professional development: Toward better conceptualizations and measures. *Educational Researcher, 38,* 181–199.

DuFour, R., DuFour, R., Eaker, R., & Many, T. (2010). *Learning by doing: A handbook for professional learning communities at work* (2nd ed.). Bloomington, IN: Solution Tree.

Dwyer, B. (2010). *Scaffolding Internet reading: A study of a disadvantaged school community in Ireland.* Unpublished doctoral dissertation, University of Nottingham, Nottingham, UK.

Goldman, S. R., Wiley, J., & Graesser, A. C. (2005, April). *Learning in a knowledge society: Constructing meaning from multiple information sources.* Paper presented at the annual meeting of the American Educational Research Association, Montreal, Quebec, Canada.

Greenhow, C., Robelia, E., & Hughes, J. (2009). Web 2.0 and classroom research: What path should we take now? *Educational Researcher, 38*(4), 246–259.

Henry, L. A. (2006). SEARCHing for an answer: The critical role of new literacies while reading on the Internet. *The Reading Teacher, 59*(7), 614–627.

Henry, L. A., Castek, J., Zawilinski, L., & O'Byrne, I. (2012). Using peer collaboration to support online reading, writing, and communication: An empowerment model for struggling readers. *Reading and Writing Quarterly: Overcoming Learning Difficulties, 28,* 279–306.

Hitlan, G. (2018). Internet/broadband fact sheet. Retrieved from *www.pewinternet. org/fact-sheet/internet-broadband.*

Hobbs, R., & Coiro, J. (2016). Everyone learns from everyone. *Journal of Adolescent and Adult Literacy, 59*(6), 623–629.

Hobbs, R., & Coiro, J. (2018). Design features of a professional development program in digital literacy. *Journal of Adolescent and Adult Literacy, 62*(4), 401–409.

Huber, C. (2010). Professional learning 2.0. *Educational Leadership, 67*(8), 41–46.

International Literacy Association (ILA). (n.d.). Literacy glossary. Retrieved March 2, 2019, from *www.literacyworldwide.org/get-resources/literacy-glossary.*

International Literacy Association (ILA). (2017). *Overcoming the digital divide: Four critical steps* (Literacy Leadership Brief). Newark, DE: Author.

International Literacy Association (ILA). (2018a). *Standards for the preparation of literacy professionals 2017.* Newark, DE: Author.

International Literacy Association (ILA). (2018b). *Improving digital practices for literacy, learning, and justice: More than just tools.* Newark, DE: Author.

International Reading Association. (2009). *New literacies and 21st century technologies: A position statement.* Newark, DE: Author.

Kuiper, E. (2007). The Web as an information resource in K–12 education: Strategies for supporting students in searching and processing information. *Review of Educational Research, 75*(3), 285–328.

Leu, D. J., Jr., Kinzer, C. K., Coiro, J., Castek, J., & Henry, L. A. (2019). New literacies: A dual-level theory of the changing nature of literacy, instruction, and assessment. In D. Alvermann, N. J. Unrau, M. Sailors, & R. B. Ruddell (Eds.), *Theoretical models and processes of literacy* (7th ed., pp. 219–236). New York: Taylor & Francis.

Leu, D. J., Jr., O'Byrne, W. I., Zawilinski, L., McVerry, J. G., & Everett-Cocapardo, H. (2009). Expanding the new literacies conversation. *Educational Researcher, 38,* 264–269.

McKenney, S., & Visscher, A. J. (2019). Technology for teacher learning and performance. *Technology, Pedagogy and Education, 28*(2), 129–132.

Moss, B., & Lapp, D. (Eds.). (2009). *Teaching new literacies in grades K–3.* New York: Guilford Press.

National Council of Teachers of English. (2018). Beliefs for integrating technology into the English language arts classroom. Retrieved March 7, 2019, from *www2.ncte. org/statement/beliefs-technology-preparation-english-teachers.*

National Governors Association Center for Best Practices & Council of Chief State School Officers (NGA & CCSSO). (2010). *Common Core Standards for English language arts and literacy in history/social studies, science, and technical subjects.* Washington, DC: Authors. Retrieved May 4, 2011, from *www.corestandards.org/ the-standards/english-language-arts-standards.*

Phillips, N. C., & Manderino, M. (2015). *Access, equity, and empowerment: Supporting digital literacies for all learners* (Policy brief). Chicago: Center for Literacy, University of Illinois at Chicago. Retrieved from *www.cfl.uic.edu/wpcontent/ uploads/2013/02/UIC_PolicyBriefBook_3.pdf.*

Prensky, M. (2001). Digital natives, digital immigrants. *On the Horizon, 9*(5), 1–2. Retrieved May 4, 2011, from *www.marcprensky.com/writing.*

Silvernail, D., & Buffington, P. (2009). *Improving mathematics performance using laptop technology: The importance of professional development for success.* Gorham, ME: Maine Education Policy Research Institute.

Wallace, R. (2004). A framework for understanding teaching with the Internet. *American Education Research Journal, 41*(2), 447–488.

Watts-Taffe, S., & Gwinn, C. B. (2007). *Integrating literacy and technology: Effective practice for grades K–6.* New York: Guilford Press.

Zhang, S., & Duke, N. K. (2011). The impact of instruction in the WWWDOT framework on students' disposition and ability to evaluate websites as sources of information. *The Elementary School Journal, 112*(1), 132–154.

Literacy Leadership in Action

Justin Aglio, EdD
*Director of Academic Achievement (K–4) and District Innovation,
Moutour School District, McKees Rocks, Pennsylvania*

THINK ABOUT THIS

1. In what ways does Justin serve as a literacy leader?
2. What lessons can be learned about the role of district administrator?
3. What questions come to mind while reading this vignette?

At the Montour School District, my leadership role is to work collaboratively with all K–4 stakeholders to fully support the educational needs for all learners. I also promote high-quality learning partnerships and explore and implement innovative best practices with all grades and content areas to better maximize learning opportunities for students and team members.

We believe that high-quality curriculum and instruction are critical to student achievement; at the same time, it is the action of the team members that has the greatest impact on student learning. Teachers are strongly encouraged every year to participate in an action research project. The action research project was introduced to teachers to encourage risk taking and promote a growth mindset in our school culture. Teachers work with a Fellow from Carnegie Mellon University's (CMU) LearnLab. They complete a literature review, collect and analyze data, and provide recommendations. At the conclusion of the project, teachers present their findings to the elementary team. Action research projects vary; for example, two first-grade teachers conducted a 6-week project on the concept of global read-alouds (GRA), using one book to make global connections. The two teachers presented their project to other team members and provided resources and tools. Now, the GRA concept, supported by the administration, has spread to other team members.

Other leadership opportunities are available. Literacy leadership committees make informed recommendations about literacy resources. Committees are supported and provided with time to meet with building and central office administration. Also, specific school team members are selected to assist the administration in supporting and coaching all school team members. Further, professionals are encouraged to participate in or seek professional development opportunities. In addition, time is provided every day at each building for teachers to plan together, and time is provided at each building for additional professional learning opportunities. Teacher teams conduct professional learning community (PLC) meet-ups every Wednesday for 30 minutes. They discuss student achievement and common assessments. For example, literacy teachers will use this time to develop common text-dependent analysis questions for their grade levels.

Montour's literacy education program also hinges on the strength of its collaborative partnerships. Teachers are encouraged, but not required, to share best literacy practice, using social media. The Twitter hashtag #MontourProud is a hub for teachers and administrators to showcase best practices. Administrators are also encouraged to showcase and support literacy best practices by capturing and sharing classroom examples. I lead efforts to develop and sustain partnerships to support the literacy program. For example, we partner with St. Vincent College's Fred Rogers Center to study simple interaction, using one-to-one adult–child interactions around technology in our primary grades, and with Harvard University to investigate promises, practices, and pedagogies of student learning. In addition, we recently opened the first-ever Brick Makerspace powered by Lego Education and Minecraft Education Lab; in this space, students create and write stories, and so on. Our goal is to create a learning culture that promotes a *student-centered . . . future-focused* environment.

As a district literacy leader, challenges do emerge. My role is to set and support core values and provide resources to develop a culture in which change is expected. Following are five tips that I have found helpful in strengthening a literacy culture:

1. Schedule frequent learning workshops with both teachers and administrators.
2. Provide time and space for teachers to share best practices.
3. Study and provide practical, teacher-friendly resources.
4. Use technology to advance learning and support the development of 21st-century skills and not as a substitute for instruction.
5. Establish, model, and support expectations.

PART III

CONTEXTS OF SCHOOLING

The chapters in Part III emphasize the many different contextual factors that influence literacy teaching and learning in schools. In Chapter 14, Scanlon, Goatley, and Spring address the key role of literacy educators and literacy instruction for learners in special education contexts. Further, they candidly discuss important policy controversies related to literacy difficulties. In Chapter 15, Walker-Dalhouse and Risko provide a research-based description and definition of culturally responsive instruction. They also describe specific instructional practices that are responsive to students' cultural and identity differences. In Chapter 16, Vogt provides key background information about English learners and who they are; she then describes what literacy leaders need to know about appropriate language, literacy, and content instruction for these learners. In Chapter 17, Paratore, Steiner, and Dougherty describe the challenges that schools face in developing productive parent–teacher partnerships and principles that can guide the planning and implementation of these partnerships. They highlight practices that support partnerships between teachers and immigrant and other marginalized families and that can also be applied universally. In Chapter 18, Woulfin and Jones describe the influence of policies on literacy instruction and then describe ways that educators have responded to these policies. In Chapter 19, DiGisi, Meltzer, Schade, and

Maze-Hsu discuss ways in which literacy leaders can work to sustain literacy practices that transform teaching and learning. They provide a matrix (using the ILA *Standards 2017*) in which they describe the contributions that various literacy leaders can make to the development of effective literacy programs. In the final chapter, Swan Dagen and Bean close the volume with a research-based discussion of professional learning practices for literacy leaders.

CHAPTER 14

Literacy Leadership in Special Education

Donna M. Scanlon
Virginia J. Goatley
Kathleen Spring

↳ In what ways does the *Standards for the Preparation of Literacy Professionals 2017* (International Literacy Association [ILA], 2018) support the role of literacy professionals in preventing long-term literacy learning difficulties?

↳ In what ways might literacy leaders collaborate with teachers to support learners in special education contexts?

↳ How might literacy leaders understand and address current policy controversies related to literacy difficulties to best support and advocate for all learners?

Special education is intended to provide supports for students who experience significant learning difficulties for a wide variety of reasons. In this chapter we discuss the role that literacy leaders have in supporting teachers and families in relation to literacy development for children who may be candidates for, or may be receiving, special education services due to literacy difficulties. Such difficulties can arise for multiple reasons, including poor early language development (Duff, Reen, Plunkett, & Nation, 2015), inadequate literacy instruction (Foorman & Al Otaiba, 2009; Scanlon, Gelzheiser, Vellutino, Schatschneider, & Sweeney, 2008), insufficient reading practice (McKenna, Shin, & Ciullo, 2015), and/or lack of background knowledge that limits an individual's ability to comprehend text (van den Broek, Mouw, & Kraal, 2016).

A key role for literacy professionals is to successfully teach learners who experience literacy difficulties. But, they have other roles as well. The following case example gives an overview of some of the many factors and community stakeholders they may influence as professionals.

CASE EXAMPLE •

THINK ABOUT THIS

1. Given the number of concerns identified by the principal, which one would you identify as being the highest priority during Tia's first year on the job and why?

2. How might Tia go about learning what's happening in classroom and intervention settings?

Tia, an experienced literacy professional, has recently taken a position as a literacy coach at a school that serves a socioeconomically diverse population. Her prior experience was in a school that served a solidly middle-class neighborhood. She has learned that approximately 25% of the children in her new school come from economically stressed homes, and many have parents who did not complete high school. Her principal has shared that many children from this background arrive in school with limited language and early literacy skills and that, although they have a response-to-intervention (RTI) program in place, many children are not responding well and, as a result, the number of students identified as needing special education supports is high. The principal also indicates that most of the children who are receiving special education support are not making the progress needed to enable them to succeed on the state's high-stakes tests. Moreover, Tia learned that several children from affluent families who have been receiving special education supports have shown limited growth in literacy over the years and that some of these families are demanding that an entirely different approach to literacy instruction be instituted. Tia is wondering what she has gotten herself into!

PREVENTING LITERACY DIFFICULTIES

In this section, we address the guiding question: In what ways does the ILA 2017 standards support the role of literacy professionals in preventing long-term literacy learning difficulties? We discuss prevention, intervention, and collaboration with families and early childhood teachers to support all learners. *Standards 2017* provides essential information about designing literacy curricula that meet the needs of all learners. The old adage "An ounce of prevention is worth a pound of cure" applies well to what has been learned about literacy difficulties. The best way to prevent such difficulties is to keep them from getting started. The strongest body of research in this regard has focused on the effects of literacy instruction in the primary grades (Fletcher, Lyons, Fuchs, & Barnes, 2019), a topic we will take up shortly. However, long before children begin their formal schooling, steps can be taken to prevent difficulties from arising and/or to reduce their severity.

Prevention Prior to Kindergarten

Opportunities to prevent literacy learning difficulties begin in infancy and continue through the early primary grades. While general health and well-being are obviously important to child development in general, for the purpose of preventing reading difficulties, a salient focus is the development of language skills. Reading and writing are language skills, and language develops through use. While there is evidence that children vary in their genetic makeup such that some acquire literacy and language skills more readily than others (Elliott & Grigorenko, 2014), there is no question that children's experiences with language in the first few years of life have a substantial impact on later school success (National Early Literacy Panel, 2008). Indeed, decades ago this relationship was well understood. For example, Anderson, Hiebert, Scott, and Wilkinson (1985) asserted that "the single most important activity for building the knowledge required for eventual success in reading is reading aloud to children" (p. 23). There has been little challenge to this assertion in the ensuing decades. Whereas literacy professionals are generally aware that speaking and reading with young children builds the language skills and background knowledge that will enable later reading comprehension, many family members and early childhood caregivers and teachers do not fully understand their role in promoting language and literacy development. Literacy professionals can take a leadership role by attempting to raise community awareness of the importance of early language skills to later school success. *Standards 2017,* Standard 5: Learners and the Literacy Environment emphasizes learner development and the need for literacy professionals to be attentive to the role that home, family and community play in literacy development.

As Anderson and colleagues assert, one of the best ways to enhance the development of young children's language skills is to engage them in shared book reading beginning at an early age. Because of the wealth of evidence in support of this claim, several organizations have developed outreach efforts and resources to increase the opportunities young children have to engage in shared book reading. These programs provide families/caregivers with guidance on how to read with children of varying ages and with resources to use in the process (e.g., lists of age-appropriate books,

books to borrow, books to own). We encourage literacy leaders to investigate whether such resources are available in their school's community and, if not, to lead efforts to either institute such programs or, at the very least, to distribute information about them to places that have contact with families with young children (e.g., clinics, child care/Head Start centers, places of worship). Figure 14.1 lists a few examples of such programs. The listed programs have informative websites that provide detail on the program and program costs. Tips for reading with young children and appropriate booklists are available at no cost. Some of the programs' websites also include videos that demonstrate the value of reading to young children and the approaches to shared reading that make it particularly productive.[iv] All of the websites reflect the findings of studies of shared book reading, as summarized by Turner, Crassas, and Segal (2015):

> Parents who made reading with their children a regular part of their lives, and who used key comprehension strategies such as asking questions, attending to illustrations and text, and making predictions, enhanced their children's print knowledge, alphabet knowledge, and reading comprehension. (p. 275)

While families and other home-based caregivers clearly play prominent roles in children's early development, the instruction offered in preschool and Head Start settings also impacts children's language and early literacy development (as detailed in Chapter 8, this volume). We suggest that the web-based resources described in Figure 14.1 could be usefully shared with teachers in these settings as well. In addition, it would be wise for literacy leaders, whenever possible, to share information, across elementary and preschool settings, about the approaches to language and literacy instruction in use in their early primary grades. There are multiple reasons for sharing such information, especially when considering children who may experience literacy difficulties. For example, some preschool settings may be amenable to incorporating some of the same instructional resources used in the primary grades. Materials used in teaching about the alphabet may be an especially useful place to start coordination efforts, because children identified as experiencing literacy difficulties in the early primary grades are generally noticed because of limited skill with the alphabetic code. At the beginning stages of learning about the code, many children rely on key words to help them remember letter–sound correspondences. When the key words in the preschool and kindergarten settings are different, children who are not yet automatic in their knowledge of letter sounds will need to learn new key words as they move from one setting to the next. This has the potential to delay the development of automaticity with letter–sound correspondences, which, in turn, can lead to subsequent delays

---

[1]For example, see *https://vimeo.com/103169733* and *https://youtu.be/5m-NqXWZsNc*.

Organization	Context	Age Group	Description
Reach Out and Read *www.reachoutandread.org*	Well-child pediatric visits	6 months to 5 years	Child receives a book at each visit. Professional briefly models shared reading.
Raising a Reader *www.raisingareader.org*	Libraries, community centers, schools, churches	Birth to 8 years	Children cycle through a set of bags of age-appropriate books to read with caregivers. Caregivers are provided with tips on how to engage their child in shared book reading.
Zero to Three *www.zerotothree.org*	Web-based resources for families and early childhood educators.	Birth to 5 years	This is a more comprehensive website that focuses on all aspects of early development and offers resources for families/caregivers, educators, and medical professionals.

FIGURE 14.1. Organizations promoting shared book reading in early childhood.

in word-solving skills, in the development of children's sight vocabularies, and, ultimately, in their ability to comprehend the texts they read.

Prevention in the Early Primary Grades

The most widely studied way to prevent long-term literacy difficulties is through the implementation of RTI approaches, in which students who are experiencing difficulties are provided with more intensive instruction to address those difficulties. Typically, there are three or four levels of intensity, referred to as *tiers,* with higher numbered tiers representing more intensive and, ideally, more responsive instruction. Models for implementing RTI vary tremendously, and in recent years RTI approaches have, in many instances, been folded into a more comprehensive framework of instructional supports, referred to as *multi-tiered systems of support* (MTSS), which include behavioral and social–emotional learning supports. In this chapter, we focus only on the literacy-related RTI component both because it has been more widely researched and because our target audience is professionals engaged in supporting children experiencing literacy difficulties. RTI approaches have been found to be especially effective when implemented in the earlier grades (Fletcher et al., 2019), probably because the gaps in skills are smaller than they would be if they went unaddressed for multiple years, and because the children have yet to develop the belief that reading and writing are beyond their capabilities.

In the implementation of RTI, children who are not meeting grade-level expectations are provided with intervention that is intended to accelerate their progress. They are periodically evaluated to determine the degree to which they are responding to these efforts. Evaluating children's response to instruction/intervention is important because, in order to close the gap with grade-level peers, students need to make more progress in a given period of time than their peers. If students do not appear to be on a trajectory that will close the gap, modifications should be made in hopes of improving the students' growth rates. Modifications may include increasing the intensity of intervention (e.g., reducing the size of the instructional group, increasing the frequency of intervention), changing the instructional foci (e.g., phonemic awareness, phonics, word-solving skills, fluency), and/or changing the person responsible for providing instruction to someone with greater expertise (e.g., a teacher with expertise in early literacy instruction/intervention).

In practice and in research contexts, the service delivery models for RTI vary considerably in terms of (1) when intervention is begun, (2) whether it is provided within or beyond the classroom, (3) who provides the intervention, (4) whether packaged/scripted programs are used, (5) the size of the instructional groups, (6) how and how often students' progress is monitored, (7) under what circumstances an instructional shift is made, and (8) whether there is a coherent relationship between the instruction offered at the classroom level and in the intervention setting(s). Fully addressing all of these variables is beyond the scope of this chapter (and Scanlon and colleagues have addressed many of these topics elsewhere: e.g., Scanlon, Anderson, & Sweeney, 2017). However, we do want to address the issue of coherence as children in intervention often receive instruction in more than one setting and/or from more than one teacher. If there is a lack of coherence between these settings and the instructional approaches employed, children who find literacy acquisition challenging are basically being asked to learn more than their classroom peers.

As noted above, the children in the primary grades who qualify for intervention generally do so because of limited skill with the alphabetic code and, relatedly, limited skill with word identification and oral reading accuracy. Effective teaching of alphabetic skills and word-solving strategies is especially important for these children. This is a place where literacy professionals' foundational knowledge plays a critical role both in the instruction they offer and in the support and guidance they offer to their colleagues. For children who find literacy learning challenging, in classroom and intervention settings, instruction around the code is more effective if it is systematic and explicit (National Reading Panel, 2000). Children need to have sufficient practice with the skills in isolation (during word work) and in applying these skills strategically in reading connected text (Scanlon et al., 2017). The ultimate goal is for the children to learn the skills and word-solving strategies to the point of automaticity, so that they can focus on meaning construction. Automaticity with these skills and strategies is important because most of the words that proficient readers can read were not explicitly taught but, rather, were learned through effective word solving while reading (Share, 1995).

In addition to individual teachers offering effective instruction, teachers who share responsibility for children's literacy learning within and across grade levels should coordinate their instruction so that it is coherent for students. We have already noted the importance of using the same key words across settings. In addition, we think it is important for teachers to use consistent language/labels in reference to aspects of the alphabetic code. For example, teachers variously refer to the silent-*e* generalization as silent-*e*, *bossy-e*, and *tricky-e*—which, to a 5-year-old, certainly would not seem to convey that they all represent the same concept. Thus, confusion can ensue. In addition, given that learning to read words is such a central focus at this point in development, we think it is important that there be coherence in the language used for word-solving strategies. Such consistency enables children to internalize the strategies so that, when they are reading independently, they can engage in more effective word solving.

Figure 14.2 presents an example of the set of word-solving strategies used in intervention studies by Scanlon and colleagues across the elementary and middle school grades (Gelzheiser, Scanlon, Hallgren-Flynn, & Connors, 2019; Scanlon et al., 2017). Note that, although the strategy list includes both code- and meaning-based strategies, it is important that children be taught to attend to as much of the code-based information as they are prepared to handle, as this ability influences the speed with which words become part of their sight vocabularies (Ehri, 2014). The meaning-based strategies are intended to enable readers to direct and check the accuracy of their word-solving attempts and to attend to text meaning more generally. Note also that, in the studies that used them, the strategies were explicitly taught and modeled, one at a time, and specific strategies were only taught when children had the alphabetic skills needed to use them.

Children's literacy development is, of course, highly dependent on the amount of reading and writing they do. Observational research suggests that children often do not spend sufficient time engaged in reading during periods set aside for such instruction. For example, in an observation study conducted in kindergartens, Kent, Wanzek, and Al Otaiba (2012) reported that children were engaged in reading instruction during only 50% of the

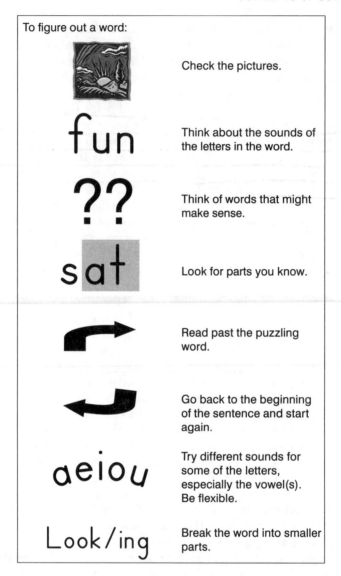

FIGURE 14.2. Interactive strategies approach word identification strategy list. Adapted from Scanlon and Anderson (2010). Copyright © 2010 International Literacy Association. Adapted by permission.

time that had been set aside for such instruction. Instead, they were engaged in activities such as transitions, games, and drawing and coloring that did not have a literacy focus. Ensuring that sufficient amounts of reading and writing occur in classroom and intervention settings is, obviously, important and provides a clear target for instructional improvement if similar patterns are identified in given classrooms.

> **THINK ABOUT THIS**
>
> 1. Is there coherence in the instructional resources and language used across classroom and intervention settings and across grade levels?
> 2. What might literacy leaders do to raise awareness of how much time learners who are experiencing difficulty with literacy acquisition actually spend engaged in literate activities that will move them forward as learners?

Another way to increase time spent in reading and writing is to enlist family support, particularly when the support is at least somewhat coherent with the children's experience in school. It may be useful, for example, to share with families the word-solving strategies that the children have learned and practiced because, often, when family members listen to young children read, their guidance around word solving is often limited to prompting children to sound out words (Compton-Lilly, 2005), even for words that are not fully decodable. This can be confusing and frustrating for children. In addition, for all children, but especially those who qualify for intervention in the early grades, providing families with information about how literacy development proceeds can be important. In informal interviews with family members, we have found that, with the best of intentions, they sometimes engage children in reading in ways that can be counterproductive. For example, when children are at a point where they are reading patterned/predictable books, it is not unusual for family members to report that they cover the pictures so that the child "has to read the words and not just look at the pictures." In response to such reports, we have prepared a small pamphlet entitled "Helping Your Child Become a Reader," which is available to download and share at *www.eltep.org/parentbooklet.cfm*.

SUPPORTING TEACHERS AND LEARNERS IN SPECIAL EDUCATION CONTEXTS

The second guiding question asks, "In what ways might literacy leaders collaborate with teachers to support learners in special education contexts?" This section provides an overview of special education processes and impacts and then offers suggestions for professional learning targets with regard to differentiating instruction for students receiving special education supports, establishing and maintaining coherence across instructional settings, and understanding/helping students to understand the relationship between practice and progress in relation to literacy skills.

Overview of Special Education

Students are identified as learning disabled (LD) if they demonstrate severe literacy (and/or math) learning difficulties despite having had "adequate" opportunities to learn and if their difficulties are unexpected in relation to their other skills and abilities. Adequate opportunity to learn, in most contexts, means that they have received multiple tiers of appropriately targeted intervention and have not demonstrated the needed level of response. A large proportion of students who are identified as LD qualify on the basis of limited literacy skills, which typically include difficulties with both reading and writing (Fletcher et al., 2019)—not surprising, given that reading and writing involve many of the same skills and knowledge sources (e.g., phonological awareness, phonics, vocabulary, meaning construction).

An individualized education plan (IEP) is developed annually for students who qualify for special education. The purpose of the plan is to describe the instructional accommodations and the differentiated instruction that should be provided, although Lemons, Vaughn, Wexler, Kearns and Sinclair (2018) indicate that these plans are often underspecified. In order to provide appropriately differentiated instruction, the person planning the instruction needs to have a solid understanding of what the student knows and can do and appropriate/logical next steps in instruction.

Legally, special education is supposed to be provided in the "least restrictive environment" that is capable of meeting students' needs. This proviso typically means that students are served in a general education classroom with additional supports and accommodations (extended time on assessments, listening to rather than reading texts, dictating rather than writing, etc.). A special educator either co-teaches the class with a general education teacher all day long or "pushes in" at some point(s) to provide students with instruction that is differentiated to meet their needs. Alternatively, students may be provided with differentiated instruction by a paraprofessional under the direction of a special educator. Or, students spend part of their day in a resource room working directly with a special education teacher or a paraprofessional. These multiple settings lead to questions about how literacy specialists might work collaboratively in these settings to further support learners' literacy development.

The Impact of Special Education

One important intent of special education is, in some ways, much like that of RTI; the goal is to accelerate students' progress through the provision of instruction that is well matched to what students are ready to learn. Unfortunately, there is little evidence that such responsive instruction is occurring on a broad scale. In summarizing observational studies of the reading instruction experienced by students identified as reading disabled, Vaughn and Wanzek (2014) concluded that "students with disabilities are often receiving inadequate instruction in reading in both general and special education settings" (p. 49). They indicated that instruction was, generally, not differentiated based on student need, that students were often taught in large groups, and that they spent too much time doing worksheets and/or working independently with little feedback. In a similar review, McKenna et al. (2015) reported that students were provided with minimal opportunities to apply the skills they were learning in connected text. Given these findings, it is perhaps not surprising that multiple studies have revealed that, at least for reading difficulties (which have been studied more thoroughly than writing difficulties), once students are placed in special education, their reading growth does not accelerate (e.g., Schulte, Stevens, Elliott, Tindal, & Nese, 2016). And, in some studies, they have been found to fall progressively further behind their peers over time (Bentum & Aaron, 2003). This is especially concerning given that low-income children, children of color, and English learners are disproportionately identified as LD (*www.ncld.org/executive-summary*).

[handwritten margin note: What needs to change]

These findings are distressing and would seem to call for major shifts, on a broad scale, in how students are supported in their classroom English language arts (ELA) program and in the intervention they receive to address their difficulties. On a local level, armed with this knowledge, literacy specialists and coaches can collaborate with special education and classroom teachers on how literacy instruction can be made more effective for and responsive to students participating in special education. Literacy specialists, as well as other educators whose preparation is aligned with *Standards 2017,* have expertise in literacy instruction that enables them to offer professional learning opportunities for their colleagues. In the next section we offer suggestions for potential targets of professional learning.

Professional Learning Targets

Differentiating Instruction

According to Fletcher et al. (2019), the majority of students who are identified as LD in reading have difficulty with the word identification aspect of the process, and this difficulty impacts their ability to comprehend grade-level texts. However, there are also students whose oral reading skills are at or close to grade level, but who do not adequately comprehend the materials that they can "read" with relative ease. These differences obviously call for very different types of instruction/intervention. In addition, as noted earlier, many students who demonstrate reading difficulties also have writing difficulties that need to be addressed. Here again, the types of difficulties experienced can range from code/mechanical-type difficulties (e.g., spelling, handwriting) to composition. There are, of course, multiple variations on these profiles. Ideally, those sharing responsibility for students with various profiles would collaborate on devising instructional plans that enable students to engage in ELA and other content-area learning in the classroom. And, again ideally, the students' more pressing literacy-related instructional needs would be addressed via responsive instruction in the intervention setting. In intervention contexts, students would, ideally, be provided with a greater amount of modeling, guidance, and feedback on needed skills and strategies and on how to apply those skills and strategies in reading and writing continuous text. Providing a substantial amount of small-group, teacher-guided instruction is clearly necessary in this regard, with instructional groups formed to enable optimal responsiveness by basing them on similarities in students' instructional profiles.

Literacy professionals who may have greater expertise in literacy than is typical of many classroom teachers and special educators, and certainly more than paraprofessionals, can play an important role in helping those who provide instruction to understand students' needs, develop and deliver instruction that is responsive to those needs, and analyze students' responses to determine next steps. Devising responsive instruction for students with diverse instructional needs is, of course, complex. This is one of the reasons we feel it is so critical to reduce the number of students who need special education supports by instituting effective early intervention. Highly effective early intervention should serve to greatly reduce the number of students who need special education supports, thus making it more feasible to provide responsive instruction for this smaller number of students.

Maintain/Promote Coherence

Much like students in early intervention, students who receive special education supports in literacy generally receive instruction from more than one person in a given day and different teachers across years. Therefore, once again, those providing instruction should coordinate to provide coherence for the students. For example, older students who, in earlier grades, learned to use particular supports to remind them of word identification, comprehension, and/or composing and editing strategies, or key words for letter–sound correspondences, would ideally continue to have access to the same supports, across grades, as needed.

Further, if students have not had the benefit of such supports at earlier points in their education, they can be usefully introduced. For example, in an intensive intervention study with middle school students, Gelzheiser, Scanlon, and Hallgren-Flynn (2010) found that students who had difficulties with word identification generally were not strategic in their

word-solving attempts and benefited when word identifica
were explicitly taught and practiced.

Efforts to create coherence can also focus on the texts
read and write in the intervention setting. While students n
read and write at grade-appropriate levels, they also need to learn the ELA,
science, and social studies content dictated by state standards. To support
this learning, whenever possible, efforts can be made to prepare students
for and/or reinforce the content that is addressed in the classroom. For
example, if students will be studying a particular genre or reading texts
set in a particular period of time in their ELA program, opportunities to
become familiar with that genre or time period could be offered in intervention, but in easier texts than those used in the classroom. This focus
should help students to develop background knowledge and vocabulary
that will make grade-appropriate texts more accessible.

An example of using the intervention setting to support content-area
learning is provided in a study by Gelzheiser, Scanlon, Vellutino, and
Deane (2019). Third- and fourth-grade students participated in a small-
group intervention in which they read thematically organized books related
to the science and social studies standards for their grade level. To build
background knowledge and vocabulary related to the topic, the books read
at the beginning of a unit were relatively easy. Subsequent books became
increasingly challenging as the theme unfolded. The goal was that the final
text for the theme would be close to a grade-appropriate level. As they
read across multiple books, students captured the new information they
acquired in writing—often using sticky notes. Reading occurred in various formats, including teacher-guided, partner, and independent reading,
depending on student need and the level of challenge posed by the text.
During teacher-guided reading, the teacher modeled note taking to capture
new information. During partner and independent reading, students did
their own note taking and, when their group came together to discuss what
they had read/learned, students often added information to a collaborative
poster. Pertinent to the issue of coherence, there was a clear connection
between what the students did in intervention and the learning expectations in the classroom. From a motivational perspective, when students had
read about a topic before it was addressed in the classroom, they were
among the topic experts in the classroom—a rare but highly motivating
experience for study participants.

Connecting Practice and Progress

Because they find reading and writing challenging, many students with literacy difficulties avoid reading and writing whenever they can. As a result,
they read and write less than their peers and have the potential to fall
further behind. One reason for this avoidance may be that they are often
asked to read and write texts that are too challenging for them (Allington,

McCuiston, & Billen, 2015). With a steady diet of texts that are too challenging, it is not surprising that some students come to believe that reading and writing will always be difficult—so why would they want to engage. Of course, if students do not engage in enough reading and writing to enable them to develop sufficient automaticity with foundational skills (e.g., word identification, spelling), they may not get to the point where they can focus primarily on the reason for reading and writing: meaning construction.

Anecdotally, we have encountered multiple students identified as LD who, during conversations in the context of evaluations, were surprised to learn that, at least for reading, the more one reads, the easier it gets. These students had developed the belief that reading would always be challenging for them and had adopted what Dweck and colleagues (see Dweck, 2017, for a summary) refer to as a fixed mindset in regard to their literacy abilities. Individuals with such a mindset, when encountering challenge, tend not to engage in the activity because they anticipate failure. In contrast, individuals with growth mindsets understand, at least implicitly, that academic abilities can grow through engagement in tasks that are initially challenging, and consequently they are far more willing to engage in ways that lead to growth.

Intervention research that is focused on helping students to adopt growth mindsets provides evidence that, at least among middle and high school students who are underperforming, such interventions are effective in improving students' academic performance both in terms of grades and high school completion rates (see Dweck, Walton, & Cohen, 2014 for a review). Although we were unable to locate any studies that focused explicitly on students receiving special education services, the effects of mindset interventions are promising. To us, the research clearly reinforces the idea that it is important to help students understand the relationship between practice and progress. Helping them to reflect on their success at learning something that was initially challenging (like riding a bike or even learning to walk) can be useful in this regard.

THINK ABOUT THIS

1. Does teachers' language clearly communicate the relationship between practice and progress?
2. Is the literacy instruction provided to students in special education appropriately differentiated?

POLICY CONTROVERSIES AND ADVOCACY

Next, we address the third guiding question, "How might literacy leaders understand and address current policy controversies related to literacy difficulties to best support and advocate for all learners?" This question draws on information from all of the standards on consulting with families, colleagues, communities, and relevant stakeholders to advocate for effective literacy practices and policies. The controversies related to literacy learning difficulties revolve around the conceptualization of dyslexia.

Most students who qualify for special education services for literacy difficulties have difficulty, sometimes severe difficulty, with the word reading (and spelling) aspects of the processes. It is generally agreed that, when such difficulties occur despite generally effective early literacy instruction, they are due to limitations in students' phonological skills, including the ability to attend to and manipulate the component sounds in spoken words (phonemic awareness) and the ability to map those sounds to their printed representations (phonics) (Fletcher et al., 2019). Difficulties in these areas lead to limited orthographic mapping that, in turn, limits growth in the number of words readers can identify on sight. Ehri (2014) defines orthographic mapping as "the formation of letter–sound connections to bond the spellings, pronunciations, and meanings of specific words in memory" (p. 5). As readers gain skill, larger orthographic patterns (e.g., syllables and whole words) are mapped to their pronunciations. This is how readers come to be able to identify words with automaticity.

Some argue that individuals with severe word reading difficulties should be identified as dyslexic on the belief that dyslexia is a type of learning difficulty/disability that is somehow categorically different from other types of difficulties that involve word-level skills. Elliot and Grigorenko (2014) have written extensively on whether and how dyslexia differs from other types of literacy learning difficulties that involve word-level accuracy and have concluded that there is no useful distinction. They note that ease of literacy learning occurs on a continuum with some students finding it easy to become literate, needing relatively little instructional support, whereas others experience severe difficulties despite otherwise effective instruction and intervention. Most students fall somewhere between the two extremes. Elliot and Grigorenko argue that reading ability is normally distributed and that there is no consensus about where to draw the line between those who are and are not disabled/dyslexic.

Readers Experiencing Severe Difficulty Do Not See Things Backward

In the general public, dyslexia is often characterized as a condition in which individuals experience literacy learning difficulties due to visual–perceptual difficulties that cause individuals to "see" things differently than do people who are not dyslexic—for example misperceiving b as d or was as saw. However, decades ago, Vellutino (1979) demonstrated convincingly that reading difficulties are not due to visual–perceptual difficulties but rather to verbal processing difficulties. The issue is not that the reader who calls a b a d sees it differently but rather that the reader can't recall whether the b is called /bee/ or /dee/. Such errors occur because, until children begin to learn about print, objects are called by the same name regardless of how they are oriented in space. (A cup is a cup no matter how it is rotated.) These confusions persist for some readers if their early confusions go uncorrected and they, essentially, practice their confusion so much that it becomes difficult to overcome them.

In recent years, substantial controversy has developed in relation to how to classify and respond to serious difficulties with word reading (and spelling) that are unexpected in relation to an individual's other skills and abilities and when the individual has had adequate instruction. The International Dyslexia Association and a parents' organization called Decoding Dyslexia have been advocates for identifying such individuals as dyslexic, and they argue that students so identified need instruction that is based on highly structured and scripted instructional programs. Others argue that dyslexia is a diagnostic category of questionable validity (Elliot & Grigorenko, 2014; ILA, 2016a) and that there is no evidence that there is one best instructional response for students with such difficulties. The Literacy Research Panel, in particular, argues that instruction should be responsive to individual need. As noted in the discussion of RTI, most children who experience early reading difficulties can, with appropriately targeted and intensified instruction, overcome their early difficulties. Members of the International Dyslexia Association and Decoding Dyslexia agree but, in many cases, would still refer to those children as *dyslexic,* albeit, compensated dyslexics, while those aligned with the position of the Literacy Research Panel of the International Literacy Association would consider them to be instructional successes.

In some settings, these differences of opinion have become quite divisive and contentious professionally, legally, and legislatively. For example, families of students who have serious reading difficulties have, in some cases, successfully sued school districts to gain access to the highly structured instructional programs advocated for by the International Dyslexia Association and Decoding Dyslexia organizations. Legislatively, these organizations have been very instrumental in convincing many state legislatures to issue laws and regulations that variably mandate that all students be screened for dyslexia, all schools have dyslexia specialists who are trained in the diagnosis and "treatment" of dyslexia, all teachers be trained in at least one of a small number of highly structured programs that place very heavy emphasis on teaching the alphabetic code, and/or that teacher preparation programs should abide by the teacher certification standards of the International Dyslexia Association (2018). (The status of legislative action for various states can be found at *www.dyslegia.com.*) Some states also allow "dyslexia specialists" to be certified to diagnose and "treat" dyslexia with remarkably limited "training" and, in at least one instance

(Texas), no requirement that they have any other educational credentials. In addition, these organizations argue that *all* students would benefit from what they refer to as *structured literacy* instruction. Programs such as Wilson, Fundations, and other Orton–Gillingham derivatives are examples of structured literacy programs. Although there is no question that some children need expert instruction to develop the necessary skill with the alphabetic code, as well as other aspects of literacy, we were unable to locate any scientific evidence that supports the preferential use of Orton–Gillingham-based programs. The advocacy groups also make strong claims about the incidence of dyslexia, arguing that one in five people is dyslexic and that schools have failed to appropriately identify and respond to the problem (*https://dyslexiaida.org*). However, most of the research places the estimate of long-term, serious reading difficulties at much lower points. For example, Fletcher et al. (2019) put the estimate at closer to 1 or 2% when early intervention is in place.

Due to concerns with the positions taken by these advocacy groups, in 2016a the ILA's Literacy Research Panel issued a Research Advisory in which they reviewed the research on literacy difficulties and interventions. With regard to the use of dyslexia as a diagnostic category, the panel concluded, much like Elliot and Grigorenko, that there is no agreement among researchers as to the criteria to use to identify individuals as having reading difficulties significant enough to qualify them as reading disabled/dyslexic. The Literacy Research Panel also noted that the term *dyslexia* tended to be used interchangeably with the term *reading disability* in the research literature. Further, the panel noted that the highly scripted (and unresponsive) instructional programs advocated by the International Dyslexia Association and Decoding Dyslexia groups have no clear scientific evidence of efficacy and therefore, clearly, no evidence that the programs are *more* effective than other approaches to intervention and instruction that are more responsive to individual needs.

Moreover, there are concerns about several of the recommended instructional practices that are implemented in these programs (see Figure 14.3). Further, it is important to note that, in a review of multiple studies of various reading interventions across grades 4–12, Wanzek et al. (2013) found only small improvements in reading outcomes. They suggested that the limited impact may be due to the use of "one-size-fits-all" programs, in which some students are taught skills and concepts they already know, while others are taught skills and concepts they are not ready to learn. In both cases, it is a waste of instructional time. The Wanzek et al. finding suggests that there is clearly still much to be learned about how to accelerate the progress of literacy learners who experience difficulty, especially those in the middle elementary grades and beyond. Indeed, Wanzek et al.'s summary would seem to make clear that there is simply no justification for advocating for programs that fall under the *structured literacy* umbrella,

Recommended Practice	Concern with the Practice
Some programs that fall under the structured literacy umbrella advocate for instruction to be scripted and sequenced identically for all program participants.	Such practices risk boredom and disengagement when students are taught skills and concepts they already know, and frustration when instruction is focused on skills and concepts students are not ready to learn.
Instruction should be multisensory (e.g., having children trace sand paper cutouts of letters and words with a finger while naming the item).	There is no evidence that programs that include this practice are more effective than those that do not. Having children write the letters and words while naming them would likely be more effective.
Dissuade children from relying on meaning (including pictures) and syntax as an assist to word identification.	Many written words are not fully decodable based on the decoding skills typically taught. Students need to use meaning to direct and check their decoding attempts.
Teach details of the orthographic system (such as the six syllable types).	This method makes literacy learning more challenging than is necessary and knowing such details does not always assist in the decoding process. Most literate adults do not know such details.
Make heavy use of decodable texts for readers at early points in development.	Some opportunity for readers to apply the phonics skills they are learning in context is useful, but a heavy diet of highly decodable texts has the potential to turn children's attention away from the meaning-making purpose of reading.

FIGURE 14.3. Recommended instructional practices in programs supported by dyslexia advocacy groups and concerns about those practices.

especially because, as noted, there is no scientific research that demonstrates the superiority of such programs and barely any research of any sort in this regard. At best, there is justification for conducting high-quality scientific research to test the programs' efficacy in relation to other approaches.

It is important that those in leadership roles know that the research to support the claims made by the International Dyslexia Association and Decoding Dyslexia groups simply does not exist. However, as Gabriel (2018) has argued, it is important for those who are uncomfortable with the International Dyslexia Association/Decoding Dyslexia position on instruction to be clear about exactly what they oppose. Some of the most concerning practices are described in Figure 14.3. Gabriel also urges those who are uncomfortable with the International Dyslexia Association/Decoding Dyslexia instructional approach to be certain that all stakeholders, including those aligned with the International Dyslexia Association/Decoding Dyslexia position, are providing instruction that addresses all aspects of literacy development that are identified as instructional foci by the International Dyslexia Association (*https://dyslexiaida.org/what-is-structured-literacy*). For the most part, the concern is more about the approach to instruction rather than the desired outcomes of instruction.

Going forward, we encourage literacy professionals to keep abreast of, and ideally take a stand on, legislation around reading difficulties/dyslexia. Both the ILA and the International Dyslexia Association are concerned that the best interests of students who struggle are served. By definition, those who qualify for special education would seem to deserve instruction that is truly special, which, according to Zigmond (2001), involves "monitoring each student's progress and taking responsibility for changing instruction when the monitoring data indicate that sufficient progress is not being made. It means providing students who have learning and behavioral disorders with something truly special" (p. 73). Prescribing highly scripted and routinized programs would seem to be the antithesis of what special education is intended to be.

In the literacy domain, it is individuals with in-depth knowledge about literacy instruction who have the expertise to guide the instructional modifications called for by Zigmond (2001), be they literacy professionals, special educators, or classroom teachers. In this context, modifications in instruction need to be based on more than the oral reading accuracy, fluency, and/or decoding assessments that are in common use. Although such assessments are informative to a degree, they do not provide the information needed about students' processing skills—or what they do at the point of difficulty while reading (i.e., what they do to solve unfamiliar words). Such information is especially important in guiding modifications in instruction.

CONCLUSION

Literacy professionals have the potential to positively influence the literacy development of children who may be at risk of experiencing literacy learning difficulties before they enter elementary school, by communicating with families and other caregivers about the importance of promoting the development of language skills and the knowledge base upon which comprehension depends. They have an even larger role to play in preventing literacy difficulties in the early elementary grades through their work with classroom teachers and interventionists to ensure that instruction is appropriately targeted, explicit, coherent, responsive, and provided with enough intensity to promote an optimal effect. The goal is to reduce the number of children who fall so far behind in their literacy skills that they qualify for special education services. For those who do qualify, literacy professionals, in collaboration with special educators and classroom teachers, can still strive to optimize the students' instructional experiences so that they experience accelerated growth in literacy skills. As discussed, in our opinion, such acceleration is more likely when instruction is responsive to student need rather than highly structured and scripted.

ENGAGEMENT ACTIVITIES

1. With your colleagues, investigate and evaluate available programs in your community that promote shared book reading in early childhood (see Figure 14.1). Discuss how your school could promote and/or expand such programs for young children in your district.

2. With the special education colleagues at your school, discuss the ways in which they collaborate with classroom teachers and specialized literacy professionals to provide literacy instruction for students. Consider instructional practices such as amount of time reading/writing, consistent instructional use of language/labels, and support for the use of strategies across settings.

3. Consider how you and your school view literacy instruction practices for students experiencing difficulty. Read the ILA's dyslexia research advisory,[2] the International Dyslexia Association's response,[3] and the ILA addendum that responds to the association's response.[4] Discuss the available research and how you might optimize learning for children in a comprehensive literacy framework, drawing on *Standards 2017*.

ANNOTATED RESOURCES

Gelzheiser, L. M., Hallgren-Flynn, L., Connors, M., & Scanlon, D. M. (2014). Reading thematically-related texts to develop knowledge and comprehension. *The Reading Teacher, 68*(1), 53–63.

This article describes an approach used to develop thematic units related to grade-level science and social studies topics for use in the context of reading intervention for middle elementary through middle school levels. The article provides examples of thematic units and details procedures used in identifying and sequencing texts within a set. The sequencing is designed to engage students first in reading

---

[2] Available at *www.literacyworldwide.org/docs/default-source/where-we-stand/ila-dyslexia-research-advisory.pdf?sfvrsn=411ba18e_6*.

[3] Available at *https://dyslexiaida.org/ida-urges-ila-to-review-and-clarify-key-points-in-dyslexia-research-advisory*.

[4] Available at *www.literacyworldwide.org/docs/default-source/where-we-stand/ila-dyslexia-research-advisory-addendum.pdf?sfvrsn=85bca08e_4*.

easy texts to develop background knowledge and vocabulary and gradually pro-
gresses to texts that are more grade-appropriate.

Scanlon, D. M., Anderson, K. L., & Sweeney, J. M. (2017). *Early intervention for
reading difficulties: The interactive strategies approach* (2nd ed.). New York:
Guilford Press.

This resource provides information on experimentally validated approaches
to early literacy instruction and intervention that have demonstrated positive
impacts on early literacy learning, when implemented by classroom teachers and in
small-group and one-to-one intervention settings.

Trelease, J. (2013). *The read-aloud handbook* (7th ed.). New York: Penguin Books.

This book provides a cogent and accessible review of the research on the
impact of read-alouds, which, as noted above, are powerful influences on early
language and literacy development. The book also provides guidance on how to
engage children of various ages in read-alouds and age-appropriate books.

REFERENCES

Allington, R. L., McCuiston, K., & Billen, M. (2015). What research says about text
complexity and learning to read. *The Reading Teacher, 68*(7), 491–501.

Anderson, R. C., Hiebert, E. H., Scott, J. A., & Wilkinson, I. (1985). *Becoming a
nation of readers*. Washington, DC: National Institute of Education.

Bentum, K. E., & Aaron, P. G. (2003). Does reading instruction in learning disability resource rooms really work?: A longitudinal study. *Reading Psychology, 24*,
361–382.

Compton-Lilly, C. (2005). "Sounding out": A pervasive cultural model of reading. *Language Arts, 82*(6), 441–451.

Duff, F. J., Reen, G., Plunkett, K., & Nation, K. (2015). Do infant vocabulary skills
predict school-age language and literacy outcomes? *Journal of Child Psychology
and Psychiatry, 56*(8), 848–856.

Dweck, C. S. (2017). The journey to children's mindsets—and beyond. *Child Development Perspectives, 11*(2), 139–144.

Dweck, C. S., Walton, G. M., & Cohen, G. L. (2014). Academic tenacity: Mindsets
and skills that promote long term learning. Retrieved from *www.edutopia.org/
resource/mindset-research.*

Ehri, L. C. (2014). Orthographic mapping in the acquisition of sight word reading,
spelling memory, and vocabulary learning. *Scientific Studies of Reading, 18,* 5–21.

Elliott, J. G., & Grigorenko, E. L. (2014). *The dyslexia debate*. New York: Cambridge
University Press.

Fletcher, J. M., Lyons, G. R., Fuchs, L. S., & Barnes, M. A. (2019). *Learning disabilities: From identification to intervention*. New York: Guilford Press.

Foorman, B. R., & Al Otaiba, S. (2009). Reading remediation: State of the art. In K.
Pugh & P. McCardle (Eds.), *How children learn to read: Current issues and new
directions in the integration of cognition, neurobiology and genetics of reading
and dyslexia research and practice* (pp. 257–274). New York: Psychology Press.

Gabriel, R. (2018). Preparing literacy professionals: The case of dyslexia. *Journal of
Literacy Research, 50*(2), 262–270.

Gelzheiser, L. M., Scanlon, D. M., & Hallgren-Flynn, L. (2010). Spotlight on RTI for adolescents: An example of intensive middle school intervention using the interactive strategies approach—extended. In M. Y. Lipson & K. K. Wixson (Eds.), *Successful approaches to RTI: Collaborative practices for improving K–12 literacy* (pp. 211–230). Newark, DE: International Reading Association.

Gelzheiser, L. M., Scanlon, D. M., Hallgren-Flynn, L., & Connors, M. (2019). *Comprehensive reading intervention in grades 3–8: Fostering word learning, comprehension, and motivation.* New York: Guilford Press.

Gelzheiser, L. M., Scanlon, D. M., Vellutino, F. R., & Deane, G. (2019). *The effects of a comprehensive and responsive intervention on the reading comprehension of intermediate grade struggling readers.* Manuscript in preparation.

International Dyslexia Association. (2018). *Knowledge and practice standards for teachers of reading.* Baltimore: Author.

International Literacy Association (ILA). (2016a). *Dyslexia* (Research advisory). Newark, DE: Author.

International Literacy Association (ILA). (2016b). *Dyslexia: A response to the International Dyslexia Association* (Research Advisory Addendum). Newark, DE: Author.

International Literacy Association (ILA). (2018). *Standards for the preparation of literacy professionals literacy professionals 2017.* Newark, DE: Author.

Kent, S. C., Wanzek, J., & Al Otaiba, S. (2012). Print reading in general education kindergarten classrooms: What does it look like for students at-risk for reading difficulties? *Learning Disabilities Research and Practice, 27*(2), 56–65.

Lemons, C. J., Vaughn, S., Wexler, J., Kearns, D. M., & Sinclair, A. C. (2018). Envisioning an improved continuum of special education services for students with learning disabilities: Considering intervention intensity. *Learning Disabilities Research and Practice, 33*(3), 131–143.

McKenna, J., Shin, M., & Ciullo, S. (2015). Evaluating reading and mathematics instruction for students with learning disabilities: A synthesis of observation research. *Learning Disabilities Quarterly, 38,* 195–207.

National Early Literacy Panel. (2008). *Developing early literacy.* Washington, DC: National Institute for Literacy.

National Reading Panel. (2000). *Teaching children to read: An evidence-based assessment of the scientific research literature on reading and its implications for reading instruction: Reports of subgroups.* Washington, DC: National Institute of Child Health and Human Development.

Scanlon, D. M., & Anderson, K. L. (2010). Using the interactive strategies approach to preventing reading difficulties in an RTI context. In M. Y. Lipson & K. K. Wixson (Eds.), *Successful approaches to RTI: Collaborative practices for improving K–12 literacy* (pp. 20–65). Newark, DE: International Reading Association.

Scanlon, D. M., Anderson, K. L., & Sweeney, J. M. (2017). *Early intervention for reading difficulties: The interactive strategies approach* (2nd ed.). New York: Guilford Press.

Scanlon, D. M., Gelzheiser, L. M., Vellutino, F. R., Schatschneider, C., & Sweeney, J. M. (2008). Reducing the incidence of early reading difficulties: Professional development for classroom teachers vs. direct interventions for children. *Learning and Individual Differences, 18,* 346–359.

Schulte, A. C., Stevens, J. J., Elliott, S. N., Tindal, G., & Nese, J. F. T. (2016). Achievement gaps for students with disabilities: Stable, widening, or narrowing on a statewide reading comprehension test? *Journal of Educational Psychology, 108*(7), 925–942.

Share, D. L. (1995). Phonological recoding and self-teaching: Sine qua non of reading acquisition. *Cognition, 55,* 151–218.

Turner, J. D., Crassas, M. E., & Segal, P. H. (2015). Family matters: Home influences and individual differences in children's reading development. In P. Afflerbach (Ed.), *Handbook of individual differences in reading: Reader, text, and context* (pp. 273–285). New York: Routledge.

van den Broek, P., Mouw, J. M., & Kraal, A. (2016). Individual differences in reading comprehension. In P. Afflerbach (Ed.), *Handbook of individual differences in reading: Reader, text, and context* (pp. 138–150). New York: Routledge.

Vaughn, S., & Wanzek, J. (2014). Intensive interventions for reading for students with reading disability: Meaningful impacts. *Learning Disabilities Research and Practice, 29*(2), 46–53.

Vellutino, F. R. (1979). *Dyslexia: Theory and research.* Cambridge, MA: MIT Press.

Wanzek, J., Vaughn, S., Scammacca, N. K., Metz, K., Murray, C. S., Roberts, G., et al. (2013). Extensive reading interventions for students with reading difficulties after grade 3. *Review of Educational Research, 83*(2), 163–195.

Zigmond, N. P. (2001). Special education at the crossroads. *Preventing School Failure, 45*(2), 70–74.

CHAPTER 15

Culturally Responsive Literacy Instruction

Doris Walker-Dalhouse
Victoria J. Risko

GUIDING QUESTIONS

→ What is culturally responsive instruction and what implications can be drawn from research investigating its impact on students' engagement and literacy development, and teachers' professional learning?

→ What barriers must be mitigated if we expect to construct new realities of culturally responsive instruction and meet the goals of diversity and equity as outlined in the *Standards for the Preparation of Literacy Professionals 2017* (International Literacy Association [ILA], 2018a)?

→ What specific instructional practices support diversity and equity and are responsive to students' cultural and identity differences?

→ How can literacy leaders lead and guide school- and districtwide efforts to both advance culturally responsive and equity-based instructional practices and advocate for students?

This chapter examines culturally responsive instruction and the lessons that can be learned about its effectiveness in promoting students' literacy engagement and achievement while optimizing students' identities, life experiences, and cultural and linguistic diversity. We describe barriers that often prevent students from realizing their literacy potential and identify specific instructional practices that can mitigate such barriers.

EXPECTATIONS FOR CULTURALLY RESPONSIVE INSTRUCTION

Culturally relevant pedagogy (Ladson-Billings, 1995) and *culturally responsive pedagogy* (Gay, 2018) are terms that are often used interchangeably. The emphasis for both is on centering students' cultural practices as essential for learning. *Culturally relevant instruction* is built upon academic indicators of students' achievement, their cultural competence, their ability to be grounded in their own culture and identities while acquiring knowledge and skills to interact effectively with people of different cultures, and their sociopolitical consciousness. Fixed notions of culture that do not acknowledge the fluidity or the changing nature of groups through the influence of other cultural groups, have resulted in a misuse of culturally relevant pedagogy (Ladson-Billings, 1995).

The goal to develop students' sociopolitical consciousness focuses on encouraging them to take actions as agents of change while examining critically issues of diversity and social justice (Ladson-Billings, 2014). Teachers' inability to encourage students to develop critical perspectives related to policies and practices that have a direct effect on their lives and communities has been found to be problematic in the implementation of culturally relevant pedagogy (Ladson-Billings, 2014).

Culturally responsive instruction is predicated more on a way of being as opposed to specific teaching practices (Ladson-Billings, 2014). Culturally responsive teaching has been described as making the educational experiences of students more visible and meaningful by utilizing their identities, cultural knowledge, prior experiences, frames of reference, and their performance styles in their instructional routines. Cultural affirmation and validation occur during the process of teaching both to and through students' strengths. Positive outcomes are reported when teachers believe in their students, hold expectations for their achievement, and know how to make connections to students' funds of knowledge, including their linguistic histories (Lopez, 2016).

Paris (2012) extended the work of culturally responsive instruction by reenvisioning what it means to foster equality and cultural pluralism. He coined the term *culturally sustaining pedagogy* (CSP) for this iteration or extension of the theory and believes that it "requires that instructional support be given to young people in sustaining the cultural and linguistic competence of their communities, while simultaneously offering access to dominant cultural competence" (p. 95). Paris believes that the use of the word *relevant* in the term *culturally relevant pedagogy* omits explicit support in maintaining culture and critiquing social issues. A more pluralistic and critical approach to education, in contrast to focusing on a mere acknowledgment of students' cultures, is advocated (Paris, 2012). Paris and others advocate for a broader or extended view of culture that moves beyond ethnicity to include various types of culturally affected concepts

such as *youth,* what is considered *popular/contemporary,* and what constitutes *local cultures* (Machado, 2017). It also involves supporting the integration of languages, dialects, and the social use of language in formal
and informal contexts, and creating culturally sustaining classrooms that
provide a "mirror" in which students can see themselves, a "window" to
understand the perspective of others, and a "doorway" through which to
consider new paths and possibilities (ILA, 2017).

To meet the goals of this chapter, we use the term *culturally responsive*
to signal our inclusion of the cultural, linguistic, and ethnically diverse
views associated with teaching to students' assets and the added broad view
of culture that moves beyond ethnicity to include a wide range of cultural
concepts, as described by Paris (2012) and others. Additionally, culturally
responsive teaching, as developed in this chapter, is characterized as being
validating, multidimensional, empowering, transformative, emancipatory,
humanistic, normative, and ethical (Gay, 2018).

Our broad view of culturally responsive instruction is consistent with
ILA's Standard 4 and its components, with its specific emphasis on diversity and equity. The argument for *diversity and equity* embedded in Standard 4 is situated in multiple theories and reviews of empirical research.
As stated in Standard 4, literacy leaders are expected to have foundational
knowledge of and make application to pedagogy in areas such as critical
race theory, second language theories, sociocultural theories, third space,
and transgender and queer theories. These theories as a whole draw to the
forefront the importance of making known students' resources as the infor-
mant for making instructional decisions (ILA, 2018a).

In this chapter, we draw on these theories and related research to identify principles, instructional practices, and examples with our goal of creating a vivid picture of instructional practices that are intended to disrupt
inequities—inequities that too often are associated with literacy instruction
that is far removed from engaging students in meaningful learning.

BARRIERS TO THE REALITY OF CULTURALLY RESPONSIVE INSTRUCTION

Culturally responsive instruction is guided by evidence that substantiates
the importance of making visible students' resources as funds of knowledge
(Moll, 2015) and acknowledging these as funds of identity that students use
to define themselves (Esteban-Guitart & Moll, 2014), their families, and
their communities. Although such evidence has been cited for at least three
decades, students continue to "fail"—not because of their attributes but
because schools and literacy instruction, in particular, have failed them.
Will *Standards 2017* be the impetus for changing that conclusion of failure
and redirecting efforts to support students—*all* students—by drawing on

and maximizing their strengths? A positive answer to this question requires a new vision, new professional learning opportunities for literacy leaders, and bold actions that are grounded in a determination by literacy leaders to support students in ways that maintain their "cultural competence" and sociopolitical consciousness, while ensuring academic success (Puzio et al., 2017). In the following section, we identify existing barriers to the goal of achieving equity.

A Deficit View Is the Coin of the Realm

Dudley-Marling and Lucas (2009), providing a provocative analysis of research reports that take narrow views of students' cultural competence and prior knowledge, argued that a lack of knowing is a fatal flaw that too often is repeated by investigators and curricular developers. For example, they disagree with Hart and Risley (1995), who claimed that poor children lack the rich and varied vocabulary needed to succeed in school. Dudley-Marling and Lucas concluded that these researchers failed to consider the language of poor families on "its own terms" (i.e., identifying attributes of language exchanges that, while different from a White or mainstream culture, had its own value and richness).

Similarly, how literacy leaders and teachers respond to differences depends on whether they view these differences as *assets* or as *deficiencies*. As Puzio and his coauthors (2017) indicate, educators and the curricula in place too often favor mainstream cultural values and norms without regard to students whose experiences and histories hold their own richness while differing from a mainstream view.

Misunderstandings Spawn Loss of Identity, Culture, and Language

Numerous investigators describe a paucity of actions by teacher educators or professional learning leaders in making explicit personal beliefs and potential biases that inhibit culturally responsive instruction (Milner, 2011). Yet when coursework or professional learning sessions address issues such as race, class, gender, culture, language, identity. and methods that teach for social justice, the results are quite striking. For example, with such professional learning in place, teacher educators report outcomes of prospective teachers' beliefs moving from deficit views of their students to views that acknowledge differences as resources. Further, they describe prospective teachers' developing abilities to teach to students' assets and adapt restrictive curricula to support diverse learners (International Literacy Association & National Council of Teachers of English, 2017).

Monolingual teachers often encounter challenges in working with English learners (ELs), given a lack of preparation for teaching them and a limited history of interacting with culturally and linguistically diverse students (Walker-Dalhouse, Sanders, & Dalhouse, 2009). McBrien (2005), in a study of instruction provided for refugee students, described multiple obstacles that derive from a lack of leadership by literacy professionals in offsetting biases that are inherent in the actions of teachers and school leaders (e.g., teachers' low expectations, unwelcoming school community, peer discrimination, lack of respect for cultural differences). These obstacles intruded on students' assimilation into the school and classroom and contributed to cross cultural misunderstandings, marginalization, depression, emotional exhaustion, and a loss of students' first language(s) and culture.

Similarly, Daniel (2018) identified a loss of refugee youths' funds of knowledge, the very knowledge that was needed to support a *blending* of their identities across "borders—of home, school, community and their use of multiple literacy modes (e.g., written text, websites, videos) and multilingual repertoires" (p. 2). In too many classrooms, students with different languages or funds of knowledge have few opportunities to leverage their strengths to make sense of what they are learning (Skerrett, 2015).

Political and Legislative Decisions Deter Positive Actions

The question has been asked, "Do children have a right to literacy?" Chief Justice Earl Warren said, in the *Brown v. the Board of Education of Topeka Kansas* ruling, that "Education [is a] right which must be made available to all on equal terms." *Brown v. Board of Education of Topeka* case, in 1954, was a landmark Supreme Court case that declared that state laws establishing separate schools for Black and White children were unconstitutional because they violated the Equal Protection clause of the Fourteenth Amendment. The case has legal and moral implications in talking about equity. Subsequently the Brown II 1955 case ordered that schools be integrated "with all deliberate speed."

More recently, a class action suit was filed on behalf of students in the Detroit Public Schools. This suit contended that decades of disinvestment and deliberate indifference in the school system by state officials responsible for administration and oversight of public education have denied students access to literacy and are in violation of their rights under the Fourteenth Amendment to the U.S. Constitution and Title VI of the Civil Rights Act of 1964.

On June 29, 2018, the judge in the case questioned whether it is the responsibility of states to provide a "minimally adequate education" that ensures a child attains literacy. Although the judge acknowledged that literacy is of "incalculable importance," he ruled that access to literacy is not a fundamental right because neither the word *school* nor *education* appears in the U.S. Constitution. This federal court failed to establish access to an adequate education as a fundamental right (Mangan, 2016).

In response to that suit and a growing awareness of less than equitable conditions for student learning, the ILA advocates strongly for access to literacy as a right. In its recent publication, *The Case for Children's Right to Read* (ILA, 2018b), the ILA expressed the belief that "Children have the basic human right to read" (p. 4). The justification provided in support of this right is that "the ability to read truly represents the difference between inclusion and exclusion from society. If we acknowledge that, then we must also acknowledge that ensuring children's rights to read is an issue of equity. It's an issue of equality of opportunity. It's an issue of quality of instruction. In short, it's an issue of social justice" (ILA, 2018b, p. 4).

The above barriers require literacy professionals to take bold actions that will lead to constructing a new reality for students and all literacy professionals.

INSTRUCTIONAL PRACTICES SUPPORTING EQUITY AND DIVERSITY

Consistent with the theoretical framing and research supporting culturally responsive instruction, we identify these evidence-based practices that share the following principles and characteristics.

Access and Actualize Students' Funds of Knowledge

Identifying, making visible, and teaching to students' assets requires intentional and informed actions by literacy professionals. These assets include multiple layers of students' capabilities and knowledge, their language histories, and their forms and styles of language interactions, interests, and home and life experiences (Risko & Walker-Dalhouse, 2019).

We share three examples of culturally responsive instruction that address students' funds of knowledge and pride in their cultural identities.

Cultural Modeling

As designed by Lee and her colleagues (Lee, Rosenfeld, Mendenhall, Rivers, & Tynes, 2004), cultural modeling makes explicit connections to the literacy practices of African American middle and high school students: for example, choices of music, involvement in digital composing, and their vernacular and rhetorical patterns of conversational language. Engaged in critical analysis of content and symbolism of music, Lee and her colleagues (2004) report enhanced text comprehension and student-generated problem solving and questioning. Use of their own vernacular and language patterns was viewed as especially important for supporting students' connections between their linguistic and cultural knowledge, lived experiences, and the school's instructional goals.

Translanguaging

Translanguaging describes how bilingual and multilingual students communicate and make meaning by drawing on and "intermingling linguistic features" of the languages that are in their repertoire (Garcia, 2009, p. 51). As a school practice, translanguaging engages students in the use of their home language(s) and English, frequently meshed together to advance students' literacy development and communication skills. Students are engaged in translating school texts and negotiating meanings with their peers during small-group collaborative efforts (Jiménez, 2015). Negotiation with teachers, often those who speak only English, continues to expand language repertoires and deepen knowledge development. For example, asking middle school students to translate selected sections of English-language texts resulted in students' deepening knowledge of text concepts, while also increasing their metalinguistic awareness of both their home language(s) and English (Jiménez et al., 2015).

Student-Centered Approaches

A third example is associated with implementing student-centered approaches, in which students generate the issues and questions that often are derived from their life experiences to serve as anchors for learning and instruction. An example is a social justice collaborative education project developed between the University of Arizona and the Tucson United School District. The goal for students, including a large Latino population, was to learn and apply research and critical thinking skills to inform their writing and speaking about inequities (e.g., the action by state legislators to eliminate ethnic studies in their school curriculum) (Cammarota, 2008). Among the reported outcomes were increased engagement, increased school attendance, increased achievement scores, and a rise in the number of students who graduated and went on to college. Embedded in these student-centered projects is students' realization of the powerful impact that student advocacy and civic engagement have on their learning and their role as change agents.

Sustain and Take Advantage of Multiple Out-of-School Cultural Communities

An important understanding associated with teaching to students' cultural knowledge and identities comes from Alim and Paris (2017), who remind us of the goal to sustain the "lifeways of communities" (p. 1) that too often are erased within and through schooling. Students' cultural ways of knowing and participating in literacy practices are not monolithic, but instead continue to grow and change in dynamic ways. It would be a mistake to think of these as fixed or to allow them to go unnoticed as internal inconsistencies that come with youth culture and development. The range of cultural enactments both in and out of school hold even more promise for diversifying instruction to promote equity across race, gender, sexuality identities, and socioeconomic class (Smith, 2016).

Perhaps the most obvious reasons for making out-of-school and in-school connections is to demonstrate to students that they matter in life and in school, that their identities are valued by the school, and that their knowledge and experiences are anchors for learning. Additionally, a larger purpose is that of sustaining the pluralism of identities and cultural communities as a "necessary good" for an equitable and democratic society (Alim & Paris, 2017, p. 1).

Daniel (2018) demonstrated how three refugee teens leveraged their multilingual (i.e., translanguaging) and multimodal (e.g., use of Internet and social media) literacy "funds of strategies" to aid their completion of English language arts and social studies homework assignments. Similarly, Machado, Vaughan, Coppola, and Woodard (2017) reported how a poetry instructional unit implemented within an urban school engaged seventh-grade students in examining their own lives and the lives of their peers, deepening knowledge of perspectives and literacy practices across multiple cultural groups. The authors recommend practices such as incorporating videos, student writing, and technological tools (i.e., blogs, podcasts, posts) to demonstrate that literacy practices go beyond what is typically characterized as school-based reading and writing.

Baines, Tisdale, and Long (2018) situated the learning of multiple concepts and information within rich explorations of musical literacies as literate acts with both teachers and students sharing their histories, interpretations, and connections. In her classroom, for example, Tisdale connected students and their Black heritage with the goal of celebrating students' cultural and racial histories as associated with musical histories. Multiple outcomes were observed in these classrooms, including students' musical compositions and use of music and drawings with written texts to speak about social justice issues, and the students' recognition that "Black History is our History" (p. 73).

RESISTING AND ADAPTING RESTRICTIVE CURRICULA TO AFFIRM DIVERSITY

The ILA Standard 4, Diversity and Equity, specifies that teacher candidates should situate diversity as a core asset in planning, teaching, and selecting texts and materials. Candidates are encouraged to engage students in literacy/disciplinary content to examine stereotypes in text, media, and literature (ILA, 2018a). Gay (2018) believes that to improve culturally diverse curriculum content, it is important that teachers learn ideological and content analysis of curriculum content pertaining to ethnic and cultural subject matter. She also recommends that university teachers and candidates conduct research independently and collectively to determine the effect of the presentation of curriculum content sources (i.e., textbooks, mass media, trade books) on the knowledge, attitudes, and behaviors toward ethnic and cultural diversity. We also believe that this lens should be expanded to examining text and media across *all* forms of diversity.

Literacy leaders must reshape the curriculum by developing integrated units around universal and authentic concepts and by exposing students to alternative viewpoints about topics (Schulz, Hurt, & Lindo, 2014). Journell and Castro (2011), for example, found that high school Latinx students' civic disposition and political awareness were increased when they integrated the topic of immigration into the social studies curriculum and involved students in discussions of the U.S. political process. Transforming the curriculum also means creating a democratic curriculum in which students take the initiative in identifying issues that are relevant to their in- and out-of-school lives and learning from each other in the process of advocating for change (Schultz, 2008).

Text Sets

A culturally responsive teaching/planning framework such as Quad Text sets is one way to build students' knowledge of social justice issues, exposing them to multiple perspectives and background knowledge required for critical engagement. Four components of Quad Text sets include video clips, pieces of artwork, and musical selections as background materials; an informational text; and two complex canonical or contemporary young-adult (YA) books, one as a target text and the other to extend students' understanding of the issues (Lewis & Flynn, 2017).

CASE EXAMPLE •

> **THINK ABOUT THIS**
>
> 1. In what ways does Mrs. Miller demonstrate teaching in a culturally responsive way and what other resources might she use?
> 2. What other resources might a teacher use to differentiate instruction and provide culturally responsive instruction for students experiencing reading difficulties?

Applying the Quad Text strategy, Mrs. Miller, a fifth-grade teacher, decides to explore the issues of conflict, migration, and refugees by using the book *Refugee* (Gratz, 2017) as the target text and *Give Me Shelter: Stories about Children Who Seek Asylum* (Bradman, 2007) as the extension text. Background knowledge might be developed using a multimedia presentation such as Unpacked: Refugee Baggage (*www.unpackedrefugee.com*);

paintings by Joel Bergner (aka Joel Artista) focused on the refugee crisis and social action, as well as other materials that can be accessed through Google searches. Similarly, Mrs. Miller might draw on another resource, such as the use of bilingual musical selections designed to comfort children who have been separated from their parents at the U.S./Mexican border in the album "Singing You Home: Children's Songs for Family Reunification" (*www.ghostlightrecords.com*).

Exposing children to literature in which they see images of themselves and content that values their lives and experiences results in individual valuing and self-affirmation (Bishop, 1990). As students acquire knowledge about their culture-based ways of knowing society, they are able to extend their understanding of the larger or broader knowledge and cultural ways of knowing of others in the world. This is known as *cultural competence* (Ladson-Billing, 2001). Students who are lesbian, gay, bisexual, transgender, or gender questioning (LGBTQ) are often invisible in the classroom. By incorporating children's literature about LGBTQ students in the classroom and promoting discussion about student difference and oppression faced by underrepresented students, teachers can create inclusive classrooms that embrace the tenets of culturally responsive teaching (Ryan & Hermann-Wilmarth, 2018). Black adolescent girls in urban classrooms have also benefited from instruction that combined multicultural literature with curriculum orientation, literacy instruction, culturally relevant pedagogy (Baxley & Boston, 2009), and from the use of a multicultural curriculum coupled with antiracist education (Wiggan & Watson, 2016).

Some teachers do not feel prepared to engage in culturally responsive teaching. Content-area teachers have reported feeling ill prepared to work with ELs (Nutta, Mokhtari, & Strebel, 2012). Community-based service learning, an alternative field-based experience, can be incorporated within teacher education programs to build prospective teachers' knowledge about culturally and linguistically diverse students and communities, and has been identified as an effective practice for preparing elementary teachers to engage in culturally responsive instruction and address equity and access to educational opportunities (Tinkler, Tinkler, Gerstl-Pepin, & Mugisha, 2014).

Milner (2011) believes that teachers need to build their cultural competence in order to develop culturally relevant pedagogy in their classrooms, especially in urban school settings. In his study of Mr. Hall, a White middle school science teacher, Milner found that to become culturally competent, teachers must engage in self-examination of their beliefs, attitudes, and histories as a prerequisite to impacting changes in institutional policies and curriculum. Teachers must begin by questioning their implicit biases about diverse students, their perceptions about the knowledge and expertise of the families of their students, the impact of their own language (asset-based or deficit-based) when talking with and about students and their families, and the ways in which they position some students and not others for success (Baines et al., 2018).

Build Positive Identities

Individuals' identities are multiple in nature and changeable by interactions with others and institutions and the larger society (McCarthy & Moje, 2002). Individuals' names are key to developing a sense of self and often reflect ties to racial, ethnic, cultural, linguistic, and family identities and histories. The names of students of color are often Anglicized or mispronounced, or in some instances students are renamed, which has been perceived as a type of micro-aggression that represents a lack of respect for students' identities and thus conveys a message of exclusion from the classroom (Marrun, 2018). Drawing attention to the importance of students' names, Marrun recommends that teachers in PreK–2 implement multiculturalism and culturally responsive teaching practices, such as having students and teachers read and discuss articles, share stories about their names, and view multimedia presentations on the topic. The My Name, My Identity Campaign, created in 2016 by the Santa Clara County Office of Education in California, is open to teachers across the country and provides numerous teacher and student resources useful for creating an awareness about students' names and their school identity.

The use of biography-driven instructional strategies is another approach to teaching and learning that is potentially effective in using the identities of students to provide culturally responsive instruction for second-language learners at the elementary and secondary levels and to guide teachers in making instructional decisions (Herrera, 2010). Students' culture and languages are used in three interrelated phases of instruction: The activation phase (before instruction), the connection phase (during), and the affirmation phase (after) (Pérez, Holmes, Miller, & Fanning, 2012).

Engaging students in open-dialogic conversation also provides spaces within the classroom curriculum for students to use classroom talk about issues affecting their community and to examine their impact on their multiple identities. Tucker-Raymond and Rosario (2017) found that seventh graders living in an urban community who were provided with classroom space and an opportunity to use a critical sociohistorical lens to examine the impact of gentrification and displacement, its impact on their racial and ethnic identities, and the identity of their urban community benefited from the opportunity to connect their life experiences to both the school curriculum and to disciplinary content presented in their class.

Develop a Home–School–Community Mutually Enabling Culture

As we discussed previously, the language and literacy practices of students' families and communities provide a wealth of information that is frequently overlooked during instruction.

Listening to families, as reported by Compton-Lilly (2011), is important for breaking through stereotypes and misconceptions that too many teachers hold (e.g., "Parents don't care"; "How can we expect these students to learn to read when their parents don't know how to read?").

Similar to Johnson (2010), who conducted life history interviews with three generations of an African American family, Compton-Lilly (2011) found that her students' families engaged in multiple and varied literacy practices (e.g., reading and rereading favorite books, valuing computers and advances in digital technology for learning). Listening to and getting to know families and communities require literacy professionals to address their own biases and develop narratives that are counter to their own prior and limited assumptions (Lopez-Robertson, Long, & Turner-Nash, 2010). Equally important, Baines et al. (2018) argue, is learning how to be allies of families. This involves opening multiple ways to engage in two-way communication, with teachers explaining their goals and worries and asking parents to do the same. Insights from families are respected and acted on, and when acted on in meaningful ways, literacy professionals are demonstrating their belief in families and that their goals and opinions are valued and shared.

Additionally, home–school relationships are strengthened when family and community knowledge is made public and relevant to the curriculum. For example, Baines and her colleagues (2018) describe the power of a project in which their first-grade students interviewed and developed oral histories of elders living in their community. As Ms. Myers, a community elder, described her experience, the book that was written about her was "amazing" and "really inspiring" (p. 79). Both students and community members came to know that they had something important to say about their community and that their histories and experiences were honored. Preparing for interviews, conducting the interviews, drawing and writing the oral histories—all were situated within a curriculum that celebrated the community and their heritage. Complex texts and vocabulary and numerous English language arts and social studies skills and concepts were embedded in each of the recorded oral histories, producing texts that were read and reread by these young children. These texts were highly valued by the students and their families because of the connections to their community and their own history and heritage. And as these educators explained, such connections motivated the children to read because these texts "mattered to them" (p. 87). See Chapter 17, this volume, for more information about parent and community engagement.

Build Advocacy and Civic Engagement

One of the assumptions underlying Standard 4 of *Standards 2017* is that specialized literacy professionals and teachers must "prepare students to engage in critiques of social inequity and promote and involve them in active citizenship to redress areas of inequity and privilege" (ILA, 2018a, p. 15). Investigating authentic issues can lead to civic engagement and advocacy by students. Daniel (2015) describes an art-based event in which undocumented adolescent refugee and immigrant students and preservice teachers deliberated about the issue of immigrant policies, immigration reform, and attitudes about immigration in the United States. Students began the Immigration Deliberation Project by discussing the issue of immigration before creating visual displays of poems and paintings to communicate their perspectives on this issue. The visuals created were then displayed at a gallery event held at the university, during which opportunities were provided for oral discussion of the displays and through online tweets. The author believed that the project provided an opportunity to engage secondary school students civically. It also broadened preservice teachers' understanding about the immigration process and the perspectives of undocumented adolescent refugee and immigrant students.

School-based social activism projects can position students as agents of social and community change. For example, Schultz (2008) describes his experience as a teacher who, with his fifth-grade students, co-constructed a yearlong integrated, authentic, and transformative curriculum focused on a social-justice-oriented project to replace their inadequate school building. Schultz built upon his knowledge of his students' problem and critical thinking skills, used to function daily in their home communities, to transcend his scripted lessons while helping students understand governmental operations and effectuate changes. Although the students' efforts did not result in getting a new school, several rewarding moments occurred in the form of the validation of their feelings and efforts in the process. A follow-up article appeared in *The Chicago Tribune* in 2007, featuring five students who attested to the important impact of the curriculum on their lives. The result of the school actions, however, was that the Chicago Board of Education voted to close their school permanently due to gentrification of the neighborhood. High-priced condominiums and townhouses were taking over the neighborhood with a plan to sell the school building for some of the same development. As residential buildings were demolished and replaced, families were forced to move to more affordable neighborhoods. Students were displaced and relocated to different schools within the district.

LITERACY LEADERS TAKING THE INITIATIVE TO ADVANCE EQUITY

Literacy leaders include prospective and practicing K–12 classroom teachers, reading/literacy specialists, literacy coaches, literacy coordinators/supervisors, district and school administrators, and teacher educators. Each has a responsibility, engaging in collective and collaborative efforts, to become an agent of change that enables equitable learning conditions for all students and to energize systems for wide-ranging effectiveness (Milner, 2015). To achieve such outcomes, we offer the following recommendations that are aligned with *Standards 2017,* specifically Standard 4:

1. Build knowledge to support literacy leaders understanding of:
   - their own histories, biases, and cultural competence and how they influence their teaching decisions, as a prerequisite to working as change agents.
   - the political contexts within schools, community, and at the national and international levels, and how to use this information to contest inequitable practices and promote their students' understanding of the larger social world.
   - research, theories, and pedagogies that address equity and diversity.
   - how to recruit students' linguistic, social, and cognitive resources for instruction.
   - culture as it reflects the changing nature of groups, families, communities, and individuals (teachers and students) and as different from a monolithic or fixed entity.
   - instruction as an opportunity for shared learning and teaching decisions.
2. Hold the difficult conversations:
   - that make explicit problems and issues that literacy leaders are confronting and must address along the pathway of enacting optimal culturally responsive instruction.
   - by asking questions such as, "Will you commit to justice in and through your teaching?" (Ryan & Hermann-Wilmarth, 2018).
   - that make explicit conversations about poverty and race and how these relate to school practices (Milner, 2015).
3. Address explicitly personal beliefs and biases by:
   - scrutinizing teachers' assumptions about diverse students and how these assumptions might position students for either success or failure, their perceptions about the knowledge held by students and their families, and the language they use when talking with or about students and their families (Baines et al., 2018).
   - building understandings of how personal cultural and linguistic experiences of literacy leaders may differ significantly from their students and that this can create a void of knowledge about how to differentiate and provide responsive instruction.
   - developing teacher narratives and students' literacy biographies to increase metacognitive awareness of the essential role of critical literacies in instruction and student learning.
4. Teacher educators, in particular, must develop rigorous teacher preparation programs that prepare prospective teachers with expertise in culturally responsive instruction, and that include:
   - multiple authentic field-based experiences linked to course content and well mentored in diverse school and community settings (e.g., yearlong community project described by Reyes, DaSilva Iddings, & Feller, 2015).
   - high-quality preparation programs that hold high expectations

for rich and well-defined content and content pedagogical knowledge and preparation to teach the students that will be in their classrooms (Risko & Reid, 2019).

CONCLUSION

We believe that all children should have an equal right to succeed as readers and writers. The barriers impeding our progress in assuring equitable outcomes for our diverse students must become a priority: As literacy leaders, we can do no less than provide optimal education for all students. The practices and recommendations identified in this chapter are grounded in powerful research accounts primed for literacy leaders to embrace and implement widely, with sustained effort, and with a desire to make a difference for all students.

ENGAGEMENT ACTIVITIES

1. On a two-column chart provide the following information: In the first column, set up at least three rows identifying three of your assets (e.g., ethnicity, cultural history, linguistic history, gender, religion, identity); in the second column, explain how these assets might influence your teaching decisions and/or your interactions with your students and their families.

2. Initiate classroom discussions focused on authentic topics (e.g., immigration policy reform, gun violence, health care, political language). Work with students to investigate ways in which these issues are portrayed in the media and ways to impact change on an individual, group, and/or community level.

3. Read about the activity titled Instructional Conversations Pedagogy (Mellon, Portes, Straubhaar, Balderas, & Ariail, 2018), develop a lesson plan (i.e., objectives, procedures, evaluation), and implement this conversation with a small group of your colleagues. Evaluate its effectiveness and recommend future changes.

ANNOTATED RESOURCES

Bottiani, J. H., Larson, K. E., Debnam, K. J., Bischoff, C. M., & Bradshaw, C. P. (2018). Promoting educators' use of culturally responsive practices: A systematic review of inservice interventions. *Journal of Teacher Education, 69*(4), 367–385.

A systematic review of empirical research with the goals of analyzing (1) the features and impact of culturally responsive practices (CRP) interventions for K–12 teachers and administrators, (2) the quality of the research. and (3) classifying the measures and outcomes.

Powell, R., Chambers-Cantrell, S., Malo-Juvera, V., & Correll, P. (2016). Operationalizing culturally responsive instruction: Preliminary findings of CRIOP research. *Teachers College Record, 118*(1), 1–44.

A preliminary study examines the Culturally Responsive Instruction Observation Protocol (CRIOP) as a multidimensional tool to guide teacher professional development in implementing culturally responsive instruction in these domains: classroom relationships, family collaboration, assessment, curriculum/planned experiences, instruction/pedagogy, discourse/instructional conversation, and sociopolitical consciousness/diverse perspectives.

Ryan, C. L., & Hermann-Wilmarth, J. M. (2018). *LGBTQ-inclusive literacy instruction in the elementary classroom.* New York: Teachers College Press.

Provides strong support for inclusive literacy instruction for LGBTQ students and practical instructional examples to guide teachers in expanding their curriculum to include LGBTQ themes and materials to validate students' existence and identities.

REFERENCES

Alim, H. S., & Paris, D. (2017). What is culturally sustaining pedagogy and why does it matter? In D. Paris & H. S. Alim (Eds.), *Culturally sustaining pedagogies: Teaching and learning for justice in a changing world.* New York: Teachers College Press.

Baines, J., & Tisdale, C., & Long, S. (2018). *"We've been doing it your way long enough": Choosing the culturally relevant classroom.* New York: Teachers College Press.

Baxley, T. P., & Boston, G. H. (2009). Classroom inequity and the literacy experiences of black adolescent girls. *Education and Society, 27*(2), 77–89.

Bishop, R. S. (1990). Mirrors, windows, and sliding glass doors. *Perspectives, 1*(3), ix–xi.

Brown v. Board of Education, 347 U.S. 483 (1954).

Cammarota, J. (2008). The cultural organizing of youth ethnographers: Formalizing a praxis-based pedagogy. *Anthropology and Education Quarterly, 39*(1), 45–58.

Compton-Lilly, C. (2011). Listening to families over time: Severn lessons learned about literacy in families. *Language Arts, 86*(6), 449–457.

Daniel, S. M. (2015). Engaging youth and pre-service teachers in immigration deliberations. *Journal of Education for Teaching, 41*(3), 321–323.

Daniel, S. M. (2018). Resettled refugee youth leveraging their out-of-school literacy practices to accomplish schoolwork. *Mind, Culture, and Activity, 25*(3), 263–277.

Dudley-Marling, C., & Lucas, K. O. (2009). Pathologizing the language and culture of poor children. *Language Arts, 86*(5), 362–370.

Esteban-Guitart, M., & Moll, L. C. (2014). Funds of identity: A new concept based on the funds of knowledge approach. *Culture and Psychology, 20*(1), 31–48.

Garcia, O. (2009). *Bilingual education in the 21st century: A global perspective.* Malden, MA: Wiley-Blackwell.

Gay, G. (2018). *Culturally responsive teaching: Theory, research, and practice* (3rd ed.). New York: Teachers College Press.

Hart, B., & Risley, T. R. (1995). *Meaningful differences in the everyday experiences of young American children.* Baltimore: Brookes.

Herrera, S. (2010). *Biography-driven culturally responsive teaching.* New York: Teacher College Press.

International Literacy Association (ILA). (2018a). *Standards for the preparation of literacy professionals 2017.* Newark, DE: Author.

International Literacy Association (ILA). (2018b). *The case for children's rights to read.* Newark, DE: Author.

International Literacy Association (ILA). (2017). *Characteristics of culturally sustaining and academically rigorous classrooms* (Literacy leadership brief). Newark, DE: Author.

International Literacy Association & National Council of Teachers of English. (2017). *Literacy teacher preparation* (Research advisory). Newark, DE/Urbana, IL: Authors.

Jiménez, R. T. (2015). Translanguaging to bridge the gap with English learners. *Literacy daily.* Retrieved from *www.literacyworldwide.org/blog/literacy-daily/2015/10/29/translanguaging-to-bridge-the-gap-with-english-learners.*

Jiménez, R. T., David, S., Fagan, K., Risko, V., Pacheco, M., Pray, L., et al. (2015). Using translation to drive conceptual development for students becoming literate in English as an additional language. *Research in the Teaching of English, 49*(3), 248–271.

Johnson, A. S. (2010). The Jones family culture of literacy. *The Reading Teacher, 64*(1), 33–43.

Journell, W., & Castro, E. L. (2011). Culturally relevant political education. *Multicultural Education, 18*(4), 10–17.

Ladson-Billings, G. (1995). Toward a theory of culturally relevant pedagogy. *American Educational Research Journal, 32*(3), 465–491.

Ladson-Billings, G. (2001). *Crossing over to Canaan: The journey of new teachers in diverse classrooms.* San Francisco: Jossey-Bass.

Ladson-Billings, G. (2014). Culturally relevant pedagogy 2.0: a.k.a. the remix. *Harvard Educational Review, 84*(1), 74–84.

Lee, C. D., Rosenfeld, E., Mendenhall, R., Rivers, A., & Tynes, B. (2004). Cultural modeling as a frame for narrative analysis. In C. Dauite & C. Lightfoot (Eds.), *Narrative analysis: Studying the development of individuals in society* (pp. 39–62). Thousand Oaks, CA: SAGE.

Lewis, W., & Flynn, J. E. (2017). Below the surface level of social justice: Using Quad Text sets to plan equity-oriented instruction. *ALAN Review, 45*(1), 22–31.

Lopez, F. A. (2016). Culturally responsive pedagogies in Arizona and Latino students' achievement. *Teachers' College Record, 118*(5), 1–42.

Lopez-Robertson, J., Long, S., & Turner-Nash, K. (2010). First steps in constructing counter narratives of young children and their families. *Language Arts, 88*(2), 93–103.

Machado, E. (2017). Culturally sustaining pedagogy in the literacy classroom. *Literacy Daily.* Available at *www.literacyworldwide.org/blog/literacy-daily/2017/05/31/culturally-sustaining-pedagogy-in-the-literacy-classroom.*

Machado, E., Vaughan, A., Coppola, R., & Woodard, R. (2017). "Lived life through a colored lens": Culturally sustaining poetry in an urban literacy classroom. *Language Arts, 94*(6), 367–381.

Mangan, D. (2016, November 30). Is literacy a constitutional right?: The battle over Detroit schools. *Literacy Leadership.* Retrieved from *www.literacyworldwide.*

org/blog/literacy-daily/2016/11/30/is-literacy-a-constitutional-right-the-battle-over-detroit-schools.

Marrun, N. A. (2018). Culturally responsive teaching across PK–20: Honoring the historical naming practices of students of color. *Journal of Culture and Education, 17*(3), 6–25.

McBrien, J. L. (2005). Educational needs and barriers for refugee students in the United States: A review of the literature. *Review of Educational Research, 75*(3), 329–364.

McCarthy, S., & Moje, E. (2002). Identity matters. *Reading Research Quarterly, 37*(2), 228–237.

Mellon, P., Portes, P. R., Straubhaar, R., Balderas, C., & Ariail, M. (2018). "They come with nothing": How professional development in a culturally responsive pedagogy shapes teacher attitudes towards Latino/a English language learners. *Teaching and Teacher Education, 71*, 98–107.

Milner, H. R., IV. (2011). Culturally relevant pedagogy in a diverse urban classroom. *Urban Review, 43*, 66–89.

Milner, H. R., IV. (2015). *Rac(e)ing to class: Confronting poverty and race in schools and classrooms*. Cambridge, MA: Harvard University Press.

Moll, C. (2015). Tapping into the "hidden" home and community resources of students. *Kappa Delta Pi Record, 51*(3), 114–117.

Nutta, J. W., Mokhtari, K., & Strebel, C. (2012). *Preparing every teacher to reach English learners*. Boston: Harvard Press.

Paris, D. (2012). Culturally sustaining pedagogy: A needed change in stance, terminology and practice. *Educational Researcher, 41*(3), 93–97.

Pérez, D., Holmes, M., Miller, S., & Fanning, C. A. (2012). Biography-driven strategies as the great equalizer: Universal conditions that promote K–12 culturally responsive teaching. *Journal of Curriculum and Instruction, 6*(1), 25–42.

Puzio, K., Newcomer, S., Pratt, K., McNeely, K., Jacobs, M., & Hooker, S. (2017). Creative failures in culturally sustaining pedagogy. *Language Arts, 94*(4), 223–233.

Reyes, I., DaSilva Iddings, A. C., & Feller, N. (2015). Promoting a funds of knowledge perspective: Preservice teachers' understanding about language and literacy development of preschool emergent bilinguals through family and community interactions. *Journal of Early Childhood Literacy, 15*(2) 1–26.

Risko, V. J., & Reid, L. (2019). What really matters for literacy teacher preparation? *The Reading Teacher, 72*(4), 423–429.

Risko, V. J., & Walker-Dalhouse, D. (2019). Best practices to change the trajectory of struggling readers. In L. Morrow & L. Gambrell (Eds.), *Best practices in literacy instruction* (6th ed., pp. 104–126). New York: Guilford Press.

Ryan, C. L., & Hermann-Wilmarth, J. M. (2018). *Reading the rainbow: LGBTQ-inclusive literacy instruction in the elementary classroom*. New York: Teachers College Press.

Santa Clara County Office of Education. (2016). My name, my identity: A declaration of self. Retrieved from *www.mynamemyidentity.org*.

Schultz, B. D. (2008). *Spectacular things happen along the way*. New York: Teachers College Press.

Schulz, L., Hurt, K., & Lindo, N. (2014). My name is not Michael: Strategies for promoting cultural responsiveness in schools. *Journal of School Counseling, 12*(2), 1–35.

Skerrett, A. (2015). A framework for literacy education in multicultural, multilingual, and multiliterate classrooms. *Multicultural Education Review, 7*(1–2), 26–40.

Smith, M. D. (2016). *Invisible man, got the whole world watching: A young black-man's education*. New York: Nation Books.

Tinkler, A., Tinkler, B., Gerstl-Pepin, C., & Mugisha, V. M. (2014). The promise of a community-based, participatory approach to service-learning in education. *Journal of Higher Education, Outreach and Engagement, 18*(2), 209–232.

Tucker-Raymond, E., & Rosario, M. L. (2017). Imagining identities: Young people constructing discourses of race, ethnicity, and community in a contentious context of rapid young development. *Urban Education, 52*(1), 32–60.

Walker-Dalhouse, D., Sanders, V., & Dalhouse, A. D. (2009). A university and middle school partnership: Preservice teachers' attitudes toward ELL students. *Literacy Research and Instruction, 48*(4), 337–349.

Wiggan, G., & Watson, M. (2016). Teaching the whole child: The importance of cultural responsiveness, community engagement, and character development in high-achieving African American students. *Urban Education, 48*, 766–798.

CHILDREN'S LITERATURE

Bradman, T. (2007). *Give me shelter: Stories about children who seek asylum*. New York: Lincoln Children's Books.

Gratz, A. (2017). *Refugee*. New York: Scholastic Press.

Literacy Leadership in Action

Valerie Kinloch, PhD
*Renée and Richard Goldman Dean, School of Education,
University of Pittsburgh, Pittsburgh, Pennsylvania*

THINK ABOUT THIS

1. In what ways does Valerie serve as a literacy leader?
2. What lessons can be learned about the role of a School of Education Dean?
3. What questions come to mind while reading this vignette?

My parents, Virginia and Louis Kinloch, from the U.S. rural South, were born and raised at a time in this country that did not embrace Black life, Black love, and Black literacies. I am of an extended working-class family who has sought ways to interrupt cycles of generational poverty and inaccessible educational opportunities. Hence, when I think about my story of literacy leadership, this is where I begin: a place in which I recognize and honor my familial foundation; a place of struggle and (un)intentional silences; a place of love and perseverance. This is also a place that has nurtured me to believe that I can learn and lead in loving and liberating ways. Thus I come to my current professional position as the Renée and Richard Goldman Dean of the School of Education at the University of Pittsburgh. It is a position in which I am the first Black woman to serve as dean of any school or college on this university's campus. I name this reality because as daughter, sister, cousin, aunt, and friend of loved ones from the segregated South, I understand that my identity and literacy leadership work are connected to *of whom* I am and *from whom* I was cultivated.

As dean, I set and enact a vision for igniting learning, engaging in educational excellence, fostering collaboration, forging engaged partnerships, and committing to educational transformation. This means that I work *with* colleagues to center equity and justice in how we recruit and retain caring faculty, staff, and students; how we teach and research; how we co-create sustainable educational partnerships with communities and schools; and in how we approach learning as intertwined with health, wellness, and human development.

In the School of Education, I am excited about how we shape practice and policy, and how we influence education through equitable, engaging approaches. One example is our P.R.I.D.E. program (Positive Racial Identity Development in Early Education) in the Office of Child Development. This program affirms racial identity in Black children and supports their sense of belonging and academic success. It offers parenting classes, community arts education festivals, professional development for educators, and a yearlong teacher cohort initiative on racial identity and culture. Another example is our Heinz Fellows Program in the Center for Urban Education. This yearlong initiative pairs fellows (postundergraduate students) with school and community leaders to support the academic and socioemotional growth of students attending urban schools. Our fellows mentor, tutor, teach, and facilitate participatory action research projects with elementary, middle, and high school students and educators across the city. They participate in a variety of professional development experiences, from education forums to brown bags, seminars, and conferences, and they work with families, school leaders, and community organizers.

Literacy leadership is also central to other initiatives in our school. From our work in teacher education, professional development, and quality of life and health across the lifespan, we are always questioning: How can we support innovative literacy collaborations among students, teachers, and families? In what ways can we ground literacy leadership in equity, health, and wellness? What kinds of larger relations exist between literacy leadership and students' learning and engagement? This last question takes me to our involvement with the Homewood Community Engagement Center (*www.pittwire. pitt.edu/news/front-door-pitt-opens-homewood*) and Museumlab™ (*https:// pittsburghkids.org/about/in-the-community/museumlab*). Partnering with these two new community-based initiatives encourages us to be more intentional with our commitment to learning with and listening to kids, youth, and families on expanded meanings of literacy leadership and engagement. These initiatives align well with *Standards 2017* and its emphasis on issues of diversity, equity, and literacy partnerships.

To think, this Black woman from the South, now Dean of Education, gets to facilitate these types of literacy leadership engagements! My advice to others: Commit to the work and to being in community with others in ways that push you to dream and act boldly. When you do, then a culture of collaboration will be nurtured, and a disruption and transformation of inequitable educational structures will become possible.

CHAPTER 16

Academic Language and Literacy Development for English Learners

MaryEllen Vogt

- Who are the English learners in our schools?
- What do literacy leaders need to know about appropriate language, literacy, and content instruction for English learners that integrates academic language and academic content instruction?
- In what ways do the *Standards for the Preparation of Literacy Professionals 2017* (International Literacy Association [ILA], 2018) address language, literacy, and content instruction for English learners?
- How can literacy leaders elevate and support teachers' language and literacy instruction for English learners?

This chapter focuses on what literacy professionals can do to provide English learners with more equitable, appropriate, and effective language, literacy, and content instruction. *Standards 2017* is discussed within the context of supporting those who are responsible for (1) teaching English learners, (2) organizing and providing professional learning opportunities for those who teach English learners, and (3) leading efforts to improve instruction in language, literacy, and academic content for English learners.

WHO ARE THE ENGLISH LEARNERS IN OUR SCHOOLS?

Currently, there are several labels used for identifying students in U.S. schools who are acquiring English as a second or additional language (Short, Vogt, & Echevarria, 2017) (see Figure 16.1).A For this chapter, I use the designation *English learners* to refer to students whose home language differs from the language of instruction in their schools. Like all other students, English learners are individuals with their own unique talents, abilities, needs, personalities, cultural backgrounds, varied educational experiences, and dreams for the future. Some English learners are gifted and talented, some have learning disabilities, some are recent immigrants, and many others are native-born. Some English learners are fully literate in their home language (L1), able to transfer their language and literacy skills to reading and learning in English (L2). Others have few, if any, language and literacy skills in their L1, making learning to read especially challenging since they are also learning to speak a new language at the same time. There are other sociocultural, emotional, and economic factors that contribute to English learner diversity, including parents' educational background; poverty; mobility; exposure to trauma, violence, abuse; and refugee or asylee status (Vogt, 2014).

Literacy leaders must identify and build upon English learners' assets, often called *funds of knowledge* (Moll, 1994), that each brings to the classroom, whether the assets are academic, personal, sociocultural, or experiential. Focusing and building on a learner's assets is a more positive and useful way of viewing diversity, than is the deficit orientation that has been prevalent in schools for many years, especially as related to English learners. This deficit view, coupled with the difficulty of distinguishing language and

English language learners (ELLs) English learners (ELs)	Fully (or fluent) English proficient (FEP)
Language minority students	English as a new language (ENL)
English speakers of other languages (ESOL)	Long-term English language learners (LTEL/LTELL)
Limited English proficient (LEP)	Students with interrupted formal education (SIFE)

FIGURE 16.1. Designations used for English learners.

learning disability from language differences, has resulted in both over- and underrepresentation of English learners in special education programs (Echevarria, Richards-Tutor, & Vogt, 2015; Echevarria, Vogt, & Short, 2017).

In contrast, the following are examples of language assets that many English learners may have developed (Short & Echevarria, 2016, p. 13):

- *Native language and literacy knowledge.* Aspects of reading that can transfer to a new language are phonemic awareness, phonics, vocabulary, cognates, knowledge of affixes and roots, and reading/ listening comprehension strategies.
- *Out-of-school literacies.* No English learner comes to school as a blank slate. Some enter school with well-honed skills developed while assisting their parents, working at a job, or caring for children or other family members.
- *Language brokering.* This is the term that describes the mediation and negotiating that English learners often do, in English, for their parents and other family members who speak little to no English. Interestingly, a child's ability to broker effectively in two languages has been suggested as a possible identifier of giftedness in students who are English learners (Brookes & Angelleli, n.d.).
- *Sociolinguistic and sociocultural practices.* English learners learn the norms for using their L1 in a variety of contexts, from informal (at home) to formal (giving a speech in class). For some English learners, the language norms of their L1 differ considerably from those of their L2 (English). These differences must be carefully navigated in some instances to avoid misunderstandings, disagreements, or embarrassment.
- *Codeswitching.* This is the practice of seamlessly moving from one language to another, when a word in the target language is forgotten or isn't deemed as appropriate as the word in the L1. Codeswitching is often a strategic resource for English learners.
- *Individual factors* that also can be assets are prior schooling, social identity, age, motivation, personality, and learning style.

Standards 2017, "Standard 4: Diversity and Equity," includes three components that are especially relevant for the preparation of literacy leaders to work with English learners. These components urge teachers and coaches to be knowledgeable about a student's funds of knowledge; his or her linguistic differences, such as dialect; and a student's cultural capital, such as bilingualism, mobility, educational background, and out-of-school experiences (ILA, 2018). If we are to hold high expectations for all students, we must first value who they are as individuals, before making decisions about their language and literacy needs.

CASE EXAMPLE •

THINK ABOUT THIS

1. What are Bilan's out-of-school literacy assets that you can identify in her story? How can her teacher use these assets to help improve Bilan's literacy skills in English?

2. Collaboration between a coach and teachers is especially important when "leveraging English learners' native language proficiencies" (ILA, 2018, p. 49). What native language proficiencies that Balin demonstrates might a teacher and coach leverage to help her reach her goal of becoming a better reader of English?

Bilan, in grade 4, attends an elementary school in Idaho. Her town is an immigration center, and dozens of languages are spoken by the students in the PreK–12 district. Bilan's parents are legal immigrants with refugee status from Somalia, and they have been in the United States for 4 years. Bilan has competent conversational language skills in Somali, but she hasn't learned how to read or write in her home language. She started school in the United States in first grade, and although she is comfortable communicating socially in English with her friends and teacher, she has struggled from the beginning with reading and writing in English.

Frequently, Bilan helps her parents navigate everyday tasks by speaking English for them and/or interpreting for them. As the oldest child in her family, she also has responsibility for watching her two younger siblings when she gets home from school, until her parents arrive home from work. She regularly accompanies her mother for their weekly grocery shopping, and she recognizes the words of many food products that they buy regularly. As a result of the chores that Bilan is expected to do at home, she has learned a variety of valuable skills, such as speaking conversationally in English to doctors, pharmacists, grocery clerks, and teachers; writing weekly grocery lists for her mother; categorizing the canned goods and other items that Bilan puts away on the kitchen shelves; translating from English into Somali the recorded phone messages from school, government offices, and the medical building where she accompanies her parents and siblings for doctors' appointments. Bilan is eager to learn to read better in English so she can teach her parents to read and write the language of their new country.

English Learner Demographics

According to the National Center for Education Statistics (U.S. Department of Education, 2018), in 2000, 8.1% or 3.8 million students were designated as English learners. In the fall of 2015 (the most recent data available at the time of this writing), 9.5% or 4.8 million students were designated as English learners in the United States. The percentage of English learners has increased in all but eight states between 2000 and 2015. The states with the most English learners as of fall 2015 were California (21.4%), Texas (16.8%), Nevada (16.8%); New Mexico (15.7%), Alaska (11.5%), Kansas (10.5%), Washington (10.4%), Florida (9.6%), Minnesota (8.2%), and New York (8.0%). The states with the fewest English learners were Vermont (1.6%), New Hampshire (2.3%), and Maine (2.8%). Interestingly, the state with the largest percentage of increase between 2000 and 2015 was Kansas with a 7.5% increase in English learners. It is clear from these data that the population of English learners in our schools is likely to continue expanding.

Home Languages Spoken by English Learners

Approximately 77% of English learners speak Spanish as their home language (McFarland, 2016). The next two largest language groups are Arabic (2.4%) and Chinese (2.1%). Two percent may not seem like many students whose home language is Chinese, but in real numbers the total is 101,347 students (as of 2015).

It is estimated that approximately 180 native languages are spoken by English learners in U.S. schools. Los Angeles Unified School District has over 164,000 English learners who speak 94 languages. To meet the needs of this growing number of students, it is imperative that all literacy leaders and administrators understand second-language acquisition, levels of English language proficiency, and how to differentiate instructionally for the strengths and needs of the English learners in their schools (Sanchez, 2017).

Academic Performance Gaps of English Learners

Education reforms in the past two decades in the United States have had both a positive and a negative impact on English learners. On the positive side are the following (Short, Vogt, & Echevarria, 2017):

- Enhanced services for English learners are included in school improvement plans for providing improved educational opportunities for this population of students.
- Educators, teachers, and administrators alike regularly examine school data and monitor English learners' language proficiency data, adjusting programs and instruction as needed.
- Professional learning opportunities are made available through federal and state funding to improve academic language and content instruction for teachers of English learners.
- The adoption of the Every Student Succeeds Act (ESSA) in late

2015 requires more accountability from states. Federal legislation holds schools accountable for the success of all students through standards for mathematics, reading language arts, English language development, and science.

- As of 2018, 41 states and the District of Columbia have adopted the Common Core State Standards (CCSS; National Governors Association Center for Best Practices & Council of Chief State School Officers, 2010) for language arts and mathematics, and other states have adapted the CCSS or developed their own rigorous standards; 17 states plus the District of Columbia have adopted the Next Generation Science Standards (NGSS). The expectation is that all students will meet these rigorous literacy and content standards, including English learners.
- *Standards 2017* (ILA, 2018) includes attention to English learners throughout the document, with a focus on linguistic diversity in Standard 4: Diversity and Equity. This standard requires that teacher education programs prepare literacy professionals who understand issues of second-language acquisition, as well as how to create linguistically relevant curriculum and instructional programs for English learners at all grade levels.

Despite these positive efforts, the literacy achievement of English learners continues to lag far behind that of their native-speaking peers. The Nation's Report Card for Reading (2017) indicated that the scaled scores were essentially flat for all grade 4 students in comparison to the past few years. However, in comparison to nearly all subgroups, English learners' scores were substantially below the basic level of proficiency. The only subgroup with slightly lower reading scores than English learners were students with disabilities.

CASE EXAMPLE ·

THINK ABOUT THIS

1. What literacy assets does Fausto have? What might be some reasons for his lack of growth in academic language proficiency in English? How could his teacher help him break through the academic language barriers that he's experiencing before he gets to high school?

2. *Standards 2017* suggests that literacy leaders need to apply knowledge of language acquisition to literacy learning. How might a literacy coach and teacher collaborate to assess Fausto's levels of both Spanish and English language proficiency? Why is it important to know both proficiency levels (home language and target language), and what can they do with this information to develop an appropriate plan to improve Fausto's academic reading and writing in English?

> **3.** How might the collaboration between a coach and teacher, as described in the previous question, be implemented in your school?

Fausto is in grade 7 and attends school in a small town in central Iowa. His parents both work at a regional tractor manufacturing plant, and they have recently become proud citizens of the United States. Fausto was born in Iowa and has attended school in the same district since kindergarten. He is a competent, conversational speaker of both Spanish and English, and he easily switches from one language to the other with friends and family. Both of Fausto's parents speak conversational English, but Spanish is spoken in the home. Fausto began receiving English as a second language (ESL) services in kindergarten, and although he no longer receives ESL support, he has not been redesignated as a fluent English speaker. His knowledge and use of academic English are limited, and he struggles with reading and writing in each of his academic classes. Despite all the help Fausto has received, he is now considered to be a long-term English learner, and his teachers and parents are concerned about whether he'll be able to handle high school level academic work.

· · · · · · · · · · · ·

Fausto represents a large percentage of students in the United States who have not been redesignated as fluent English speakers and who continue to struggle with academic reading and writing. There are many reasons why these English learners perform poorly on the NAEP and other standardized measurements of reading, including reading ability, educational background, exposure to standardized testing methods, and lower levels of English language proficiency.

However, there may also be a reason that is more problematic for literacy leaders and other educators: Many teachers and coaches have not been adequately prepared to meet the academic and language development needs of English learners. Despite the growing numbers of language minority students, as of 2014, only 11 states (Arizona, California, Florida, Indiana, Massachusetts, Missouri, New Mexico, New York, Pennsylvania, Virginia, Washington) require all preservice teachers to have preparation in second-language acquisition and instructional methods for teaching English learners (Education Commission of the States, 2018). Some states, such as New Hampshire, New Mexico, and Texas, require professional development postcertification. Thirty states require no preparation at all in second-language acquisition or instructional methods for teaching English learners. Therefore, we have a large cadre of teachers across this country with little or no preparation in how to meet the language, literacy, and academic content needs of English learners who, it is estimated, will be more than one-quarter of our total student population in the United States by 2025 (National Clearinghouse for English Language Acquisition, 2010).

WHAT DO LITERACY LEADERS NEED TO KNOW ABOUT APPROPRIATE LANGUAGE, LITERACY, AND CONTENT INSTRUCTION FOR ENGLISH LEARNERS?

Appropriate *Language* Instruction for English Learners

If you have learned a second language in school or through immersion in another country, you know that it is not an easy process, and it takes a significant amount of time and effort. English learners need to develop reading, writing, listening, and speaking in English, along with subtleties that must be learned to use English effectively. For example, language learners must understand situational uses of English (pragmatics), such as using language for different purposes (e.g., greeting or requesting); changing language to fit the needs of the speaker (e.g., speaking at home vs. speaking at school); and following rules for conversations (e.g., staying on topic and turn taking) (Short, Vogt, & Echevarria, 2017, p. 26). Couple these demands with the language demands of school, especially with the CCSS and NGSS, and you begin to understand how stressful it can be to learn a new language at the same time that you are trying to learn challenging academic content.

Therefore, before teachers can begin to plan appropriate language instruction for English learners, they must understand some of the basics of second-language acquisition. First, it is important to recognize the important differences between acquiring social language and academic language in the L2. Note the differences in a teacher's use of English with her students:

- *Social language:* "Hi, everybody! Happy Monday! Did you all have a good weekend? Can somebody tell me one fun thing you did?"
- *Academic language:* "Look carefully at the household chemicals in the little cups on your table. Some cups contain acids; others contain bases. Compare and contrast the liquids by their function, their consistency, and the color of the litmus paper after you dip one strip in each cup. Orally share with your lab partner one hypothesis about each type of chemical."

In a nutshell, social language is used with friends and family, and with teachers during social conversations in the classroom. Social language is more concrete than abstract, and it usually has contextual supports, such as facial expressions and body language. Therefore, learning conversational language is relatively easy, and it can occur within a few weeks or months.

Academic language, on the other hand, represents the range of language that we use in academic settings. It is more challenging and more abstract, especially for students who are acquiring English at the same time they are learning academic content. Therefore, it can take several years of study to be on equal footing with native English-speaking peers, especially without supportive, appropriate instruction and practice (Echevarria, Vogt, & Short, 2017; Short & Echevarria, 2016; ILA, 2017). Simply put, academic language is a second language for all students, including native English speakers (Short & Echevarria, 2016, p. 2).

At present, 39 states determine students' levels of English proficiency with the WIDA English language proficiency standards (see *https://wida.wisc.edu* for more information). The WIDA Consortium at the University of Wisconsin–Madison developed the levels of English proficiency to assist educators in estimating students' developing English acquisition. (WIDA is the abbreviation for *World-Class Instructional Design and Assessment*.) The stages or phases of English language acquisition are fluid rather than rigid. The descriptions of these levels follow (Short, Vogt, & Echevarria, 2017, pp. 18–19):

- *Level 1:* Essentially no English proficiency. Students are often new-comers and need extensive pictorial and nonlinguistic support. Students with interruptions in their educational backgrounds of more than 2 years (SIFE) are often placed in a Level 1 newcomer program. These students need to learn basic oral language and literacy skills in English.

- *Level 2:* Students are beginners and can use phrases, simple questions, and short sentences. They should be introduced to general content vocabulary and lesson tasks. They generally need targeted ESL or English literacy development (ELD) classes along with sheltered instruction (see SIOP overview in this chapter) or bilingual classes.

- *Level 3:* Students can use general and specific language related to the content areas; they can speak and write sentences and paragraphs, although with some errors, and they can read with instructional supports. They, too, benefit from targeted ESL/ELD classes, although they need less time per week than Levels 1 and 2 students, along with sheltered or bilingual classes.

- *Level 4:* Viewed as an intermediate level of proficiency. Students use general academic and specific language related to the content areas. They have improved speaking and writing skills and stronger reading comprehension skills (compared to Level 3). In some cases, they are no longer scheduled into ESL/ELD classes, but are in sheltered classes where attention is given to furthering their academic English, sometimes with an ESL teacher who acts as a co-teacher. If Level 4 students are in a bilingual program, they typically have some content classes taught in the native language and others taught in English.

- *Level 5:* Viewed as an advanced intermediate or advanced level of proficiency. Students use general academic and technical language of the content areas. They can read and write with linguistic complexity. In some states, students at this level exit the ESL or ELD program, but their language and academic performance is still monitored. They may be placed in general education or sheltered classes depending on their academic performance.

- *Level 6:* At or close to grade-level proficiency. Students' oral and written communication skills are comparable to those of native English speakers at their grade level. Students at this level have exited the ESL or ELD program, but their language and academic performance is still monitored.

As you examine these levels, think about the earlier vignettes of Bilan and Fausto. Obviously, assessment is needed to confirm any language level, but as an estimate, Bilan might be at Level 3, while it appears that Fausto seems stuck somewhere between Level 3 and Level 4. Without appropriate, explicit, and supported instruction by a teacher knowledgeable in second-language acquisition, these two English learners may not make much progress with either their English development or reading and writing skills.

CASE EXAMPLE ·

THINK ABOUT THIS

1. Contrast Mykalo's experiences as an immigrant to the United States with Bilan's and Fausto's. How would you describe his assets/funds of knowledge? How do you think they have impacted his acquisition of academic English? What level of English language development would you estimate for Mykalo, based on this brief profile?

2. In the ILA (2017) Literacy Brief, *Second-Language Learners' Vocabulary and Oral Language Development,* the authors state, "While many of these students [English learners] might be conversant in the target language and speak comfortably in social settings, they still may struggle with academic language (p. 2)." Why do you think that this quote applies to Bilan and Fausto, but not to Mykalo? What accounts for the differences in their academic language and literacy development?

Mykalo's parents, two older sisters, and a younger brother are immigrants from Ukraine. His family left their home country for Sacramento, California, after the revolution of 2014 because, at the time, his father worked with the government under the deposed president, Viktor Yanuckovych. Mykalo's parents are both college-educated, and he and his siblings were in private schools at the time of the uprising. At the time he immigrated, Mykalo was 13 years old, fully literate in Ukranian, and he had studied French for 2 years in school. Now in grade 10, Mykalo is fluent in social English and with continuing ESL support, he is now at Level 4 (expanding) of English acquisition. Because of his strong academic background in Ukraine, Mykalo has been able to transfer knowledge and learning strategies from his home language to English. He is thoroughly enjoying high school, is in a program for gifted students, and he and his father recently visited California State University, Sacramento, to investigate its offerings in political science, an area of interest for Mykalo.

Appropriate *Literacy* Instruction for English Learners

As illustrated in Mykalo's vignette, many language and literacy experts believe that teaching students to read in their first language promotes higher levels of reading achievement in English because skills and other knowledge about literacy transfer across languages (Bauer, 2009; Cummins, 1981). Goldenberg (2008) explains, "If you learn something in one language you either already know it in another language, or you can more easily learn it in another language" (p. 15). However, in most U.S. schools, it is impossible for all English learners to learn to read in their L1, and studies have shown that English learners can develop adequate literacy skills and strategies in English-only classrooms given appropriate, modified instruction (August & Shanahan, 2008; Echevarria, Short, & Powers, 2006).

Although the five core reading elements (phonological awareness, phonics, reading fluency, vocabulary, comprehension), as identified by the National Reading Panel (2000), are the same elements that English learners must master (August & Shanahan, 2006), the development of and practice with oral language is also of critical importance (ILA, 2017). Therefore, core reading instruction and intensive, small-group intervention, based on assessment data, should focus on the five core components *plus* oral language development.

High-quality vocabulary instruction should be provided to English learners throughout the elementary and secondary school day, with a focus on essential content words, language processes, and language functions. Additionally, instructional time should be allotted for teaching common words, phrases, and expressions in English. In the ILA's (2017) *Second-Language Learners' Vocabulary and Oral Language Development*, teachers are encouraged to explicitly teach and provide practice with unusual words and phrases, such as words with multiple meanings, homophones, and idioms. Clearly, it is not enough for English learners to just learn "English words." Rather, students will benefit from explicit instruction in topic-specific vocabulary; cross-curricular words and phrases (e.g., *explain, define, provide evidence*); language functions (e.g., how to ask questions in English) and English grammar and structure (Echevarria et al., 2017; Shearer, Carr, & Vogt, 2019).

The ILA literacy brief (2017) includes practical recommendations to literacy leaders about providing language and literacy instruction for English learners, with a focus on academic vocabulary and oral language development. As an example, and to further support English learners' developing oral language proficiency, sentence starters and language frames can serve as a scaffold during class discussions. Figure 16.2 shows examples of each of these (Short & Echevarria, 2016, pp. 80, 82).

In addition, predictable classroom routines should be maintained so that English learners can depend on a degree of consistency throughout their day, including easy-to-read daily agendas, posted and reviewed content and language objectives for each lesson, procedures for transitioning between subjects, and so forth. Redundancy of key information can be provided with visual cues, pictures and diagrams, modeling, physical gestures, and graphic organizers.

Some Considerations for Secondary English Learners

Whereas the instructional recommendations made in the previous section are applicable for both elementary and secondary English learners, there are additional challenges for students and teachers alike at the secondary level. These include:

- Long-term English learners like Fausto, who have been educated exclusively in the United States, have not developed adequate academic English proficiency or the reading and writing skills that would prepare them for success in secondary schools, in part because of the reading demands required by the CCSS or other equally rigorous state standards. For English learners to be successful, secondary content teachers must be able to teach and reinforce the academic language of their content concurrently with the content concepts.

- Many adolescent classrooms are not aligned with students' interests and out-of-school literacies. Students who are highly engaged in searching on the Internet, participating regularly on Instagram, Twitter, and other social media sites, may be the same students who are disengaged from school literacy practices. With native-speaking adolescents, disengagement

Story Starters	Language Frames
What does _____ mean?	If _____ happens, then _____.
My opinion/view is _____.	Because of _____, then _____.
I agree with _____ and would add _____.	_____ is better than _____ because _____.

FIGURE 16.2. Examples of story starters and language frames.

may be perceived as apathy and frustration. With adolescent English learners, it may be thought of as a lack of ability. Unfortunately, adolescents needing intensive reading intervention typically outnumber the support personnel, such as reading specialists, who are available to provide it (Echevarria, Richards-Tutor, et al., 2015).

• Most adolescent English learners who have reached an intermediate level of English proficiency receive little or no ESL or language development instruction in secondary schools. These are the students who are generally labeled *long-term English learners.* The problem with this label is that it implies an "end-to-road," which is inappropriate and unnecessary.

• The configuration of many secondary schools results in no one teacher "owning" students, as contrasted to the elementary grades with one teacher per classroom. Many English learners with poor literacy skills can easily slip through the cracks until they come to the attention of a counselor when they are already experiencing academic failure.

• The assessment of English learners' language and literacy skills continues to be a challenge, especially for non-Spanish-speaking students. While assessments of Spanish-speaking students' language and literacy are readily available, for those students who speak other languages, determining their first language and literacy competencies is more difficult. Community members who speak a student's language can serve as a resource, as can texts in the home language at varied reading levels. It is important to access whatever resources you can to estimate a student's language and literacy proficiency in his or her home language.

It is incumbent on secondary literacy leaders to develop appropriate and flexible program options for adolescent English learners. In addition, modifying instructional practices to accommodate students' language, literacy, learning, and experiential backgrounds is of utmost importance.

Appropriate *Content* Instruction for English Learners

Since 1995, Echevarria et al. (2017) have been conducting research to develop and refine the SIOP model, based on the Sheltered Instruction Observation Protocol. Sheltered instruction is a means of integrating academic language and content in elementary and secondary lessons that are comprehensible for English learners while they are developing English proficiency. At the time of this writing, SIOP is the only empirically validated model of sheltered instruction that exists (Echevarria, 2012; Echevarria, Richards-Tutor, Canges, & Francis, 2011; Echevarria et al., 2006; Short, Fidelman, & Louguit, 2012).

From the research on SIOP as a model of sheltered instruction, we have learned that consistent, systematic implementation of effective

Lesson Preparation	Teachers plan lessons carefully and include content and language objectives (or goals); appropriate grade-level content; supplemental materials; adaptation, as needed, of instructional materials; meaningful activities.
Building Background	Teachers make explicit links to their students' background experiences, knowledge, and past learning; teach and emphasize key academic vocabulary.
Comprehensible Input	Teachers use a variety of techniques that make instruction understandable, such as including speech appropriate to students' language proficiency levels.
Strategies	Teachers provide regular practice with language and learning strategies, support instruction with a variety of scaffolds, and promote higher-order thinking in lessons.
Interaction	Teachers provide frequent opportunities for student interaction, sufficient wait time for processing, and clarification in the home language, if possible.
Lesson Delivery	Teachers implement lessons that clearly support content and language objectives, and use appropriate pacing, resulting in high levels of student engagement.
Review and Assessment	Throughout lessons, teachers provide reviews of key concepts and vocabulary, provide specific academic feedback, and assess student comprehension of lesson concepts.

FIGURE 16.3. The Sheltered Instruction Observation Protocol (SIOP) model.

sheltered techniques in academic language and content lessons can result in significant academic and language gains for English learners (Echevarria, Richards-Tutor, Chinn, & Ratleff, 2011; Echevarria, Vogt, & Short, 2015a, 2015b, 2017; Vogt, 2009). The features of the SIOP model are mostly familiar instructional techniques that organize instruction for English learners purposefully, consistently, and systematically. A brief overview of the eight components of the SIOP model is offered in Figure 16.3.

HOW CAN LITERACY LEADERS ELEVATE AND SUPPORT TEACHERS' LANGUAGE AND LITERACY INSTRUCTION FOR ENGLISH LEARNERS?

As suggested by the ILA *Standards 2017*, literacy leaders can support linguistically and culturally responsive classrooms with purpose and determination, not just with lip service. This means actively doing the following:

- As a literacy leader, ensure that all teachers and administrators in your school understand first- and second-language acquisition and the importance of developing students' oral language proficiency.

- Move beyond a "heroes and holidays" mentality, where the entire school celebrates Cinco de Mayo and thinks that's enough support for English learners. Instead, as a literacy leader, work with your staff to ensure that all teachers, literacy coaches, and administrators are well prepared to support effectively students' second (or additional) language acquisition, as well as the integration of academic language and content instruction in every lesson every day. It means understanding, honoring, and valuing the linguistic and cultural differences among the students, teachers, and administrators in classrooms and schools.

- Provide assistance and support for differentiated classroom instruction for English learners, including those who are gifted and those who struggle with learning or language or both.

- An important step that leaders can take in implementing effective literacy instruction for English learners is to require appropriate assessment of all English learners' language proficiency in the L1, if possible, and in English.

- Examine the data on students who have been exited from the ESL/ELD program by passing the state test, but have not been redesignated as language proficient because they haven't met reading and/or math standards. Another aspect to consider is whether the students who have been redesignated falter academically once they are placed in mainstream classes. The data may point to the lack of language development classes, ineffective language and academic assessments, a lack of a comprehensive plan for teaching English learners, and/or teachers who have not been adequately prepared to teach their content to this population of students.

- Create a professional learning plan with opportunities for teachers, coaches, and administrators to learn about appropriate assessment and effective academic language and content instruction for English learners. Take an inquiry stance with professional learning that is substantive; dynamic, intense (ongoing, over time); collaborative; situated (teachers' own classrooms with their own students); and personal (see Risko & Vogt, 2016).

- Assist teachers, reading specialists, literacy coaches, and special educators in making effective use of adopted reading programs. Most states require that the programs include provisions for working with English learners. However, the suggestions in the teacher's edition may be superficial, focusing more on how the teacher should explain something, rather than involving students in generating, practicing, and applying what they are learning about English.

- Become an advocate for English learners, both those who are native born and those who are immigrants. These students deserve effective instruction that is appropriate for their language, literacy, and other academic strengths and needs.

CONCLUSION

Some time ago, I had the opportunity to interview some adolescent English learners about what makes learning in English either easy or difficult in their various high school classes. These astute teens didn't hesitate to tell me their thoughts. "One teacher does everything she can to make us understand. She'll explain something and then will give examples, draw pictures, even slide across the floor to show us what 'slippery' means. She doesn't give up until we get it. Other teachers just tell us to do stuff and then we're supposed to do it. It doesn't seem like they really expect us to understand it . . . just get it done."

My final question for these students was, "If you could tell teachers one thing that they could do to make it easier for you as an English learner, what would it be?" A young woman from India said, "Don't just talk to the kids who speak English. Talk to us, too." A boy from Ukraine (the inspiration for Mykalo) said, "Tell us what to do in the order we have to do it." Finally, a girl from Guatemala paused and then quietly added, "I would tell them to not forget we're here."

Bilan, Fausto, and Mykalo are just three individual students who are trying to learn English while they are learning the curriculum of the elementary, middle, and high schools they attend. They represent the hundreds of thousands of other English learners, who, like them, are just trying to make it in this diverse, unique, and challenging country. By assessing and understanding your English learners' language and literacy needs and strengths, you and your colleagues can develop your students' interests, talents, abilities, and English proficiency. Your students who are English learners, like their native-English-speaking peers, will thus have a better chance of becoming literate, capable, contributing adults.

ENGAGEMENT ACTIVITIES

1. How could you use the *Standards 2017* document as a roadmap for a school improvement or other plan to improve instruction and support for English learners?

2. Reflect and discuss these questions with colleagues in your present educational context (e.g., school, district office, county office, university, or other workplace): What do you see as obstacles or challenges to providing effective language,

literacy, and content instruction for English learners? What would it take to overcome these obstacles or challenges?

3. What similarities are there in the implications suggested in Chapter 15 (this volume), on culturally relevant instruction, and this chapter? What are the differences, if any, between culturally relevant pedagogy and linguistically relevant pedagogy? See the background information on Standard 1: Foundational Knowledge of *Standards 2017* to help you answer this question.

ANNOTATED RESOURCES

Echevarria, J., Vogt, M. E., & Short, D. J. (2017). *Making content comprehensible for English learners: The SIOP model* (5th ed.). Boston: Pearson

This text, also available in elementary and secondary editions, is a widely used resource for teachers of English learners, and for those who plan and administer programs for them. Based on a federally funded study and 20+ years of research, the authors offer a comprehensive, empirically validated model of sheltered instruction for English learners and other students. The SIOP model focuses on the integration of developing students' subject-matter knowledge and academic language concurrently and consistently throughout content lessons.

International Literacy Association. (2017). *Second language learners' vocabulary and oral language development* (Literacy leadership brief). Newark, DE: Author.

This ILA literacy leadership brief describes effective instruction for language minority students, with an emphasis on building vocabulary and developing oral proficiency. This overview is appropriate for educators as well as administrators and policymakers.

TESOL International Association (Short, D. J., Becker, H., Cloud, N., Hellman, A. B., Levine, L. N., & TESOL Team Writers). (2018). *The 6 principles for exemplary teaching of English learners: Grades K–12*. Alexandria VA: TESOL Press.

With a Foreword by Jim Cummins, this book is the first in a series published by the TESOL International Association that includes research and practical information about six key principles for effectively teaching English learners. Examples of the principles include "#3. Design High-Quality Lessons for Language Development" and "#5. Monitor and Assess Student Language Development."

REFERENCES

August, D., & Shanahan, T. (2006). *Developing literacy in second-language learners: Report of the National Literacy Panel on Language-Minority Children and Youth*. Mahwah, NJ: Erlbaum.

August, D., & Shanahan, T. (Eds.). (2008). *Developing reading and writing in second-language learners: Lessons from the Report of the National Literacy Panel on Language-Minority Children and Youth*. New York: Routledge; Newark, DE:

International Reading Association; Washington, DC: Center for Applied Linguistics.

Bauer, E. B. (2009). Informed additive literacy instruction for ELLs. *The Reading Teacher, 62*(5), 446–448.

Brookes, H., & Angelleli, C. (n.d.). *What educators need to know about bilingual children interpreting and translating: Practitioners Guide: A9816.* Storrs, CT: National Research Center on the Gifted and Talented. Retrieved from *www.gifted.uconn.edu/nrcgt.*

Cummins, J. (1981). The role of primary language development in promoting educational success for language minority students. In C. F. Leyba (Ed.), *Schooling and language minority students: A theoretical framework* (pp. 3–49). Los Angeles: California State University—Evaluation, Dissemination, and Assessment Center.

Echevarría, J. (2012). *Effective practices for increasing the achievement of English learners.* Washington, DC: Center for Research on the Educational Achievement and Teaching of English Language Learners. Retrieved from *www.cal.org/create/resources/pubs.*

Echevarría, J., Richards-Tutor, C., Canges, R., & Francis, D. (2011). Using the SIOP model to promote the acquisition of language and science concepts with English learners. *Bilingual Research Journal, 34*(3), 334–351.

Echevarría, J., Richards-Tutor, C., Chinn, V., & Ratleff, P. (2011). Did they get it?: The role of fidelity in teaching English learners. *Journal of Adolescent and Adult Literacy, 54*(6), 425–434.

Echevarria, J., Richards-Tutor, C., & Vogt, M. E. (2015). *Response to intervention (RTI) and English learners: Using the SIOP Model* (2nd ed.). Boston: Pearson.

Echevarría, J., Short, D., & Powers, K. (2006). School reform and standards-based education: An instructional model for English language learners. *Journal of Educational Research, 99*(4), 195–210.

Echevarría, J., Vogt, M. E., & Short, D. (2015a). *Making content comprehensible for elementary English learners: The SIOP model* (3rd ed.). Boston: Pearson.

Echevarría, J., Vogt, M. E., & Short, D. (2015b). *Making content comprehensible for secondary English learners: The SIOP model* (3rd ed.). Boston: Pearson.

Echevarría, J., Vogt, M. E., & Short, D. (2017). *Making content comprehensible for English learners: The SIOP model* (5th ed.). Boston: Pearson.

Education Commission of the States. (2018). *50-state comparison: What ELL training, if any, is required for general education students?* Denver, CO: Author. Retrieved from *http://ecs.force.com/mbdata/mbquestNB2?rep=ELL1415.*

Goldenberg, C. (2008). Teaching English language learners: What the research does and does not say. *American Educator, 32*(2), 8–23, 42–44. Retrieved from *www.aft.org/pubs-reports/american-educator/index.htm.*

Institute of Education Sciences/National Center for Education Statistics. (2018, May). Reading performance. Retrieved from *https://nces.ed.gov/programs/coe/indicator_cnb.asp.*

International Literacy Association (ILA). (2017). *Second language learners' vocabulary and oral language* (Literacy leadership brief). Newark, DE: Author.

International Literacy Association (ILA). (2018). *Standards for the preparation of literacy professionals 2017.* Newark, DE: Author.

McFarland, J. (2016). Diversity in home languages: Examining English learners in U.S. public schools. NCES Blog: National Center for Education Statistics. Retrieved October 14, 2018, from *https://nces.ed.gov/blogs/nces/post/diversity-in-home-languages-examining-english-learners-in-u-s-public-schools.*

Moll, L. C. (1994). Literacy research in communities and classrooms: A sociocultural approach. In R. B. Ruddell, M. R. Ruddell, & H. Singer (Eds.), *Theoretical models and processes of reading* (4th ed., pp. 179–207). Newark, DE: International Reading Association.

National Clearinghouse for English Language Acquisition. (2010). Frequently asked questions. Retrieved from *www.ncela.gwu.edu/faqs*.

National Governors Association Center for Best Practices & Council of Chief State School Officers. (2010). *Common Core Standards for English language arts and literacy in history/social studies, science, and technical subjects.* Washington, DC: Authors.

National Reading Panel. (2000). *Teaching children to read: An evidence-based assessment of the scientific research literature on reading and its implications for reading instruction.* Washington, DC: National Institute of Child Health and Human Development, National Institutes of Health.

Nation's Report Card. (2017). *2017 NAEP mathematics and reading assessments highlighted results at grades 4 and 8 for the nation, states, and districts.* Washington, DC: National Assessment of Educational Progress (NAEP). Retrieved from *www.nationsreportcard.gov/reading_math_2017_highlights*.

Risko, V. J., & Vogt, M . E. (2016). *Professional learning in action: An inquiry approach for teaches of literacy.* New York: Teachers College Press.

Sanchez, C. (2017). English language learners: How is your state doing? Retrieved from *www.npr.org/sections/ed/2017/02/23/512451228/5millionenglish-language-learners-a-vast-pool-of-talent-at-risk*.

Shearer, B. A., Carr, D. A., & Vogt, M. E. (2019). *Reading specialists and literacy coaches in the real world* (4th ed.). Long Grove, IL: Waveland Press.

Short, D. J., & Echevarría, J. (2016). *Developing academic language with the SIOP model.* Boston: Pearson.

Short, D. J., Fidelman, C., & Louguit, M. (2012). Developing academic language in English language learners through sheltered instruction. *TESOL Quarterly, 46*(2), 333–360.

Short, D. J., Vogt, M. E., & Echevarría, J. (2017). *The SIOP model for administrators* (2nd ed.). Boston: Pearson.

U.S. Department of Education, Institute of Education Sciences/National Center for Education Statistics. (2018, April). *English language learners in public schools.* Washington, DC: Author. Retrieved from *https://nces.ed.gov/programs/coe/indicator_cgf.asp*.

Vogt, M. E. (2009). Teachers of English learners: Issues of preparation and professional development. In F. Falk-Ross, S. Szabo, M. B. Sampson, & M. M. Foote (Eds.), *Literacy issues during changing times: A call to action* (pp. 23–26). Oak Creek, WI: College Reading Association.

Vogt, M. E. (2014). Reaching linguistically diverse students. In S. B. Wepner, D. S. Strickland, & D. J. Quatroche (Eds.), *The administration and supervision of reading programs* (5th ed., pp. 182–189). New York: Teachers College Press.

Literacy Leadership in Action

Celia Banks, MEd
Literacy Coordinator, School District U-46,
Elgin, Illinois

THINK ABOUT THIS

1. In what ways does Celia serve as a literacy leader?
2. What lessons can be learned about the role of literacy coordinator?
3. What questions come to mind while reading this vignette?

Currently, I serve as Coordinator of Elementary Literacy and Libraries, K–6 Bilingual, for School District U-46, which spans 11 communities in Chicago's northwest suburbs and is the second largest school district in Illinois. More than 39,000 preschool through 12th-grade students attend the district's 57 schools and programs. Over 50% of our students are Hispanic, and more than 10,000 students are developing their bilingual and biliteracy skills in our award-winning dual-language program. Our dual-language philosophy is that no student should have to lose a language in order to learn a new one. Our dual-language program services our English learners as well as English-speaking students who choose to enroll in kindergarten and first grade in order to also become bilingual and biliterate.

As the Coordinator of Elementary Literacy and Libraries, I collaborate with the Coordinator of Secondary Literacy. Together, we provide professional development for literacy across the district, facilitate curriculum-writing teams, serve on various district committees, collaborate with all content areas and programs, assist in the selection of literacy resources, and support classroom instruction. We do this to ensure that all of our students have the experiences they need to graduate from U-46 prepared with the skills necessary to compete and succeed in a global society.

In U-46, we believe that teachers need to be included in curriculum writing and resource selection. Five years ago, when I first started as Coordinator of Elementary Literacy, I sent out a call for a committee to begin curriculum writing for our K–5 literacy program. The committee was formed with representation from each grade level, including dual language and specialized student services. This committee used the Common Core State Standards, adopted by Illinois, to create a framework of units with essential questions, enduring understandings, academic vocabulary, and learning objectives for language arts. Suggestions for formative and summative assessments were also included in the units. Once the units were complete, they were presented to our Instructional Council and then Board of Education for approval. Following their approval, a plan was put together to provide professional development along with a copy of the units to our approximately 800 elementary teachers.

As you can imagine, providing professional development to so many teachers at one time is a challenge. In our district, an effort is made to encourage school professionals to assume leadership roles in providing professional learning activities and then ongoing support in their schools. The district offers professional learning sessions to help prepare our teachers to present literacy content to adult learners, including a follow-up session to get feedback on a presentation before it "goes live." This practice has greatly benefited our large district, though there is still much to be done to encourage more teachers to participate.

Throughout the almost 25 years I have worked in U-46, I have learned the importance and impact of building relationships. As I moved from a classroom teacher to a reading specialist to a district coach to my current position of Coordinator of Elementary Literacy and Libraries, I have always had a network of teachers with which to collaborate and upon whom I can rely to support the work of the literacy department. In the past few years, as I learn more about trauma-informed care, mindfulness, positive behavior supports, and social and emotional learning, it has become more and more evident that one of the most important things for nurturing a lifelong love of learning and success in life for our students and teachers is starting with the foundation of a trusting relationship.

CHAPTER 17

Developing Effective Home– School Literacy Partnerships

Jeanne R. Paratore
Lilly M. Steiner
Susan M. Dougherty

GUIDING QUESTIONS

➥ What should literacy leaders do to achieve strong home–school partnerships, and how is this effort aligned with the *Standards for the Preparation of Literacy Professionals 2017* (International Literacy Association [ILA], 2018)?

➥ What are the challenges to productive parent–teacher partnerships for families of marginalized groups, and specifically for immigrant families?

➥ What principles can guide the planning and implementation of partnerships that align with *Standards 2017* and support teachers and parents in their work together to increase children's opportunities to learn? What types of initiatives make the guiding principles "come alive"?

➥ What do we know about practices that support productive partnerships between teachers and immigrant (and other marginalized) families?

In the previous edition of this book, we argued that "there is robust evidence of a strong, positive relationship between parent involvement and children's school success" (Paratore, Steiner, & Dougherty, 2012, p. 317). We based this claim on consistent, compelling evidence of a relationship between higher levels of parent involvement and higher rates of student motivation and engagement, school attendance, achievement test scores, and high school graduation. In the intervening years, new evidence has lent further support to these overall findings (e.g., Jung & Zhang, 2017). Given the strength and stability of the evidence, in this revision, we have chosen to turn the lens a bit and focus on the particular needs of immigrant families, a group that continues to grow in the United States and is often not well served by traditional parent involvement initiatives.

As we do so, however, we do not mean to suggest that the evidence and related practices hold merit only for immigrant families. Although negotiating relationships with partners who have different cultures and languages may create special challenges, the more general challenge of relationship building clearly is not limited to teachers' interactions with immigrant parents. Rather, building a relationship with any family is rooted in finding common ground even in the face of uncommon circumstances. Differences and difficulties may arise as a challenge in teachers' interactions with *any* parent or caregiver, as a result of an underrecognized situation (e.g., two working parents with little time, a noncustodial parent) or a marginalized group (e.g., low-income, homeless, LGBTQ). Through a particular focus on immigrant families, we hope to gain insight into types of teaching and leadership actions that have the potential to support relationship building, and in turn, productive partnering, with *any* family that may not respond as expected, for myriad reasons, to traditional notions of family involvement. As you read, then, we ask that you keep in mind the *broad* implications of the findings related to immigrant families, and consider them in the context of the families in your particular classroom or community.

In the sections that follow, we review the ILA's *Standards 2017* with specific attention to those sections related to parent engagement. With the standards as a backdrop, next we examine what we know about the actions immigrant families take (and don't take), and the teaching and leadership actions that are especially productive in forming trusting relationships with immigrant and other marginalized families. We then use this information to formulate a few guiding principles intended to help literacy leaders act on the evidence and make *Standards 2017* "come alive." Finally, we provide a few examples of initiatives that enact the principles, and we offer a brief conclusion.

DEVELOPING HOME–SCHOOL PARTNERSHIPS

Standards 2017 offers a foundation for literacy leaders to meet their responsibilities to collaborate with parents in positive and productive ways. The standards position parents as literacy partners, on a par with internal partners (e.g., special educators, English learner [EL] teachers) and other external partners (e.g., community agencies). Further, *Standards 2017* emphasizes an asset-based approach to parent interactions, specifically calling on leaders to acknowledge and respect families' existing resources and also to seek ways to exchange information (i.e., "support" and "learn from") rather than transmit information:

- Literacy professionals . . . must use culturally responsive strategies that respect and appreciate the linguistic, cultural, and family resources students bring to literacy development from their homes and communities. (Standard 4) (ILA, 2018, p. 108)
- Literacy leaders have a responsibility to . . . support all literacy partners' knowledge of literacy development; likewise, there is a need to respect, advocate, and learn from their partners. (Standard 6) (ILA, 2018, p. 108)

Even as *Standards 2017* emphasizes the importance of building on families' existing linguistic, cultural, and community resources as a foundation for teaching and learning, the standards also guide literacy leaders to recognize that family literacies may *differ* from school literacies, and to understand that these differences may call for explicit support to introduce children to literacy behaviors and practices that will be helpful to their success in school. Related to this idea, *Standards 2017* identifies three particular home-based literacy practices that have been shown to positively influence children's literacy knowledge: (1) having a variety of print and using it in different ways, (2) having a large collection of books, and (3) reading frequently with a child. Finally, the expectation that literacy leaders will "respect, advocate, and learn from their partners" (ILA, 2018, p. 108) effectively encompasses literacy leaders' responsibility to understand the barriers to parents' participation in school-based activities and events and search for alternatives that will enable parent participation without compromise.

With knowledge of the actions literacy leaders are expected to take to engage parents as partners in their children's schooling, we next review what we know about immigrant parents' engagement in children's schooling and the specific challenges they face.

DEVELOPING HOME–SCHOOL PARTNERSHIPS WITH IMMIGRANT FAMILIES

Immigrant parents and their children represent nearly a quarter of all children in U.S. public schools; in classrooms throughout the United States, at least one in ten children is likely to reside in a family holding immigrant status, more in several U.S. cities (National Center for Education Statistics, 2018). At times, the changing demography of families served by U.S.

schools has challenged educators' understandings of what it means to be "involved" in children's education. For many, parent involvement has long meant parental compliance with a collection of specified practices enacted for the particular purpose of supporting children's school-based learning. This understanding leads teachers and administrators to plan and implement an approach to parent engagement intended to *transmit* school-based knowledge, independent of out-of-school knowledge. Educators with this view largely perceive parent engagement as a "scripted role to be 'performed,' rather than as unrehearsed activities that parents and other family members routinely practice" (López, 2001, p. 417). This often leads to a search for *specific* and familiar literacy practices in home settings, and in turn, may lead one to ignore or simply not see other, potentially valuable, literacy practices.

Others, though, view parent engagement in an entirely different light: as a process of home–school interaction that is fundamentally reciprocal. That is, they approach engagement with parents as an opportunity to *exchange* information about children's learning opportunities both at home and school. Educators who hold this view engage in a search for "household funds of knowledge" (Moll & Greenberg, 1990) that surround daily routines and traditions; they perceive household funds of knowledge as rich sources of capital just waiting to be uncovered, connected to, and integrated within school-based learning (e.g., González, Moll, & Amanti, 2005).

It is this latter approach that is endorsed within the previously described *Standards 2017,* and on the surface, this seems like a logical and straightforward approach to parent engagement. However, as our classrooms have increased in diversity, teachers' knowledge of "typical" background experiences has become substantially less secure, making such an approach seem challenging and perhaps even a bit intimidating to classroom teachers. How does a teacher unfamiliar with a family's culture, language, and traditions recognize, acknowledge, and build on existing literacies, and lay a foundation for entering into trustworthy and meaningful partnerships with parents? In the remainder of this section, we examine why it's important for teachers to learn how to do so and also how knowledgeable teachers accomplish it.

Let's start with what we know about current family involvement practices. We know that many families, and in particular, immigrant families, are less likely to participate in forms of parent involvement that require parents' presence at school, such as back-to-school nights and classroom or field trip volunteers (e.g., Jung & Zhang, 2017; Maríñez-Lora & Quintano, 2009; Mena, 2011; Valdés, 1996). Some reported reasons for reluctance to participate in on-site activities cross immigrant and nonimmigrant backgrounds (e.g., work schedules, transportation, child care), whereas others are specifically related to immigration status, including language differences, and more recently, a concern that schools may serve as contexts for enforcing immigration policies (addressed more fully below). In addition, like many of their native-born counterparts (e.g., Lapp, Fisher, Flood, & Moore, 2002), immigrant parents may not believe they are able to provide academic support in the home, at least partially because they lack (or believe they lack) requisite content knowledge to comply with teacher expectations (Schneider & Arnot, 2018).

When traditional forms of parent engagement are the predominant focus of a home–school partnership effort, teachers may conclude that a low rate of parent participation means that parents are unconcerned or uninvolved in their children's education. Some teachers even choose not to reach out to immigrant parents, assuming their efforts will be ignored or met with resistance (e.g., López-Robertson, Long, & Turner-Nash, 2010). Schneider and Arnot (2018) described parent engagement efforts such as these as "pathologizing parents from marginal groups as 'failed parents'" (p. 11). Over time, these efforts can lead teachers to develop a "fixed mindset" (Dweck, 2016, p. 8) that creates an expectation of failure and limits both the scope and effectiveness of actions intended to engage parents in collaborative activities.

Notably, this mindset is refuted by findings from several studies (e.g., Delgado-Gaitan, 1996; Valdés, 1996) that show that, despite their reluctance to participate in these types of activities, immigrant parents (and parents from other marginalized groups) are deeply concerned with and engaged in their children's learning in other ways. Across studies, findings show that although some parents rarely attend school events, they perceive themselves as very involved in their children's schooling, raising their children to be "good and well-behaved human beings" (Valdés, p. 166) and encouraging them to do well in school. Henderson and Mapp (2002) provided an apt summary of findings from this collection of studies:

> Families of all cultural backgrounds, education, and income levels encourage their children, talk with them about school, help them plan for higher education, and keep them focused on learning and homework. In other words, all families can, and often do, have a positive influence on their children's learning. (p. 34)

Specifically related to literacy learning, several studies document an array of literacy practices embedded within families' daily lives. Dougherty and Paratore (2018) summarized findings from pivotal studies as follows:

> . . . young children are routinely encouraged to write and read in myriad ways. They read grocery lists, coupons, recipes, notes, logos and words on food packaging and games, and books, including children's books and the bible. They create notes, lists, drawings, letters to family members, and labels of various types. They listen to, learn, and memorize stories, songs, prayers,

riddles, and rhymes, and they recite them for themselves, family, and friends. In some families, they are taught letters of the alphabet and words; and they see family and community members reading and writing. Overall, prior to school entry, most children have had some experience with varied forms of literacy, and as such, have had opportunities to develop both language and concept knowledge, and also emerging identities as readers and writers. (p. 271)

Of course, household funds of knowledge and routine literacy practices vary from culture to culture and from family to family. So, how do concerned teachers learn about the funds of knowledge and literacy routines within the families of the children in their classrooms? Numerous studies (e.g., Compton-Lilly, 2017; González et al., 2005; O'Brien et al., 2014; Purcell-Gates, Lenters, McTavish, & Anderson, 2014) tell us that the answer (1) resides in an asset-based approach to parent engagement that acknowledges that *both* parties have valuable information to share and (2) seeks to engage parents in co-constructing a *shared* agenda. This approach is grounded in a belief that parents' knowledge about their children's out-of-school lives, when combined with teachers' knowledge of children's in-school lives, will lead to a more accurate representation of what children already know and do. When all of this knowledge is considered, it will lead to expanded learning landscapes for children and more relevant opportunities to learn.

Even so, these *different* literacies (e.g., Purcell-Gates, 1996)—valuable in their own right and made even more so when recognized and connected to classroom curriculum—may be an insufficient substitute for specific literacy experiences that are known to support school-based literacy achievement. That is, when children's home experiences include plenty of parent–child talk, opportunities for shared storybook reading, and interaction with all print in a variety of places for a variety of purposes, children are better prepared for school success (e.g., Sénéchal & Young, 2008). In other words, productive partnerships may demand more than joining two sources of knowledge; they may require developing new knowledge for both parents and teachers.

In sum, taken together, evidence confirms that immigrant families, and families from other marginalized groups, are generally unlikely to participate in traditional forms of parent involvement, such as back-to-school meetings and volunteer activities; and they may feel unprepared to adequately respond to requests to support specific skill learning or monitor homework completion. On the other hand, immigrant parents (and parents from other marginalized groups) have a deep interest in and concern about their children's academic success—a concern that is enacted in ways not always visible to teachers, including emphasizing the importance of education to their lifelong goals, encouraging their children to do their best in school, demanding that they treat teachers (and classmates) with respect, and arriving at school on time and well rested. Moreover, although parents and children may not engage in school-specific learning activities, there are various learning experiences that frame their daily lives, and these activities result in children's development of varied literacies and important knowledge about their world. Finally, specific literacy practices known to be important to school-based success may be absent. Supporting parents in the development and use of these literacies can support children's academic success.

In short, conceptualizing home–school partnerships as an opportunity to exchange information such that teachers learn about varied household funds of knowledge and parents learn about important school-based forms of knowledge is likely to support the development of mutual trust and respect, and, over time, long-term and sustained home–school partnerships. These, in turn, are likely to contribute to expanded learning opportunities for children.

Immigrant Parents' Fear of Schools as Surveilling Contexts

Even as school leaders work to understand and act on evidence about ways in which immigrant parents are engaged in their children's education, they are now faced with a potentially far more consequential challenge to productive parent involvement. In a recent study of immigrant families, Ee and Gándara (2019) found that parent involvement in their children's schooling had diminished because of parents' fear of immigration policy enforcement. Parents' fears not only kept them from coming to school, but also from signing forms necessary for school services (e.g., individualized education plans [IEPs], special services, field trips, free lunch) due to worry that the "documentation could somehow be used against them" (p. 21). Parents' fear of schools as surveilling contexts appears to be well founded. Despite a policy prohibiting engagement in immigration enforcement in schools (U.S. Department of Homeland Security, 2018), numerous incidents have been reported (Rein, Hauslohner, & Somashekhar, 2017). In one example, a planned enforcement action was carried out during morning drop-off "in plain view of students and families" (Phillips, 2017). The potential reach of these concerns is substantial. Ee and Gándara (2019) estimated that more than 5 million children in U.S. cities reside with parents affected by U.S. immigration policies, and they reported that 53% of respondents who completed their survey ($N = 3,800$) reported parental fear of immigration enforcement authorities as a barrier to parent involvement.

These recent developments are a sobering reminder of the challenges immigrant families face on a daily basis as they try to navigate their own and their children's lives in and out of school. With this context as a backdrop, exactly what should we expect of parents and of the teachers who share responsibility for their children's learning? What actions can literacy leaders take to support parents and teachers as they try to make a difference? In the remaining sections of this chapter, we aim to answer that question.

ACTING ON THE EVIDENCE: GUIDING PRINCIPLES

How do we act on what we know to make *Standards 2017* come alive? In the next sections, we provide a few guiding principles to answer these questions.

Principle 1: Words Matter

As we consider how to engage families meaningfully, let's step back briefly to consider the words we use. Are the phrases *parent involvement programs* and *parent–teacher partnerships* interchangeable? Do they mean the same thing? More than two decades ago, Shockley, Michalove, and Allen (1995) argued that these two labels prescribe substantially different actions:

> Programs are implemented; partnerships are developed. Programs are adopted; partnerships are constructed. Parent involvement programs as America's schools have implemented them have serious problems. By their very nature, most programs have steps, elements or procedures that become static. A program cannot constantly reinvent itself, change each year, be different in every classroom, and for every teacher–family–child relationship. Yet schools and parents have a shared and vested interest in children that almost demands some kind of collaboration. We believe, along with an increasing number of home and school educators, that this shared responsibility be a genuine partnership. (p. 91)

Shockley et al. explained that developing a genuine partnership is dependent on five conditions: (1) respect for parents and a belief that they are interested in and dedicated to supporting their children's education; (2) understanding that different family cultures and traditions dictate different ways of collaborating; (3) an assumption that parents and teachers have something to learn from each other; (4) an understanding that parents may need explicit instruction in particular types of activities that are known to benefit children; (5) an understanding that making home–school connections is beneficial to children, and that children's out-of-school experiences should be used, at least partially, as the basis for in-school learning.

The principle here is clear: As we initiate parent outreach, let's be sure to do so using words and labels that convey our intention to expand children's learning landscapes by both seeking and providing information about how children learn, and then by creating the conditions necessary for genuine partnerships to take hold. At the outset, describing these efforts using words such as *partnership, collaboration,* and *exchange* may help participants frame the actions and interactions necessary to realize anticipated outcomes.

Principle 2: Families' Cultural, Linguistic, and Community Resources Enrich the Classroom Curriculum

To enact this principle, we first need to get to the bottom of the meaning of culturally responsive teaching (CRT) and explore what it looks like in the context of home–school partnerships. This important and complex body of work merits extensive treatment on its own. For our purposes here, we draw (briefly) on the work of Ladson-Billing (1995) and Gay (2013) to identify three specific actions especially pertinent to home–school partnership building: (1) Use knowledge of students' cultural backgrounds and experiences to guide curricular and instructional decision making (e.g., search for and integrate familiar materials and experiences common in classrooms *and also* in students' homes and communities as important curricular and instructional resources); (2) recognize and build on the social nature of learning by situating instructional experiences within collaborative contexts in which students can share their own ideas and experiences, question and challenge the ideas of others, and co-construct meaning and understanding; and (3) create opportunities to practice and apply new understandings in meaningful contexts in *and* out of school.

To implement these three action-based ideas, teachers must be intentional and deliberate, seeking opportunities to uncover families' experiences, interests, achievements, problems and challenges, and to share children's classroom and school experiences. This exchange of knowledge will support collaboration among teachers, family, and community members so that students' learning in and out of school is coherent and purposeful, deepening their understanding of important ideas.

Principle 3: Parents May Need Guidance to Support School-Based Practices

The extent to which parents implement specific school-based practices relates to two factors: parental role construction and parental self-efficacy (e.g., Hoover-Dempsey et al., 2005; Tang, 2015). *Parental role construction* refers to parents' beliefs about the appropriateness of their involvement in their children's education. *Parental self-efficacy* relates to parents' perception of their ability to appropriately implement the recommended practice. Studies (e.g., Jeynes, 2012; Sénechal & Young, 2008) indicate that when parents are provided with explicit guidance in implementing specific literacy practices, they develop requisite expertise, and their work with their children makes a difference. In the particular area of literacy learning, Sheldon and Epstein (2005) cautioned that leaving parents on their own to create a supportive home environment for reading and literacy has the potential to lead to inequities between the children of parents who are more familiar with school-based literacy practices and those who require explicit support in learning how to support their children's schooling. The overarching takeaway is that productive home–school partnerships include a plan for explicitly guiding parents' implementation of specific literacy practices.

Principle 4: Parents' Concerns about Schools as Surveillance Sites May Be Mediated by Seeking Alternatives to School-Based Meetings

At present, engaging parents in their children's schooling may be complicated by parents' fear that both attendance at school and even completion of school forms will compromise parents' safety in the community. These concerns are widespread and have eroded parents' sense of trust in the teachers and administrators in their children's schools (Gándara & Ee, 2018; Sanchez, Freeman, & Martin, 2018). This circumstance is especially challenging because it holds the potential to diminish *all* collaborative efforts—asset-based or not. That is, no matter how respectful and collaborative the effort, parents who fear for their own or their children's safety are unlikely to take a risk.

To understand how school leaders respond to these concerns, Kugler (2017) interviewed 25 school leaders, teachers, and support staff. She found that they employed four common, productive strategies: (1) They use a variety of practices to develop trust, including monthly coffee visits, on or off school premises, home visits, and specialized services to support new immigrant students; (2) their interaction with families is persistent and sustained; (3) they connect families to resources and legal advice, essentially serving as a trusted source of information; and (4) they help parents develop emergency plans (akin to fire safety plans) in the event of deportation. Notably, even as educators help parents manage their concerns about immigration enforcement, they continue to emphasize their importance to their children's learning, sharing salient information about school and offering opportunities for parents to increase their skills relative to their own and their children's education.

In the following section, we present a case example addressing how a grade-level team attempts to act on guiding principles.

CASE EXAMPLE •

> **THINK ABOUT THIS**
>
> 1. Is the project in this example a parent involvement program or a partner-
>   ship? Was there anything that they could have done to make it more of a
>   partnership?
> 2. Does the project design help teachers learn about and build on children's
>   cultural, linguistic, or community resources? If so, how? Does the project
>   incorporate guidance for families about literacy learning? If so, how? What
>   modifications would strengthen either of these aspects of partnering with
>   families?
> 3. Does the project account for families who might be reluctant or unable to
>   attend the meeting at the school? If so, how?

Marissa, a reading specialist, and two third-grade teachers co-planned a writing unit on "how to" books. They agreed to use parent expertise to help the children develop book topics and content. First, Marissa and the teachers called the parents and invited them to a meeting to talk about the project. They scheduled the meeting immediately before school, with an option to attend virtually (using Google HangOut). (At the meeting, they received permission of those in attendance to video-record it. They later posted the video on their classroom website so that parents who did not attend could access the information.) At the start of the meeting, the teachers described "how to" writing topics and shared a few examples (making Grandma's pound cake, knitting a scarf, digging for fishing worms). That led to a conversation about parents' own talents or family traditions that they could share with their children. Next, the teachers explained what children would be expected to do: First, interview a family member about a talent or tradition, and then write the steps in a "how to" essay.

Teachers distributed the interview form, and, as parents looked at it, one asked if children could use their phone to audiorecord the conversation so they would "get all of the steps right." Teachers agreed that was a great idea. At the end of the meeting, Marissa and the teachers were excited by parents' enthusiastic responses. Parents who attended the meeting were excited too, and shared the information with others who were not there, prompting quite a few to view the session video. In the days that followed, as they came to school with their interview notes and recordings, children worked on their books with observable pride, and it was evident that parents had followed through. At the end of the project, teachers were as enthusiastic about what they had learned about the families' cultures and experiences as they were about the children's books! They deemed this effort as one that was both worthy and enjoyable for them and their students.

GUIDING PRINCIPLES IN ACTION

In this section, we share a few initiatives from the published literature that, in our view, effectively respond to the evidence and help literacy leaders meet *Standards 2017* for developing productive home-school partnerships. These initiatives vary in scope and purpose, some requiring relatively little time and effort and others a lot of time and effort. Our intent is not to suggest that any one should be replicated. In fact, doing so would violate the very notion that effective partnerships are co-constructed and co-implemented. Rather, we strive to provide examples of the *types* of initiatives that can lead parents and teachers to exchange information in ways that are meaningful, purposeful, and respectful, and as such, expand children's learning landscapes.

Example 1: Digital Tools as a Pathway to Developing Home–School Partnerships

A particular challenge for many school leaders is how to "get the message out"—a phrase that, by itself, seems at odds with the underlying idea of establishing partnerships with parents grounded in exchanging rather than transmitting information. Yet, as we reviewed Gustafson's (2018) recommendations for "high-tech, low-tech, and no-tech" (p. 27) ways to share information, we agreed with his characterization of them as "refreshingly relational" (p. 27), with each having the potential to promote both parent and student voices. We also thought the opportunity to attend various events remotely, without the necessity of being present on the school site, might be an especially helpful response to immigrant parents' fears, while also bringing accessibility to parents who may be unable to attend for a variety of reasons. In brief, here are a few of the ideas.

One school uses Facebook Live for student-led morning announcements, such as, "creating scripts, introducing special guests, and connecting directly with their parents" (Gustafson, 2018, p. 28). Another school uses a parent ambassador program to amplify parents' voices and increase responsiveness to concerns and needs, including the use of blogs and podcasts. School leaders emphasize that it's not the "tech-savvy" nature that makes the difference, but rather leaders' willingness to listen and respond honestly to parents' concerns. Yet another school uses Twitter (#WeAre-Whitt) to build community: "We have student tweeters, we have pictures taken by students that we share, and we have students who will come grab that tripod to record what's happening in our classroom" (p. 29). The shared comments become the basis for discussion with families at monthly "Think Tank" meetings that focus on "the good, the bad, and the in-between" (p. 29). Gustafson cautioned that there is "no one 'right' way to create engagement and no single technology—new or old—that holds the key" (p. 30), but suggested these ideas as a way to "build trust, encourage student efficacy, and further your school's initiatives" (p. 30).

Example 2: Fluency and Comprehension at Home Program

Fluency and Comprehension at Home was a 7-week at-home reading partnership (Hindin, Steiner, & Dougherty, 2017). The goals were two-fold: to encourage parent–teacher communication and familiarize parents with the context of the school, and to inform teachers of the ways that parents work with literacy in the home. Each week, parents were provided with books and specific strategies to support their children's decoding and comprehension. Parents audiorecorded home reading sessions. The audio recordings were studied by the researchers to document parents' support and children's reading performance. Parents reported that they successfully used the suggested tasks surrounding the texts and gained increased confidence in assessing their children's reading progress. They also expressed a belief that participation in the program impacted their children's literacy learning and their understanding of their children's progress, and they interpreted the initiative as affirmation that teachers welcomed their involvement in their children's learning.

Example 3: A Summer Reading Program

Compton-Lilly, Caloia, Quast, and McCann (2016) aimed to collaborate with students and their families during a summer reading program. Using their knowledge of books and topics of general interest to rising second graders in the program, and the results of running record assessments to determine each child's reading level, the authors assembled a bag of five books for each child to take home at the end of the school year. During the summer months, the school's reading specialist visited each home three or four times, chatting with parents and children about reading and their favorite books, listening to the children read aloud, encouraging children to write or illustrate in response to the books, and delivering a few new books. At the end of the project, the researchers shared three important observations. First, they noticed that the home visits were treated as social events, with parents and siblings present and engaged during almost every visit, as parents read with their children and younger and older siblings read together. Some parents even indicated that they used the books to support their own learning, for example, practicing English. Second, parents were observed using social networks (extended family, secondhand stores, garage sales) and school resources (library, book fairs) to access additional books. Third (and especially interesting!), children experienced reading gains, but these did *not* show up at the beginning of the fall term—in fact,

a few children even seemed to fall behind when tested i[n]
spring testing, six of the seven children were reading at c[ ]

Example 4: Restructuring Sharing Time

Protacio and Edwards (2015) explored the ways in w[ ]
common in many classrooms, could be used to develop meaningful interactions between immigrant children, parents, and teachers. Parents were
invited to plan a sharing time presentation, during which they would share
a family artifact and explain why it is meaningful to them. Parents were
given examples of artifacts (e.g., currency used in a country, a national
costume) and guidance in choosing the artifacts they would share. Parents carefully prepared their presentations, including charts with images
and details about the artifacts. During the presentations, children were
observed to be engaged and excited as they asked questions and shared
their thoughts, often making connections to their own cultural experiences. Protacio and Edwards noted that, as a predominantly "mainstream
Western practice" (p. 420), sharing time is largely unfamiliar to immigrant
parents. They concluded that the opportunity to participate in this way
provided (1) parents with a meaningful way to join in and connect to an
otherwise unfamiliar and perhaps confusing activity; (2) a means for the
teacher to learn about previously unknown aspects of the families' cultures
and traditions; and, unexpectedly, (3) children's increased interest in and
curiosity about their own cultural heritage.

Example 5: Bilingual Picture Books by English Learners

Louie and David-Welton (2016) implemented a picture book writing project for K–6 students. At the root of the project, family members shared
personal or cultural stories with their children, and then, with teachers'
assistance, the children transformed the stories into picture books written
by the children in the families' native languages and in English, and also
illustrated by the children. Picture book writing was framed as a five-step
process that began with story gathering (in partnership with parents, other
family or community members) and culminated in children's presenting
their books to a class and to families in a Family Literacy Night Celebration. The published books, which represented "a rich oral language tradition of stories passed down from generation to generation, honored students' families' cultural heritages and traditions" (Louie & David-Welton,
2016, p. 597). The broad reach of the project was evident in one teacher's
reflection: "Not only did my parent communication skills improve, but
also the ways I interact with and relate to my students. . . . I learned a lot
from [them] and we communicated about what was going well in school"
(p. 604).

CLUSION

Literacy leaders who are knowledgeable about factors that influence productive home–school partnerships and are skillful at helping colleagues to acquire and use a repertoire of strategies for forging effective relationships with parents are in a position to provide valuable support. The challenge, though, is to resist the sometimes tidal-like force that pulls us toward the traditional practice of interactions with parents that support a predetermined school agenda, and instead move toward practices that lead to authentic partnerships grounded in shared decision making and agenda setting (Bertrand, Freelon, & Rogers, 2018). In this chapter, our purpose was to help literacy leaders effectively assume this latter role by describing ways they can act on evidence of effective home–school partnerships. Our hope is that in the studies cited within the chapter, readers will find many examples of events, activities, and projects that, when selected and modified through collaboration among local literacy leaders, teachers, and families, will have the desired outcomes.

ENGAGEMENT ACTIVITIES

1. Work with your colleagues to develop a list of actions school leaders and classroom teachers might take to become knowledgeable about families' household funds of knowledge and, then, how they might use what they learn to connect children's in-school and out-of-school learning.

2. Imagine that you are about to meet with teachers who have had largely negative experiences in their efforts to develop home–school partnerships. What information from this chapter might you use to build an argument that, if you work together to design an assets-based approach to partnering with parents, they are likely to meet with better success? Develop two or three PowerPoint slides that frame your argument.

3. In schools with effective home–school partnership efforts, teachers and literacy leaders are especially active in working with parents. What types of professional learning opportunities might help teachers with whom you work develop a deeper understanding of "effective practices" in developing home–school partnerships?

ANNOTATED RESOURCES

Edwards, P. (2016). *New ways to engage parents.* New York: Teachers College Press.

Provides teachers and school leaders meaningful and authentic ways to involve parents and caregivers in children's education. Focuses on schools' increasingly diverse landscapes and offers strategies for communicating with parents and engaging parents in school-based activities, while honoring and recognizing parental constraints.

International Literacy Association. (2017). *Early literacy learning for immigrant and refugee children: Parents' critical roles* (Literacy leadership brief). Newark, DE: Author.
www.literacyworldwide.org/docs/default-source/where-we-stand/ila-early-literacy-learning-immigrant-refugee-children.pdf?sfvrsn=b60ca58e_10.

Provides teachers and administrators with a brief description of ways teachers can build on families' rich reservoir of knowledge and experiences and draw on them to support parent engagement.

Thiers, N. (2017). Unlocking families' potential: A conversation with Karen L. Mapp. *Educational Leadership, 75*(1), 40–44.

Provides brief, practical, to-the-point answers to teachers' frequently asked questions about parent engagement. (This article appears in a themed issue of *Educational Leadership* on building productive home-school partnerships. The entire issue is a great resource.)

REFERENCES

Bertrand, M., Freelon, R., & Rogers, J. (2018). Elementary principals' social construction of parents of color and working-class parents: Disrupting or reproducing conflicting and deficit orientations of education policy? *Education Policy Analysis Archives, 26*, 1–33.

Compton-Lilly, C. (2017). *Reading students' lives: Literacy learning across time.* New York: Routledge.

Compton-Lilly, C., Caloia, R., Quast, E., McCann, K. (2016). A closer look at a summer reading program: Listening to students and parents. *The Reading Teacher, 70*(1), 59–67.

Dougherty, S. M., & Paratore, J. A. (2018). Family literacy: Is it really all about storybook reading? In C. M. Cassano & S. M. Dougherty (Eds.), *Pivotal research in early literacy foundational studies and current practices* (pp. 257–278). New York: Guilford Press.

Dweck, C. (2016). *Mindset: The new psychology of success.* New York: Ballantine Books.

Ee, J., & Gándara, P. (2019). Impact of immigration enforcement on the nation's schools. *American Educational Research Journal, 20*, 1–32.

Gay, G. (2013). Teaching to and through cultural diversity. *Curriculum Inquiry, 43*(1), 48–70.

González, N., Moll, L. C., & Amanti, C. (2005). *Funds of knowledge: Theorizing practices in households, communities, and classrooms.* Mahwah, NJ: Erlbaum.

Gustafson, B. (2018). Reaching families in the digital age. *National Association of Elementary School Principals, 98*(1), 26–30.

Henderson, A. T., & Mapp, K. (2002). *A new wave of evidence: Impact of school, family, and community connections on student achievement.* Austin, TX: National Center for Family and Community Connections with Schools.

Hindin, A., Steiner, L. M., & Dougherty, S. (2017). Building our capacity to forge successful home–school partnerships: Programs that support and honor the contributions of families. *Childhood Education, 93*(1), 10–19.

Hoover-Dempsey, K. V., Walker, J. M. T., Sandler, H. M., Whetsel, D., Green, C. L.,

Wilkins, A. S., et al. (2005). Why do parents become involved?: Research findings and implications. *Elementary School Journal, 106*(2), 105–130.

International Literacy Association (ILA). (2018). *Standards for the preparation of literacy professionals 2017*. Newark, DE: Author.

Jeynes, W. (2012). A meta-analysis of different types of parental involvement programs for urban students. *Urban Education, 47*(4), 706–742.

Jung, E., & Zhang, Y. (2017). Parental involvement, children's aspirations, and achievement in new immigrant families. *Journal of Educational Research, 109*(4), 333–350.

Kugler, E. G. (2017). Supporting families in a time of fear. *Educational Leadership, 75*(1), 26–32.

Ladson-Billing, G. (1995). Toward a theory of culturally relevant pedagogy. *American Educational Research Journal, 32*(3), 465–491.

Lapp, D., Fisher, D., Flood, J., & Moore, K. (2002). "I don't want to teach it wrong": An investigation of the role families believe they should play in the early literacy development of their children. *National Reading Conference Yearbook, 51*, 276–287.

López, G. (2001). Redefining parental involvement: Lessons from high-performing migrant-impacted schools. *American Educational Research Journal, 38*(2), 253–288.

López-Robertson, J., Long, S., & Turner-Nash, K. (2010). Constructing counter narratives of young children and their families. *Language Arts, 88*(2), 93–103.

Louie, B., & David-Welton, K. (2018). Family literacy project: Bilingual picture books by English learners. *The Reading Teacher, 69*(6), 597–606.

Maríñez-Lora, A. M., & Quintana, S. M. (2009). Low-income urban African-American and Latino parents' school involvement: Testing a theoretical model. *School Mental Health, 1*, 212–228.

Mena, J. A. (2011). Latino parent home-based practices that bolster student academic persistence. *Hispanic Journal of Behavioral Sciences, 33*, 490–506.

Moll, L. C., & Greenberg, J. B. (1990). Creating zones of possibilities: Combining social contexts for instruction. In L. C. Moll (Ed.), *Vygotsky and education: Instructional implications and applications of sociohistorical psychology* (pp. 319–348). Cambridge, UK: Cambridge University Press.

National Center for Education Statistics. (2018). Condition of education (Report No. 2018144). Retrieved from *https://nces.ed.gov/pubsearch/pubsinfo.asp?pubid= 2018144*.

O'Brien, L., Paratore, J. R., Leighton, C., Cassano, C., Krol-Sinclair, B., & Green, J. (2014). Examining differential effects of a family literacy program on children with varying vocabularies. *Journal of Literacy Research, 46*(3), 383–415.

Paratore, J. R., Leighton, C., Cassano, C., Krol-Sinclair, B., & Green, J. (2014). Examining differential effects of a family literacy program on language and literacy growth of linguistically diverse children with varying vocabularies. *Journal of Literacy Research, 46*(3), 383–415.

Paratore, J. R., Steiner, L. M., & Dougherty, S. (2012). Developing effective home-school literacy partnerships. In R. M. Bean & A. Swan Dagen (Eds.), *Best practices of literacy leaders* (pp. 331–336). New York: Guilford Press.

Phillips, N. (2017, April 6). Mayor Hancock tells ICE: Back off arrests in courthouses and near schools. *Denver Post*. Retrieved from *www.denverpost.com/2017/04/06/ denver-ice-agents-courthouse-school-raids*.

Protacio, M. S., & Edwards, P. A. (2015). Restructuring sharing time for English learners and their parents. *The Reading Teacher, 68*(6), 413–421.

Purcell-Gates, V. (1996). Stories, coupons, and the *TV Guide*: Relationships between home literacy experiences and emergent literacy knowledge. *Reading Research Quarterly, 31*(4), 406–428.

Purcell-Gates, V., Lenters, K., McTabish, M., & Andersons, J. (2014). Working with different cultural patterns and beliefs: Teachers and families learning together. *Multicultural Education, 21*(3–4), 17–22.

Rein, L., Hauslohner, A., & Somashekhar, S. (2017, February 11). Federal agents conduct immigration enforcement raids in at least six states. *Washington Post*. Retrieved from *www.washingtonpost.com/national/federal-agents-conduct-sweeping-immigration-enforcement-raids-in-at-least-6-states/2017/02/10/4b9f443a-efc8-11e6-b4ff-ac2cf509efe5_story.html*.

Sanchez, S., Freeman, R., & Martin, P. (2018). *Stressed, overworked, and not sure whom to trust: How public-school educators are navigating recent immigration enforcement*. Los Angeles: University of California, Los Angeles Civil Rights Project.

Schneider, C., & Arnot, M. (2018). Transactional school–home–school communication: Addressing the mismatches between migrant parents' and teachers' views of parental knowledge, engagement and the barriers to engagement. *Teaching and Teacher Education, 75*, 10–20.

Sénéchal, M., & Young, L. (2008). The effect of family literacy interventions on children's acquisition of reading from kindergarten to grade 3: A meta-analytic review. *Review of Educational Research, 78*, 880–907.

Sheldon, S. B., & Epstein, J. L. (2005). School programs of family and community involvement to support children's reading and literacy development across the grades. In J. Flood & P. Anders (Eds.), *Literacy development of students in urban schools: Research and policy* (pp. 107–138). Newark, DE: International Reading Association.

Shockley, B., Michalove, B., & Allen, J. (1995). *Engaging families: Connecting home and school literacy communities*. Portsmouth, NH: Heinemann.

Tang, S. (2015). Social capital and determinants of immigrant family educational involvement. *Journal of Educational Research, 108*, 22–34.

U.S. Department of Homeland Security. (2018). U.S. immigration and customs enforcement. Retrieved from *www.dhs.gov/topic/immigration-and-customs-enforcement*.

Valdés, G. (1996). *Con respecto: Bridging the distances between culturally diverse families and schools*. New York: Teachers College Press.

Literacy Leadership in Action

Shawna Zervos, MA, NBCT

Prekindergarten Teacher, McNinch Primary School, Moundsville, West Virginia

THINK ABOUT THIS

1. In what ways does Shawna serve as a literacy leader?
2. What lessons can be learned about the role of a PreK teacher?
3. What questions come to mind while reading this vignette?

Since 2008, I have been employed as a West Virginia universal prekindergarten (UPK) teacher. My classroom is housed in a public primary school serving over 450 students in grades PreK–2. I am one of two PreK teachers in the building. Three years ago, I participated in a statewide grant initiative with other PreK teachers from around the state as we worked toward National Board Certification. Though I have always considered reflection a huge part of who I am as a teacher, the ongoing reflection and daily writing I was required to do to successfully complete the certification has tremendously influenced my role as a literacy leader.

As I think about the 4-year-old students in my class today, the lack of access and exposure to books outside of school stands out as a problem. Many of my students come from low socioeconomic backgrounds, and in many homes, there appears to be a lack of reading materials. Additionally, many of the parents of my students have had experiences in school that shaped them, often in a negative way. As a classroom teacher and certified reading specialist, I take advantage of every opportunity to expose them to books: I read aloud to my students and have created an inviting, quiet book center with a wide selection of reading materials.

As a literacy leader, I set out to create a bridge between school activities and those that children experience at home. I implemented the "Brown Bear Book Club," for which my students receive a book to read with their families each month. I try to purchase the books using Scholastic Book Club points. This past year, with my principal's support and encouragement, I wrote a grant to assist in funding the program. I carefully select the books based on what we are currently reading in our classroom, and always begin with *Brown Bear, Brown Bear, What Do You See?* (1967). Throughout the year, we are reading classic, rich, timeless books such as *Blueberries for Sal* (1948) or popular books like *Pete the Cat: I Love My White Shoes* (2010) I enjoy working with parents to teach them how to enjoy a read-aloud with their child and see the deep benefits of reading aloud. My students get to keep the books and by the end of the year, they have amassed their own beginning library! As a result, we are looking to expand the program, making it available in my co-teacher's classroom; we are hoping to move it into the kindergarten classrooms as well. I have been told that some students ask their kindergarten teacher about the book club.

Last year I took exposing students to books one step further for them. Rather than inviting a guest reader in only on designated days like "Read Across America" day, students heard from a variety of community voices throughout the entire year. My students are still talking about visits from the high school football coach and three players, all of whom came equipped with their favorite childhood books. We are looking forward to our next reader—a local fireman. By listening to people in the community talk about books and read aloud, students want to talk about their favorite book or "read" a beloved story from school. We are all then talking about books, and the students feel as though there is a literacy leader in all of us. As a classroom teacher and literacy leader, I am an advocate for my students, my school, and my community.

Children's Literature References

Litwin, E., & Dean, J. (2010). *Pete the cat: I love my white shoes.* New York: Harper-Collins.

Martin, B., & Carle, E. (1967). *Brown bear, brown bear, what do you see?* New York: Holt.

McCloskey, R. (1948). *Blueberries for Sal.* New York: Viking Press.

CHAPTER 18

Enactment of Reading Policy
Leading and Learning for Literacy and Equity

Sarah L. Woulfin
Britney Jones

GUIDING QUESTIONS

⮞ What is the current understanding of leaders' and teachers' role in policy implementation and how does *Standards for the Preparation of Literacy Professionals 2017* (International Literacy Association [ILA], 2018) inform the work of teachers and leaders?

⮞ How do current educational policies influence leadership for learning and equity?

⮞ How can literacy leaders improve their enactment of systems and practices for learning and equity?

LANDSCAPE OF LITERACY POLICY AND PRACTICE

Over the past 20 years, a barrage of policies that intends to change the quality of instruction has reached into schools and classrooms. These policies include rules, ideas, and resources affecting the work of literacy leaders in substantial ways. As noted by Woulfin and Coburn (2011), "Today's policymakers and education reformers place reading instruction squarely at the center of their efforts to improve instruction and close the achievement gap" (p. 337). First, No Child Left Behind (2002) dramatically raised the stakes for student performance on standardized tests in reading. This policy placed heavy pressure on states, districts, schools, and teachers to improve achievement. Consequently, reading instruction and achievement have been prioritized by many state- and district-level accountability policies (Coburn, Pearson, & Woulfin, 2010; Coburn & Woulfin, 2012; Mintrop & Trujillo, 2007; Woulfin, 2015b).

The ascendance of evaluation systems and Common Core State Standards (CCSS) after 2009 encouraged districts and schools to alter the supervision of teachers and leaders and to adopt new content and pedagogy for both English language arts and math (National Governors Association Center for Best Practices & Council of Chief State School Officers [NGA & CCSSO], 2010; Donaldson & Woulfin, 2018). On the one hand, state and district evaluation models used rubrics and ratings in systematic ways while observing instruction and measuring teacher quality (Donaldson & Woulfin, 2018; Gabriel & Woulfin, 2017). On the other hand, CCSS put forth ambitious visions of teaching and learning with a particular emphasis on reading expository text and engaging in close reading activities (Polikoff, 2017; Sawchuk, 2018). Many states and districts across the United States have adopted new reading programs and then linked them with pacing guides, targeted professional development, and progress monitoring assessments to comply with federal and state accountability policies post-Race to the Top (U.S. Department of Education, 2009).

Throughout the accountability policy era, guidance on literacy instruction has become increasingly specified, moving from broad principles and objectives, as in the case of standards, to promoting mandated curriculum accompanied by pacing guides, assessments, and monitoring for fidelity. Notably, the Every Student Succeeds Act (ESSA), passed in 2015, shifted responsibility toward districts. As such, district leaders now allocate resources and time toward the design and implementation of instructional programs in the domain of literacy (Heitin, 2018). Further, district leaders must construct professional learning opportunities for principals, coaches, teachers, and other instructional staff on literacy curricula and assessments.

ESSA encourages comprehensive literacy instruction, multi-tiered systems of support, professional development for educators, and evidence-based strategies (ILA, 2016). ESSA's attention toward multi-tiered systems of support indicates that response to intervention (RTI) should be used to meet the literacy learning needs of each student. As such, it is crucial for literacy leaders to consider the structure and activities related to RTI in their sites. The quantity of policy related to literacy instruction, along with the use of increasingly aggressive policy levers, makes it important to understand the relationship between instructional policy and the work of literacy leaders and teachers. Paying attention to how and why policy is translated into practice in schools illuminates opportunities and challenges for improving teachers' literacy instruction and students' literacy achievement.

While encountering and coping with this blizzard of reforms, teachers and literacy leaders may want to look to their guiding professional organizations for support. Thus, this chapter leans on the work of the ILA, specifically their newly released *Standards 2017* document. We grapple with literacy leaders' roles and responsibilities in addressing policy mandates while advancing equity, promoting leadership and professional learning, and deploying curriculum and assessments. We share research on literacy policy implementation because literacy leaders' advocacy is vitally important and because it is necessary for leaders and teachers to be aware of current policies and their influence on instruction. This chapter incorporates vignettes to reveal obstacles and successes in literacy reform in different contexts. Moreover, the chapter raises questions and provides evidence-based recommendations for practitioners at multiple levels of the education system. We conclude with engagement activities for reflecting and analyzing existing practices associated with literacy reform in various educational organizations.

OVERVIEW OF LITERACY POLICY IMPLEMENTATION

Current policies in the domain of literacy expect that teachers will use challenging texts; address foundational skills, vocabulary, and comprehension; and expand literacy instruction across content areas (NGA & CCSSO, 2010). It is important to unpack how and why educators respond to these policies. Scholars have determined that individual, social, and policy factors shape the implementation of instructional policy from legislation to classrooms (Coburn, 2001; Spillane, Reiser, & Reimer, 2002; Woulfin & Coburn, 2011). As depicted in Figure 18.1, educators' response to literacy policy is shaped by the interaction among (1) individual knowledge, beliefs, and dispositions; (2) the school and district context; and (3) features of the policy itself (Woulfin & Coburn, 2011).

First, prior knowledge, beliefs, and dispositions influence how educators come to understand and enact instructional policy inside schools (Spillane et al., 2002; Coburn, 2001). As Spillane et al. (2002) explain, "Individuals must use their prior knowledge and experience to notice, make sense of, interpret, and react to incoming stimuli—all the while actively constructing meaning from their interactions with the environment, of which policy is part" (pp. 393–394). For example, a coach's beliefs about effective writing instruction shapes how he or she responds to a new spelling program. Further, educators' advocacy efforts are affected by their knowledge of literacy policies.

Second, social interaction with colleagues and school and district leaders matters for how educators implement literacy policies in their workplace (Woulfin & Rigby, 2017). More specifically, literacy leaders' interactions

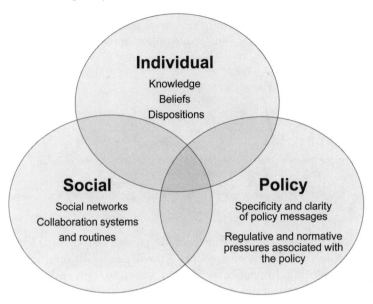

FIGURE 18.1. Factors influencing literacy policy implementation.

with colleagues influence how they come to understand the meaning and implications of a new policy. The social networks of literacy leaders and teachers matter for how they respond to reforms across the state, district, and school levels (Coburn & Russell, 2008). Notably, a school's structures and systems for collaboration affect when, where, how, and why educators work together to comprehend and enact literacy policies and programs.

Third, the design and characteristics of policy matter in relation to its implementation (Matland, 1995). Researchers have reported that the clarity and specificity of policy messages influences educators' understandings of and responses to instructional programs. For example, a highly prescribed reading program will influence teachers' changes in practice differently than open-ended guidelines on literacy instruction. Additionally, some initiatives, particularly in the accountability policy era, are coupled with strict mandates and monitoring activities. These regulative features of reforms steer leaders' and teachers' enactment in different ways than reforms accompanied solely by regulative pressure.

This chapter illuminates how several types of literacy policy are enacted by teachers and leaders. Specifically, we focus on implementation issues tied to four ILA leadership standards: (1) diversity and equity, (2) professional learning and leadership, (3) curriculum and instruction, and (4) assessment. While exploring these strands of literacy policy, we pay close attention to the people doing the work of implementation in the context of districts and schools. In this way, we shed light on the potential for literacy leaders to positively—and strategically—influence policy implementation.

DIVERSITY AND EQUITY

CASE EXAMPLE •

THINK ABOUT THIS

1. How could these teachers collaborate on issues of culturally relevant pedagogy?
2. What are some inclusive ways to involve families in students' literacy development?

Kristin and Vanessa are two fourth-grade teachers at Green Elementary with differing conceptions on students' knowledge, skills, and interests in reading and writing. In particular, Kristin aims to design and teach in culturally responsive ways; this means that she goes beyond displaying multicultural books. She has high expectations for her students and incorporates multiple means of assessing student learning. Kristin also uses literacy content to encourage students to engage in critical reflection and to empower students to enact change in their own lives/communities. For example, after reading *Percy Jackson and the Lightning Thief* (Riordan, 2005), she had students consider how the story might be different if it drew upon mythology from other ancient societies. She also led students in a discussion about why Greek mythology was so prevalent compared to mythology from other cultures. In contrast, Vanessa frequently reminds other teachers of their major goals on district interim assessments as well as state-mandated standardized tests. Her assessment tools mirror the state and interim assessments, and she rarely monitors student performance in alternative ways. Vanessa also focuses on basic comprehension skills and does not push her students to think critically about the assigned reading material.

Additionally, within a single school, these two educators frame the expectations and roles of students' families in strikingly different ways, with Vanessa presuming that many of the families of her English learner students don't have the time or inclination to support literacy development. Kristin strives to understand and acknowledge families' use of and appreciation for literacy, and she also supports parents in better understanding the nature of reading and writing instruction in her classroom. Finally, the two teachers position student achievement in noticeably different ways. When student achievement goals are not met in Kristin's class, she reflects upon the lessons within the unit and brainstorms ways to make content more engaging and relevant for students. When student performance goals are not met in Vanessa's class, she tends to blame students with statements like "These standards are just too hard for them" or "In these kinds of neighborhoods it's just harder to meet these achievement goals."

Scholarship on Diversity and Equity for Literacy

Increased focus on diversity and equity within *Standards 2017* is reflective of research in the field of educational policy that pushes for culturally relevant pedagogy in literacy education. Literacy leaders can ensure that classrooms are equitable and inclusive by demonstrating their understanding of pedagogies that consider culturally and linguistically diverse students. Culturally relevant pedagogy and critical literacy are two such pedagogies that value the knowledge, experiences, and academic success of students from diverse backgrounds. It is not enough for principals and coaches to acquire a deep understanding of strategies for diversity and equity; they must also be able to impart such knowledge to teachers. In the vignette on Green Elementary School, it is apparent that instructional leaders failed to demonstrate their commitment to diversity and equity or present teachers with a clear a vision for how to accomplish such goals.

Culturally relevant pedagogy (CRP) has become one of the most prominent frameworks/strategies for attending to claims for diversity and equity. This form of pedagogy calls for teachers to consider the ways in which they can foster academic success, cultural competence, and sociopolitical consciousness among students (Ladson-Billings, 1995). Teachers and school leaders who effectively engage in CRP are mindful of their conceptions of themselves and others, social relations, and knowledge. That is, they consider how identity impacts students and teachers, how teacher-to-student and student-to-student interactions play out, and how social constructs influence what knowledge and skills are deemed valuable in traditional spaces. *Critical literacy* (Fisher, 2005; Lopez, 2011) is a social-justice-oriented pedagogy that helps teachers deconstruct issues of power within texts and encourages students to view texts as tools of empowerment. Lopez (2011) notes that teachers may engage in this form of pedagogy by asking students to consider, deconstruct, and then reconstruct their views around certain types of literature, while also exploring and questioning which types of literature tend to be privileged in English classrooms. Further, Ladson-Billings (1992) calls for educators to treat literacy instruction as a political act in which they take up a sociocultural approach by capitalizing on the funds of knowledge (González, Moll, & Amanti, 2006) students bring into the classroom and empowering students to effect change in their own lives.

Taking a culturally relevant or critical approach is a political endeavor, and it is important to be explicit about the practices and strategies associated with these forms of pedagogy. Here we illustrate some of the ways literacy educators can implement culturally relevant, critical practice in their schools and classrooms. One strategy that educators can employ is the use of texts that are culturally appropriate (Toppel, 2015) and varied. Research by Souto-Manning (2009) suggests that teachers go beyond required texts/ textbooks with happy endings and incorporate literature from multiple sources and perspectives. For example, a unit on the civil rights movement might include texts written from the perspective of marginalized people and newspaper articles from the time period to create a more holistic picture. These types of activities allow students to examine literature critically and urge teachers to reconsider how content is traditionally presented. Toppel (2012) magnifies the importance of incorporating students' culture and making content culturally relevant. She advocates for using personal alphabets in which students are asked to connect letters and sounds to personal stories, and even encouraged to use other languages. This approach creates space for students to learn about one another while also building cultural competence. The goal of these strategies for facilitating diversity and equity should always be increased engagement, inclusion, educational success, and student empowerment.

Implications for School Literacy Improvement

Literacy professionals must understand and accept the variety of ways in which students communicate and learn and then strive to make literacy content accessible for an increasingly diverse student body (Toppel, 2015). Taking up CRP or critical literacy requires educators to dismiss the inclination to force students to assimilate or fit in (Ladson-Billings, 1992). Teachers, along with their students, must challenge the status quo by using literature and the literacy classroom to critically examine the world and promote change. If teachers are to do this challenging work, teacher leaders must advocate for culturally relevant and critical pedagogy by creating a school environment that facilitates a social justice orientation toward learning (Theoharis & O'Toole, 2011).

In these types of spaces teachers should be encouraged to first learn about their students' backgrounds and assets, then use that knowledge to inform instruction (Villegas, 1991). They should also carefully reflect on their own identity and biases. This means that teacher leaders must consider opportunities for teacher learning around diversity and equity, develop ways to monitor teacher progress toward these goals, and create a culture and climate that supports culturally relevant, critical pedagogy. School systems also need to increase the diversity of the teacher workforce, so it more closely matches student/community demographics.

This is complex work because teachers, literacy leaders, and school leaders are charged with the tasks of centering marginalized students and critically interrogating curriculum in school systems that may be resistant to this kind of teaching (Lopez, 2011). However, if the goal is to increase diversity and equity, researchers, policymakers, and practitioners alike must position themselves and students as change agents. Literacy professionals, in particular, must remain committed to consistently deconstructing curriculum and curriculum materials in ways that foster critical understandings (Larson & Marsh, 2005). Finally, literacy professionals should serve as advocates for culturally responsive and sustaining programs, materials, and instruction.

PROFESSIONAL LEARNING AND LEADERSHIP

CASE EXAMPLE •

Clinton Elementary School's principal, assistant principal, literacy coach, and lead teachers meet weekly for instructional leadership team meetings. However, these meetings rarely focus upon literacy instruction or achievement. Instead, the group discusses schedules, plans events, and completes reports for district administrators. Members of this team hold different sets of beliefs about quality literacy instruction and priorities for improvement. Specifically, the assistant principal and two lead teachers tend to be concerned about student behavior, while the principal and literacy coach are more concerned about teachers' lesson planning and students' opportunities to read and write. This team rarely engages in in-depth, evidence-based planning of professional learning opportunities for Clinton's teachers. Consequently, many of the school's teachers feel disappointed—and even frustrated—that professional development is disconnected from their pressing problems and overly relies on dull PowerPoint presentations and announcements.

Scholarship on Leadership

Research in the field of educational policy highlights the role of leadership in developing and supporting teachers, thereby braiding together professional learning and leadership. District and school leaders control working conditions as well as the structure and content of professional learning opportunities. More specifically, school leaders can advance implementation by prioritizing components of literacy programs and strategically framing how these programs will benefit the school, teachers, and students (Coburn, 2006; Woulfin, 2015a). That is, principals and coaches can teach teachers about facets of reforms. However, in the vignette on Clinton Elementary, instructional leaders failed to align their framing of literacy instruction— with consequences for educator learning and improvement efforts.

In addition to principals and coaches catalyzing reform, teacher leaders play multiple roles during the reform process. Teacher leaders can serve as models, facilitating the formation of shared understandings among teachers and staff on the content and pedagogy of instruction (Coburn, 2001; Woulfin & Rigby, 2017). Wenner and Campbell (2017) highlight that teacher leaders "are uniquely positioned to promote change within schools because they are well versed in the complexities involved with teachers" (p. 134). Moreover, these authors encourage researchers, reformers, and administrators to treat "teacher leaders as not just influencing individual teachers, but also having the capability to influence the entire school, community, and profession" (p. 140). Thus, we underscore that literacy leaders can influence implementation by supporting professional learning on literacy instruction and programs.

Over the past decade, teacher leadership has become a popular strategy for addressing literacy deficiencies, but it's still necessary to unpack *how* teacher leaders catalyze literacy improvement. For instance, teacher leaders can open their classroom doors so that other teachers can see the nature of their instruction and learn from modeling and sharing feedback (Aguilar, 2013; Woulfin & Rigby, 2017). In addition, teacher leaders can communicate ideas on a literacy program so that teams of teachers can gain a shared conceptualization of how and why to change. This type of communication, which prioritizes some elements of the reform to draw attention to important shifts, matters during implementation because it facilitates the alignment of teachers' beliefs and practices with a reform.

In the context of her work, Little (1995) declares that "teacher leaders find themselves caught in the collision" (p. 50) between enacting *commitment strategies,* which wield incentives for leading and collaboration, and *bureaucratic controls,* including teacher evaluation and curriculum alignment. Depending upon district and school contexts, teacher leaders may juggle these strategies in their literacy improvement efforts (Deussen, Coskie, Robinson, & Autio, 2007; Little, 1995). For example, many literacy leaders facilitate teacher collaboration to support educator development while also working to raise the consistency of instruction to match district priorities and curricula.

Implications for School Literacy Improvement

To foster conditions for significant and sustainable improvements in literacy instruction, system leaders should create conditions in which school leaders can serve as literacy leaders. For instance, district leaders could manage additional aspects of school operations so that principals could devote additional attention to issues of literacy instruction. And, perhaps more importantly, district leaders should develop the capacity of principals, coaches, and teacher leaders on literacy reforms and adult learning so that these school-based leaders can increase the capacity of educators. We propose that system leaders need to boost trust between actors in central office and schools, enabling coordination and collaboration among district administrators, principals, and coaches (Mangin & Stoelinga, 2008). These trusting relationships could help raise coherence and catalyze literacy improvement.

We underscore the point that teacher leaders can serve in both formal and informal ways to motivate changes in literacy instruction. As such, teachers should reach out to school leaders to take on important leadership activities tied to literacy. Finally, we emphasize that teachers teaching teachers about literacy instruction is a lever for school change. Thus, when teachers mentor new teachers, collaborate during meetings (or even over lunch and in the hallways!), and discuss news stories or books regarding literacy, they can shift outcomes across the school.

CURRICULUM

Scholarship on Curricular Policies

Curriculum has become a central tool for reforming literacy instruction because it can influence patterns of classroom practice and student outcomes (Correnti & Rowan, 2007; Xu, 2015). State and district leaders have adopted new curricular programs and instructional materials to steer teachers' work toward CCSS-aligned English language arts (ELA) instruction. They have also adopted intervention programs to be used as part of RTI systems to differentiate literacy instruction. Some researchers have devoted attention toward analyzing the strengths and limitations of curricula. For instance, Correnti and Rowan (2007) surfaced the way in which a school's reading program influenced the balance of phonics, reading comprehension, and writing instruction in teachers' classrooms. Brenner and Hiebert (2010) studied the volume of text in third-grade core reading programs, finding that popular programs contained, on average, words per day and minutes of reading per day that were *lower than* recommended levels. They point out that they "provide a realistic estimation of opportunities to read in classrooms in which teachers are attempting to use a core reading program with mandated fidelity" (p. 359). Thus, the nature of curriculum shapes classroom practice.

Literacy leaders play roles in selecting, creating, and implementing curricula (Bean, 2004; Coburn & Woulfin, 2012; Deussen et al., 2007). Across the United States, many districts now distribute curriculum reform tasks to teacher leaders and coaches. This means that teacher leaders and coaches spend time writing and refining literacy curricula and assessments. Further, coaches, as one type of literacy leader, can catalyze teachers' use of new instructional programs and pedagogical models that may be part of district initiatives. Woulfin (2015b) articulated literacy coaches' role in emphasizing certain elements of a district-mandated reading workshop reform. In particular, coaches addressed certain facets of the new reading program, such as mini-lessons and independent reading, while downplaying others. Specifically, only 16% of messages addressed conferencing with students. As compared to other dimensions of the district's reading reform, teachers only occasionally encountered messages telling them to conference with students as a way to provide differentiated instruction. Yet conferencing is a challenging pedagogical move that matters in RTI and in meeting the needs of students at different instructional levels. In sum, this study's findings illuminate that curricula are multidimensional, targeting various aspects of classroom practice.

Implications for School Literacy Improvement

There is mounting evidence that leaders should carefully select curricula, support their adoption, and assess their implementation. While selecting curricula, leaders should consider how they address various facets of literacy (i.e., phonics, fluency, comprehension, vocabulary, writing) and how they provide opportunities for students to engage in sustained reading, encounter culturally responsive texts, and permit teachers to differentiate teaching material to meet all students' needs. Further, literacy leaders should determine whether instructional materials are educative in nature, providing ideas to teachers so they understand the rationales for why they should teach in particular ways. Literacy leaders should also clearly frame instructional materials so that teachers and coaches understand the aims of curricular adoptions and are motivated to use the curriculum in appropriate ways.

To advance literacy instructional improvement, district and school leaders should support teachers in learning about multiple facets of curricula. This could include various opportunities for groups of teachers to study lessons from a curriculum and observe other teachers' enactment of a curriculum. This process could also entail collecting and analyzing evidence on the limitations as well as the strengths of current programs. Again, we emphasize that literacy leaders should apply tenets of adult learning so that teachers experience high-quality professional learning on particular programs. This type of professional learning has the potential to advance the implementation of literacy policies.

ASSESSMENT

CASE EXAMPLE ·

West School District mandates that all elementary teachers administer the Fountas and Pinnell benchmark assessment system three times per year. This assessment involves teachers listening to each student's reading, one on one, to ascertain his or her reading level, thereby relying on educators to make objective judgments and ratings of students' reading abilities. Concomitantly, as part of West's teacher evaluation system, teachers must set one student learning objective that is measured by the Fountas and Pinnell assessment. Literacy coaches recently shared with district administrators that a few teachers across their schools imprecisely scored their Fountas and Pinnell assessments to game the evaluation system. That is, teachers rated students as reaching higher levels on the reading assessment to reach their evaluation target.

. . . .

These inaccurate assessment results represent gaming of the evaluation system, in which educators purposefully inflate evaluation results while under accountability pressure (Donaldson & Woulfin, 2018). These inaccurate measurements of students' reading also influence classroom practice and students' experiences. In light of these issues, district leaders pressed for coaches to model the administration and scoring of Fountas and Pinnell assessments and to be more closely involved in teachers' goal setting, so that they set reasonable, attainable goals. District leaders also warned principals and teachers that they could audit any teacher's reading assessment results. These steps are meant to obviate the inflation of assessment results plus teacher evaluation ratings.

Scholarship on Assessment

Assessments play a potent role in current educational policies and practices. However, assessments hold multiple and, at times, conflicting purposes for a variety of stakeholders (Afflerbach, 2017). ELA assessments can focus on particular dimensions of teaching and learning, measuring knowledge and skills in particular ways (Afflerbach, 2016). As such, some assessments provide more relevant and useful information at particular grade levels, on particular strands of literacy instruction, or for making particular decisions. Afflerbach (2017) declares that "a useful assessment would be one that allows teachers to gather accurate and usable information about students' reading" (p. 34). Afflerbach also states that educators benefit from reading assessments that provide formative and summative information, attend to the processes and products of student reading, and "that are sensitive to the breadth and depth of students' accomplishments in reading at different levels of reading achievement" (p. 36). In sum, the features of assessments matter for their influence on teaching, and leaders must understand the purposes and attributes of assessments and make decisions accordingly.

In most districts, high-stakes standardized testing has become deeply institutionalized. Politicians, reformers, educators, and even parents now take for granted that standardized tests will be administered and that their scores will be reported with consequences at the system, school, and even individual levels. These tests may be used to rate schools, evaluate teachers, and determine whether to retain students (International Reading Association, 2014). Scholars and practitioners articulate that using assessments for accountability aims has serious consequences; teachers' responses in the West District vignette reflect the negative consequences of linking reading assessment results with evaluation. During the accountability policy era, scholars have grappled with the (un)intended consequences of assessments. Linn (2003) declares that "attaching high stakes to test results in an accountability system leads to a narrowing of the instructional focus of teachers and principals" (p. 4). This narrowing of the curriculum alters schools as places where educators work and students learn, and includes "a restriction in the creative and enjoyable activities engaged in by teachers and students" (Berliner, 2011, p. 287).

Regardless of the structure or aim of any assessment, it must be scored and the results analyzed and interpreted by educators—in individual and group formats (Boudett, City, & Murnane, 2005; Huguet, Marsh, & Farrell, 2014). Huguet et al. (2014) note that although "teachers appreciate having access to various types of data—including metrics from classroom assessments, common grade assessments, teacher observations, interim or benchmark assessments, state tests—they often struggle to use data due to a lack of skills and knowledge to formulate questions, select indicators, interpret results, and develop instructional responses" (p. 3). As a consequence, coaches are often deployed to raise teachers' capacity to appropriately analyze results from ELA assessments and plan changes in literacy instruction.

Coaches play a pivotal role in "connecting teachers with student data, interpreting data, applying new information to classroom practice, facilitating constructive dialogue, and identifying instructional responses" (Huguet et al., 2014, p. 3). Literacy coaches can meet with teams of teachers to examine results from different forms of assessments, ranging from phonemic awareness screenings and developmental reading assessment (DRA) to district writing assessments with standards-aligned rubrics. In this manner, coaches educate teachers about assessment policy and practice and, in turn, influence the implementation of accountability policies that hinge on assessments (Farrell, 2015; Huguet et al., 2014).

Implications for School Literacy Improvement

System and school leaders should be aware of the promises and pitfalls of various assessments. Leaders should put in place systems and activities that develop the assessment literacy of literacy leaders and teachers. This effort would include explaining how and why educators administer various assessments. Additionally, since data analysis and improvement planning necessitate time and space for collaboration, leaders should set up conditions for teachers to thoughtfully analyze data and, more importantly, discuss how to improve instruction achievement. We propose that literacy leaders should draw on multiple sources of evidence on student progress and literacy instruction while making decisions. Finally, we acknowledge that educators should consider multiple ways to advocate for—or against—assessments and testing systems that influence schooling and instruction in powerful ways.

CONCLUSION

While exploring the role of literacy leaders in instructional improvement efforts, this chapter concentrates on structures and practices related to the implementation of literacy policy. We have delved into recent scholarship on how and why policies associated with diversity and equity, leadership and professional learning, curriculum, and assessments are enacted. We surface key implications for school improvement in each of these policy domains and acknowledge that these improvements will require changes at the district, school, and/or individual levels. We note that ESSA shifts responsibility toward district leaders, and that they can play key roles in selecting and promoting evidence-based literacy programs and aligned professional learning opportunities for coaches and principals as well as teachers.

It is obvious that future waves of reform will once again attempt to change the nature of literacy instruction. To realize their aims and facilitate much-needed systemic change, these reforms must tackle issues of diversity, inclusion, and equity. Further, while acknowledging current gaps in literacy instruction for historically marginalized groups, reforms include the goal of teaching educators how to reach equity-oriented goals. Additionally, policies regarding literacy instruction should carefully consider how adults learn, devoting sufficient resources toward the educative-oriented (in addition to the accountability-oriented) dimensions of implementation. For instance, curricular reforms should include short- and long-term plans on professional learning opportunities for district administrators, principals, coaches, teachers, and support staff. Likewise, reforms focusing on altering teacher leaders' role should include ongoing, contextualized professional development and support for teacher leaders and principals. In this reform environment, it is vital for literacy leaders to remain aware of policies at the national, state, and district levels and to advocate for structures and practices that benefit teaching and learning.

This chapter also identifies implications for educator preparation programs and state and district leaders on literacy policy implementation. First, teacher and leader preparation programs should work to raise the capacity of future teachers and leaders to critically analyze and use instructional programs and assessments. Second, state and district leaders should create conditions that enable the ongoing professional learning of literacy leaders on topics, such as CRP, curriculum, assessments and data use, and leadership. This professional learning could support educators as advocates on literacy instruction and school improvement. Finally, we note that many questions remain about literacy leaders' roles in enacting policies and programs. Thus, researchers should collect a variety of data to answer pressing questions on literacy leaders' interpretations of and responses to a range of reforms. Researchers should also strive to partner with practitioners to design studies and transmit evidence and findings that improve literacy-related outcomes for schools and communities.

ENGAGEMENT ACTIVITIES

1. **Equity audit.** Walk around your school and take note of symbols and activities that are more or less culturally responsive. In particular, look for representations of people of color and listen for references to people of color. What are the assumptions and biases reflected in those representations and references? You should also look for the manner in which people of color are portrayed in the ELA curriculum and instructional materials. What does this portrayal reveal about the match (or mismatch) between the curriculum and the students, families, and community served by your school?

2. **Learning about diversity.** Toppel (2015) describes a strategy for increasing engagement among marginalized students who may be identified as struggling. Teachers are encouraged to learn about these students and develop culturally relevant plans/strategies for engaging them in content. She also encourages other teachers to observe teachers and their focal students to provide nonevaluative feedback on the nature of literacy instruction. We suggest that teachers should partner to help each other observe and check on focal students' levels of engagement. We also recommend that teacher leaders incorporate this strategy and form of observation into their coaching routine. Observations with the goal of better understanding how focal students are engaged can be a fruitful means of shifting school culture toward greater diversity and equity.

3. **Analysis of professional learning opportunities.** Reflect on professional development that you have experienced over the past year and complete the following chart. How did each session tie into literacy instructional improvement? To what degree was each session contextualized? Aligned to current district and school priorities? Job-embedded? Ongoing in nature? Finally, note whether and how the professional development contributed to shifts in practice.

Professional development session	Connection to literacy instructional improvement	Contextualized	Job-embedded	Ongoing	Shifts in practice
District professional development on new writing program	Addressed aspects of teaching the new writing program	Matched district initiative to improve students' writing skills and achievement	No, a 3-day summer workshop	Yes, school-based coaches have facilitated additional learning on the writing program	Yes, I'm using the writing program 3 days per week

4. Download the ILA's Advocacy ESSA Toolkit (see Annotated Resources). Discuss with colleagues how this toolkit might impact your school literacy program.

ANNOTATED RESOURCES

Advocacy ESSA Toolkit: *www.literacyworldwide.org/docs/default-source/where-we-stand/ila-essa-toolkit.pdf*

The toolkit document summarizes important information on the history and pillars of ESSA, including descriptions of the major objectives of ESSA to develop the knowledge and awareness of literacy leaders striving to advocate for changes to policy and practice.

Gabriel, R. G., & Woulfin, S. L. (2017). *Making teacher evaluation work: A guide for literacy teachers and leaders.* Portsmouth, NH: Heinemann.

This book explains the multiple purposes of teacher evaluation, providing suggestions for collaboration between leaders and teachers so that evaluation aligns with quality literacy instruction. This text can be used to learn more about elements of evaluation systems and to create routines and tools that develop and support teachers.

Wenner, J. A., & Campbell, T. (2017). The theoretical and empirical basis of teacher leadership. *Review of Educational Research, 87*(1), 134–171.

This article reviews existing research on teacher leadership. In so doing, it summarizes important aspects of teacher leaders' roles and responsibilities in school and instructional improvement.

REFERENCES

Afflerbach, P. (2016). Reading assessment. *The Reading Teacher, 69*(4), 413–419.

Afflerbach, P. (2017). *Understanding and using reading assessment.* Newark, DE: International Reading Association.

Aguilar, E. (2013). *The art of coaching: Effective strategies for school transformation.* San Francisco: Jossey-Bass.

Bean, R. M. (2004). *The reading specialist*. New York: Guilford Press.

Berliner, D. (2011). Rational responses to high-stakes testing: The case of curriculum narrowing and the harm that follows. *Cambridge Journal of Education, 41*(3), 287–302.

Boudett, K. P., City, E. A., & Murnane, R. J. (2005). *Data wise*. Cambridge, MA: Harvard Education Press.

Brenner, D., & Hiebert, E. H. (2010). If I follow the teachers' editions, isn't that enough?: Analyzing reading volume in six core reading programs. *Elementary School Journal, 110*(3), 347–363.

Coburn, C. E. (2001). Collective sensemaking about reading: How teachers mediate reading policy in their professional communities. *Educational Evaluation and Policy Analysis, 23*(2), 145–170.

Coburn, C. E. (2006). Framing the problem of reading instruction: Using frame analysis to uncover the microprocesses of policy implementation. *American Educational Research Journal, 43*(3), 343–379.

Coburn, C. E., Pearson, P. D., & Woulfin, S. L. (2010). Reading policy in an era of accountability. In M. Kamil, P. D. Pearson, E. Moje, & P. Afflerbach (Eds.), *Handbook of reading research* (Vol. 4, pp. 561–593). Mahwah, NJ: Erlbaum.

Coburn, C. E., & Russell, J. L. (2008). District policy and teachers' social networks. *Educational Evaluation and Policy Analysis, 30*(3), 203–235.

Coburn, C. E., & Woulfin, S. L. (2012). Reading coaches and the relationship between policy and practice. *Reading Research Quarterly, 47*(1), 5–30.

Correnti, R., & Rowan, B. (2007). Opening up the black box: Literacy instruction in schools participating in three comprehensive school reform programs. *American Educational Research Journal, 44*(2), 298–339.

Deussen, T., Coskie, T., Robinson, L., & Autio, E. (2007). *"Coach" can mean many things: Five categories of literacy coaches in Reading First*. Washington, DC: U.S. Department of Education, Institute of Education Sciences, National Center for Education Evaluation and Regional Assistance, Regional Educational Laboratory Northwest.

Donaldson, M. L., & Woulfin, S. L. (2018). From tinkering to going "rogue": How principals use agency when enacting new teacher evaluation systems. *Educational Evaluation and Policy Analysis, 40*(4), 531–556.

Farrell, C. C. (2015). Designing school systems to encourage data use and instructional improvement: A comparison of school districts and charter management organizations. *Educational Administration Quarterly, 51*(3), 438–471.

Fisher, M. (2005). From the coffee house to the school house: The promise and potential of spoken word poetry in school contexts. *English Education, 37*(2), 115–131.

Gabriel, R. G., & Woulfin, S. (2017). *Making teacher evaluation work*. Portsmouth, NH: Heinemann.

González, N., Moll, L. C., & Amanti, C. (Eds.). (2006). *Funds of knowledge: Theorizing practices in households, communities, and classrooms*. New York: Routledge.

Heitin, L. (2016). ESSA reins in, reshapes federal role in literacy. Retrieved from *www.edweek.org/ew/articles/2016/01/06/essa-reins-in-reshapes-federal-role-in.html*.

Huguet, A., Marsh, J., Farrell, C. (2014). Building teachers' data-use capacity: Insights from strong and developing coaches. *Education Policy Analysis Archives, 22*(52), 1–31.

International Literacy Association (ILA). (2016). Advocacy toolkit: Every Student Succeeds Act. Newark, DE: Author.

International Literacy Association (ILA). (2018). *Standards for the preparation of literacy professionals 2017.* Newark, DE: Author.

International Reading Association. (2014). *Using high-stakes assessments for grade retention and graduation decisions* (Position statement). Newark, DE: Author.

Ladson-Billings, G. (1992). Reading between the lines and beyond the pages: A culturally relevant approach to literacy teaching. *Theory into Practice, 31*(4), 312–320.

Ladson-Billings, G. (1995). Toward a theory of culturally relevant pedagogy. *American Educational Research Journal, 32*(3), 465–491.

Larson, J., & Marsh, J. (2005). *Making literacy real: Theories and practices for learning and teaching.* London: SAGE.

Linn, R. L. (2003). *Accountability: Responsibility and reasonable expectations* (CSE Report 601). Los Angeles: Center for the Study of Evaluation, National Center for Research on Evaluation, Standards, and Student Testing, Graduate School of Education and Information Studies, University of California, Los Angeles. Retrieved from *www.cse.ucla.edu/products/reports/r601.pdf.*

Little, J. W. (1995). Contested ground: The basis of teacher leadership in two restructuring high schools. *Elementary School Journal, 96*(1), 47–63.

Lopez, A. E. (2011). Culturally relevant pedagogy and critical literacy in diverse English classrooms: A case study of a secondary English teacher's activism and agency. *English Teaching: Practice and Critique, 10*(4), 75–93.

Mangin, M. M., & Stoelinga, S. R. (Eds.). (2008). *Effective teacher leadership: Using research to inform and reform.* New York: Teachers College Press.

Matland, R. E. (1995). Synthesizing the implementation literature: The ambiguity–conflict model of policy implementation. *Journal of Public Administration Research and Theory, 5*(2), 145–174.

Mintrop, H., & Trujillo, T. (2007). The practical relevance of accountability systems for school improvement: A descriptive analysis of California schools. *Educational Evaluation and Policy Analysis, 29*(4), 319–352.

National Governors Association Center for Best Practices & Council of Chief State School Officers (NGA & CCSSO). (2010). *Common Core Standards for English language arts and literacy in history/social studies, science, and technical subjects.* Washington, DC: Authors. Retrieved from *www.corestandards.org/ELA-Literacy.*

No Child Left Behind Act of 2001, P.L. 107-110, 20 U.S.C. § 6319 (2002).

Polikoff, M. S. (2017). Is Common Core "working"? *AERA Open, 3*(1). Retrieved from *https://journals.sagepub.com/doi/full/10.1177/2332858417691749.*

Sawchuk, S. (2018). The state of Common Core reading and writing in 5 charts. Retrieved from *http://blogs.edweek.org/edweek/curriculum/2018/07/the_state_of_common-core_reading_5_charts.html.*

Souto-Manning, M. (2009). Negotiating culturally responsive pedagogy through multicultural children's literature: Towards critical democratic literacy practices in a first-grade classroom. *Journal of Early Childhood Literacy, 9*(1), 50–74.

Spillane, J. P., Reiser, B. J., & Reimer, T. (2002). Policy implementation and cognition: Reframing and refocusing implementation research. *Review of Educational Research, 72*(3), 387–431.

Theoharis, G., & O'Toole, J. (2011). Leading inclusive ELL: Social justice leadership for English language learners. *Educational Administration Quarterly, 47*(4), 646–688.

Toppel, K. (2012). Phonics instruction with a culturally responsive twist: Three approaches to transforming curriculum. *Multicultural Perspectives, 14*(2), 99–102.

Toppel, K. (2015). Enhancing core reading programs with culturally responsive practices. *The Reading Teacher, 68*(7), 552–559.

U.S. Department of Education. (2009). Race to the top. Retrieved from *www2.ed.gov/programs/racetothetop/factsheet.html.*

Villegas, A. M. (1991). *Culturally responsive pedagogy for the 1990s and beyond* (Trends and Issues Paper No. 6). Washington, DC: ERIC Clearinghouse on Teacher Education.

Wenner, J. A., & Campbell, T. (2017). The theoretical and empirical basis of teacher leadership. *Review of Educational Research, 87*(1), 134–171.

Woulfin, S. L. (2015a). Catalysts of change: An examination of coaches' leadership practices in framing a reading reform. *Journal of School Leadership, 25*(3), 526–557.

Woulfin, S. L. (2015b). Highway to reform: The coupling of district reading policy and instructional practice. *Journal of Educational Change, 16*(4), 535–557.

Woulfin, S. L., & Coburn, C. E. (2011). Policy implementation: The pathway from reading policy to classroom practice. In R. Bean & A. Dagen (Eds.), *Best practices of literacy leaders in schools* (pp. 337–354). New York: Guilford Press.

Woulfin, S. L., & Rigby, J. G. (2017). Coaching for coherence: How instructional coaches lead change in the evaluation era. *Educational Researcher, 46*(6), 323–328.

Xu, Z. (2015). A first look at student outcomes for Common Core State Standards. Retrieved from *www.air.org/resource/first-look-student-outcomes-common-core-state-standards.*

CHILDREN'S LITERATURE

Riordan, R. (2005). *The lightning thief: Percy Jackson & Olympians* (Vol. 1). New York: Hyperion Books.

Literacy Leadership in Action

Sean Kottke, PhD

Education Consultant Manager, Michigan State
Department of Education, Lansing, Michigan

THINK ABOUT THIS

1. In what ways does Sean serve as a literacy leader?
2. What lessons can be learned about the role of a state department of education official?
3. What questions come to mind while reading this vignette?

As manager of the Michigan Office of Educator Excellence's Educator Preparation Unit, it is my privilege to supervise a team of consultants who lead the development and implementation of Michigan's educator certification standards and assessments, as well as the review, approval, and accreditation of all educator preparation programs in our state. My specialized role on this team is as senior consultant for literacy teacher preparation policy. In simplest terms, my daily work is to identify the people in our state with the greatest expertise in literacy education and teacher preparation, bring them together, and serve as a conduit for ensuring their deepest concerns and best ideas are reflected in statewide policies governing teacher preparation and professional learning.

Our motto is "Beyond compliance." Although traditionally responsible for enforcement of regulations around the preparation and placement of certified educators, our work in the post-NCLB (No Child Left Behind) era has shifted toward supporting Michigan's education community in considering the needs of children first and recognizing the wisdom of our most effective educators in supporting ecosystems of educator preparation and professional growth. This ethos is best exemplified in our efforts to raise literacy achievement in

Michigan through effective and sustainable systems of preservice and inservice professional learning for all stakeholders who participate in children's literacy development.

Dissatisfied with the statewide portrait of literacy achievement and the inevitability of legislative mandates for retention of students who do not demonstrate achievement of third-grade reading benchmarks, we convened a task force to identify a core set of "essential instructional practices" to guide inservice teacher professional learning in literacy instruction. Representatives from all sectors of Michigan's literacy education community participated in this effort, and the result is a series of research-informed "Literacy Essentials" documents and professional learning modules around effective literacy practices across the PreK- through 12-grade span (check them out at *www.literacyessentials.org*).

Concurrently with the task force's work, my team led efforts to redefine Michigan's teacher certification structure with narrower grade bands and an increased emphasis on preparation to provide early literacy instruction. As a participant in the task force, I committed to affirming the Literacy Essentials by carrying them forward into preservice teacher preparation. Leveraging professional networks established through the task force and through my leadership of the Michigan Reading Association, I assembled teams of literacy researchers, teacher educators, and master teachers representing the geographic and ideological diversity of Michigan's education community to draft new teacher preparation standards for literacy instruction in PreK–3 and 3- through 6-grade bands.

With strong first principles of putting children's needs first and ensuring that every standard had a solid research base, these diverse teams created new standards that give proper emphasis both to skills-focused approaches to teaching reading and to integrated approaches emphasizing reciprocal development across the language arts. Central to accomplishing this monumental task was securing permission to use drafts of the International Literacy Association's *Standards for the Preparation of Literacy Professionals 2017* as a source document. The ILA standards provided a strong framework around essential facets of literacy teacher preparation, which our drafting teams reinforced with details from the Literacy Essentials documents and the latest research. These standards were adopted by the State Board of Education in November 2018, and thus their impact won't be visible in statewide data for some years to come. Nevertheless, this represents the first time in Michigan's history that the full spectrum of stakeholders (i.e., literacy partners) has come together to articulate a consensus vision of effective literacy instruction and foundational knowledge and skills necessary for achieving that vision in our PreK–12 schools.

CHAPTER 19

Sustaining Literacy Practices That Transform Teaching and Learning

Lori Lyman DiGisi
Julie Meltzer
Lynn Schade
Stephanie Maze-Hsu

GUIDING QUESTIONS

➥ In order to sustain literacy practices that transform teaching and learning, how do literacy leaders[1]:

➥ Develop and sustain a clearly articulated, shared vision?

➥ Develop and sustain a culture that promotes collaboration, conversation, risk taking, and ongoing learning?

➥ Develop and sustain mutual accountability for ongoing improvements in literacy teaching and learning?

Starting a literacy improvement initiative is a large undertaking; sustaining one is an even greater challenge. As described throughout this book, if the goal is to improve literacy teaching and learning, literacy leaders have key roles to play in providing planning, ongoing advocacy, and support

---

[1]Throughout the chapter we refer to *literacy leaders*. In this term, we include teacher leaders, literacy coaches, principals, district leaders, library media specialists, literacy specialists, outside consultants, and classroom teachers—everyone who takes on leadership roles in forwarding literacy teaching and learning during a literacy improvement initiative.

for implementation. Fixsen, Naoom, Blase, Friedman, and Wallace (2005) define "discernible stages in implementing research-based practices: exploration and adoption, program installation, initial implementation, full operation, innovation, and sustainability" (p. 15). Unfortunately, many programs and practices do not make it through all these stages, or reach full operation for only a year or two, never leading to ongoing improvements in student achievement as readers, writers, and thinkers. In this chapter, we discuss why sustainability is so difficult to achieve, the core components of sustainability, and what literacy leaders can do to optimize the chances that effective literacy practices will continue beyond the initial stages.

As researchers and practitioners, we believe in the promise that literacy has the power to change lives. We accept the premise that the education system is the best vehicle to ensure that all students develop the literacy skills they need to be successful. And, we bemoan the fact that actual experience shows very few places where the vision, culture, and accountability around effective literacy practices are deeply shared and sustained long enough to deliver on this promise.

Why is that? Fixsen, Blase, Naoom, and Wallace (2009) claim that sustainability in service fields such as education is "far more complex than any other industry" (p. 531) because in human services "the practitioner is the intervention" (p. 532). In other words, practices and programs may be effective, but people must implement them, and schools are dynamic systems where people and personnel are constantly changing (Fixsen et al., 2005). The result is that without active processes in place for sustaining the initiative, there is little likelihood of visible long-range results.

We contend that sustainability of a literacy improvement initiative requires (1) a shared vision of literacy improvement that is consistently nurtured, (2) a culture of skilled collaboration and risk taking, and (3) mutual accountability among professionals. This vision of sustainability means that literacy leaders—teachers, literacy coaches, teacher leaders, curriculum directors, principals, library/media specialists, and district administrators—discuss on an ongoing basis how they will collaboratively address and take aligned action in each of these three areas. Further, because these areas are not exclusive but are heavily interdependent (see Figure 19.1), this is a complex endeavor; yet one that is critical to success.

If this is a viable definition of sustainability, what gets in the way? What do we mean by *vision, culture,* and *mutual accountability* in the context of a literacy improvement initiative? And what are the specific roles and actions that literacy leaders can take to ensure that these components of sustainability are in place and actively nurtured? Throughout this chapter, we paint pictures, provide practical approaches, and showcase the critical roles literacy leaders can and must play relative to vision, culture, and accountability. We provide specific examples of how the *Standards for the Preparation of Literacy Professionals 2017* (International Literacy Association

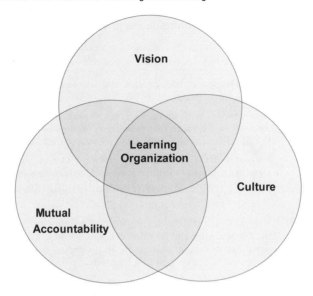

FIGURE 19.1. Interrelationship of vision, culture, and mutual accountability in a sustainable learning organization.

[ILA], 2018) identify the actions and skills literacy professionals can use to implement a common vision, collaborative culture, and mutual accountability in Table 19.1.

Many issues impact sustainability. Two in particular pose significant challenges to ongoing implementation of successful literacy improvement efforts: frequent administrative turnover and competing mandates. Frequent leadership and initiative changes disrupt teaching and learning in ways that do not benefit students or teachers. Either can thwart ongoing efforts to establish and sustain literacy transformation in complex school systems.

School administrators—superintendents, curriculum leaders, and principals—frequently change positions. "Half of the superintendents said that they did not plan to be on the job by the end of five years" (Domenech, 2017, p. 1). With many superintendents holding 2- or 3-year contracts, it is uncommon for these individuals to stay in their roles long enough to build and sustain structures that create and maintain change, even when their intention is to improve student achievement. Without sustained implementation, stakeholders often doubt the potential efficacy of any proposed change. As described in Fixsen et al. (2009) and stated in Fullan and Quinn (2016):

Achieving coherence in a system takes a long time and requires continuous attention. The main threat to coherence is turnover at the top with new leaders who come in with their own agenda. It is not turnover per se that is the problem, but rather discontinuity of direction. (p. 128)

TABLE 19.1. Literacy Leaders' Contributions to Vision, Culture, and Accountability

Literacy leaders	Contribution to vision, culture, and accountability
District Director of curriculum	*Vision:* Develop a shared vision and goals for literacy that reflect evidence-based practices (p. 56).
	Culture: Work with literacy leaders to evaluate initiatives ensuring a literacy-rich climate that promotes continuous improvement, risk taking, reflection, and steadfast focus on student learning (p. 61).
	Accountability: Collaboratively develop and evaluate a districtwide assessment system to inform and evaluate teaching and learning. Facilitate discussions to interpret and analyze patterns in data (p. 57).
School Principal	*Vision:* Engage staff in developing and refining a shared vision for effective teaching and learning of literacy that is standards-based, relevant to diverse student needs and interests, evidence-based, and focused on high expectations for student performance (p. 97).
	Culture: Structure frequent and ongoing opportunities for instructional staff to meet regularly to reflect on student progress, examine systemic inequities, and implement and align successful literacy practices across classrooms (p. 96).
	Accountability: Distribute leadership for professional learning across all personnel rather than positioning it tightly within a limited few. Ensure that all teachers see themselves as responsible for meeting the literacy goals of all their students (p. 99).
School Literacy coach and/or literacy specialist	*Vision:* Facilitate/participate in efforts to develop a vision and goals for literacy (p. 46). Participate in the vision and development of curricula that are horizontally and vertically aligned across the school (p. 35).
	Culture: Collaborate with teachers to create, analyze, transform, and implement culturally responsive learning experiences linked to school and community literacy knowledge (p. 49). Demonstrate the skills, knowledge, and dispositions to work with teachers effectively and collaboratively (p. 33); create classrooms that are inclusive and affirming (p. 38) and foster a positive climate (p. 39).
	Accountability: Facilitate professional learning and school improvement and use knowledge of assessment tools to monitor student progress to inform schoolwide interventions (p. 47). Select and use appropriate assessment tools to screen, diagnose, and measure student literacy achievement; inform instruction and evaluate interventions; assist teachers in their understanding and use of assessment results; advocate for appropriate literacy practices to relevant stakeholders (p. 37).
School Library/media specialist	*Vision:* Share innovative ways to use technology to improve literacy teaching and learning (p. 110).

(continued)

TABLE 19.1. *(continued)*

Literacy leaders	Contribution to vision, culture, and accountabili
School Library/media specialist *(continued)*	*Culture:* Share, promote, and support powerful u. online reading and writing that connect to the cur students' interests and passions. *Accountability:* Empower students to be critical th......rs, enthusiastic readers, skillful researchers, and ethical users of information (p. 109).
School All teachers	*Vision:* Examine, design, adapt, implement, and evaluate instructional approaches and materials to provide a coherent, integrated, and motivating literacy program (p. 69). *Culture:* Participate in inquiry and professional learning communities (p. 75). Recognize how their own cultural experiences affect instruction; celebrate the diversity of families and community (p. 72). *Accountability:* Use observations and results of student work to determine students' literacy and language strengths and needs. Select and administer assessments appropriate for measuring language and literacy development (p. 71). Reflect upon practice; use ongoing inquiry to improve professional practice; advocate for students and families to enhance students' literacy learning (p. 74).

Note. Page references are to the ILA (2018) *Standards for the Preparation of Literacy Professionals 2017.*

Discontinuity can also be fostered when both new and veteran leaders are given mandates—sometimes from the state, district, or school—as a result of new research or new technology, or because of the adoption of a program, approach, or product. Implementation of the "new" frequently disrupts or fragments practices that are in place. For teachers, this results in initiative fatigue (Reeves, 2006) or overload (Fullan & Hargreaves, 1996), a condition in which teachers become disheartened and disengaged due to the frequent changes in the district's priorities, direction, and programs. Failure to adequately nurture new and promising initiatives prevents teachers from developing instructional expertise and comfort with the new approach.

Occasionally, however, despite changes in leadership and programming, expertise is developed and successfully sustained in ways that improve literacy outcomes for students while supporting their development as readers, writers, presenters, and thinkers. This led us to ask, what factors are in place when improvement efforts succeed and thrive?

USTAINABILITY IN THE CONTEXT OF LITERACY IMPROVEMENT INITIATIVES

A well-designed literacy improvement initiative can successfully develop students' confidence and competence as readers, writers, presenters, and thinkers if given enough time to be fully implemented vertically across grade bands and horizontally across content areas (e.g., Meltzer, 2015). However, without purposeful attention to developing key components of sustainability, it may be difficult to see lasting evidence of changes in literacy teaching and learning when the grant runs out, the mandate is lifted, or when a key literacy leader leaves.

In *Visible Learning for Literacy*, Fisher, Frey, and Hattie (2016) introduce their ideas about surface learning, deep learning, and transfer. We build on the components described in Fixsen et al. (2005) and apply Fisher, Frey, and Hattie's (2016) research idea to the stages of a literacy initiative where the ultimate goal is for the organization to sustain and extend the improvements made to literacy teaching and learning. Table 19.2 describes each phase: *Imagine It, Try It, Own It.*

We contend that **vision, culture,** and **mutual accountability** can be sustained throughout the phases of an initiative, although development can occur in phases.

Development of vision in Phase 1 of a literacy initiative (*Imagine It*) involves initial professional development, instructional coaching, and needs assessment to understand what type of literacy teaching and learning is needed within the school (the *what*) and to develop the vision of what literacy teaching and learning should be. There is surface learning of new strategies and practices during which the vision is refined and reinforced.

Development of culture occurs in Phase 2 of the initiative (*Try It*). During this phase, participants connect the ideas to the larger vision of teaching and learning espoused by the school, ask teachers to evaluate student work and agree on the types of feedback or instructional response that would be helpful, provide time for lesson study, and link the expectations in the initiative to supervision and evaluation (the *how*). Professionals transfer the learning to their own practice.

Development of mutual accountability in Phase 3 (*Own It*) involves the development of the school into a true learning organization that articulates the gains made thus far, learns from them, reflects on them, and transforms the practices into the work of a learning organization that sustains and extends the initial practices (the *why*). Professionals are able to transfer their learning to new situations and adjust their practice based on new data. Phase 3 embodies a commitment to the "new way we do business" as people see that the practices are effective, spurring determination in all professionals to keep learning and supporting one another as the work continues. The phases we describe reflect the components present in the research

TABLE 19.2. Tools and Processes to Support Literacy Leaders

What can leaders do to sustain improvements in literacy?	Description of tool/process
Phase 1: Envision → Plan → Launch ("Imagine It")	
Instructional leadership teams	Gather stakeholders from within the school and community; leaders are able to gather multiple perspectives and share common values.
Needs assessment	Collect data on current practices, strengths, and needs. Use protocols to discover beliefs, clarify thinking, share ideas. See the School Reform Initiative protocols to support this work: *www.schoolreforminitiative.org/protocols.*
Vision statement (with input from multiple stakeholders)	Create a vision statement and develop a literacy action plan. Declare the district's objectives, beliefs, and priorities (short, clear, precise).
Launch event/kick off	Promote the vision, inspire and ignite the community, and lay out the long-term plan for learning and implementation via meetings, workshops, and other venues.
Phase 2: Learn → Practice → Implement → Monitor ("Try It")	
Lab classrooms and peer observation	Teachers volunteer to work with a literacy coach or consultant and try out new instructional practices, and to open their classrooms to others as a learning laboratory. Peers participate in structured observations to learn from and with the lab classroom teachers.
Guided observation	Structured visits to other districts/schools that have exemplary literacy programs.
Coaching cycles (1:1 and teams)	An ongoing coaching process consisting of collaborative goal setting, demonstration and co-taught lessons, observation and feedback, reflection and action planning.
List of look fors/non-negotiables	Clear statement or list that describes an observable teaching or learning behavior, strategy, outcome, or procedure. Observers search for "look fors" during classroom visits or when examining student work: *https://pdo.ascd.org/LMSCourses/PD13OC010M/media/Leading_Prof_Learning_M6_Reading2.pdf.*
Inquiry groups/professional learning communities	Formation of teacher-led professional development in which groups of educators pose questions and then study and investigate together to deepen their collective understanding, identify possible solutions, and refine improvement efforts.
Modified lesson study	Collaborative learning process in which teachers work together (with or without a coach) to conceptualize, design, and co-construct one exemplary lesson. After rehearsing the lesson, they each take one small part and teach their lesson to one group of students. Then they meet to reflect, review, and revise the lesson.

(continued)

TABLE 19.2. *(continued)*

What can leaders do to sustain improvements in literacy?	Description of tool/process
Phase 3: Reflect → Refine → Innovate → Institutionalize ("Own It")	
Focused learning walks	A team of teachers, coaches, and school leaders visit classrooms looking for evidence of specific improvements in literacy practices. The team summarizes areas of strength and next steps, and provides feedback to teachers.
Teachers as literacy leaders groups	Teachers volunteer to study teacher leadership, team facilitation, professional development, and the process of change in schools. They design and implement a "Change Project" related to the school's vision and improvement goals, and collect data to measure impact.

of McLaughlin (1990), Fixsen et al. (2005, 2009), and McLaughlin and Talbert (2010), and mirror the results we have seen in our own work. Based on our review of the research and combined work as practitioners, we observe that sustainability of a literacy initiative depends on the ability of the school or district to nurture, extend, deepen, and revisit the goals, practices, and outcomes of its own efforts to improve literacy and learning. We assert that thinking about sustainability cannot be an "add on" but needs to be woven into the implementation of a literacy initiative from the beginning.

Sustainability is increasingly defined as a dynamic process that involves the key components of environment, population, policies, and data change (Shelton, Cooper, & Stirman, 2018). We maintain that sustainability depends on the interconnectedness of and coherence across the three areas of vision, culture, and mutual accountability. This sustainability defines a key role for literacy leaders and educators engaged in the implementation of transformational literacy initiatives: to cultivate the transformation of schools and districts into learning organizations.

Learning Organizations That Sustain Literacy Improvement

A *learning organization* can be thought of as a well-integrated self-educating system. According to Garvin (1993), "A learning organization is an organization skilled at creating, acquiring, and transferring knowledge, and at modifying its behavior to reflect new knowledge and insights" (p. 3). McLaughlin and Talbert (2010) report that learning organizations grow through professional learning communities where leaders and teachers share mutual accountability in addition to ongoing cycles of collaboration around data, using the feedback to continually create questions and solve problems of practice. One can conclude, therefore, that in order for schools to sustain transformative teaching practices leading to ongoing positive outcomes for students, they must become learning organizations.

Research into schools that showed sustained gains in literacy achievement past initial grant funding, the end of a professional development initiative, or after changes in leadership verifies that such schools are able to become learning organizations. They are clear about their fundamental components and are able to "maintain the effectiveness in the context of a changing world" (Fixsen et al., 2005, p. 23). Research on the sustainability of programs after the Reading First funding ended supports this point. It shows that schools that persisted in demonstrating an increase in the number of third graders who were proficient readers continued to maintain the systems and structures that had demonstrated success. Further, they continued to improve by using instructional data to improve instruction (Bean, Dole, Nelson, Belcastro, & Zigmond, 2015). Factors that contributed to sustainability were stability in school leadership, ongoing teacher learning, and teachers' and leaders' commitment to the work (p. 47). That is, each of the schools that sustained gains became an "organized system of elements in dynamic interaction with one another" (Bryk, Sebring, Allensworth, Luppescu, & Easton, 2010, p. 66). Although the focus on these components may vary from organization to organization, depending on the people, core components such as staff involvement from the onset; data systems to support decision making; administrative supports, interventions, recruitment, and selection of staff; pre- and inservice training on practice; and coaching to provide ongoing feedback and support all work together to implement and sustain evidenced-based programs (Fixsen et al., 2009; Mclaughlin, 1990).

Individual case study research confirms that a systemic and dynamic set of factors contribute to sustained improvements in literacy outcomes for students. For example, Francois (2014) found that "each of these elements—instructional leadership, teacher agency, time and space, and a commitment to constant improvement—operated in a complex, interdependent relationship to affect improvement in school practices and also necessitated a significant commitment to instructional improvement" (p. 600). A comprehensive review of case studies in middle and high schools across the country led to the development of the multicomponent Leadership Framework for Improving Adolescent Literacy (Irvin, Meltzer, & Dukes, 2007), which summarizes consensus on a set of interrelated factors to which attention is needed in order to sustain improvements in literacy and learning. This framework has also been successfully applied to elementary schools across the country. A recent synthesis of case studies from preschool to grade 3 reports that effective improvements in elementary literacy programs result when there is an interrelationship between research-based practices, professional learning communities, coaching, teacher voice, training, feedback, and planning to support the ongoing work (U.S. Department of Education, 2016).

This research strongly suggests that the roles of literacy leaders need to be focused on three interrelated domains within the context of a learning organization to ensure sustainability:

- A *shared vision* that guides the purpose, work, and decision making of students, teachers, and administrators and drives resource allocation, including staffing, funding, time, materials, and celebration of effort.
- A *collaborative culture* that creates common practices, routines, collaboration, coaching, and ongoing learning.
- A *deep sense of mutual accountability* that reaches far beyond supervision and evaluation to an embedded continuous improvement cycle that includes everyone.

CASE EXAMPLES

In the following subsections, we examine each of these three interrelated domains and illustrate them with case examples from different schools. All teachers and students in the examples are composites based on the many educators and students with whom we have worked through the years.

Vision

THINK ABOUT THIS

1. How do these scenes make visible each school's vision of an active culture of literacy?
2. Where do you see students enacting a strong vision of literacy and learning in your school or district?
3. Ask educators in your school or district to describe the vision for literacy learning. Is the message consistent across principals, educators, parents?

At the end of the day, two boys linger to discuss *Michael Vey: The Final Spark* (Evans, 2012) from the Michael Vey series. Further down the hall, a student pulls her friend into the open space of a teacher's classroom, points to the books in the classroom library, and says, "Ms. Saras, Isabella has NEVER read a dystopian book! She likes fantasy, but I think she would really like dystopia. What do you think she would like?" The teacher recommends *Legend* by Marie Lu (2013). It turns out that Ella has never read it either. Fortunately, the teacher has two copies. Both girls sign out the books and are out the door laughing and giggling as they leave, chatting about their books.

Pairs of students are scattered around the room in chairs side by side. In each pair there is a fourth grader reading the book he or she recently finished writing to a kindergartener, who listens intently. The books were carefully researched and proudly written by the older students, and each contains features of nonfiction text: a table of contents, labeled illustrations, an index. Down the hall, third graders surround a teacher reading J. K. Rowling's (1997) *Harry Potter and the Philosopher's Stone*. After they discuss the use of vivid language, each retrieves the book they are currently reading from desks, shelves, and lockers. Settling into beanbag chairs, at desks, or sprawled on the rug, each starts reading, paying attention to how the author of their book uses specific word choice to paint pictures. The teacher quietly confers with individual students who eagerly share what they have found.

• • • • • • • • • • •

Schools and districts that successfully support improved student achievement over time point to "shared vision" as a key component of sustainability (e.g., Fullan, Rincon-Gallardo, & Hargreaves, 2015; Spillane, Haverson, & Diamond, 2001). Fullan et al. (2015) assert that "[i]nviting the participation of teachers and school leaders to shape, lead, and, over time, review and renew the overall vision and standards of practice will increase the likelihood of ownership, a better solution, and sustainability" (p. 8). In a school where there is distributed leadership for literacy and many people contribute to and affirm a common vision for literacy and learning, the gains initially achieved are much less at risk when a leader moves on to a new position. There are ongoing roles for all literacy leaders to play in developing, communicating, enacting, affirming, and revisiting a collective vision that guides the work.

To get a sense of why a shared vision is important, consider what it looks like when a coherent vision does not exist, is blurry or fuzzy, or is held by the leader but is not shared. When a vision of change is not clear and is not shared, there is little or no buy-in from others. People cannot see where the initiative is going, why this is the initiative that was chosen, how this initiative connects to anything else in the school, or how they can contribute.

Solutions from Research and the Field

The core of a shared vision has to be a sincere belief that all students can learn to read and write at high levels, and that it is the responsibility of the entire school community to believe in high achievement for each student (Fountas & Pinnell, 2018, p. 8). It is critical, even if there is a thoughtful, well-written vision, to revisit it with stakeholders regularly. It is helpful to begin by collectively generating ideas about what should be seen and heard in classrooms during the literacy block or content area instruction: *What should teachers be doing? What should students be doing? What should the environment include?* (See Table 19.2.) Once a shared vision is established, it is easier to get down to the question of *"How can we make this vision a reality in every classroom, every day?"*

Shafer (2018) contends that beliefs and values will translate into action when stakeholders communicate in multiple ways, both directly and indirectly. The act of communicating and opening up lines of communication is essential to actualizing a shared vision. Following are steps for literacy leaders to take in developing and invigorating a vision to guide the work:

- *Engage a representative group of stakeholders* in a careful process of clarifying values and core beliefs, data analysis, and envisioning excellence. Use this input to draft a short vision statement articulating what is valued in terms of literacy teaching and learning.

- *Distribute the draft of the vision statement to the broader community* and request suggestions for further revision. Reconvene the original group to revise the vision statement so that it incorporates the ideas from community members.

- *Collapse the vision statement into a few powerful words.* Develop a plan to disseminate the complete vision—and the sound-bite version—through meetings, presentations, print and social media, etc. Say those words at meetings, post those words on signs, make those words part of your letterhead and website, print them on pens and T-shirts and coffee mugs. Let the whole world know your vision!

- *Search for exemplars that best reflect your vision, as well as variations.* Visit other schools where the practices are implemented, read case studies, prepare scenarios and examples of practice to share. Early on, select a set of videos that show what it will look like in classrooms if the vision is visibly driving the work. Over time, replace these with videos created internally. Use video when communicating with parents, new teachers, and the community to keep the work aligned with the vision as you have defined it.

- *Revisit and refine the vision based on data.* Use data collected from inside and outside your organization to acknowledge what is going well and what needs attention. Determine if the goal is to expand good practices that are already happening or if there are new programs or practices that need to be implemented. Periodically convene a group of stakeholders to revisit the vision statement.

- *Develop an action plan and prioritize the use of resources.* Once the vision is agreed upon and shared, identify funding sources, professional development, and an accountability process. How will participants share and make visible the work that they are doing? How will it be safe for teachers to describe what is and is not working? Discuss how each member of the school community—literacy directors, coordinators, coaches, principals and teachers, parents and students—can be involved in the work. Determine when the team will reconvene to examine and discuss progress on the action plan and make course corrections as necessary. Ensure that resources are allocated or found as needed to implement the action plan.[2]

- *Ongoing communication and celebration are important.* Determine how the message and progress will be disseminated to all community members. Schedule celebrations so that preliminary steps, growth, and ongoing data can be shared and celebrated.

- *Facilitate innovation.* It is important to create and sustain safe places where the work happens; where "early adopters" are free to experiment, try out new ideas, collaborate with colleagues, and reflect on student learning. These are the teachers who are willing to try something new, to open their classrooms, and to accept suggestions and feedback from coaches and consultants. Facilitating innovation ensures that the new initiative has a good chance to take root and blossom.

- *Connect the vision* to ongoing initiatives, mandates, the district's vision statement, and to the superintendent's priorities. Because it is easy to get distracted in the life of schools, it is important to show people how the work connects to other work being done in the district. It is also helpful to continually show how the literacy initiative is and is not like other work that is going on.

Culture

THINK ABOUT THIS

1. When and where in your school or district do teachers talk about literacy and learning?
2. How can literacy leaders foster frequent conversations about the literacy initiative underway?
3. When and where are there opportunities for teachers to share literacy practices?

A teacher walks up to the outside consultant and says, "You're going to think we've become nerds, but every day at lunch, one person on my team reads aloud from a new children's book—and then we talk about how we can use those books as mentor texts for writing craft lessons. We haven't talked about our fights with our kids and spouses in weeks!"

---

[2]For resources you can use to develop a literacy action plan, see *Taking the Lead on Adolescent Literacy: Action Steps for Schoolwide Success* (Irvin et al., 2010).

A new teacher asks to observe in another teacher's room. "Come in any time!" is the response. Teachers sit down to discuss practice. Someone asks, "Can we talk about how people set up partnerships for reading and writing?" A long conversation ensues.

• • • • • • • • • • • •

These examples from schools where we have worked are evidence of teachers taking ownership of their shared learning and expanding the effects across the school culture (see Table 19.1). This notion of ownership parallels Fullan and Quinn's (2016) idea of coherence as continuity combined with innovation. Teachers who successfully use new practices to improve students' literacy and learning are proud of their craft knowledge. They are eager to become more expert, to share, and to collaborate. A collaborative professional culture develops over time, requiring ongoing nurturing, self-awareness, and recognition.

However, when ownership of a literacy initiative is not widely shared, the initiative does not get past a small group of early adopters or is not embedded deeply enough into practice to sustain once attention shifts. If a committed culture exists only in pockets, there will be little to show when the mandate or leadership changes or the initiative is perceived as "over."

There are many ways that literacy initiatives, even those met with initial enthusiasm, can flounder because the enactors never reach a state of commitment to sustaining an ongoing implementation of transformative practice (e.g., poor implementation, insufficient resources, leadership that is not "on board"). Irvin et al. (2007) suggest eight reasons why teachers may not buy in and may resist literacy improvement efforts: (1) fear of not "doing it right," (2) feeling overwhelmed, (3) preferring the comfort of the familiar, (4) a conviction that "This, too, shall pass," (5) lack of support or resources, (6) unclear expectations, (7) misaligned belief systems, and (8) inadequate professional development (pp. 196–197). When teachers and leaders see these hampering conditions as reasons not to engage, they do not invest the energy needed to sustain the literacy improvement initiative

Solutions from Research and the Field

Fountas and Pinnell (2018) argue that success happens when leaders realize that all initiatives "operate within a culture that supports continuous study and improvement" (p. 7). When schools establish "a coherent vision for literacy learning, educators can act in unison to ensure high literacy outcomes for every child" (p. 7)—which, after all, is the reason for implementing a new literacy initiative in the first place.

In *Cultivating Coaching Mindsets,* Bean and Ippolito (2016) describe the case of Brookline High School where a group of teacher leaders came together to support their most struggling readers through a multipronged approach to disciplinary literacy. This effort resulted in a collaborative project undertaken with teachers, teacher leaders, administrators, and community members. The effectiveness of the initiative grew as teachers supported one another to develop solutions to address student learning needs, learning together within a context of continuous improvement.

A professional teaching and learning culture is sustained through changes in leadership when there are shared routines, practices, and knowledge related to literacy teaching and learning. Such a culture supports professional conversations, collaboration, and risk taking and simultaneously reinforces common practice while supporting reflection, innovation, and ongoing learning.

PROFESSIONAL CONVERSATION AND COLLABORATION

In our experience, literacy leaders in schools with purposefully collaborative cultures engage in ongoing, solution-focused conversations across stakeholders about what is and is not working. Principals and other literacy leaders communicate and reinforce the vision when they visit classrooms, share positive messages, and communicate how the initiative looks in action. Teachers actively seek experiences to deepen and further their learning and to see one another as a source of ideas and expertise, requesting time to meet during the school day or finding funding to meet outside of the school day.

It is critical to provide time for teachers to share current practice, reflect on teaching and learning, and openly discuss adjustments that need to be made based on student data. In many schools, protocols are used to elevate the analysis of student work and facilitate safe opportunities for coaches, teachers, and specialists to learn from one another (see Table 19.2).

Teachers report that the information presented in professional development makes more sense when they collaborate to read professional books, attend conferences together, observe and debrief classroom observations in pairs or small groups, and/or work with one another to collaboratively design lessons. These teachers willingly share with stakeholders, including with their students, when they implement strategies or approaches learned from one another. Talking about the work—what they want to achieve, what they are learning, what they are wondering about—becomes the norm, not the exception.

RISK TAKING TO LEARN MORE

In schools where it is OK to take risks—some of which will result in failures—teachers feel safe to try out new approaches because they know professional development and coaching will be ongoing. Literacy leaders set an expectation that teachers will implement new professional learning but acknowledge that there will be a growth curve and that ongoing improvement, not instantaneous perfection, is the goal. Release time is provided so that teachers can observe one another or observe outside consultants working with students in another classroom, making every classroom into a "lab site." Collaborative lesson design and instruction, such as lesson study, supports greater coherence in instruction across classrooms (see Table 19.2).

In schools where peer coaching (from literacy coaches, outside partners, mentor teachers, colleagues) becomes part of the school culture, there is an increased likelihood of deeper, sustained implementation. Teachers are more likely to commit to ongoing collaboration as a vehicle for developing deep knowledge and greater expertise, becoming collectively more able to share and enact a vision of high-quality literacy instruction. The specific role of each literacy professional in this work can be seen in Table 19.1.

Mutual Accountability

THINK ABOUT THIS

1. Where are the opportunities for educators to strengthen accountability to student learning with one another?
2. How do literacy leaders use ongoing opportunities to focus the conversation on literacy improvement?

When Principal Jim Bailey began his faculty meeting to open the school year, he shared the research on classroom libraries with his teachers. Then he reached into his pocket and pulled out a stack of $100 gift cards to Barnes and Noble and announced, "We are spending the rest of the professional development day at Barnes and Noble, and I have $100 for each of you to spend on your classroom library" (Bailey, 2018).

The middle school ELA teachers in one district decided that it would be helpful to have standards-aligned reading rubrics to help them assess students' level of comprehension and understanding of the choices authors make. They asked for permission to use professional development time to develop these. Several months later, the group came back together and shared how they each used the rubrics and decided to create speaking and listening rubrics as well. When asked how the rubrics were working, one teacher laughed and said she thought the rubrics were more for the teachers than the students—creating them together was a great way to make sure the teachers were all on the same page with what seventh-grade reading and writing should look like across the schools! Others agreed.

· · · · · · · · · · · ·

Inherent in sustaining literacy improvement over time is a requirement of mutual accountability for student success. For us, that means that the district is accountable to teachers and building leaders; that teachers are accountable to one another, building leaders, students, and parents; and building leaders are accountable to teachers, to the district, and to the community. Without this web of accountability, schools do not, and really cannot, fulfill their accountability to improve student teaching and learning. Furthermore, as Fountas and Pinnell (2018) suggest, "the language naturally shifts from *my* students and my classroom to *our* students, our classrooms" (p. 9) as literacy leaders, administrators, and community members work together toward the shared goal and vision.

Often, the community, the district, and policymakers view students' scores on publicized, state-mandated standardized tests as the primary measure of accountability. However, test scores measure only a small part of literacy achievement at a point in time. Although some state assessments show growth, most only report the percentage of students meeting benchmark. Test scores against benchmarks can provide important information. However, it is limited information and does not inform daily instruction. The mandate to "raise test scores" in a high-stakes environment does not inspire teachers to improve their practice, especially when one of the following exists:

- Teachers do not see the test scores as correlating with the work they see students doing in the classroom, and/or the test results are not reported in a timely way or in an easily understood format, making the data "beside the point" in the minds of teachers.
- Most students in the district fall into the extremes of failing or exceeding. When most students are succeeding, there is no sense of urgency. When most students are failing, districts may respond with sweeping reforms such as ousting leaders, changing programs midstream, or flooding schools with initiatives, leaving teachers overwhelmed and frustrated.

It is clear that mutual accountability for improving student literacy and learning has to be about much more than standardized test scores. We define mutual accountability as the ongoing engagement with the vision through complex processes of collaboration, including learning, reflecting, and giving and accepting feedback, within an atmosphere of trust and support.

Solutions from Research and the Field

School and district leaders engaged in work to redesign multifaceted accountability systems know that this is a complex task that requires commitment, skill, and focus across stakeholders. Through a comprehensive self-study of contributions to improved student outcomes, a consortium of urban districts in Massachusetts identified teacher learning as an integral part of this model, noting that mutual accountability is key (Famularo,

French, Noonan, Schneider, & Sienkiewicz, 2018). Based on their work, DuFour and Mattos (2013) insist, "The most powerful strategy for improving both teaching and learning . . . is not by micromanaging instruction but by creating the collaborative culture and collective responsibility of a professional learning community" (pp. 34, 40).

Learning organizations that sustain effective literacy practices maintain accountability to the vision, culture, and improving student outcomes in the forefront of their work. Literacy leaders emphasize practices that relate to the vision, promote continuous collaboration and communication among the staff, support distributed leadership, and pay sustained attention to student learning, using ongoing data from formal and informal assessments.

ACCOUNTABILITY TO THE VISION

Keeping the focus on literacy practices that transform teaching and learning raises the likelihood that the entire staff can collaboratively enact the vision. Aligning professional evaluations, hiring, decisions about what to take on, professional development, and ongoing reflection on teaching and learning with the vision is a multifaceted strategy to sustain effective literacy practices (Schmoker, 2018; Bryk, Gomez, Grunow, & LeMahieu, 2017; Gabriel, 2005; Bean & Dagen, 2012). Such a strategy sets up the school to systematically provide children with literacy teaching and learning practices that match the vision (Fountas & Pinnell, 2018).

A critical task for leaders of learning organizations is "staying the course" and saying no to initiatives or grants that would pull teachers away from the vision. Leaders who successfully sustain focus on the vision keep their staff from the overload caused by new or multiple initiatives every year that are not related to the improvement of literacy teaching and learning (Fullan & Hargreaves, 1996). When hiring, one principal we know hands out the school's mission and value statement to teacher candidates when they come in for interviews. It states the school's beliefs and commitments explicitly so that any potential hire understands the centrality of the mission to teaching and learning.

ACCOUNTABILITY TO THE CULTURE

Literacy leaders commit to building and sustaining relationships with teachers in ways that nurture collaboration, professional growth, and communication. Just as with students, relationships matter. In creating a collaborative culture within a learning organization, literacy leaders provide differentiated professional learning and support that responds to a range of diversity, expertise, and engagement of professionals (ILA, 2018). They may follow a theory such as Blanchard, Zigarmi, and Nelson's (1993) situational leadership and provide highly directive and highly supportive guidance to less experienced teachers and provide less directive support and more delegation to experienced teachers who are ready to teach others a practice, open their classroom, or facilitate peers in a discussion. Through differentiated support, teachers begin to own and help others become accountable for implementation of new literacy practices. Eventually, teachers become collectively accountable because the culture is so powerful that "members reach a shared paradigm about how to work together to be successful. They keep doing what they've been doing because it works . . . it satisfies that particular organization's priorities and values" (Horn & Staker, 2015, p. 251).

Dale Carnegie's (1948) phrase that leaders "inspect what they expect" translates to literacy leaders visiting classrooms and positively commenting on teaching and learning practices that are associated with the stated goals. Literacy leaders establish trust through frequent visits to classrooms, in both a nonevaluative and evaluative capacity, providing opportunities for frequent dialogue about effective literacy practices. Literacy leaders continue to engage in professional dialogue during the supervision and evaluation process for the purpose of supporting teachers' ongoing growth and development. In this context, evaluation procedures become opportunities for collaboration, self-assessment, goal setting, and reflection (Bean & Ippolito, 2016; Danielson, 2016; Saphier & Marshall, 2008; ILA, 2018).

Through these observations and discussions about student learning, literacy leaders create systems where the work of engaging in effective literacy practices belongs to the collective organization. Each teacher is individually responsible for learning and using effective literacy practices, and each teacher feels responsible for supporting his or her colleagues' ongoing learning and growth.

ACCOUNTABILITY FOR IMPROVING STUDENT OUTCOMES

In a system of mutual accountability, ongoing formative assessment on teaching and learning is key. Teachers openly discuss student learning as well as pedagogical successes and challenges, working collaboratively to design solutions. Literacy leaders design structures and systems so that teachers and leaders together can maintain a careful balance between (1) deliberate use of ongoing forms of formative data (e.g., student writing, running records, benchmark assessments, listening to book circle conversations) to inform instruction and improve student learning, and (2) active support for ongoing improvement of instruction through observation, feedback, discussion, and professional development. With individual and collective accountability, all teachers are prepared to analyze the data and have regular discussions about what it says and what it means about student learning (Gabriel, 2005; McLaughlin & Talbert, 2010).

Critical to this work is that literacy leaders monitor student data regularly to ensure that all students are showing growth. Effective literacy leaders are explicit with the teachers, district leaders, and community members about what they expect to see when observing teaching and learning. In this context, literacy leaders consider walk-throughs, informal conversations, and the teacher evaluation system as opportunities to have conversations about student learning, to learn where individual teachers need support to meet student needs, and to make explicit the literacy vision and expected outcomes. Leaders use all of these strategies for discussion to build coherence across grade levels and subject areas. Feedback, reflection, and assessments become part of the ongoing conversations between and among teachers and leaders to support ongoing learning (see Table 19.1).

In a learning organization, literacy leaders also evaluate the assessments, keeping the ones that provide the most useful information about students as readers and writers, discarding assessments that don't provide effective information, and finding new ones that provide the information needed (Zemelman, Daniels, & Hyde, 2012). In order to do this work, literacy leaders themselves need support to develop the systems, practices, and conversations that lead to a learning organization. Table 19.2 provides a list of tools and processes that support literacy professionals in this work.

CONCLUSION

Throughout this chapter we describe how a shared vision, a collaborative culture, and mutual accountability are key to the sustainability of a literacy improvement initiative. We identify some of the problems associated with sustaining effective literacy teaching and learning practices in schools. We provide solutions from research and the field showing how literacy leaders can develop their schools into learning organizations able to sustain rich literacy teaching and learning over time. Sustainability, in our experience, is more likely to happen when it is part of the intentional planning at the outset. The three components of sustainability—vision, culture, and mutual accountability—need to be deliberately nurtured by literacy leaders so that ongoing improvements to literacy teaching and learning continue beyond the mandate, through changes in leadership, and despite lack of grant funding.

ENGAGEMENT ACTIVITIES

1. Refer to Table 19.1. Thinking about the interrelated domains of vision, culture, and mutual accountability as defining sustainability, identify the actions taken regularly by the literacy leaders in your district or school. Which of these domains are being strongly supported? Which might need further attention?

2. In Table 19.2, we share practices that build a collaborative culture. We list and define lab classrooms, peer observations, guided observation, coaching cycles, look fors, inquiry group, professional learning communities, and modified lesson study. How can you use one of these practices to establish safe spaces for teachers to try new innovations with support?

3. In this chapter, we discuss that when literacy initiatives are sustainable, there is mutual accountability to the vision, the culture, and student outcomes. Using a protocol in Table 19.2, engage in a discussion with literacy professionals about where and how leaders demonstrate mutual accountability.

ANNOTATED RESOURCES

Bean, R. M., & Ippolito, J. (2016). *Cultivating coaching mindsets: An action guide for literacy leaders.* West Palm Beach, FL: Learning Sciences.

This text provides step-by-step guidelines, resources, and examples to support literacy leaders and coaches in doing this work. This is an excellent resource for Phase 2: *Try It* (Table 19.2).

Fountas, G., & Pinnell, S. (2018). Every child, every classroom, every day: From vision to action in literacy learning. *The Reading Teacher, 72*(1), 17–19.

This article provides a broad-based systems approach to improving literacy and sustaining those improvements. The authors describe four critical and connected elements for long-term, systemic change: shared vision and set of core values; common goals, common language, and collective responsibility; a high level of teacher expertise; and a culture of continuous professional learning.

Irvin, J., Meltzer, J., & Dukes, M. (2007). *Taking action on adolescent literacy: An implementation guide for school leaders.* Alexandria, VA: ASCD.

This book describes a leadership model for improving adolescent literacy. The model describes four systemic areas that require attention if the goal is to improve adolescent literacy: student motivation, engagement, and achievement; integration of literacy and learning across the content areas; intervention for struggling readers and writers; and sustainability through school, parent, community, and district support. Chapters are devoted to the actions that literacy leaders need to take to put these in place: developing an action plan, supporting teachers, ongoing use of data, building leadership capacity, and allocating resources.

A NOTE OF GRATITUDE

We are grateful to all of the literacy leaders and school districts with whom we have worked over the years. Your commitment to providing the highest quality of literacy instruction to students and to building sustainable learning organizations inspires us. In particular, we would like to thank the Wayland Public Schools in Massachusetts, the Mount Desert Island Regional School System in Maine, and the many teachers, coaches, principals, and district administrators who have partnered with Teaching and Learning Alliance, Inc., over the years. We would also like to thank Susi Leeming, TLA

Staff Writer and Curriculum Developer, for all of her assistance with copyediting and manuscript preparation.

REFERENCES

Bailey, J. (2018, August 4). A classroom library: If you build it, they will read it (Web log posted by CbethM). Retrieved from *https://nerdybookclub.wordpress.com/2018/08/04/a-classroom-library-if-you-build-it-they-will-read-by-jim-bailey.*

Bean, R. M., & Dagen, A. (Eds.). (2012). *Best practices of literacy leaders: Keys to improvement.* New York: Guilford Press.

Bean, R. M., Dole, J. A., Nelson, K. L., Belcastro, E. G., & Zigmond, N. (2015). The sustainability of a national reading reform initiative in two states. *Reading and Writing Quarterly, 31*(1), 30–55.

Bean, R. M., & Ippolito, J. (2016). *Cultivating coaching mindsets: An action guide for literacy leaders.* West Palm Beach, FL: Learning Sciences.

Blanchard, K. H., Zigarmi, D., & Nelson, R. B. (1993). Situational leadership after 25 years: A retrospective. *Journal of Leadership Studies, 1*(1), 21–36.

Bryk, A. S., Gomez, L. M., Grunow, A., & LeMahieu, P. G. (2017). *Learning to improve: How America's schools can get better at getting better* (5th ed.). Cambridge, MA: Harvard Education Press.

Bryk, A. S., Sebring, P. B., Allensworth, E., Luppescu, S., & Easton, J. Q. (2010). *Organizing schools for improvement: Lessons from Chicago.* Chicago: University of Chicago Press.

Carnegie, D. (1948). *How to stop worrying and start living.* New York: Simon & Schuster.

Danielson, C. (2016, April 20). Charlotte Danielson on rethinking teacher evaluation. *Education Week, 35*(28), 20–24. Retrieved from *www.edweek.org/ew/articles/2016/04/20/charlotte-danielson-on-rethinking-teacher-evaluation.html?print=1.*

Domenech, D. (2017). AAAS status check on the superintendency. Retrieved from *www.aasa.org/SchoolAdministratorArticle.aspx?id=17184.*

DuFour, R., & Mattos, M. (2013, April). How do principals really improve schools? *Educational Leadership, 70*(7), 34–40. Retrieved from *www.ascd.org/publications/educational-leadership/apr13/vol70/num07/How-Do-Principals-Really-Improve-Schools%C2%A2.*

Evans, R. P. (2017). *Michael Vey: The final spark.* New York: Simon Pulse/Mercury/Simon & Schuster.

Famularo, J., French, D., Noonan, J., Schneider, J., & Sienkiewicz, E. (2018). *Beyond standardized tests a new vision for assessing student learning.* Boston: Center for Collaborative Education. Retrieved from *http://cce.org/paper/beyond-standardized-test-white-paper.*

Fisher, D., Frey, N., & Hattie, J. (2016). *Visible learning for literacy: Implementing the practices that work best to accelerate student learning grades K–12.* Thousand Oaks, CA: Corwin Press.

Fixsen, D. L., Blase, K. A., Naoom, S. F., & Wallace, F. (2009). Core implementation components. *Research on Social Work Practice, 19*(5), 531–540. Retrieved from *https://journals.sagepub.com/doi/10.1177/1049731509335549.*

Fixsen, D. L., Naoom, S. F., Blase, K. A., Friedman, R. M., & Wallace, F. (2005). *Implementation research: A synthesis of the literature* (FMHI Publication No. 231). Tampa: University of South Florida, National Implementation Research Network. Retrieved from *https://nirn.fpg.unc.edu/sites/nirn.fpg.unc.edu/files/resources/NIRN-MonographFull-01-2005.pdf.*

Fountas, G., & Pinnell, S. (2018). Every child, every classroom, every day: From vision to action in literacy learning. *The Reading Teacher, 72*(1), 17–19.

Francois, C. (2014). Getting at the core of literacy improvement: A case study of a secondary school. *Education and Urban Society, 46*(5), 580–605.

Fullan, M., & Hargreaves, A. (1996). *What's worth fighting for in your school?* New York: Teachers College Columbia.

Fullan, M., & Quinn, J. (2016). *Coherence.* Thousand Oaks, CA: Corwin Press.

Fullan, M., Rincon-Gallardo, S., & Hargreaves, A. (2015). Professional capital as accountability. *Education Policy Analysis Archives, 23*(15), 8.

Gabriel, J. G. (2005). *How to thrive as a teacher leader.* Alexandria, VA: ASCD.

Garvin, D. (1993, July/August). Building a learning organization. *Harvard Business Review.* Retrieved from *https://hbr.org/1993/07/building-a-learning-organization.*

Horn, M. B., & Staker, H. (2015). *Blended: Using disruptive innovation to improve schools.* San Francisco: Jossey-Bass.

International Literacy Association (ILA). (2018). *Standards for the preparation of literacy professionals 2017.* Newark, DE: Author.

Irvin, J., Meltzer, J., & Dukes, M. (2007). *Taking action on adolescent literacy: An implementation guide for school leaders.* Alexandria, VA: ASCD.

Lu, M. (2013). *Legend.* New York: Speak/Penguin.

McLaughlin, M. W. (1990). The RAND change agent study revisited: Macro perspectives and micro realities. *Educational Researcher, 19*(9), 11–16.

McLaughlin, M. W., & Talbert, J. E. (2010, Spring). Professional learning communities: Building blocks for school culture and student learning. *V.U.E.,* pp. 35–45. Retrieved from *www.researchgate.net/publication/265655002.*

Meltzer, J. (2015). Differentiated professional development: Supporting substantive change in writing instruction in one district. *Journal of Maine Education, 31,* 17–25. Retrieved from *http://publications.catstonepress.com/i/567263-journal-2015.*

Reeves, D. (2006). *Leading change in your school.* Alexandria, VA: ASCD.

Saphier, J., & Marshall, K. (2008, July). Jon Saphier and Kim Marshall on supervision and evaluation. Retrieved from *https://marshallmemo.com/articles/Saphier%20Marshall%20confluence%202008.pdf.*

Schmoker, M. (2018). *Focus: Elevating the essentials.* Alexandria, VA: ASCD.

Shafer, L. (2018, July 23). What makes a good school culture? (Web log). Retrieved from *www.gse.harvard.edu/news/uk/18/07/what-makes-good-school-culture.*

Shelton, R. C., Cooper, B. R., & Stirman, S. W. (2018). The sustainability of evidence-based practices in public health and health care. *Annual Review of Public Health, 36,* 55–75.

Spillane, J. P., Halvorson, R., & Diamond, J. B. (2001, April). Investigating school leadership practice: A distributed perspective. *Educational Researcher, 30*(3), 23–38.

U.S. Department of Education, Office of Planning, Evaluation, and Policy Development. (2016). *Case studies of schools implementing early elementary strategies: Preschool through third grade alignment and differentiated instruction.* Washington,

DC: Policy and Program Studies Service. Retrieved from *www2.ed.gov/rschstat/eval/disadv/p-3-alignment-differentiated-instruction/report.pdf.*

Zemelman, S., Daniels, H., & Hyde, A. (2012). *Best practice: Bringing standards to life in America's classrooms* (4th ed.). Portsmouth, NH: Heinemann.

CHILDREN'S LITERATURE

Evans, R. P. (2012). *Michael Vey 7: The final spark*. New York: Simon Pulse/Mercury/Simon & Schuster.

Lu, M. (2013). *Legend*. New York: Speak/Penguin.

Rowling, J. K. (1997). *Harry Potter and the philosopher's stone*. London: Bloomsbury.

CHAPTER 20

Schools as Places of Learning

The Powerful Role of Literacy Leaders

Allison Swan Dagen
Rita M. Bean

GUIDING QUESTIONS

⇀ How have past research findings on features of effective professional development contributed to a new framework for collaborative professional learning opportunities for PreK–12 educators?

⇀ In what ways do contemporary tenets on professional learning align with current standards about professional learning, including those in *Standards for the Preparation of Literacy Professionals 2017* (International Literacy Association [ILA], 2018b)?

⇀ In what ways can schools implement professional learning experiences that support overall organizational improvement, benefit student learning, and encourage teachers' growth as lifelong learners?

⇀ How can literacy leaders work with others to establish a culture of collaborative teacher professional learning and transform schools into places of learning for teachers and students?

One of the themes that can be found in the chapters in this book is the need for quality teaching, not only by the classroom teacher, but also by other professionals (e.g., specialized literacy professionals [SLPs]) who also have teaching responsibilities. Such quality teaching requires that schools support a climate and culture in which lifelong learning is encouraged (Bean, 2015). In previous chapters, authors address professional learning (PL) needs related to specific topics (e.g., technology, assessment, disciplinary literacy); the goal in this chapter is to summarize key research findings about PL, in general, to guide literacy leaders in establishing an environment that encourages teacher learning and in designing, implementing, and evaluating PL experiences in their schools.

We begin by presenting a fictionalized example to illustrate one literacy leader's effort to guide change efforts in schoolwide literacy instruction. From there, we share key ideas of past research on professional development (PD) to set the stage for a vision of teacher learning and growth anchored in collaborative PL. We address both the need for enhancing organizational, schoolwide growth, and also for attending to needs and interests of individual teachers in the school. In the final section, we return to the scenario described at the beginning of the chapter and share insights on what literacy leaders might consider when planning PL to support implementation and sustainability efforts. Last, we provide a description of multiple PL opportunities in Appendix 20.1 (see pp. 425–434).

In the case that follows, we describe a situation that illustrates a decision-making challenge faced by Mrs. Campbell, a literacy coordinator who is leading an effort to select a new literacy program for the elementary grades. Mrs. Campbell thinks about what she wants to do to make sure this work involves teachers so that they not only buy in to the decision, but also have a sense of ownership of the selected program. She is also aware of, and begins immediately to think about, how to organize the necessary PL experiences so that there will be successful implementation and sustainability. As this example suggests, meeting the needs of individuals and schools within a complex school system (e.g., districts, counties, parishes) is a challenge.

CASE EXAMPLE ·

THINK ABOUT THIS

1. In what ways does Mrs. Campbell lay the groundwork to support engagement in the program selection process?

2. What are your thoughts about Mrs. Campbell's three-stage process of PL for the teachers in the three schools? In what ways is she addressing both organizational goals and individual needs?

As a literacy coordinator, Mrs. Campbell has been given the green light from district administration to select a new literacy series to be used for Tier 1 instruction, replacing the very dated program currently in use in the district's three elementary schools. She knew there were variations in the beliefs and assumptions about literary learning in the three schools. For example, the reading/literacy specialists and teachers in one school seemed to support a balanced literacy approach to teaching literacy that included an emphasis on integrated writing instruction. In the second school, a Title I school with large numbers of students experiencing reading difficulties, there appeared to be a preference for instruction with leveled materials and a greater emphasis on phonics instruction. And in the third school, with a large English learner (EL) population, teachers and specialized literacy professionals were focused on the need for instruction that provided support for this population. Obviously, there was variability in beliefs as well as in student needs in the individual schools.

In consultation with district's SLPs, Mrs. Campbell created a needs assessment instrument to distribute to the K–5 regular and special education teachers in all three schools to get teachers' input about current reading instruction and student learning: specifically, in what ways was it meeting or not meeting student needs and the goals in the district's comprehensive literacy plan? Mrs. Campbell also asked each of the schools' SLPs to be prepared to share their schools' annual data on reading and writing achievement. She worked with the SLPs to identify possible teacher and parent representatives from each school to serve on a working committee, which she planned to chair. Because she wanted principal representation, she asked the three principals if one of them would be willing to serve on the committee, share information, and get input from the other two.

Although identification of criteria for selecting the program was a necessary first step, as was the development of a process for committee work, Mrs. Campbell also began thinking about the PL experiences and opportunities that teachers might need once the program was adopted. Mrs. Campbell realized that the publishers might offer some support at little to no additional cost, but she wanted to be certain that there were opportunities specific to each school that would address the unique needs of students and teachers. She began thinking of a three-stage process that would work if the talents and expertise of the SLPs and teachers at the various schools could be actualized.

First, would be general sessions in which all teachers would receive information necessary to understand the new program; she was sure that the publisher would help with this. But she realized she would need to do more than to "transmit" information to the teachers. In the second phase, specialists, coaches, and teacher leaders would facilitate school-based teams, perhaps differentiated for the primary and intermediate teachers. She saw these small-group meetings as ones in which teachers could address the specific needs and challenges in their school and take ownership of the program. Third would be the follow-up sessions for individual teachers who would identify their own individual learning needs as well as student needs. Teachers would work with literacy coaches to identify an area of focus that would help them address student needs in their classrooms.

Mrs. Campbell saw this implementation plan as a 3-year effort, in which she would listen to and learn from the teachers and her literacy team about what worked and what would need to be modified to meet the goals of each school. Mrs. Campbell understood that much more was needed than a new core reading program if the school were to apply a comprehensive literacy program. There would need to be some changes in attitudes and beliefs about students and what they brought to their learning, and about literacy development and instruction. She was hopeful that digital resources from various professional organizations might be useful in providing personalized PL activities for teachers. She expected, through this process, to address other aspects of the reading program (e.g., support for ELs, Title I, writing instruction). She was looking forward to the challenge of this task and knew that if she could get teachers excited about and committed to this opportunity to learn and grow through this adoption process, she would be successful.

FROM PROFESSIONAL DEVELOPMENT TO PROFESSIONAL LEARNING

Mrs. Campbell understands the importance of developing the school as a place of learning where all are encouraged to work collaboratively to create exemplary literacy learning experiences for students. She knows that when PL is authentic and situated in teachers' own classrooms, they will value such learning and that these experiences will result in changes in teaching practices, not only in individual classrooms but in the school. Mrs. Campbell wants to support teachers in making transformational changes in their teaching practices, and she realizes that there is a need for some changes in how the school operationalizes its PL experiences if this is to happen.

Since the publication of the first edition of *Best Practices of Literacy Leaders* (Bean & Swan Dagen, 2012), we have witnessed a shift from the term *professional development,* a model that seemed to reflect "something done to teachers" (ILA, 2018a), replaced by *professional learning,* reflecting a process where teachers instead "embrace their own agency" (ILA, 2018a, p. 3) and have opportunities for identifying their own knowledge needs and how to address them. Kragler, Martin, and Sylvester (2014) suggest that this shift in terminology is one of many changes in how teacher learning has been addressed over time: from inservice (1950s–1960s) to staff development (1970s–1980s) to professional development (1990s–2000s) and now to professional learning (2000–present). The goal of PL, as we view it today, is to enhance learning by engaging teachers in identifying and solving problems that are pertinent to their own context or situation.

Next we highlight key findings of research on PD, given its historical value and impact on the field. When describing these seminal pieces, we use the term *PD;* later we switch to the term *PL* as we discuss some of the implications of this new approach to teacher learning.

Teacher Learning Is Important:
Key Ideas from Past Research on Professional Development

As highlighted in the research, quality teaching is the single most important variable contributing to student learning (Darling-Hammond, Wei, Andree, Richarson, & Orphanos, 2009; Hanushek, 1992; Rivkin, Hanushek, & Kain, 2005). Further, PD can make a difference in teaching quality and student learning (Blank & de las Alas, 2009; Bryk, Sebring, Allensworth, Luppescu, & Easton, 2010; Darling-Hammond, Hyler, & Gardner, 2017; Desimone, Porter, Garet, Yoon, & Birman, 2002; Garet, Porter, Desimone, Birman, & Yoon, 2001; Yoon, Duncan, Lee, Scarloss, & Shapley, 2007). In 2010, the National Staff Development Council (now Learning Forward) defined PD as "a comprehensive, sustained, and intensive approach to improving teachers' and principals' effectiveness in raising student achievement" (p. 16). Below we summarize eight widely accepted, essential elements of effective PD (American Education Research Association, 2005; Darling-Hammond et al., 2017; Learning Forward, 2010). Effective PD must:

- Focus on content.
- Focus on student learning.
- Use models of effective practice.
- Support collaboration.
- Provide for active learning.
- Provide support through coaching.
- Provide opportunities for feedback and reflection.
- Be of sustained duration.

Content and Pedagogical Knowledge in a Collaborative Culture

The American Education Research Association (AERA; 2005) described iterations of PD in two waves. The first wave, beginning in the 1960s, centered around teachers' knowledge of generic teaching skills, such as instructional routines, grouping, and pacing. The second wave, based on research in the 1990s, shifted focus from teacher knowledge to student learning (e.g., student problem solving). This wave emphasized the importance of the teachers' content-area knowledge in improving student learning. In this publication, AERA summarized important notions of the PD research conducted during these "waves of research" and called for a focus on evaluating PD, focusing on changes in teaching practices and student learning.

Extending this metaphor, Swan Dagen and Bean (2014) proposed a third wave in which school culture and collaboration serve as drivers of PL experiences. This third wave describes PL as involving "experiences that take place within a collaborative culture of shared leadership, that increase educators' knowledge about content and pedagogy, and enable them to use that knowledge to improve classroom and school practices that improve student learning" (Swan Dagen & Bean, 2014, p. 44). Specifically, teachers together have a key role in establishing literacy goals for their students, deciding how to achieve those goals, and participating in decision making about what learning experiences they themselves need to achieve those goals (see Figure 20.1). A primary goal of this third wave is to view PL through a lens that focuses on the impact of the collective capacity of teachers in a school. As such, this model addresses ways of providing structures through which a collective group of professionals learns and solves problems. While collaboration has been cited as a key component of PD over time (Anders, Hoffman, & Duffy, 2000; Byrk et al., 2010; Darling-Hammond et al., 2017; Desimone et al., 2002; Wei, Darling-Hammond, & Adamson, 2010), only recently has there been an emphasis on systematic, intentional approaches to nurture such collaborative engagement.

Support for the importance of a collaborative culture in schools comes not only from the research about shared leadership but from the research findings of Leana and Pil (2006, 2017) about the importance of social capital in schools. They found that, although teachers' experiences and knowledge (human capital) were important, the interactions among teachers and others (social capital) served as the glue for creating schools in which professionals and staff work together to identify and then solve challenges they face. Their work identifies the importance of moving beyond the individual

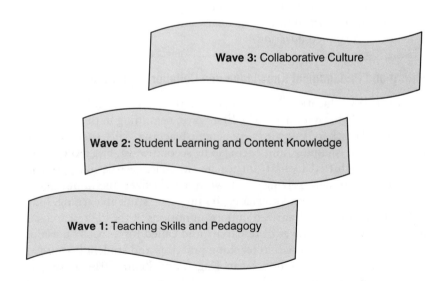

FIGURE 20.1. Waves of professional development. From Swan Dagen and Bean (2014). Copyright © 2014 The Guilford Press. Reprinted by permission.

level; specifically, selecting or promoting "star" teachers is not enough to ensure school change. Their work reinforces the notion that school faculty members must work together if they are to create overall and sustainable changes in teaching practices and student learning. Thus, although we acknowledge the importance of providing support for individual growth, the emphasis in this chapter is on PL that assists in transforming the school as a whole.

Professional Learning

In this section, we focus on exploring some nuances found in contemporary literature on PL. Learning Forward (formerly National Staff Development Council), an organization that has been committed to this work for decades, published its *Standards for Professional Learning* (2011), a document that provides an analytical overview, denoting an increased emphasis on educators taking an active role in their own PL. Their core standard determinants include learning communities, leadership, resources, data, learning design, implementation, and outcomes (*www.learningforward. org*). PL is also a focal point throughout ILA's *Standards 2017,* but specific to "Professional Learning and Leadership" (Standard 6). As described in that standard, PL opportunities are a necessity for all role types (e.g., SLPs, classroom teachers, principals) who work directly and indirectly with PreK–12 students. Across all six roles, ILA suggests these experiences be based in high-quality content (e.g., literacy); include elements of inquiry, responsiveness, reflection, and advocacy; be ongoing in duration and structure; based on needs of students, teachers, and the organization; grounded in research, and collaborative in nature (ILA, 2018b). There is a great degree of overlap between Learning Forward's *Standards for Professional Learning* (2011) and ILA's *Standards 2017* (2018b).

In the *What's Hot in Literacy 2018 Report* (ILA, 2018c), 2,000 survey participants from 91 countries identified "professional learning and development in literacy instruction" as seventh in importance of the 17 categories (e.g., digital literacy, assessment, family engagement) used in this survey research. In addition to the placement in overall rank, 81% of participants indicated that PL/D was an extremely or very *important* topic. Further, 47% of these same participants identified PL/D as an extremely or very *hot* topic. In their report, ILA emphasizes access to high-quality, well-prepared literacy teachers as a "matter of equity" (2018c).

The shift in terminology and justification for the shift was further outlined in a literacy leadership brief titled "Democratizing Professional Growth with Teachers" (ILA, 2018a). This brief begins with a description of key differences between PD and PL and then focuses on PL practices. Similar to the comparisons made by Risko and Vogt (2016), ILA describes PD as something done *to* teachers, by experts or organizations, in short duration, reflecting what is commonly known in the field as an isolated "hit-and-run" or "one-shot" approach. This type of experience—one that almost every reader of this chapter has likely experienced at one point in their teaching career—leaves teachers feeling less confident, more isolated, and less supported, This is not to say that all PD offered by schools, organizations, or consultants is bad or ineffective. PD initiatives aligned with effective design elements (see the list on p. 415), as identified above, can most certainly be transformative (Swan Dagen & Bean, 2007).

Key research supports a shift toward PL, which considers the teacher's own expertise and background, personal goals for growth, and agency/experiences. As stated in the ILA brief, PL should provide for choice of content; be designed around active engagement; make connections between new and known knowledge, be co-constructed by the teachers (i.e., not conveyed to teachers), connected to their daily work, and include opportunities for reflection and collaboration (ILA, 2018a). As evident, some recommendations for PL do align with many components of research-based PD (e.g., active engagement, focus on content). A critical difference is the involvement of teachers themselves, acting as agents of their own learning. Risko and Vogt (2016) present an inquiry model where teachers are involved in their own learning by solving authentic problems, setting goals, proposing solutions to teaching problems, and responding and transforming their teaching practices. This authentic, inquiry-based model, self-directed by teachers, provides a roadmap for solving issues around teacher instruction and students' success. In Appendix 20.1 (see pp. 425–434), we provide descriptions of various opportunities, with books and resources for further study, which schools might want to consider as they develop PL plans and processes.

Educators as Lifelong Learners

Although our primary focus in this chapter is on PL that supports school-wide goals and vision for literacy, we also recognize that in addition to opportunities organized and directed by schools, teachers themselves play a critical role in their own leaning. Individual teachers have often sought learning experiences on their own: They attend graduate classes, sometimes working on advanced certifications, read professional books, or attend conferences or workshops. Joyce and Showers (1995) described ways that teachers might differ in how they approach learning. They categorize some as gourmet omnivores who strive to learn all they can about their craft, "giv[ing] and tak[ing] energy from their peers" (p. 151). Others may be more passive or reticent to engage in learning opportunities, although they can respond in a positive way to well-designed PL activities in a climate that promotes collaboration among peers.

In today's digital world, technology also provides teachers with a vast array of learning opportunities. These opportunities can be accessed either during or outside the school day. Teachers can download lesson plans, observe examples of practice, attend classes, and connect with other educators. For example, teachers often use social media (e.g., Twitter, YouTube, Pinterest) as a source of individual learning. Engagement in professional learning networks (PLNs), defined as "informal gatherings in digital spaces" (ILA, 2018a, p. 6), bring together educators from a variety of roles (e.g., preservice teachers, professors, researchers, grant administrators). As well, on-demand opportunities are plentiful and offered by organizations (e.g., webinars), individuals (e.g., YouTube channel), schools (e.g., literacy coaching), PLNs (e.g., informal or formal), and groups of educators focusing on specific topics (e.g., Decoding, Dyslexia). Engagement in these PLNs can involve synchronous participation (e.g., being a panel member for a podcast recording or participating in an evening Twitter chat) or asynchronous attendance (e.g., listening to a recorded podcast during a commute to work or reading the Tweets and responses from the aforementioned Twitter chat during a prep period).

A key to benefiting from PLNs is active participation, although "lurking" is learning too! Further, by collaborating within these PLNs, teachers may receive support, feedback, and/or coaching or provide support and feedback to others. To formalize this process, educators can create personal learning goals and record new learning in a personal journal or blog. Many of these technological resources can also be useful as teachers work collaboratively to achieve school goals. As always, though, the value and credibility of these various resources must be evaluated for their accuracy and authenticity. Nevertheless, these digital resources can provide schools as well as individual teachers with more access to PL activities, often less expensive, and personalized to meet the needs of teachers as well as the school.

Schools as Places of Learning

We circle back to Mrs. Campbell and her long-range plan to facilitate the adoption of a core literacy program for the district. She considers this adoption to be an adaptive rather than a technical challenge for the three schools (Heifetz & Linsky, 2002). In order to achieve the goal of designing a literacy program that meets the goals of all students, changes will be necessary, not only in instruction but also in teacher attitudes, beliefs, and priorities. Although the actual selection of the core program might be somewhat more technical in nature (i.e., a clearly defined task), the implementation efforts in these three schools with their different populations will require teacher leadership, involvement, and a willingness to make changes that transform literacy instruction.

Mrs. Campbell sees her role as one of providing the structure and resources to accomplish this long-range goal. She is designing opportunities for teachers to work collaboratively to develop their own leadership skills and ultimately to build school capacity. She believes that this process, while addressing school goals, has the flexibility to provide teachers with choice in both what and how they learn. She recognizes that although SLPs will individually coach and support teachers, there will also be a need for group experiences, such as walk-throughs or study groups. For example, she can envision teachers in the school with many EL students, reading and discussing articles that develop their knowledge and skills of culturally responsive instruction. She also plans to ask the SLPs to set up a network so that they and the teachers can talk informally with SLPs and teachers at surrounding districts, through social media, to learn more about how these districts have addressed the challenges of changing their literacy program. In sum, she is supporting teachers in their efforts to develop collective responsibility for ensuring "that all students have access to the best teaching in a grade level, subject matter, or entire school . . . [and that] teachers can tap the internal expertise among their colleagues" (Hirsh, 2010, p. 5).

As the literacy coordinator, Mrs. Campbell understands that there will be some challenges and barriers to the implementation plan. Some challenges are institutional in nature: resources (e.g., extensive time for teachers to meet and for staff to support them) and limited administrative support. Others relate to helping teachers understand why changes are occurring and supporting them as they move through the change process. She wrote the following on her list of "to-dos":

- Develop teachers' and specialized literacy professionals' abilities to lead and work effectively in groups (e.g., norms, active listening).
- Use the four Ps to help teachers make a transition from where they are to where they need to be (Bridges & Mitchell, 2008):
  - Purpose (Why?)
  - Picture (What will it look and feel like?)
  - Plan (How will we get there?)
  - Part (What can you do to help us get to where we want to be?)
- Create a risk-taking environment (questions and ideas are encouraged).
- Celebrate the progress (even the baby steps).
- Be creative in providing opportunities for SLPs and teachers to work collaboratively during the school day (e.g., use various technological resources from organizations, webinars, blogs). Encourage individual teachers to seek out-of-school experiences.
- Keep reminding myself and teachers that change is a long-term process and that individual teachers are at different places.

Mrs. Campbell is aware that, given the differences among the teachers, students, and administration at the three schools, there may be differences in the pace and emphasis of program implementation. Teacher leaders at these three schools will negotiate how this program will unfold and what it will look like in practice. In other words, she is aware of what McLaughlin (1976, 1990) calls "mutual adaptation": that is, the effect of local or individual school dynamics and characteristics on the implementation of a policy initiative. As Santee Siskin (2016, p. 2), indicates, mutual adaptation is the "process where local adopters do change their own practices, but at the same time make modifications in the design to suit their particular organizational context." This principle provides room for schools to participate in inquiry work and empowers them to make decisions that address their local needs rather than be held to prescriptive fidelity. If schools are to become places of learning, they must have the skill and will to identify and carry through with adaptations. It is hard for policy to change practice without recognizing the importance of local-level factors (McLaughlin, 1990). As Santee Siskin (2016) indicates, we might think of this mutual adaptation as "perpetual beta testing," whereas "designs are strengthened by the designers' willingness to try, test, and adapt based on the experiences of real users" (p. 16). Those schools that systematically address how a new initiative can be adapted to meet their needs have the best chance for real reform. Effective literacy leaders recognize that context matters and use formative and ongoing feedback to make essential modifications not only in the implementation of the initiative, but in the PL necessary to support it.

CONCLUSION

Ensuring quality learning for students—and teachers—requires an equitable school effort, particularly within a larger school system, that is based on collaboration and shared leadership, and that fosters collective responsibility among school personnel. In this edition of *Best Practices of Literacy Leaders*, this notion is exemplified throughout all chapters, including those that describe roles, program development, implementation and evaluation, and contexts of schooling. In this final chapter, we have presented a discussion on the possibilities for transforming teacher PL, highlighting the importance of designing a culture of collaboration. To sustain a vision of schools as places of learning, we must do so through both a system lens (Chapter 19) and a people lens (Chapter 6). Results of research have helped educators understand the importance of job-embedded PL, anchored in teacher agency, which builds school capacity and enables educators to provide the best education for all the students they serve.

The greatest resource in schools is its educators; as such, they need opportunities to think, learn, and reflect if they are to become effective professionals. Such PL opportunities should be focused on the ultimate goal of schooling: that of improving student learning. And such PL opportunities should occur in an environment that respects and values the contributions of each educator in the school. When school personnel recognize that PL is an integral part of every school day, they take the first step on the journey toward developing schools that are places of learning for both PreK–12 students and for teachers!

ENGAGEMENT ACTIVITIES

1. Revisit the scenario at the beginning of this chapter describing Mrs. Campbell. Discuss with peers the types of barriers you have encountered in your own school's implementation or PL initiatives and prepare some strategies for success (like Mrs. Campbell's to-do list, p. 420).

2. See Appendix 20.1 (pp. 425–434). Discuss the 13 activities described with other literacy leaders in your school; think about which of these might be helpful in meeting the goals and vision that your school has established for the literacy program. What opportunities do you have to share this plan with the person or team within your district or school that creates the PL days' agenda or content? Try to learn more about how and why PL is designed and become an advocate for yourself and peers in this process schoolwide.

3. *Standards 2017* asserts that PL includes learning, inquiry, reflection, collaboration, and advocacy. Create a map, table, or Sketchnotes of your own personalized learning goals for the upcoming school year using these five categories as headers. Revisit these notes throughout the year and record your experiences with school-based PL and your own on-demand engagement outside of school.

4. Identify an organization that serves as a source of information for the content of your literacy instruction (e.g., ILA, National Council of Teachers of English). Explore their websites for information on upcoming events, how to receive notifications of events, free or low-cost PL opportunities (e.g., blogs, unconferences). Sign up for their listservs or use your social media platforms to "follow" these organizations so that you are informed.

ANNOTATED RESOURCES

International Literacy Association (ILA). (2018). *Democratizing professional growth with teachers: From development to learning* (Position statement). Newark, DE: Author.

This position statement describes the concept of shifting from professional development to professional learning. This is not simply a shift in word choice; rather it is a rebranding situating professional learning as growth-based opportunities addressing teachers' needs for inquiry, critical thinking, and problem solving.

Risko, V., & Vogt, M. (2016). *Professional learning in action: An inquiry approach for teachers of literacy.* New York: Teachers College Press.

This book provides an action plan for assessing, creating, evaluating, and sustaining an inquiry approach to professional learning. A literacy-focused vignette spans across all chapters, providing readers with an opportunity to follow as the action plan unfolds in a school.

REFERENCES

American Education Research Association. (2005). *Research points: Teaching teachers–professional development to improve student achievement* (Vol. 3, Issue 1) (Brochure). Washington, DC: Author. Retrieved from *www.aera.net*.

Anders, P., Hoffman, J., & Duffy, G. (2000). Teaching teachers to teach reading: Paradigm shifts, persistent problems, and challenges. In M. Kamil, P. Mosenthal, P. D. Pearson, & R. Barr (Eds.), *Handbook of reading research* (Vol. 3, pp. 721–744). Mahwah, NJ: Erlbaum.

Bean, R. M. (2015). *The reading specialist: Leadership for the classroom, school, and community* (3rd ed.). New York: Guilford Press.

Bean, R. M., & Swan Dagen, A. (Eds.). (2012). *Best practices of literacy leaders: Keys to school improvement*. New York: Guilford Press.

Blank, R. K., & de las Alas, N. (2009). *Effects of teacher professional development on gains in student achievement: How meta-analysis provides scientific evidence useful to education leaders*. Washington, DC: Council of Chief State School Officers.

Bridges, W., & Mitchell, S. (2008). Leading transition: A new model for change. In F. Hesselbein & A. Shrader (Eds.), *Leader to leader: Enduring insights on leadership* (pp. 246–255). San Francisco: Jossey-Bass.

Bryk, A. S., Sebring, P. B., Allensworth, E., Luppescu, S., & Easton, J. Q. (2010). *Organizing schools for improvement: Lessons from Chicago*. Chicago: University of Chicago Press.

Darling-Hammond, L., Hyler, M. E., & Gardner, M. (with Espinoza, D.). (2017). *Effective teacher professional development*. Palo Alto, CA: Learning Policy Institute.

Darling-Hammond, L., Wei, R. C., Andree, A., Richardson, N., & Orphanos, S. (2009). *Professional learning in the learning profession: A status report on teacher development in the United States and abroad*. Palo Alto, CA: Stanford University.

Desimone, L. M., Porter, A. C., Garet, M., Yoon, S. K., & Birman, B. F. (2002). Effects of professional development on teachers' instruction: Results from a three-year longitudinal study. *Educational Evaluation and Policy Analysis, 24*(2), 81–112.

Garet, M. S., Porter, A. C., Desimone, L., Birman, B. F., & Yoon, S. K. (2001). What makes professional development effective?: Results from a national sample of teachers. *American Educational Research Journal, 38*(4), 915–945.

Hanushek, E. A. (1992). The trade-off between child quantity and quality. *Journal of Political Economy, 100*(91), 84–117. Retrieved from *www.jstor.org*.

Heifetz, R., & Linsky, M. (2002). *Leadership on the line: Staying alive through the dangers of leading*. Cambridge, MA: Harvard Business School Press.

Hirsh, S. (2010, Fall). Teacher evaluation: An opportunity to leverage learning at all levels. *Learning System, 1*, 4–5.

International Literacy Association (ILA). (2018a). *Democratizing professional growth with teachers: From development to learning* (Position statement). Newark, DE: Author

International Literacy Association (ILA). (2018b). *Standards for the preparation of literacy professionals 2017*. Newark, DE: Author.

International Literacy Association (ILA). (2018c). *What's hot in literacy?: 2018 report*. Newark, DE: Author.

Joyce, B., & Showers, B. (1995). *Student achievement through staff development* (3rd ed.). Alexandria, VA: ASCD.

Kragler, S., Martin, L. E., & Sylvester, R. (2014). Lessons learned: What our history and research tell us about teachers' professional learning. In L. E. Martin, S. Kragler, D. J. Quatroche, & K. L. Bauserman (Eds.), *Handbook of professional development in education: Successful models and practices, PreK–12* (pp. 483–505). New York: Guilford Press.

Leana, C. R., & Pil, F. K. (2006). Social capital and organizational performance: Evidence from urban public schools. *Organization Science, 17*(3), 353–366.

Leana, C. R., & Pil, F. K. (2017.) Social capital: An untapped resource for educational improvement. In E. Quintero (Ed.), *Teaching in context: How social aspects of schools and school systems shape teachers' development and effectiveness* (pp. 113–130). Cambridge, MA: Harvard University Press.

Learning Forward. (2010). Key points in Learning Forward's definition of professional development. *Journal of Staff Development, 31*(6), 16–17.

Learning Forward. (2011). Standards for professional learning. Retrieved from *https://learningforward.org/standards-for-professional-learning*.

McLaughlin, M. W. (1976). Implementation as mutual adaptation: Change in classroom organization. *Teachers College Record, 77*(3), 339–351.

McLaughlin, M. W. (1990). The Rand Change Agent Study revisited: Macro perspectives and micro realities. *Educational Researcher, 19*(9), 11–16.

Risko, V., & Vogt, M. (2016). *Professional learning in action: An inquiry approach for teachers of literacy*. New York: Teachers College Press.

Rivkin, S. G., Hanushek, E. A., & Kain, J. F. (2005). Teachers, schools and academic achievement. *Econometrica, 73*(2), 417–458.

Santee Siskin, L. (2016). Mutual adaptation in action. *Teachers College Record, 118*(13), 1–18.

Swan Dagen, A., & Bean, R. M. (2007). Providing professional development to improve literacy instruction: Tinkering or transforming? *Pennsylvania Reads, 8*(1), 27–40.

Swan Dagen, A., & Bean, R. M. (2014). High-quality, research-based professional development: An essential for enhancing high-quality teaching. In L. Martin, S. Kragler, D. Quatroche, & K. Bauserman (Eds.), *Handbook of professional development in education* (pp. 42–63). New York: Guilford Press.

Wei, R. C., Darling-Hammond, L., & Adamson, F. (2010). *Professional development in the United States: Trends and challenges*. Dallas, TX: National Staff Development Council.

Yoon, K. S., Duncan, T., Lee, S. W., Scarloss, B., & Shapley, K. (2007). *Reviewing the evidence on how teacher professional development affects students' achievement* (Issues & Answers Report, REL 2007-NO. 033). Washington, DC: U.S. Department of Education, Institute of Education Sciences, National Center for Education Evaluation and Regional Assistance, Regional Educational Laboratory Southwest. Retrieved from *www.ies.ed.gov/ncess/edlabs*.

Activities for Developing Professional Learning in Schools

School leaders might consider the following activities or approaches to PL as they develop plans for individuals and groups. Each can be helpful in promoting collaborative work in schools. For each of the suggested activities, we provide a brief description and resources that may be helpful to those interested in using them as part of their PL plan.

ANALYZING AND REFLECTING ON DATA

Although data analysis has become a common activity in many schools, too often once data are analyzed, little is done to modify or change instruction in the classrooms. Part of the problem lies in the process of considering student data in a vacuum without analyzing other aspects of how the school functions. For example, looking across student data, a teacher can determine an area of need for her third-grade students (e.g., student writing lacks organization); however, without resources in place (e.g., opportunities to develop their own background about the topic; having access to a co-teacher or literacy coach to model lessons), teachers may be left wondering what to do with this information. Mokhtari, Rosemary, and Edwards (2007) present a framework that literacy leaders can use called the *data analysis framework for instructional decision making.* The tool focuses on student performance data but also analyzes data on PL (e.g., How does the school literacy coach function?) and classroom instruction data (e.g., teacher lesson plans, student grouping) to provide an overall view for decision making.

Resources

Doing Data Right. (2015, November). *Educational Leadership, 73*(3) [issue].
Mokhtari, K., Rosemary, C., & Edwards, P. (2007). Making instructional decisions based on data: What, how, and why? *The Reading Teacher, 61*(4), 354–359.

CLASSROOM OBSERVATIONS OR WALK-THROUGHS

A useful approach to promoting a sense of community is that of making teaching public. Teachers observe one another to share their approaches to teaching and to learn from each other. Too often in a school, there is great variability in how teachers are implementing an innovation or approach (e.g., guided reading, discussion groups). By participating in peer observations, teachers can become familiar with how others view and implement these approaches and develop guidelines for how the approach can be implemented schoolwide to promote consistency for students. City, Elmore, Fiarman, and Teitel (2009) discuss a form of PL known as *instructional rounds networks*. They contend that in most schools, individual teachers have a set way of teaching, and that what is needed in schools is shared practices. They promote instructional rounds as a means for school personnel to learn from each other, using a four-step process: "identifying a problem of practice, observing, debriefing, and focusing on the next level of work" (p. 6). Such rounds can help teachers develop a common language: What do we mean by *active learning*? Effective classroom management? And what is the evidence that we would consider for identifying such aspects in the classroom? In some schools, the peer observation process may be one that is developed collaboratively by the principal and the leadership team. In such cases, the purpose for the observations as well as the procedures for debriefing or giving feedback are developed.

Resources

City, E. A., Elmore, R. F., Fiarman, S. E., & Teitel, L. (2009). *Instructional rounds in education: A network approach to improving teaching and learning.* Cambridge, MA: Harvard Education Press.

Grim, E., Kaufman, T., & Doty, D. (2014). Rethinking classroom observations. *Educational Leadership, 71*(8), 24–29.

Ippolito, J., & Bean, R. M. (2018). *Unpacking coaching mindsets: Collaboration between principals and coaches.* West Palm Beach, FL: Learning Sciences International.

Protheroe, N. (2009, March/April). Using classroom walkthroughs to improve instruction. *Principal, 88*(4), 30–34.

COACHING

Bean and Ippolito (2015) define coaching as "a process of facilitated inquiry that enables teachers to make decisions, solve problems, and set and achieve both individual goals and the goals of the organization" (p. 5). The art of coaching can be formal or informal, carried out by literacy coach or a peer. Coaching includes high-quality elements of PL: (1) adequate time or duration, (2) activities that build knowledge and theory, and (3) ongoing support and feedback.

A trusting relationship creates a solid basis for coaching. Those who choose to coach informally should be cognizant of adult learning theory and peers' readiness for coaching. Ippolito and Bean (2015) suggest a four-part framework for coaching mindsets: coach as leader, coach as facilitator, coach as designer, and coach as advocate. ILA (2018) describes three models of coaching or change: coaching to conform (e.g., fidelity to a practice or initiative), coaching into practice (e.g., reflective classroom teaching), and coaching for transformation (e.g., change in practice followed by change in systems). An effective coaching program requires that district leadership decide upon a framework, goals, and expectations for coaching and share those with teachers.

Resources

Bean, R. M., & Ippolito, J. (2015). *Cultivating coaching mindsets: An action guide for literacy leaders.* West Palm Beach, FL: Learning Sciences International.

International Literacy Association. (2018). *Literacy coaching for change: Choices matter.* Newark, DE: Author.

COLLABORATION WITH PROFESSIONAL ORGANIZATIONS

Another sort of activity that can enhance collaboration with peers is engaging with electronic resources found on the Internet. Many professional organizations have created high-quality materials available at little or no cost to educators. For example, the International Literacy Association has developed opportunities for teacher or groups of teachers to use technology resources (e.g., webinars, lesson plans, podcasts, and listserves) for ongoing teacher PL. They have also developed a series of position statements and briefs that can be read by individual teachers or serve as a basis for study or discussion groups.

Possible organizations as resources for literacy leaders include:

International Literacy Association (*www.literacyworldwide.org*)
National Center for Families Learning (*www.familieslearning.org*)
National Council of Teachers of English (*www.ncte.org*)
Public Broadcasting System (*www.pbs.org*)
Reading Rockets (*www.readingrockets.org*)
Teach to Lead (*http://teachtolead.org*)

ENGAGEMENT WITH EDU-BLOGGERS

At the 2019, SXSW EDU Conference, education blogger Jennifer Gonzalez (one of our favorites) from Cult of Pedagogy gave an inspiring talk titled "The

Aerodynamics of Exceptional Schools."[1] Gonzalez, a former National Board Certified middle school language arts teacher, has created a "cult" audience exploring the art of teaching through her insightful blog posts, witty videos, and podcasts with of educators, literacy leaders, and teachers in the field who are influencers in their own right. Our recommendation to "engage with an edu-blogger" doesn't mean to follow whomever we recommend (although this would be fine), but instead we suggest that you follow someone who aligns with your philosophy, experiences, and learning needs. Following is a sample of a few of the contemporary activities for PL, outlined in a Cult of Pedagogy blog titled "OMG Becky. PD is Getting So Much Better!!" (*www.cultofpeda-gogy.com/pd*), for you to consider. Examples of how schools carried out these types of activities are linked from the blog post.

> *Unconferences.* A gathering where the academic agenda is developed by the participants in a spontaneous manner. In these gathering, the "experts" are the participating educators.
> *Voluntary piloting.* As the name indicates, this option allows interested participants to volunteer to pilot or try out new ideas, programs, or structures. In this model, many times the volunteer becomes the coach or leader if/when full implementation takes place.
> *Micro credentials.* Teachers participate in activities for PL around a given topic and earn "badges" to represent their learning/expertise.
> *Choice boards.* Fashioned to look like a tic-tac-toe board or àla carte menu, teachers are provided with variations of PL opportunities and can *choose* what and how to engage within a certain time frame.

CURRICULUM DEVELOPMENT

Teachers at specific grade levels, those who teach a specific subject (e.g., 10th-grade literature), or those at a specific school meet to set learning goals and to develop or select curriculum and evaluative tools to measure accomplishment of the goals. These are often temporary committees or teams that have a specific goal to achieve and are terminated when they achieve those goals. These task-oriented groups give teachers an opportunity to work together on an authentic task and to increase their learning as they address an issue or task.

Resources

Design Thinking for Educators (*https://designthinkingforeducators.com*).
National Governors Association Center for Best Practices & Council of Chief State School Officers. (2010). *Common Core Standards for English language arts and literacy in history/social studies, science, and technical subjects.* Washington, DC: Authors.

---

[1] Available at *www.sxswedu.com/news/2019/watch-jennifer-gonzalez-on-the-aerodynamics-of-exceptional-schools-video.*

LESSON STUDY

Stigler and Hiebert (1999) describe the notion of lesson study as a process for collaborative work by teachers to systematically study and improve their pedagogy. Essentially, a topic or instructional issue of importance is selected; as a group, teachers plan a lesson and then one teacher volunteers to teach that lesson. Others can watch or the lesson can be videotaped. As a group, teachers discuss the lesson and its effect on student learning; the lesson is then revised and taught again, generally to another class. And the process begins again. Variations to this concept can be made; for example, teachers might *select* rather than develop a specific lesson from the core reading program and then go through the described process. Such an approach allows teachers to reflect on the appropriateness of the lesson for the many students in the classroom who have different skills and needs. Another approach is to ask teachers to discuss the assignments or feedback rubrics they give to students as a means of facilitating learning. The following are examples of what three secondary social studies teachers might ask their students to do after reading a political cartoon: write a paragraph explaining the message of the cartoon; write a letter to the editor indicating their reaction to the political cartoon; or work with a partner to draw a cartoon that takes a view different from the one expressed in the original cartoon. Each of these assignments presents a different type of learning challenge for students. Additionally, teachers may discuss how feedback is provided to students by reviewing student rubrics. By sharing and comparing assignments, teachers can get a better sense of the variation in their expectations for students and discuss ways to improve the quality of those assignments.

Resources

Organization: Read, Write Think (ILA/NCTE) (*www.readwritethink.org*)
Organization: The Responsive Classroom (*www.responsiveclassroom.org*)
Stigler, J. W., & Hiebert, J. (1999). *The teaching gap: Best ideas from the world's teachers for improving education in the classroom.* New York: Free Press.

PARTNERSHIPS WITH EXTERNAL PARTNERS

A key component to these high-quality partnerships is shared collaboration and commitment for ongoing support. Some find that these partnerships are rewarding given that these associations sometimes take place outside of school or that teacher participation is more voluntary in nature. An example of high-quality school-based working partnership is West Virginia University's (WVU) PK–20 Collaborative. This partnership, which began in the 1990s, housed in WVU's College of Education and Human Services, focused on collaborating to improve student learning by promoting simultaneous renewal for all stakeholders (e.g., university faculty, public school teacher, and administrators). University faculty, working in a variety of capacities (e.g., Collaborative Faculty in Residence, action research mentor, professional development provider, school liaison) became members of school teams. Consequently, teachers from participating elementary, middle, and high schools worked in varying roles with WVU personnel (e.g., adjunct and clinical instructors). These boundary-spanning opportunities (Stevens, 1999) allow stakeholders to experience different perspectives as they walk in each other's shoes. This partnership generated a deeper understanding of PK–20 education that has been maintained as a part of the ongoing PL for all who engage in this collaborative work.

Resources

Burns, R., Jacobs, J., Baker, W., & Donahue, D. (2016). Making muffins: Identifying core ingredients of school–university partnerships. *School–University Partnerships, 9*(3), 81–95.

PROFESSIONAL LEARNING COMMUNITIES

Although there is much written about the importance of PLCs, there is less clarity about what this means and less research about what it takes to make such efforts meaningful for teachers and students. We define PLCs broadly: These are initiatives by schools for all staff members to work collaboratively as learners to achieve a common goal, that of improving student learning. As such, staff members are provided with the time and resources they need to function as members of that community. In other words, there are many different ways of organizing the school so that it functions effectively as a community or organization of learning. An individual school must decide the specific journey it will take, and that path will be dependent on the expertise, knowledge, and needs of the staff as well as those of students. The five essential characteristics of PLCs, as identified by Vescio, Ross, and Adams (2008), provide critical insights about this professional learning effort. These include (1) development of shared values and norms, (2) a focus on student learning, (3) reflective dialogue among teachers, (4) making teaching public, and (5) collaboration among educators at the school.

Resources

DuFour, R., DuFour, R. B., Eaker, R., Many, T., & Mattos, M (2016). *Learning by doing: A handbook for professional learning communities at work* (3rd ed.). Bloomington, IL: Solution Tree.
ILA Position Statements: A short synthesis and action plan for variety of literacy topics (*www.literacyworldwide.org/get-resources/position-statements*).
Vescio, V., Ross, D., & Adams, A. (2008). A review of research on the impact

of professional learning communities on teaching practice and student learning. *Teaching and Teacher Education, 24,* 80–91.

PROFESSIONAL LEARNING NETWORKS

Professional learning networks (PLNs) are defined as "informal gatherings in digital spaces" (ILA, 2018, p. 6). Within this new model of professional collaboration, educators with different job titles and opinions, from all types of schools and geographic locations, come together to talk, learn, collaborate, and engage. Laskowski (2018) interviewed six edu-Twitter influencers for advice on creating online PLNs. These educators, with 250,000-plus combined followers, are principals, authors, and teachers, and have one thing in common: They are all leaders in the field of education. When asked why they became engaged on Twitter, responses include to connect, for inspiration, for idea sharing, to promote a new book, and to have hard conversations. Although none said *to influence,* this is exactly what they do. When creating a PLN on Twitter, the influencers offered the following newbie advice: Follow people and educators you respect, use hashtags, be honest, be respectful, provide high-quality information, and position yourself as a leader.

Resources

International Literacy Association. (2018). *Democratizing professional growth with teachers: From development to learning (Position statement).* Newark, DE: Author.

Laskowski, T. (2018). Secrets of the edu-Twitter influencers. *Educational Leadership, 76*(3), 44–48.

Organization: International Society for Technology in Education (ISTE) (*www.iste.org/learn/about-iste-plns*).

Podcast: What is an educator mastermind and why should you join one (*www.cultofpedagogy.com/educator-mastermind*).

STUDY GROUPS

Over the last two decades, teacher study groups have become an emerging best practice for teacher learning. The purpose of study groups is to provide a collaborative learning experience that is guided by teacher inquiry, choice, and ownership. At their core, "study groups read articles and books together and discuss the implications of the text's ideas" (Lambert, 2002, p. 38). When teachers can discuss, debate, and analyze facets of their teaching practices and beliefs, they grow in a variety of ways. Teachers who participate in teacher study groups voluntarily spend time together aimed at PL, share quality reading (fiction and nonfiction) with colleagues, model lifelong reading pleasure, explore their own literacy, gain experience and confidence with book discussion, and may transfer this new learning to the classroom.

Walpole and Beauchat (2008) discuss criteria for instituting study groups: (1) Participants should have an opportunity to choose the subject or topic for study; (2) opportunities for making connections to classroom practice are essential; and (3) participation should be voluntary if the group meets after school hours. Allen (2016) describes how she successfully started a teacher study group at her school, in her first year as literacy leader. Her practical tips for a successful meeting include maintaining a 1-hour time limit, meeting in a relaxed environment, establishing a consistent format, end on time, and embrace the "discovery through inquiry" (p. 55) model for teacher participants.

Resources

Allen, J. (2016). *Becoming a literacy leader: Supporting learning and change.* Portland, ME: Stenhouse.

Walpole, S., & Beauchat, K. A. (2008). *Facilitating teacher study groups.* Denver, CO: Literacy Coaching Clearinghouse.

TEACHER RESEARCH

Given the schoolwide emphasis on data-driven decision making, teacher research, sometimes called *practitioner* or *action research,* is another example of an activity for schoolwide PL. Teacher research comprises multiple elements of inquiry, including identifying a question, collecting data, analyzing data, and modifying or refining instruction. Risko and Vogt (2016) suggest the following steps: (1) building knowledge, (2) generating specific questions, (3) collecting data, (4) allocating time for research, (5) planning for observations and dialogue, (6) addressing validity and ethical issues, (7) reporting of findings, and (8) reflecting on what has been learned from the research. The last step of the model is the first step to planning change in practice. Within this model are multiple opportunities for peer collaboration. This type of inquiry-based learning can be carried out in individual classroom or collectively (schoolwide) and should include teacher collaboration. This is a systematic way to understand issues about teacher instruction and student learning.

Resources

Fichtman, D. N., & Yendol-Silva, D. (2003). *The reflective educator's guide to classroom research: Learning to teach and teaching to learn through practitioner inquiry.* Thousand Oaks, CA: Corwin Press.

Risko, V., & Vogt, M. (2016). *Professional learning in action: An inquiry approach for teachers of literacy.* New York: Teachers College Press.

TEAMS OF LEARNERS (GRADE LEVEL, ACADEMIC DEPARTMENTS)

One of the most common and important means of building communities of learners is that of forming specific teams of teachers who have something in common: teaching the same grade or subject or teaching the same students. Generally, these teams are facilitated by one of the teacher leaders on the team or a literacy or instructional coach. The leader of the team must understand how to facilitate a group meeting, be an active listener, and encourage participation by all members. Leaders must also know how to help members to problem-solve and to address issues related to decision making. Leading a group takes much skill and patience. Kaner, Lind, Toldi, Fisk, and Berger (1996) talk about the fact that any group goes through a "groan zone" as it moves from divergent to convergent thinking. Leaders must recognize this time of potential conflict or they will become discouraged with what they see as group members' inability to work together effectively. The following websites provide ideas for protocols that can be used by leaders to help groups learn to work more effectively:

Learning Forward (*www.learningforward.com*)
School Reform Initiative (*www.schoolreforminitiative.org*)

Resources

Bean, R. M. (2015). *The reading specialist: Leadership and coaching for the classroom, school, and community* (3rd ed.). New York: Guilford Press.

References

Allen, J. (2016). *Becoming a literacy leader: Supporting learning and change.* Portland, ME: Stenhouse.

Bean, R. M. (2015). *The reading specialist: Leadership for the classroom, school, and community* (3rd ed.). New York: Guilford Press.

Bean, R. M., & Ippolito, J (2015). *Cultivating coaching mindsets: An action guide for literacy leaders.* West Palm Beach, FL: Learning Sciences International.

Burns, R., Jacobs, J., Baker, W., & Donahue, D. (2016). Making muffins: Identifying core ingredients of school–university partnerships. *School–University Partnerships, 9*(3), 81–95.

City, E. A., Elmore, R. F., Fiarman, S. E., & Teitel, L. (2009). *Instructional rounds in education: A network approach to improving teaching and learning.* Cambridge, MA: Harvard Education Press.

DuFour, R., DuFour, R. B., & Eaker, R. (2008). *Revisiting professional learning communities at work: New insights for improving schools.* Bloomington, IL: Solution Tree.

Fichtman, D. N., & Yendol-Silva, D. (2003). *The reflective educator's guide to classroom research: Learning to teach and teaching to learn through practitioner inquiry.* Thousand Oaks, CA: Corwin Press.

Grim, E., Kaufman, T., & Doty, D. (2014). Rethinking classroom observations. *Educational Leadership, 71*(8), 24–29.

International Literacy Association. (2018). *Literacy coaching for change: Choices matter.* Newark, DE: Author.

Ippolito, J., & Bean, R. M. (2018). *Unpacking coaching mindsets: Collaboration between principals and coaches.* West Palm Beach, FL: Learning Sciences International.

Jacobs, H. H., & Johnson, A. (2009). *The curriculum mapping planner: Templates, tools, and resources for effective professional development.* Alexandria, VA: ASCD.

Joyce, B., & Showers, B. (2002). *Student achievement through staff development* (3rd ed.). Alexandria, VA: ASCD.

Kaner, S., Lind, L., Toldi, C., Fisk, S., & Berger, D. (1996). *Facilitator's guide to participatory decision-making.* Philadelphia: New Society.

Lambert, L. (2002). A framework for shared leadership. *Educational Leadership, 59*(8), 37–40.

Laskowski, T. (2018). Secrets of the edu-Twitter influencers. *Educational Leadership, 76*(3), 44–48.

Mokhtari, K., Rosemary, C., & Edwards, P. (2007). Making instructional decisions based on data: What, how, and why? *The Reading Teacher, 61*(4), 354–359.

National Governors Association Center for Best Practices & Council of Chief State School Officers. (2010). *Common Core Standards for English language arts and literacy in history/social studies, science, and technical subjects.* Washington, DC: Authors.

Protheroe, N. (2009, March/April). Using classroom walkthroughs to improve instruction. *Principal, 88*(4), 30–34.

Stevens, D. D. (1999). The ideal, real, and surreal in school–university partnerships: Reflections of a boundary spanner. *Teaching and Teacher Education, 15,* 287–299.

Stigler, J. W., & Hiebert, J. (1999). *The teaching gap: Best ideas from the world's teachers for improving education in the classroom.* New York: Free Press.

Vescio, V., Ross, D., & Adams, A. (2008). A review of research on the impact of professional learning communities on teaching practice and student learning. *Teaching and Teacher Education, 24,* 80–91.

Walpole, S., & Beauchat, K. A. (2008). *Facilitating teacher study groups.* Denver, CO: Literacy Coaching Clearinghouse.

Index

Note. f or *t* following a page number indicates a figure or a table.

INTERNATIONAL
LITERACY
ASSOCIATION

The International Literacy Association (ILA) is a global advocacy and membership organization dedicated to advancing literacy for all through its network of more than 300,000 literacy educators, researchers, and experts across 146 countries. With more than 60 years of experience, ILA has set the standard for how literacy is defined, taught, and evaluated. ILA's *Standards for the Preparation of Literacy Professionals 2017* provides an evidence-based benchmark for the development and evaluation of literacy professional preparation programs. ILA collaborates with partners across the world to develop, gather, and disseminate high-quality resources, best practices, and cutting-edge research to empower educators, inspire students, and inform policymakers. ILA publishes *The Reading Teacher, Journal of Adolescent & Adult Literacy*, and *Reading Research Quarterly*, which are peer reviewed and edited by leaders in the field. For more information, visit *literacyworldwide.org*.